Important Dates in the Lives of Jesus and Mary

Important Dates in the Lives of Jesus and Mary

by
Ronald L. Conte Jr.

"For a thousand years before your eyes are like
the days of yesterday, which have passed by,
and they are like a watch of the night, which was held
for nothing: so their years shall be." (Psalm 89:4-5)

Important Dates in the Lives of Jesus and Mary
Revised Edition

All quotations from Sacred Scripture are from the Catholic Public Domain Version, Original Edition, translated, edited, and published by Ronald L. Conte Jr.

Chronology: This book took over four years to research and write. The first edition was first published as an electronic book (ISBN 0-9707993-3-0) in March of 2002. This revised edition was first published in June of 2007 as a print-on-demand book (no ISBN). The revised edition changes the quotes of Sacred Scripture from the RSV to the Catholic Public Domain Version, Original Edition, and makes a few minor edits to the text. The current printing (January, 2008), with an ISBN-13, changes the layout to a different size book, but the text remains the same.

Written, edited, and published by: Ronald L. Conte Jr.

ISBN-13: 978-0-9802249-2-4

Dedication

May the most Sacred Heart of Jesus
be adored and loved
in the true Holy Eucharist
at every Mass
throughout the world
until the end of time.

May the most Sacred Heart of Jesus
be adored and loved
in the true Holy Eucharist
in every tabernacle
throughout the world
until the end of time.

May the most Sacred Heart of Jesus
be adored and loved
in the true Holy Eucharist
by the heart of every Christian
throughout the world
until the end of time.

May the most holy, most sacred,
most adorable, most mysterious
and unutterable Name of God
be always praised, blessed,
loved, adored and glorified,
in Heaven, on earth and under the earth,
by all the creatures of God,
and by the Sacred Heart of Our Lord Jesus Christ
in the most holy Sacrament of the altar.

Table of Contents

Table of Contents – Appendices

Author's Foreword

This book was written for both the ordinary Christian and the Biblical scholar. I ask the indulgence of those who know Biblical chronology well, for there are many things explained at length in this book which the Biblical scholar does not need explained at all. There is also some repetition of certain points; this is done so as not to leave behind anyone who is unaccustomed to following a complex chronological argument.

Those who are new to the ideas of Biblical chronology may find the glossary in the back of the book helpful. I would also recommend, to anyone who is serious about understanding these ideas, several other books: *Handbook of Biblical Chronology*, revised edition, by Jack Finegan (Hendrickson Publishers); the works of the ancient historians Josephus, Dio, Suetonius, and Tacitus (various editions are available); *Chronos, Kairos, Christos*, (volumes I and II), edited by Vardaman and Yamauchi; and *The History of the Church*, by Eusebius.

To the Biblical scholar, I say: "Keep an open mind!" There are many new and controversial ideas in this book. Do not reject these ideas prima facie. There is much evidence in support of this revised chronology, see especially chapters 12, 13, 14, and 17.

The chronology in this book refutes the underlying assumptions of modern-day Biblical chronology. Those assumptions consist mainly in the almost universally-accepted dates for the reigns of the Roman emperors. My conclusions undermine the very foundations of the chronological arguments of every other modern-day Biblical chronologist. Therefore, I expect that some Biblical chronologists and other scholars will attempt to quickly dismiss this book, without examining or refuting the arguments and conclusions found therein. For if they cannot find a way to cast off this book, before it is thoroughly examined by students and scholars, their own theories and conclusions will be in danger of being refuted and of becoming irrelevant. If the conclusions of this book are accepted, then many of the theories of present-day Biblical chronologists will crumble to the ground.

Suppose that someone, researching and studying in any field of knowledge, finds some new conclusions which advance that field by a fraction of a step. Such conclusions would be likely to find wide acceptance. Other persons studying in that same field will see such results as a kind of validation and advancement of their own work. This happens when the new results compliment previous results.

Now suppose that someone finds new conclusions, which advance a field of knowledge by leaps and bounds. Such conclusions are unlikely to find immediate and widespread acceptance among researchers in the same field. It is too much for them to accept all at once. They would have to revise their own ideas to a great extent, rather than to a small extent, in order to accept the new conclusions.

Finally, suppose that someone finds new conclusions which contradict, refute, and thoroughly undermine the work of all contemporary researchers in the same field. These researchers will be unlikely to admit that their life's work is riddled with false assumptions and erroneous conclusions. They will not want to step down from the role of teacher and take the role of student, in the very field of knowledge where they are considered an expert. They will not want to do the extensive work needed to completely revise their own theories to conform to the new conclusions. It is easier for them to simply dismiss the new conclusions.

But they will have to dismiss these new conclusions without examining them closely and without making a logical or scholarly argument. If they argue against these new conclusions in a scholarly fashion, by closely examining the evidence and arguments presented, then they will be admitting, in effect, that these ideas have merit. They will not want to examine these ideas closely, for fear that they might be understood to be correct. Thus, their approach will be to ridicule, rather than to refute.

If almost everyone believes something, is that something necessarily true? If every expert in a field of knowledge believes the same conclusion, is that conclusion certainly correct? No, not so. It happens from time to time, in any field of knowledge, that experts believe things which later turn out to be incorrect. It is the same in the field of Biblical chronology. Nearly every Biblical chronologist firmly believes numerous conclusions which this book shows are incorrect.

I expect that the ideas in this book will, at first, be widely rejected by scholars. However, the truth is like a city on a hill—it cannot be kept hidden. There must be at least a few present-day scholars who are sincerely dedicated to truth. These will examine and eventually accept the conclusions of this book. And the next new generation of students and scholars of the Bible and of Biblical chronology will be more likely to accept the new ideas in this book. I expect that eventually the conclusions of this book will be generally-accepted, both by the ordinary Christian and the Biblical scholar. I think it will take at least a generation for such acceptance to occur.

This book of Biblical chronology was written with faith in God and for those who have faith in God. The Bible is a book of faith, inspired by God, written down in faith, transmitted in faith, preserved in faith, and lived out in the lives of countless faithful souls. Anyone who claims that faith should be absent from Biblical research is an idiot.

Chapter 1
Guidelines

Sound Premises

A conclusion is only as sound as the premises on which it is based. Logical arguments proceed from various premises to one or more conclusions. A conclusion that Jesus was born in a particular year, or that He was crucified in a particular year, is based on a set of premises. Each premise must be examined and supported, in one way or another. This chapter examines some of the most basic premises upon which the chronological arguments in this book rest.

1. Sacred Scripture is the inspired Word of God and is entirely without error.
2. The writings of Blessed Anne Catherine Emmerich contain reliable chronological information from God about the lives of Jesus and Mary, but may also contain some human errors and misunderstandings.
3. The writings of ancient historians, such as Josephus, Dio, Tacitus, and others, contain reliable chronological information, but may also contain some human errors and misunderstandings.
4. The generally-accepted dates for events in the first century B.C. and first century A.D. cannot be assumed to be correct. Each date for any event must be examined and supported.
5. Modern astronomy can provide reliable information about the moon's phases and other celestial events, such as solar and lunar eclipses.
6. Ancient records of comet observations provide reliable information which can be helpful in dating certain historical events.

Sacred Scripture

The most important premise relied upon for the chronology in this book is that Sacred Scripture was written by God and so must be entirely without error. This premise is also an article of faith. It is an essential and indisputable teaching of the Christian faith that the Bible was written by God. All faithful Christians believe that the Bible is the inspired Word of God. God chose to write the books of the Bible through many different human persons, who were both fallible and sinful, yet by God's Providence and Grace, God is the sole True Author of the Bible. The Bible contains all those things and only those things which God wills. God is infallible, therefore the Bible must also be infallible. God's Sacred Scripture is accurate and true, completely free from imperfection and error, including errors of omission.

Many commentators speak as if the Bible were merely a human book, as if, for example, Luke's Gospel could contain only Luke's imperfect understanding of events; this idea is contrary to the Christian understanding of Sacred Scripture. The Bible is inspired by God, and therefore must contain more than its human authors' imperfect understanding of events. The Bible is fundamentally different from other books and must not be treated as if it were one of many fallible historical documents.

Some theologians have even developed interpretations of the Bible which have as their premise or conclusion that the Bible contains some kind of error. Such ideas must be rejected because they are contrary to the Christian faith. We must follow our faith to be able to arrive at the whole truth. God wrote the Bible, and since God is infallible, there cannot possibly be any errors in the Bible. This book, *Important Dates in the Lives of Jesus and Mary*, begins with the belief that the Bible was written by God and is entirely without flaw, omission, or imperfection.

Some theologians and scholars claim to find errors in the Bible. And where are those supposed errors?—wherever Sacred Scripture conflicts with their own ideas and theories. If the theory of any theologian or scholar conflicts with Sacred Scripture—if both cannot be true—then the theory is in error and must be changed.

The original human authors of the various books of the Bible were guided by the inspiration of the Holy Spirit, so that their writing is God's writing, entirely and without exception. Thus the original books of the Bible are without error. And neither could any error enter into the Bible by an error of transmission, when the text of the Bible is copied and reprinted from one time period to the next. It is true that there have been particular editions of the Bible which contained typographical errors, or (in the time before the modern printing press), the copying errors of scribes. However, no such error could enter into the text of the Bible in such a way that every existing edition would have an error in the same place and the original text be lost. If so, then the reliability and infallibility of Sacred Scripture would be lost, and any one who disliked a particular passage could claim that the passage was added or altered at a later date and was not a part of the original text. Some have made this claim, for example, about John 6:51b-58, yet verse 59 plainly states that Christ did teach this doctrine in a synagogue at Capernaum.

God not only guided the original human authors of the Sacred Scripture, but He also continues to protect the true text and true meaning of Sacred Scripture throughout Time. Otherwise, faith would lose its certitude. We do not have the original manuscripts from any of the books of the Bible. If these original manuscripts are the only ones said to be without error, so that every subsequent copy could be said to all contain the same errors, then the Bible would not be an entirely true and reliable basis for faith. Such a theory would make the inspiration of Sacred Scripture effectively null and void, since any part of the text could be said to be the result of an error introduced sometime after the text was written.

As an example, one theory in biblical chronology claims to find a particular error in the text of one of Paul's letters. Paul explains that his second visit to Jerusalem occurred "after fourteen years" (Gal 2:1). This presents a certain chronological problem which some have attempted to solve by claiming that Saint Paul originally wrote "four years" and a copying error by a scribe turned the "four" into "fourteen." Then they also claim that this error made its way into every existing version of the Letter of Paul to the Galatians, except for one copy of Galatians from the Middle Ages, which does say "four years."[1]

The above theory is unacceptable, firstly because it holds that there is an error in Sacred Scripture. Secondly, how could a copying error make its way into every ancient edition of the Letter to the Galatians, but not in a much later edition from the Middle Ages? If every older copy of Galatians had the same error, the later edition could not obtain the correct wording. Obviously, the copying error was made in the later version. One scribe at that time must have mistakenly wrote "four years," instead of "fourteen years." If many witnesses tell the same story, and only one witness says the opposite, the case will be decided in favor of the many.

Another example of a supposed error in Sacred Scripture involves the question as to whether Jesus was crucified on the Preparation day of the Passover, which is the 14th of the Jewish month of Nisan, or on the next day, the first day of Passover itself, which is the 15th of Nisan. The Gospel of John clearly states that Jesus was crucified on "the preparation day of the Passover" (Jn 19:14) and a Friday (Jn 19:31). John's Gospel also says that the Jewish leaders had not yet eaten the Passover supper (Jn 18:28). The Passover lamb is sacrificed in the afternoon on Nisan 14, and the Passover supper is eaten after sunset later that day. So, John's Gospel tells us that the Jewish leaders were going to eat the Passover supper later that day (after Jesus had died). Yet the Gospels of Matthew, Mark, and Luke each describe Jesus and the Apostles eating the Passover supper on the previous evening, a Thursday.

A common approach to solving this problem is to claim that either the synoptic Gospels (Matthew, Mark, Luke) or the Gospel of John contains a chronological error. This approach is contrary to the teaching of the Christian faith that the Bible is the inspired Word of God. Since there cannot be any kind of error in Sacred Scripture, the correct explanation of this chronological problem must be in agreement with all four Gospels. The solution to this problem is presented in chapter 2 of this book.

A Lamp for Our Feet

God's Holy Infallible Scripture is a certain source of knowledge about the life of Jesus Christ. Many scholars treat the various statements in the Bible that refer, directly or indirectly, to dates and times, as if these words could be mistaken. Some scholars put more faith in their own ideas than in the words of Sacred Scripture. Without faith, how can they discern the correct dates for important events in the life of Jesus Christ? Faith is the lamp that lights the path to true knowledge. "Your word is a lamp to my feet and a light to my paths." (Psalm 118:105). It is true that faithful Christians do not need to know the exact dates of events in the life of Christ. Yet, at the same time, it is faith that reveals these dates.

One of the main premises of this book is that the Bible can be relied upon for true historical information about the dates and times of events in the lives of Jesus Christ and the Virgin Mary. This premise is based on faith. Whoever attempts to build a chronology of the life of Jesus Christ not based on faith in the words of Sacred Scripture is certain to fail. The things of faith cannot be proved from science and historical evidence alone.

Even though Sacred Scripture is entirely without error, any individual's understanding and interpretation of Sacred Scripture is subject to error. The possibility that one might misunderstand the meaning of the Bible is clear from the many disagreements which have occurred throughout the centuries among devout Christians about various ideas in Christian theology. Therefore, some devout Christians might piously disagree with some of my interpretations of Sacred Scripture concerning dates and times of various events in the life of Christ.

Blessed Anne Catherine Emmerich

The ideas in this book are not based solely on Sacred Scripture. The dates given in this book are also based on the visions given by God to Blessed Anne Catherine Emmerich and, to a certain extent, Saint Bridget of Sweden (especially in the chapter on the Dormition of the Virgin Mary). Some of the information presented in this book about the dates and times of various events in the lives of Jesus and Mary comes from the visions of Blessed Anne Catherine Emmerich. This book is based partly on the belief that Blessed Anne Catherine's visions are true visions from God.

Blessed Anne Catherine lived from 1774 to 1824, and spent most of her adult years as a nun in an Augustinian convent. She had the stigmata, the wounds of Jesus Christ, in her body, and she suffered many times with Christ while meditating on His Passion.[2] She was certainly a devout disciple of Jesus Christ. And the Catholic Church has declared Anne Catherine Emmerich to be Blessed, that is, to be an example of holiness for faithful Christians to emulate.

Blessed Anne Catherine had many visions from God about the lives of Jesus and Mary. Since she was close to God, had the stigma, and suffered much for Christ, she must have been telling the truth about her visions from God. These visions from God are not merely the meditations of a pious nun. Blessed Anne Catherine clearly and repeatedly spoke of these visions as having come from God.

God is infallible. Everything that God does and says is infallible. Therefore, the visions which God gave to Blessed Anne Catherine, and the visions which God gives to many different holy persons throughout the ages, are infallible. However, the understanding which Blessed Anne Catherine had of these visions is fallible, and the writing down of the visions is also fallible. For this reason, books about visions which God has given to the saints do not have the infallibility of Sacred Scripture.

The Bible is infallible because both the meaning of the Bible and the writing down of that meaning was God's infallible work. But the visions given to Blessed Anne Catherine were private revelation, and so were subject to misunderstandings and errors when these were written down. Sacred Scripture is Divine Revelation given to all, and is entirely true and accurate. Private revelation is subject to errors, introduced through the human fallibility of those who receive and transmit such private revelations. Notice here that Divine Revelation must be in some way infallible in its transmission, or it would quickly become no more authoritative than private revelation (because of the possibility of numerous errors introduced during transmission).

Many of the important dates in this book depend on my own understanding and interpretation of Sacred Scripture and on the writings of Blessed Anne Catherine. My interpretation of Sacred Scripture, and of private revelation given to the saints, is subject to possible errors or misunderstandings on my part. However, in this book I only write those things which I understand and believe to be true with a reasonable degree of certainty.

There are no errors in the Bible, but there are a few errors in the writings of Blessed Anne Catherine Emmerich. Firstly, there are a few errors where she misunderstood the meaning of the visions given to her. For example, she thought that the length of Christ's life was to be counted from His Birth, but the vision about the length of Christ's life came during other visions on the Incarnation. The length of the life of Jesus Christ should certainly be counted from His Holy Conception, for life begins at conception. There are other examples of her misunderstandings which will be presented later in this book.

Secondly, there are a few errors introduced by Clemens Brentano, who wrote down Blessed Anne Catherine's visions as they were told to him. For example, in one place he concludes that Jesus was born on the 12th of Kislev (by the Jewish calendar).[3] In another place, he states it was the 10th of Kislev.[4] Yet Blessed Anne Catherine never gives the date of the 10th or 12th of Kislev as having come from her visions. This was merely a conclusion drawn by Clemens Brentano. She herself says only, "I think Christ was born in the month Kislev."[5]

Despite the possibility of error in Blessed Anne Catherine's writings, I consider her writings to be at least as reliable as the writings of ancient historians, such as Josephus, Dio, Tacitus, and others. Her source for her assertions is her visions from God. Josephus lived in the last half of the first century and was not a direct witness to most of the events which he chronicled. Dio lived at an even later time (late second century A.D.). These ancient historians were not generally eye witnesses to most of what they wrote. They based their histories on various sources (most of which are unknown to us today). Therefore, there could be errors in their source material, as well as errors in their understanding of their sources.

On the other hand, Blessed Anne Catherine's visions came from God, Who is Infallible. By means of her visions from God, Blessed Anne Catherine was in a sense a witness to these events she describes. She could misunderstand the information given to her by God, but her source of information is sure. Even so, this book looks at Blessed Anne Catherine's chronological statements with a critical eye. Her visions are subject to various interpretations, as are the writings of Josephus and other ancient historians. Each of her chronological statements is evaluated by comparison with other statements she made, with the chronological information given in Sacred Scripture, and with other sources.[6]

Ancient Historians

Jesus Christ was born during the reign of Caesar Augustus (Lk 2:1) and His ministry took place during the reign of Tiberius Caesar (Lk 3:1). But ancient historians, such as Josephus, Dio, and Tacitus, lived at a later time, years after Tiberius' reign had ended. They were not themselves eyewitnesses to events during the reigns of Augustus and Tiberius. Most of what these ancient historians wrote was based on source material which we do not have available to us today. Since we cannot examine the source material of these ancient historians, we must admit the possibility that their source material, or their conclusions based on their source material, may have contained some chronological errors. That such errors were sometimes present is clear from certain contradictions in their histories, such as the varying dates given by Josephus for the rebuilding of the Temple.[7] Some errors could have been introduced by a misunderstanding on the part of the historian, but other errors could certainly have come from their source material.

Generally-accepted Dates

In sincere pursuit of the truth, we cannot merely assume that the generally-accepted dates for events during the reigns of Augustus and Tiberius are correct. Every historian today would, I think, give 44 B.C. as the year of Julius Caesar's death and A.D. 14 as the year of Caesar Augustus' death. Yet if we build a chronology on the premise that the generally-accepted dates for events of this time period are correct, any conclusions reached would be limited by such assumptions. This book does not begin with the unexamined premise that the generally-accepted dates for events during the first century B.C. and first century A.D. are necessarily correct.

In recent years, some scholars have challenged some of the most widely-accepted dates for historical events during this time period. For example, Dr. E. Jerry Vardaman makes the argument, based on archaeological evidence, that Pilate's reign over Judea occurred about ten years earlier than is generally believed.[8] Also, the dates given by various scholars specifically for the Birth and Crucifixion of Christ vary widely. There is, in fact, no general agreement among scholars or theologians as to the dates for various events in the life of Jesus Christ. *Handbook of Biblical Chronology*, by Jack Finegan, clearly illustrates this point by presenting the wide range of opinions among various scholars on almost every issue in Biblical chronology.[9] While some books present certain Biblical dates, such as the year of the Crucifixion, as if there were no difference of opinion, this is not true. There is no general agreement on most dates in Biblical chronology.

There is much uncertainty among scholars as to when events described in the Bible actually occurred partly because the calendar systems used to keep track of the years has changed over time. The current system using the terms "B.C." and "A.D." was not developed until hundreds of years after the Birth of Christ. Assigning a year B.C. or A.D. to an event is therefore not a simple and straightforward task. No one during the first century A.D. wrote the number of the year as we would write it today. They numbered the years by the reigns of various rulers (e.g. Lk 3:1). Consequently, we should not accept, as an unexamined premise, that Augustus died in A.D. 14, or that Herod died in 4 B.C., or that any other event occurred in a particular year. Each premise must be supported by sufficient evidence. Any premise for an argument in Biblical chronology, which is supported merely by the statement that "most scholars agree" on a particular date, is an unexamined premise, and one that may very well turn out to be false.

Insights from Astronomy

The science of astronomy provides information which is helpful in determining the dates of certain events in the first century B.C. and first century A.D. In the writings of ancient historians, there is mention of certain celestial events, including lunar eclipses, solar eclipses, and the sightings of various comets. Modern astronomy can determine, using computer software, not only the dates of each lunar and solar eclipse, but also detailed information about where the eclipse was visible, how long it lasted, and its general appearance.

In this book, the software program *RedShift 3* was used to obtain information about lunar and solar eclipses.[10] *RedShift 3* not only provides the date, time, and duration for each eclipse, but also displays a realistic view of the sky from any point on earth, at any point in time stretching back for thousands of years. One can use this software to watch an eclipse much as it might have been seen from Jerusalem, or Rome, or some other location.

Data on solar and lunar eclipses was also obtained from Fred Espenak's Eclipse Home Page at the NASA/GSFC Sun-Earth Connection Education Forum: (http://sunearth.gsfc.nasa.gov/eclipse).[11] This web site provides both a *Five Millennium Catalog of Solar Eclipses* and a *Five Millennium Catalog of Lunar Eclipses* containing detailed data on each eclipse.[12] A comparison of the dates and times for these eclipses given by the NASA/GSFC web site and by *RedShift 3* software correlate well (see chapter 17).

Astronomy is also useful in reconstructing the Jewish calendar, which is based on the phases of the moon. The moon's lunar cycle begins with the new moon. The astronomical new moon occurs when the moon passes a line drawn between the earth and the sun. On those occasions when the moon, in passing such a line, also passes directly between the sun and the earth, the moon's shadow falls upon the earth in a solar eclipse. Notice that solar eclipses only occur about the time of the new moon. Thus, if data on the dates and times of solar eclipses is accurate, then similar calculations used to determine the dates and times of astronomical new moons will also be accurate.

The same NASA/GSFC web site also offers a *Five Millennia Catalog of Phases of the Moon.*[13] This data on the moon's phases also correlates well with the data from *RedShift 3* software. (Further details on determining astronomical new moons and the start of various months in the Jewish calendar can be found in chapter 17.)

The evidence of two or three witnesses is needed to decide a case (Mt 18:16; Deut 17:6; 2 Cor 13:1). Since the data from both the NASA/GSFC web site and *RedShift 3* software are in close agreement, we can have confidence in this data and use it to assist in determining the dates of events in the first century B.C. and first century A.D.

Information on Ancient Comets

Ancient historians also occasionally mention sightings of comets in association with important historical events. The Romans believed that comets were a sign from the gods foreshadowing some important event, such as a war or the death of an emperor. One of the most famous examples of this is a comet seen shortly after the death of Julius Caesar. The Roman people believed that this was a sign that Julius Caesar had taken his place among the gods. For this reason, ancient coins and images of Julius Caesar often show a comet above his head.

How can modern astronomy determine which comets appeared when in ancient times? For the most part, it cannot; however, independent verification of comet sightings is provided by ancient Chinese and Korean astronomers, who observed the stars closely and kept careful records of the date and location of comets. Since the ancient Chinese calendar system (a lunar calendar) is unrelated to the B.C./A.D. system, this provides a way to verify the sightings mentioned by the Roman historians.

The best modern source for information on these ancient comet sightings is undoubtedly *Cometography, A Catalog of Comets, Volume 1,* by Gary W. Kronk. This book covers every ancient comet from 675 B.C. to A.D. 1799, and consolidates all of the often quoted sources for ancient comet data, such as the *Hou Han shu* (an ancient Chinese text), J. Williams, Ho Peng Yoke, A. G. Pingré, and others. Treatment is even given to brief mentions of comets found in ancient Roman texts.

Comets are typically visible (with the naked eye) for a period of a few days or weeks to, at most, several months. They travel in an arc around the sun and should be visible, at some point in their path, from both Europe and China. Thus, any noted comet in Roman history would likely have been observed and mentioned by the ancient astronomers of China. It should then be possible, in a given chronology for dates in the reigns of Roman emperors, to match the mention of comets in Roman texts to those in Chinese texts. Comet data is examined in chapter 13 of this book, along with a revised chronology of the reigns of the Roman emperors in the first century A.D.

Scholars Are Uncertain

In 525 A.D., Pope St. John I, asked a Roman Catholic abbot named Dionysius Exiguus to determine the dates of Easter for future years. Dionysius was a well-known theologian, who also excelled at mathematics and astronomy. The date for Easter is determined by astronomy.[14] In determining these dates, Dionysius objected to the then-current system of numbering the years from the time of the emperor Diocletian, (third century A.D.), under whose reign there was a great persecution of Christians.[15] Instead, he devised a calendar system where the years are numbered according to the Incarnation of Jesus Christ, *ab incarnatione Domini* ('from the Incarnation of the Lord').[16] Today, we use the abbreviation "A.D.," which stands for *Anno Domini* ('in the year of the Lord'), but the numbering of the years is according to Dionysius.[17]

Dionysius numbered the first full year after the Incarnation and Birth of Christ as A.D. 1. Thus, in A.D. 1, according to Dionysius, Christ would have completed one year of life since the Incarnation (early in the calendar year), and one year of life since His Holy Birth (late in the calendar year). The number of the year should reflect the age of Christ in this system. The custom of referring to the years before A.D. 1 as "B.C." ('before Christ') did not develop until a later time. However, Dionysius did believe that Christ was born in the year before A.D. 1, which we now call 1 B.C.

Even though this new system of numbering the years was accepted by the Church, and by much of society, there is today no agreement among historians, Biblical scholars, theologians, or Church leaders that Dionysius chose the correct year to call A.D. 1. In other words, there is no general agreement that Christ was born in 1 B.C. It is not the official teaching of the Catholic Church, nor of any other Christian Church of which I am aware, that Jesus Christ was necessarily born in 1 B.C., as was the opinion of Dionysius.

Since hundreds of years had passed between the Birth of Christ and the time of Dionysius, he could well have been mistaken about which year was the year of Christ's Birth. Also, he numbered the years as his reference point using the Roman dating system A.U.C., *ab urbe condita,* (from the founding of the city of Rome). So, any errors in the Roman system of dating the years would have affected his determination as to in which year Christ was born. As we shall see in chapter 13 of this book, Dionysius would have been correct as to the year of Christ's Birth, except for some errors in the Roman histories upon which Dionysius depended.

The Teaching of the Church

The Catholic Church has no official teaching as to the year of the Birth or Crucifixion of Jesus Christ. And, even though we celebrate the Birth of Jesus Christ on December 25, the Church does not teach that this was necessarily the day on which Our Savior was born. Nor does the Catholic Church have any teachings about other dates or times for events in the life of Jesus, except what is stated in Sacred Scripture. For example, the Gospels reveal that Jesus died on a Friday and rose from the dead on a Sunday. We also know from Sacred Scripture that Jesus died on "the preparation day of the Passover" (Jn 19:14). Since these teachings are found in the Word of God, these are included in the teaching of the Catholic Church. But, beyond what is taught by the Bible, there is no official teaching as to the year, or even the month and day in the Christian calendar, when various events occurred.

In general, Christian doctrine does not teach or require belief in particular dates, even for important events in the life of Christ. Some members of the faithful have their own opinions as to which are the correct dates, but these are opinion, not doctrine. Likewise, the statements made in this book are opinions, not required beliefs. The only statements about dates and times which are required beliefs are the statements of Sacred Scripture (and any future declarations which might be made by the teaching authority of the Catholic Church).

Certitude

I am absolutely certain that Jesus Christ was born our Savior and Lord. I am less certain as to when Christ was born. I am absolutely certain that Jesus Christ was crucified, died, and rose from the dead for our salvation. I am less certain as to when Christ died and rose from the dead. The certitude of faith always exceeds the certitude of human knowledge. However, as far as mere human knowledge is concerned, I am quite certain that I have found the correct dates for the Birth of Christ, for His Crucifixion and Resurrection, and for other important events in the lives of Jesus Christ and the Virgin Mary.

Chapter 2
The Crucifixion of Jesus Christ

The Jewish Day

The Jewish Sabbath, and every day in the Jewish calendar, begins and ends at sunset (cf. Lev 23:32).[18] The Jewish Sabbath is Saturday, but that day begins on Friday at sunset and ends on Saturday at sunset. This method of counting the beginning and end of each day worked well in ancient times. People did not have watches and clocks in their homes. Yet they had to know when the day began and ended in order to keep the Sabbath and to mark the beginning of certain feasts and holy days. Sunset was a clear and convenient starting and ending point for each calendar day.

It is clear from Sacred Scripture that the Jewish calendar day ends at sunset. For example, in the Gospel of Mark, Jesus taught and healed in the synagogue on the Sabbath (Mk 1:21-28). "Then, when evening arrived, after the sun had set, they brought to him all who had maladies and those who had demons. And the entire city was gathered together at the door." (Mk 1:32-33). The people saw Jesus heal in the synagogue hours earlier, but they did not bring the sick to Him until after sundown. The reason is that, on the Jewish Sabbath, it was prohibited to travel more than a short distance, or to do work, such as carrying something heavy (or someone heavy). The Sabbath ended at sundown on that day (Saturday), and then they were permitted to bring the sick to Him.

Jesus Died on a Friday

"And when evening had now arrived (because it was the Preparation Day, which is before the Sabbath) there arrived Joseph of Arimathea, a noble council member, who himself was also awaiting the kingdom of God. And he boldly entered to Pilate and petitioned for the body of Jesus." (Mk 15:42-43).

God's Holy Infallible Scripture clearly indicates that the Crucifixion of Jesus Christ occurred on a Friday. The Jewish Sabbath is Saturday, a day on which devout Jews would do no work. The day of Preparation is the day before the Sabbath, that is, Friday. On that day, devout Jews prepare what they need for the next day, so that they can keep the Sabbath as a day of rest. All four Gospels tell us plainly that Jesus died on the day before the Jewish Sabbath, on Friday (Mk 15:42; Mt 27:62; Lk 23:54, 56; Jn 19:31, 42).

"Then the Jews, because it was the preparation day, so that the bodies would not remain upon the cross on the Sabbath (for that Sabbath was a great day), they petitioned Pilate in order that their legs might be broken, and they might be taken away." (Jn 19:31).

The Jews wanted those who had been crucified to be removed from the crosses before the beginning of the Sabbath. Since the Sabbath begins on Friday at sunset, they asked Pilate to have their legs broken, so that they would die more quickly on their crosses and could be removed before the Sabbath began. When the soldiers went to break the legs of those who had been crucified, they found that Jesus was already dead, so they did not break His legs (Jn 19:32-33). Jesus died well before sunset, on a Friday. It is an indisputable teaching of Sacred Scripture that Jesus died on a Friday.

Passover Began at Sunset on the Day Jesus Died

The feast of Passover begins on the evening of the 14th day of the first month of the Jewish sacred calendar (Exodus 12:1-14). That month in the Jewish calendar is called Nisan and it falls in early springtime. The first day of Passover is the 15th day of Nisan (which begins at sunset, at the end of Nisan 14).

The Gospel of John refers to the day that Jesus was crucified as "the preparation day of the Passover" (Jn 19:14). The 14th of Nisan is the day on which Jews prepare for the beginning of Passover (Ex 12:6). Therefore, Jesus died on Nisan 14 by the Jewish calendar.

Jesus died on Friday, the Preparation day of the Sabbath, and that day was also the Preparation day of the Passover (Nisan 14). The next day, Saturday, was both the Sabbath and the first day (Nisan 15) of Passover. The Gospel of John makes a point of stating that this particular Sabbath was special, "for that Sabbath was a great day" (Jn 19:31). Every Sabbath is a holy day, but Sacred Scripture distinguishes this Sabbath from other Sabbaths as a special day because it was also the beginning of the Jewish Passover. The year that Jesus died, Passover began on the Sabbath (Saturday), so that the day of Preparation for the Sabbath (Friday) was also the day of Preparation for the Passover.

The year that Jesus died, Passover began on a Saturday (that is, on Friday at sunset). Passover began at sunset, a few hours after Jesus' death on the Cross. Jesus died on the day of Preparation of the Passover because that is the day on which the Passover lamb is sacrificed and Jesus is the Passover Lamb. The sacrificing of the Passover Lambs began at the ninth hour. Jesus died on the day, and at the time of day (Mk 15:33-34), when the Passover lambs were being sacrificed.[19] Saint John the Baptist was referring to Jesus' sacrificial death when he said, " 'Behold the Lamb of God.' " (Jn 1:36; cf. 1 Cor 5:7).

The Fourteenth Day of Nisan

In the early Church, there was a controversy as to which day should be celebrated as the day of the Crucifixion of Christ. Most Christians kept the observance of the day Christ died for us on a Friday, no matter which day of the month it was. But many Christians in Asia Minor kept the observance of the Crucifixion on the 14th day of the lunar month, i.e. the Jewish month of Nisan.[20] This group of Christians were called "quartodecimans," a name which means "the fourteeners." Eventually, the Church decided to keep the observance of this day always on a Friday, hence the name Good Friday. This controversy tells us something about the day of the Crucifixion.

This decision, whether to keep the observance always on a Friday or always on the 14th day of Nisan, had to be made by the Church because Jesus was crucified on Friday, Nisan 14, but Nisan 14 does not always fall on a Friday. So, in subsequent years when Nisan 14 and Friday did not coincide, Christians had to decide on which day to observe the Crucifixion. Notice that there was no one arguing to observe the day of Christ's Crucifixion on the 15th day of Nisan, nor did any one argue in favor of observing the

Crucifixion always on some other particular day of the week. Early Christians understood that Christ died on a Friday and on Nisan 14, that is why there was no dispute about whether Christ died on Nisan 14 or 15, nor any dispute about on which day of the week Christ died. Modern-day theories which claim that Christ died on Nisan 15 or on some day of the week other than Friday were absent then (and should be absent still).

The Solution to the Synoptic Problem

"Then the day of Unleavened Bread arrived, on which it was necessary to kill the Pascal lamb. And he sent Peter and John, saying, 'Go out, and prepare the Passover for us, so that we may eat.' " (Lk 22:7-8).

"Then they led Jesus from Caiaphas into the praetorium. Now it was morning, and so they did not enter into the praetorium, so that they would not be defiled, but might eat the Passover." (Jn 18:28).

The Gospels of Matthew, Mark and Luke clearly tell us that Jesus celebrated the Passover supper with his disciples (cf. Mt 26:17-19; Mk 14:12-16). And the Gospel of John tells us that the Jewish leaders who delivered Jesus to Pilate, early on Friday morning, had not yet eaten the Passover supper. How can these two teachings of God's Holy Infallible Scripture be reconciled?

The solution to this problem is to believe that all of these teachings of Sacred Scripture are true. Those who have faith in Jesus Christ also have faith that the Bible is without error. Sacred Scripture teaches us that Jesus died on a Friday before sunset. The Gospel of John indicates that Passover began the day Jesus died at sunset. The synoptic Gospels clearly describe Jesus celebrating the Passover supper with His disciples the night before He died. All of these things are true.

Since the first day of Passover, Nisan 15, began that year on Friday at sunset (which is the beginning of Saturday in the Jewish calendar), most Jews ate the Passover supper on Friday evening. So then, why did Jesus and His disciples celebrate the Passover a day early on Thursday evening? The answer is found in the writings of Blessed Anne Catherine Emmerich. She describes how Jesus was brought before the Jewish leaders and accused of various offenses.

"Some said that he had eaten the Pascal lamb on the previous day, which was contrary to the law.... Nicodemus and Joseph of Arimathea were called up, and being commanded to say how it happened that they had allowed him to eat the Pasch on the wrong day in a room which belonged to them, they proved from ancient documents that from time immemorial the Galilaens had been allowed to eat the Pasch a day earlier than the rest of the Jews.... The reason was this: the sacrifices would not have been finished by the Sabbath if the immense multitudes who congregated together for that purpose had all been obliged to perform the ceremony on the same day...."[21]

There is no contradiction between the synoptic Gospels and the Gospel of John. Jesus and His disciples celebrated the Passover meal a day early, on Thursday evening. Divine Providence arranged events so that Jesus could both celebrate the Passover supper with His disciples on Thursday evening and also be the Passover Lamb sacrificed on the Cross on Friday. Only those who are lacking in faith will believe that any part of Sacred Scripture could ever be in error.

The Jewish Hour

In ancient times, the Jews kept track of the hours of each calendar day by dividing the daylight hours into 12 parts and the night hours into 12 parts. There were 24 hours in each calendar day, but the length of each hour depended on the total amount of time of darkness or light. In the winter, when the daytime is short and the nighttime is long, an hour during daytime would be shorter than what we today would call an hour (60 minutes). In the summer, an hour during daytime would be longer than 60 minutes.

Passover occurs after the spring Equinox, in late March or in April. At that time of year, if the daylight hours are counted from sunup to sundown, the number of minutes of daylight is greater than 12 times 60. In other words, there are more than 60 of our minutes to a Jewish daytime hour. In early April, the increase makes each Jewish hour about 3 minutes longer than what we would call an hour. The length of each daylight hour increases as summer approaches, and decreases as winter approaches, so the length of an hour depends on the day of the year.

The observation of the sun was used in daylight hours to determine the time. The first hour of the daylight time began at sunrise. The sixth hour was when the sun reached its highest point in the sky, midway between sunrise and sunset. One might call the sixth hour "noon," but, in modern time-keeping, 12:00 noon does not usually mark the exact time when the sun is highest in the sky. (Rather, this depends on the time of year and on one's distance from the center of each time zone.) But, when keeping track of time by the sun, noon would refer to the time when the sun is at its highest point in the sky (the technical term for this is "apparent solar noon"). The twelfth hour of the day ends at sunset, in the ancient Jewish way of keeping track of time. Astronomers refer to the method of keeping track of time by observation of the sun's position in the sky as "apparent solar time," sometimes called "solar time" or "sun time."[22] The times of day given by Blessed Anne Catherine are according to sun time, since the modern time-zone standard had not yet been invented during her lifetime.[23]

The Hour of the Scourging

"Then he released Barabbas to them. But Jesus, having been scourged, he handed over to them, so that he would be crucified." (Mt 27:26).

"The dreadful scourging had been continued without intermission for three quarters of an hour...."[24] Blessed Anne Catherine Emmerich tells us, based on her visions from God, that the scourging of Jesus lasted about 45 minutes. "It was not more than nine o'clock a.m. when the scouring terminated."[25] Her statement that the scourging ended about 9 a.m. agrees with Sacred Scripture (as explained below). So the scourging began roughly a quarter after 8 a.m.

The Hour of the Crucifixion

"Then Pilate, wishing to satisfy the people, released Barabbas to them, and he delivered Jesus, having severely scourged him, to be crucified." (Mk 15:15).

"Now it was the third hour. And they crucified him." (Mk 15:25).

Now, the vast majority of Jews and Romans at that time had no time-keeping devices to keep track of the hours, exact to the minute, as we do.[26] However, certain hours of the daytime could be determined more easily than others. The first hour began at sunrise, a time easily determined by observation. The sixth hour was the midpoint between sunrise and sunset, when the sun reaches its highest point—also easily determined by observation. The third hour was not a certain number of minutes after sunrise, for there was no way for the ordinary person to keep count of the minutes. Rather, the third hour was the approximate midpoint between sunrise and the sixth hour (noon sun time). Thus, the third hour referred to by Sacred Scripture was the midpoint between sunrise and noon, or mid-morning. The third hour by sun time would be called 9:00 a.m.[27]

The Gospel of Mark counts the Crucifixion as having begun immediately after the scourging, when Pilate delivered Jesus to be crucified, at the third hour. Pilate intended to scourge Jesus, even if he did not decide to hand Him over to be crucified (Lk 23:16, 22). That is why Sacred Scripture, in the Gospel of Mark, counts the Crucifixion as beginning at the third hour, after the scourging. Sacred Scripture says that Jesus was crucified at the third hour, referring to the whole process of crucifixion, including when Jesus was carrying His Cross.

"Now it was the preparation day of the Passover, about the sixth hour." (Jn 19:14).

The Gospel of John counts the Crucifixion as beginning at about the sixth hour because Jesus was on the Cross from about the sixth hour to the ninth hour (Mt 27:45-50; Mk 15:33-37; Lk 23:44-46).[28] The Gospel of Mark counts the whole process of Crucifixion, including when Jesus was crowned with thorns and when Jesus was carrying His Cross. But the Gospel of John counts only the hours when Jesus was actually on the Cross, that is, the Crucifixion itself. These hours were the worst of the worst of Jesus' suffering.[29] Thus there is no contradiction between the Gospels of Mark and John as to when Jesus was crucified.

The Nailing to the Cross

"It was about a quarter past twelve when Jesus was crucified; and at the moment the cross was lifted up, the Temple resounded with the blast of trumpets, which were always blown to announce the sacrifice of the Paschal Lamb."[30]

Blessed Anne Catherine Emmerich gives the time that Jesus was crucified as several minutes after noon. She states this after describing the nailing of Jesus to the Cross, but before describing the raising of the Cross. She says "about a quarter past twelve" to indicate that this is not an exact time.

Some people assume that important events in the lives of Jesus and Mary must have happened exactly on the hour (and by our way of counting the hours). But it is not necessary to God's plan that everything happen exactly on the hour. The Gospel of John places the Crucifixion of Jesus at "about the sixth hour." Even Sacred Scripture does not reveal the exact time to the minute of various important events in the life of Christ. The phrase "about the sixth hour" does not mean exactly at noon.

The nailing of Jesus to the Cross, as is clear from Blessed Anne Catherine's description, was time-consuming and extraordinarily painful.[31] It may have taken anywhere from 15 to 45 minutes to complete the whole process of nailing Jesus to the Cross. Then, about a quarter past noon, the Cross, with Jesus on it, was raised up.

Jesus was first nailed to the Cross, then the Cross was raised up. So the length of time that Jesus was on the Cross, if we include the time which passed as Jesus was being nailed to the Cross, was likely between 3 hours and 3½ hours. The nailing to the Cross began sometime between 11:30 a.m. and noon (sun time).[32]

The Three Hours of Darkness

"And when the sixth hour arrived, a darkness occurred over the entire earth, until the ninth hour." (Mk 15:33).

The three hours of darkness began about the sixth hour (noon sun time) and ended about the ninth hour (3 p.m. sun time).[33] From about noon until 3 p.m. there was darkness over the whole land. This was not caused by a natural event, such as an eclipse. Eclipses of the sun last only for a few minutes, not for 3 hours.[34] Also, Jesus was crucified at the beginning of Passover, about the time when the moon is full. Eclipses of the sun only occur about the time of the new moon. When the moon is full, it is on the opposite side of the earth from the sun and cannot pass between the earth and the sun to cause a solar eclipse.

The three hours of darkness when Jesus was on the Cross was not an act of nature, it was a supernatural act of God. This event was foreshadowed by the three days of darkness which occurred when God, through Moses, freed the Israelites from slavery in Egypt. God gave the Egyptians three days of darkness as one of many afflictions which caused the Egyptians to let the Israelites go free (Ex 10:21-23).

The three days of darkness marked the end of the slavery of God's people in Egypt. The suffering and death of Jesus on the Cross frees us from the slavery of sin. The three hours of darkness, when Jesus was on the Cross, marked the end of our slavery to sin and the beginning of our freedom as the people of God.

After describing words exchanged between Jesus and the good thief (while they were both on their crosses), the Gospel of Luke tells us: "Now it was nearly the sixth hour, and a darkness occurred over the entire earth, until the ninth hour." (Lk 23:44). God covered the entire earth in darkness to mark the time of Jesus' greatest suffering. And so, Jesus was on the Cross for about three hours.

Some commentators have suggested that the 3 hours of darkness was caused by a dust storm, not by a supernatural act of God. Which is more likely, that God brought about a natural event, such as a dust storm, to darken the sky when Jesus was on the Cross, or that God darkened the sun by a supernatural act, when Jesus was on the Cross as a sign to the whole world?

When God interacts with this world, He is not limited to guiding natural events, He can also act beyond the limits of nature. Some people argue for a natural explanation for nearly every event described in the Bible. God does guide natural events with His Providence, but God also intervenes more directly in human events, through miraculous acts. Every faithful Christian believes in such miraculous interventions, for example, in the Virgin Conception of Jesus Christ, His Resurrection from the dead, and His Ascension to Heaven. A natural explanation cannot be found for every event described in the Bible. So then, at the time of the very death of God's only Son Jesus Christ, God darkened the whole land, or the whole earth, by miraculous means, and not merely by guiding natural events.

The Hour of Jesus Christ's Death

"And at the ninth hour, Jesus cried out with a loud voice, saying, 'Eloi, Eloi, lamma sabacthani?' which means, 'My God, My God, why have you forsaken me?'.... Then Jesus, having emitted a loud cry, expired."
(Mk 15:34.37).

The ninth hour is about 3:00 p.m. sun time.[35] The ninth hour is also the midpoint between the sixth hour, when the sun is at its highest point in the sky, and sunset. The ninth hour is the middle of the afternoon.

Blessed Anne Catherine Emmerich tell us, based on visions she received from God, "It was about three o'clock when Jesus expired."[36] And Saint Faustina Kowalska refers to the three o'clock hour as the hour of great Mercy, because it was at that hour that Jesus died for our salvation.[37] God has revealed the hour of Jesus' death, through Sacred Scripture and the saints, because God wants us to know at what time of day Jesus died. Through Saint Faustina Kowalska, Jesus asked us to remember His Passion and death at 3 o'clock every day.[38]

The Gospel of Mark tells us that at the ninth hour Jesus cried out to God. Next, someone ran to get a sponge soaked with vinegar, placed it on a reed, and offered it to Jesus. Then Jesus cried out to God again and died (Mk 15:34-37). Sacred Scripture does not say that Jesus died at exactly the ninth hour, but rather, that at the ninth hour Jesus cried out to God, then a few more things happened, and then Jesus died.

We do not know the exact time to the minute of the death of Jesus Christ. However, Sacred Scripture indicates that Jesus died at about 3 o'clock in the afternoon. Jesus died about 3 p.m. (sun time) on a Friday, on the preparation day of Passover (the 14th of Nisan).[39]

The Length of the Passion of Jesus Christ

The Passion of Jesus Christ ended with His death on the Cross for our salvation at about 3 p.m. on Friday, Nisan 14. Perhaps we should mark the beginning of the Passion of Jesus Christ at His agony in the garden of Gethsemane on the previous evening. His suffering at that time was most intense, as shown by the words of Sacred Scripture. "And he took Peter, and James, and John with him. And he began to be afraid and wearied. And he said to them: 'My soul is sorrowful, even unto death. Remain here and be vigilant.' " (Mk 14:33-34). Blessed Anne Catherine describes the great suffering of Christ in the garden in detail.[40] Christ must have suffered at the Last Supper, when He spoke of Judas Iscariot's betrayal (Mk 14:17-21), and again when He spoke of the Apostles falling away and of Peter's denial (Mk 14:27-31). However, there were other sufferings of this kind at other times in Christ's Ministry. I would count the beginning of the Passion from the intense sufferings of Jesus when he was at prayer in the garden of Gethsemane.

"It was about nine o'clock when Jesus reached Gethsemani with his disciples. The moon had risen, and already gave light in the sky, although the earth was still dark."[41] According to Blessed Anne Catherine, the agony of Jesus in the garden began about 9 p.m. She obviously counts the Passion of Jesus Christ as beginning at that time, since she later remarks that the Passion of Christ lasted about 18 hours. She describes a talk that the Apostle Saint Peter gave sometime after the Resurrection, but before the Ascension. "He told them, as I still remember, that Jesus, during His Passion of eighteen hours, had borne insult and outrage from the whole world."[42] Here Blessed Anne Catherine is saying that Peter counted the length of Christ's Passion as 18 hours. Since Christ died about 3 p.m., the 18 hours would be counted from about 9 p.m. of the previous evening, the time that Christ entered the garden of Gethsemane. This length of time is approximate.

The Opening of the Side of Christ

"Therefore, the soldiers approached, and, indeed, they broke the legs of the first one, and of the other who was crucified with him. But after they had approached Jesus, when they saw that he was already dead, they did not break his legs. Instead, one of the soldiers opened his side with a lance, and immediately there went out blood and water." (Jn 19:32-34).

The soldiers were breaking the legs of those who had been crucified, so that they would die more quickly (Jn 19:31). But Jesus was already dead, so they did not break His legs. The piercing of the side of Jesus occurred after His death, sometime after 3 p.m. sun time.

According to Blessed Anne Catherine Emmerich, the soldier who pierced the side of Christ with his spear was named Cassius. He was inspired by the grace of God to pierce the side of Christ.

"But Cassius...was suddenly illuminated by grace, and being quite overcome at the sight of the conduct of the soldiers, and the deep sorrow of the holy women, determined to relieve their anxiety by proving beyond dispute that Jesus was really dead. The kindness of his heart prompted him, but unconsciously to himself he fulfilled a prophecy."[43]

The soldiers who had broken the legs of the others were still uncertain whether Jesus was really dead. The holy women who were at the foot of the Cross were afraid that the soldiers might do violence to the dead body of Christ on the Cross. So Cassius proved that Jesus was really dead by piercing His side with his spear. But God had a greater plan, unknown at that time to Cassius, to have the blood and water flow from the side of Christ, in fulfillment of Sacred Scripture (Jn 19:36-37), as the symbol and source of the Sacramental life of the Church. The suffering and death of Christ, the blood and water from the side of Christ, is the fountain of the seven Sacraments of Christ.

"He seized his lance and rode quickly up to the mound on which the Cross was planted, stopped just between the cross of the good thief and that of our Lord, and taking his lance in both hands, thrust it so completely into the right side of Jesus that the point went through the heart, and appeared on the left side."[44]

The soldiers broke the legs of the others who were crucified so that the bodies would not remain on the crosses when the Sabbath and the first holy day of Passover began that same Friday evening at sunset. So the piercing of Christ's side must have occurred between about 3 p.m. sun time and sunset. Christ's body had to be taken down from the cross, washed and prepared for buried with spices, wrapped in linen cloths and placed in a tomb, all before the Sabbath and Passover began at sunset that day (cf. Jn 19:39-42). There had to be sufficient time after the piercing of Christ's side, but before sunset, to accomplish all of these tasks.

Sunset is by definition 6:00 p.m. sun time, and on that day, April 7, sunset also happened to coincide with 18:00 hours or 6 p.m. by Jerusalem Standard Time.[45] Sunset on that day was also about 6 hours and 19 minutes after the sixth hour (apparent solar noon). There were about 3 hours and 9 minutes between the sixth hour and the ninth hour, and the same length of time between the ninth hour and sunset.

The piercing of Christ's side occurred between 3 p.m. and 6 p.m., but closer to 3 p.m., since there was so much to do afterwards. According to Blessed Anne Catherine, the piercing of Christ's side and the surrounding events, occurred sometime before 4 p.m. "All these events took place near the Cross, at a little before four o'clock, during the time that Joseph of Arimathea and Nicodemus were gathering together the articles necessary for burial of Jesus."[46]

The Year of the Crucifixion of Jesus Christ

The Catholic Church has no official teaching telling us in which year Christ died and rose from the dead. And, as far as I know, no Christian denomination has an official teaching on the year of the Crucifixion. I believe that the year can be determined, based on information given in Sacred Scripture, along with additional information from other, non-canonical sources. The conclusion as to which year saw the Crucifixion and Resurrection of Christ is not a part of essential Christian teaching, and so, does not have the same certitude as the articles of faith. I am absolutely certain that Jesus Christ died for our salvation, but I am less certain as to when He died for us. Even so, as far as the certainty of mere human knowledge (as opposed to Divine Revelation) can go, I am convinced of my conclusion as to the year of the Crucifixion of Jesus, and the years of other important events.

Below you will find two separate lines of reasoning, each of which can stand on its own without the other, and each of which arrives at the same conclusion as to the year of the Crucifixion. Both depend, in part, on the words of God's Sacred Infallible Scripture. One line of reasoning also depends on the words of Blessed Anne Catherine Emmerich. The other argument depends on a new chronology for the reigns of various Roman emperors and rulers (presented in detail in chapters 12, 13, and 14). Either line of reasoning can stand on its own, without any reference to the other, except of course that both make use of Sacred Scripture.

The Length of the Ministry of Jesus Christ

There is no plain statement in the Gospels as to the length of Jesus' Ministry. However, there are some clear indications in Sacred Scripture that His Ministry lasted about 3½ years.

"Then he said: 'Amen I say to you, that no prophet is accepted in his own country. In truth, I say to you, there were many widows in the days of Elijah in Israel, when the heavens were closed for three years and six months, when a great famine had occurred throughout the entire land. And to none of these was Elijah sent, except to Zarephath of Sidon, to a woman who was a widow.' " (Lk 4:24-26; cf. James 5:17-18; 1 Kings 17).

Jesus was teaching in a synagogue in his own country, in Nazareth, when He said these words (Lk 4:16). He was not only comparing Himself to the prophet Elijah, but was also comparing His Ministry to the time of 3½ years of famine during Elijah's ministry. Jesus came to Israel in a time of spiritual famine, when the people were in great need of true spiritual food; and He fed them with His teaching and His life. Elijah's ministry during the time of drought and famine was a foreshadowing of Jesus' Ministry.

In this passage from the Old Testament, Elijah refers to the drought as lasting three years (1 Kings 17:1). Jesus did not have to mention any length of time when comparing His Ministry to the ministry of Elijah during the drought. But Jesus mentions the length of time and gives us the more specific information that the full length of the drought was 3½ years for a reason, because the length of this drought matches the length of His Ministry, which was about 3½ years.[47]

"He spoke another parable to them: 'The kingdom of heaven is like leaven, which a woman took and hid in three measures of fine wheat flour, until it was entirely leavened.' " (Mt 13:33).

The leaven represents the teaching of Christ Jesus (cf. Mt 16:12), and the three measures of meal represents the three years of the Ministry of Jesus. These three years were the beginning of the establishment of the kingdom of heaven on earth, the beginning of the Christian Church. This parable reflects the understanding of Jesus that His Ministry would last about 3 years.

"And he also told this parable: 'A certain man had a fig tree, which was planted in his vineyard. And he came seeking fruit on it, but found none. Then he said to the cultivator of the vineyard: "Behold, for these three years I came seeking fruit on this fig tree, and I have found none. Therefore, cut it down. For why should it even occupy the land?" ' " (Lk 13:6-7).

The three years that the fruit tree stood without bearing fruit represent the three years of Jesus' Ministry. Many rejected Jesus during His Ministry, many turned away and refused to accept Him (cf. Jn 1:10). Part way into the fourth year of His Ministry, Jesus died for us on the Cross, and the fruit of His teaching and His Ministry finally bore fruit in the establishment of the Christian Church (cf. Jn 12:24). If Christ had not suffered and died, would His Ministry still have born fruit? If Christ taught for three years but did not die for us, would the Christian Church even exist? Again, the length of the Ministry of Jesus is revealed in His teaching, in the form of a parable.

"And the woman fled into solitude, where a place was being held ready by God, so that they might pasture her in that place for one thousand two hundred and sixty days." (Rev 12:6).

The great suffering of the Church described in the book of Revelation, and predicted by the prophets of Sacred Scripture, will last about 3½ years (cf. Rev 11:3; 13:5; Dan 7:25; 9:7; 12:7, 11, 12). These 3½ years of trials for the Church have the same length as the Ministry of Jesus. Just as Jesus nourished the nascent Church for the 3½ years of His Ministry, so also will Jesus again nourish the Church, for the same length of time, during the Church's time of great suffering.[48]

Blessed Anne Catherine Emmerich also confirms that the Ministry of Jesus lasted about 3½ years. She places the Baptism of Jesus by John in the autumn, in early

October.[49] All four Gospels mark the Baptism of Jesus by John as the beginning of Jesus' Ministry (e.g. Lk 3:21-23). Jesus died and rose from the dead at the time of the Passover, which is in the spring. So, the total length of Jesus' Ministry, ending with His Crucifixion, Resurrection, and Ascension in the springtime, could not be a whole number of years, but must include a half year.

Also, Blessed Anne Catherine relates how Jesus, at the beginning of His Ministry, knew that His Crucifixion would occur 3½ years from that time.[50] Shortly after Jesus was baptized by John in the Jordan river, Jesus was speaking to some people who lived in that area. They complemented Jesus on His appearance. "Jesus remarked that, three and a half years hence, they would see no beauty in Him, they would not even recognize Him so disfigured would He be."[51] Jesus was referring to His Crucifixion. This conversation occurred soon after Jesus was baptized, that is, soon after His Ministry began.

The Ministries of John the Baptist and Jesus

"And he will convert many of the sons of Israel to the Lord their God. And he will go before him with the spirit and power of Elijah, so that he may turn the hearts of the fathers to the sons, and the incredulous to the prudence of the just, so as to prepare for the Lord a completed people."" (Lk 1:16-17; cf. Is 40:3).

"As it has been written by the prophet Isaiah: 'Behold, I send my Angel before your face, who shall prepare your way before you. The voice of one crying out in the desert: Prepare the way of the Lord; make straight his paths.' " (Mk 1:2-3).

How much time passed between the beginning of the ministry of John the Baptist and the beginning of the Ministry of Jesus Christ? There is no plain statement in Sacred Scripture which explicitly answers this question. However, there are some indications in Sacred Scripture that this length of time was relatively brief.

Matthew's Gospel begins its description of John's ministry at Mt 3:1, and first mentions Christ's Baptism at Mt 3:13. Only 12 verses are used to describe John's ministry before Christ's Baptism. In the Gospel of Mark, only 7 verses are given to this same period of time. John's ministry begins at Mk 1:2, and the Baptism of Jesus begins at Mk 1:9. The Gospel of John first mentions the Baptism of Jesus in the past tense, at Jn 1:32-34. The number of verses which refer to John before this point are few: Jn 1:6-8, 15, 19-31 (a total of 17 verses). Luke's Gospel gives the greatest number of verses, 20, to this length of time, from Lk 3:1 to 3:20. None of the Gospel writers devotes even a whole chapter to the space of time from the start of John's ministry to the start of Jesus' Ministry. In this way, Sacred Scripture indicates that this length of time was relatively brief.

Luke's Gospel gives us some further indication of the specific length of the time between the beginning of John's ministry and the beginning of Christ's Ministry. The Gospel of Luke was not merely written by Luke; all of Sacred Scripture was first and foremost written by God. Thus God can explain to us, through the Gospel of Luke, truths which even Luke did not understand when he wrote his Gospel. And, unlike any other writer, God can speak to us though events, which were guided and preordained by God's Providence and Wisdom. The arrangement of the events themselves, as well as the words which describe those events, contain God's message to us.

Zechariah and Elizabeth were childless; Elizabeth was called "barren" by some people (Lk 1:36). They were able to conceive a child only by the intervention of God, who sent an angel to announce this to Zechariah. Therefore it was God who decided when John the Baptist would be conceived and born.

Mary of Nazareth was a virgin. She was betrothed to a man named Joseph (Lk 1:27). But when the angel Gabriel told Mary that she would bear a son, she did not assume that her husband Joseph would be the father; instead she asks, " 'How shall this be done, since I do not know man?' " (Lk 1:34). The Virgin Mary had no husband in the usual sense of the word, because she had no intention of giving up her virginity. Thus the Virgin Mary had no plans to bear any children—until God revealed His plan to her through the angel Gabriel. Mary did not choose when the Incarnation would occur, she merely accepted God's plan. God chose the timing of the Virgin Conception of Jesus Christ.

God could have had John the Baptist be conceived and born at a later or earlier time. John could have been years older, or years younger, and still completed the task of his ministry—to prepare the way of the Lord. But God chose to have the conception and birth of John precede the Holy Conception and Birth of Jesus by between 5 and 6 months (for details, see chapter 5).

The Gospel of Luke repeatedly refers to the length of time between John's conception and the Incarnation of Christ. Sacred Scripture reveals that after Elizabeth conceived, "she hid herself for five months" (Lk 1:24) and then the angel Gabriel announced Christ's Virgin Conception to Mary (Lk 1:26). The words of the angel Gabriel reveal the timing between John's conception and Jesus' Incarnation: "And this is the sixth month for her who is called barren." (Lk 1:36). The angel Gabriel's words mean that it is sometime during the sixth month, not that six full months had been completed. So the length of time from John's conception to Jesus' conception was more than 5 months and less than 6 months, i.e., 5 months plus some number of days.

Sacred Scripture, in the words of the angel speaking to Zechariah, says that John the Baptist would "go before" Jesus to prepare for his arrival (Lk 1:17). Again, in the Gospel of Mark, God tells us that John would prepare the way for Jesus (Mk 1:2). The ministry of John the Baptist prepared the way for the Ministry of Jesus Christ. John went before Jesus as His messenger and herald.

God wanted John the Baptist to "go before" Jesus, not only in his ministry, but also even from the very beginning of John's life, because John's entire life was dedicated to preparing for Christ Jesus. Sacred Scripture emphasizes that John's conception occurred between 5 and 6 months before the Incarnation because this timing is a part of John's call to "go before" Jesus Christ to prepare His way. John the Baptist was conceived and born for that very purpose, to go before Christ, and so it was fitting that, even in his conception and birth, John prepared the way for Christ Jesus.

God chose to place noticeable emphasis in Luke's Gospel on the length of time between John's conception and the Holy Conception of Christ. Perhaps the reason for this emphasis is that the length of time between John's conception and the Incarnation foreshadows the length of time between the start of John's ministry and the start of Christ's Ministry. The order and timing of these events was chosen by God and is full of meaning. Sacred Scripture tells us that the conception of John the Baptist preceded the Holy Conception of Jesus Christ by just over 5 months. This indicates that the ministry of John the Baptist also preceded the Ministry of Jesus Christ by about the same length of time, about 5 to 6 months. (The words of Blessed Anne Catherine also support the idea that the Baptism of Jesus occurred only a few months after John began his ministry; see chapter 7 for more on this point.)

The Ministry of Jesus lasted about 3½ years and Jesus died at Passover, which is in the springtime. So, the Ministry of Jesus must have begun in the autumn, along with His baptism by John (as Blessed Anne Catherine also says).[52] If John the Baptist's ministry began about 5 or 6 months before Jesus' Ministry, then John's ministry must have begun in the springtime of that same year. The Gospel of Luke reveals that the ministry of John the Baptist began: "Then, in the fifteenth year of the reign of Tiberius Caesar...." (Lk 3:1). Therefore, the Ministry of Jesus Christ also began later that same calendar year.

Christ's Age at His Death

The age of Jesus Christ at His Crucifixion can be determined from Sacred Scripture, though not precisely. The Gospel of Luke reveals that Jesus was about 30 years old when He began His Ministry (Lk 3:23). (More on this point is found in chapter 7 of this book.) And, as stated above, there are several clear indications in Sacred Scripture that Christ's Ministry lasted about 3½ years. Therefore, according to Sacred Scripture, Jesus was approximately 33 years old when He died and rose from the dead.

The exact age of Christ Jesus on the day of His Crucifixion was explained to Blessed Anne Catherine Emmerich in a vision she received from God. "Christ reached the age of thirty-three years and three times six weeks. I say three times *six*, because that figure was in that moment shown to me three times one after the other."[53] She interprets her vision to mean that Jesus died when He was 33 years and 18 weeks old. However, this is not the correct interpretation of the vision.

God showed Blessed Anne Catherine the numbers 33 and 6, because Jesus was 33 years and 6 weeks old at the time of His death. Her error in interpreting the vision comes from her expectation that the age of Jesus Christ would be calculated from His birth to His death. Instead, the true age of Jesus Christ must be determined beginning with His Holy Conception, the Incarnation of God. When we think about the age of Jesus Christ, we cannot forget about the nine months that Jesus was in the womb of the Virgin Mary. Human life begins at conception. Christ's human life began at the Incarnation.

Also, Blessed Anne Catherine was shown her vision of the length of the life of Jesus Christ during the time that God was giving her visions of the Incarnation, not the birth, of Christ. "That night, as I contemplated the Mystery of the Incarnation, I was taught many things."[54] God gave Blessed Anne Catherine the vision of numbers 33 and 6 at that time, because the age of Jesus is counted from the first moment of His life as a human being, as God made man, at the Incarnation. Therefore, the age of Jesus Christ at the time of His death was 33 years and 6 weeks, but this is counted from His conception, not His birth.[55]

Blessed Anne Catherine herself admitted that she sometimes misunderstood the visions which God gave to her. For example, she describes a vision about the Virgin Mary, which she had once thought was a vision of the Annunciation, but later realized was a vision of an earlier event. "This was not the Annunciation, for I saw that happen later in Nazareth. I must, however, once have thought that I saw the appearance of an angel here too, for in my youth I often confused this vision with the Annunciation and thought that I saw the latter happening in the Temple."[56]

Counting from the Incarnation then, Jesus Christ was 33 years and 6 weeks old on the day of the Crucifixion. His Ministry lasted about 3½ years. Therefore, counting from conception, Jesus was just over 29½ years old, was closer to 30 years of age than to 29, and was in His 30th year of life, at the beginning of His Ministry.

The Day and Month of the Crucifixion

Sacred Scripture teaches that Jesus Christ was crucified on a Friday, the 14th of Nisan, (the day on which Passover begins at sunset). Blessed Anne Catherine Emmerich's visions from God tell us that the length of Christ's life, from His Holy Conception to His Crucifixion, was 33 years and six weeks. We can therefore determine the day of the month on which Jesus died, if we know the day and month of His Holy Conception.

"[On March 25th, 1821, Sister Emmerich said:] Last night I saw the Annunciation as a Feast of the Church, and was once more definitely informed that at this moment the Blessed Virgin had already been with child for four weeks. This was expressly told me because I had already seen the Annunciation on the 25th of February, but had rejected the vision and had not related it."[57]

Blessed Anne Catherine often received visions on the actual day of the month that the event in the vision occurred. She also received visions of the same events on the day of the month that the Church celebrates the event. Thus she received the vision of the Annunciation on February 25, the actual day and month of the Annunciation, as well as on March 25, the date of the liturgical celebration of the Annunciation.

Jesus Christ was conceived by the power of the Holy Spirit in the womb of the Virgin Mary on February 25. This holy event, the Incarnation of Jesus Christ, occurred about midnight, at the start of February 25.[58] Jesus completed His 33rd full year of life (from His Holy Conception) at midnight between the 24th and the 25th of February. In our culture today, we mark the anniversary of our births as if it were the completion of another year of life, but in truth, it is the anniversary of one's conception which marks the completion of each year of life.

If we count forward 6 weeks (42 days) in the calendar from the day of the Incarnation, we arrive at April 7 as the day of Christ's death.[59] This date of April 7, for the death of Christ Jesus is exactly 33 years and 6 weeks from the date of His Holy Conception, in agreement with the vision given to Blessed Anne Catherine Emmerich. February 25 is counted as the 1st day of the 6 weeks because Jesus was conceived about midnight at the very beginning of the 25th of the month. So then, February 25 of each year is the first day of each new year of Jesus' human life.

The date of April 7 for the Crucifixion is also supported by a vision Blessed Anne Catherine had about the number of days (not counting the years) from the Ascension of Christ to the death of the Virgin Mary. The number of days was revealed to her as 13 days plus two full months. Adding 13 days to the date of Christ's Ascension only brings one to the end of a month, (so that two whole months could then be added), if Christ died on April 7. His Ascension to Heaven took place then on May 18, on the 40th day from His Resurrection, inclusive. Adding 13 days to May 18 brings us to the end of May (see chapter 10).

An Unlucky Day

Nikos Kokkinos points out that April 7 was considered an unlucky day by the Romans, particularly for court judgments. The Romans avoided certain types of court judgments on that day. He counts this as evidence against a date of April 7 for the Crucifixion.[60]

On the contrary, I must ask why the Romans avoided court judgments on that one day of the year. The most likely answer is that on that day, April 7, at some point in Roman history, a court judgment was made by the Roman government which was later considered to be a serious error.

A similar situation occurred after the death of Julius Caesar. The Roman Senate voted that the day on which Julius Caesar was killed, the Ides of March, "be called the Day of Parricide, and that a meeting of the senate should never be called on that day."[61] An event occurred on March 15 in the Roman Senate, which was considered to be a serious error (parricide refers to killing one's father), and so the Senate decided never again to hold a meeting on that day.

Now, we do not know for certain which event led to the April 7 admonition. One plausible explanation, though, is that Jesus Christ was condemned to death on April 7 by a Roman government official, Pontius Pilate. As the Christian faith spread throughout the Roman empire, more and more Roman citizens (and some government officials) accepted the faith. The day of the Crucifixion was then seen in retrospect as an unlucky day for Roman court judgments, since it was on that day that the Romans gave a court judgment against their Savior Jesus Christ. Of course, a negative version of this explanation is also possible. Perhaps those Romans who saw the Christians as trouble for the Roman way of life regretted the Crucifixion of Christ only because it was the starting point of Christianity. In either case, the outcome would be that the Romans decided never again to hold a similar type of court session on that day.

The Julian and Gregorian Calendars

The calendar system currently used by Catholics and most Christians in the West, and which is in general use in many countries (including the United States), is called the Gregorian calendar. This calendar places the Spring Equinox, when the length of the daytime is about the same as the length of the nighttime, on or about March 20 GMT (Greenwich Mean Time).

The Gregorian calendar has 365 days in a year, except in leap year, when an extra day (February 29) is added. Leap years typically occur every four years, in any year which is evenly divisible by 4, except in centennial years, (years evenly divisible by 100). A centennial year is only a leap years if it is evenly divisible by 400. So, the year 1900 is not a leap year, but the year 2000 is a leap year.

The Gregorian calendar is a revised version of the Julian calendar, an older calendar system. The Julian calendar was created under the direction of Julius Caesar and was used throughout the Roman empire. Several centuries after the death of Jesus Christ, when Christianity became the dominant religion, the terms A.D. and B.C. were added to the Julian calendar system.

The Julian calendar is nearly the same as the Gregorian calendar, except that every four years is a leap year without exception. This leads to a year which is, on average, slightly longer than the true solar year (the time it takes the earth to revolve around the sun). The result is that the Julian calendar adds 3 days too many every 400 years, which causes the date of the Spring Equinox to slowly recede through the calendar. The Julian calendar is still used today, primarily by Orthodox Christians.

At the time of Christ's life, the Spring Equinox fell on March 22 or 23, by the Julian calendar. Currently, in the Julian calendar, the Spring Equinox falls on March 7 or March 8 GMT. The date given to the Spring Equinox moves approximately 3 days earlier every 400 years in the Julian calendar. By the 1500's the date of the Spring Equinox had shifted to March 11.

To correct this problem, in 1582, Pope Gregory XIII issued a papal bull which removed ten days from the calendar, placing the Spring Equinox of 1583 at March 21. He also instituted the current formula for determining leap years, which has 3 fewer leap years every 400 years. This change effectively keeps the Spring Equinox on March 20 in most years, even though in 1583 the Spring Equinox happened to fall early on March 21. This new calendar system, which is only a slightly modified version of the Julian calendar, was then called the Gregorian calendar. The Gregorian calendar first came into use in October of 1582. Currently, the Gregorian calendar is 13 days ahead of the Julian calendar.

Blessed Anne Catherine Emmerich lived during the late 1700's and early 1800's. The Gregorian calendar was in use at that time. However, the Julian calendar, not the Gregorian calendar, was in use during the time of Christ's life. So then, are the dates which God revealed to Blessed Anne Catherine in her visions dates from the Julian or Gregorian calendar?

There are a couple of reasons for believing that the dates given by Blessed Anne Catherine Emmerich refer to the Julian calendar. First, the Julian calendar was in use at the time of Christ's life. The Julian calendar was used by the Roman empire, which had conquered and was occupying Israel during the Ministry of Jesus. The Gregorian calendar was not in use anywhere until A.D. 1582.

Second, Blessed Anne Catherine, in her visions from God, was shown numbers referring to dates as Roman numerals (I, II, III, IV, V, etc.), not in Arabic numerals (0, 1, 2, 3, 4, 5, etc.). Yet she understood Arabic numerals well and Roman numerals poorly.[62] "(It is remarkable that Catherine Emmerich was not shown numbers with our ordinary Arabic figures, with which she was familiar, but never saw anything but Roman figures in her visions.)"[63] God showed Blessed Anne Catherine these numbers as Roman numerals because the numbers refer to dates in the Roman (Julian) calendar, not the modern Gregorian calendar.

Three Requirements for the Year

Jesus Christ was crucified on April 7, a Friday, which was also Nisan 14 in the Jewish calendar. Nisan 14 does not always fall on a Friday, as on the day of Christ's death.

Much less often does the date of April 7 in the Christian calendar coincide with Nisan 14 in the Jewish calendar. Rarely is the same day a Friday and Nisan 14 and April 7. Any proposed year for the Crucifixion must meet these three conditions.

Passover does not always begin on a Friday at sunset. The 14th of Nisan can fall on other days of the week, such as Monday or Wednesday. There are quite a few years from A.D. 1 to A.D. 50 when Passover fell on a Friday. There is some uncertainty as to how the start of Passover in the ancient Jewish calendar was determined. (For details, see chapter 17.) In any case, there are only two possible years when Passover could have fallen on a Friday and Nisan 14 and April 7 — A.D. 19 and A.D. 30 (See Appendix I, Chart 1).[64]

Thus the dates of April 7, A.D. 19, and April 7, A.D. 30, agree with the three conditions for the date of Christ's death revealed by Sacred Scripture and Blessed Anne Catherine Emmerich. These are the two possible dates for the Crucifixion of Jesus Christ which must be considered based on Sacred Scripture and the visions of Blessed Anne Catherine. (For details on the probability that Passover began on April 7 in A.D. 19, or on April 7 in 30 A.D., see chapter 17.)

First Conclusion

The words of Sacred Scripture, together with the visions of Blessed Anne Catherine, lead us to the conclusion that Jesus was about 33 years old at the time of His Crucifixion. More specifically, Jesus completed 33 years and 6 weeks of life from His Incarnation to His Crucifixion, (counting from His Birth it would be 32 years and 19 weeks). If the Crucifixion of Jesus Christ occurred in A.D. 19, then the Incarnation would have occurred 33 years earlier, in 15 B.C. But if the Crucifixion of Jesus Christ occurred in A.D. 30, then the Incarnation would have occurred 33 years earlier, in 4 B.C. (By comparison, a date of A.D. 33 for the Crucifixion would place the Incarnation and Birth of Jesus in 1 B.C., a year which in no way fits the information on the Birth of Christ presented later this book.)

As chapter 4 relates in detail, the chronological information given by Blessed Anne Catherine confirms the year 15 B.C. as the year of Christ's Birth. This supports the conclusion that the Crucifixion and Resurrection of Jesus Christ occurred in A.D. 19.

A Variation on the First Conclusion

The conclusion that Christ was crucified in A.D. 19 does not necessarily depend on the idea that Christ died on April 7, exactly 6 weeks after the date Blessed Anne Catherine gives for the Incarnation (Feb. 25). We could consider every year within a range of dates approximately 33 years after the year of Christ's Incarnation and Birth (15 B.C.). Then, we can choose between the years in that range based on which years had a Nisan 14 coinciding with a Friday.

The only year which fits the information given by Blessed Anne Catherine Emmerich for the year of Christ's Birth is 15 B.C. (see chapter 4). If Christ was about 30 years old when He began His Ministry, and His Ministry lasted about 3½ years, then the Crucifixion occurred about 33 years after the year of the Incarnation and Birth of Christ. Counting forward 33 years from 15 B.C. brings us to A.D. 19. A reasonable range of dates would be plus or minus 2 years, which allows for one year error in either direction for both the age of Christ and the length of His Ministry. The range of dates is then A.D. 17 to A.D. 21, inclusive.

The Jewish calendar adds a leap year, containing 13 months rather than the usual 12 months, every 2 or 3 years, to prevent the Passover and the month of Nisan from occurring too early in the year (i.e. too long before the Spring Equinox). In ancient times, the decision to add a leap year (which adds the 13th month of AdarII just prior to Nisan) was also based partly on whether or not the crops were ready to be harvested and presented to God as the first fruits of the field.[65] In a typical year, the crops would be ready as early as mid to late March. However, if the weather was unfavorable, being too dry or too cold, and the Passover that year fell in mid to late March, then the crops would not be ready and a leap year would be declared (adding the month AdarII before Nisan). The addition of the leap month of AdarII would then delay the start of Nisan by one lunar month. In some cases, a delay of this kind in the start of the month of Nisan would affect whether or not Nisan 14 will coincide with a Friday.

In A.D. 21 and A.D. 18, Nisan 14 could not have fallen on a Friday and the date for Passover is late enough to preclude a delay due to the addition of a leap year. In A.D. 17, Nisan 14 would not have fallen on a Friday, unless the Passover and the month of Nisan were delayed due to immaturity of the crops and the start of the month of Nisan was determined by observation, rather than calculation (see Appendix I, Chart 1). This book, however, concludes that calculation, not observation, was used to determine the calendar months during this time period (see chapter 17). In A.D. 20, the Passover would have fallen on a Friday, only if the Passover was not delayed and the months were determined by observation, or, if the Passover was delayed due to immaturity of the crops. Thus, even if we place the Crucifixion within a range of dates approximately 33 years after the Incarnation of Christ, the year A.D. 19 is still the most probable year when Nisan 14 would coincide with a Friday.

This line of reasoning can be summarized as follows. Christ was born in 15 B.C. and was about 33 years old at the time of the Crucifixion. The Passover of A.D. 19 is 33 years after the year of Christ's Incarnation in 15 B.C. Other years, within 2 years plus or minus of A.D. 19, most probably did not have Nisan 14 coinciding with a Friday. Therefore, Christ died and rose from the dead in the year A.D. 19.

Second Argument and Conclusion

A second line of reasoning can be used to determine the year of the Crucifixion of Jesus Christ. This second argument does not rely on the visions of Blessed Anne Catherine, but rather on a new chronology of the reigns of various Roman rulers, especially Caesar Augustus, Tiberius Caesar, and Pontius Pilate. This revised chronology for the reigns of various Roman rulers is presented in detail in chapters 12, 13, and 14 of this book, but is also briefly summarized below (see also Appendix II, Section B).

Tiberius Caesar

"Then, in the fifteenth year of the reign of Tiberius Caesar...the word of the Lord came to John, the son of Zechariah, in the wilderness." (Lk 3:1-2).

This passage from the Gospel of Luke has often been used in attempts to date the beginning of the Ministry of Jesus Christ. Two main questions arise in assigning a year to the Ministry of Jesus based on these words. First, which year is to be counted as the first year of the reign of Tiberius Caesar? Second, since this passage from Sacred Scripture refers to the beginning of the ministry of John the Baptist, how much later was the beginning of the Ministry of Jesus Christ?

Tiberius Caesar succeeded Caesar Octavian Augustus as emperor of Rome. Historians generally date the death of Augustus to A.D. 14.[66] Tiberius was proclaimed emperor by the Roman senate soon after the death of Augustus. On this basis, many scholars have drawn the conclusion that the 15th year of the reign of Tiberius Caesar occurred in either A.D. 28 or 29 (depending on whether A.D. 15 is counted as Tiberius' first or second year). This date for the beginning of John the Baptist's ministry is consistent with a date of A.D. 33 for the Crucifixion. And Nisan 14 did fall on a Friday in A.D. 33.

About two years before Caesar Augustus died, Tiberius Caesar ruled the Roman provinces jointly with him in a power-sharing arrangement.[67] Consequently, some scholars date the beginning of the Tiberius Caesar's reign from about A.D. 12, not A.D. 14.[68] The count of the 15 years of Tiberius Caesar's reign does not necessarily begin when Augustus died, for Tiberius had considerable power before he became emperor of Rome. Counting forward 15 years from A.D. 12 or 13 brings us to A.D. 26 or 27 (depending on which year is counted as the first year of Tiberius' reign). This date for the beginning of John the Baptist's ministry is consistent with a date of A.D. 30 for the Crucifixion. Since scholars generally hold that Nisan 14 could have coincided with Friday, April 7 in A.D. 30, this year is considered a possible year for the Crucifixion.

Dr. E. Jerry Vardaman points out a third possible starting point for the count of the 15 years of Tiberius Caesar's reign.[69] About ten years before the death of Caesar Augustus, a grandson of Augustus named Gaius, who had been chosen by Augustus to be the next emperor of Rome, died.[70] Another of Augustus' grandsons, named Lucius, had also died a couple of years earlier. Tiberius was somewhat in disfavor in the years before the deaths of Lucius and Gaius. He was in voluntary exile on the island of Rhodes and had little power in the Roman empire.[71] But after their death, Augustus chose Tiberius as his successor, adopted him as his son, and gave him a ten-year decree of power.[72] According to the ancient Roman historian, Dio Cassius: "Augustus... not only adopted Tiberius, but also sent him out against the Germans, granting him the tribunician power for ten years."[73] And about ten years later, Augustus died and Tiberius succeeded him as emperor of Rome.

During the ten years preceding the death of Augustus, Tiberius was the chosen successor and adopted son of the emperor of Rome. He had a great deal of power in the Roman empire. He was in charge of a large portion of the Roman army (which was the practical guarantor of the power of the leaders of Rome).

When Tiberius was named successor to the emperor, he received the name of Caesar. From his birth, his name was Tiberius Claudius Nero. When he was adopted as the son of Augustus (he was actually Augustus' stepson) and chosen as his successor, his name was changed to Tiberius Julius Caesar. Later, when he finally became emperor, his name was changed again to Tiberius Caesar Augustus.[74] Tiberius was given the name Tiberius

Julius Caesar to indicate to everyone that he was to be the next emperor of Rome. His new name was an indication of the new power he was given in the Roman empire.

Also, during the ten years between the adoption of Tiberius and the death of Augustus, Augustus was undoubtedly feeling the effects of his advanced age. According to Dio, Augustus died at the age of 75 years, 10 months and 26 days.[75] So Augustus was about 65 years old when he chose Tiberius as his successor (about ten years before his death). Dio also tells us that Augustus adopted Tiberius and gave him power partly because he needed the assistance of a successor and supporter.

"Later, when a German war broke out and Augustus was worn out in body, by reason of old age and illness, and incapable of taking the field, he yielded...and not only adopted Tiberius, but also sent him out against the Germans.... After this he took courage, feeling that he had successors and supporters...."[76]

Notice that Augustus placed Tiberius in command of the war against the Germans, when previously it was Augustus himself who had that role. Tiberius had a great deal of power during the ten years preceding the death of Augustus, partly because, at his age, Augustus could not rule the entire Roman empire without strong support from a chosen heir.

At that time in history, it was not uncommon for rulers to date the beginning of their reigns from as early a date as possible. They believed that great leaders had long reigns: the longer the reign, the greater the leader. So each king or emperor sought to count the beginning of his reign from as early a date as possible.[77] This practice is called "antedating." Therefore, it is possible that Tiberius Caesar also counted the beginning of his reign as emperor from the earliest possible date, from about the time that he was chosen as the heir to the throne and given the name of Caesar. Many scholars hold that Tiberius did antedate his reign, but to a point in time two years before the death of Augustus. So, the idea that Tiberius may have antedated his reign already has some degree of acceptance among scholars.

The generally-accepted date of A.D. 14 for the death of Augustus would place Tiberius Caesar's adoption as son and heir about the year A.D. 4, and Tiberius' 15th year could then be counted as A.D. 18 or 19. However, if we begin with the assumption that the generally-accepted historical dates for this time period are correct, every idea about the date of the Crucifixion would be limited by that assumption. In chapters 12, 13, and 14 of this book, I argue that the generally-accepted dates for the reigns of various Roman emperors and rulers during this time period are in error. My conclusion is that Augustus Caesar died in A.D. 10, not A.D. 14, and that a complete revision of the dates for the reigns of first century Roman emperors is required (see Appendix II, Section B for a summary of dates).

If Augustus died in A.D. 10, then Tiberius' sudden rise to power began in mid 1 B.C. Tiberius was adopted as heir to Augustus on June 26.[78] The 15th year of Tiberius Caesar's reign would then be A.D. 15, with A.D. 1 counted as the first full year of Tiberius' Caesar's reign.

If the first partial year (1 B.C.) of Tiberius' reign was counted as a full year, then Tiberius' 15th year would be A.D. 14. This method was commonly used by the Jews in counting the years of a king's reign. They counted the first partial year of a king's reign the same as full years.[79] However, it was the Romans who numbered the years by the reigns of the Roman emperors, and they did not count a partial year as a whole year, as did the Jews. Since God chose, in the Gospel of Luke, to tell us the time of the beginning of John the Baptist's ministry by means of the reigns of various Roman rulers, the method of counting the years would be according to Roman practice. Roman historians often counted the years of a rulers reign beginning with the first whole calendar year.[80] So the first full year of Tiberius' reign would be A.D. 1 (with the first partial year not being counted),[81] and the 15th year of Tiberius' reign would be the full year of A.D. 15.[82]

Since it was the Roman practice to count the first year of an emperors reign from the first full year, Tiberius' first year would then be A.D. 1. John the Baptist's ministry began during Tiberius' 15th year, about 5-6 months before Christ's Ministry began. Christ's Ministry was 3½ years long, ending in spring and therefore beginning in the fall. Therefore, John the Baptist's ministry began in spring of A.D. 15. This date for the beginning of John the Baptist's ministry is consistent with a date of A.D. 19 for the Crucifixion. In that year, Nisan 14 coincided with a Friday, in agreement with the Gospel of John's description of the Crucifixion (Jn 19:14, 19:31).

Pontius Pilate

"Then, in the fifteenth year of the reign of Tiberius Caesar, Pontius Pilate being procurator of Judea...the word of the Lord came to John, the son of Zechariah, in the wilderness." (Lk 3:1).

Sacred Scripture tells us that Pilate was ruler over Judea at the beginning of John the Baptist's ministry. Pilate also handed over Jesus to be crucified (Lk 23). So, the Ministry of Jesus took place during the reign of Pilate over Judea. The time frame of Pilate's rule over Judea is sometimes used to help ascertain the year of the Crucifixion. However, there is some disagreement as to the time frame of Pilate's reign. The majority of scholars date the reign of Pontius Pilate over Judea from about A.D. 26 to 36.[83] This range of years is consistent with a date of A.D. 30 or 33 for the Crucifixion. However, Vardaman places the beginning of Pilate's rule over Judea as early as A.D. 14.[84]

In chapter 13 of this book, I present a reasoned argument and substantial evidence in support of a new chronology for the years of Tiberius Caesar's reign. In this chronology, the first year of Tiberius' reign is counted as A.D. 1. This chronology places Pilate's first year as ruler of Judea in late A.D. 11 (or early A.D. 12), with his ten year rule ending in the winter of A.D. 21/22, shortly before the death of Tiberius Caesar in March of A.D. 22.[85] Eusebius, in agreement with Josephus, also tells us that Pilate began his reign over Judea in the 12th year of Tiberius Caesar.[86]

The ministry of John the Baptist began during Pilate's reign over Judea (Lk 3:1). The Ministry of Jesus began shortly thereafter, lasted for about 3½ years, and began and ended under Pilate's reign. So, in this line of reasoning, the Crucifixion could not have occurred any earlier than A.D. 16, nor any later than Pilate's last spring in Judea, which was A.D. 21. But in A.D. 21, the Passover did not begin on a Friday (See Appendix I, Chart 1). Therefore Christ was crucified sometime between A.D. 16 and A.D. 20 inclusive. In A.D. 18, the Passover did not begin on a Friday, so the remaining possibilities are A.D. 16, 17, 19, and 20.

As concluded above, the start of John the Baptist's ministry was in spring of A.D. 15. Christ's Ministry began later that year in the fall of A.D. 15, and lasted 3½ years. This places the Crucifixion in spring of A.D. 19. The years A.D. 16 and 17 are too close to the time of the start of John's Ministry for either to be the year of Jesus was crucified. The year A.D. 20 is a year too late to be the year of the Crucifixion. Also, the years A.D. 17 and 20 would only have had a Nisan 14 Friday if the start of each month was determined by observation, not calculation (See Appendix I, Chart 1). I am convinced that dates in the Jewish calendar were determined by calculation during this time period (see chapter 17).

The year A.D. 20 could have had a Nisan 14 coinciding with a Friday, if the month of Nisan was delayed due to the insertion of a leap month (the month of AdarII, added during Jewish leap years). But such a calendar change would only have taken place in A.D. 20 if the previous winter had unfavorable weather (colder or drier than usual) which delayed the maturity of the grain and fruit crops. The grain crop in particular had to be ready in time for the offering of the first fruits of grain which takes place during the Passover. If the crops were not ready, the Passover and the month of Nisan would have to be delayed by the insertion of the leap month of AdarII (just prior to Nisan).[87] A.D. 20 was not the usual year scheduled to have a leap year to prevent the Passover from falling before the Spring Equinox. So, for this reason also, A.D. 20 was most likely not the year of the Crucifixion.

Second Conclusion

In this revised chronology, the 15th year of Tiberius Caesar's reign coincides with A.D. 15, and the reign of Pontius Pilate coincided with about the last ten years of Tiberius' reign (A.D. 12 to 21, inclusive). This correction of the dates for the reigns of these Roman leaders rules out the usual range of dates given for the Crucifixion (A.D. 27 to 36), and give us a new range of dates for the Crucifixion, from A.D. 16 to 21. This new chronology also gives us the date of A.D. 15 for the start of the ministry of John the Baptist (Lk 3:1). Christ's Ministry began about 5 to 6 months later in fall of A.D. 15. The Ministry of Christ, from Baptism to Crucifixion, lasted about 3½ years. This places the Crucifixion in the spring of A.D. 19. In that year Nisan 14 coincided with a Friday, in agreement with the Gospels. Therefore, the Crucifixion and Resurrection of Jesus Christ occurred in the year A.D. 19.

Final Comments

Above are two different lines of reasoning, both of which point to the year A.D. 19 as the year when Jesus Christ died for us. The first line of reasoning is based, to a large extent, on the words of Blessed Anne Catherine Emmerich, and leads to the conclusion that Jesus Christ died in a year when Nisan 14 coincided with a Friday and with April 7, and that the Crucifixion occurred 33 years after the Incarnation. The second line of reasoning does not depend at all on the writings of Blessed Anne Catherine. This second argument depends on a new chronology for the reigns of the Roman emperors, which establishes A.D. 15 as the 15th year of the reign of Tiberius Caesar (cf. Lk 3:1). This second argument has substantial historical evidence supporting a revised chronology of the Roman emperors. Each of these two lines of reasoning can stand on its own without the other. And each reaches the same conclusion: the Crucifixion of Christ occurred in A.D. 19.

Similarly, the year for the Birth of Jesus Christ can be also established by the writings of Blessed Anne Catherine Emmerich, and, separately, by this revised chronology for the reign of Roman rulers. In both lines of reasoning, the words of Sacred Scripture are essential to a proper understanding of the dates of important events in the lives of Jesus Christ and the Virgin Mary. And both of these arguments conclude that the Birth of Jesus Christ occurred in 15 B.C. (see chapter 4).

Many other dates for important events in the lives of Jesus and Mary are presented in this book. These dates are based in large part on the conclusion that Jesus was born in 15 B.C. and died in A.D. 19. But the dates for these other events also give additional support to the dates for the Birth and Crucifixion of Jesus, because all these dates fit together in a seamless whole. The date for the Immaculate Conception fits the chronology of the rebuilding of the Temple and the date for the beginning of Jesus' Ministry. The dates for the 3 days that Jesus was lost and found in the Temple (at age 12) are in harmony with the dates for His Birth and His Crucifixion. This new chronology for the lives of Jesus and Mary is all the more compelling because the various dates all make sense in relation to one another.

Chapter 3
Resurrection, Ascension, Pentecost

The Resurrection of Jesus Christ from the Dead

"Now on the morning of the Sabbath, when it began to grow light on the first Sabbath, Mary Magdalene and the other Mary went to see the sepulcher. And behold, a great earthquake occurred. For an Angel of the Lord descended from heaven, and as he approached, he rolled back the stone and sat down on it." (Mt 28:1-2).

When the two women see the angel of the Lord, he tells them that Jesus has risen from the dead, and instructs them to inform the disciples. But, before they can reach the disciples, Jesus meets them.

"And behold, Jesus met them, saying, 'Hail.' But they drew near and took hold of his feet, and they adored him." (Mt 28:9).

The two women meet Jesus, confirming the angel's word that Jesus had risen from the dead. They are able to take hold of His feet, therefore, He is not a ghost. And they worship Him, because they realize that He is the Son of God.

The Jewish Sabbath is Saturday, the seventh day of the week (cf. Gen 2:1-3). The day after the Jewish Sabbath is Sunday, the first day of the week. Jesus rose from the dead on the first day of the week, Sunday. As shown in chapter 2 of this book, Jesus died on Friday, April 7 of A.D. 19, and so He rose from the dead on the following Sunday. The three days from His Crucifixion to His Resurrection are counted inclusively, where a part of a day counts as a day. The three days from His Crucifixion to His Resurrection do not total 3 times 24 hours. Instead, the Jewish custom to count inclusively, where a part counts for the whole, is followed.[88] Jesus rose from the dead on Sunday, April 9 of A.D. 19.

The Order of Events

The order of events on the day of the Resurrection of Jesus Christ is not immediately obvious from the different descriptions given in the four Gospels. As often occurs in the Gospels, one Gospel gives us one set of details, and another gives us a different set of details. Each Gospel tells the one true story in its different parts. We are then left to put together the order and meaning of the events.

The writings of Blessed Anne Catherine Emmerich are a useful guide to discovering the order of events on that first Easter Sunday, for she described the events of that day in great detail based on her visions from God. Even so, the words of Sacred Scripture are far above the words of even the holiest of saints. God's Sacred Infallible Scripture is first among all writings.

The Time of Day

"Now on the morning of the Sabbath, when it began to grow light on the first Sabbath, Mary Magdalene and the other Mary went to see the sepulcher." (Mt 28:1).

According to the Gospel of Matthew, Mary Magdalene and "the other Mary" went to the sepulchre "when it began to grow light." We can readily see from the expression "when it began to grow light" that it was not yet dawn, in other words, the sun had not yet risen above the horizon. The sky begins to brighten well before the visible disc of the sun appears above the horizon. The sky becomes progressively lighter as much as an hour or more before sunrise, especially in the eastern sky, where the sun will later rise. On Sunday, April 9 of A.D. 19, sunrise occurred at approx. 05:21 a.m. Jerusalem Standard Time (JST).[89]

"And very early in the morning, on the first of the Sabbaths, they went to the tomb, the sun having now risen." (Mk 16:2).

The Gospel of Mark states that the women went to the tomb "very early in the morning," when the sun had risen. This statement does not contradict the statement in Matthew's Gospel that they went to the tomb "when it began to grow light" because there is obviously a length of time needed for the women to set out from their homes and travel to the garden of the Holy Sepulchre. Thus the sun must have risen at some point in time during the visit of the women to the tomb.

The Gospel of Luke describes the women going to the tomb at "at very first light." This expression could well refer to the brightening of the sky before the sun rises.

"Then on the first Sabbath, Mary Magdalene went to the tomb early, while it was still dark, and she saw that the stone had been rolled away from the tomb." (Jn 20:1).

Here the Gospel of John adds another detail, that it was still dark when Mary Magdalene went to the tomb. The expression "while it was still dark," however, does not necessarily mean that the sky was as dark as in the middle of the night. The sky may be called dark before the sun rises, even though it is beginning to brighten in the eastern sky in the hour before dawn. Still it is clear that Mary Magdalene reached the tomb before sunrise. Here again, as in the other Gospels, we see that the women visited the tomb beginning before dawn.[90]

Mark's Gospel implies that the sun rose at some point during their trip to the tomb, and the other Gospels have the women traveling to the tomb just before dawn. So, the women must have begun their trip to the tomb before dawn, while it was still fairly dark out. And, since the Gospel of Mark places the rising of the sun during this trip to the tomb (Mk 16:2), dawn must have occurred at about the time of their arrival at the tomb. The differing statements of the Gospels must be interpreted in some way so that every passage will be understood as true. No part of Sacred Scripture can ever be in error (Jn 10:35).

The Time of the Resurrection

In the Gospel of Matthew, the stone is rolled away from the entrance to the tomb, and the angel sitting on the stone tells the women that Jesus has risen from the dead (Mt 28:2-6). The angel speaks in the past tense about the Resurrection, and tells the women that Jesus "is not here" (Mt 28:6). The women at the tomb do not see Jesus as He is rising from the dead. They see Jesus only after He has risen (Mt 28:9-10; Jn 20:14-18). Therefore, Jesus had already risen from the dead before the stone was rolled back from the tomb. And, in the Gospel of John, when Mary Magdalene went to the tomb, "while it was still dark," she saw that the stone had been rolled away from the tomb (Jn 20:1). So, Jesus rose from the dead before the stone was rolled away from the tomb, and the stone was rolled away before dawn. Therefore, Jesus rose from the dead before the sun rose above the horizon on that very first Easter Sunday.

Blessed Anne Catherine Emmerich tells us that the women set out for the tomb "When the morning sky began to clear with a streak of white light...."[91] These words are in harmony with the words of Sacred Scripture that the women went to the tomb just before dawn. And, according to Blessed Anne Catherine, it was not until sometime later, when the women arrived at the gate to the garden of the sepulchre, that Jesus rose from the dead. "The holy women, when the Lord arose from the dead, were near the little gate belonging to Nicodemus."[92] So then, Jesus rose from the dead after the sky began to brighten, but before the sun actually rose above the horizon.

The sky begins to lighten about an hour or so before dawn. On the day of the Resurrection, April 9 of A.D. 19, sunrise occurred about 05:21 a.m. Jerusalem Standard Time. Therefore, Jesus rose from the dead sometime during the hour before sunrise, between about 04:20 a.m. and 05:20 a.m., a time that the Jews call the twelfth hour of the night.

The Four Holy Women

Blessed Anne Catherine describes the visit of the holy women to the tomb of Our Lord. She both agrees with Sacred Scripture and provides additional details, which clarify some of the differences in each Gospel's description of the events.

"When the morning sky began to clear with a streak of white light, I saw Magdalen, Mary Cleophas, Johanna Chusa, and Salome, enveloped in mantles, leaving their abode near the Coenaculum....and one of them had a lighted lantern."[93]

Four holy women went to tomb the morning of the Resurrection of Jesus Christ. One was Mary Magdalene; she alone of the four is mentioned by John's Gospel. Her story at the tomb is also recounted by Matthew, Mark, and Luke.

Joanna is mentioned only by Luke's Gospel. "Now it was Mary Magdalene, and Joanna, and Mary of James, and the other women who were with them, who told these things to the Apostles." (Lk 24:10). Luke tells us that Joanna was among those women who reported the Resurrection to the Apostles. This group of women included Mary Magdalene and Mary the mother of James, whom Mark tells us were at the tomb after the Resurrection (Mk 16:1-2). However, Luke's Gospel does not name the women who were at the tomb, nor the women who were at the cross; these women are described simply as "the women who had followed him from Galilee" (Lk 23:49; cf. 23:55).

The Gospel of Luke describes Joanna as someone who had been healed by Jesus: "And it happened afterwards that he was making a journey through the cities and towns, preaching and evangelizing the kingdom of God. And the twelve were with him, along with certain women who had been healed of evil spirits and infirmities: Mary, who is called Magdalene, from whom seven demons had departed, and Joanna, the wife of Chuza, Herod's steward, and Susanna, and many other women, who were ministering to him from their resources." (Lk 8:1-3).

Joanna's husband, Chuza, had a fairly important position, so that Joanna and her husband must have had some wealth. Joanna and other women were able to provide for Jesus and his disciples.

Blessed Anne Catherine tells us that Joanna was at the tomb with the other women, but the Gospels neither confirm or deny this. Some of the other women with them, who went to tell the apostles, might have not been at the tomb, but might have only joined the holy women after they left the garden of the sepulchre. On the other hand, there is no reason, based on Sacred Scripture, to disbelieve Blessed Anne Catherine's statement that Joanna was at the tomb with Mary Magdalene and the other Mary.

Blessed Anne Catherine describes Mary Cleophas as accompanying Mary Magdalene to the tomb at the time of the Resurrection. None of the Gospels uses the exact name 'Mary Cleophas.' However, the synoptic Gospels each mention another Mary, besides Mary Magdalene.

Matthew's Gospel tells us that several women were present at the Crucifixion of Jesus Christ, including "Mary the mother of James and Joseph" (Mt 27:56). Matthew's Gospel then says that Mary Magdalene and "the other Mary" went to the tomb before and after the Resurrection (Mt 27:61; 28:1). This "other Mary" must be Mary the mother of James and Joseph, for she is mentioned just a few verses earlier along with Mary Magdalene.

Mark's Gospel calls this same Mary, "Mary the mother of James the younger and of Joseph" (Mk 15:40). Joses is another way of saying the name Joseph. Later, Mark's Gospel calls her simply "Mary the mother of Joseph" (Mk 15:47), and also, "Mary the mother of James" (Mk 16:1). Luke's Gospel also refers to Mary as the mother of James (Lk 24:10). By saying "James the younger," Mark's Gospel is clearly referring to one of the Twelve Apostles, who is often called 'James the Less.' Earlier in the Gospel, Mark refers to this same Apostle as "James of Alphaeus" (Mk 3:18).

But who is this Mary, the mother of James the Apostle and the wife of Alphaeus? According to Blessed Anne Catherine, she was the daughter of Mary of Heli and a man named Cleophas, which is why she was called Mary Cleophas.[94] Mary of Heli was the eldest daughter of Saint Joachim (also called Heli, as in Lk 3:23) and Saint Ann. Mary of Heli was the Virgin Mary's older sister, and so Mary Cleophas was the Virgin Mary's niece.[95]

The Gospel of John bears witness to the truth that the Virgin Mary had a sister. "And standing beside the cross of Jesus were his mother, and his mother's sister, and Mary of Cleophas, and Mary Magdalene." (John 19:25). In this passage from John's Gospel, "Mary of Cleophas" [or 'Clopas'] is not a fourth woman, but a description of "his mother's sister." Clopas is a different spelling of the name Cleophas. Mary Cleophas was the daughter of Clopas (Cleophas) and of Mary of Heli, the Virgin Mary's sister.

Blessed Anne Catherine tells us that Salome was among the four holy women who went to the tomb after the Resurrection. She also says that this Salome was not the same Salome who was the mother of the Apostles John and James, the sons of Zebedee, but another Salome.[96] She says that this other Salome was a rich lady of Jerusalem who helped to pay for the spices that the women brought to the tomb. However, Sacred Scripture leads us to a different conclusion.

There is no direct statement in the Gospels which contradicts Blessed Anne Catherine's assertion that the Salome at the tomb was not the Salome who was the mother of the sons of Zebedee. But Matthew's Gospel plainly says that the mother of the sons of Zebedee was present at the Crucifixion of Jesus with Mary Magdalene and Mary the mother of James.

"And in that place, there were many women, at a distance, who had followed Jesus from Galilee, ministering to him. Among these were Mary Magdalene and Mary the mother of James and Joseph, and the mother of the sons of Zebedee." (Mt 27:55-56).

Notice that the women named here were from Galilee. The mother of the sons of Zebedee was from Galilee, as is clear from the occupation of her husband and sons—fishermen on the sea of Galilee (Matthew 4:18-22). On the other hand, the other Salome mentioned by Blessed Anne Catherine was a rich lady from Jerusalem, not a fisherman's wife from Galilee.

Now, Matthew's Gospel does not specifically say that the mother of the sons of Zebedee helped to buy the spices, or that she went to the tomb with the other women. However, Mark's Gospel tells us that a women named Salome was with Mary Magdalene and Mary the mother of James at the Crucifixion, and that these women were from Galilee (Mk 15:40-41). This Salome was from Galilee, not Jerusalem. And this Salome is again named, with Mary Magdalene and Mary the mother of James, as one of the women who obtained the spices and went to the tomb (Mk 16:1).

Sacred Scripture does not specifically tell us that the mother of the sons of Zebedee was named Salome, and that she was the one who bought spices and went to the tomb with the other women. But Mark's Gospel gives the name Salome with Mary Magdalene and Mary the mother of James in the same description, of the women looking upon the Crucifixion, where Matthew's Gospel tells us that the mother of the sons of Zebedee was with Mary Magdalene and Mary the mother of James. And Mark's Gospel is clear that this Salome was from Galilee, not Jerusalem. Therefore, the Salome who bought spices and went to the tomb with Mary Magdalene and the other Mary was the mother of the sons of Zebedee.

The Trip to the Tomb

Blessed Anne Catherine describes how four holy women, Mary Magdalene, Mary Cleophas, Johanna Chusa, and Salome, began their trip to the tomb very early, when "the morning sky began to clear with a streak of white light,"[97] and again, "As soon as a faint glimmering of dawn appeared in the east...."[98] The sun had not yet risen, but the sky was beginning to brighten, which occurs about an hour or so before sunrise. They carried a lighted lantern with them, and so it must have been still quite dark out (cf. Jn 20:1).

Even though none of the Gospels names all four of these women as traveling to the tomb together, Matthew and Mark name three of the four: Mary Magdalene, Mary the mother of James (=Mary Cleophas), and a third woman, whom Matthew calls the mother of the sons of Zebedee and whom Mark names as Salome. The fourth holy woman, Johanna Chusa, is named by Luke's Gospel as being among this company of women, though Luke does not specifically state that she was at the tomb. Thus this description of events by Blessed Anne Catherine finds significant support in Sacred Scripture.

The four holy women brought spices with them to anoint the dead body of Jesus Christ. Clearly, none of the women expected Jesus to be risen from the dead on this day.

The trip to the tomb began near the Cenaculum (the Cenacle) in Jerusalem. Jesus was buried in a garden not far from the place of the Crucifixion (cf. Jn 19:42). "This garden was at least seven minute's distance from Mount Calvary, near the Bethlehem gate, and on the height that sloped down to the city wall."[99] The length of time it took the women to travel to the tomb is uncertain, but the tomb was most likely less than half an hour's walk away. Thus, the sun would still not have risen when the women arrived at the garden. This timing agrees with the Gospels of Matthew, Luke, and John, which each use different wording to tell us that the women went to the tomb before the sun rose (Mt 28:1; Lk 24:1; Jn 20:1).

The Resurrection of Jesus Christ

"The holy women, when the Lord arose from the dead, were near the little gate belonging to Nicodemus."[100] The sun had not yet risen, but it was beginning to be light outside. The women had not yet entered the garden of the holy sepulchre. They did not yet know that the Resurrection had taken place.

"Now I saw the Lord floating in glory up through the rock. The earth trembled, and an angel in warrior garb shot like lightning from Heaven down to the tomb, rolled the stone to one side, and seated himself upon it."[101] Jesus rose from the dead and left the tomb before the angel rolled back the stone. Jesus did not need to have the stone rolled back to leave the tomb; rather, the stone was rolled back so that holy persons could enter the tomb and give witness to the Resurrection. The angel seated himself on the stone; the guards at the tomb fell to the ground, stunned, as if dead. Only after these events did the holy women enter the garden. They did not see the stone being rolled back from the tomb, nor did they witness the Resurrection as it actually occurred.[102]

The Gospel of Matthew does not state that the women saw the stone being rolled back, but only that the women spoke to the angel after the stone was rolled back. The Gospel of John tells us that Mary Magdalene "saw that the stone had been rolled away from the tomb" (Jn 20:1), which implies that she arrived after the stone had been rolled back. Mark and Luke also indicate the same, that the stone was already rolled away when the women arrived (Mk 16:4; Lk 24:2). Since Jesus rose from the dead before the stone was rolled back, He rose from the dead before the holy women arrived at the tomb.

At the Tomb

According to Blessed Anne Catherine Emmerich, the events at the tomb of Our Lord were as follows. As the four holy women approached the tomb, they saw the fallen guards and their lanterns. They became frightened, and two of them, Mary Cleophas and Joanna Chusa, did not enter the garden immediately, but went a short distance beyond it. Mary Magdalene hurried into the garden, and Salome followed a short distance behind her.[103]

Mary Magdalene and Salome approached the tomb and saw that the stone had been rolled back. Magdalene entered and saw the empty burial cloths of Jesus Christ. She then ran to the Apostles to inform them of what she had seen. Salome also entered the tomb, after Magdalene had left, and she also saw the burial cloths and the place where the body of Jesus had lain. But while Magdalene was on her way to inform the Apostles, Salome left the garden to inform the other women of the empty tomb.[104]

Cassius was also in the garden of the holy sepulchre. He was a Roman soldier, the same soldier who pierced the side of Jesus with a lance, after Jesus had died on the Cross.[105] He saw the angel roll back the stone, and he entered the tomb first (before the holy women), to see the burial cloths and the empty place where the body of Jesus had lain.

Cassius had hoped to see the risen Lord Jesus, but when he did not see Jesus, he left the garden to inform Pilate of these events. After leaving the garden, on his way towards the city, he met the holy women (Salome, Mary Cleophas, Joanna) and encouraged them to go in and see the tomb.[106]

Salome, Mary Cleophas, and Joanna therefore decided to enter the garden and approach the tomb. They entered the sepulchre and saw two angels, who spoke to them and told them of the Resurrection of Jesus Christ. The angel told them to inform the disciples of these events. These three holy women left the tomb and the garden, but they did not go to the disciples, as the angel had instructed them. They were full of joy, but also very afraid. They started back towards the city, but they did not tell anyone what happened yet (Mk 16:8).[107]

In the mean time, Mary Magdalene was in Jerusalem. She went to the door of the Cenaculum where the Apostles were staying, but she did not go inside. Peter and John answered the door and she told them that someone had taken the body of Jesus from the tomb. She did not yet understand that Jesus had risen from the dead. Mary Magdalene then immediately returned to the garden of the sepulchre.[108]

Peter and John went back inside and spoke to the other disciples. Then they followed after Magdalene towards the tomb. She reached the tomb well before John and Peter, because they had gone back inside and so had left for the tomb after she was already well on her way.[109]

When Mary Magdalene went into the tomb for the second time, she saw the same two angels that the three other holy women had seen. One of them spoke to her, and she left the tomb in search of Jesus. While wandering in the garden, Magdalene came upon Jesus, but at first she did not recognize Him. She mistook Him for the gardener. When Jesus spoke her name, she at once recognized Him and approached Him. Jesus spoke to her, and then disappeared.

Next Mary Magdalene ran to the tomb for the third time. Again she saw the two angels, and they spoke to her just as they had spoken to the three other holy women. She then left the garden to look for Mary Cleophas, Joanna, and Salome. As Magdalene was leaving the garden, John and Peter entered it.[110]

John had outrun Peter and reached the tomb first. He looked into the tomb and saw the linen clothes which had once held the body of Jesus Christ. Peter now arrived at the tomb and entered first; John followed after him. John immediately believed in the Resurrection, as did Peter (Jn 20:4-8). Peter took the linen clothes which had covered the body of Jesus in the tomb, and they both returned to the city.[111]

The guards who were at the tomb revived about this time. They went into the city to report the empty tomb to Pilate.[112]

On her way back towards Jerusalem, Mary Magdalene met the three other holy women. She told them what she had seen and heard. Then she left them to go into the city.

The three women, Mary Cleophas, Joanna, and Salome, then went towards the garden. There they saw the risen Lord Jesus. He spoke to them and showed them His Sacred Wounds. Now the women went to the disciples to report all that they had seen and heard. Not until they had met Jesus did they find the courage to report these incredible events to the disciples. But the disciples did not believe them. And when Peter and John returned and also reported the Resurrection of the Lord to them, the disciples were dumbfounded.[113]

Peter and John, after leaving the Cenaculum where the disciples were gathered, met the Apostles James and Thaddeus. They had seen the risen Lord Jesus a short time earlier. According to Blessed Anne Catherine, as Peter and John were walking, Peter also saw the risen Lord Jesus, but John perhaps did not see Jesus at that time. She does not clearly state whether Peter saw Jesus before or after James and Thaddeus saw Him.[114]

The Gospel of Matthew

Matthew's Gospel mentions only Mary Magdalene and "the other Mary" (Mt 28:1) as visiting the tomb on the morning of the Resurrection. The other Mary is Mary the mother of James and Joseph (Mt 27:56). Everything written in Sacred Scripture is entirely true and without error. However, not every detail is presented in every passage. Matthew does not mention the other women, but they were present, as evidenced in the Gospels of Mark and Luke.

After saying that the two Marys went to the tomb, Matthew tells us that an angel rolled back the stone (Mt 28:1-4). Sacred Scripture does not say that the women saw the angel roll back the stone. And Blessed Anne Catherine's description tells us that they did not see this event.

Matthew tells us that the angel spoke to the women, then they ran with fear and joy to inform the disciples. But before they went to the disciples, they first met Jesus. "Then Jesus said to them: 'Do not be afraid. Go, announce it to my brothers, so that they may go to Galilee. There they shall see me.' " (Mt 28:10). Notice that Jesus tells them not to be afraid, immediately before telling them to go to the disciples. The women wanted to tell the disciples what they had seen, but they were hesitant out of fear. Meeting Jesus strengthened them for the task of going to inform the disciples.

Matthew's Gospel simplifies the events surrounding the angel speaking to the women. Blessed Anne Catherine describes an angel speaking first to three of the women, while Magdalene was on her way to inform Peter and John that the body of Jesus was missing. An angel later spoke to Mary Magdalene about the Resurrection, but not until she returned to the tomb after meeting Jesus. Matthew sums up in one description (of an angel speaking to the women), events which actually occurred in stages.

The fact that the angel spoke to Magdalene sometime after he had spoken to the other women can be inferred from what the other Gospels tell us. Mary Magdalene ran and told Peter and John that someone had taken Jesus' body from the tomb (Jn 20:2), because she had not yet met the risen Jesus, and not yet heard the angel speak about the Resurrection.

The Gospel of Mark

Mark's Gospel adds additional information not presented in Matthew's Gospel. Mark tells us that the two Marys were accompanied to the tomb by Salome (Mk 16:1). Mark's Gospel also clarifies the point that the women did not see the stone being rolled back; it was already rolled back when they arrived (Mk 16:3-4).

The Gospel of Mark tells us that the women were afraid after hearing the angel speak of the Resurrection: "And they said nothing to anyone. For they were afraid." (Mk 16:8). The Gospel of Mark describes the women as remaining silent, whereas the Gospel of Matthew describes the women as informing the disciples of the Resurrection. Yet these two different accounts of these events are both true. Mark tells us that the women "said nothing to anyone" because the women at first did not follow the angel's instruction to inform the disciples of the Resurrection—they were too afraid. And Matthew's Gospel adds that the women were able to overcome their fear after they met Jesus. After meeting the angel, the women were at first afraid and unwilling to tell anyone of these events. That is why Jesus tells the women not to be afraid when He instructs them to go inform His disciples. The women's fear was preventing them from following the angel's instruction to tell the disciples of the Resurrection,—until they met Jesus.

"But he, rising early on the first Sabbath, appeared first to Mary Magdalene, from whom he had cast out seven demons. She went and announced it to those who had been with him, while they were mourning and weeping. And they, upon hearing that he was alive and that he had been seen by her, did not believe it." (Mk 16:9-11).

Here the Gospel of Mark begins the story of the Resurrection a second time. Mary Magdalene meets the risen Lord, then informs the disciples, "while they were mourning and weeping." (Mk 16:10). They are mourning and weeping partly because they were previously informed that the body of Jesus was not in the tomb. (It was Magdalene who informed them that Jesus' was missing, as we learn in John's Gospel.) But when Mary Magdalene now tells them that Jesus is alive and has appeared to her, they do not believe (Mk 16:11). They did not yet believe that Jesus had risen; they were mourning and weeping because He died and because His body was missing. Thus the Gospel of Mark implies the disciples were informed of these events twice, just as the Gospel of John also reveals (Jn 20:2, 18).

The Gospel of Luke

Luke's Gospel explains to us that the women who visited the tomb are the women who accompanied Jesus from Galilee (Lk 23:55). They found the stone already rolled away from the tomb, and they saw two angels (who seem to them like men) who informed them of the Resurrection (Lk 24:1-7). All this is in agreement with the other Gospels and the account given by Blessed Anne Catherine.

The Gospel of Luke gives the names of the women who went to the apostles to inform them of the Resurrection. These include Mary Magdalene, Mary the mother of James, and Joanna (Lk 24:10). Luke's Gospel does not mention Salome, but adds that there were other women with them who also informed the apostles of these events. Does this mean that more than four women visited the tomb that wonderful morning? No other women than those four are named in Sacred Scripture, and Blessed Anne Catherine does not mention any other women at the tomb. Therefore, those four holy women were not accompanied by other women. However, Luke's Gospel states plainly that there were other women with Mary Magdalene, Mary Cleophas and Joanna. Since the word women is plural, Salome could not have been the only other woman referred to here. Thus those four holy women were not accompanied by any other women when they went to the tomb early on the Resurrection morning, but they must have been joined by other women when they went to inform the Apostles.

The Gospel of John

The Gospel of John gives us a detailed account of Mary Magdalene at the tomb. She finds the tomb empty, but does not yet know of the Resurrection. She informs Peter and John only that the body of Jesus is missing (Jn 20:2). Later, she returns to the tomb, sees the angels (just as the other women had seen) and meets the risen Lord Jesus (Jn 20:11-17). Then Mary Magdalene goes to the disciples a second time and tells them of the Resurrection (Jn 20:18). Their reaction is revealed in Mark's Gospel: they did not believe her (Mk 16:11).

The Gospel of Luke briefly describes Peter running to the tomb after the Resurrection (24:12). Peter looks in the tomb and sees the empty grave clothes: "...and he went away wondering to himself about what had happened." (Lk 24:12).

John's Gospel describes this same event in greater detail. Peter was not alone when he ran to the tomb, "the other disciple, whom Jesus loved" was with Peter (Jn 20:2). This other disciple was certainly one of the Twelve Apostles, for he reclined at table next to Jesus at the Last Supper (Jn 21:20; 13:23). And this other disciple was the author of John's Gospel, as Sacred Scripture tells us: "This is the same disciple who offers testimony about these things, and who has written these things. And we know that his testimony is true." (John 21:24). Therefore, it was John the Apostle and Gospel writer who ran with Peter to the tomb.

The Gospel of John describes Mary Magdalene's second visit to the tomb, and her meeting with Jesus, after describing John and Peter at the tomb (Jn 20:1-18). However, Blessed Anne Catherine states that Magdalene arrived at the tomb before John and Peter.[115] Sacred Scripture does not specifically state who arrived first, Magdalene or John and Peter. Events are not necessarily described in Sacred Scripture in the order in which they occurred. Blessed Anne Catherine's explanation is that after Magdalene told John and Peter of the empty tomb, she immediately ran back to the tomb, whereas John and Peter first went and talked to some of the other disciples.[116]

Sometimes events in Sacred Scripture are given in the order that is best for the meaning being presented, but not the order in which the events occurred. Now if Sacred Scripture tells us that certain events did occur in a particular order, then without doubt that is the order in which the events occurred. But when Sacred Scripture places events out of chronological order and does not tell us that the events happened in the order in which they are described, there is still no error or falsehood in Sacred Scripture—the events of a true story do not need to be told in the exact order in which they occurred.

In this case, Sacred Scripture describes John and Peter running to the tomb, then describes Magdalene at the tomb. However, Sacred Scripture does not use any language to indicate which occurred first. And Blessed Anne Catherine tells us that God revealed to her that Magdalene arrived first. Therefore, Magdalene arrived at the tomb (for the second time) before John and Peter.

Who Saw Jesus First?

"But he, rising early on the first Sabbath, appeared first to Mary Magdalene, from whom he had cast out seven demons." (Mk 16:9).

After the Resurrection, Jesus appeared first to Mary Magdalene. Our Lord did not appear first, after the Resurrection, to His Holy Mother, the Virgin Mary. Instead, He appeared first to a sinful woman who had seven serious vices (which were being cultivated in her life by seven demons). Why would Jesus appear first to a great sinner, rather than to the most pure and sinless Virgin Mary? Notice that Sacred Scripture says that Jesus had cast out those seven demons. Mary Magdalene was not merely a great sinner; she was a great sinner who had greatly repented. Jesus died and rose from the dead in order to bring sinners to repentance; that is why Jesus appeared first to Mary Magdalene. She was a fitting example of the fruit of Jesus' Crucifixion and Resurrection—the repentance of sinners.

Why did Jesus not appear first to Peter, who was first among the Apostles and first in authority over the Church which Jesus established on earth? Those who are first in authority in the Church are not first in everything. Sometimes it is the humble, faithful servant of Christ (who has no authority in the Church) who understands first, and the leaders understand afterwards. An example of this is found in the book of the prophet Jonah.

"And the men of Nineveh believed in God. And they proclaimed a fast, and they put on sackcloth, from the greatest all the way to the least. And word reached the king of Nineveh. And he rose from his throne, and he threw off his robe from himself and was clothed in sackcloth, and he sat in ashes. And he cried out and spoke: 'In Nineveh, from the mouth of the king and of his princes, let it be said: Men and beasts and oxen and sheep may not taste anything. Neither shall they feed or drink water.' " (Jonah 3:5-7).

The people of Nineveh believed and repented first. Only afterwards did the king follow their example and make an official proclamation of a fast. But the people were already fasting. In the same way, within the Body of Christ, sometimes the least among the faithful understand something first—such as Magdalene understanding the Resurrection—and the leaders understand afterwards. Thus the Apostles and disciples did not believe Magdalene at first (Mk 16:11); only later did they realize that she spoke the truth.

Pope John Paul II once expressed the opinion that the Virgin Mary was the first to know that Jesus had risen from the dead. This opinion does not contradict the teaching of Sacred Scripture that Jesus appeared first to Mary Magdalene after the Resurrection. The Virgin Mary *knew* first, but Mary Magdalene met and saw Jesus first, after He rose from the dead. Jesus appeared first, in person (not merely in a vision) and in His Resurrected body, to Mary Magdalene.

The Empty Tomb

According to Blessed Anne Catherine, the Roman soldier who had pierced the side of Jesus on the Cross with a lance (Jn 19:34) was named Cassius and was present at the tomb with the other guards.[117] The other guards were not Roman soldiers, they were temple guards under the direction of the chief priests and Pharisees (Mt 27:65). Cassius was not under the direction of the Jewish leaders, but was appointed by Pilate to keep him informed of the events at the tomb.

Immediately after the angel rolled back the stone from the tomb, the temple guards fell to the ground, stunned or unconscious (Mt 28:4).[118] But Cassius remained conscious and alert. He saw the angel roll back the stone. He entered the tomb first, before Mary Magdalene, the other women, and Peter and John. Cassius saw and touched the empty grave clothes of Jesus Christ. But he did not see Jesus.[119] Cassius went and informed Pilate of what he had seen. Cassius believed in the Resurrection and told Pilate so.[120] Cassius believed in the Resurrection before the Apostles, even though he was but a Roman soldier, not a Jew or a disciple. The Apostles were chosen by Jesus Christ for their appointed roles and tasks, but they were not chosen for every role, nor for every task (1 Cor 12:4-31). It is just so, even today, within the Body of Christ.

What happened to Cassius in later years? Blessed Anne Catherine tells us that, at the time of the Crucifixion, he was 25 years old and an officer in the Roman army.[121] She also states that he was soon after baptized with the name 'Longinus,' and that he eventually became a deacon.[122] Interestingly, Josephus mentions a Cassius Longinus in his work *The Antiquities of the Jews.* This Cassius Longinus was chosen by Claudius to be the successor to Marcus as president of Syria.[123]

It is possible that the Cassius Longinus described by Josephus is the same Cassius Longinus who pierced Christ's side with a lance. By the time that Cassius was appointed president of Syria, about the fourth year of Claudius' reign (A.D. 29), the Cassius of the Crucifixion would have been about 35 years old and have served as an officer in the Roman army for over ten years (if he remained in the Roman army). There was another Cassius who lived, over 75 years earlier, during the time of Julius Caesar and Herod the great. That Cassius was for a time ruler over Syria.[124] Since the Romans often named the child after the father or the grandfather, Cassius Longinus could well be the grandson (or other relative) of that earlier Cassius. The Romans often chose rulers in part based on their parentage (for example, Claudius wanted to immediately put Herod Agrippa II in charge of Herod Agrippa I's kingdom, even though he was still quite young).[125] Thus Cassius Longinus would have been a suitable choice to govern Syria for Rome, both because of his experience as a Roman soldier and because his relative formerly ruled Syria. Of course, it is also possible that these were two different men named Cassius Longinus (who were perhaps related to one another).

Who Saw Jesus When?

Mary Magdalene saw Jesus first after the Resurrection (Mk 16:9). Then, according to Blessed Anne Catherine, the three holy women, Mary Cleophas, Joanna, and Salome, met the risen Lord Jesus.[126] The next to see Jesus was either Peter, or, James and

Thaddeus. Blessed Anne Catherine tells us that James the Less and Thaddeus saw the Lord, then she tells us that she once saw Peter startled by seeing the Risen Lord, but she does not say in which order these two events happened.[127] "Once I saw Peter, as they went along, suddenly start and tremble, as if he had just got a glimpse of the risen Savior."[128] Sacred Scripture, in the first letter of Saint Paul to the Corinthians, places Christ's appearance to Peter ("Cephas") before His appearance to the Twelve Apostles (1 Cor 15:3-8). However, this passage does not definitively rule out a prior appearance of Jesus to James and Thaddeus, for Jesus could have appeared to those two, then to Peter, then to the Twelve.

This appearance of the risen Lord Jesus to Peter is also mentioned in the Gospel of Luke. "And rising up at that same hour, they returned to Jerusalem. And they found the eleven gathered together, and those who were with them, saying: 'In truth, the Lord has risen, and he has appeared to Simon.' " (Lk 24:33-34). Simon is Simon Peter (cf. Lk 5:1-11), the leader of the Apostles.

The Road to Emmaus

"But after these events, he was shown in another likeness to two of them walking, as they were going out to the countryside. And they, returning, reported it to the others; neither did they believe them." (Mk 16:12-13).

The Gospel of Mark mentions another appearance of the risen Christ Jesus, which occurred after His appearance to Magdalene (Mk 16:11). This appearance could not be the one spoken of by Blessed Anne Catherine, when Jesus appeared to James and Thaddeus. Jesus appeared to them when they were in the city "near the Coenaculum,"[129] whereas Jesus appeared to these other two "as they were going out to the countryside" (Mk 16:12). And so, this appearance, described briefly by Mark, is almost certainly the one described in much greater detail by the Gospel of Luke.

"And behold, two of them went out, on the same day, to a town named Emmaus, which was the distance of sixty stadia from Jerusalem." (Lk 24:13).

Jesus appeared to two of His disciples as they were walking into the country, to Emmaus. These two were among Jesus' disciples, for Mark says that they went back and "reported it to the others," meaning the rest of the disciples. In Luke's Gospel, one of them says that the women who went to the tomb were "certain women from among us" (Lk 24:22). And he also states his belief in Jesus Christ, using these words: "But we were hoping that he would be the Redeemer of Israel." (Lk 24:21).

The name of one of these two disciples is given by the Gospel of Luke as "Cleopas" (Lk 24:18). According to Blessed Anne Catherine, this man was not the husband of "Mary of Cleophas" (Jn 19:25). But rather, he was "a grandson of Mary Cleophas' paternal uncle."[130] The spelling of the two names, Clopas and Cleopas, is different in these two Gospels, which may be Sacred Scripture's way of indicating that these were two different men, who were relatives of one another.

The name of the other disciple is not given by the Gospel of Luke. Notice that Luke recounts this story in great detail, including a fair amount of dialogue, whereas Mark gives the account in only two verses (Mk 16:12-13). What was Luke's source for the detailed information on this event? According to Blessed Anne Catherine, Luke himself was the other disciple.[131] Luke does not mention his own name in writing this story in the Gospel of Luke, just as John does not use his own name in mentioning himself in the Gospel of John (Jn 21:20-24).

When the two disciples, Cleopas and Luke, returned to Jerusalem and informed the apostles and disciples that they had met the risen Christ Jesus, some among the Apostles and disciples reply: " 'In truth, the Lord has risen, and he has appeared to Simon.' " (Lk 24:34). Here we see that some of the Apostles and other disciples believed that Jesus had risen from the dead, based on the testimony of Simon Peter and others. However, not all the Apostles and disciples believed, even after hearing from the women and Peter and others. That is why Mark's Gospel tells us that the testimony of the two disciples, Cleopas and Luke, was not believed (Mk 16:13). A few believed, but many still did not. Some even continued to doubt after they saw the risen Jesus (Mt 28:17).

Saint Paul the Apostle

"For I handed on to you, first of all, what I also received: that Christ died for our sins, according to the Scriptures; and that he was buried; and that he rose again on the third day, according to the Scriptures; and that he was seen by Cephas, and after that by the eleven. Next he was seen by more than five hundred brothers at one time, many of whom remain, even to the present time, although some have fallen asleep. Next, he was seen by James, then by all the Apostles. And last of all, he was seen also by me, as if I were someone born at the wrong time." (1 Cor 15:3-8).

Sacred Scripture, in Paul's first letter to the Corinthians, gives us the order of some of the appearances of Jesus Christ after the Resurrection. This list of appearances is not complete; it leaves out appearances to Mary Magdalene, the other holy women, and other appearances. However, Sacred Scripture is clearly stating an order to the appearances that are listed there.

Jesus appeared to Peter, as is also mentioned in the Gospel of Luke (Lk 24:34). Then, Jesus appeared to the Twelve Apostles. Notice that Paul counts the apostles as twelve, even though Judas Iscariot was dead (Mt 27:5), so that there were only Eleven Apostles at this time (Mt 28:16; Mk 16:14; Lk 24:9, 33). Why then does Sacred Scripture, in Paul's letter, say that Jesus appeared after His Resurrection to the Twelve? The twelfth apostle must be Matthias, who was chosen, between the Ascension and Pentecost, to be the Apostle replacing Judas Iscariot (Acts 1:26). Matthias was chosen partly because he was among the disciples of Christ from the beginning, as Peter himself says: " 'Therefore, it is necessary that, out of these men who have been assembling with us throughout the entire time that the Lord Jesus went in and out among us, beginning from the baptism of John, until the day when he was taken up from us, one of these be made a witness with us of his Resurrection.' " (Acts 1:21-22). Therefore, Matthias was among the Apostles and disciples of Christ from the beginning, and must have been with the Eleven Apostles when Jesus appeared to them. Sacred Scripture, in the words of Saint Paul, refers to Matthias as one of the Twelve, at the time of Jesus' appearances after the Resurrection, even though he was not chosen and enrolled as one of the Twelve Apostles, replacing Judas Iscariot (Acts 1:20), until after Jesus' Ascension.

Appearances on the Christian Sabbath

When did the risen Lord Jesus appear to all twelve of the Apostles? It was not on the first day of the Resurrection, for the Apostle Thomas was not present that first evening when Jesus appeared to the Apostles (Jn 20:19,24). "Now Thomas, one of the twelve, who is called the Twin, was not with them when Jesus arrived." (John 20:24). It was not until eight days later, on the first Sunday after the Resurrection, that Jesus appeared to Thomas for the first time (Jn 20:25-26). Therefore, the appearance of Jesus to all of the Twelve Apostles, as stated by Saint Paul, did not occur until that day.

Jesus appeared to ten of the Apostles on the evening of the first day of the Resurrection (and perhaps Matthias was present also). But Jesus did not appear to all eleven Apostles (twelve including Matthias) until the following Sunday, the eighth day of the Resurrection. Thus, when the Gospel of Mark tells us that Jesus appeared to the eleven Apostles, this describes the eighth day of the Resurrection, not the first day. "Finally, he appeared to the eleven, as they sat at table. And he rebuked them for their incredulity and hardness of heart, because they did not believe those who had seen that he had risen again." (Mk 16:14).

Appearance on the Road to Emmaus

The Gospel of Luke describes the days from the Resurrection to the Ascension in condensed form. When the two disciples returned from Emmaus, they discussed the events of Emmaus with the apostles and other disciples (Lk 24:35). "Then, while they were talking about these things, Jesus stood in their midst, And he said to them: 'Peace be with you. It is I. Do not be afraid.' " (Lk 24:36). The phrase "while they were talking about these things" tells us that Jesus appeared to the Apostles and disciples while they were still discussing the events of Emmaus and other appearances of the risen Christ. There was a length of time between the disciples return from Emmaus and the appearance of Jesus that evening, which may have been as long as a few hours.

Notice that the Eleven Apostles were gathered together when the two disciples returned from Emmaus (Lk 24:33), but Thomas, one of the Eleven, was not present when Jesus appeared later that same evening, the first day of the Resurrection (Jn 20:19-29). Thus, Thomas must have departed sometime between the return of the disciples from Emmaus and the appearance of the risen Christ that same evening. Blessed Anne Catherine adds that Thomas did leave the company of the other Apostles that day, to go to "some little place near Samaria with a disciple from that part of the country."[132]

Those Who Saw and Those Who Believed

The first appearance to the Apostles, on the evening of the first day of the Resurrection, is described in the Gospel of Luke in verses 36 and following (Lk 24:36ff). At this point in time, some of the Apostles still did not believe that Jesus had risen from the dead; they considered whether they might be seeing a ghost (Lk 24:37). Not all of the Apostles reacted this way, as is clear from the earlier statement in Luke's Gospel: " 'In truth, the Lord has risen, and he has appeared to Simon.' " (Lk 24:34). Clearly the

Apostle Peter believed in the Resurrection of Jesus Christ, even before Christ appeared to the Apostles that first evening.

"Then the other disciple, who had arrived first at the tomb, also entered. And he saw and believed. For as yet they did not understand the Scripture, that it was necessary for him to rise again from the dead." (Jn 20:8-9).

The Apostle and Gospel writer John also believed in the Resurrection before seeing the risen Christ (Jn 20:8). Verse 9 does not mean that John and Peter disbelieved in the Resurrection, but only that they had not understood references to the Resurrection of Christ in Sacred Scripture (Jn 20:9). Their belief was, at that time, based on seeing the tomb and grave clothes, and not based on their understanding of Sacred Scripture. Until that time, they had not understood what Sacred Scripture foretold about the Resurrection of Christ. If they had understood, they would have been expecting the Resurrection, but not so.

Blessed Anne Catherine says that John and Peter understood the meaning of Sacred Scripture concerning the Resurrection only after they saw the empty tomb and empty grave clothes. "John instantly believed in the Resurrection, and they both understood clearly the words addressed to them by Jesus before his Passion, as well as the different passages in Scripture relating to that event, which had until then been incomprehensible to them."[133] Once they saw the evidence of the empty tomb and the empty grave clothes, they both believed in the Resurrection (because of what they saw) and, finally understood the references to the Resurrection in Sacred Scripture.

Even though Peter and John believed, many of the other Apostles, by the end of that same day, still did not believe in the Resurrection. That is why Jesus showed them His hands and His feet, invited them to touch Him, and ate something in front of them (Lk 24:38-43). Jesus showed those Apostles who did not yet believe that He had truly risen from the dead and was not merely a spirit. The Gospel of John tells us that when Jesus appeared again on the eighth day of the Resurrection, He spoke similarly to Thomas and showed him His wounds, inviting Thomas to touch His wounds (Jn 20:26-29). However, the description given by the Gospel of Luke (Lk 24:36-43), in which Jesus also shows His wounds to the Apostles, occurred on the evening after the Resurrection (Sunday evening). The Gospel of John tells us that Jesus showed His wounds to the Apostles that first Sunday, when Thomas was absent (Jn 20:20). Then, on the following Sunday, Jesus showed again His wounds specifically to Thomas (Jn 20:24-29). The Apostles were startled and frightened at the appearance of Christ (Lk 24:37), because this occurred on Resurrection Sunday and was the first appearance of Jesus to most of them. Also, many of the Apostles at this point in time did not yet believe in the Resurrection, so Jesus invited them to touch Him as proof to them of His Resurrection. If this description was of the second appearance to the Apostles (as a group) on the eighth day after the Resurrection, they would not have been as startled and frightened and disbelieving, because they would have seen Jesus on the previous Sunday and would have had a week to take it all in.

The next passage of the Gospel of Luke, however, may have taken place the following Sunday, on the eighth day of the Resurrection. This section begins with the words, "And he said to them ...." (Lk 24:44). At first glance, it might seem that this discourse is a continuation of the previous verses, but unless Sacred Scripture tells us that one event occurred after another, we should not assume that they did.

A clear example of this is found a few verses further in the Gospel of Luke. "Then he led them out as far as Bethania. And lifting up his hands, he blessed them. And it happened that, while he was blessing them, he withdrew from them, and he was carried up into heaven." (Lk 24:50-51). After describing the words of Jesus to the Apostles (Lk 24:36-43 and 44-49), the Gospel of Luke next describes the Ascension of Jesus into Heaven. But we know that the Ascension did not occur that same day, neither on the Sunday of Jesus' first appearance to the Apostles, nor on the following Sunday. There were further appearances of Jesus to the Apostles and disciples, and the Ascension occurred on the 40th day (Acts 1:3), not on the eighth day. Therefore, the discourse in Luke 24:44-49 could have occurred a full week after the events of Luke 24:36-43.

Divine Mercy Sunday

The first Sunday after Easter is celebrated by many faithful Catholics as Divine Mercy Sunday. Jesus Christ revealed to Saint Faustina Kowalska that the first Sunday after Easter is to be celebrated as the Feast of Divine Mercy. Pope John Paul II established the Feast of Divine Mercy, as an official part of the Church's liturgical calendar, at the canonization of Saint Faustina on April 30 of A.D. 2000. But God established the Feast of Divine Mercy on the first Divine Mercy Sunday, which was the eighth day from the day of Christ's Resurrection. The Feast of Divine Mercy was established by the Crucifixion and Resurrection of Jesus Christ, and began on the first Sunday after the Resurrection.

The Mercy of God is poured out on all creation through the suffering, death, and Resurrection of our Lord Jesus Christ. That is why the Feast of Divine Mercy is placed on the first Sunday after the Resurrection of Jesus Christ. And the very first Feast of Divine Mercy occurred on that first Sunday after the Resurrection of Christ. On the first Sunday after the Resurrection, the eighth day since Christ rose from the dead, Jesus appeared to the Eleven Apostles (Mk 16:14-18; Lk 24:44-49; Jn 26-29). Matthias, who was later chosen as the twelfth Apostle (Acts 1:26), must also have been present (Acts 1:21-22; 1 Cor 15:5). That Sunday, the eighth day from the Resurrection, was the first Feast of Divine Mercy.

Sacred Scripture reveals to us a number of events which occurred on that day:

"Finally, he appeared to the eleven, as they sat at table. And he rebuked them for their incredulity and hardness of heart, because they did not believe those who had seen that he had risen again." (Mk 16:14).

In the Gospel of Mark, we learn that Jesus corrected the Apostles for their lack of faith and their unresponsiveness to God's grace. On the Feast of Divine Mercy, God offers us correction, through His Mercy and Love, because of our lack of faith and hardness of heart. Jesus was merciful to the Apostles, despite their sinfulness and lack of faith. So also is Jesus merciful to us, despite our sins and our lack of faith.

"And he said to them: 'Go forth to the whole world and preach the Gospel to every creature. Whoever will have believed and been baptized will be saved. Yet truly, whoever will not have believed will be condemned.' " (Mk 16:15-16).

The Feast of Divine Mercy is not only for Catholics, and not only for Christians, it is for the whole world and all of creation. When Catholics receive the Sacrament of Reconciliation with sincere repentance from their sins, and receive the Sacrament of

Holy Communion with faith and prayer, on the first Sunday after Easter, they participate most fully in the Feast of Divine Mercy. But, on this day of great mercy, God pours out His Mercy, Love, and Grace on the whole world, even on those who do not yet believe and do not yet understand.

When we participate in the Feast of Divine Mercy, we not only receive God's tender Mercy, we also become God's pitiful little assistants to bring God's unfathomable Mercy to the whole world. Just as Jesus Christ, on the first Feast of Divine Mercy, gave the command to His Twelve Apostles to "preach the Gospel to every creature" (Mk 16:15), so also does Jesus Christ, on the Feast of Divine Mercy, give us poor sinners the command to preach the gospel to all creation by being merciful even to the worst of sinners.

On that first Feast of Divine Mercy, Jesus Christ also reminded His followers that some will not believe, some will reject Christ and the Gospel, some will reject the Mercy of God—such as these will be condemned (Mk 16:16). The incomprehensible Mercy of God is not an excuse to refuse to repent and to refuse to follow Christ on the Way of the Cross. Those who reject the Mercy of God by refusing to repent and by refusing to be merciful to others, will be condemned by the Justice of God (cf. Mt 24:45-51; 25:1-13; 25:31-46).

"Then he opened their mind, so that they might understand the Scriptures. And he said to them: 'For so it is written, and so it was necessary, for the Christ to suffer and to rise up from the dead on the third day, and, in his name, for repentance and the remission of sins to be preached, among all the nations, beginning at Jerusalem. And you are witnesses of these things.' " (Lk 24:45-48).

Here in Luke's Gospel, we again find the words of Jesus to the Apostles on the first Feast of Divine Mercy. Jesus taught the Apostles that His suffering, death, and Resurrection from the dead are the source of repentance and forgiveness for the world. And on this day, Jesus taught that repentance and forgiveness should be preached to the whole world. And still today, Jesus teaches us, through the Feast of Divine Mercy, that His Crucifixion and Resurrection are the source of repentance and forgiveness for even the worst of sinners, and that we should spread God's Mercy to the whole world. Those who receive the Mercy of God are witnesses to God's Mercy. How wonderful and surprising and incomprehensible is the Mercy of God!

"Next, he said to Thomas: 'Look at my hands, and place your finger here; and bring your hand close, and place it at my side. And do not choose to be unbelieving, but faithful.' Thomas responded and said to him, 'My Lord and my God.' " (Jn 20:27-28).

On the first Feast of Divine Mercy, Jesus Christ had mercy on Thomas, to help him believe in His Resurrection and Divinity. Thomas was one of the Twelve chosen Apostles; he was with Jesus for many of His signs and miracles. Thomas was taught by Jesus over the course of Jesus' 3½ year Ministry. Yet Thomas still did not believe and still did not understand that Jesus is God and so is able to rise from the dead. Despite Thomas' lack of faith and understanding, Jesus showed him the Mercy of God by helping him to believe.

Notice that once Thomas believes, he also understands. As soon as Thomas believes in the Resurrection, he calls Jesus, God, because now he understands that Jesus is

Divine. It is the same with us today. Those who lack faith in the True Holy Teaching of the Catholic Church also lack understanding. Those who believe will also understand.

Even today, when people lack faith in God and in the True Holy Teaching of Jesus Christ, Jesus is ready to help them to believe and so to understand. One of the special graces given in abundance on the Feast of Divine Mercy is the grace of true faith in the Sacred Infallible Teaching of the Holy Catholic Church. " 'Ask, and it shall be given to you. Seek, and you shall find. Knock, and it shall be opened to you.' " (Mt 7:7).

The Sea of Tiberius

"After this, Jesus manifested himself again to the disciples at the Sea of Tiberias.... This was now the third time that Jesus was manifested to his disciples, after he had resurrected from the dead." (Jn 21:1,14).

The first time that Jesus appeared to the Apostles and other disciples after His Resurrection was the day of the Resurrection (April 9, A.D. 19). The second time was eight days later, on the first Feast of Divine Mercy (April 16, A.D. 19). The third appearance of the risen Christ to the Apostles and other disciples was at the Sea of Tiberius. By the end of even the first day of the Resurrection, Jesus had appeared more than three times to various persons, but this was the third time that He had appeared to a group of Apostles and other disciples. It was also the third day on which appearances occurred to the Apostles and other disciples. The first day included several appearances on Resurrection Sunday, the next day on which Christ appeared to the disciples was a full week later, on Divine Mercy Sunday. The third day was that described by the Gospel of John (Jn 21:1-14).

Christ did not appear to a group of Apostles and other disciples between Resurrection Sunday and Divine Mercy Sunday. Yet Blessed Anne Catherine describes Christ appearing to some individual persons, and her description is given between her account of events on Resurrection Sunday and on Divine Mercy Sunday. She does not specifically state when these appearances occurred. However, she does not say that Christ appeared to a group of Apostles and other disciples during this time period. Thus, these appearances may have occurred during that first week after the Resurrection, to individual disciples (but not to a group which included Apostles and other disciples), without any contradiction of Sacred Scripture.

"I saw Jesus appearing in many places during these days, and lastly in Galilee, in a valley across the Jordan in which was a large school. Many people were standing together, speaking about Him and expressing their doubts upon the report of His Resurrection. He appeared among them, and vanished again after some words. I saw Him appearing in this way in different localities."[134]

I think that Christ did make such appearances throughout the 40 days, because He had such a short time to complete this work before His Ascension to Heaven. Christ's appearance at the Sea of Tiberius was the third time He appeared to the Apostles as a group, and the third day on which he made appearances to the Apostles and others among His closest disciples. But it was not the third appearance all together. This third appearance must have occurred not long after Jesus' second appearance (on Divine Mercy Sunday), for He continued to appear to the Apostles and disciples on other occasions over the course of the 40 days from His Resurrection to His Ascension (cf. Jn 20:30; Acts 1:1-3; 1 Cor 15:6-7).

The Apostles and disciples who were present for this third appearance of the risen Christ were seven. "These were together: Simon Peter and Thomas, who is called the Twin, and Nathanael, who was from Cana of Galilee, and the sons of Zebedee, and two others of his disciples." (Jn 21:2). The sons of Zebedee are John the Gospel writer and James the Greater (Mt 4:18-22). According to Blessed Anne Catherine Emmerich, the two other disciples were John Mark and Silas. These two disciples are mentioned repeatedly in Acts of the Apostles (e.g. Acts 15:22-41).

The More Than Five Hundred

"Next he was seen by more than five hundred brothers at one time, many of whom remain, even to the present time, although some have fallen asleep. Next, he was seen by James, then by all the Apostles." (1 Cor 15:6-7).

Saint Paul the Apostle names further occasions when Jesus appeared to the Apostles. These appearances must have occurred after the appearance at the Sea of Tiberius, for Sacred Scripture counts the appearance at the Sea of Tiberius as only the third to a group of Apostles and disciples. Saint Paul's letter to the Corinthians mentions the appearance to the five hundred brethren only briefly. However, some details are given by Blessed Anne Catherine, based on her visions from God.

According to Blessed Anne Catherine, the Apostles and many other disciples gathered on a hilltop near the Sea of Tiberius (also called the Sea of Galilee). The Virgin Mary was also present, along with Saint Veronica and the holy women (including those holy women who went to the tomb, I suppose). Peter and the Apostles taught the hundreds of people who were gathered there. Then Jesus appeared and taught the people. Jesus began to teach that His followers must endure sufferings and persecutions, and that they must love Him more than their own relatives (cf. Mt 10:16-23, 34-39). "About two hundred of His hearers withdrew when they heard him talking of such things."[135] Even after the Crucifixion and Resurrection of Jesus Christ, some people rejected the teaching of Christ and abandoned Him. (It is the same today. Many people have abandoned Christ because they find some of His Church's teachings unacceptable.)

Saint Paul does not say that there were five hundred present for this appearance, but rather that there were "more than five hundred brothers" (1 Cor 15:6). Did this group of more than five hundred include the two hundred or so who left because they would not accept Christ's words? Since Sacred Scripture calls these more than five hundred, "brothers," this number must refer to those who did not abandon Christ, but remained a part of the brothers, the community of believers. Thus, there were perhaps 700 or more persons gathered at the onset, but about 200 departed because they took offense at Christ's teaching.

When Jesus finished teaching the people, he vanished miraculously. He did not simply walk to another place. "Jesus vanished. His disappearance was like a light suddenly extinguished in their midst."[136] Sacred Scripture also indicates that Jesus appeared and disappeared miraculously after the Resurrection. "And their eyes were opened, and they recognized him. And he vanished from their eyes." (Lk 24:31). Jesus also appeared among the disciples though the doors were shut (or locked) out of fear of the Jews (Jn 20:19).

The appearance of the risen Christ to the more than five hundred brethren on a hilltop near the Sea of Tiberius was likely Jesus' fourth appearance to the Apostles and other disciples as a group. This appearance took place near the third appearance, which was at the Sea of Tiberius. Blessed Anne Catherine also tells us that the Apostles gathered on this hilltop soon after Jesus' appearance to a few of them on the shores of the Sea of Tiberius.[137]

The appearance of Jesus to the more than 500 does not seem, at first glance, to be mentioned in the Gospels. However, there is a passage, at the very end of the Gospel of Matthew, which describes an appearance of Jesus to the Eleven Apostles in Galilee.

"Now the eleven disciples went on to Galilee, to the mountain where Jesus had appointed them. And, seeing him, they worshipped him, but certain ones doubted. And Jesus, drawing near, spoke to them, saying: 'All authority has been given to me in heaven and on earth. Therefore, go forth and teach all nations, baptizing them in the name of the Father and of the Son and of the Holy Spirit, teaching them to observe all that I have ever commanded you. And behold, I am with you always, even to the consummation of the age.' " (Mt 28:16-20).

This appearance could not have occurred at the time of Jesus' Ascension to Heaven. Jesus met with His disciples in Galilee after the Resurrection (Mt 28:7; Mk 16:7; Jn 21:1). But He ascended to Heaven from "the mountain, which is called Olivet, which is next to Jerusalem, within a Sabbath day's journey." (Acts 1:12).

This appearance in Galilee likely occurred during the earlier part of the 40 days between the Resurrection and the Ascension, for some of the Eleven Apostles still have their doubts (Mt 28:17). Also, the first verse of this passage (Mt 28:16) indicates that the Eleven were not yet in Galilee; they had to go there to arrive at the mountain where they then saw Jesus.

Blessed Anne Catherine tells us that the appearance to the more than 500 occurred on a hill, which was located on a plateau or elevated region. She also uses the word "mountains" to describe that region. This region overlooked the Sea of Galilee (also called the Sea of Tiberius).[138] The descriptions of the location in the Gospel of Matthew and in the visions of Blessed Anne Catherine are in agreement. Thus, the appearance of Jesus on the mountain in Galilee (Mt 28:16-20) could well have been the same as His appearance to the more than 500 brethren (1 Cor 15:6).

James and All the Apostles

"Next, he was seen by James, then by all the Apostles. And last of all, he was seen also by me, as if I were someone born at the wrong time. For I am the least of the Apostles...." (1 Cor 15:7-9).

After mentioning the appearance of Jesus to the more than five hundred brethren, Saint Paul tells us that Jesus continued to appear to the Apostles. Jesus appeared to James, then to "all the Apostles." The name "James" could refer to one of the Twelve Apostles, either "James the son of Zebedee," called James the Greater, or "James the son of Alphaeus," called James the Less (Mt 10:2-3). Or, perhaps "James" refers to another disciple of Christ.

According to Blessed Anne Catherine, Jesus appeared to James the Less "alone on the mountain in Galilee...."[139] The first appearances of Jesus to the apostles and disciples were in Jerusalem and the surrounding area. Then the disciples went to Galilee, where a few of them saw Jesus at the sea of Tiberius, and more than 500 saw Him on the mountain overlooking the sea of Tiberius. Paul places the appearance to James after the appearance to the more than 500, so this appearance to James likely occurred in Galilee also. Thus the appearance of Jesus to James the Less alone on the mountain in Galilee is most likely the same appearance to James mentioned by Saint Paul.

When Paul uses the word "Apostles" in this passage, he is not referring solely to the eleven Apostles. Earlier in this passage, Paul refers to the Apostles as "the eleven" (1 Cor 15:5). But in the verses that follow, he includes himself as one of the apostles. Therefore, when Sacred Scripture tells us that Jesus appeared to James, then to "all the Apostles," this was not an appearance only to the eleven Apostles, but to a larger group of preachers of the Word of God, whom Paul refers to as apostles. However, since Paul states that this group included "all the Apostles," the eleven Apostles must also have been present.

Further Appearances of the Risen Christ

"He also presented himself alive to them, after his Passion, appearing to them throughout forty days and speaking about the kingdom of God with many elucidations." (Acts 1:3).

During the 40 days between the Resurrection and the Ascension, Jesus appeared to His disciples and to those who were not yet disciples. Most of these appearances are not specifically mentioned in Sacred Scripture. Blessed Anne Catherine Emmerich spoke of some of those additional appearances.

"Jesus communicated with the Apostles quite naturally in those last days. He ate and prayed with them, walked with them in many directions, and repeated all that He had before told them. He appeared also to Simon of Cyrene as he was working in a garden.... Jesus appeared also in other places, Bethlehem and Nazareth for instance.... He scattered blessings everywhere, and they that saw Him believed and joined the Apostles and disciples."[140]

The Ascension of Jesus Christ to Heaven

"But he, rising early on the first Sabbath, appeared first to Mary Magdalene, from whom he had cast out seven demons." (Mk 16:19).

"Then he led them out as far as Bethania. And lifting up his hands, he blessed them. And it happened that, while he was blessing them, he withdrew from them, and he was carried up into heaven. And worshiping, they returned to Jerusalem with great joy. And they were always in the temple, praising and blessing God. Amen." (Lk 24:50-53).

"Then they returned to Jerusalem from the mountain, which is called Olivet, which is next to Jerusalem, within a Sabbath day's journey." (Acts 1:12).

The Gospel of Mark mentions the Ascension briefly in a single verse (Mk 16:19), but does not give any information as to the time and place of the Ascension. The Gospel of Luke and the Acts of the Apostles provide the most information about the time and place of the Ascension.

According to the Acts of the Apostles, the Ascension occurred from the Mount of Olives; Acts clearly describes the Apostles returning from the Mount of Olivet after the Ascension (Acts 1:12). This mount is located across the Kidron valley, a Sabbath day's journey (a short walk) from Jerusalem. A sabbath day's journey was considered to be 2,000 cubits[141] (which is approx. one half to two thirds of one mile, or about one kilometer).[142] The Gospel of John tells us that Jesus and the Apostles crossed the Kidron valley to get to the garden where the Passion of Jesus began (Jn 18:1). This garden was on the Mount of Olives (Lk 22:39; Mk 14:26; Mt 26:30).

Though Jesus met with His disciples in Galilee after the Resurrection, the Ascension of Jesus Christ occurred near Jerusalem, not in Galilee. The Gospel of Matthew ends with an event in Galilee, but this event was not the Ascension (Mt 28:16-20). This passage does not describe Jesus being raised up to Heaven, but instead ends with the words of Jesus teaching the Apostles and giving them the authority to continue His ministry.

The Gospel of Luke and the Acts of the Apostles were both written by Saint Luke (cf. Lk 1:1-4 and Acts 1:1-2). But in the Gospel of Luke, the only place mentioned in association with the Ascension is Bethany (i.e. Bethania). Luke tells us that Jesus led the disciples out "as far as Bethania," that he blessed the disciples, and that the Ascension of Jesus Christ to Heaven occurred while Jesus was blessing them (Lk 24:50-53). And Luke tells us in Acts that Jesus Ascended to Heaven from the Mount of Olives.

"And it happened that, when he had drawn near to Bethphage and Bethania, to the mount which is called Olivet, he sent two of his disciples, saying: 'Go into the town which is opposite you. Upon entering it, you will find the colt of a donkey, tied, on which no man has ever sat. Untie it, and lead it here.' " (Lk 19:29-30).

The town of Bethany was not far from Jerusalem; the center of Bethany was less than two miles to the east from the city walls of Jerusalem.[143] The Mount of Olives is also to the east of Jerusalem, across the Kidron Valley. The town of Bethany was located on the eastern slopes of the Mount of Olives.[144] The Ascension of Jesus occurred from the top of the Mount of Olives, and not from the center of the town of Bethany. However, the top of the Mount of Olives may well have been considered a part of the town, since it was certainly located on the outskirts of the town of Bethany. Similarly, Jesus was born in a cave on the outskirts of the town of Bethlehem, not in the center of the town where most of the buildings were located. Yet we still truly say that Christ was born in Bethlehem.[145]

That is why Sacred Scripture tells us that Jesus and His disciples went out of Jerusalem "as far as Bethania" at the time of the Ascension of Jesus to Heaven. They went as far as the outskirts of the town of Bethany, on the Mount of Olives, but not to the center of the town. There was a huge crowd of disciples gathered around Jesus at the time of the Ascension. "The multitude that here surrounded Jesus was so great that I could no longer count them."[146] So then, there were disciples gathered over a large area of the Mount of Olives, and certainly also down the east side, approaching Bethany.

The Month and Day of the Ascension

"He also presented himself alive to them, after his Passion, appearing to them throughout forty days and speaking about the kingdom of God with many elucidations." (Acts 1:3).

The number of days from the Resurrection to the Ascension of Jesus Christ was 40 days. Sacred Scripture tells us that Jesus appeared to the disciples after His Resurrection over the course of 40 days. Jesus certainly appeared to His disciples on the day of the Resurrection and on the day of the Ascension. Therefore, the 40 days is to be counted inclusively, so that the day of the Resurrection is counted as day 1 and the day of the Ascension is counted as day 40.

Jesus rose from the dead on a Sunday. Counting inclusively 40 days from any Sunday will bring us to a Thursday, so that Jesus must have ascended to Heaven on a Thursday. And it is on Thursday that the Church celebrates the Ascension of Jesus Christ, sometimes called "Ascension Thursday."

Jesus was crucified on Friday, April 7 of A.D. 19, and He rose from the dead on Sunday, April 9 of A.D. 19. The Ascension of Jesus Christ to Heaven, on the 40th day of the Resurrection, must then have occurred on Thursday, May 18 of A.D. 19.

The Time of Day of the Ascension

Sacred Scripture does not tell us at what time of day the Ascension of Jesus to Heaven occurred. Blessed Anne Catherine Emmerich, based on her visions from God, indicates that the Ascension happened sometime in late morning, but she does not give an exact time.

First, Jesus and the Eleven Apostles, the Virgin Mary, and other disciples left the house of the Last Supper at dawn on the day of the Ascension. Jesus walked through the streets of Jerusalem, retracing the path He traveled during His Passion, and teaching the disciples at some length. The crowd grew, and Jesus and the disciples left the city and went to the Mount of Olives. Jesus stopped along the way and continued to teach the crowd for some time. Jesus then continued up the Mount, towards its summit.[147]

"The crowd followed as in a procession, ascending by the different paths that encircled the mount.... Jesus at each instant shone more brightly and His motions became more rapid. The disciples hastened after Him, but it was impossible to overtake Him. When He reached the top of the mountain, He was resplendent as a beam of white sunlight. A shining circle, glancing in all the colors of the rainbow, fell from Heaven around Him.... Jesus Himself shone still more brightly than the glory about Him. He laid the left hand on His breast and, raising the right, turned slowly around, blessing the whole world."[148]

"And now the rays of light from above united with the glory emanating from Jesus, and I saw Him disappearing, dissolving as it were in the light from Heaven, vanishing as He rose.... He disappeared as it were in a cloud of light."[149]

After Jesus ascended to Heaven, two angels appeared and spoke to the disciples (Acts 1:10-11). The disciples remained on the Mount of Olives for some time, talking with one another and wondering at the miraculous event that had just occurred.[150] "It was past noon before the crowd entirely dispersed."[151] Here Blessed Anne Catherine gives us an indication that the Ascension occurred before noontime, and that the crowd remained until sometime in the afternoon. If the Ascension had occurred at or after noon, she would have had no reason to remark that the crowd remained on the Mount of Olives until after noontime—they would not have had to remain any additional length of time to disperse after noontime.

Jesus and the disciples began their walk to the Mount of Olives at about dawn, and according to Blessed Anne Catherine's description, they spent a considerable time retracing part of the Way of the Cross, and additional time listening to Jesus teach on the Mount of Olives.[152] All these events must have filled up the early morning hours. Therefore, the Ascension of Jesus Christ to Heaven occurred sometime in mid to late morning, but before noontime.

Between the Ascension and Pentecost

"And dining with them, he instructed them that they should not depart from Jerusalem, but that they should wait for the Promise of the Father, 'about which you have heard,' he said, 'from my own mouth. For John, indeed, baptized with water, but you shall be baptized with the Holy Spirit, not many days from now.' " (Acts 1:4-5).

The Apostles did not travel about the country preaching the Word of God until after the descent of the Holy Spirit at Pentecost. Instead, they remained in Jerusalem and devoted themselves to prayer (Acts 1:14). Blessed Anne Catherine tells us that, during the days following the Ascension of Christ to Heaven, the Apostles stayed in the same building where the Last Supper was held. "On the following days I saw the Apostles always together and the Blessed Virgin with them in the house of the Last Supper."[153] The "upper room" mentioned by Acts as the place where the Apostles gathered (Acts 1:13) was the same upper room mentioned in the Gospel of Luke as the place of the Last Supper (Lk 22:12). This place was called the Cenacle, a word meaning "a small dining room, usually on an upper floor."[154]

"And they appointed two: Joseph, who was called Barsabbas, who was surnamed Justus, and Matthias.... And they cast lots concerning them, and the lot fell upon Matthias. And he was numbered with the eleven Apostles." (Acts 1:23, 26).

Matthias became one of the Twelve Apostles, replacing Judas Iscariot. Matthias was with the Apostles and disciples from the beginning of Jesus' Ministry, from the baptism of John to the Ascension (Acts 1:21-22). Yet, during all that time, no one but Jesus knew that Matthias was to be one of the Twelve Apostles. He was among the Apostles as one of many other disciples, with no authority or distinction given to him until his appointment as an Apostle, which occurred between the Ascension and Pentecost.

According to Blessed Anne Catherine, it was Peter who suggested Joseph Barsabbas and Matthias as the two candidates to replace Judas Iscariot. Neither of these two men had ever considered becoming one of the Twelve. Some of the other disciples had entertained such a desire, but none of these were chosen.[155]

Blessed Anne Catherine also tells us that Peter put forward Barsabbas and Matthias as the two candidates on one day, but they waited until the following day to cast lots to decide between the two. In Sacred Scripture, the verse telling us which two were put forward as candidates (Acts 1:23) is followed by two verses saying that the Apostles and disciples prayed for God to reveal to them whom God had chosen to be an Apostle (Acts 1:24-25). Then the next verse describes the casting of lots to choose Matthias (Acts 1:26). In this way, Sacred Scripture indicates a period of prayer between the choosing of the two candidates and the choice of Matthias as one of the Twelve.

The length of that period of prayer is not stated, for Sacred Scripture does not always tell us on which days various events occurred. The absence of words indicating a change from one day to the next does not necessarily mean that the events being described all happened on the same day. In the same way, when a series of parables from the teaching of Christ are placed one after the other in Sacred Scripture, we should not assume that those parables were all taught on the same day.

Notice that Joseph had two other names: Barsabbas and Justus. These were not his last or middle names; they were nicknames. The name 'Justus' means 'just' or 'one who is just.' This Josephus was not only considered to be a just man, but had a reputation for being just which resulted in his being called 'Justus.' The name 'Barsabbas' means 'son of the Sabbath.' The word 'bar' in Hebrew means 'son,' as in 'bar mitzvah,' meaning 'son of the commandments,' and "Simon Bar-Jona," meaning 'Simon son of John' (cf. Mt 16:17 to John 21:15). The word 'sabbas' is merely an alternate spelling for the word Sabbath. Josephus was called 'son of the Sabbath,' most likely because he kept the Sabbath strictly and devoutly. And perhaps there was also some other connection between this Joseph and the Sabbath (or possibly the Sabbatical year).

Now this Joseph was well known to be a just man who kept the Sabbath devoutly, so well known that he was given the surnames of Justus and Barsabbas. Yet God chose the other just and devout man, Matthias, who was not so well known, to be the Twelfth Apostle. They chose Matthias by lot. But if they had decided between the two by voting, Joseph would likely have won the election, since he was more well known as a disciple of Christ.

Pentecost

"And when the days of Pentecost were completed, they were all together in the same place. And suddenly, there came a sound from heaven, like that of a wind approaching violently, and it filled the entire house where they were sitting. And there appeared to them separate tongues, as if of fire, which settled upon each one of them. And they were all filled with the Holy Spirit. And they began to speak in various languages, just as the Holy Spirit bestowed eloquence to them." (Acts 2:1-4).

The descent of the Holy Spirit occurred on the same day as the Jewish feast of Pentecost, which is also called Shavuot, or the Feast of Weeks. This feast is celebrated by the Jews on the 50th day from the second day of Passover (Nisan 16). Counting forward 50 days from Nisan 16 brings us to the 6th of the Jewish month of Sivan. The Feast of Weeks begins on Sivan 6 and continues for a second day on Sivan 7.

This Jewish feast is called Pentecost, meaning fiftieth, because it occurs on the 50th day from the second day of Passover. Pentecost is also called the Feast of Weeks because it begins on the day following the completion of 7 full weeks, or 50 days (Lev 23:9-21). The first fruits of the harvest of grain were brought by the Jews to the priests of the Temple of Jerusalem as an offering to God, during the Passover. Even though Sacred Scripture says that this was done on the morning after the first Sabbath after the harvest began (which would be during Passover), Jewish tradition eventually developed so that the first fruits of the grain harvest were offered to God always on the morning after the first holy day of Passover (that day is a kind of Sabbath). The year that Christ died, the first day of Passover was a Saturday, the Jewish Sabbath (Jn 19:14, 31). So the first fruits of the harvest were offered that year, in complete fulfillment of Sacred Scripture, on the morning after the Sabbath, which was also the morning after the first day of Passover.

The day after the Jewish Sabbath is Sunday and counting forward, inclusively, 50 days brings us also to a Sunday, the first day of the Jewish feast of Pentecost and the very first Christian Pentecost.

The Month and Day of Christian Pentecost

Jesus Christ rose from the dead on Sunday, April 9 of A.D. 19, which was Nisan 16 in the Jewish calendar. Nisan 16 is also the first day in the count of the 50 days until the Feast of Weeks (the Jewish feast of Pentecost). On the 40th day from the Resurrection, Jesus ascended to Heaven. Counting 40 days, beginning with the Resurrection on April 9, brings us to May 18, a Thursday, the day of Jesus' Ascension to Heaven. Ten days later the Jewish feast of Pentecost began, on the 50th day from Nisan 16, which was also the 50th day from the Resurrection.

When two days of the calendar occur 50 days apart, counting inclusively, they will coincide with the same day of the week. And since there are 50 days from Nisan 16 to Sivan 6 (the first day of Jewish Pentecost), those two days will always fall on the same day of the week. According to Sacred Scripture, the first day of the Jewish feast of Pentecost was to be celebrated on the morning after the seventh Sabbath. So the first day of the 50 days was to be the morning after the first Sabbath of Passover, and the last day of the 50 days was to be the morning after the seventh Sabbath (Lev. 23:15-16). The first of the seven Sabbaths, though, was not the first Sabbath of Passover, but the next Sabbath, the seventh day in the count of 50 days, (see chapter 7 for an explanation of 'the second first Sabbath'). The Jews at the time of Jesus' Ministry had developed a tradition of counting the 50 days from the second day of Passover (Nisan 16) to the 6th day of Sivan (50 days later), regardless of whether these days coincided with the morning after a Sabbath. However, the Jews at one time must have counted the 50 days from Sunday to Sunday (the Jewish Sabbath is Saturday, the morning after the Sabbath is Sunday).

The book of Leviticus in the Old Testament was written after the Jewish people had been delivered out of slavery in Egypt and had begun to live the teachings of God given to them by Moses. The Jewish people first lived these teachings, then handed them down from generation to generation by a tradition of words and of continued practice in their lives—a living tradition. The book of Leviticus was written afterwards, a written record of that living tradition. Therefore, when Sacred Scripture says that the 50 days was to be counted from the morning after the Sabbath to the morning after the seventh Sabbath (Sunday to Sunday), this must once have been the case. Only later did some Jewish religious leaders develop a new tradition of beginning the 50 days on the second day of Passover regardless of the day of the week.

Yet, by God's Providence, in the year that Christ died, the 50 days began and ended on a Sunday, according to the instruction of Sacred Scripture and the practice of the Jews in earlier times. Thus did Sacred Scripture instruct the Jews to live the feast of Passover in preparation for the Resurrection of the Christ and the Descent of the Spirit of God. The Descent of the Holy Spirit on Pentecost occurred on the 50th day from the Resurrection, on Sunday, May 28 of A.D. 19.

Chapter 4
The Virgin Birth of Jesus Christ

The Day of the Week

"Just before the close of the Sabbath Joseph went into Bethlehem, and as soon as the sun had set, he quickly bought a few necessary things—a stool, a little low table, a few little bowls, and some dried fruit and grapes."[156]

Here Blessed Anne Catherine Emmerich describes the sunset before the Birth of Christ. The Jewish Sabbath begins on Friday at sunset and ends on Saturday at sunset. Devout Jews would neither buy nor sell on the Sabbath. Joseph went into town to buy some things to prepare for the imminent birth of Jesus Christ, but he would not buy anything until after sunset. Joseph waited until the end of the Sabbath to buy the things he and Mary needed. Since the Sabbath ends at sunset on Saturday, it was on Saturday evening after sunset that Joseph bought these items.

"Mary had told St. Joseph that to-night at midnight would be the hour of the child's birth, for then the nine months since the Annunciation would have been completed."[157]

That very night, the night between Saturday and Sunday, Christ was born about the midnight hour. Blessed Anne Catherine repeatedly mentions the Jewish Sabbath as she describes in detail the events of the day before the birth of Christ.[158] She tells us how Joseph and Mary said their Sabbath prayers together. They also went for a short Sabbath walk, but spent most of the day in prayer and meditation. Christ was born late that night, after the Jewish Sabbath, at the beginning of the Christian Sabbath, which is Sunday. It was fitting that Jesus should be born just after the Jewish Sabbath and at the beginning of the Christian Sabbath, Sunday. For Jesus is the completion of the Promises made to the Jews and the fulfillment of the Jewish faith, and He is the beginning (and the end) of the Christian faith.

Blessed Anne Catherine Emmerich clearly taught, based on her visions from God, that Jesus was born very early on Sunday, before dawn. The word midnight, in its usage today, refers to 24:00 hours, that is, 12:00 a.m. The Virgin Mary informed Joseph that her Son Jesus would be born that night at midnight, but she was not using the word midnight as we use it today. The Jews divided the day into 12 hours and the night into 12 hours (no matter how long or short the night). So, midnight more likely meant approximately the middle of the night, about halfway between sunset and sunrise, (the sixth hour of the night). Jesus, the Light of the world, was born in the middle of the night.

The Birth of Our Lord occurred in a cave on the outskirts of Bethlehem. This cave was often used by shepherds, and had been a place of refuge and prayer for Joseph when he was young.[159] They laid the Child Jesus in a manger (Lk 2:16) within the cave.[160] And shepherds from the surrounding area came and worshipped the Christ Child (Lk 2:8-20).[161]

The Month and Day of Christ's Birth

"The reason why the Church keeps the feast exactly a month later than the actual event is because at one time, when an alteration in the calendar was made, some days and seasons were completely omitted."[162]

The Church currently celebrates the Birth of Our Lord on December 25. However, the Church does not teach that Christ was born in December. There is no date given in Christian doctrine for the Birth of Jesus. Furthermore, it is not necessary to faith or salvation to know the exact date of the Birth of Our Lord. It is enough to know that the Savior was born.

However, God did reveal to Blessed Anne Catherine Emmerich the exact day and month of the Birth of Jesus Christ. In her visions, she saw the Birth of Jesus as occurring on November 25: "she dated the day of Christ's birth a month earlier, that is to say on November 25...."[163] God often gave Blessed Anne Catherine visions of events in the life of Jesus on the same day and month as each event actually occurred. In this way, God clearly revealed to her the true dates of important events in the lives of Jesus and Mary.

God also gave Blessed Anne Catherine visions of these same events on the day specified for each event in the liturgical calendar of the Church. God wants His people to know the true dates of these important events, but He also wants us to follow the current liturgical calendar of the Church. In teaching Blessed Anne Catherine the true dates, God nevertheless did not allow her to ignore the liturgical calendar to follow the true dates.

The same reasoning applies today. God wants us to know the true dates of these important events, but we must continue to follow the Church's liturgical calendar, for the Christian Church is Christ's Church. However, I believe that the Church will eventually make changes to the liturgical calendar to bring these true dates into practice throughout the universal Church (see chapter 15).

"The actual date of Christ's Birth, as I always see it, is four weeks earlier than its celebration by the Church; it must have happened on St. Catherine's feast-day. I always see the Annunciation as happening at the end of February."[164]

St. Catherine of Alexandria's feast-day is November 25. In this case, when Blessed Anne Catherine says "four weeks," she does not mean 28 days, but rather a full month. The actual date of the Birth of Jesus Christ, as revealed to Blessed Anne Catherine, was November 25, a full month earlier than the date in the liturgical calendar of the Church.

The date of November 25 for the Birth of Jesus Christ agrees with the date revealed to Blessed Anne Catherine for the Incarnation of Christ (the Annunciation). She saw the Annunciation as occurring on February 25. And she states that it was a full nine months from the Incarnation to the Birth of Christ. "Mary had told St. Joseph that to-night at midnight would be the hour of the child's birth, for then the nine months since the Annunciation would have been completed."[165]

The Year of Christ's Birth

The year of the Birth of Jesus Christ can be determined using two separate lines of reasoning. The first is based on the visions given to Blessed Anne Catherine Emmerich. The second is based on a new chronology of the reigns of various Roman rulers.

Blessed Anne Catherine Emmerich does not reveal the year of Christ's Birth by the B.C./A.D. calendar system. However, she gives us much information, which can be used to determine the year of the Birth of Jesus Christ. First, as stated above, Jesus was born in a year when November 25 fell on a Sunday. But November 25 did not fall on a Sunday in any of the years most commonly given for the Birth of Our Lord (see Appendix I, Chart 2). From 20 B.C. to A.D. 7, inclusive, the only years in which November 25 coincided with a Sunday are **15 B.C., 4 B.C.,** and **A.D. 3**. Most of the more commonly proposed years for Christ's Birth, in the range of 3 B.C. to A.D. 1 and 12 B.C. to 5 B.C., are then ruled out.[166] So, without referring to the conclusions of chapter 2, we begin with 15 B.C., 4 B.C., and A.D. 3 as possible years for the Birth of Christ.

Seven Years Earlier

Blessed Anne Catherine Emmerich tells us that the dates which are typically given for events around the time of the Birth of Jesus are offset from the actual dates. "Afterwards people forgot the period of three years and a portion of a year ... and then reckoned our new era as beginning four years later, so that Christ was born seven years and a portion of a year earlier than according to our reckoning."[167] She never stated the actual year of Christ's Birth, but she did clearly say that Christ was born 7 years earlier than was generally believed. (Blessed Anne Catherine adds "and a portion of a year," which is consistent with her date of November 25, instead of December 25, for the month and day of Christ's Birth.)

The phrase "according to our reckoning" refers to some date for the Birth of Christ that was generally accepted during Blessed Anne Catherine's lifetime (late 1700's to early 1800's), but she never states which year that was. Even so, there has never been a generally-accepted date for the Birth of Christ in any year later than 1 B.C. Many scholars have suggested various dates for the Birth of Christ, but these dates generally range from 12 B.C. to 1 B.C.[168] Therefore, the generally-accepted date for the Birth of Christ, (from which Blessed Anne Catherine counts back 7 years to the true date for the Birth of Christ), can be no later than 1 B.C., and the true date of Christ's Birth can be no later than 8 B.C. Also, the generally-accepted date can be no earlier than 12 B.C., making the actual date no earlier than 19 B.C. On this basis, the range for the year of Christ's Birth must be between 19 B.C. and 8 B.C., inclusive.

Many scholars believe that Christ was born sometime in the range of 6 B.C. to 1 B.C., but none of these dates are seven years earlier than any year that was reckoned as the year of Christ's Birth during Blessed Anne Catherine's lifetime. Even in the earliest days of the Church, it was generally believed that Christ was born in some year during the period of time which was later called "B.C.".[169] On this basis, any year for the Birth of Jesus Christ later than 8 B.C. is too late to be reconciled with her statement that "Christ was born 7 years and a portion of a year earlier" than people generally believed during her lifetime. Therefore, the years 4 B.C. and 3 A.D. do not agree with the chronological information given by Blessed Anne Catherine Emmerich.

Which year was generally-accepted during Blessed Anne Catherine's lifetime as the year of Christ's Birth? The year 8 B.C. was long considered a possible year for the Birth of Christ. For example, an article in an older edition of the reference book *Catholic Commentary*, suggested 8 B.C. as a likely year for Christ's Birth.[170] And historians have long held that there was a census of some kind conducted in 8 B.C. (Though it now appears that the census of 8 B.C. did not apply to the Jews, this was probably not known during her lifetime.) If the seven years is to be counted from this commonly-held date for the Birth of Christ, then counting back from 8 B.C. brings us to 15 B.C. The year 15 B.C. fits well with the information from Blessed Anne Catherine about the Birth of Jesus Christ.

Christ was born on Nov. 25 and on a Sunday. From 20 B.C. to A.D. 7, the only years in which Nov. 25 fell on a Sunday are 15 B.C., 4 B.C., and A.D. 3. But these last two years, 4 B.C. and 3 A.D., are too late to fit Blessed Anne Catherine's statement that Christ was born 7 years earlier than a commonly-held date for the Birth of Christ. Therefore, Christ was born on Sunday, Nov. 25 of 15 B.C.

From the Birth to the Crucifixion

The length of Jesus Christ's life from the Incarnation to His Crucifixion was 33 years and six weeks (as explained in chapter 2). Christ was born Nov. 25 of 15 B.C. and His Incarnation occurred Feb. 25 of that same year. Counting forward 33 years and six weeks from Feb. 25 of 15 B.C. brings us to exactly April 7 of 19 A.D. That day coincided with Nisan 14 and a Friday, in agreement with what the Gospel of John states about the Crucifixion. Therefore, Christ died on April 7 of A.D. 19, and Christ rose from the dead on April 9 of A.D. 19.

Notice that the above date for the Birth of Christ was determined independent of the date for the Crucifixion. Yet, these two dates are in perfect agreement, exact to the day, with the age of Christ given by Blessed Anne Catherine. Furthermore, Blessed Anne Catherine did not know that this information fit together so well. There is no indication whatsoever that she knew in which years Nov. 25 was a Sunday, nor in which years Nisan 14 was a Friday. She never states the year in B.C. or A.D. of any event in Christ's life. She only gives separate pieces of chronological information derived from her visions from God. Yet it all fits together so well because it is true.

These dates for the Birth, Crucifixion, and Resurrection of Jesus are significantly earlier than the dates given by other scholars for these events. Further evidence in support of this early chronology is given, not only in the chapters on the Birth and Crucifixion of Jesus, but throughout this book. An examination of the chronology for other events in the lives of Jesus Christ and the Virgin Mary lends additional support to this chronology. For example, Blessed Anne Catherine's comments about the Holy Family's flight to Egypt also support the year 15 B.C. as the year of Christ's Birth. And the chronology of the rebuilding of the Second Temple of Jerusalem fits the information given by Blessed Anne Catherine about the Immaculate Conception of the Virgin Mary.

Additional Information

Blessed Anne Catherine Emmerich presents some additional details about events surrounding the Birth of Jesus Christ. Though we have already determined the year of Christ's Birth from the information above, these additional details clarify the situation in Israel at the time of Our Lord's Birth. She gives interesting information about the census which brought Joseph and Mary to Bethlehem, about the role of the scribes and Jewish religious leaders in collecting the Roman tax, about the date for the death of king Herod, and about the Christmas Star. This information is not essential to establishing the year of the Birth of Jesus Christ, but it does lend additional support to the chronology.

The Day and Month in the Jewish Calendar

In 15 B.C., Nov. 25 coincided with Kislev 5 in the Jewish calendar.[171] (See the chapter 17 for details on determining dates in the ancient Jewish calendar.) The Jewish date of Kislev 5 for the Birth of Christ is also consistent with the conclusions of chapter 5 of this book, on the date of the Incarnation.

Clemens Brentano, the man who wrote down Blessed Anne Catherine's visions, commented in one place that Jesus must have been born on Kislev 12,[172] but in another place he states it was Kislev 10.[173] These dates were conclusions drawn by Clemens Brentano. Blessed Anne Catherine herself said only, "I think Christ was born in the month Kislev." [174]

The sources of Clemens Brentano's error in determining the Jewish date for the Birth of Christ is probably the statement of Blessed Anne Catherine that Hanukah (Kislev 25) that year coincided with Dec. 8 (beginning the previous evening on Dec. 7). However, in 15 B.C., the new moon occurred **after** noontime on Nov. 20, at 12:39 p.m. Jerusalem time (10:39 UT), making Nov. 21 the first day of Kislev (by calculation). Nov. 25 would then be Kislev 5, and Dec. 8 would be Kislev 18. Hanukah fell exactly a week later (Dec. 15 in 15 B.C.) than Blessed Anne Catherine thought.

When speaking about the days following the Birth of Jesus Christ, Blessed Anne Catherine also said that the feast of Hanukah on Kislev 25 (the "Feast of the Consecration of the Temple") would have coincided with a Sabbath that year, and so was postponed a day (to avoid a conflict between the Sabbath day of rest and the celebration of Hanukah).[175] In 15 B.C., Kislev 25 (by calculation) would have fallen on a Saturday, and so Hanukah that year may well have been postponed until Sunday. Her statement that Hanukah fell on a Saturday (but was moved to Sunday) agrees with her other chronological statements.

A Note About The Taxation

Joseph traveled to Bethlehem with the Virgin Mary at the time of the Birth of Jesus Christ (Lk 2:1-7), in order to take part in a Roman census (or enrollment). Blessed Anne Catherine tells us that this enrollment was for the purpose of taxation.

"This taxation has been going on for several months.... Joseph came rather late to the tax office, but was treated in quite a friendly way. He has not paid anything yet, but was asked about his means, and stated that he had no land and lived by his handicraft and by the assistance given him by his wife's mother.... Only the people who are not resident anywhere and have no land on which they can be taxed have to present themselves at their birthplace." [176]

"There are a great number of scribes and high officials in many of the rooms.... There are also present Pharisees and Sadducees, priests, elders and every kind of official and scribe, both Jewish and Roman."[177]

Here she describes the place in Bethlehem where the taxes were collected during the Roman taxation and enrollment at the time of the Birth of Jesus. Notice that the Jewish religious leaders are present to assist the Romans with the process of enrollment and taxation. As Joseph is being questioned by the tax officials, they consult genealogical records on long scrolls.

"They are asking him who he is and are referring to long scrolls of which a great many are hanging on the walls. They unroll them and read aloud to him his ancestry and also Mary's: he did not seem to know that she also descended so directly from David through Joachim...."[178]

The Jewish priests and scribes must have kept detailed genealogical records (cf. Nehemiah 7:5ff). Keeping records of who was descended from whom was a religious duty. They knew that the Messiah would be a descendant of David. If no genealogical records were kept, then how would they know who was descended from David? They would then lose one of the signs indicating the Messiah.

These detailed genealogical records were used by the Jewish religious leaders to assist the Romans in identifying the Jewish people for the enrollment and taxation. According to Blessed Anne Catherine, the tax was divided into three installments. One installment went to Caesar Augustus and to Herod. Another went to some kind of debt, related to the building of the Temple.[179]

"The third installment is intended for widows and poor people, who have had nothing for a long time, but of all this little reaches the right people, just as happens to-day. The money is meant for nothing but good causes, and yet remains in the hands of the great."[180]

The Jewish religious leaders assisted in the collection of the tax by making their genealogical records available, thus helping the Romans to identify the Jews for the enrollment and taxation. In return, the Jewish religious leaders received a portion of the tax money, for the relief of the poor. Yet, according to Blessed Anne Catherine, that tax money remained mostly in the hands of the Jewish leaders, though they were supposed to dispense the money to the poor among their own people. These Jewish leaders took money intended for widows, orphans, and the poor, and kept most of it for themselves.

Years later, Jesus was asked whether or not the Jews should pay the Roman tax. "So in response, Jesus said to them, 'Then render to Caesar, the things that are of Caesar; and to God, the things that are of God.' And they wondered over him." (Mk 12:17). Jesus is here criticizing the Pharisees for receiving and keeping part of the tax money. He is saying that the tax money, paid in Roman coinage, could be lawfully paid to the Romans, but it was not right for the Pharisees and other religious leaders to receive and keep a portion of the money. The things of Caesar, the tax money, should only go to Caesar, not to the religious leaders. The Jewish religious leaders were supposed to belong only to God.

The Pharisees were hypocritical in the matter of the taxation. They helped collect the tax by providing genealogical and other information to the Romans about the Jewish people, and they even kept some of the tax money for themselves, yet they despised those among their own people who dirtied their hands by actually collecting the money

(Lk 15:1-2; 18:10-11). They must have understood the answer which Jesus gave about taxation as being, in part, a criticism of their hypocrisy concerning the tax money.

The Death of King Herod

As explained in chapter 12, Herod died in early 8 B.C. Blessed Anne Catherine places the death of Herod about the sixth year of Christ's life. "He died about the time of Christ's sixth year."[181] By these words, she could mean when Jesus was six years old, in other words, when Jesus had completed just over six years since His Birth. Or, she could mean when Jesus was five years old, since he would have completed five full years since His Birth, and would then be in His sixth year.

In another place, she states the age of Christ at Herod's death differently. "(I am not sure whether it was in His fifth or seventh year).... I saw two angels appearing to Him and announcing the death of Herod the Great."[182] If Herod died after Christ's sixth birthday, then Christ would have been in His seventh year since Birth at that time. And if his death occurred only a little while after Christ's sixth birthday, then the statement the Herod died "about the time of" Christ's sixth year would also be a good approximation. This interpretation also agrees with the conclusion of chapter 12, that Herod died in early 8 B.C. So, despite Blessed Anne Catherine's uncertainty on this point, Jesus was about six years old at the time of Herod's death.

The usual assumption of Biblical chronologists is that Herod died about 2 years after the Birth of Christ, shortly after the Massacre of the Holy Innocents. The Gospel of Matthew does not mention any events between the death of the Holy Infants and Herod's death (Mt 2:18, 19). However, the assumption that Herod died soon after his attempt to kill the Christ Child is unwarranted. Sacred Scripture indicates only that Herod was still alive about 2 years after the Birth of Christ. There is no plain statement in the Gospel of Matthew as to the total number of years from the Birth of Christ to the death of Herod.

When telling a story about a series of events, it is neither necessary nor usual to describe the events of every period of time from the start of the story to the end. Ordinarily, the events important to the story are related in some detail, and any events that are not relevant to the story are omitted—no matter what the length of time. Just because there is no mention of the period of time between two events does not mean that the events occurred immediately one after the other.

Notice here that, of the three years which we initially considered as possible years for the Birth of Jesus Christ—15 B.C., 4 B.C., A.D. 3—only the year 15 B.C. makes sense, if Herod died about 6 years after the Birth of Christ. If Christ was born in 4 B.C., then He would have reached His sixth birthday in late A.D. 3, placing Herod's death much later than can be accounted for by the historical evidence (see chapters 12 and 13). And, for much the same reasons, the year A.D. 3 is also too late to be the year of Christ's Birth.

The Christmas Star

"And so, when Jesus had been born in Bethlehem of Judah, in the days of king Herod, behold, Magi from the east arrived in Jerusalem, saying: 'Where is he who was born king of the Jews? For we have seen his star in the east, and we have come to adore him.' " (Mt 2:1-2).

In attempting to determine the year of Christ's Birth, many scholars have examined astronomical evidence in search of the Christmas Star. Various natural phenomena have been considered as possible explanations for the star, including comets, supernovae, and the conjunction of two planets.[183]

Blessed Anne Catherine Emmerich gives a detailed description of the Christmas Star. She describes the star as having a tail: "...always following the star, whose long tail reaches down to earth."[184]

"The star which led them was really like a round ball with light streaming out of it as from a mouth. It always seemed to me as if this ball, which was as it were swinging on a shaft of light, was guided by the hand of a supernatural being. In the daytime I saw a light brighter than daylight going before them."[185]

She repeatedly describes the Christmas Star as one would describe a comet. These descriptions rule out the idea that the Christmas Star could have been a conjunction of planets or a supernova. Comets have long tails, but supernovae and planets do not. However, there is more to the Christmas Star than can be attributed to any mere comet.

Natural, Yet Supernatural

"...And behold, the star that they had seen in the east went before them, even until, arriving, it stood still above the place where the child was." (Mt 2:9).

Sacred Scripture clearly describes a supernatural aspect to the Christmas Star. Comets, stars, supernovae, and the conjunction of planets do not both move across the sky and then stop above one small place on earth. If the event was merely a natural phenomenon, the wise men would not have been able to find the exact location of the Christ Child, in a cave on the outskirts of Bethlehem. Thus, if the Christmas Star was a comet, it was not merely a comet. It was guided by the hand of God, appearing at a time chosen by God, and more. Though a comet appeared in the heavens as a sign of the Birth of Christ, there was a supernatural light which also appeared and which guided the three wise men (the Magi).

Blessed Anne Catherine testifies to this supernatural aspect of the Christmas Star. "The star which went before them was not the comet, but a shining brilliance borne by an angel. By day they followed the angel."[186] It is possible for a comet to be bright enough, and close enough to the earth, so that it would be visible even in the daytime.[187] But this would not provide enough information for the Magi to navigate to a precise location within Israel and within the area of Bethlehem. So many miracles happened during the Ministry of Jesus Christ, is it so hard to believe that the Christmas Star could have a miraculous aspect? The three kings were able to find the exact place of the Birth of Jesus Christ by this miraculous sign.

"...the kings saw the star appear bright and clear above the hill where the Cave of the Nativity was, the light that streamed from it descending in a vertical line on to the hill. The star seemed to grow larger as it drew near until it became a body of light which looked to me as big as a sheet. I saw them at first gazing at it in great astonishment."[188]

The Christmas star was also miraculous in that it grew brighter or dimmer, not by nature, but by the hand of God. "I did not see the star always shining brightly before them; sometimes it was quite dim. It seemed to shine more brightly in places where good people lived...."[189] The Christmas Star brightened in areas where the people were more devout and holy, but dimmed in places where the people were less devoted to God. When they arrived in the city of Jerusalem, the star was very dim. And when they went to see Herod, the Christmas Star had vanished from their sight.[190] After hearing what the three wise men had to say, Herod himself searched the night sky to see the Star, but could not find it.

This disappearance of the Star was a sign to them that Herod was wicked and not to be trusted. They had perhaps made a mistake in going to Herod at all. Since the Star had been lost to their sight for a time, the three wise men were overjoyed to see the Christmas Star again, after they left Herod. "Then, seeing the star, they were gladdened by a very great joy." (Mt 2:10). The Star had reappeared to show them they were again on the right path. This disappearance and reappearance of the Star is another indication that the Christmas Star was partly miraculous.

Who Could See the Star?

Some commentators have suggested that only the three kings could see the Christmas Star, because it was wholly miraculous and only given to them to see. On the contrary, Blessed Anne Catherine relates that the three kings "awoke the inhabitants living near to show them the star."[191] They saw the Star in wonder, but did not understand its meaning.[192]

Also, she mentions that the shepherds, to whom the angels announced the Birth of Christ (Lk 2:8-20), also saw the Christmas Star above the cave where Jesus was born. "They looked about them, and were astonished to see a wonderful radiance over the place where the Cave of the Nativity was." [193]

Thus, the star could be seen by many people, but it's meaning was open only to those who were open to the Spirit of God. The three kings, when they interpreted the stars and the Christmas Star, found meaning partly in the arrangement and patterns in the actual stars, but more so through the inner guidance of the Holy Spirit. The Christmas star was a real object, a comet, but it had a supernatural aspect to it.

One Becomes Two

According to Blessed Anne Catherine, when Christ was born of the Virgin Mary, the three wise men saw the Christmas Star split in two, forming an image which they interpreted as a picture of a virgin and her child. She describes what the three wise men saw in this heavenly sign. "They were on a pyramid-shaped tower looking through long tubes at the Star of Jacob, which had a tail. The star split asunder before their eyes, and I saw a great shining virgin appear therein, before whom a radiant child hovered in the air."[194]

The splitting of the comet, the Christmas Star, was an actual event seen in the sky which symbolized the Birth of Jesus Christ. Comets do split into pieces in nature,[195] as has been seen in recent years with the Shoemaker-Levy comet, which split into several pieces before colliding with Jupiter. However, the splitting of the Christmas Star was an act of God signifying the Birth of the Savior, not a mere coincidence of nature.[196]

Halley's Comet

The Christmas Star could not have been Halley's Comet. Halley's Comet was visible from late August to mid October in 12 B.C.[197] But, according to Blessed Anne Catherine, the Magi did not begin their journey until the night of Christ's Birth, very early on November 25, and they ended their journey about December 23, at the end of the day.[198] The time frame for the appearance of Halley's Comet does not match the time frame for the journey of the Magi. Therefore, they could not have been guided by Halley's Comet.

The three wise men began their journey because they saw the Christmas Star split in two. If Halley's Comet had split into two pieces, then its orbit around the sun would have been significantly altered and it would not return each time after the usual 75 to 77 year length of time. Halley's Comet appeared in 87 B.C., in 12 B.C. and again in A.D. 66, which is a period of about the same length of time.[199] Also, there is no record of Halley's comet splitting in two in 12 B.C.

Observers of the Stars

" 'Where is he who was born king of the Jews? For we have seen his star in the east, and we have come to adore him.' " (Mt 2:2).

The Magi were observers of the stars. Their interpretation of signs they saw in the night sky led them to understand that the Messiah, the long-promised king of the Jews had been born. They came from the East, not looking for any mere human king, but a king who was Divine, for they came to worship Him (cf. Mt 2:11). Guided by the grace of the Holy Spirit, they understood signs in the stars, which were not understood even by the religious leaders of the Jews. The chief priests and scribes of the Jews knew where the Messiah would be born, but not when (Mt 2:4-6). Herod had to find out from the Magi when the star first appeared (Mt 2:7).

Some commentators have suggested that the Magi could have arrived many months after the Birth of Jesus Christ. This theory is contradicted by the visions of Blessed Anne Catherine Emmerich, who stated that the wise men started their journey the day of the Birth of Jesus Christ (November 25) and arrived about a month later (December 23).[200] Sacred Scripture also makes it clear that the Magi arrived after the birth of Jesus, not before. Notice that the wise men ask where is "he who was born," (Mt 2:2) indicating that they knew from the signs in the stars that the Messiah had already been born.

Other Theories

There was a comet seen in 5 B.C., but this comet was seen early in the year, as early as March and no later than June.[201] The Magi made their journey, following the star, in the latter part of the year, from late November to late December. Since Jesus was born late in the calendar year, following this comet would not have brought the Magi to Bethlehem at the time of Christ's Birth.

There was a triple conjunction of the planets Jupiter and Saturn in 7 B.C. From the point of view of an observer on earth, the planets Jupiter and Saturn appeared to move close to one another and then move apart three times in 7 B.C.—on May 27, October 6, and December 1. Some commentators have suggested that this triple conjunction was the sign in the stars which the Magi interpreted to mean that the Messiah was born.[202]

On the contrary, Blessed Anne Catherine Emmerich repeatedly describes the Christmas Star as having a long tail, and in one place she actually refers to it as a comet. She further explains that the Magi saw patterns, which they interpreted as pictures, in the Christmas star. The appearance of a comet's tail will vary greatly from one comet to another. The appearance of the comet's tail is affected by the location of the sun relative to the direction of the comet. As viewed from earth, the shape and direction of a comet's tail will change as the comet moves through its orbit around the sun. Thus, a comet with a long tail can have an appearance which is complex enough to be interpreted as a picture—one that changes with time,—but a conjunction of planets cannot.

Also, if the Magi had seen the first conjunction of Jupiter and Saturn, and had begun their journey at that time, they would have arrived too early. But if they did not see the first conjunction as such a remarkable event that it signified the Birth of a great King, why would the same event occurring in October, or again in December, be interpreted as having so much more significance? And the Magi could not have been guided through their long journey by such a brief event, which lasts but a single evening (in three different months).

In February of 6 B.C., there was a massing of the planets Mars, Jupiter, and Saturn. This event is sometimes erroneously called a triple conjunction.[203] In any case, this event occurred too early in the year to coincide with the Birth of Jesus Christ. And again, such a brief event could not have led the three wise men to Israel during the course of a long journey.

In the years 3 B.C. and 2 B.C., there were also notable celestial events, including a conjunction of Jupiter and Venus in June of 2 B.C., and a triple conjunction of Jupiter with the star Regulus (Sept. 14 of 3 B.C., Feb. 17, and May 8 of 2 B.C.).[204] Yet how could the Magi have followed the Star to the Christ Child, if the Star was not an object, but an event, such as a conjunction, which lasts only a few hours? Also, the detailed descriptions given repeatedly by Blessed Anne Catherine Emmerich tell of an object with a tail; conjunctions do not appear to have a tail. Conjunctions of planets and other brief celestial events could not have been the Christmas Star that led the Magi to the Messiah.

The Magi must have been much more than casual observers of the stars, for they left their home and their country to travel to a distant land based mainly on their understanding of what they saw in the night sky. They watched the night sky constantly and found great importance in the celestial events there.[205] They must have seen many different conjunctions throughout their years of star watching; the conjunction of planets with other planets and with the moon and certain bright stars are very common events.[206] Why would one particular conjunction be given so much more importance than all the others?

On the other hand, a comet which is bright enough to be seen with the naked eye, and which splits in two, would be very unusual. It would present a pattern in the sky complex enough to be interpreted as a picture with certain meanings, (especially when seen against the pattern of stars in the background). Also, from ancient times and in many lands, comets have been considered to be signs associated with great kings.[207]

A Natural Comet with Supernatural Aspects

The Christmas Star was most likely not an actual star, but a comet with supernatural aspects, that is, a comet which was accompanied by a supernatural light and guided by God. Only a supernatural event could completely explain all of the details about the Christmas Star given in Sacred Scripture and in the visions of Blessed Anne Catherine Emmerich. One might take the view that the Christmas Star was entirely supernatural, yet it was evidently able to be seen in the sky by many people, even by those who saw in it no special meaning, such as the inhabitants of certain towns through which the three wise men passed.[208]

On the other hand, any explanation which attempts to explain the Christmas Star as solely a natural event, merely coincidental to the Birth of the Son of God, is both insufficient and false. Many scholars have written about the Christmas star as if it were merely a naturally-occurring event, which happened to coincide with Christ's Birth. Such events as comets, supernovae, and the conjunction of planets happen again and again throughout human history. The reigns of earthly kings and their battles have often been considered to have been marked by comets and other events in the night sky.[209] But God would not mark the Birth of the Son of God and Savior of humanity merely by a coincidental natural event, the likes of which has occurred and would occur again many times. The unique supernatural aspects of the Christmas Star testify to the Divine Nature of the Christ Child.

Finding the Christmas Star

Ancient Chinese and Korean astronomers observed novae (new stars) and comets and kept detailed records of their observations. There is no record, from these ancient astronomers, of the observation of a comet in 15 B.C.[210] However, there appear to be gaps in the extant records of these ancient astronomers. Some records may have been lost as the centuries passed, or there may have been periods of time when these astronomers (perhaps because of political or social changes) were not active in observing comets and keeping records. Roman historians also made note of comets and other celestial events, but with less detail than the Chinese and Korean astronomers. Also, Roman historians tended to mention comet observations only when these coincided with some important event in Roman history, such as the death of a leader, or the beginning of a war.

The Roman historian Dio Cassius records the observation of a comet at the time of the death of the Roman general Agrippa. "The star called the comet hung for several days over the city and was finally dissolved into flashes resembling torches....These were the events connected with Agrippa's death."[211] The exact time of year when this comet was observed is not given by Dio. However, the sequence of events which he describes is as follows.

In the year when P. S. Quirinius was consul, my revised date of 16 B.C. (usually dated as 12 B.C.), Agrippa had returned from Syria to Rome. Caesar Augustus conferred on him tribunician powers for a five year term, then sent him to Pannonia to quell a rebellion there. "And Agrippa set out on the campaign in spite of the fact that the winter had already begun (this was the year in which Marcus Valerius [Messala] and Publius Sulpicius [Quirinius] were the consuls); but when the Pannonians became terrified at his approach and gave up their plans for rebellion, he returned, and upon reaching Campania, fell ill."[212] Notice that Agrippa went to Pannonia in early winter in 16 B.C. (12 B.C., usual date). He was there only a short time because the Pannonians gave up their plans to rebel against the Romans. He then went to Campania and fell ill.

Dio then tells us that Augustus was presiding over the gladiatorial contests at the festival of Quinquatrus (the Panathenaic festival in Athens), when he heard of Agrippa's illness.[213] The Roman festival of Quinquatrus occurs from March 19-23.[214] Augustus then traveled to Campania to visit Agrippa, but before he arrived Agrippa had died. Since this was the March festival after the winter which began in late 16 B.C. (12 B.C., usual date), Agrippa must have fallen ill and died in spring of 15 B.C. (11 B.C., usual date).

Cassius Dio states that a comet was seen at about the time of Agrippa's death.[215] He does not say exactly when the comet was observed, but he does places his description of the comet after his statement that Agrippa died. Also, he does not say that the comet was an omen seen before the death of Agrippa, as he does for other comets (such as the comet seen before the death of the emperor Vespasian).[216] He states merely that it was one of many events "connected with Agrippa's death."[217] Therefore, the comet was most likely seen after the death of Agrippa, sometime in mid to late 15 B.C.

Dio gives an unusual description of this particular comet. He says that it "dissolved into flashes resembling torches."[218] Other comets described by Dio and other Roman historians are not similarly described as dissolving into flashes of light.[219] This particular comet did something that the other comets did not do. Perhaps this comet is the same comet described by Blessed Anne Catherine as splitting into two parts and forming a complex pattern in the sky. Dio did not describe this comet as merely dissolving, as if it had disappeared in the sky. Rather, he describes the comet as dissolving, in the sense of separating, into flashes of light resembling torches. He does not say how many torch-like lights the comet separated into, nor for how long the separate lights lasted. But the description has unusual parallels to the Christmas Star as described by Blessed Anne Catherine.

I believe that this comet, seen in 15 B.C. (my revised date) was the Christmas Star. This comet was seen in the same year as the census/taxation and so also the same year as the Birth of Christ. And the unusual description of this comet fits the description given in the writings of Blessed Anne Catherine Emmerich. Though we cannot be certain, it is well worth considering that this comet may have been the Christmas Star, since it coincided with the census under Augustus and Quirinius (cf. Lk 2:1-2), as explained below.

A Second Line of Reasoning

A second argument can be made for the year of Christ's Birth, without relying on the words of Blessed Anne Catherine Emmerich. This argument is based on a revision of the generally-accepted dates for the reigns of Roman rulers (details in chapters 12, 13, and 14). As with the two arguments for the date of the Crucifixion presented in chapter 2, each of these two arguments can stand on its own without the other. The argument above, based on the writings of Blessed Anne Catherine, does not make use of the revised chronology for the reigns of the Roman emperors, nor does the argument below make use of the information given in the visions of Blessed Anne Catherine. Each can stand on its own, yet, because their conclusions agree, each one supports the other.

The Enrollment

"And it happened in those days that a decree went out from Caesar Augustus, so that the whole world would be enrolled. This was the first enrollment; it was made by the ruler of Syria, Quirinius. And all went to be declared, each one to his own city. Then Joseph also ascended from Galilee, from the city of Nazareth, into Judea, to the city of David, which is called Bethlehem, because he was of the house and family of David, in order to be declared, with Mary his espoused wife, who was with child. Then it happened that, while they were there, the days were completed, so that she would give birth." (Lk 2:1-6).

Saint Joseph and the Virgin Mary went to Bethlehem because of this census (or enrollment), and while they were there, Christ our Savior was born. Determining the date of this census will help us determine the year of the Birth of Jesus Christ.

There is no agreement among scholars as to the date of this census or enrollment. Several different enrollments are known to have occurred. There was a census of Roman citizens in 28 B.C. and also in 8 B.C. (the usual dates given for these).[220] For some time it was thought by many scholars that Christ was likely born in 8 B.C., because of this census. However, modern scholars now believe that these enrollments were for Roman citizens only, and did not apply to the Jewish people, nor to other nations conquered by the Roman empire.[221] The enrollment described by the Gospel of Luke applied to "the whole world," in other words, to the entire Roman empire, not merely to Roman citizens.

The census described in the Gospel of Luke was the first carried out under the authority of Quirinius. "This was the first enrollment; it was made by the ruler of Syria, Quirinius." (Lk 2:2). It was not necessarily the first enrollment of the Jews since the Roman occupation, but the first under Quirinius. The statement that this enrollment was the first implies that there was a second. The second enrollment is described in detail by Josephus, and is usually dated to A.D. 6.[222]

The enrollment of A.D. 6 (usual date) included a taxation of Syria and Judea. This census of the Jewish people is described by the ancient Jewish Roman historian Flavius Josephus.[223] He states that Caesar Augustus sent Cyrenius (Quirinius),[224] to Syria and Judea to make a taxation, and that one of the Jews from Galilee, named Judas, started a rebellion against this taxation.[225] This rebellion is mentioned in Sacred Scripture, in the Acts of the Apostles: "After this one, Judas the Galilean stepped forward, in the days of the enrollment...." (Acts 5:37). This enrollment of A.D. 6 was clearly a taxation, under Quirinius, who also had authority over Syria at that time.

If this was the second census under Quirinius, when did the first census under Quirinius take place? According to Dr. E. Jerry Vardaman, the census under Caesar

Augustus was taken every 17 years in the provinces (the occupied territories, including Israel). He places the first census under Quirinius in 12 B.C., 17 years before the second census of A.D. 6.[226]

Microletters on the Lapis Venetus

Dr. E. Jerry Vardaman also offers archaeological evidence in support of the conclusion that the 12 B.C. census was the census of Luke 2:2. A census is mentioned on an ancient tombstone called "Lapis Venetus" (stone of Venice). The tombstone was for a Roman officer who, under orders from Quirinius, made a census of Apamea, a city in Syria. Vardaman uses microletters on the tombstone to date the tombstone itself to 10 B.C.[227]

Microletters on the tombstone also state that the census of Apamea took place in the year that Quirinius was a Roman consul: "LA CONS P.S.QVIRINI"[228] This text means "year one of the consulship of P.S. Quirini." The letter 'L' is the abbreviation for 'year,' the letter 'A' stands for the number one. Letters were used in ancient Greek and Latin to stand for numbers. In the Greek number system, the first letter represented the number 1, the second letter represented 2, etc. The abbreviation "CONS" stands for "consul" or "consulship." And "P.S.QVIRINI" is the Quirinius mentioned in Luke 2:2. He is also mentioned by Josephus[229] and by Dio,[230] both of whom state that Quirinius was a Roman consul. The usual year given for the consulship of P.S. Quirinius is 12 B.C. Based on this and other considerations, Vardaman dates this census to 12/11 B.C.[231]

Vardaman's discovery of this microletter inscription on the Lapis Venetus provides important archaeological evidence concerning the year of the Birth of Christ. This inscription places the census at the time of Christ's birth beginning in the first year of the consulship of Quirinius.

The Census Under Quirinius

The Gospel of Luke states that the first census was carried out, not only in Israel, but in "the whole world," (Lk 2:2) meaning in the whole Roman empire. In agreement with this point, the 12 B.C. census is also known to have occurred in other parts of the Roman empire, including Gaul (France).[232]

According to Josephus, at the time of the second census, Quirinius was sent by Caesar Augustus to Syria "to be judge of that nation...." and the area of Judea in Israel was also put under his authority.[233] Quirinius is known to have been governor of Syria during the second census.[234] But the Gospel of Luke says that Quirinius was also governor of Syria during the first census, at the time of Christ's Birth (Lk 2:2).

According to Dio, at the time of the earlier census in 12 B.C. (usual date), Quirinius was a Roman consul (a position at the head of the Roman Senate).[235] As consul, Quirinius had a position of considerable power in the Roman empire, but most scholars do not believe that he was governor of Syria as early as 12 B.C. However, Vardaman writes that Quirinius may have ascended from the position of Roman consul to governor of Syria in 12 B.C.[236]

On the other hand, it is not necessary to this chronological argument for Quirinius to have held the title of governor of Syria twice. Quirinius may have had authority over

Syria and Israel as a result of his assignment to conduct a census, and may not have had the official position of governor of Syria. The Gospel of Luke refers to Pontius Pilate as "governor of Judea" (Lk 3:1; RSV), even though Pilate did not have the official Roman title of governor. Pilate was the governor of Judea in the sense of being ruler over Judea, but not as an official title (his title was Procurator). In the same way, the Gospel of Luke may be saying merely that Quirinius was one of the rulers over Syria, not necessarily its official governor.[237] Quirinius certainly did have much authority at this time, since he was both a Roman consul and in charge of the census in Syria and Israel.

A Revised Chronology

The above argument, concerning Quirinius and the first census, falls within the range of ideas put forward by various scholars in the current debate over the year for the Birth of Jesus Christ. However, at this point, I must depart from the usual arguments to introduce a new idea into the chronology of this time period. I have reached the conclusion that the usual dates given for events during the reign of Caesar Augustus, including the dates for the above mentioned censuses (stated as 12 B.C. and A.D. 6), are off from the true dates by 4 years. A lengthy argument in support of this conclusion is given in chapters 12, 13, and 14 of this book. The result is that the census of 12 B.C. actually began in 16 B.C. and the census of A.D. 6 actually began in A.D. 2.

Though a census is usually referred to by the year in which the census began, each census took two years to complete. According to Vardaman, the taking of the census began with a public announcement in May or June, and the people then had 12 months to "file their returns."[238] The first 12 months of the census overlapped two calendar years, which is why the year for a census is sometimes written with both calendar years, e.g. 12/11 B.C.

Nikos Kokkinos adds that, after the initial 12 period for census-taking, there was a second 12 month period for collecting the tax.[239] Thus the census of 16 B.C. would cover a 2-year period of time: the first year, from mid 16 B.C. to mid 15 B.C., and the second year, the collecting year, from mid 15 B.C. to mid 14 B.C. This is written as: 16/15 B.C. – 15/14 B.C. (Note that Kokkinos wrote that the census at the time of Christ's Birth—his date is 12 B.C.—was a local census undertaken by Herod, not an empire-wide census.) [240]

No Other Census

Whether one accepts my revised chronology or not, there is no other census under Quirinius which could possibly fit the description of the Gospel, other than the 12/11 B.C. census (my revised date is 16/15 B.C.). The census of A.D. 6 (A.D. 2, revised) is too late to be the census at the time of Christ's Birth. The Gospel of Matthew indicates that the death of king Herod occurred as long as 2 years or more after the Birth of Christ (Mt 2:16-19). Some scholars present arguments placing the death of Herod as late as 1 B.C., but there is no support for a date for the death of Herod later than A.D. 1.[241]

Josephus describes an event occurring about 3–2 B.C. (the usual date), in which the Jewish people were required to take an oath to Caesar.[242] Some scholars have tried to equate this oath-taking with the census or enrollment described in the Gospel of Luke (Lk 2:1-2). However, the 3-2 B.C. 'census' was only for the purpose of taking an oath of allegiance to Caesar, not for taxation. Josephus records that some Pharisees refused to take the oath, and so had to pay money to Caesar, but only as a fine.[243] One can infer from the text that, if they had taken the oath, they would not have had to pay anything.

Furthermore, Justin Martyr (A.D. c. 114-165) described the census at the time of Christ's Birth as a taxation, not an oath-taking. "Now there is a village in the land of the Jews, thirty-five stadia from Jerusalem, in which Jesus Christ was born, as you can ascertain also from the registers of the taxing made under Cyrenius, your first procurator in Judaea."[244]

The second census under Quirinius was clearly a taxation, as Josephus describes it.[245] But Sacred Scripture, in saying that the census at the time of Christ's Birth was the first under Quirinius, implies not only that there was a second census, but also that the first was like the second. Otherwise, they would not be seen as being related, and the census of Luke 2:2 would not have been called the first. Thus, the first census (of Lk 2:2) must also have been a census for the purpose of taxation.

Also, there seems to be no reason why such an oath-taking would require people to return to their place of birth. Whereas, if the census was for purpose of taxation, people would have had to return to their place of birth, because there the local religious leaders, and the genealogical records they kept, could be used to identify each person and their degree of wealth. Thus any proposed year for the Birth of Jesus Christ in the first several years B.C. has no census/taxation associated with it, as required by the Gospel of Luke (Lk 2:1-7).

There was a census about 8 B.C. (usual date), but this census only affected Roman citizens.[246] It would not have applied to Joseph and Mary, nor to the majority of Jews. This census was also not a taxation of the Roman provinces (the occupied lands, which would include Israel and Syria). Nor would it have required large numbers of persons in the occupied lands (such as Judea and Galilee) to return to their place of birth. The only census during this time period, which could possibly be the census of Luke 2:1-2, is the census of 12/11 B.C. (my revised date is 16/15 B.C.).

The Taxation during Christ's Ministry

Under Caesar Augustus, taxations were held 17 years apart, but under Tiberius Caesar, there were 14 years between taxations.[247] The taxation at the time of Christ's Birth, the first under Quirinius, occurred 17 years before the second taxation under Quirinius. But the next taxation, under Tiberius, occurred only 14 years later. Thus, the length of time from the taxation at Christ's Birth to the taxation under Tiberius was about 31 years (17 + 14 = 31). Jesus was about 31 years old, counting his age from birth, at the time of the taxation under Tiberius.

The Gospels clearly and repeatedly mention tax collectors and the Roman taxation during the time of Christ's Ministry. The Pharisees sent their disciples to ask if it was permitted under Jewish religious law to pay the Roman tax (Mt 22:15-22). They were even able to show Jesus one of the coins used to pay the tax (a denarius with the name and face of Caesar on it). Jesus sat at table and ate with tax collectors (Mk 2:15-16).

Matthew, one of the Twelve Apostles, (also called Levi) was a tax collector (Mt 10:3; Lk 5:27), as was a disciple named Zacchaeus (Lk 19:1-10). And Jesus repeatedly spoke of tax collectors in His teachings and parables (Lk 18:9-14; Mt 5:46; 21:28-32). Therefore, the Ministry of Jesus Christ coincided with a taxation during Tiberius Caesar's reign (Lk 3:1).

Jesus was born during a census/taxation under Caesar Augustus. Sometime during the Ministry of Jesus Christ, there was a taxation under Tiberius Caesar. Taxations under Augustus were 17 years apart, but under Tiberius they were 14 years apart.[248] The second census/taxation under Quirinius occurred 17 years after the first. But the next taxation (after the second under Quirinius) occurred, when Tiberius was emperor, 14 years later. Thus, the length of time from the first census/taxation under Quirinius to the taxation under the emperor Tiberius is 31 years (17 + 14 = 31). Since Christ was born at the time of the first census/taxation under Quirinius, there must have also been a taxation about the time of Christ's 31st year since birth.

Jesus was about 30 years old when He began His Ministry (Lk 3:23). And His Ministry lasted about 3½ years (see chapter 2). So, the taxation occurring about the time of Christ's 31st year must have also occurred during His Ministry. Since the census/taxation took 2 years, a large portion of Christ's 3½ year Ministry coincided with the taxation.

This line of reasoning fits perfectly with the Gospel accounts of a taxation during the Ministry of Jesus Christ. Only in this way can the Gospel accounts of a census/taxation, both at the time of Christ's Birth and during His Ministry, find agreement with the historical evidence.

The Year of Christ's Birth

From the above information, it becomes clear that Jesus was born during the first census/taxation under Quirinius, which began in 16 B.C. (my revised date). But the process of taxation lasted 2 years, from mid 16 B.C. to mid 15 B.C., the first year, plus a second "collecting year" from mid 15 B.C. to mid 14 B.C. Can we determine, within this time frame, the year and time of year of Christ's Birth?

The approximate time of year of Christ's Birth can be determined from statements in the Gospel of Luke. The Incarnation of Christ occurred during both Elizabeth's sixth month (Lk 1:36) and the sixth month of the Jewish calendar (Lk 1:26). If Christ was born approximately 9 months later,[249] then He must have been born sometime during the Jewish months of Heshvan, Kislev, or Tevet, (months 2, 3, and 4 of the Jewish civil calendar) depending on whether a Jewish leap month intervened and on the length of time from conception to birth (this argument is explained in detail in chapter 5). These months of the Jewish calendar correspond to the last few months of the Christian calendar. Thus, according to this interpretation of Sacred Scripture, Christ was born during the late fall or early winter. (A more exact date for the Birth of Christ, based on this line of reasoning, can be given if one also knows the year of Christ's Birth, and this is presented in chapter 5.)

Since Christ was born in the last few months of the calendar year, He must have been born in either late 16 B.C. or late 15 B.C., during either the first or second year of the census/taxation, which ran from mid 16 B.C. to mid 14 B.C. Without referring to the words of Blessed Anne Catherine Emmerich, the choice between late 16 B.C. and late 15 B.C. is less than certain. However, the Gospel of Luke does indicate that the city of Bethlehem was crowded at the time of Christ's Birth, since there was no room for the Holy Family at the inn, and the only place left for the Christ-Child was in a manger (Lk 2:7). People at that time in history, as is much the same today, preferred to pay their taxes later, rather than sooner.[250] Also, because communication was not as fast and widely available as it is today, after a census/taxation decree was issued by the government in Rome, it took many months for word of this to spread among the people, and then longer for the people to make the trip to the place of their birth. Thus, it is more likely that Bethlehem would be so crowded in the second year of the taxation (the "collecting year"), when people are up against a deadline for paying their taxes. In this line of reasoning then, 15 B.C. is preferred over 16 B.C. as the year of Christ's Birth.

Conclusion

Two different lines of reasoning have now led us to the same conclusion, that Christ was bon in the year 15 B.C. First, according to the chronological information given by Blessed Anne Catherine Emmerich, Christ was born in a year when Nov. 25 was a Sunday, and was born 7 years earlier than some generally-accepted year for the Birth of Christ. The only year which fits this criteria is 15 B.C.

Further support for this conclusion comes from her statement that Jesus was in about His sixth year at the time of Herod's death. Scholars generally date Herod's death no later than 1 B.C. This makes the other years when Nov. 25 was a Sunday (4 B.C., A.D. 3) too late to account for Herod dying in Christ's sixth year.

The second line of reasoning puts aside the writings of Blessed Anne Catherine and looks at the date of the census under Caesar Augustus and Quirinius mentioned by the Gospel of Luke (Lk 2:1-2).

The historical and archaeological evidence cited above makes the first census under Quirinius, usually dated to 12/11 B.C., the only reasonable fit to the description of the census given in Sacred Scripture. And the revision of the dates of the reigns of Augustus and Tiberius, supported by chapters 12, 13, and 14 of this book, place that census in 16/15 B.C. The great crowds gathered in Bethlehem for the census kept the Holy Family from staying at the inn, and at any usual place of lodging in the city itself, so that the Christ-Child had only a manger for His bed. The large number of people indicates that the census was nearer to its close than to its beginning, so that this was late fall/early winter of 15 B.C., not 16 B.C.

The time of year for the Birth of Christ, sometime during the last months of the Roman calendar, can be established from Sacred Scripture. This argument is described briefly above, and in greater detail in chapter 5 of this book. The conclusion is less precise than the information given by Blessed Anne Catherine, but is in harmony with her statements.

Further support for this conclusion comes from a revised chronology for the reigns of various Roman rulers. The date for Herod's death in this new chronology is 8 B.C., which rules out any date for Christ's Birth later than about 10 B.C. Chapter 12, 13, and 14 provide ample support for this revised chronology.

The first argument above for the year of Christ's Birth, the one based on Blessed Anne Catherine's words, is used in chapter 2 to help determine the year of Christ's Crucifixion. The first argument in chapter 2 for the year of the Crucifixion is based on Blessed Anne Catherine's writings and not on the revised Roman chronology.

The second argument above for the year of Christ's Birth, the one based on a revised set of dates for the reigns of various Roman rulers, is independent of the conclusions of chapter 2. The date for the Crucifixion of Christ, based on a revised Roman chronology, does not depend on this chapter's date for the Birth of Christ. However, once we have established both the date for the Birth of Christ, and, independently, the date of the Crucifixion, we can consider whether the length of time between those two dates is correct, lending additional support to these dates.

The Length of Time from Birth to Crucifixion

Jesus was about 30 years old when He began His Ministry (Lk 3:23). And, as explained in chapter 2, Sacred Scripture indicates that the Ministry of Jesus Christ lasted about 3½ years. Therefore, Jesus was about 33 years old when He was crucified. Counting back 33 years from A.D. 19 brings us to 15 B.C.

Blessed Anne Catherine Emmerich gives a more specific age for Christ at the Crucifixion. At the time that she was receiving visions from God about the Incarnation, she was shown the age of Christ as 33 plus 6, meaning 33 years plus 6 weeks. She interpreted this to mean that Christ was 33 years and 18 weeks old counting from His Birth to the Crucifixion because she was shown the vision 3 times (3 x 6 = 18), and because she generally counted a person's age from birth. However, I interpret this to mean that Christ was 33 years and 6 weeks old counting from the Incarnation to the Crucifixion, with the vision being shown 3 times for emphasis, not so as to multiply the numbers. Christ's human life began at His Incarnation, not His Birth.

Both Sacred Scripture and the visions of Blessed Anne Catherine agree that the Crucifixion occurred about 33 years after the year of Christ's Incarnation and Birth. The age of Jesus at the Crucifixion fits the dates given in this book for the years of His Birth and Crucifixion, because these dates are the correct number of years apart. Any set of dates for the Birth and Crucifixion of Christ which are not 33 years apart cannot be correct. The fact that 15 B.C. and A.D. 19 are 33 years apart adds additional support to these dates.

The evidence of two witnesses, or three, is needed to decide a case (Mt 18:16; Deut 17:6; 2 Cor 13:1). The same can be said for the conclusions of this book. Two separate arguments are given in support of the conclusion that Christ was born in 15 B.C. These are, in effect, two witnesses for the year of Christ's Birth. Two separate arguments are given in support of the conclusion that Christ was crucified in A.D. 19. These are two witnesses for the year of Christ's Crucifixion. There are, in effect, two witnesses for each conclusion.

A third line of reasoning provides additional support for these conclusions. These dates are spaced the correct length of time apart, 33 years. The space between these dates agrees with the age of Christ at the Crucifixion. Here then is a kind of third witness, so that every case may be decided by the evidence of two witnesses, or three. These witnesses agree in their testimony that these are the true dates for these events in the life of Jesus Christ.

Chapter 5
The Virgin Incarnation of God

Zechariah in the Temple

"Then it happened that, when he was exercising the priesthood before God, in the order of his section, according to the custom of the priesthood, the lot fell so that he would offer incense, entering into the temple of the Lord. And the entire multitude of the people was praying outside, at the hour of incense. Then there appeared to him an Angel of the Lord, standing at the right of the altar of incense." (Lk 1:8-11).

Luke's Gospel begins, after a brief introductory passage, with the story of Zechariah and Elizabeth. Zechariah is burning incense in the Temple when the angel announces to him that he and Elizabeth will conceive a son (Saint John the Baptist). Luke's Gospel tell us that "the entire multitude of the people" were gathered outside praying. Since all the people were gathered for this event, it was not merely the daily burning of incense of any day of the year (Ex 30:7-8).

The phrase, "the entire multitude of the people," is a superlative expression which cannot be interpreted as referring merely to any large crowd. Other expressions are used in the Gospel of Luke to indicate a large crowd of people, but without using the phrase "the entire multitude of the people." For example: "as the crowds were quickly gathering" (Lk 11:29), "as great crowds were standing so close that they were stepping on one another" (Lk 12:1), "he also said to the crowds" (Lk 12:54), and "Now great crowds traveled with him" (Lk 14:25), are all used to refer to a large gathering of people. But the expression "the entire multitude of the people" differs from these other expressions in that the words "entire" and "of the people" indicate that this very large crowd was representative of the whole Jewish people. This type of crowd would not be gathered outside the Temple every day of the year, but only at the time of important religious celebrations, such as the Feast of Passover, the Feast of Weeks, or the Feast of Tabernacles (Deut 16:16). At such feasts, devout Jews traveled from every part of the nation, and even from other countries, to worship at the Temple of Jerusalem. Therefore, the service of Zechariah in the Temple must have coincided with a major feast of the Jewish faith.

There are only three major feasts in the Jewish faith: the Feast of Passover, the Feast of Weeks and the Feast of Tabernacles. Passover occurs in early spring (March-April), in the Jewish month of Nisan. The Feast of weeks occurs in late spring (May-June), in the Jewish month of Sivan. The Feast of Tabernacles is the only major feast that occurs in the autumn (Sept.-Oct.), in the Jewish month of Tishri.

Blessed Anne Catherine Emmerich also taught that Zechariah was serving in the Temple at the time of a feast. She explains that Zechariah was teaching in his home town about an impending feast. Shortly thereafter, Zechariah left his home to go to the Temple. And a few days later, while serving in the Temple, he saw the angel, who told him that he and Elizabeth would conceive the child John.[251]

Saint John Chrysostom believed that Zechariah was serving in the Temple about the time of the Day of Atonement (Yom Kippur) and the Feast of Tabernacles (Lev 23; Num 29), when people from every part of Israel would be gathered in Jerusalem for these holy days.[252] Yom Kippur is the 10th of Tishri and is considered the holiest day of the year. The Feast of Tabernacles follows soon after and lasts for 8 days, from the 15th to the 22nd of Tishri. Tishri is the first month of the Jewish civil calendar and occurs in the autumn. The Feast of Tabernacles (also called 'the feast of booths') is one of the three holy feasts of the year (Deut 16:16).

In the Sixth Month

"Then, in the sixth month, the Angel Gabriel was sent by God, to a city of Galilee named Nazareth, to a virgin betrothed to a man whose name was Joseph, of the house of David; and the name of the virgin was Mary." (Lk 1:26-27).

"And this is the sixth month for her who is called barren." (Lk 1:36).

The "sixth month" is mentioned twice in Luke's account of the Annunciation. Is the Gospel of Luke telling us twice within the same passage that this was the sixth month of Elizabeth's pregnancy? No, rather Luke's Gospel is giving us important additional information about the timing of the Annunciation.

"In the sixth month" means the sixth month of the Jewish civil calendar, which is called Adar (or AdarI). Sacred Scripture contains many references to the months of the Jewish calendar which use the same phrasing, "in the nth month." For example, "in the sixth month" is found in Ezek 8:1 and Haggai 1:1, 15. And there are many other examples of the expression "in the nth month" in the Old Testament. In this passage from the Gospel of Luke, the same expression is used. Sacred Scripture is telling us that the Annunciation and the Incarnation of Jesus Christ occurred in the sixth month of the Jewish calendar.

In the Old Testament, the expression "in the nth month" refers to the sacred calendar, which begins in the spring with the month of Nisan. However, this passage from Luke's Gospel refers to the sixth month of the Jewish civil calendar, which begins with the month of Tishri. The Jewish civil calendar is used here, rather than the sacred calendar because the announcement by the angel to Zechariah of the conception of John the Baptist coincided with Tishri, the first month of the civil calendar.

Another reason the Gospel uses the civil calendar here is that this particular civil calendar year was a Sabbatical year (see chapter 16; see also Appendix I, Chart 7). The Sabbatical year at this time in Jewish history was counted from the month of Tishri. The Sabbatical year is a holy year, like the holy day of the Sabbath, a time of rest and worship of God. So Sacred Scripture begins the Gospel narrative with the annunciation to Zechariah in the first month of the Sabbatical year and continues with the Annunciation to Mary and Incarnation of Christ in the sixth month of the Sabbatical year.

Saint Luke places the story of Zechariah and Elizabeth at the beginning of his Gospel, and that event occurred at the beginning of the Jewish civil calendar. The story then continues, in the sixth month of that calendar, with the announcement by the angel to Mary of the Virgin Conception of Jesus Christ. The true story that Luke is telling about God's plan began at the beginning of the Jewish civil calendar, a calendar which is based on Sacred Scripture and is a part of God's plan. Saint Luke points out the alignment of these events with the Jewish civil calendar by telling us that Jesus was conceived in the 6th month of the calendar, and also during Elizabeth's sixth month. In this way, Luke marks the passage of time from the announcement about John the Baptist, at the beginning of the civil calendar, to the Announcement of the Incarnation of Christ. Saint John Chrysostom was correct; Zechariah was serving in the Temple of Jerusalem during the month of Tishri.

The Incarnation of Jesus Christ occurred "in the sixth month" (Lk 1:26) of the Jewish civil calendar, and also in the sixth month of Elizabeth's pregnancy, as is clear from the words of the angel Gabriel to the Virgin Mary, "And this is the sixth month for her who is called barren." (Lk 1:36). However, the angel does not tell the Virgin Mary that Elizabeth has completed six full months, but rather that it is now sometime **within** her sixth month. Thus there was some degree of overlap between the sixth month of the Jewish civil calendar and Elizabeth's sixth month.

Notice that Sacred Scripture says that after Elizabeth conceived, "she hid herself for five months," not for six months (Lk 1:24). If Sacred Scripture had said that she hid her pregnancy for six months, and that in the sixth month the Annunciation had occurred, then the time given would be at the end of Elizabeth's sixth month. But Sacred Scripture says that she hid herself for five months, and then, **during** the sixth month, the Annunciation occurred. The Annunciation and the Incarnation of Christ occurred after the completion of Elizabeth's fifth month, but before the end of her sixth month.

Counting back 5+ months from the sixth month of the Jewish civil calendar (AdarI) brings us to the first month of the calendar (Tishri), or possibly the latter part of the previous month (Elul, the month before Tishri). If the Incarnation occurred near the end of AdarI (sixth month), then the conception of John the Baptist occurred, at the latest, near the end of Tishri, or, at the earliest, near the start of Tishri. If the Incarnation occurred near the start of AdarI, then John's conception occurred in late Elul or early Tishri.

The annunciation to Zechariah, about the soon-to-occur conception of John the Baptist, occurred at the time of a gathering of "the entire multitude of the people" (Lk 1:10). During the months of Elul and Tishri, only the time of the Day of Atonement and the Feast of Tabernacles would bring such a large crowd representative of the whole people. The conception of John occurred after the annunciation to Zechariah, and so must have occurred sometime during the month of Tishri.

Christ was born in 15 B.C. (see chapter 4). Christ's Incarnation occurred about 9 months before His Birth. The conception of John the Baptist occurred 5+ months before the Incarnation of Christ. This places the conception of John the Baptist about 14 – 15 months before the Birth of Christ. Since John was conceived sometime late in the month of Tishri (early autumn), Christ must have been born in late autumn/early winter, about a year and 2 to 3 months after the conception of John. And, since Christ was born in 15 B.C., John must have been conceived in 16 B.C., soon after the Feast of Tabernacles.

That particular Feast of Tabernacles, in 16 B.C., occurred at the beginning of a Sabbatical year (see chapter 16; see also Appendix I, Chart 7). There are two prevalent views on the occurrence of Sabbatical years during this time frame. Zuckermann and Blosser have the Sabbatical year beginning in Tishri of 17 B.C. and ending in Tishri of 16 B.C., whereas Wacholder has the Sabbatical year beginning in Tishri of 16 B.C. and ending in Tishri of 15 B.C.[253] In chapter 16, I conclude that the cycle of Sabbatical years in Wacholder's chronology is generally correct. The list of Sabbatical years would then include the Jewish civil calendar year beginning in Tishri of 16 B.C. and ending in Tishri of 15 B.C. So the month of Tishri in 16 B.C. was the beginning of a Sabbatical year.

"And he instructed them, saying: 'After seven years, in the year of remission, at the Feast of Tabernacles, When all Israel assembles together, so as to appear before the sight of the Lord your God in the place which the Lord will have chosen, you shall read the words of this law before all of Israel, in their hearing.' " (Deut 31:10-11).

In the book of Deuteronomy, the Israelites are commanded to assemble, during the Sabbatical year and during the Feast of Tabernacles, to hear the Law of Moses read. Now the text says "After seven years," however, this cannot mean at the end of the seventh year. The Law must be read during the seventh year and during the Feast of Tabernacles. That feast occurs at the beginning of the Sabbatical year (when the Sabbatical year was counted beginning in the month of Tishri). Thus the text does not mean the end of the seventh year, but rather the end of the cycle of seven years, that is, during the last of the seven years.

Zechariah was serving in the Temple during the month of Tishri in 16 B.C., at the beginning of the Sabbatical year of 16/15 B.C. During that month, the people of Israel were gathered in Jerusalem, not only for the holy days of the Day of Atonement and the Feast of Tabernacles, but also to hear the Law read during the Feast of Tabernacles of the Sabbatical year. Josephus also describes this practice of hearing the Law read at that time.[254] A particularly large crowd would gather in Jerusalem at the beginning of a Sabbatical year, to hear the Law read as well as to worship God during the Day of Atonement and the Feast of Tabernacles. The crowd may have been even larger than usual in a Sabbatical year, since this particular Sabbatical year was followed by a Jubilee year (see chapter 16; see also Appendix I, Chart 7). The annunciation to Zechariah (of the future conception of John the Baptist) occurred at such a time, and so Sacred Scripture tells us, "And the entire multitude of the people was praying outside...." (Lk 1:10).

The Conception of John the Baptist

"And it happened that, after the days of his office were completed, he went away to his house." (Lk 1:23).

Each division of priests began their duty in the Temple on the Sabbath, and they continued in the service of the Temple for eight days, from Sabbath to Sabbath, so that each term of service included two Sabbaths.[255] Each term of service, then, overlapped with both the previous division's term and with the subsequent division's term. In this way, there would always be two divisions of priests on duty on the Sabbath, when the priests were most needed.

But on the three great feasts of the year, the Feast of Passover, the Feast of weeks and the Feast of Tabernacles, all of the priestly divisions were on duty at the same time.[256] Every priest was needed because of the huge numbers of worshipers who came to the Temple during those feasts. Without doubt, Zechariah's division was on duty at the time of the Feast of Tabernacles, because every division was on duty for that feast. Thus it may have been during the Feast of Tabernacles that the angel told Zechariah the good news that he and Elizabeth would conceive a son.

It is possible, though, that the angel visited Zechariah in the Temple on the Day of Atonement (Tishri 10), the week before the Feast of Tabernacles. Zechariah may have been on duty that week also, as part of the regular schedule for his division of priests. As concluded above, an exceptionally large crowd, representative of the whole nation of Israel, were gathered at Jerusalem for the Day of Atonement and the Feast of Tabernacles at the start of this Sabbatical year (autumn of 16 B.C.). Since "the entire multitude of the people" were gathered outside the Temple praying when Zechariah received the annunciation by the angel, that day was either the Day of Atonement or one day during the Feast of Tabernacles.[257] On other days, fewer people would be gathered outside the Temple and the phrase "the entire multitude of the people" would not apply.

Consequently, there are two likely scenarios for the timing of John's conception suggested by the available information.

1) Blessed Anne Catherine states that Zechariah had to wait four days, after arriving in Jerusalem, for his turn to sacrifice.[258] It was on the day that Zechariah was chosen to offer sacrifice (the sacrifice of burning incense) that the angel appeared to him. In the year 16 B.C. (the calendar year before the Incarnation), Tishri 10 fell on a Wednesday, four days after the Sabbath (Saturday).[259] Thus, if Zechariah began his term of service on Saturday, Tishri 6, his turn to sacrifice would have coincided with the Day of Atonement on Wednesday, Tishri 10.[260] In this case, Zechariah would have completed his week of service the following Saturday, on Tishri 13.[261] But if Zechariah was serving in the Temple during the week containing the Day of Atonement, when would he have returned to his home?

Sacred Scripture tells us that, even though he had been left mute by his encounter with the angel, Zechariah did not go home until his time of service in the Temple had ended (Lk 1:20, 23). If Zechariah had tried to go home immediately after his time of service, the soonest he could have departed would be on Saturday, after sunset. He had to complete his term of service in the Temple on the Sabbath, and also, devout Jews would not travel more than a short distance on the Sabbath, (about one half to two thirds of a mile).

Blessed Anne Catherine Emmerich states that Zechariah and Elizabeth lived a short distance from Hebron, in Jutta.[262] Hebron is about 20 miles from Jerusalem, and Jutta is another 5 miles or so further south.[263] Zechariah's home was more than a Sabbath's walk away. Since Zechariah was "advanced in years" (Lk 1:7), his home was some distance from Jerusalem, and he could not depart before sunset on Saturday, he probably could not have arrived at his home until sometime late in the day on Sunday, at the earliest. Yet Monday (Sunday at sunset) was the 15th of Tishri, the first day of the Feast of Tabernacles, a day of solemn rest, when Zechariah would not be able to travel (Lev 23:35). He would have had to arrive home before sunset on Sunday. And once home, he would not have had time to return to Jerusalem before the Feast began.

Even if he would have been able to arrive home before sunset on Sunday, Zechariah nevertheless would have had to remain in Jerusalem to attend the Feast of Tabernacles. He would not have had sufficient time or opportunity to return home until the feast had ended. The Feast of Tabernacles is one of the three holiest feasts of the year, and he was one of the Temple priests. Every division of the priests was required to be on duty at that time. And Sacred Scripture tells us that, even though he had been struck mute by the angel, he still completed his service in the Temple (Lk 1:23). Being a priest and a devout Jew, he had to remain in Jerusalem to attend the Feast of Tabernacles, before going home to his wife.

Also, Zechariah would have wanted to fulfill the commandment of God in Sacred Scripture: "Three times a year all your males shall appear in the sight the Lord your God in the place which he will have chosen: at the Feast of Unleavened Bread, at the Feast of Weeks, and at the Feast of Tabernacles." (Deut 16:16). (The Feast of Tabernacles is also called the Feast of Booths.) Sacred Scripture tells us that Zechariah and Elizabeth kept all of God's commandments. "Now they were both just before God, progressing in all of the commandments and the justifications of the Lord without blame." (Lk 1:6). Therefore, Zechariah must have remained in Jerusalem until after the Feast of Tabernacles (which ended on Tishri 22), even if it was on the Day of Atonement (Tishri 10) when the angel appeared to him.

2) The other possibility is that Zechariah's term of service mentioned in the Gospel of Luke, "when he was exercising the priesthood before God, in the order of his section" (Lk 1:8), was simply the usual duty of every division of priests to serve during the Feast of Tabernacles. In this case also, Zechariah would have waited until the feast had ended before returning home. As a priest of the Temple, he would not have left Jerusalem in the middle of the feast (Lk 1:23).

The Feast of Tabernacles ends on the eighth day (Tishri 22), and that day is a day of solemn rest (Lev 23) on which traveling more than a short distance was not permitted. Zechariah's earliest opportunity to set out for home was at the end of Tishri 22 (which in 16 B.C. was a Monday), at sunset. If he departed in the evening, he could have traveled some distance before spending the night somewhere, then spent most of the next day (Tishri 23; a Tuesday that year) in travel. In this way, he could have arrived home late in the day on Tishri 23. Since Tishri 24, (like any day in the Jewish calendar), begins at sunset, the earliest opportunity for Zechariah and Elizabeth to have conceived John the Baptist would be Tishri 24 (which began after sunset at the end of Tuesday, Tishri 23).

Or, if Zechariah, who was "advanced in years," took a little longer in getting home, he would have arrived a day later on Tishri 24 before sunset (which would be Tishri 25, if after sunset). Either way, the conception of John the Baptist would most likely have occurred at the end of Tishri. In the year 16 B.C., Tishri 24 fell on September 27. The conception of John the Baptist, then, occurred at the end of September in 16 B.C.

In both of these above scenarios, the conclusion would be the same, that the earliest opportunity for the conception of John would be in the last week of Tishri, on or after Tishri 24. Zechariah and Elizabeth were both looking forward to having a child (Lk 1:13, 25). They were also both God-fearing, devout Jews who followed God's commands (Lk 1:6). So, when God sent an angel to reveal to them that it was God's will that they conceive a holy child, they would not have added any unnecessary delay. Zechariah and Elizabeth conceived their child, John the Baptist, soon after Zechariah returned from God's service at the Temple.

John the Baptist's conception was not miraculous or virginal. However, God did grant to Zechariah and Elizabeth His miraculous and grace-filled assistance in conceiving a child. By a miracle of God, Zechariah and Elizabeth became fertile and so were made able to conceive a child in the usual way.

Notice that the verse which describes the hour of incense, when Zechariah was in the Temple praying, is the 10th verse (Lk 1:10), and it is on Tishri 10 that the holy day of Yom Kippur (the Day of Atonement) occurs. This was possibly the day when Zechariah saw the angel of God and received the promise of a son. Also, it is the 23rd verse which states that Zechariah went home after his term of service (Lk 1:23), and the Feast of Tabernacles concludes with a holy day on Tishri 22, so that people would be returning to their homes on the following day, Tishri 23. And it is the 24th verse (Lk 1:24) which tells us that Elizabeth conceived her child, John. The first opportunity for Zechariah and Elizabeth to conceive a child was likely Tishri 24 . So, by God's Providence, the verse numbers of this passage from Sacred Scripture give us an indication of the days when these event occurred.

Blessed Anne Catherine says that Zechariah had to wait four days before the day on which he offered sacrifice in the Temple and received the announcement from the angel. The Day of Atonement that year fell on the fourth day after the Sabbath. Zechariah began his term of service on the Sabbath. The Day of Atonement was a fitting time for such an announcement about John the Baptist, because John the Baptist's life was like one long Day of Atonement and of calling others to Atonement. Therefore, the most likely time for the angel's announcement to Zechariah was the Day of Atonement, rather than the Feast of Tabernacles. In the year 16 B.C., the Day of Atonement (Tishri 10) fell on September 13.[264]

Though the earliest date for the conception of John the Baptist is Tishri 24, his conception could not have occurred later than the end of Tishri. Sacred Scripture tells us that the Incarnation occurred in the sixth month of the Jewish civil calendar (Lk 1:26) and during the sixth month that Elizabeth was with child (Lk 1:36). If Elizabeth conceived after the month of Tishri (first month), then even the last day of the month of AdarI (sixth month) would not be within her sixth month, but rather her fifth month. If Elizabeth conceived in the month of Heshvan (second month), then the sixth month of the calendar, AdarI, would be her fifth month, not her sixth. Therefore, John the Baptist was conceived sometime on or after Tishri 24, but before the end of Tishri.

I believe that John was conceived on the night of Tishri 24, because Zechariah and Elizabeth would not have added any unnecessary delay to the doing of God's will, and because the verse of Sacred Scripture referring to the conception of John is the 24th verse (Luke 1:24). However, the arguments below take into account the possibility that John was conceived later than Tishri 24.

The Incarnation of Jesus Christ

The sixth month of the Jewish civil calendar (AdarI) and Elizabeth's sixth month both contained the day of the Incarnation of Christ (Lk 1:26, 36). But the conception of John the Baptist by Zechariah and Elizabeth could have occurred no earlier than Tishri 24 and no later than the end of Tishri. So Elizabeth's first month began near the end of Tishri, the first month of the Jewish civil calendar. Her second month began near the end of the second month of the calendar, and so on. Elizabeth's sixth month began near the end of the sixth month of the Jewish civil calendar, AdarI. Since the Incarnation occurred during both Elizabeth's sixth month and the sixth month of the calendar (AdarI), the Incarnation must have occurred during the last few days of AdarI, on or after the 24th of the month.

The Incarnation of Jesus Christ also occurred in that same Sabbatical year (16/15 B.C.), a year of special blessings from God. The Jewish faith was designed to prepare for the coming of the Messiah, and the Sabbatical years and Jubilee years were a foreshadowing of the Blessing from God, Jesus Christ. How fitting then that the Messiah should begin His human life during a Sabbatical year. The year following that Sabbatical year was a Jubilee year (see chapter 16; see also Appendix I, Chart 7). The Jubilee year begins in the autumn in the month of Tishri. The Sabbatical year of 16/15 B.C. was followed by the Jubilee year of 15/14 B.C. (Tishri of 15 B.C. to Tishri of 14 B.C.). The Incarnation of Christ occurred during a Sabbatical year and the Birth of Christ occurred during a Jubilee year. The Jubilee year was associated in ancient Jewish thought with the coming of the Messiah.[265]

From the Incarnation to the Birth of Christ

The above time frame for the Incarnation (between AdarI 24 and AdarI 30) is based on my interpretation of the Gospel of Luke.[266] Now, without using the information given to us by Blessed Anne Catherine, we can determine the approx. date of the Birth of Christ. The normal length of time from conception to birth is 266 days, plus or minus 2 weeks; 90% of all children today are born within that time frame.[267] Nine lunar months is 266 days, so that the ninth lunar month from the time frame of AdarI 24-30 is Heshvan 24-30. Adding and subtracting two weeks to this time frame gives us Heshvan 10 to Kislev 14 as the most probable time frame for the Birth of Christ. In 15 B.C., Heshvan 10 coincided with Oct. 31 and Kislev 14 coincided with Dec. 4.[268] Using this determination, Christ was born sometime between Oct. 31 and Dec. 4, inclusive, in 15 B.C. The date of Dec. 25 is three weeks beyond the usual time frame for birth and six weeks past the usual calculation for the due date of birth. The date of Dec. 25 is too late in the calendar year to fit the above date for the Incarnation. Christ was not born on December 25.

The Day and Month of the Incarnation

"Last night I saw the Annunciation as a Feast of the Church, and was once more definitely informed that at this moment the Blessed Virgin had already been with child for four weeks. This was expressly told me because I had already seen the Annunciation on the 25th of February, but had rejected the vision and had not related it."[269]

Blessed Anne Catherine Emmerich received visions from God about the Annunciation, both on the actual day of the Annunciation, February 25, and on the day in the liturgical calendar when the Church celebrates the Annunciation, March 25. She at first rejected the vision given to her on February 25, because she had assumed that the Annunciation and Incarnation occurred on the same day as it is celebrated by the Church, March 25. But God informed her that the actual day of the Incarnation was four weeks earlier, on Feb. 25th.

The Incarnation occurred sometime during the last few days of the month of AdarI. And Blessed Anne Catherine places the Incarnation on February 25. In the year 15 B.C., February 25 fell during the last few days of the Jewish month of AdarI, on AdarI 28.[270] Sacred Scripture tells us that the Incarnation occurred during Elizabeth's sixth month. So, on or before AdarI 28, Elizabeth must have begun her sixth month. The earliest opportunity for the conception of John by Zechariah and Elizabeth was probably Tishri 24. And now we see that the conception of John must have occurred no later than Tishri 28, so that beginning of Elizabeth's sixth month would occur by AdarI 28.

This count of the months refers to lunar months, used in the Jewish calendar, of 29-30 days each. Normal human gestation is considered to be 38 weeks (266 days), counting from the day of conception.[271] Thirty-eight weeks is almost exactly 9 lunar months (29.5306 days x 9 = 265.78). So if Elizabeth's first month began on Tishri 24, one can reasonably call AdarI 24 the start of her sixth month.

Jesus was conceived on Feb. 25, and so His Virgin Birth, on Nov. 25, occurred fully nine months after the Incarnation (see chapter 4). The time that Jesus was in the womb of the Virgin Mary was nine months, by the Christian calendar, and 273 days, rather than nine lunar months (266 days). Of all children born today, 90% are born within a four week time frame of 266 days from conception, plus or minus 2 weeks.[272] So, a time frame of 273 days (266 days plus 1 week) for the time from the Incarnation to the Birth of Christ is within normal limits.

According to Blessed Anne Catherine, the year of Christ's Birth was a leap year in the Jewish calendar.[273] 15 B.C. was a Jewish leap year in the sense that the 13th month of the Jewish calendar occurred during early 15 B.C. AdarI 28 fell on February 25 that year, and the first day of the following Jewish month, AdarII, would have been Feb. 28.[274] If it had not been a leap year, then the next month would have been Nisan, and Passover would have begun about March 13—significantly before the Spring Equinox. Since the Jews of that time period did not permit the Passover to begin much before the Spring Equinox (March 22 or 23, by the Julian calendar during that time period), 15 B.C. must have been a Jewish leap year, with a 13th month, called AdarII. The addition of a 13th month was needed every 2 or 3 years in the Jewish calendar, so as to delay the month of Nisan and keep the Passover celebration in the spring. (The modern Jewish calendar still uses this method of adding a 13th "leap month" every 2 or 3 years.)

Counting forward nine lunar months from AdarI 28 brings us to Heshvan 28 (including the leap month of AdarII in the count).[275] Now we know from Blessed Anne Catherine that the Birth of Jesus Christ occurred on Nov. 25, which is 39 full weeks (273 days) after the Incarnation on Feb. 25. This date for the Birth of Christ is 266 days plus one week from the Incarnation, and so is within the usual time frame for birth of 266 days, plus or minus 2 weeks, from conception. In 15 B.C., Nov. 25 coincided with Kislev 5. Blessed Anne Catherine stated that Jesus was born sometime in the month of Kislev. "I think Christ was born in the month Kislev."[276]

The Day and Hour of the Incarnation

Blessed Anne Catherine tells us that the Holy Conception of Jesus Christ occurred about midnight at the beginning of February 25. After describing the Virgin Conception of Jesus in the womb of the Virgin Mary, she states, "It was at midnight that I saw this mystery happen."[277] Recall that she also saw the Birth of Jesus occurring at midnight.

Blessed Anne Catherine tells us that the Birth of Jesus Christ occurred on a Sunday, November 25. In any year of the Christian calendar (the Julian calendar), February 25 will fall on the same day of the week as November 25, except in a leap year. 15 B.C. was not a leap year in the Christian calendar, and so February 25 and November 25 both fell on a Sunday. Therefore, the Incarnation of Jesus Christ occurred on a Sunday, the same day of the week as Christ's Birth. Jesus was both conceived and born about midnight on a Sunday, the beginning of the Christian Sabbath. (By comparison, March 25 and December 25 never fall on the same day of the week. December 25 always falls two days of the week later than March 25. When March 25 is a Sunday, December 25 is a Tuesday. When March 25 is a Friday, December 25 is a Sunday.)

The Betrothal of Joseph and Mary

In Israel, during Biblical times, the customs surrounding marriage were different than today. In our present society, couples who decide to marry are engaged first, and the engagement might last 6 months, or a year, or longer. Then, after the wedding ceremony, they immediately begin their married life together. But in ancient times in Israel, when a man and woman decided to marry, there was a betrothal ceremony, which marked the beginning of the marriage. There was no long engagement period during which the couple dated. Then, after the betrothal ceremony, there was a space of time before the couple moved in together and began their married life.

The Jewish Law of the Old Testament clearly indicates that marriage began with a betrothal, and that the couple often did not move in together until some length of time afterwards. Consider the following three cases from the book of Deuteronomy. If a man lies with another man's wife, he is stoned to death for adultery (Deut 22:22). But if a man lies with a virgin who is not betrothed, he is not put to death, but has to give her father a sum of money and marry her. He has sinned, but his sin is not adultery (Deut 22:28-29). In the third case, if a man lies with a betrothed virgin, he is stoned to death. She is another man's wife, so he is given the punishment for adultery (Deut 22:24). Notice that the woman of the third case has been betrothed, but is still a virgin—she is married, but has not yet moved in with her husband. The marriage began with the betrothal ceremony, but the couple did not move in together until some time had passed. This was the custom of that culture and time period.

How was Joseph chosen to be the husband of Mary? Blessed Anne Catherine tells us that unmarried men of the house of David were brought to the Temple and each inscribed his name on a branch with a closed flower blossom. After a number of prayers and sacrifices were offered, and after an interval of time passed, none of the flowers opened. The Temple priests then searched the land for more candidates and found Joseph. When his branch was brought before the altar, the flower blossomed, and so Joseph was recognized as God's choice to be betrothed to the Temple Virgin, Mary of Nazareth.[278]

Other ancient accounts, from apocryphal sources, claim that it was a dove, not the blossoming of a flower, which miraculously came from the branch.[279] The apocryphal story, involving a dove coming out of a branch, is clearly fictitious. Why would the Jewish priests choose Mary's husband using a method that required such an incongruous miracle? This story has not been accepted by the Christian community in any generation. Miracles do occur in salvation history, but this story has a miracle seemingly unrelated to the event. It does not make sense that the Jewish priests would expect God to miraculously cause a dove to come out of a branch, as a way to choose a husband for a Temple virgin.

On the other hand, Blessed Anne Catherine's account is much more plausible. Her account does not require the Jewish priests to have expected a miracle, but rather to have relied upon the Providence of God, merely expecting flowers to naturally open. Even so, the event could have been miraculous, in that Joseph's branch is sometimes said to have been "a dry rod blooming."[280] Joseph's branch may have been a dry dead branch, incapable of blooming naturally.[281]

In any case, her account fits the Jewish tradition of making important choices by lot, that is, by some type of chance event subject to the guidance of God's Providence (e.g. Joshua 14:2ff; Judges 7:4-7; Jonah 1:7). Blessed Anne Catherine's account of the event is also not unique to her writings. Saint Joseph is often depicted carrying a branch with a flower on it, as a reference to this ancient story.[282] Thus, this account has found some acceptance in the Christian community. Blessed Anne Catherine's account also provides chronological information, which fits well with the chronology of related events.

A flowering tree branch is most likely from a fruit tree. The purpose of the flower is to produce fruit. Fruit trees were cultivated in ancient Israel. The Jewish liturgical calendar even marked a New Year for Trees, celebrated in the month of Shevat (in winter).[283] The first fruits of the crop from fruit tree cultivation were offered as a sacrifice to God. A delay in the maturity of the crop from fruit trees was one of three factors in determining whether or not to delay the start of Passover (in spring), by adding the leap month of AdarII to the calendar.[284] So, the fruit crop was expected to reach maturity before Passover. The cultivation of fruit trees was connected with religious ritual. Thus, Blessed Anne Catherine's account of the Temple priests' method for choosing a husband for a favored Temple Virgin makes sense within the religious and cultural context.

Fruit trees produce flower buds, which grow to a point where they are nearly ready to open as flower blossoms. After pollination, the flowers become fruit, and the fruit grows to maturity. A skilled gardener can tell when a flower blossom is nearly ready to open. This skill is used, even today, to hand-pollinate various types of garden plants.[285]

In Israel, the only appreciable rainfall occurs from late fall, through winter, until early spring, that is, from November to March, inclusive.[286] The fruit trees could not have produced buds until sometime after the rains began in November. The buds then grew to maturity, and opened as flower blossoms, probably about the month of December. With any species of fruit tree, there are variations from one variety to the next, and even from one year to the next (depending on weather conditions), as to when the tree will flower, and when it will produce fruit.[287] But, in general, the fruit trees in Israel could not have blossomed before November, because of a lack of rain, and had to have blossomed and been pollinated well before the fruit crop would reach maturity in late winter/early spring.

If the Temple priests wanted to use a fruit tree branch as a religious test, not so different from the Old Testament practice of casting lots (Num 26:55; 1 Sam 14:42), they could only do so at a time when the fruit tree branches were close to blooming, which, in Israel, would be more or less the month of December. Earlier than that, the fruit tree buds would be too immature, later than that and the blossoms would already be opened, or would have been replaced by growing fruits.

Therefore, the time of year when Joseph was chosen to be the husband of Mary, Virgin of the Temple, was in early winter, about the month of December. This timing agrees with Blessed Anne Catherine's description of new Temple virgins being chosen in November (see chapter 9). The older Temple virgins had to be dismissed about that same time, to make room for the new. This timing also agrees with her statement that Joseph and Mary were betrothed in late January (see below). Mary returned to Nazareth, after being dismissed from the Temple, about the month of November. Joseph was chosen from among several candidates to be the husband of the Temple Virgin, Mary of Nazareth, about the month of December. And the betrothal ceremony was held in late January, after people had been notified and the betrothal preparations had been made.

"Now the procreation of the Christ occurred in this way. After his mother Mary had been betrothed to Joseph, before they lived together, she was found to have conceived in her womb by the Holy Spirit. Then Joseph, her husband, since he was just and was not willing to hand her over, preferred to send her away secretly." (Mt 1:18-19).

In this passage, Sacred Scripture indicates that the betrothal ceremony was the beginning of the marriage of Joseph and Mary. They "had been betrothed," meaning that the betrothal ceremony had already taken place. The phrase "before they lived together," means before they began to live in the same dwelling together. Here again is a reflection of the custom that the betrothed couple did not move in together until some length of time after the betrothal ceremony. Yet Sacred Scripture still calls Joseph "her husband," because the betrothal was the beginning of the marriage. And these three things: they were betrothed, they had not yet moved into the same house, and they were already considered married, are mentioned together in the same sentence. The Virgin Mary was a betrothed virgin.

"And for seven days they feasted, and all were rejoicing with great joy." (Tobit 11:21).

Blessed Anne Catherine describes the betrothal celebration of Joseph and Mary as lasting about 7 or 8 days, and occurring in late January, in Jerusalem.[288] She also repeatedly refers to their betrothal as a wedding. If the betrothal celebration began on Jan. 23, as Blessed Anne Catherine suggests,[289] and lasted seven days, then Mary would have started her journey back to Nazareth at the end of January.

The journey from Jerusalem to Nazareth is about 65 miles when measured straight on a map, and perhaps 70 – 75 miles when traveled by the roadways of the time. Mary traveled on foot,[290] so the journey itself may have taken at least 4 or 5 days, and perhaps longer. The journey of Mary and Joseph from Nazareth to Bethlehem is described as taking about 9 days, plus one day when they rested on the Sabbath and did not travel.[291] Bethlehem is only a short distance from Jerusalem, about 5 miles. Therefore, Mary's journey from Jerusalem to Nazareth after her wedding may have taken, at most, 8 or 9 days. The Virgin Mary arrived at Nazareth after her betrothal to Saint Joseph sometime in early February.

After the betrothal ceremony, the Virgin Mary went to Nazareth, but Joseph went to Bethlehem to see about an inheritance, or some family matter.[292] Joseph must have spent some length of time in Bethlehem, where his family lived, before returning to Nazareth. The Incarnation of Jesus Christ took place on February 25 of that year (15 B.C.), before Joseph had returned to Nazareth to live there permanently. And Blessed Anne Catherine tells us that Joseph had not yet moved into the same house with the Virgin Mary, when, after the Incarnation, they journeyed to Hebron to visit Elizabeth and Zechariah (Lk 1:39, 56).

"Mary's Annunciation took place before Joseph's return. He had not yet settled at Nazareth when, with Mary, he started on the journey to Hebron."[293]

"Some days after the Annunciation St. Joseph returned to Nazareth and made further arrangements for working at his craft in the house; he had never lived in Nazareth before and had not spent more than a few days there."[294]

In this way, Blessed Anne Catherine details what is also mentioned in Sacred Scripture, that the Annunciation and the Incarnation occurred soon after Joseph and the Virgin Mary were married, but before they came to live in the same house. The Virgin Mary received Jesus, the Inheritance of Israel, after her marriage ceremony, but before Joseph had arrived at the house in Nazareth.

Why did the Incarnation take place after the marriage of Saint Joseph and the Virgin Mary, not before?—because the Promise to the Israelites was that the Messiah would be born a descendent of David. Sacred Scripture tells us that Joseph was a descendent of David (Mt 1:6-16), as was the Virgin Mary (Lk 3:23-31).[295] Even though Joseph was not the biological father of Jesus, he was legally the father of Jesus (under Jewish religious law), because he was lawfully married to the Virgin Mary before the Incarnation occurred. In this way, the Promise that the Messiah would be a descendent of David was fulfilled both through Joseph's lineage (by the law) and through the Virgin Mary's lineage (by the flesh). And so it was important that the betrothal of Joseph and Mary take place before the Incarnation, so that the Promise would be doubly fulfilled, through Joseph by the law, and through the Virgin Mary by the flesh.

The Visitation of Mary and Elizabeth

"And in those days, Mary, rising up, traveled quickly into the hill country, to a city of Judah. And she entered into the house of Zechariah, and she greeted Elizabeth. And it happened that, as Elizabeth heard the greeting of Mary, the infant leaped in her womb, and Elizabeth was filled with the Holy Spirit. And she cried out with a loud voice and said: 'Blessed are you among women, and blessed is the fruit of your womb. And how does this concern me, so that the mother of my Lord would come to me?' " (Lk 1:39-43).

Sacred Scripture does not say that the Virgin Mary left for the house of Zechariah and Elizabeth immediately after the Incarnation. The phrase "In those days" simply means 'in that time period,' and does not imply immediate action. The phrase "traveled quickly" does not mean that Mary started her journey right away, but only that, when it was time to leave, she traveled quickly.

"When the Blessed Virgin felt that the Word was made Flesh in her, she was conscious of a great desire to pay an immediate visit to her cousin Elisabeth at Jutta near Hebron, whom the angel had told her was now six months with child. As the time was now drawing near when Joseph wished to go up to Jerusalem for the Passover, Our Lady decided to accompany him in order to help Elisabeth in her pregnancy."[296]

According to Blessed Anne Catherine, the Virgin Mary waited until the time of Passover to leave Nazareth. She and Joseph traveled to Jerusalem, attended the Passover feast, and then went to visit Zechariah and Elizabeth. The day before Mary and Elizabeth met, Zechariah returned from the Passover feast to Elizabeth. The following day, Joseph and the Virgin Mary arrived at Jutta, where Zechariah and Elizabeth lived.[297] Joseph and Mary arrived after Zechariah, perhaps because they took a longer route in order to avoid the crowds.[298]

On what day did the Visitation of the Virgin Mary and Elizabeth occur? The Passover of 15 B.C. began with the Preparation Day on Nisan 14, which was April 11 and a Wednesday.[299] The first day of Passover is Nisan 15 (a Thursday that year), so the seventh and last day of Passover would then have been the following Wednesday, April 18. The seventh day of Passover, Nisan 21, is a holy day on which devout Jews do no work (Ex 12:16-18). A devout Jew would not travel far on such a day. So Zechariah, a Jewish priest, could not have set out from the Passover to his home in Jutta, about 25 miles away, until Wednesday evening, April 18, when the day ended at sunset, at the earliest.

How long did it take to travel from Jerusalem to Jutta? This distance is about 25 miles, as a straight line on a map, but a traveler might have to take a somewhat longer route, in order to follow roads or avoid geographical obstacles. As stated above, it may have taken Zechariah more than a day of travel. If he left on Wednesday evening, when the day ended at sunset, he could travel several miles, then rest for the night. The next day, he would still have over 20 miles to travel, a distance which could be walked in a single day. Thus, he may have arrived home as early as Thursday evening, April 19, or at the latest on Friday before sunset, April 20. Since the Sabbath begins on Friday at sunset, Zechariah, would have wanted to arrive home before the Sabbath began. He could not have traveled on the Sabbath, because he was both a priest and a devout Jew, so he could not have arrived home on the Sabbath (Saturday). So Zechariah could have arrived home on Thursday, April 19, or on Friday, April 20.

However, Joseph and Mary arrived on the next day after Zechariah arrived home. They were also devout Jews and would not have traveled on the Sabbath.[300] They arrived at Zechariah and Elizabeth's home on the day after Zechariah returned, so they must have been traveling during that day. The day they arrived could not have been a Saturday, because Joseph and the Virgin Mary would not have broken the Sabbath by traveling on that day. Therefore Zechariah did not arrive at his home on Friday, April 20, because the next day was the Sabbath, a day on which Joseph and Mary would not have traveled. Zechariah must have arrived home on Thursday, April 19, so that Joseph and Mary arrived on the following day, Friday, before the Sabbath began at sunset. Therefore, the Visitation of the Virgin Mary and Elizabeth occurred on Friday, April 20, before sunset.

Zechariah would not have taken longer to travel from Jerusalem to his home in Jutta. He was a priest in service at the Temple in the Jerusalem and was used to traveling this particular route. People in that time period were accustomed to traveling on foot and would be able to walk 20 miles or more in a day. Zechariah was traveling alone and so could travel as quickly as he wanted. Also, he most likely wanted to arrive home before the Sabbath, since he was a Jewish priest. On the other hand, Joseph was traveling with a young wife and so took longer to make the same journey. Also, Blessed Anne Catherine tells us that Joseph and Mary took a longer route to avoid the crowds.[301] Thus they arrived a day later.

The Birth of Saint John the Baptist

"Then Mary stayed with her for about three months. And she returned to her own house." (Lk 1:56).

Sacred Scripture tells us that the Virgin Mary remained with Elizabeth for "about three months." Since the word "about" is used, this is not the exact length of time. As with the verse from Luke's Gospel which tells us that Jesus began His ministry when he was "about thirty years old" (Lk 3:23), God's Holy Infallible Scripture would not have used the word "about" if this was the exact length of time. So then, the Virgin Mary did not stay with Elizabeth for exactly 3 months, but for some number of days more or less than three months.

Sacred Scripture does not tell us whether or not the Virgin Mary remained for the birth of John the Baptist. The birth of John is mentioned in the verse immediately following the statement that Mary returned home from visiting Elizabeth (Lk 1:56-57). However, this does not necessarily mean that Mary left before John was born.

According to Blessed Anne Catherine, the Virgin Mary went to visit Elizabeth to help her during her pregnancy, and she did remain with Elizabeth until after the birth of John. "The Blessed Virgin returned home to Nazareth after John's birth and before his circumcision."[302] It makes sense that Mary would remain until after John was born, since she went to assist Elizabeth during the latter part of her pregnancy, which was the time when Elizabeth would be most in need of assistance.

Since John was conceived on or after Tishri 24, a day which began at sunset on Sept. 26 of 16 B.C.,[303] he would most likely have been born about nine months later in late June of 15 B.C. A full term pregnancy is considered to be 38 weeks (266 days) from conception. In our society today, 90% of births occur within a time frame of 266 days, plus or minus 2 weeks, from conception.[304] If John was conceived the night of Sept. 26/27 (at the start of Tishri 24), then 266 days would be completed on June 19 (Sivan 24 in the Jewish calendar).[305] The most probable time period for the birth of John the Baptist would then be a four-week period of time from June 6 to July 3, inclusive.[306] If John was conceived a day or more after Tishri 24, then the probable time frame for his birth would be moved forward by that number of days. However, John's conception could not have taken place later than about Tishri 28, because Elizabeth had begun her sixth month on or before AdarI 28, the date of the Incarnation. Therefore, the 4-week probable time frame for the birth of John could be moved forward no more than 4 additional days, to July 7. This consideration gives us a slightly larger probable time frame for John's birth of June 6 to July 7, inclusive.

This time frame for the birth of John can be narrowed down by examining the circumstances surrounding his birth. The Incarnation of Jesus Christ occurred on Feb. 25

and near the beginning of Elizabeth's sixth month. The Virgin Mary waited until after the Passover to visit Elizabeth, so that her visit began on April 20. Since Elizabeth was in her sixth month by Feb. 25, she would be in her 8th month by April 25, about the time of the beginning of the Virgin Mary's visit. Yet Sacred Scripture tells us that Mary stayed with Elizabeth for about three months. And Blessed Anne Catherine adds that Mary left after the birth of John, but before his circumcision on the eighth day. If the Virgin Mary had stayed with Elizabeth for more than three months, she would have stayed from April 20 to sometime after July 17 (three lunar months). But this date is too many days past the time frame for John's birth to fall between John's birth and his circumcision (on the 8th day). So the exact length of Mary's stay with Elizabeth must have been somewhat less than three full months. But if the Virgin Mary had left after a period of time closer to two months than to three, then Sacred Scripture would not have said "about three months."

Following this line of reasoning, July 2 is the mid-point between 2 and 3 months from the beginning of Mary's visit with Elizabeth. (April 20 to July 2 is 74 days, inclusive; 2.5 lunar months is just under 74 days.)[307] So Mary's visit must have lasted until sometime after July 2, so that the length of time for her visit would be closer to 3 months than to 2 months.

Now, Mary departed after the birth, but before the circumcision, of John, so John was born no sooner than June 27, which is 7 days before the earliest possible date for Mary's departure (July 3). This earliest date for John's birth is arrived at by taking the earliest date for Mary's departure which could still be called "about three months" by Sacred Scripture, July 3, and subtracting the longest possible time between the birth of John and the departure of Mary. Mary departed before the circumcision, which was held on the eighth day from birth, inclusive; so that Mary could have left as late as the seventh day from John's birth. That seventh day could have occurred no earlier than July 3, and so John the Baptist could have been born no earlier than June 27.

The above argument gives us a narrower time frame for the birth of John the Baptist: June 27 to July 7, inclusive—a time frame of only eleven days. The birth of John could not have occurred earlier, because the Virgin Mary's visit with Elizabeth lasted closer to three months than to two months. The birth of John could have occurred later than July 7, but only if he was born more than 40 weeks after conception, that is, more than 2 weeks after Elizabeth's due date. Such a late date for the birth of any child is very unlikely. Therefore, the date of John's birth very likely occurred within the above time frame, sometime from Wednesday, June 27 to Saturday, July 7, inclusive, in 15 B.C. In the Jewish calendar, in 15 B.C., June 27 coincided with Tammuz 2, and July 7 coincided with Tammuz 12.[308] The summer solstice that year occurred early in the day on June 25.[309]

Chapter 6
The Divine Childhood

The Eighth Day

"And after eight days were ended, so that the boy would be circumcised, his name was called JESUS, just as he was called by the Angel before he was conceived in the womb." (Lk 2:21).

Jesus was circumcised on the eighth day from His birth according to Jewish Law and custom. Since Christ was born about midnight at the beginning of Nov. 25, the first day would be Nov. 25. The eighth day would then be December 2. Sacred Scripture specifies that the circumcision took place "after eight days were ended," but this does not mean at the end of the eighth day, but rather at the end of an eight day period of time.

The Circumcision of the Christ-child took place on the last of the eight days in accordance with Jewish Law. The eighth day was also the earliest practical date for any circumcision, because Jewish women were considered unclean for the first seven days from the birth of a male child (Lev 12). People could not gather for this ceremony, which must of course involve the mother, during the days when she was considered unclean.

Blessed Anne Catherine Emmerich received visions from God about this event in Christ's life. She tells us that Jesus was circumcised at dawn on Sunday, Dec. 2.[310]

Even though the angel gave him the name Jesus before He was conceived, He was not formally given His name until the eighth day (Lk 2:21). Thus the ceremony on the 8th day was not only for circumcising the child, but also for giving the child a name. The same practice of waiting until the 8th day to give the child his name is also seen with the circumcision of John the Baptist (Lk 1:59-63). This Jewish practice is not so different from the Christian practice of giving the child a name at the time of the ceremony of Baptism (sometimes called a "Christening"). Similarly in the Jewish faith, the eighth day was both the day for circumcision and the day for naming the child. (See chapter 9 for details about a similar naming ceremony for female children.)

The Presentation of Jesus Christ in the Temple

"And after the days of her purification were fulfilled, according to the law of Moses, they brought him to Jerusalem, in order to present him to the Lord, just as it is written in the law of the Lord, 'For every male opening the womb shall be called holy to the Lord,' and in order to offer a sacrifice, according to what is said in the law of the Lord, 'a pair of turtledoves or two young pigeons.' " (Lk 2:22-24).

"Speak to the sons of Israel, and you shall say to them: A woman, if she has received the seed to bear a male, shall be unclean for seven days, just as in the days of separation due to menstruation. And on the eighth day, the little infant shall be circumcised. Yet truly, she herself shall remain for thirty-three days in the blood of her purification. She shall not touch anything holy, nor shall she enter into the Sanctuary, until the days of her purification are completed. But if she will bear a female, she shall be unclean for two weeks, according to the custom of her monthly flow, and she shall remain in the blood of her purification for sixty-six days. And when the days of her purification have been completed, for a son or for a daughter, she shall bring to the door of the tabernacle of the testimony, a one-year-old lamb as a holocaust, and a young pigeon or a turtledove for sin, and she shall deliver them to the priest." (Lev 12:2-6).

Although the Gospel of Luke does not explicitly say that the Presentation occurred on the 40th day from the Birth of Christ, it is clear that Joseph and Mary went to the temple with the infant Jesus in fulfillment of Jewish law (Lk 2:22, 23, 27). Formerly, I concluded that the Presentation must have occurred on the 40th day in order to fulfill the Law. But Leviticus 12 does not require the presentation of a male child **on** the 40th day. Notice that the text of Leviticus specifies that the circumcision take place on the eighth day. But as to the Presentation, it is only required sometime after the days of her separation (7 days for a male child, including the day of birth) and her purification (33 days for a male child). The total number of days is 40 days including the day of birth, so the 40th day after the birth would be the first opportunity for the Presentation in the Temple. But there is no reason to assume that all mothers presented their newborns, after a possibly long trip to Jerusalem, on the 40th day. In fact, it is more reasonable to conclude that most mothers did not do so, because of the difficulty of travel, and the ease with which a newborn might take ill. Also, while a woman is in her days of separation, it would be difficult to travel and remain separate. And, given the uncertainties of travel in ancient Israel, it would be difficult to ensure arrival in Jerusalem on any chosen day.

In the particular case of the Christ-child and the Virgin Mary, they were staying in Bethlehem, which is near Jerusalem, at the time. The trip to Jerusalem was about 5 to 7 miles, depending on the route and also on the exact location of the cave in which they were staying, on the outskirts of Bethlehem. This is not too long a trip. However, the time of year was winter, and mothers prudently keep their newborns from cold temperatures and undue risks. Mary had confidence in God, but she was still prudent in her decision and actions, as was Joseph. Therefore, it is possible that the Presentation in the Temple occurred relatively soon after the days of separation and purification were completed, but perhaps not on the 40th day. Still, there seems to be no indication in Scripture, that would tell us the exact day.

Jesus was born on Sunday, November 25 of 15 B.C. The 40th day inclusive from November 25th was then Thursday, January 3 of 14 B.C. But the first opportunity for the Presentation would have been the next day, i.e. the 40th day after, not the 40th day inclusive of the day of the Birth. Note that the Church currently celebrates the Presentation on February 2 is because that date is the 40th day from Christmas (Dec. 25). But the count used there for the 40 days is inclusive, in other words, the day of the Birth is counted as day one, and the day of the Presentation is counted as day 40 in the liturgical calendar. Now it may be that the Jews in ancient times counted the days inclusively, or perhaps not. But this point is not crucial to this discussion, since the 40th day was probably not typically the day for this ceremony in any case.

Turning to private revelation for some guidance, the words of Blessed Anne Catherine lend some support to a date in early January for the Presentation. "In the night of Sunday, December 30th, to Monday, December 31st, I saw Joseph and Mary with the Child visiting the Cave of the Nativity once more and taking leave of that holy place."[311] She further states that the Virgin Mary and Saint Joseph set out from the Cave of the

Nativity in Bethlehem, "At dawn on Monday, December 31st...." to travel to Jerusalem for the Presentation. Although she received the visions of these events about the time of the Church's celebration of the Presentation of the Lord (Feb. 2), she clearly states that the trip from Bethlehem to Jerusalem for the Presentation began on the morning of Dec. 31. After describing the beginning of their journey on Dec. 31, Blessed Anne Catherine describes a second day of travel, which brought them to an inn just outside Jerusalem. They stayed at this inn for their visit to Jerusalem at the time of the Presentation.[312]

Why did it take two days to travel from Bethlehem to Jerusalem? Bethlehem is a short distance from Jerusalem, but Joseph and the Virgin Mary were traveling from the Cave of the Nativity, not from the center of the town, so there was an additional distance to travel. Joseph and the Virgin Mary traveled slowly, for they had the newborn infant Jesus with them. Also, the inn where they were staying was not necessarily directly between Bethlehem and Jerusalem. Joseph and Mary may have had to travel some distance around the city of Jerusalem to arrive at the inn. The route from the Cave of the Nativity to the inn outside Jerusalem may have been somewhat circuitous, and not a straight line from the center of Bethlehem to the outskirts of Jerusalem.

After two days of travel (Dec. 31, Jan. 1), Joseph, Mary, and Jesus rested for a day at the inn outside Jerusalem (Wed., Jan. 2). On the next day, January 3, Joseph and the Virgin Mary presented the infant Jesus to God in the Temple at Jerusalem. Although Blessed Anne Catherine does not explicitly state on which day the Presentation occurred, she does state plainly that the journey began on the morning of Dec. 31, and she describes two days of travel (Dec. 31, Jan. 1) and a day of rest (Jan. 2) before the day of the Presentation.[313] However, in another place, she contradicts this apparent chronology when she states that the Presentation occurred on the 43rd day from the Birth of Christ.[314]

Time of Day of the Presentation

"This morning, while it was still dark, I saw the Holy Family...going to Jerusalem to the Temple with the baskets of offerings...."[315]

"The Presentation must have ended about nine o'clock this morning, for it was at this time that I saw the departure of the Holy Family."[316]

According to Blessed Anne Catherine, the ceremony of the Presentation of Jesus in the Temple and of the Purification of the Virgin Mary took place in the morning. The Holy Family went to the Temple before dawn, and the ceremony ended by about mid morning.

The Offering

The Presentation of the Lord is also sometimes called the Purification of the Virgin Mary, because on the 40th day from the birth of a son, the mother was required by the law to bring a sacrifice to the Temple of Jerusalem for her purification. The offering required by the law was a lamb and either a turtledove or a young pigeon (Lev 12:6). However, if the mother could not afford a lamb, she was required instead to offer two of the birds, the additional bird taking the place of the lamb. According to Sacred Scripture, the Virgin Mary did offer two turtledoves or two young pigeons (Lk 2:24), therefore,

Joseph and Mary must have been poor. Blessed Anne Catherine says that Mary offered two doves.[317]

The reason Sacred Scripture specifies turtledoves or young pigeons is that these birds were white. Turtledoves are white at any age, but pigeons are only white when they are young. That is why only the pigeons were required to be young.

The usual meaning given to this offering was as a purification for the mother after giving birth. The Most Pure Virgin Mary did not need to be purified by the sacrifice of a lamb or a dove, for she had already been purified by the sacrifice of the Lamb of God and by the Holy Spirit (symbolized by a dove). This sacrifice required by all Jewish women was merely a foreshadowing of the one true sacrifice of Jesus the Lamb of God, which purifies us from all sin. So, when the Virgin Mary made her offering of two turtledoves, the meaning in this case was not to obtain purification, but to offer it. The two white doves symbolize the purity of the two holy souls of the Virgin Mary and Jesus Christ. These doves were offered as a sacrifice to God to symbolize the offering of the souls of Mary and Jesus to God, a perfect and most pure sacrifice through which God offers purification to all.

The Return to Nazareth

"And after they had performed all things according to the law of the Lord, they returned to Galilee, to their city, Nazareth. Now the child grew, and he was strengthened with the fullness of wisdom. And the grace of God was in him." (Lk 2:39-40).

According to Sacred Scripture, the Holy Family returned to Nazareth after the Presentation in the Temple of Jerusalem. Blessed Anne Catherine also describes the return to Nazareth as occurring after the Presentation.[318] And so, it is clear that the Holy Family did not flee into Egypt immediately. Herod was likely still searching for and worrying over the new-born king of the Jews (cf. Mt 2:2-3), but had not yet devised his plan to kill all the young children in the Bethlehem area.

The Flight to Egypt

"And after they had gone away, behold, an Angel of the Lord appeared in sleep to Joseph, saying: 'Rise up, and take the boy and his mother, and flee into Egypt. And remain there until I tell you. For it will happen that Herod will seek the boy to destroy him.' And getting up, he took the boy and his mother by night, and withdrew into Egypt. And he remained there, until the death of Herod, in order to fulfill what was spoken by the Lord through the prophet, saying: 'Out of Egypt, I called my son.' " (Mt 2:13-15).

The Gospel of Matthew does not mention the Holy Family's stay in Nazareth between the departure of the wise men and the flight to Egypt. However, the Gospel of Luke does plainly say that the Holy Family returned to Nazareth after the Presentation (Lk 2:39-40). The Holy Family left Jerusalem for Nazareth, after the Presentation in the Temple (Jan. 3), which took place on the 40th day after Christ's Birth (Nov. 25). Then, sometime after their return to Nazareth, the Holy Family fled to Egypt.

"Then Herod, seeing that he had been fooled by the Magi, was very angry. And so he sent to kill all the boys who were in Bethlehem, and in all its borders, from two years of age and under, according to the time that he had learned by questioning the Magi." (Mt 2:16).

There are several indications that the flight to Egypt occurred well over a year after the Birth of Jesus Christ. The Holy Family's flight to Egypt occurred because Herod was about to try to destroy the Christ Child (Mt 2:13). Before the wise men realized that Herod had evil intentions, they had given him knowledge of when the Christmas Star first appeared (Mt 2:7). So Herod had some idea of when Christ was born. But Sacred Scripture tells us that Herod ordered the death of all the male children in Bethlehem and the surrounding area who were two years old or younger. Herod's soldiers could have easily distinguished between a one year old and a two year old, since two year olds can walk and run about fairly well, whereas one year olds can barely walk. Yet Herod chose to have children 2 years old or younger killed, rather than children one year old or younger.

If the flight to Egypt had taken place just a few months after Christ's Birth, Herod would have ordered the death of male children one year old and younger. Herod was a cruel and evil man, but he would not have ordered the death of these children if it did not accomplish his purpose. For example, he ordered the death only of the male children, since he knew that the Child King of the Jews would be male; ordering the death of female children would not have fit his purpose. In the same way, Herod would not have ordered the death of male children as old as two years, unless he thought the Christ Child could have been as old as two years. Therefore, the flight to Egypt took place over a year after the Birth of Jesus Christ.

In addition, according to Blessed Anne Catherine, the flight to Egypt began on February 29th. The writer of her visions, Clemens Brentano, asked her, on February 10, if that was the day when Joseph fled to Egypt. " 'Was it to-day that Joseph started for Egypt?' to which she answered clearly and decisively: 'No, the day he started on the flight was what is now February 29th.' "[319]

Of course, February 29 only occurs on a leap year. In the years beginning with A.D. 4, leap years in the Julian calendar occur in every year which is evenly divisible by 4. So the leap years were A.D. 4, 8, 12, 16, etc. But if we count backwards four years from A.D. 4, we arrive at 1 B.C. as the leap year immediately prior to A.D. 4 (because there is no year zero). Thus, in the years B.C., the leap years would be 1, 5, 9, 13, 17, 21, 25, 29 and 33 B.C., etc. Whether or not the Romans kept the leap years every fourth year from the very earliest years of the Julian calendar is debatable, which is perhaps why Blessed Anne Catherine says "what is now February 29th." In any case, the flight to Egypt began in a year which we now consider a leap year.

Jesus was born in late 15 B.C.; the next leap year in the Julian calendar was 13 B.C. The date of February 29 of 13 B.C. falls more than one year and less than two years after the Birth of Christ. This date fits the time frame indicated by the Gospel of Matthew because Herod ordered the deaths of the male children 2 years or younger, not one year or younger. On February 29 of 13 B.C., Jesus was just over 15 months old counting from birth.

The flight to Egypt could not have occurred in Feb. of 14 B.C., just a few months after the Birth of Christ (Nov. of 15 B.C.), because that year was not a leap year and because the Christ-Child was much less than one year old. So the Holy Family must have fled to Egypt the following year, in 13 B.C., on February 29.

This chronology of the Flight to Egypt provides additional support for the conclusion that Christ was born in 15 B.C. Herod killed the children two years of age or younger, so the flight to Egypt must have occurred between one and two years after the Birth of Christ. It could not have occurred only a few months after Christ's Birth, or Herod would not have killed children as old as two years. But the flight to Egypt also could not have occurred more than two years after Christ's Birth, or Herod would have killed children older than two years. Also, Blessed Anne Catherine described the Christ Child as being, at most, between one and two years old at the time of the flight to Egypt.[320] So, since the flight to Egypt took place in a leap year on Feb. 29, any proposed year for the Birth of Christ must be followed by a non-leap year and then a leap year. The only year which fits this line of reasoning, and has Nov. 25 falling on a Sunday, is 15 B.C. The year 4 B.C. is too long before the leap year of 1 B.C. to have been the year of Christ's Birth. And Nov. 25 of A.D. 3, which was a Sunday, is only a few months from Feb. 29 of A.D. 4. Other years which are two years prior to a leap year do not fit the criteria for the year of Christ's Birth, nor do they fit the criteria for the year of Christ's death 33 years later.

Blessed Anne Catherine's description of the Child Jesus during the flight to Egypt indicates that Jesus was just over 1 year old at that time. "Once she said: 'The Child may well be more than a year old, I saw Him playing about by a balsam-bush at one of the halting-places on the journey, and sometimes His parents led Him by the hand for a little way.' "[321]

There was some confusion, though, on the part of Blessed Anne Catherine about the age of Christ at the time of His flight to Egypt. She gives conflicting information about whether the flight to Egypt occurred in the calendar year after Christ's Birth, or a year later. Though she describes the Child Jesus as walking while His parents held His hand during the journey, in another place, she asserts that Jesus was at this time only about 12 weeks old. "The Child was twelve weeks old. I had seen three times four weeks."[322] This statement conflicts with her description of the Child Jesus being able to walk.

Her statement that Christ was 12 weeks old also conflicts with her descriptions of the young Saint John the Baptist. "Little John had nothing on but a lamb's skin; although scarcely eighteen months old, he was sure on his feet and could run and jump about."[323] We know from Sacred Scripture that John was conceived just over 5 months before the Incarnation (see chapter 5). If John was born about 5 months or so before Christ was born, then he was born in late June or early July. Since the flight to Egypt began at the very end of February, John must have been about 20 months old. John's 18th month occurred about December (14 B.C.), and his 20th month occurred about February (13 B.C.). If John was able to run and jump about, he must have been about 20 months old, not the 8 months old that he was in late February of the previous year. Therefore, the Christ Child was about 15 months old, and not 3 months old (12 weeks), when the flight to Egypt began.

So then, why would God show Blessed Anne Catherine three times four weeks? Perhaps this was an indication of the month when the flight to Egypt began, but not the year. In this way, the three times four weeks means that the flight began at the end of February, about three months after the Birth of Jesus Christ. A similar misunderstanding occurred regarding the time of the Virgin Mary's death, where Blessed Anne Catherine interprets 13 plus 2 months to mean 13 years and 2 months, whereas an interpretation of

13 days plus 2 months is a much better fit for the information which she herself gives (see chapter 10).

The Holy Family's flight to Egypt began on February 29 of 13 B.C. In that year, February 29 coincided with Saturday, AdarI 24 in the Jewish calendar.[324] Devout Jews would not travel more than a short distance on Saturday, because it is the Sabbath. But the Holy Family fled in the evening, as is clear from Sacred Scripture: "And getting up, he took the boy and his mother by night, and withdrew into Egypt." (Mt 2:14). And Blessed Anne Catherine tells us: "It was not yet midnight when they left the house."[325] Since the Sabbath day ends at sunset on Saturday, the beginning of the Holy Family's flight to Egypt did not conflict with their obligation to rest on the Sabbath. By the Jewish calendar each day ends at sunset, so the Holy Family's flight to Egypt actually began on Sunday (AdarI 25), but by the Roman calendar it was near the end of Saturday on February 29.[326]

Blessed Anne Catherine describes a worship ceremony occurring the evening before the evening the flight to Egypt began.[327] The evening of February 28 of 13 B.C. was a Friday; the Jewish Sabbath begins at sunset on Friday. So the worship ceremony she described was for the Sabbath. The Holy Family fled for Egypt not that night, but the next, after the Sabbath had ended. The descriptions of events given by Blessed Anne Catherine fit well with a date of February 29 of 13 B.C., after dark, for the start of the Holy Family's flight to Egypt.

The Path to Egypt

Blessed Anne Catherine tells us that the entire trip from Nazareth to Egypt took about 20 days. "They had been ten days in the Jewish country and ten days in the desert."[328] The ten days in the desert must refer to the Sinai desert, which the Holy Family had to cross to enter Egypt. Since they left Nazareth late in the evening on Feb. 29, they entered the desert about Mar. 10, and they entered Egypt about Mar. 20, of 13 B.C.

The distance from Nazareth to the border between Israel and the Sinai is about 120 miles, as measured on a map, and perhaps as much as 140 to 150 miles when traveling by various roadways on a less than direct route.[329] In Israel, the Holy Family traveled from Nazareth, by an inland route, passing near Jerusalem and Hebron.[330] The distance from the border between Israel and the Sinai, near the Mediterranean Sea, to Egypt by way of the coastline is also about 120 miles on a map, and not too many miles more than that for the actual journey, since the way is fairly direct. The Holy Family most likely traveled along the coastline, since the rest of the Sinai is mountainous and rugged terrain.

Blessed Anne Catherine says that the journey took 10 days in Israel and 10 more days in the Sinai. The Holy Family left for Egypt on Saturday after sunset (which is the start of Sunday in the Jewish calendar). So, of the first 10 days they traveled, there was one Sabbath day of rest.[331] And on the next 10 days, there was also one Sabbath day of rest. If they arrived in Egypt on the 20th day, then the 21st day would be the Sabbath. So their journey began after a Sabbath, included two more Sabbaths, then ended just before the fourth Sabbath.

If the trip from Nazareth to the Sinai was about 140 miles, and the trip across the Sinai was about 130 miles, then the total was about 270 miles. To arrive in Egypt in 20 days time, less 2 days for rest on the Sabbath, means that the Holy Family traveled an average of roughly 15 miles per day (15 x 18 = 270). This distance is not too great for a small family to travel on foot and with a donkey.

The Massacre of the Holy Innocents

"Then what was spoken through the prophet Jeremiah was fulfilled, saying: 'A voice has been heard in Ramah, great weeping and wailing: Rachel crying for her sons. And she was not willing to be consoled, because they were no more.' " (Mt 2:17-18).

Sacred Scripture does not say how soon the Massacre of the Holy Innocents occurred after the Holy Family fled to Egypt. However, it probably occurred shortly after the flight to Egypt, since that was why they fled from Israel. The angel said to Saint Joseph: " '...flee into Egypt. And remain there until I tell you. For it will happen that Herod will seek the boy to destroy him.' " (Mt 2:13). Jesus was about 15-16 months old at the time of the flight to Egypt, and the Massacre likely occurred within a few months of the flight.

"Then Herod, seeing that he had been fooled by the Magi, was very angry. And so he sent to kill all the boys who were in Bethlehem, and in all its borders, from two years of age and under, according to the time that he had learned by questioning the Magi." (Mt 2:16). So the Massacre must have occurred under two years after the Birth of Christ. Herod did not know the exact date of Christ's Birth, for the wise men avoided him after the Birth of Christ (Mt 2:12), but he had some idea of the time, based on what the wise men had told him previously (Mt 2:7,16). Herod was so determined to kill the Christ Child that he would not have taken any unnecessary chance of missing his opportunity by choosing too low an age for the children to be killed. If Herod thought that the Child Jesus had been born two full years earlier, he would have set the age of those to be killed higher than two years. Therefore, Christ was probably at least a few months younger than 2 full years at the time of the Massacre of the Holy Innocents.

According to Blessed Anne Catherine Emmerich, the Massacre of the Holy Innocents occurred when Jesus was nearly 18 months old and John the Baptist was about 2 years old. "John the Baptist was two years old when it happened.... Jesus was nearly eighteen months old and could already run about."[332] And in another place she tells us: "Both Mary and Joseph were deeply grieved, and the Child Jesus, who was now able to walk, being a year and a half old, shed tears the whole day."[333] Again, she tells us: "...the Massacre of the Innocents was in His second year."[334] (Notice that the "second year" is not the year following Jesus' second birthday, but rather, the year between His first and second birthdays. A person's second birthday marks the end, not the beginning of their second year of life since birth.)

Jesus was born Nov. 25 of 15 B.C., and so He completed His 18th month since His Birth at the end of May in 13 B.C. Blessed Anne Catherine says that Jesus was "nearly" 18 months old, indicating that the Massacre happened before the end of May.

However, she also states that John was two years old when the Massacre happened. John was born in late June or early July of 15 B.C. and was about 5 months older than Jesus. John completed his second year from birth in late June or early July of 13 B.C.; he would have been not quite 2 years old in May. So the Massacre could have happened as late as June or July.

On the other hand, Blessed Anne Catherine received her visions about the Massacre of the Holy Innocents on March 9. She usually received her visions on either the actual day of the event, or on the day of the Church's celebration of that event. The Church's celebration of the Martyrdom of the Holy Innocents is held on Dec. 28. So, perhaps the actual day of the Massacre occurred on the day that she received the vision, which was March 9.

In 13 B.C., the Passover was most likely held from April 18 to 25.[335] If the Passover was held in March, it would have started before the Spring Equinox. Huge numbers of Jews came to Jerusalem for the Passover. Herod would not have put so many Jewish children to death just before or during the Passover, for fear of the crowds. The Jewish feast of Pentecost (the Feast of Weeks) begins on the 50th day (Sivan 6; June 8 that year) from the second day of Passover. Since huge crowds also came to Jerusalem for the Feast of Weeks, Herod would likely have avoided killing the Holy Innocents at that time. So, the Massacre of the Holy Innocents could have occurred in early March, well before the late April Passover. Or, it could have occurred in early May, after the Passover crowds had left the area. Or, it could have occurred in mid to late June or in July, after the Feast of Weeks had ended.

Based on various statements by Blessed Anne Catherine, the Massacre most likely occurred sometime between March and July of 13 B.C. The exact date of the Massacre of the Holy Innocents is not certain. However, within this time frame, I favor the date of March 9. Early March is not long after the Holy Family fled to Egypt; in fact, they were still in transit at that time. They fled to Egypt to avoid the Massacre, so a date closer to the date of their flight is preferable. Also, March 9 was the date on which Blessed Anne Catherine received her visions of the event.

The number of infants killed in the Massacre, according to Blessed Anne Catherine, was probably about 700. "Their number was shown to me, but I have no clear recollection of it. I think it was 700, and another number with 7 or 17 in it."[336] These children were taken, not only from Bethlehem and the adjacent towns, but also from other towns in Judea. There would not have been so many infants killed if only the male infants from Bethlehem and the immediate area were taken.

Herod sent his soldiers out to various towns around Jerusalem, even those some distance from Bethlehem. "Under various pretexts he dispatched soldiers to different places round Jerusalem, such as Gilgal, Bethlehem, and Hebron, and ordered a census of the children to be made."[337] Bethlehem is only a few miles from Jerusalem, but the town of Hebron is about 20 miles south of Jerusalem. And the town of Gilgal is over 15 miles northeast of Jerusalem, just north of Jericho.[338] Blessed Anne Catherine also tells us: "The children were massacred in seven different places."[339] Herod would not have needed 7 different places to kill the children if they were taken from only one small area around Bethlehem.

Sacred Scripture also indicates that the Holy Innocents were taken from a large area: "all the boys who were in Bethlehem, and in all its borders...." (Mt 2:16). The phrase "and in all its borders" is a broad generalization, which does not limit the area spoken of to one immediate location, but extends it to a larger area. Also, Sacred Scripture tells us that the Massacre of the Holy Innocents was a fulfillment of a prophecy of Jeremiah that refers to Ramah. " 'A voice has been heard in Ramah, great weeping and wailing: Rachel crying for her sons. And she was not willing to be consoled, because they were no more.' " (Mt 2:18). Bethlehem is about 5 miles south of Jerusalem, but the town of

Ramah is about 7 miles north of Jerusalem.[340] In this way, Sacred Scripture indicates that the Holy Innocents were taken from a larger area, not only from Bethlehem and the adjacent towns.

The Holy Family in Egypt

According to Blessed Anne Catherine, the Holy Family arrived in Egypt after a journey of about 20 days.[341] Since they departed Nazareth on the evening of February 29 of 13 B.C., they probably arrived in Egypt on Friday, March 20. They traveled into Egypt and a few days later settled in Heliopolis.[342] This town was located a little to the east of the present-day city of Cairo, Egypt. Heliopolis is also called "On." It was located about 15 miles north of the city of Memphis, on the eastern side of the Nile river, at the southern tip of the Nile Delta (a fertile region).[343]

"After staying in Heliopolis for a year and a half, until Jesus was about two years old, the Holy Family left the city because of lack of work and various persecutions."[344] The Holy Family arrived in Egypt in March of 13 B.C., when Jesus was about 16 months old. Heliopolis was the first town they settled in. So, if the Holy Family remained there for about a year and a half, then Jesus would have been about 34 months old, when they moved to another town. Blessed Anne Catherine says that Jesus was 2 years old when the Holy Family left Heliopolis, but He must have been nearly 3 years old.

The Holy Family moved from Heliopolis to a nearby town which is called Matarea.[345] This move likely occurred in late autumn of 12 B.C., which is about a year and a half after they arrived in Egypt. They lived in Matarea for several years.[346] During the time that the Holy Family lived in Matarea, Jesus was told by an angel about the death of Herod. Blessed Anne Catherine says: "I am not sure whether it was in His fifth or seventh year."[347] (The conclusion that Herod died during Jesus' seventh year, between His sixth and seventh Birthdays, when He was just over six years old, is explained in chapter 12, and also below in the section on the Return from Egypt.)

The Childhood of John the Baptist

"I was shown how Elisabeth, warned by the angel, once more fled into the desert with the little John to escape the Massacre of the Innocents."[348]

"When she went home, an Essene from the community on Mount Horeb came to the boy in the wilderness, brought him food, and gave him all the help he needed....but in a short time John no longer needed help, for he was soon more at home in the wilderness than among men. It was ordained by God that he should grow up in the wilderness without contact with mankind and innocent of their sins. Like Jesus, he never went to school; the Holy Ghost taught him in the wilderness."[349]

John was staying in the wilderness in southern Israel, between Hebron and the Dead Sea.[350] The Essene who lived on Mount Horeb visited him "as first every eight days."[351] The Essenes lived a very simple and poor life, so the Essene who visited John most likely traveled by walking. Mount Horeb would then be only a day or two's walk from southern Israel. If it were three or four day's walk from Mount Horeb to the place in Israel where John was staying, then it would be 6 to 8 days round trip. The Essene would not have spent three or four days in travel from where John was to his home, only to have to turn around again within a day or so to travel for another three or four days to visit John again.

Also, the "eight days" probably refers to the length of time from one day of the week to the same day of the following week. For example the time from one Saturday to the next Saturday is counted as 8 days inclusive. Inclusive counting was commonly used among the Jewish people. So the Essene likely visited John on the same day of the week each time.

Would the Essene have celebrated the Sabbath with John or with His community? Most likely with His community. He may have had religious obligations within his community. The Essenes lived a very strict and devout life, in seclusion even from most other Jews. But in any case, he would not have spent the Sabbath traveling to or from visiting the child John. Perhaps he traveled after the Sabbath on Sunday and Monday, and before the Sabbath on Thursday and Friday, visiting John about mid-week.

So, according to the words of Blessed Anne Catherine, Mount Horeb, where Moses saw the burning bush and received the Ten Commandments, must be located within a day or two's walk from southern Israel. But the generally-accepted view is that Mount Horeb, also called Mount Sinai, is that mountain called Jabal Musa and located in the southern part of the Sinai (over 200 miles from Hebron).[352] That location is too far from southern Israel to fit Blessed Anne Catherine's description.

On the other hand, Dr. Gerald E. Aardsma has proposed a theory, based on historical evidence, that Mount Yeroham in Southern Israel is Mount Horeb, where Moses and the Israelites received the Ten Commandments.[353] This location for Mount Horeb is within a day or two's walking distance of the area where the child John the Baptist hid in the wilderness. This location fits Blessed Anne Catherine's description well. I believe that Dr. Aardsma is correct in his conclusion that Mount Yeroham is the true Mount Horeb.

Blessed Anne Catherine tells us that Jesus never went to school. In our culture today, it would be unusual for a child not to attend school. However, during that period of history, attendance at school was probably neither mandatory nor widespread. There were some schools, run mainly by the Jewish priests (see below, on the Finding in the Temple), but most children did not receive much of a formal education.

Of course, Jesus Christ did not need a formal education. The Divine Nature of Jesus Christ taught the Human Nature of Jesus Christ. True and pure knowledge flowed within Jesus Christ, from His Divine Nature to His Human Nature. In this way, Jesus taught Himself. It is also true that the Holy Spirit taught Jesus in His Human Nature.

During the time that the Holy Family lived in Egypt, John the Baptist lived in the wilderness of Israel. He received visits and support from his mother and from a member of the Essenes, but he lived and grew up mostly alone.[354] It is as if his whole life, even from his earliest days, had only one purpose: "Prepare the way of the Lord." (Mt 3:3).

The Essenes were a community of Jews living a very strict and devout life in the wilderness, away from society in general, and even away from other Jews. According to Blessed Anne Catherine, they were very prayerful and holy.[355] "The real Essenes who lived in chastity were indescribably pure and devout."[356] She speaks about them at length in connection with the ancestors of Saint Anne and the Virgin Mary.

The Essenes were also mentioned by Josephus, the ancient Jewish Roman historian, who also held them in very high esteem.[357] Modern-day writers have often pondered the possible connections between John the Baptist and the Essenes. The community of Jews who lived at Qumran, and who wrote the Dead Sea Scrolls, are believed to have been Essenes.

According to Blessed Anne Catherine, the child John spent some length of time in early childhood living in secret with his parents at Jutta (near Hebron). But he returned again to the wilderness at about the age of four or five.[358] So, John did not live entirely in the wilderness during his childhood.

Sometime after Herod died, the Holy Family returned to live at Nazareth. But John the Baptist continued to live in the wilderness, even after the danger had passed. John remained in the wilderness until the time of his ministry began, a few months before the beginning of the Ministry of Jesus Christ, for this was the will of God.

The Martyrdom of Zechariah and Elizabeth

"...there had been much talk in the land about John ever since his early days. It was well known that wonders had attended his birth, and that he was often seen surrounded by light, for which reasons Herod was particularly suspicious of him."[359]

Even though Herod had killed hundreds of infants in his attempt to kill the Christ-child, he remained uneasy about the prophecy of a newborn king of the Jews. The Holy Family did not return from Egypt after the Massacre of the Holy Innocents, but they waited until Herod's death (cf. Mt 2:13-15). There was still danger from Herod, so Jesus remained in Egypt and John remained in hiding in the wilderness.

Herod did not know that the Christ-child had fled to Egypt, nor did he know to which family the newborn king of the Jews belonged. If he had known, he would not have killed so many children in his useless attempt to kill the Christ-child. Since John the Baptist showed great holiness, even at an early age, Herod was suspicious of him. Perhaps Herod thought that John might be the future king of the Jews, spoken of by both the wise men and Sacred Scripture (Mt 2:1-6).

Herod tried to find little John the Baptist, probably intending to kill him like the Holy Innocents, by questioning John's father, Zechariah. "He had caused Zecharias to be questioned several times as to the whereabouts of John...."[360] Zechariah did not reveal John's hiding place to Herod. And, according to Blessed Anne Catherine, Zechariah never visited John in the wilderness, "so that he might truthfully say, if asked by Herod where his son was, that he did not know."[361]

On one occasion, when Elizabeth was visiting John in the wilderness, Zechariah went to the Temple at Jerusalem: "...as he was on his way to the Temple, he was attacked by Herod's soldiers...These soldiers, who had been lying in wait for him, dragged him brutally to a prison on the slope of the Hill of Sion.... The old man was here subjected to ill-treatment and even torture, in order to force from him a confession of his son's whereabouts. When this had no effect, he was, by Herod's soldiers, stabbed to death."[362] Zechariah was martyred because of Herod's continued attempts to find and kill the Christ-child. In this way, Zechariah's martyrdom was like the martyrdom of the Holy Innocents, who also died because of Herod's desire to kill the Christ-child.

According to Blessed Anne Catherine, the martyrdom of Zechariah occurred when John was about six years old.[363] Since John was born in late June or early July of 15 B.C., he would have reached his sixth birthday about that time of year in 9 B.C. (Herod must still have been alive at this time, since he was responsible for Zechariah's murder.) Zechariah's death likely occurred sometime in 9 B.C., before Herod's death (in early 8 B.C.) and before the Holy Family returned from Egypt (late 7 B.C.).

"On reaching home Elisabeth heard the terrible news of the murder of Zecharias. She grieved and lamented so sorely that she could find no peace or rest at home, and so left Jutta for ever and hastened to join John in the wilderness. She died there not long after, before the return of the Holy Family from Egypt."[364]

Elizabeth was not killed by Herod's soldiers; however, it can be truly said that she died of a broken heart in consequence of the martyrdom of Zechariah. Her great sorrow at her husband's death eventually brought about her own death. Elizabeth shared in her husband Zechariah's martyrdom in much the same way that the Virgin Mary shared in the martyrdom of her Divine Son Jesus Christ. Both Mary and Elizabeth grieved greatly at the suffering and death of someone they loved, and each suffered more than they would have suffered had they been killed in place of the one they loved. Zechariah and Elizabeth were both martyrs.

Elizabeth's death occurred after Zechariah's death and before the Holy Family returned from Egypt. This places her martyrdom sometime from 9 B.C. to 7 B.C. Since Blessed Anne Catherine says that she died "not long after" her husband's death, she may have died in 9 B.C., the same year as her husband, or sometime in 8 B.C.

The Return from Egypt

"Then, when Herod had passed away, behold, an Angel of the Lord appeared in sleep to Joseph in Egypt, saying: 'Rise up, and take the boy and his mother, and go into the land of Israel. For those who were seeking the life of the boy have passed away.' And rising up, he took the boy and his mother, and he went into the land of Israel." (Mt 2:19-21).

Sacred Scripture tell us that the Holy Family returned from Egypt to Israel after the death of Herod. However, Sacred Scripture does not tell us the length of time between Herod's death and the Holy Family's return from Egypt. We should not assume that the length of time was very short, merely because the two events are mentioned one after the other.

Notice also that the angel uses the plural "those who sought the child's life are dead." In this way, Sacred Scripture indicates that there were others, in addition to Herod, who sought to kill the Christ Child. The use of the plural ("those") leaves open the possibility that Herod was not the last to die of those who sought to kill the Child Jesus.

Blessed Anne Catherine said that Jesus was in His fifth or seventh year when two angels appeared to Him to announce the death of Herod.[365] "He knelt down to pray on the way, and I saw two angels appearing to Him and announcing the death of Herod the Great. Jesus said nothing of this to His parents, why I do not know, whether from humility or because the angel had forbidden Him to, or because He knew that the time had not yet come for them to leave Egypt."[366]

The death of Herod could not have occurred in Jesus' fifth year. Blessed Anne Catherine tells us that Herod had Zechariah put to death when John the Baptist was six years old.[367] John was only about five months older than Jesus, and he turned six years old about late June or early July of 9 B.C. Jesus was then five years old, which was Jesus' sixth year, not His fifth year. A person completes their fifth year of life since birth on their fifth birthday, so that the year which follows is their sixth year (but they are called 'five years old'). Also, Herod died in the winter after an eclipse of the moon visible from Jerusalem. The next lunar eclipse after John turned six years old (i.e. after June/July of 9 B.C.) was on Nov. 28 of 9 B.C., which was after Jesus turned six years old and had begun His seventh year of life since His Birth. Therefore, Herod died in Jesus' seventh year, not His fifth.

"I saw the Holy Family's departure from Egypt. Herod was long since dead, but danger still threatened and they could not return."[368]

Blessed Anne Catherine Emmerich tells us that the Holy Family did not return from Egypt immediately upon the death of Herod. Herod died in early 8 B.C., but the Holy Family did not return to Israel that year.

"The return from Egypt happened in September. Jesus was nearly eight years old."[369]

Jesus was born Nov. 25 of 15 B.C., and so He completed eight years of life from birth in November of 7 B.C. In September of 7 B.C., Jesus was nearly eight years old. Therefore, the Holy Family returned from Egypt in September of 7 B.C. The return from Egypt happened well over a year after the death of Herod. Jesus was then seven years old, and in His eighth year of life since birth.

"At the age of eight years, Jesus went for the first time with His parents to Jerusalem for the Pasch, and every succeeding year He did the same."[370]

Jesus did not have the opportunity to attend the Passover in Jerusalem while the Holy Family was in exile in Egypt. The first time that He had the opportunity to attend the Passover in Jerusalem was the Passover following their return from Egypt. If the Holy Family returned from Egypt in 7 B.C., then Jesus could attend the Passover in Jerusalem for the first time in 6 B.C., when He was eight years old counting from birth, (but nine years old counting from the Incarnation).

The length of time that the Holy Family spent in Egypt was about 6½ years, from March of 13 B.C. to September of 7 B.C. This is about the same length of time as the future time of great suffering for the Church revealed in the book of Daniel (cf. Dan 9:24, 27; 8:14) and the book of Revelation. The suffering of the Holy Family in Egypt foreshadows the suffering of the Church during that future time of great suffering, the Passion of the Church, described in Sacred Scripture.[371]

Lost and Found in the Temple

"And his parents went every year to Jerusalem, at the time of the solemnity of Passover. And when he had become twelve years old, they ascended to Jerusalem, according to the custom of the feast day. And having completed the days, when they returned, the boy Jesus remained in Jerusalem. And his parents did not realize this." (Lk 2:41-43).

Sacred Scripture states plainly that Jesus was 12 years old at the time of this particular Passover. Later in the Gospel of Luke, Sacred Scripture gives the age of Jesus at the beginning of His ministry as "about thirty years old." (Lk 3:23). The word 'about' is not used in the earlier passage referring to the Child Jesus in Jerusalem, but is used in the later passage concerning the beginning of Jesus' ministry. And so, when Sacred Scripture tells us that Jesus was 12 years old, the meaning cannot be that Jesus was about 12, for the word 'about' is deliberately not used in this instance. Therefore, Jesus was 12 years old when He was lost and found in the Temple of Jerusalem.

Jesus was conceived on February 25, and born on November 25, of 15 B.C. He completed 12 years of life, counting from conception, in February of 3 B.C., but He completed 12 years of life from birth in November of 3 B.C. At the Passover of 3 B.C., Jesus was 12 years old from conception and 11 years old from birth. At the Passover of 2 B.C., Jesus was 13 years old from conception and 12 years old from birth. Does Sacred Scripture here count the age of Jesus from His Holy Conception or from His Holy Birth?

First, the true age of Jesus in His humanity should be counted from conception, since that was the beginning of His life as a human person. God became a man at the time of the Incarnation of Jesus Christ. Therefore, Sacred Scripture is referring to the Passover of 3 B.C., when Jesus was 12 years old from conception.

Second, further support for this conclusion is found in the meaning of this event. Jesus was lost to His parents, who were in great distress at this loss, and he was found on the third day in the Temple of Jerusalem. This event was a great foreshadowing of the Crucifixion, death, and Resurrection of Jesus, which occurred many years later. At His Crucifixion and death, Jesus was lost to His disciples (cf. Jn 13:36), and they were in great distress at this loss. On the third day, Jesus was found in the Temple of His Body. The Finding of Jesus in the Temple was a foreshadowing of the Resurrection of Jesus from the dead.

In 3 B.C., the month of Nisan began on March 17, so that the Passover began on the evening of Nisan 14, which was March 30.[372] Passover ends on the evening of Nisan 21 (Ex 12:18), on the seventh day (the eighth day, if you include the Preparation day of the Passover). In 3 B.C., Nisan 21 fell on April 6, a Saturday.[373] If the Holy Family left Jerusalem the day after Passover ended, then April 7 was the first day that Jesus was lost to His parents.

"But, supposing that he was in the company, they went a day's journey, seeking him among their relatives and acquaintances. And not finding him, they returned to Jerusalem, seeking him." (Luke 2:44-45).

Since they had gone a day's journey away from Jerusalem before they turned around, the Virgin Mary and Saint Joseph had to travel another day's journey back towards Jerusalem. According to Blessed Anne Catherine, they sought Jesus everywhere along the way back to Jerusalem, and everywhere in the city itself.[374] "And it happened that, after three days, they found him in the temple, sitting in the midst of the doctors, listening to them and questioning them." (Lk 2:46). The third day would then be April 9 of 3 B.C.

Jesus died on April 7, and rose from the dead on April 9, in the year A.D. 19 (see chapter 2). Jesus was lost and then found in the Temple from April 7 to April 9 of 3 B.C. The meaning of this event and its dates correspond to the meaning and dates of the Crucifixion and Resurrection of Jesus Christ. The Finding of Jesus Christ in the Temple foretold, not only of the meaning of the Resurrection, but also of its date.

In 2 B.C., the Passover began on Friday, April 18 and Nisan 14.[375] Passover ended on the evening of Friday, April 25. The last day of Passover is a day of solemn rest (Lev 23:8). The last day of Passover that year was also a Friday; the Jewish Sabbath beings on Friday at sunset and ends on Saturday at sunset. Since devout Jews would not travel more than a short distance on the Sabbath, nor on any day of solemn rest, the Holy Family could not have traveled away from Jerusalem on Friday or Saturday that year. If the Finding in the Temple had occurred in 2 B.C., the three days would have begun on April 27 and ended on April 29. These dates do not correspond to any proposed dates for the death and Resurrection of Jesus Christ in any year.

Third, Blessed Anne Catherine refers to this as Jesus' 12th year: "...wherein they had recorded all that had happened in the Temple to Jesus, the Son of Mary, in His twelfth year." [376] A person's 12th year from birth begins on their 11th birthday and is completed on their 12th birthday. Each birthday is numbered according to the years which have been completed. In 3 B.C., Jesus had completed just over 11 years from birth, and so was in His 12th year from birth.

Fourth, at the time of the first Passover of Jesus' Ministry, in spring of A.D. 16, Blessed Anne Catherine tells us that Jesus spoke about the time when He taught in the temple as a child. "He said: 'It is now about eighteen years ago since a little *bachir*' (by which Jesus must have meant a young scholar) 'argued most wonderfully with the Doctors of the Law who, in consequence, were filled with wrath against the Child.' And then He related to them the teachings of the little *bachir*."[377] Since these words were said at the first Passover of Jesus' ministry in A.D. 16, counting back 18 years brings us to the Passover of 3 B.C. Here again is support for the conclusion that the Child Jesus was lost to Joseph and Mary on April 7 of 3 B.C., and then found in the Temple on the third day, April 9 of 3 B.C.

Fifth, the true age of Jesus, in His humanity, must be counted from His Incarnation, when the Word took flesh and became a man. "And the Word became flesh, and he lived among us, and we saw his glory, glory like that of an only-begotten son from the Father, full of grace and truth." (Jn 1:14).

But the Jewish people during the time of Christ did not count a person's age from conception. How is it, then, that they considered Jesus to be 12 years old at the time of that Passover in 3 B.C.?

Blessed Anne Catherine describes a feast which took place in Saint Ann's house at Nazareth for Jesus after the Passover. She mentions that the reason for the feast may have been that is was "customary upon the completion of a son's twelfth year."[378] The time of the Passover was considered to be the completion of Christ's 12th year, even though He was conceived in February (AdarII) and born in November (Kislev). How could the Jews have considered Jesus to be 12 years old at this time, when He was past 12 years old from conception and nowhere near 12 years old from birth?

This Passover (of 3 B.C.) was the 12th Passover of Jesus' life since birth (14 B.C. was the first). I believe it was the custom among the Jews of that time to keep track of a person's age by the number of Passovers since birth. (The counting of the years since the completion of the rebuilding of the Temple of Jerusalem was also according to the number of Passovers. See chapter 8 for details).

Keeping track of the number of Passovers since a child's birth would have been easy and well in keeping with the lives of the Jewish people. Jewish religious law required all adult Jewish males to attend the Passover (Deut 16:16). Many Jews traveled a significant distance for several days or longer to arrive in Jerusalem for the Passover. Such an event would be easy to mark in one's memory, as would also the number of Passovers since a child's birth. One would not need a calendar to keep track of this important yearly event.

Furthermore, this method of counting the years of a child's birth parallels the Jewish method of counting the years of a king's reign. Passover occurs in the Jewish month of Nisan, in the spring. It was certainly the custom of the Jews at that time to keep track of the years of a king's reign from the month of Nisan. So then, even if a king ascended to the throne in the fall, each year of the king's reign was counted from the beginning of the month of Nisan. Any portion of a year from the beginning of the king's reign to the first of Nisan was counted as the king's first year, so that a few months, or even a few days, were counted as if a whole year.[379] If the Jewish people counted the years of a person's life as with the years of a king's reign, then each year the start of the month of Nisan would be counted as the completion of one year of age and the beginning of the next year of age.

The month of Passover occurs in the middle of the month of Nisan. Counting the years from the celebration of Passover, in the middle of Nisan, rather than from the start of Nisan, would be more convenient and more meaningful. The importance of the Passover in Jewish life and worship carried over into the counting of the years of a person's life; a person's age was counted by the number of Passovers since their birth. So, if the Jewish people at that time in history counted the years of a person's life by the number of Passovers, the first Passover of a person's life since birth would be counted as the completion of the first year, even though that year was a partial year.[380] We see this same principle (of the part counted as the whole) applied to the count of the 3 days from the death to the Resurrection of Jesus Christ. That amount of time is not 3 full days (24 hours x 3), but rather one full day, Saturday, and two partial days, Friday and Sunday.

An example of this method of counting a person's age is found in Jack Finegan's *Handbook of Biblical Chronology, Revised Edition.* He quotes from commentary by Rabbi Avadyah on the Mishna: "Like a man whose son is born on passover. He has fulfilled his first year of life on passover of the next year."[381] Finegan interprets this quote to mean that each year of a person's life is counted as the completion of 12 full months of the Jewish calendar (or 13 in a leap year) since the day of their birth. However, I suggest that the choice of the Passover to illustrate the counting of a person's age was not arbitrary. Thus, a man whose son is born on any day of the year would count his son's first year as being completed on the very next Passover. In this way, the number of Passovers since birth would be the count of a person's age.

Now we see why Sacred Scripture omits the word "about" when telling us Christ's age at this particular Passover, but uses the word "about" in telling us Christ's age when His Ministry began (Lk 2:42; 3:23). The start of Christ's Ministry was in the fall, but the Passover is in the spring. Christ's age is called "about thirty years," not exactly thirty years, because His Ministry did not begin at the time of the Passover in the spring. But the passage from the Gospel of Luke telling us that Christ was 12 years old (without using the word "about") refers to his trip to Jerusalem for the Passover; the exact time of year when the Jews counted the completion of one year of age and the start of the next. Christ's age at the 12th Passover since His Birth was counted by the Jews as the completion of His 12th year exactly (with the first partial year, from Birth to Passover, counted as year one).

The Twelfth Year

I believe that Jesus chose this particular year to stay behind and teach in the Temple of Jerusalem for a reason. Today among the Jews, a boy's 13th year is the time of his bar mitzvah, when he takes greater responsibility for his faith. But I believe that in ancient times a Jewish boy's 12th year was the time when he would begin to take a greater role in his faith. The number 12 has great significance in the history of the Jewish people, but the number 13, less so. In this way, Jesus followed the principles of the Jewish faith, a faith designed from its very core to prepare the way for Himself, the Messiah. "From His twelfth year, Jesus was always like a teacher among His companions."[382]

Chapter 7
The Divine Ministry of Jesus Christ

Before the Ministry of Christ Began

"And he went down with them and came to Nazareth, and was obedient to them; and his mother kept all these things in her heart. And Jesus increased in wisdom and in stature, and in favor with God and man." (Lk 2:51-52).

After Jesus was found in the Temple, when He was 12 years old, He returned to Nazareth with the Virgin Mary and Saint Joseph, and was obedient to them. In His human nature, Jesus increased in wisdom and stature (he grew up) and in the grace of God. The Divine Nature of Jesus Christ, Second Person of the Most Holy Trinity, is perfect and unchangeable. But in His humanity, Christ could grow and change. The humanity of Christ was always perfect, yet Christ could still increase in grace in His humanity. More is expected of an adult than of a child; a perfect child is less than a perfect adult. Jesus also increased in favor among other people, though not with everyone.

Blessed Anne Catherine gives us some additional information about the life of Jesus after He returned to Nazareth from the Passover of His 12th year. "He said also to one of the youths, a relative of His own named Nathanael: 'I shall be present at thy marriage.' "[383] Jesus knew the future, even from His Childhood, and He had foreknowledge of His future Ministry. He also spoke at that time of a marriage feast where water would be turned into wine (the marriage of Nathanael at Cana, Jn 2:1-11) and a marriage feast where wine would be changed into Blood, and bread into Flesh (the first Eucharist, Lk 22:19-20, cf. Lk 5:34-35).[384] Jesus knew the course that His Ministry would take, even from His Childhood.

Jesus Christ as a Teenager

The Ministry of Jesus Christ was a public teaching Ministry, yet He taught people privately long before His public Ministry began. "From His twelfth year, Jesus was always like a teacher among His companions. He often sat among them instructing them or walked about the country with them."[385] Jesus taught the youths who were near His own age beginning about the time that He returned from the Passover of His 12th year. As a teenager, Jesus could not have been a follower or someone who joined in with whatever the other teens were doing. And He knew so much about God and the path to Heaven that He could not have refrained from sharing His knowledge and teaching by word and example. Even so, this was not the beginning of His public teaching Ministry, for He taught a limited group of people privately; He did not yet go out into the streets to offer His teaching to everyone.

Did Jesus heal anyone before His public Ministry began? He may well have done so. Any devout Jew or Christian, upon hearing that a neighbor was ill or injured, would surely pray to God on behalf of that person. So also, Jesus must have obtained (in His Humanity) and provided (from His Divinity) the healing of many, even before His public Ministry began. Yet, He must also have done this healing, for the most part, in secret and at a distance. Otherwise, He would become the center of attention and His Ministry would have begun before the appointed time.

Jesus Christ in His Twenties

Blessed Anne Catherine describes the persecution that Jesus suffered from various Jewish religious leaders, even before His public Ministry began.

"He [Joseph] had already suffered much from the persecution Jesus had had to support from the malice of the Jews from His twentieth to His thirtieth year; for they could not bear the sight of Him. Their jealousy often made them exclaim that the carpenter's Son thought He knew everything better than others, that He was frequently at variance with the teachings of the Pharisees, and that He always had around Him a crowd of young followers."[386]

These accusations made by the jealous religious leaders were actually true. Jesus did think that He knew everything better than others (and He was right); Jesus did frequently disagree with the teachings of the Pharisees (e.g. Mt 23; Lk 6:1-5). And, though His public ministry had not yet begun, He had a group of followers of about His own age or younger, whom He taught to a limited extent. The religious leaders heard about His teaching and how He was admired by many, and they were jealous and angry.

As it was when Jesus was a teenager, so also when He was in His twenties. He continued to teach a group of people about His own age, but did not yet teach publicly. Many of the Jewish leaders persecuted Jesus. "Unspeakable was the love with which Jesus in His youth bore the jealous persecution of the Jews."[387]

Jesus had followers even in His early adult years, but He did not appoint Apostles or other leaders among them. Jesus even knew some of the persons whom He later chose to be among the Twelve Apostles, but they occupied no special position at this point in time. Indeed, Blessed Anne Catherine says that some of the future Apostles, though they knew of Jesus at that time, did not take much of an interest in Him, until His public Ministry began.[388]

The Death of Saint Joseph

"As the time drew near for Jesus to begin His mission of teaching, I saw him ever more solitary and meditative; and toward the same time, the thirtieth year of Jesus, Joseph began to decline."[389]

"Joseph had of necessity to die before the Lord, for he could not have endured His Crucifixion; he was too gentle, too loving."[390]

Blessed Anne Catherine tells us that Joseph died shortly before the public Ministry of Jesus began. The death of Saint Joseph occurred during Jesus' 30th year, counting from conception.[391] Blessed Anne Catherine gave the years as God told them to her. These years must be counted from conception, because life begins at conception. So the first year of Jesus Christ's human life began with His Holy Conception, the Incarnation, on Feb. 25 of 15 B.C. And the 30th year of Jesus' human life began in Feb. of A.D. 15 and was completed in Feb. of A.D. 16. In 15 B.C., then, Jesus completed 29 years since the Incarnation and began His 30th year of human life. Saint Joseph died during the year

A.D. 15, early in Jesus' 30th year. He could not have died late in Jesus' 30th year, because he died before the Ministry of Jesus Christ began in fall of A.D. 15.

Shortly before describing the Baptism of Jesus, Blessed Anne Catherine tells us that some people commented about Jesus that " 'Three months ago, His father, the carpenter, was still alive.' "[392] This comment was made some time before the Baptism of Jesus in early October (see below). So, if the comment was made in August or September, then Joseph was still alive in about May or June of that same year (A.D. 15). Again, the death of Saint Joseph is placed before the Ministry of Christ began, at about the time when John's ministry began.

According to Blessed Anne Catherine: "Joseph was about thirty years older than Mary."[393] Since Jesus was about 15 years older than the Virgin Mary (see chapters 4, 5, 8, 9), Joseph must have been approximately 45 years older than Jesus. Joseph was about 45 years old when Jesus was born, and Joseph died at about the age of 75 years.[394]

The Beginning of the Ministry of John the Baptist

After describing the burial of Saint Joseph, Blessed Anne Catherine says that Jesus and the Virgin Mary moved to a place between Capernaum and Bethsaida. Soon after her description of Joseph's death, she mentions that John the Baptist was traveling about the countryside and preaching.[395] Based on the order of events in her description, Saint Joseph died shortly before, or at about the time of, the beginning of the ministry of John the Baptist. Joseph died in Jesus' 30th year (after the completion of 29 years since the Incarnation, but before the completion of 30 years). The ministry of John the Baptist began that same year, A.D. 15.

John was called "the Baptist" because one of the main duties of his ministry was to administer the baptism of repentance that prepared for the Divine Ministry of Jesus Christ.[396] Now the baptism of John occurred outdoors, in the waters of the river Jordan (cf. Mk 1:9). According to Blessed Anne Catherine, the person to be baptized stood in the water up to about their waist, then John baptized them by pouring water over their head.[397] Immersion in water at the baptism of John is also implied by Sacred Scripture: "And immediately, upon ascending from the water...." (Mk 1:10). This description means that Jesus was in some way immersed in the water. Blessed Anne Catherine describes the Baptism of Jesus as Jesus standing in water up to His breast and John pouring water in three streams from one shell over the head of Jesus.[398]

In the Holy Land in winter, the temperatures during the daytime can be fairly cold, even at times close to freezing. John's ministry centered around a baptism of repentance, a baptism which took place outside in the waters of a river, with the person to be baptized standing in the water. Therefore, John most likely began his ministry in the spring, when it would be warm enough outside to baptize, and when he would have a significant length of time to continue baptizing in the warm weather.[399]

From John's Ministry to Christ's Ministry

Blessed Anne Catherine indicates that the ministry of Jesus Christ began soon after the ministry of John the Baptist. In her book, *The Life of Jesus Christ and Biblical Revelations*, she does not explicitly state the amount of time between John leaving the desert and the baptism of Jesus by John. However, she gives the impression that it was a relatively short time. For example, she mentions a period of three months, prior to the baptism of Jesus, when John traveled about calling for repentance and saying that the Lord was near. And there are only a couple of paragraphs about John's ministry between her description of John leaving the desert and her statement about that three-month period of time.[400] So the time between the start of John's ministry and the start of Christ's Ministry was somewhat longer than three months, and perhaps as long as 5 or 6 months. (See chapter 2 for more on this point.)

The total length of John's ministry was certainly longer than a few months, for his ministry and the Ministry of Jesus overlapped for a period of time. Both Sacred Scripture and the writings of Blessed Anne Catherine make it clear that the ministry of John the Baptist continued even as Jesus Christ's Ministry began. Interestingly, Blessed Anne Catherine states that John stopped baptizing soon after Jesus was baptized. About that time, Jesus began to give instruction about baptism to His disciples. And, beginning early in His Ministry, Jesus supervised His disciples as they baptized many people (Jn 3:22, 4:1-3).[401]

The Beginning of the Ministry of Jesus Christ

Sacred Scripture does not plainly state the length of Jesus' Ministry. However, there are several clear indications in Sacred Scripture that Jesus' Ministry lasted about 3½ years. Some of Jesus' own parables about His Ministry give a length of time of about 3½ years. And Blessed Anne Catherine also tells us that the length of Christ's Ministry was 3½ years. (See chapter 2 for details on these points.)

Since Jesus died at the Passover of A.D. 19, in the spring, and His Ministry lasted 3½ years, His Ministry must have begun in the fall of A.D. 15. The Ministry of Jesus Christ began only a few months after the beginning of John the Baptist's ministry. So again we see that John's ministry began in the spring of that same calendar year, A.D. 15. Christ's ministry lasted about 3½ years, and John's ministry began several months earlier, so Jesus was crucified approximately 4 years after the start of John's ministry. John the Baptist's ministry began in the spring of the 15th year of Tiberius Caesar's reign (Lk 3:1) and Jesus died in the spring of the 19th year of Tiberius Caesar's reign.

All four Gospels mark the beginning of the Ministry of Christ about the time of Christ's Baptism by John in the Jordan (Mt 3:13-17; Mk 1:9-15; Lk 3:23; Jn 1:19-34). So the date of Christ's Baptism can be considered the starting date for His Ministry. Even so, Jesus was not idle before His Baptism by John. He must have done some teaching, at least to some of His followers, as is described by Blessed Anne Catherine.[402] She seems to count Christ's Ministry as beginning a little while before His Baptism, when Jesus began to travel about and teach. However, she also states that Jesus taught about the coming of the Messiah, indicating that Jesus' teaching at this time was preparatory to His Ministry.[403] Therefore, as Sacred Scripture clearly indicates, the Ministry of Jesus Christ began with His Baptism.

The Age of Jesus at the Beginning of His Ministry

"And Jesus himself was beginning to be about thirty years old…." (Lk 3:23).

Sacred Scripture does not say that Jesus was exactly 30 years old when He began His Ministry, but only that He was "about thirty years old." Why does Sacred Scripture use the word "about" in this passage?

Earlier in the Gospel of Luke, Sacred Scripture tells us the age of Jesus at another point in His life, when He stayed behind in Jerusalem after the feast of Passover. "And when he had become twelve years old, they ascended to Jerusalem, according to the custom of the feast day." (Lk 2:42). In this passage, the Gospel of Luke tells us the age of Jesus as a plain statement: "he had become twelve years old," which is not qualified by the word, "about." Thus, the meaning of this statement about age is different from the meaning of the statement about the age of Jesus at the beginning of His Ministry.

As explained in chapter 6, Jesus was 12 years old counting from His Holy Conception, at the time described by Luke 2:41-50. Life begins at conception, so the length of Christ's human life should be counted beginning with the Incarnation. Also, the custom among the Jews at that time was to count the years of a person's life according to how many Passovers occurred since that person's birth. Sacred Scripture calls Jesus 12 years old for both these reasons. Therefore, in both these passages from Luke's Gospel, Sacred Scripture is counting Christ's age from the Incarnation, or by the number of Passovers since His Birth.

In the passage about the Child Jesus being found in the Temple, the phrase telling us that Jesus "had become twelve years old" (Lk 2:42) means that Jesus had completed just over 12 years of His human life since the Incarnation. However, in the passage on the beginning of the ministry of Jesus, the phrase telling us that Jesus "was about thirty years old" (Lk 3:23) cannot mean that Jesus had completed just over thirty years since the Incarnation. The addition of the word "about" indicates a different meaning than in the previous passage on the visit of the Child Jesus to Jerusalem. So, the age referred to is not the year following the completion of Christ's 30th year since the Incarnation. During that year, A.D. 16, Christ Jesus would be called 30 years old, not "about thirty."

Again, looking at the number of Passovers since birth, Jesus completed 29 Passovers since birth by the start of His Ministry in autumn of A.D. 15. If His Ministry began at the Passover of A.D. 16, His age by this method of counting would have been 30 years of age exactly, not about 30 years. In the autumn of A.D. 15, when Christ's Ministry began, He had completed 29 Passovers since birth and was in His 30th year since the Incarnation. Also, the date of Christ's Baptism (Oct. 4; see below) is closer to the 30th year than the 29th year since the Incarnation, and about midway between His 29th and 30th Passover.

Sacred Scripture was written by God, and so must be both true and accurate. Therefore, we cannot conclude that the word "about" is used because no one knew the exact age of Jesus at that time. God told us the age of Jesus at the start of His Ministry truly and accurately. The word "about" does not indicate a lack of knowledge as to the age of Jesus at the beginning of His Ministry. Instead, the different phrasing used by adding the word "about" indicates that Jesus was near the age of 30 years. But if Jesus had just completed 30 years of age, Sacred Scripture would have used the same phrasing as in the earlier passage when Jesus was 12 years old. Jesus was near the age of 30 years, but He had not yet reached the completion of His 30th year. Therefore, Jesus was just under 30 years of age, counting from the Incarnation, when His Ministry began.

Some scholars debate the accuracy of Sacred Scripture. Some even suggest that parts of Sacred Scripture may be in error. But I believe that Sacred Scripture is both true and accurate. Therefore, I consider that, if Jesus had been closer to 31 years of age, or closer to 29 years of age, the Gospel of Luke would have said "29 years" or "about 31," rather than the phrase "about thirty years old" Jesus was under 30 years of age counting from the Incarnation when His Ministry began, and he was closer to 30 than to 29 years of age. Since Jesus was conceived Feb. 25, His Ministry must have begun sometime after August 25 (29 years plus six months after the Incarnation on Feb. 25), when He would then be closer to 30 than to 29 years of age.

Jesus Christ was about 33 years old at the time of the Crucifixion (see chapter 2), and His Ministry lasted about 3½ years. Therefore, Jesus was about 29½ at the start of His ministry. Counting back 3½ years from April 7 of A.D. 19, when Christ was crucified, brings us to early October of A.D. 15. Blessed Anne Catherine places the Baptism of Jesus by John in early October (see below).[404] Thus, the Ministry of Jesus Christ began when He was closer to 30 years old than to 29, in the 30th year since the Incarnation, between the 29th and 30th Passovers (A.D. 15, A.D. 16) since His Birth, and 3½ years before the Crucifixion.

The Baptism of Jesus by John

"Now it happened that, when all the people were being baptized, Jesus was baptized; and as he was praying, heaven was opened. And the Holy Spirit, in a corporal appearance like a dove, descended upon him. And a voice came from heaven: 'You are my beloved Son. In you, I am well pleased.' " (Lk 3:21-22).

Immediately after telling us about the Baptism of Jesus, the Gospel of Luke gives us the age of Jesus when He began His Ministry (Lk 3:23). So, the Gospel of Luke counts the Ministry of Jesus as having begun at the time of His Baptism. Each of the other Gospels also marks the Baptism of Jesus by John as the beginning of Jesus' Ministry (Mt 3:13-17; Mk 1:9-15; Jn 1:19-34).

Jesus was baptized by John the Baptist in the river Jordan (Mt 3:6; Mk 1:9; Lk 4:1; Jn 1:28). The place of Baptism must have been between the Dead Sea and the Sea of Galilee, which are connected to one another by the Jordan River. Also, Sacred Scripture tells us that those who came to be baptized were from Judea and Jerusalem (Mt 3:5; Mk 1:5). So, one place where John baptized was in the region of Judea.[405]

The Gospel of John tells us: "Now John was also baptizing, at Aenon near Salim, because there was much water in that place. And they were arriving and being baptized." (Jn 3:23). Aenon is located in Samaria, not in Judea, and is closer to the Sea of Galilee than to the Dead Sea. Thus, John baptized in more than one location.

Blessed Anne Catherine provides some additional details about the places where John baptized people.[406] She names three places along the Jordan River, between the Dead Sea and the Sea of Galilee. First John baptized at Ainon (Aenon), near Salem (Salim). Then John baptized "at On opposite Beth-Araba on the west side of the Jordan, and not far from Jericho."[407] That location is close to the north end of the Dead Sea.[408] The third place where John baptized is not given a name by Blessed Anne Catherine, but she tells us it was located "a couple of hours further north" than the second place.[409] Lastly, John returned to the first place, Aenon, to baptize for the last time before being arrested and put in prison. The Gospel of John mentions John's impending imprisonment immediately after telling us that John baptized at Aenon.

At which of these locations was Jesus baptized? The Gospel of John gives us some indication that the Baptism of Jesus by John occurred near the Dead Sea, not at Aenon, which is nearer the Sea of Galilee. The Gospel of John describes a conversation between John the Baptist and some priests and Levites sent by the Pharisees. "These things happened in Bethania, across the Jordan, where John was baptizing." (Jn 1:28). Bethany is a short distance, about a Sabbath's walk, from Jerusalem (Lk 24:50; Acts 1:12). Bethany is somewhat less than 20 miles from the Jordan river, but is over 50 miles from Aenon. The next day after the conversation at Bethany, John saw Jesus at a distance and spoke about the Holy Spirit descending on Jesus at His (recent) Baptism (Jn 1:29-34). It is not until much later in the Gospel of John (Jn 3:23) that Aenon is mentioned as a place where John baptized. Therefore, Jesus was baptized in the Jordan, in the region of Judea, not at Aenon, but at a place closer to the Dead Sea than to the Sea of Galilee.

Jesus was baptized by John in the fall of A.D. 15, after John had spent several months preparing the way for Christ's Ministry. Blessed Anne Catherine Emmerich provides some more specific information about when the Baptism of Christ occurred. When speaking a settlement of lepers that Jesus had visited, she tells us: "Jesus healed here on September 30th before His Baptism."[410] So, the Baptism of Jesus occurred on or after Sept. 30 of A.D. 15. In another place, she states: "It is the same house in which thirty years later Jesus spent the night of October 11th before the morning on which he passed near the Baptist for the first time after His Baptism."[411] So, the Baptism of Jesus occurred on or before Oct. 11 of A.D. 15.

In describing the day on which Jesus was baptized by John, Blessed Anne Catherine tells us that Jesus traveled that morning along with Lazarus, but that He walked more quickly than Lazarus and so He arrived 2 hours before him.[412] They must have both walked a long distance for Jesus to arrive so long ahead of Lazarus. Later in the day, after His Baptism, Jesus also traveled with some of His followers to a place a couple of hours away.[413] Since Jesus and Lazarus and some other disciples traveled much that day, it could not have been a Jewish Sabbath (on which Jews were not permitted to travel more than a short distance).

Now Blessed Anne Catherine describes Jesus celebrating the Feast of Tabernacles that year sometime after His Baptism.[414] And she also describes two Sabbaths between the Baptism of Jesus and the beginning of the Feast of Tabernacles.[415] That year the Jewish month of Tishri began on Thursday, Oct. 3.[416] This places the solemn fast day of Yom Kippur (the Day of Atonement) on Saturday, Oct. 12. The Feast of Tabernacles then began on Thursday, Oct. 17, and ended on Thursday, Oct. 24. The two Sabbaths that Blessed Anne Catherine describes before the Feast of Tabernacles must then have been Saturday, Oct. 5, and Saturday, Oct. 12. Since there were two Sabbaths between the Baptism of Jesus and the Feast of Tabernacles, Jesus must have been baptized before Oct. 5, but still on or after Sept. 30.

Blessed Anne Catherine also tells us that Jesus kept the Sabbath at the small town He had traveled to after His Baptism. It seems from her description that the Sabbath day was the day after Jesus arrived.[417] If so, then Jesus was baptized on a Friday. The only Friday between Sept. 30 and Oct. 5 of A.D. 15 was Friday, Oct. 4, which was also Tishri 2. Based on the chronological information in the writings of Blessed Anne Catherine, then, Jesus was baptized by John on Friday, Oct. 4 of A.D. 15.

It is unlikely that Jesus could have been baptized on Thursday, Oct. 3 and Tishri 1, because the start of any month is a Jewish holy day, Rosh Hodesh (New Moon day), and the start of Tishri 1 is Rosh Hashanah (Jewish New Year's day). The Jews during Jesus' time kept the first day of each month as a holy day of rest.[418] Jesus and his disciples would not have traveled far on that day, but they did travel far on the day of Jesus' Baptism (which must have been the following day, Tishri 2).[419]

The Baptism of Jesus marked the beginning of His Ministry. Blessed Anne Catherine states that it was about 10:00 a.m. when Jesus was baptized.[420] The length of Christ's Ministry, from His Baptism on October 4 of A.D. 15 to His Crucifixion on April 7 of A.D. 19, was 3½ years plus about 3 days.

The First Sacrament of Baptism

"And immediately, upon ascending from the water, he saw the heavens opened and the Spirit, like a dove, descending, and remaining with him. And there was a voice from heaven: 'You are my beloved Son; in you I am well pleased.' " (Mk 1:10-11).

" 'For John, indeed, baptized with water, but you shall be baptized with the Holy Spirit, not many days from now.' " (Acts 1:5).

"And he said to them, 'After believing, have you received the Holy Spirit?' But they said to him, 'We have not even heard that there is a Holy Spirit.' Yet truly, he said, 'Then with what have you been baptized?' And they said, 'With the baptism of John.' " (Acts 19:2-3).

"Jesus responded: 'Amen, amen, I say to you, unless one has been reborn by water and the Holy Spirit, he is not able to enter into the kingdom of God.' " (Jn 3:5).

John's baptism was a baptism of repentance (Mk 1:4). Anyone baptized by John had to later be baptized in the Holy Spirit (Acts 19:1-7). However, there is an exception to this rule. The Baptism of Jesus by John in the river Jordan was not a baptism of repentance, but rather the first true Sacrament of Baptism given to anyone. The Sacrament of Baptism requires water and the Spirit of God (Jn 3:5). When John baptized Jesus with water, the Holy Spirit descended upon Jesus. In this way, the Human Nature of Jesus Christ received the Sacrament of Baptism from the Holy Trinity.

"After these things, Jesus and his disciples went into the land of Judea. And he was living there with them and baptizing." (Jn 3:22).

"And so, when Jesus realized that the Pharisees had heard that Jesus made more disciples and baptized more than John, (though Jesus himself was not baptizing, but only his disciples) he left behind Judea, and he traveled again to Galilee." (Jn 4:1-3).

During the Ministry of Jesus Christ, His disciples baptized people. Was this baptism the true Sacrament of Baptism, just as it is today, or was it as yet only the baptism of repentance, a baptism like that of John's? According to Sacred Scripture, the baptism given by the disciples of Jesus was carried out under His direction and authority. The Gospel of John states: "Jesus made more disciples and baptized more than John...." This phrasing indicates that Jesus was in truth the One who was baptizing, even though the baptizing was actually carried out by Jesus' disciples (Jn 4:1-3). Here Sacred Scripture clearly counts the baptism given by the disciples of Christ just as if it had come from Christ. Sacred Scripture considers that baptism by Christ's disciples comes directly from Christ, so much so that the clear statement is made in the Gospel that "he was living there with them and baptizing." (Jn 3:22). The baptism given by the disciples of Christ during His Ministry did truly proceed from Christ, and so must have been the true Sacrament of Baptism. For when any disciple of Christ baptizes, it is Christ who baptizes. But if that baptism by the disciples were not the true Sacrament, then Sacred Scripture would not have told us it came from Christ. How could Jesus the Messiah give anyone a baptism which was lacking in the power and grace of the true Sacrament of Baptism, when all true Sacraments, and their grace and power, proceed from Jesus Christ? Therefore, the true Sacrament of Baptism was given, first to the humanity of Jesus Christ by the Holy Trinity at the baptism of John, and thereafter, by the disciples of Christ to His followers during His Ministry, even before the Crucifixion.

Furthermore, Blessed Anne Catherine describes the baptism given by Jesus' disciples in the following way.

"The spot upon which Andrew, Saturnin, and the other disciples baptized in turn upon Jesus' command, was the little island upon which He Himself had been baptized....While the disciples baptized, Jesus taught and prepared the aspirants for Baptism."[421]

"Near the place of Baptism was a kind of altar upon which lay the baptismal garments. Two of the disciples imposed hands upon the shoulders of the neophytes while Andrew or Saturnin, sometimes another, dipped the hollow hand three times into the basin and poured the water over their head baptizing them in the name of the Father and of the Son and of the Holy Ghost."[422]

According to Blessed Anne Catherine, Jesus Himself taught and prepared many of the candidates for baptism. His disciples baptized under his direction and authority. They baptized in the same place where Jesus Himself had received the first true Sacrament of Baptism. And they used a formula very similar to the one used today in the Sacrament of Baptism, including pouring water three times and using the words "in the name of the Father and of the Son and of the Holy Spirit."[423] Blessed Anne Catherine further states that both the procedure and words used by John for baptism were different than that used by the disciples of Jesus.[424] This baptism, given by the disciples of Christ under His direction and authority, was clearly and without any doubt the true and full Sacrament of Baptism. Nothing more and nothing different, of any significance, is found in the Sacrament of Baptism today. The words used by Jesus' disciples invoked the name of the Father and of the Son and of the Holy Spirit; they poured water three times over the person being baptized; and they baptized under Jesus' direction and with His help in teaching and preparing the candidates for Baptism. Therefore, the baptism given by the disciples of Jesus Christ, under His direction, and beginning soon after Jesus' baptism by John, was the true and full Sacrament of Baptism, just as it is today.

Some claim that, at that time, there was not yet a true Sacrament of Baptism, even the baptism which Sacred Scripture describes as being given by the disciples of Christ under His direction (Jn 3:22; 4:1-2), because Jesus had not yet suffered and died for our salvation. Now it is true that the power of salvation and the grace for all the Holy Sacraments of the Church proceed from the Cross of Jesus Christ. However, Time is no obstacle to God. Do you not know that whoever is saved, throughout all of Time, even going back thousands of years before the Crucifixion and Resurrection of Christ, is saved by the One True Sacrifice of Christ on the Cross? And the Church clearly teaches that the merits of Jesus Christ, which most obviously include Christ's suffering and death on the Cross, were the source of grace and power which brought about the Immaculate Conception of the Virgin Mary.[425] Therefore, under the authority and direction of Christ, the true Sacrament of Baptism (and other Sacraments) could be dispensed before the Crucifixion, in accordance with the will of God.

A clear and indisputable example of a Sacrament beginning before the Crucifixion of Christ is the first Holy Eucharist. At the Last Supper, on the night before the Crucifixion, Christ Himself established the Sacrament of Holy Communion and Christ Himself consecrated the first Eucharist. Yet the Crucifixion of Christ, that most holy event which is in truth the source of grace and power for all the Holy Sacraments, occurred the following day—for nothing is impossible to God.

Forty Days in the Wilderness

"And immediately the Spirit prompted him into the desert. And he was in the desert for forty days and forty nights. And he was tempted by Satan. And he was with the wild animals, and the Angels ministered to him." (Mk 1:12-13).

The Gospel of Mark describes the Baptism of Jesus (Mk 1:9-11), then the 40 days in the wilderness, then the arrest of John the Baptist. The Gospel of Matthew likewise gives the same order of events. Mark's Gospel uses the word 'immediately,' which might be interpreted to mean that the Baptism of Jesus was followed by the 40 days in the wilderness with little time or other events intervening. On the other hand, the Gospel of Luke places a statement that the Ministry of Jesus began when He was about 30, and an account of His ancestry (through the Virgin Mary), between the Baptism and the 40 days. The placement of a significant amount of text between the Baptism and the 40 days might be interpreted to mean that a length of time and a number of events occurred between the Baptism of Jesus and His 40 days in the wilderness.

The word 'immediately' generally means 'without delay', so that if one event occurs immediately after the other, there are no intervening events of any significance and little or no time between the occurrence of the two events. When Jesus healed the leper, Sacred Scripture says: "And after he had spoken, immediately the leprosy departed from him, and he was cleansed." (Mk 1:42). There was no delay or other events between Jesus saying "be cleansed" and the leper being healed. In the case of this healing, the entire time frame being described is quite brief, occurring over the course of probably only a few minutes, from the exchange of words to the completion of the healing (Mk 1:40-42). But in the case of a much longer series of events, (e.g. Baptism, 40 days in the wilderness, and the arrest of John), the much larger time frame imparts a somewhat different meaning to the word 'immediately'. In the context of a larger time frame, the word 'immediately' still means that one event occurred after the other, and without any significant delay, but there may have been a greater space of time between the two events, a time larger than a few minutes or hours.

Blessed Anne Catherine describes a series of events between the Baptism of Jesus and the 40 days in the wilderness. In particular, she states that, after His Baptism, Jesus celebrated two Sabbaths and then the Feast of Tabernacles, before going into the wilderness for 40 days. She does not mention the Day of Atonement (Yom Kippur) by name. However, she does say that, on the Sabbath before the Feast of Tabernacles began, Jesus taught several different groups of people, at great length, on the topics of penance, modesty, chastity, and humility before God.[426] These topics are fitting instruction for the Day of Atonement. Furthermore, the Day of Atonement in that year (A.D. 15) coincided with a Saturday (the Sabbath), in harmony with her description of events.[427]

When did the 40 days in the wilderness occur? No particular date is given in Sacred Scripture, except the indication that the 40 days occurred soon after the Baptism of Jesus by John. In the writings of Blessed Anne Catherine, she describes the 40 days soon after describing the celebration of the Feast of Tabernacles. She does not specifically state how many days occurred between the end of the Feast of Tabernacles and the 40 days in the wilderness. However, in the year A.D. 15, the Feast of Tabernacles began on Oct. 17 and ended on Oct. 24. She further states that Jesus left for the wilderness, to begin His 40 days fast, on the hour before the Sabbath began.[428] Since the Jewish Sabbath begins on Friday at sunset, the 40 days began on a Friday evening (Saturday, by the Jewish calendar), after the Feast of Tabernacles had ended.

After describing the 40 days that Jesus spent in the wilderness, Blessed Anne Catherine describes three Sabbaths celebrated by Jesus, and then the Feast of Dedication (Hanukkah).[429] In A.D. 15, the Feast of Dedication fell on Tuesday, Dec. 24 (and so actually began at sunset on Dec. 23).[430] The three previous Sabbaths would then be the Saturdays of Dec. 21, 14, and 7. So, Jesus was in the wilderness for 40 days sometime between Thursday, Oct. 24, and Saturday, Dec. 7, of A.D. 15. There are only 43 days between those two dates. And since Jesus began His 40 day fast on a Sabbath (beginning on Friday evening) after the Feast of Tabernacles, that Sabbath must have been the one from sunset on Friday, Oct. 25, to sunset on Saturday, Oct. 26, immediately following the close of the Feast of Tabernacles on Oct. 24. The 40 days in the wilderness would then be the 40 days from Saturday, Tishri 24 and Oct. 26, to Wednesday, Kislev 5 and Dec. 4, counting inclusively.

Jesus was in the wilderness for forty days from the end of Tishri, throughout the month of Heshvan, until the beginning of the month of Kislev. In choosing this time of the year to spend in the wilderness, Jesus was able to spend 40 days apart from the other Jews and not miss any important liturgical celebrations. At many other times during the year, taking 40 days to be apart from Jewish society would mean missing some important celebration, such as Passover, the Feast of Weeks, the Feast of Tabernacles, Hanukkah, Rosh Hashanah, etc. Jesus did not ignore His religious duties as a faithful Jew, even as He, the Son of God, came to establish the new covenant of Christianity.

Behold the Lamb of God

"On the next day, John saw Jesus coming toward him, and so he said: 'Behold, the Lamb of God. Behold, he who takes away the sin of the world. This is the one about whom I said, "After me arrives a man, who has been placed ahead of me, because he existed before me." And I did not know him. Yet it is for this reason that I come baptizing with water: so that he may be made manifest in Israel.' " (Jn 1:29-31).

"The next day again, John was standing with two of his disciples. And catching sight of Jesus walking, he said, 'Behold, the Lamb of God.' " (Jn 1:35-36).

"On the next day, he wanted to go into Galilee, and he found Philip. And Jesus said to him, 'Follow me.' " (Jn 1:43).

According to Sacred Scripture, John had a dispute in Bethany with some priests and Levites sent by the Pharisees (Jn 1:19-28). John saw Jesus on each of the two following days (Jn 1:29, 35), and on both days he exclaimed, "Behold, the Lamb of God." Then on the next day, which was the fourth consecutive day, Jesus decided to go to Galilee. Thereafter, Jesus called Philip, and then Nathanael, to follow him (Jn 1:43-51).

According to Blessed Anne Catherine, on the day that Jesus ended His 40 days in the wilderness, He crossed the river Jordan and traveled to a place on the opposite bank of the river from where John the Baptist was baptizing. John saw Jesus, pointed to Him, and exclaimed, "Behold, the Lamb of God who taketh away the sins of the world."[431] Then, the following day, Jesus taught in another place near the river, and some of the disciples of John were there. She does not say whether John saw Jesus again on that occasion, but that must be the case. Sacred Scripture clearly states that John saw Jesus on two consecutive days and there is no other place in Blessed Anne Catherine's description of Christ's Ministry that could fit this sequence of events. She tells us that John saw Jesus after His Baptism and before the 40 days in the wilderness, and at that time also exclaimed, "Behold the Lamb of God...."[432] However, she places the call of Philip and Nathanael, and the marriage at Cana, after the 40 days. So, the two consecutive days when John saw Jesus, described in the Gospel of John as occurring just before the call of Philip, must have occurred after Christ's Baptism and after the 40 days in the wilderness. The first time that John saw Jesus after His Baptism was before the 40 days, but the next two times were after the 40 days. Here then are three occasions when John saw Jesus after His Baptism and declared that He was the Lamb of God.

The day that Jesus left the wilderness to end His 40 days of fasting was Wednesday, Kislev 5 and Dec. 4, of A.D. 15. On each of the next two days, Thursday, Dec. 5, and Friday, Dec. 6, John saw Jesus and declared Him to be the Lamb of God.

On the next day, after John had seen Jesus two consecutive days, Jesus decided to go to Galilee (Jn 1:43). Notice that Sacred Scripture does not say that Jesus went to Galilee on that day, but only that He decided to go on that day. Since the next day after Friday, Dec. 6, was a Sabbath, Jesus would not have traveled far on that day. Blessed Anne Catherine repeatedly describes Jesus keeping a day of rest on the Sabbath, even after His Ministry began.[433] Furthermore, we are not told on which day thereafter that Jesus met Philip and Nathanael. There is no support for the assumption that Jesus met Philip on the same day that He decided to go to Galilee. According to Blessed Anne Catherine, Jesus called Philip and Nathanael, as the Gospel of John describes, sometime after the

Feast of the Dedication (Hanukah).[434] In A.D. 15, Hanukah began on Tuesday, December 24, or, more specifically, at sunset on December 23.

The Wedding at Cana

"And on the third day, a wedding was held in Cana of Galilee, and the mother of Jesus was there. Now Jesus was also invited to the wedding, with his disciples." (Jn 2:1-2).

Sacred Scripture tells us that there was a marriage at Cana in Galilee on the third day. However, this cannot be the third day counting from the day of John's dispute with the Pharisees, for Jesus did not decide to go to Galilee until the fourth day:

1. John's dispute with the Pharisees
2. John sees Jesus: "Behold the Lamb of God"
3. John sees Jesus again: "Behold the Lamb of God"
4. Jesus decides to go to Galilee.

The expression "the third day" could refer to the third day after Jesus arrived in Galilee, or the third day after the call of Nathanael, or it could even refer to the third day of the week, Tuesday.

According to Blessed Anne Catherine, the wedding at Cana lasted for 4 days.[435] She describes the order of events as follows: the feast of Hanukah began (on Tues. Dec. 24), then a Sabbath (Sat. Dec. 28), then the wedding for 4 days, then another Sabbath (Sat. Jan. 4).[436] From her description of these events, it seems that the Sabbath followed immediately after the fourth day of the wedding celebration, so that the 4 days of the wedding at Cana would be Tuesday to Friday (Dec. 31 to Jan. 3). Dec. 31 of that year was also Tevet 2, the last day of Hanukah. Now Tuesday is the third day of the week, but there must be more to the statement in Sacred Scripture: "And on the third day, a wedding was held in Cana of Galilee ...." (Jn 2:1).

Blessed Anne Catherine tells us that Jesus traveled to Cana on the day after the Sabbath; that Sabbath was the one following the start of Hanukah. Supposing that Jesus arrived in Cana that same day, Sunday, Dec. 29, then the wedding began on Tuesday, the third day after Jesus arrived at Cana in Galilee. This interpretation of these events fits the description given by Sacred Scripture. John 1:43 has Jesus deciding to go to Galilee; some events follow, including the call of Philip and Nathanael; then, on the third day that Jesus arrived at Cana in Galilee, a wedding ceremony began at Cana. Following the wedding and the subsequent Sabbath, Blessed Anne Catherine mentions a two-day fast.[437] This fast must be the fast of Tevet 10, which that year fell on Wednesday, Jan. 8.

First Passover of Christ's Ministry

"And the Passover of the Jews was near, and so Jesus ascended to Jerusalem. And he found, sitting in the temple, sellers of oxen and sheep and doves, and the moneychangers. And when he had made something like a whip out of little cords, he drove them all out of the temple, including the sheep and the oxen. And he poured out the brass coins of the moneychangers, and he overturned their tables." (Jn 2:13-15).

This passage is the first description of a Passover in the Gospel of John and is found near the beginning of the Gospel. Many scholars consider this to be the first Passover of Christ's Ministry. Blessed Anne Catherine Emmerich confirms that this Passover was the first of Christ's Ministry. She also tells us that Jesus drove the buyers and sellers out of the Temple on the first day of this Passover (Nisan 15). She describes the sacrifice of the Paschal lambs as occurring on the previous day, then the Passover supper in the evening, followed by the conflict in the Temple the next morning.[438] That evening (after the conflict), the first fruits of the grain harvest were cut, in preparation for the offering of the first fruits the next morning (Nisan 16; the morning after the first Sabbath of the Passover, cf. Lev 23:15-17).

This first day of Passover (Nisan 15) coincided with the Sabbath in that year, A.D. 16. Blessed Anne Catherine describes the first day of Nisan (earlier that month) as both the feast of the New Moon (Rosh Hodesh) and the Sabbath.[439] In A.D. 16, the new moon of March occurred on March 27 at 06:00 Jerusalem Standard Time.[440] Ordinarily, when the start of the month is determined by calculation, this would make March 27 as Nisan 1. However, in A.D. 16, March 27 was a Friday and so Nisan 1 was delayed until Saturday in order to prevent the first holy day of Passover (Nisan 15) from falling also on a Friday and interfering with the preparation day of the Sabbath. Thus, the day when Jesus drove the buyers and sellers out of the Temple was also a Saturday, Nisan 15 and April 11 of A.D. 16.

Blessed Anne Catherine correctly indicates that the first day of Nisan was a Sabbath. In A.D. 16, this could only have occurred if Jewish calendar months during that period of time were determined by calculation and with modifications from a set of rules. If the calendar was determined by observation, or by observation modified by a set of rules, the crescent new moon would not have been seen until the evening of March 28, making Sunday, March 29 the first day of Nisan. (And any delay based on a calendar rule would push the first day of Nisan forward another day, not backwards.)

The Second First Sabbath

"Now it happened that, on the second first Sabbath, as he passed through the grain field, his disciples were separating the ears of grain and eating them, by rubbing them in their hands. Then certain Pharisees said to them, 'Why are you doing what is not lawful on the Sabbaths?' ... And he said to them, 'For the Son of man is Lord, even of the Sabbath.' " (Lk 6:1-2, 5).

Knowing which Sabbath is the second first Sabbath is important to the understanding of this passage. In the book of Leviticus, God commanded the Israelites not to eat bread, parched grain, or fresh grain, taken from the harvest at the time of the Passover, until the first fruits of the harvest had been offered to God.

"...you shall not eat from the grain field, until the day when you shall offer from it to your God. It is an everlasting precept in your generations and in all of your dwelling places." (Lev 23:14).

The first fruits of the harvest, in the form of sheaves of grain, were offered to God on the morning after the Sabbath. In ancient times, this was most likely the Sabbath occurring during the Passover. In more recent times, the Jews interpreted this passage to refer to the first holy day of Passover, which is a day of solemn rest and a type of

Sabbath. In some years, the first holy day of Passover (Nisan 15) coincides with the Sabbath; this was the case in A.D. 16 and in A.D. 19.[441] The last day on which the Jews could **not** eat grain (from the spring harvest) was the Sabbath of the Passover. The first day on which they could begin to eat grain from that harvest was the day after the Sabbath, the day on which the first fruits were offered to God. That day, Sunday, was also the first day in the count of the 50 days to the Feast of Weeks (the Jewish feast of Pentecost).

"Therefore, you shall number from the day after the Sabbath, in which you offered a sheaf of the first-fruits, seven full weeks, all the way to the day after the completion of the seventh week, that is, fifty days, and then you shall offer a new sacrifice to the Lord, from all of your dwelling places: two loaves from the first-fruits, from two-tenths of leavened fine wheat flour, which you shall bake as the first-fruits of the Lord."
(Lev 23:15-17).

The first fruits of the grain harvest (barley) were offered on the Sabbath during Passover because the grain harvest in Israel begins in late March or early April, at the time of the Passover in the spring.[442] Then, 50 days later, a second offering to God, this time of loaves of bread, was made from the fruits of the same harvest. Notice that the first offering to God is sheaves of grain, taken from the beginning of the harvest, which have not been threshed or ground into flour or baked into loaves—here the harvest has just begun. Then, 50 days later, the harvesting of the fields is complete; the grain has been threshed, ground into flour, and baked into loaves. The second offering, the loaves, signals the completion of the harvest. God is thanked at the beginning and at the end of the harvest time.

The count of the 50 days is 7 full weeks (counted as 7 Sabbaths) plus one day. The first day of the 50 days is the day after the first Sabbath of the Passover. Then seven more Sabbaths are counted, which is 7 full weeks (each week ending with a Sabbath), and the 50th day, the day after the seventh Sabbath, begins the Feast of Weeks.

So, which is the first Sabbath in this counting of the Sabbaths at the time of the grain harvest? The Sabbath of the Passover is the first Sabbath used to determine the start of the count, because the following day is the first day of the 50 days. But the first Sabbath of the Passover is not one of the seven Sabbaths contained within the 50 days; it is the Sabbath before the 50 days begins. The Sabbath after the Passover has ended is the first Sabbath in the count of 7 Sabbaths to the Feast of Weeks. Thus there are two first Sabbaths: the Sabbath of the Passover and the Sabbath following the Passover. The "second first Sabbath" must therefore be the Sabbath after the Passover. There are only seven days in the Feast of Passover (not counting the preparation day), so there can be only one Sabbath during Passover. The second first Sabbath is always the Sabbath immediately after the Passover.

At no other time during the calendar year (that I know of) do the Jews count the Sabbaths. So there is no other time of the year to which the expression "second first Sabbath" could refer. Also, the passage from Luke 6:1-5 is clearly describing the time of year when the grain is harvested. The disciples are picking ears of grain and eating them from the fields because the grain is ripe and ready for harvest, but has not yet been harvested. The grain harvest in Israel occurs in the spring.[443] That is why Jewish Law requires offering the first fruits of the grain harvest during Passover and again at the

Feast of Weeks. Therefore, the time of year which is referred to by the expression "second first Sabbath" must also be in the spring.

Why does Sacred Scripture make a point of telling us that the disciples were eating grain from the fields on the "second first Sabbath," and not on some other Sabbath of the year? The previous Sabbath, that is, the first Sabbath of Passover, was the last day on which they were prohibited from eating fresh grain, because the first fruits had not yet been offered to God. The second first Sabbath, that is, the Sabbath immediately after Passover, occurred after the first fruits had been offered to God, so the disciples were permitted to eat fresh grain from the fields on that day. Sacred Scripture tells us that is was the second first Sabbath to indicate that the disciples were not breaking Jewish Law when they ate fresh grain from the fields. But the disciples would have been breaking the Jewish Law if they had eaten grain from the fields on the previous Sabbath.

John the Baptist's Arrest

In the Gospel of Matthew, John the Baptist's ministry begins in chapter 3. The Baptism of Jesus by John occurs at the end of chapter 3. Then the 40 days that Jesus spent in the wilderness follows at the beginning of chapter 4. The next passage states that John had been arrested (Mt 4:12). Jesus then continues John's message of repentance (Mt 3:2; 4:17). The Gospel of Matthew places John's arrest during the early part of Jesus' Ministry and not long after the baptism of Jesus by John. The other synoptic Gospels likewise place John's arrest soon after Jesus' baptism.

In the Gospel of Mark, John's ministry is described beginning with Mk 1:2. Next Jesus is baptized and spends 40 days in the wilderness. Then, by Mk 1:14, John has been arrested. Only a few verses cover the period of time from the baptism of Jesus to John's arrest. Here again, the arrest of John is placed early in the Gospel and early in the Ministry of Christ.

In the Gospel of Luke, John the Baptist's ministry begins in chapter 3 (Lk 3:1-2), and his arrest is mentioned in that same chapter (Lk 3:19-20). Luke places his description of the Baptism of Jesus after his description of John's arrest. This does not mean that Luke thought someone else baptized Jesus. A writer does not always place events in chronological order, but rather in whatever order is best for the telling of a story. Sacred Scripture does not always place events in chronological order, but rather in whatever order is best for teaching and explaining God's message to us. Even so, Luke's Gospel agrees with the other Gospels in placing John's arrest earlier rather than later.

In the Gospel of John, the Baptism of Jesus by John is described in the past tense (Jn 1:32-24). The 40 days in the wilderness is not described. But, after describing the wedding at Cana, the Passover at Jerusalem, and the call of Nicodemus, the Gospel of John plainly states that John was still baptizing and had not yet been put in prison (Jn 3:23-24). This passage is placed early in John's Gospel and still fairly early during Christ's Ministry, yet it is now clear that John's arrest did not occur immediately after Jesus returned from His 40 days in the wilderness.

When two events are described one after the other in Sacred Scripture, even without so much as one sentence between them, there still may have been any number of days, months, or years between the two events. If not for John's Gospel, we might incorrectly have concluded that John was arrested soon after Jesus' Baptism. Rather, we must place the arrest of John sometime after the first Passover of Jesus' Ministry. And since John baptized Jesus Christ in the autumn, the arrest of John may have occurred six months to a year after the beginning of Christ's Ministry.

Blessed Anne Catherine Emmerich provides us with more information about the timing of John the Baptist's arrest. As in the Gospel of John, she places the arrest of John the Baptist not long after the first Passover of Christ's Ministry. In her book, *The Life of Jesus Christ and Biblical Revelations*, she describes the Passover in volume 2, on pages 114-121.[444] She first mentions John's arrest on page 161, only forty pages after the first Passover of Christ's Ministry (April 10-17 of A.D. 16).

On page 145, she describes another Jewish religious ceremony, in which the Jews wore long black mantles as well as sackcloth, went barefoot, and "prayed and chanted in a mournful tone."[445] Though she does not name this ceremony, it most probably occurred during the time between Passover and the Jewish Pentecost (Feast of Weeks). That time period for the Jews is a time of partial mourning, in remembrance of the time between the Exodus from slavery in Egypt and the giving of the Law in the Sinai desert.[446] Her description of the ceremony fits that theme. Also, she places this ceremony not long after the Passover.

After this ceremony, Blessed Anne Catherine describes some additional events during Christ's Ministry, including the mention of two Sabbaths.[447] Next she details how John's disciples spoke with Jesus about John's imprisonment; this is followed by the mention of the Feast of the New Moon (which occurs at the start of each month in the Jewish calendar).[448] This places John's arrest within two Sabbaths of the time between Passover and the Feast of Weeks (Shavuot). The Feast of Weeks is celebrated on Sivan 6 and 7 (the Jewish months from Passover are: Nisan, Iyar, Sivan, Tammuz, etc.).

From her description of the Passover to her first mention of John's arrest, there are forty pages and the mention of at least four Sabbaths.[449] Thus, the Feast of the New Moon she mentions could not be Sivan 1, this is too close to the Passover for all of the Sabbaths and events, plus the arrest of John to occur before the new moon. Yet there were two Sabbaths only mentioned between the ceremony (the one related to the Passover and the Feast of Weeks) and John's arrest. Therefore John the Baptist was arrested by Herod during the month of Sivan, prior to the next Feast of the New Moon on Tammuz 1. The month of Sivan, in the year A.D. 16 began on May 26 and ended on June 22.[450]

Furthermore, Herod would have been less likely to arrest John just before or during the Feast of Weeks. Huge crowds gathered for the Feast of Weeks at Jerusalem because it was one of three feasts that all able-bodied Jewish men were required to attend (Deut 16:16). John was a popular religious figure, so there might have been a disturbance among this great crowd of people, if John were arrested at that time. Herod would have waited until the crowds left Jerusalem for their homes before arresting John. The Feast of Weeks ends in early Sivan, so the most likely time for John's arrest would be in mid to late Sivan in A.D. 16.

John was arrested in late spring of A.D. 16. Since John began baptizing in spring of A.D. 15, his ministry must have lasted for about one year, or, at most, a year and a few months, up to the point of his imprisonment. Perhaps one could say that his ministry continued even after he was imprisoned, but it was not a public ministry of preaching and baptism.

The Martyrdom of John the Baptist

John's martyrdom is described in chapter 14 of the Gospel of Matthew (Mt 14:1-12). However, this event is presented as having already occurred earlier in Matthew's timeline. Chapter 14 begins with Herod speculating that Jesus was really John the Baptist raised from the dead. Thus, by the beginning of chapter 14, John had already been dead for some time. The description of John's beheading then follows, but is clearly presented as a description of what had already taken place at some earlier time.

How long was John in prison before he was beheaded? In Matthew's Gospel, John's imprisonment begins in chapter 3 (Mt 3:12), and by chapter 11 (Mt 11:2) John is still in prison. Thus, Matthew's Gospel indicates that John was in prison for a lengthy period of time. This interpretation is supported by the description of John's beheading. Herod was reluctant to put John to death and did so because of his oath and his guests (Mt 14:9). Herod's intention was to keep John in prison without putting him to death, and perhaps to release him at some point in time.

In the Gospel of Mark, John's imprisonment is first mentioned in chapter 1 (Mk 1:14). John's martyrdom is not described until chapter 6 (Mk 6:14-29), but again it is described as having already occurred at some earlier time. Even so, Mark's Gospel does not present John's imprisonment as if it were brief.

In the Gospel of Luke, John's imprisonment is stated in chapter 3 (Lk 3:20). John's martyrdom is not described in detail by Luke, but is mentioned in chapter 9, where people are wondering if Jesus is really John the Baptist raised from the dead (Lk 9:7-9, 19). Here again John's martyrdom is referred to as a past event, making it difficult to determine when John died.

In the Gospel of John, the martyrdom of John the Baptist is not mentioned. However, in chapter 5, Jesus first says, " 'You sent to John, and he offered testimony to the truth.' " (Jn 5:33). This refers to a time when John was alive. But immediately thereafter Jesus speaks of John the Baptist in the past tense: " 'He was a burning and shining light. So you were willing, at the time, to exult in his light.' " (Jn 5:35). This implies either that John has been imprisoned, so that he could no longer continue his ministry of preaching and of baptism, or that he has died. In chapter 10, the people speak of John in the past tense, again indicating that John had either died or been imprisoned. Thus all four Gospels give some witness to John's martyrdom, but they do not reveal when John was martyred.

The Gospels clearly state that John the Baptist was beheaded by Herod the tetrarch on the occasion of Herod's birthday. If only we knew when Herod was born, we would then know the exact day of John's beheading. Since we do not have this information, we must approach the problem in a different way.

Blessed Anne Catherine provides us with some indication of the time frame for the beheading of John the Baptist. First, she clearly states that the Ministry of Jesus Christ lasted about 3½ years (see chapter 2).[451] In her book, *The Life of Jesus Christ and Biblical Revelations*, there are some 1170 pages describing Christ's Ministry, from His Baptism to the Last Supper. The average number of pages per year is approx. 334 (1170 / 3.5 years

= 334.3). The average number of pages per month is approx. 28 (1170 / 42 months = 27.9).

Blessed Anne Catherine describes John the Baptist's arrest in volume 2, pages 161-169, of *The Life of Jesus Christ and Biblical Revelations*, and his martyrdom in volume 3, pages 144 and following. There are some 455 pages of description of Christ's Ministry between those two events. This number of pages is significantly more than the average of 334.3 pages per year. This comparison indicates that the time from John's arrest to his martyrdom was more than one year. Furthermore, if we divide those 455 pages by the average of 27.9 pages per month, the result gives us a rough estimate of the time frame from John's arrest to his beheading: approx. 16 months.

Some 94 pages after the arrest of John, Blessed Anne Catherine states: "With the Sabbath, the first day of the month of Elul began."[452] Since John was arrested during the month of Sivan in A.D. 16, this mention of Elul must be in the same year.[453]

A little further on, Blessed Anne Catherine states that people were very busy with preparations for both the upcoming Sabbath and the first day of the Feast of Tabernacles, which occurred that year on the day after the Sabbath. This Feast begins on Tishri 15 and ends on Tishri 22, with both the first and last days kept as holy days of rest from work (Lev 23:33-36). In the modern Jewish calendar, Tishri 1 is not permitted to fall on a Sunday. This arrangement prevents two solemn days of rest (Tishri 15 and 22) from occurring consecutively. In the ancient Jewish calendar, all these rules for the arrangement of feasts in the calendar had not yet been developed and put into practice. Thus, Blessed Anne Catherine describes a year when Tishri 1, 15, and 22 coincided with a Sunday. Tishri 1 began on September 20 and the Feast of Tabernacles began on October 4 and ended on October 11 of A.D. 16.[454] This Feast of Tabernacles is described in volume 2 on page 373, well after John's arrest, but also well before his beheading.[455]

Some 200 pages later, in volume 3 pages 92-105, Blessed Anne Catherine describes the celebration of the Feast of Lights, Hanukkah.[456] This could not be the Hanukkah occurring 2 months later in Dec. of A.D. 16, because this Feast is placed about 200 pages after the Feast of Tabernacles of A.D. 16. The average number of pages per month is 28, not 100. Rather, this must be the following Hanukkah, occurring over a year later, in A.D. 17 (from sunset on Dec. 31 of A.D. 17, to Jan. 8 of A.D. 18).

Blessed Anne Catherine describes this Feast of Lights as encompassing two Sabbaths, including the last day of the feast. And she states that the people were celebrating the Feast of the New Moon (celebrated at the start of every month in the Jewish calendar).[457] The Hanukkah of A.D. 17/18 fits this description, but only if a leap month was added in March/April of A.D. 17 (See Appendix II, Section C). In that case, Kislev 25 would coincide with Saturday, Jan. 1 and Tevet 2 (the last day of Hanukkah) would coincide with Saturday, Jan. 8, A.D. 18.[458] This arrangement matches the description of Blessed Anne Catherine of a Hanukkah that began and ended on the Jewish Sabbath.

The adding of a leap month in A.D. 17 would not have been required to prevent the start of Passover from occurring before the spring Equinox. However, if a leap month had not been added, Passover would have begun on March 30 (Nisan 14). In the ancient Jewish calendar, the scheduling of leap years was partly a human decision, not entirely determined by astronomy and mathematics.[459] If the winter was colder or dryer than usual, the crops would grow more slowly and the grain would not be ready for the offering of the first fruits on the morning of the second day of Passover (Lev 23:15-17).[460]

An earlier date for Passover allows less time for the crops to mature. Consequently, earlier dates for Passover were more likely to be delayed due to the addition of a leap month (AdarII). For these reasons, the Passover of A.D. 17 was delayed from late March to late April, resulting in a later than usual date for the following Hanukkah.

There are a number of distinct events described by Blessed Anne Catherine between the Hanukkah of A.D. 17/18 and the beheading of John the Baptist. The exact length of time is difficult to discern. However, shortly after describing John's martyrdom, she describes a Feast of the New Moon (celebrated at the start of each and every month). This particular first day of the month was also the time for celebrating "the return of the trees to new life."[461] She likewise refers to the rising of the sap in the trees and a ritual of purification of trees at the start of this same month. This celebration is clearly the Jewish New Year for trees,[462] which falls in the Jewish month of Shevat. There is some dispute among the Jews as to whether the correct day for this celebration should be Shevat 1 or Shevat 15, but Blessed Anne Catherine places it on the same day as the Feast of the New Moon (first day of the month). In A.D. 18, following the date for Hanukkah explained above, Shevat 1 coincided with Saturday, February 5.[463]

Blessed Anne Catherine places Hanukkah before, and the New Year for trees on Shevat 1 after, John the Baptist's beheading. Hanukkah ends on Tevet 2; Shevat is the next month after Tevet. Therefore, John the Baptist was martyred sometime during the month of Tevet, in early A.D. 18. In that year, Tevet began on January 7 and ended on February 4. Some events are described between the end of Hanukkah (Tevet 2) and John's martyrdom; additional events are described between John's martyrdom and the New Year for trees (Shevat 1).[464] So, John most likely died about the middle of Tevet, and about the end of January, in A.D. 18.

Not long after describing the New Year for trees, Blessed Anne Catherine describes the Feast of Purim.[465] She states that Jesus taught in the synagogue on the Sabbath: "...for it was the Sabbath of the Purim festival."[466] Purim lasts only two days, Adar 14 and 15, and is preceded by the fast of Esther on Adar 13. If the year contains both AdarI and AdarII, Purim is placed in AdarII; otherwise it falls in Adar I. In A.D. 18, Purim coincided with the Sabbath because AdarI 14 and 15 coincided with Saturday, March 19, and Sunday, March 20.[467] Even if the leap month of AdarII were placed in A.D. 18 instead of A.D. 17, the Purim of A.D. 18 would still coincide with the Sabbath of Saturday, March 19, but the Jewish month would be called AdarII.

On the other hand, in A.D. 17, Purim fell on Tuesday, March 30, and Wednesday, March 31. This assumes the above conclusion that A.D. 17 included AdarII. If it did not, then the Purim of A.D. 17 would be one month earlier, and would occur on Sunday, Feb. 28 and Monday, March 1 (and still not on the Jewish Sabbath).

Therefore, Purim would coincide with the Sabbath in A.D. 18, but not in A.D. 17. Therefore, the Sabbath of Purim placed by Blessed Anne Catherine soon after the martyrdom of John the Baptist occurred in A.D. 18, not A.D. 17. This line of reasoning confirms the above conclusion that John was beheaded in early A.D. 18, after more than a year of imprisonment.

The astute reader of *The Life of Jesus Christ and Biblical Revelations* will notice that Blessed Anne Catherine describes only three Passovers during the Ministry of Jesus when there should be four—A.D. 16, 17, 18, and 19 (the last being the Passover of Christ's Passion). The editor of that book calls the Passover following the beheading of

John the Baptist the second Pasch, when it is in fact the third.[468] The mistake occurs because Blessed Anne Catherine does not describe all four Passovers. The four Gospels of Jesus Christ likewise do not describe, or even mention, every Passover during Christ's Ministry. Thus, there was a Passover between the arrest and the beheading of John the Baptist that is not mentioned in her book.

After writing the above chronology of the martyrdom of John the Baptist, I came across a footnote in Blessed Anne Catherine's book, *The Life of the Blessed Virgin Mary*, which reads as follows: "In 1823, when recounting Jesus' stay in Hebron during the third year of His ministry, some ten days after the death of the Baptist, Catherine Emmerich said that she saw Our Lord teaching, on Friday the 29th day of the month of Thebet [Tevet]…."[469] Comparing this new information to the above chronology of John the Baptist's martyrdom, I found that, in my chronology, Tevet 29 did coincide with a Friday in the third year of Christ's Ministry. Since Jesus was baptized at the beginning of His Ministry in Oct. of A.D. 15, the first year would be fall of A.D. 15 to fall of A.D. 16, the second year would be A.D. 16 to 17, and the third would be A.D. 17 to 18. The above chronology places John the Baptist's death in the third year of Christ's Ministry, in early A.D. 18.

Furthermore, this footnote places John the Baptist's death about ten days before Tevet 29 (Feb. 4 of A.D. 18), which would be approx. Tuesday, Jan. 25 and Tevet 19. The date is approximate because the length of time of ten days is stated as an approximation: "some ten days." But this approximate date of Jan. 25 for the death of John the Baptist is in complete harmony with my above conclusion for the time frame of John's beheading—about the middle of Tevet, and about the end of January, in A.D. 18.

This new information also lends support to my assertion that the Passover of A.D. 17 began in late April, not late March, due to the addition of AdarII, (the leap month of the Jewish calendar leap year A.D. 16/17), that year. Tevet 29 would not have fallen on a Friday in Jan. of A.D. 18 but for the addition of AdarII in the previous spring.

The Call of the Twelve Apostles

Blessed Anne Catherine gives specific information about the call of the Twelve Apostles and other disciples of Christ. For all those details, I refer the reader to her book, *The Life of Jesus Christ and Biblical Revelations*. However, one question is of particular interest: When were the Twelve Apostles chosen as a group to be more than disciples of Christ?

The Gospel of Matthew places the appointment of the Twelve Apostles in chapter 10 (Mt 10:1-15), after a significant portion of Christ's Ministry has passed. The Gospel of Mark places the call of the Twelve in chapter 6 (Mk 6:7-13). But, since Mark's Gospel is shorter than Matthew's Gospel, Mark is not placing the call of the Twelve any earlier than Matthew. However, Matthew describes John the Baptist's as being still in prison after the call of the Twelve (Mt 11:1-6), while Mark mentions the death of John the Baptist after the call of the Twelve (Mk 6:14). Did the call of the Twelve occur while John was in prison or after his beheading?

The Gospel of Luke offers a possible explanation. Luke places the call of the Twelve Apostles in chapter 6 (Lk 6:12-16). Thereafter, in chapter 7 (Lk 7:18-23), Luke describes John asking Jesus a question through John's disciples. Matthew gives us the additional information that John asked this question of Jesus through his disciples during his imprisonment (Mt 11:2-6). Then, in chapter 9 (Lk 9:1-10), Luke describes a second stage in the call of the Twelve, when they were sent out on their own and given power to cast out demons and to cure diseases (Lk 9:1). It was after the Twelve went out on their own that Herod heard about these events and considered the death of John the Baptist, as both Luke and Mark describe (Lk 9:7-9; Mk 6:14-16). Therefore, Jesus chose the Twelve Apostles during John's imprisonment, and He called them and sent them out on their own after the death of John the Baptist.

Notice here that Jesus did not choose the Twelve at the very beginning of His Ministry. First the Twelve were mere disciples of Christ, then they were chosen as Apostles, then moreover they were called and sent out on their own. The Twelve Apostles progressed through stages to become the eventual leaders of the Church.

Palm Sunday

In the liturgical calendar of the Church, Palm Sunday is celebrated on the Sunday before Easter. This celebration recalls the joyous entrance of Jesus into Jerusalem not long before His Crucifixion and Resurrection. However, an examination of Sacred Scripture and of the writings of Blessed Anne Catherine Emmerich reveals that the events of Palm Sunday actually occurred more than a week before Easter.

The Gospels do not clearly state when Palm Sunday occurred. The Gospel of Matthew describes the entrance of Jesus into Jerusalem in chapter 21 (Mt 21:1-11). Jesus later leaves the city of Jerusalem to lodge at Bethany (Mt 21:17). The subsequent passage describes Jesus cursing a fig tree in the morning. If these passages are in chronological order, then the cursing of the fig tree occurred on a day after Palm Sunday. After this, Matthew places a long series of teachings of Jesus as well as a number of disputes between Jesus and the Jewish religious leaders. There is no clear statement as to how many days contained these teachings and disputes, but they take up over four chapters out of the 28 chapters in Matthew.

Then, in chapter 26, Jesus states that the Passover is two days away: " 'You know that after two days the Passover will begin, and the Son of man will be handed over to be crucified.' " (Mt 26:2). Those two days might be counted up to the time of the Last Supper, Thursday evening, or the time of the Crucifixion, Friday afternoon, which was the Preparation day of the Passover (Jn 19:14). But they could not be counted to the first holy day of Passover, on Nisan 15 (Saturday), because two days before that day would be Thursday. Matthew describes the day of the Last Supper (Thursday) beginning with verse 17 (Mt 26:27). Before that day, Matthew describes Jesus at Bethany, where Jesus lodged at night. That event must be place sometime before the Thursday of the Last Supper (Wednesday, at the latest). And the comment, referring to two days time until the Passover, must be placed before the events that night at Bethany, either earlier on Wednesday (making two days until Friday and the Crucifixion), or on Tuesday (making two days until Thursday and the Last Supper.

The result of this analysis leaves us with three possibilities. The events of Matthew 21:18 to 26:1 may have occurred in a very short amount of time (less than three full days from Mon. to Tues. or Wed.), or most of those events occurred at an earlier time (and so are presented out of order), or the events of Palm Sunday occurred more than a week before the Sunday of the Resurrection.

After describing Palm Sunday and before describing the Last Supper, the Gospel of Luke repeatedly comments that Jesus spent days teaching in the Temple. "And he was teaching in the temple daily." (Lk 19:47). "And it happened that, on one of the days when he was teaching the people in the temple and preaching the gospel…." (Lk 20:1). "Now in the daytime, he was teaching in the temple. But truly, departing in the evening, he lodged on the mount that is called Olivet." (Lk 21:37). These passages seem to indicate that there were more than a few days between Palm Sunday and the Last Supper.

The Gospel of John, on the other hand, seems to indicate that Palm Sunday occurred on the Sunday before Easter. "Then six days before the Passover, Jesus went to Bethania, where Lazarus had died, whom Jesus raised up." (Jn 12:1). That evening, Mary anointed the feet of Jesus. Then John reveals that a crowd of people came to see both Jesus and Lazarus, but that the chief priests made a plan to put Lazarus to death (Jn 12:9-11). The events of Palm Sunday are then briefly described (Jn 12:12-19), beginning with the text: "Then, on the next day…." (Jn 12:12). This text seems to indicate that Palm Sunday occurred five days before the Passover. If the Passover is counted as beginning with the Preparation day (Nisan 14), then the previous Sunday is five days before the Passover. However, there is another possible interpretation of this passage from John's Gospel.

Not every event described in Sacred Scripture is in chronological order. Sacred Scripture is entirely without error, but where Scripture is silent (for example, as to the order of events) we cannot fill in the silence with assumptions. The phrase "six days before the Passover" (Jn 12:1) refers to Jesus visiting Lazarus, and to Mary anointing the feet of Jesus. A subsequent passage (Jn 12:10-11) states that the chief priests made a plan to kill Lazarus. The very next verse (Jn 12:12) begins with "Then, on the next day" and goes on to describe the events of Palm Sunday. The "next day" could refer, then, to the day after the chief priests made their plan to kill Lazarus. This interpretation is supported by the verses that follow, describing Palm Sunday. These verses state that the crowd went out to see Jesus enter Jerusalem because Jesus had raised Lazarus from the dead (Jn 12:18), and that the Pharisees, seeing the crowds on Palm Sunday, gave up their plan to kill Lazarus (Jn 12:19). Thus the events of Palm Sunday caused them to abandon their plan to kill Lazarus, the very plan they had made just the day before.

The above interpretation allows for the possibility that the day when the chief priests made a plan to kill Lazarus, and the next day, Palm Sunday, are described out of chronological order by the Gospel of John and actually happened well before the day called "six days before the Passover," when Jesus visited Lazarus and had his feet anointed by Mary Magdalen. John's Gospel may have described these events in a different order for the purpose of pointing out the connection between Palm Sunday and the raising of Lazarus from the dead by Jesus.

The great crowds came to Bethany, where Jesus was staying six days before the Passover, partly to see Lazarus, because Jesus had raised Lazarus from the dead (Jn 12:9). The chief priests planned to kill Lazarus because, after Jesus raised him from the dead, many Jews began to follow Jesus. Therefore, the plan to kill Lazarus most likely began at an earlier time, soon after he was raised from the dead and the chief priests saw the effect that this miracle had on the people. The next day after they made the plan was Palm Sunday. The events of Palm Sunday then caused the chief priests to abandon the plan to kill Lazarus (Jn 12:19). This is one possible chronology.

The writings of Blessed Anne Catherine Emmerich can assist us in deciding which interpretation is correct. In volume 4 of *The Life of Jesus Christ and Biblical Revelations*, on pages 11-19, she describes in detail the events of Palm Sunday.[470] Prior to this description, on page 8, she mentions a pagan carnival that occurred about five weeks before the Passover.[471] In the old Roman calendar (before Julius Caesar reformed the calendar), the year began on March 1.[472] This carnival was likely the pagan celebration at the end of the old Roman calendar year. If we count five weeks back from the week of April 7 (when Passover began), we arrive at the week of March 1 (this week includes the end of Feb.).

Next, on page 9, Blessed Anne Catherine mentions the following Jewish Sabbath, which would then be Saturday, March 4.[473] Then, on pages 10-11, she describes the events that occurred "On the following day," which would then be Sunday, March 5.[474] She tells us that Jesus predicted His triumphant entrance into Jerusalem and said that it would occur in 15 days. So there were 15 days between that day and the day of Palm Sunday. Counting the days inclusively, the 15 days would start on one Sunday and end on the Sunday two weeks later. If this chronology is correct, then there were three weeks between Palm Sunday and Resurrection Sunday, not one week, and Palm Sunday occurred on March 19, not April 2. Blessed Anne Catherine gives further details about the events between Palm Sunday and Easter Sunday, which confirm this three-week length of time.

She follows her description of Palm Sunday with the withering of the fig tree (Mk 11:12-14) and the driving out of the buyers and sellers from the Temple (Mk 11:15-19).[475] Then she describes the events of the following Sabbath.[476] If Palm Sunday was March 19, then this Sabbath was Saturday, March 25 (and Nisan 1). We can actually follow Blessed Anne Catherine's day-by-day description of events from the Sabbath after Palm Sunday to the second Sabbath after Palm Sunday.[477] This day-by-day detailed description of events includes the story of the widow's mite (Mk 12:41-44) on the Wednesday between those two Sabbaths (Wednesday, March 29).[478] We can determine that this event occurred on Wednesday by counting the number of days before and after those two Sabbaths.

On the second Sabbath after Palm Sunday (Saturday, April 1, Nisan 8), Blessed Anne Catherine tells us that Jesus spent that evening at Lazarus' house in Bethany. Sacred Scripture reveals that Mary anointed Jesus' feet six days before the Passover where Lazarus was (Jn 12:1). Six days before the Passover (counted as beginning on Friday, Nisan 14) would be Saturday, Nisan 8. Even though Blessed Anne Catherine does not mention Mary Magdalen anointing Jesus at that time, her account and the account of the Gospel of John are in harmony. She states that Jesus was at Lazarus' house on that day and that the holy women were there.[479] She also relates that Mary anointed Jesus in similar manner on repeated occasions.

Following Blessed Anne Catherine's day-by-day account of events after Saturday, Nisan 8 brings us to the Last Supper on Thursday, Nisan 13 (actually, it would be counted as Nisan 14 since it occurred after sunset). Here we see that Blessed Anne

Catherine's description of events before Palm Sunday leads us to place Palm Sunday on Sunday, March 19. And her description of events after Palm Sunday likewise places Palm Sunday on the same day. No other date for Palm Sunday can fit her detailed description of the events in the weeks before the Crucifixion. Therefore, Palm Sunday actually occurred on Sunday, March 19 of A.D. 19, three weeks before the Resurrection (not one week before the Resurrection).

Further Details

There is sufficient information in the Gospels and in the writings of Blessed Anne Catherine Emmerich for a more detailed analysis of the chronology of events during the Ministry of Jesus Christ. The interested reader should find in this chapter a sufficient starting point from which to go forward and discover many more details about what happened during the Divine Ministry of Jesus Christ. For my part, I have said enough on this topic.

Chapter 8
The Immaculate Virgin Conception of the Virgin Mary

Sacred Scripture and the Immaculate Conception

"Jesus responded and said to them, 'Destroy this temple, and in three days I will raise it up.' Then the Jews said, 'This temple has been built up over forty-six years, and you will raise it up in three days?' Yet he was speaking about the Temple of his body." (John 2:19-21).

This conversation between Jesus and some of the Jews occurred at the time of the Passover (Jn 2:13). Jesus was referring to the Temple which is His body. When Jesus said that He would raise up this Temple in three days, He was giving a prophecy of His own death and Resurrection (Jn 2:22).

The Jews did not understand what Jesus meant. They thought He was referring to the temple of Jerusalem. When they told Jesus that "This temple has been built up over forty-six years," they were speaking about the Sanctuary building. But these words of the Jews to Jesus are part of the Gospel of John, and all of Sacred Scripture is God speaking to us. Therefore, God is telling us that it has taken forty-six years to build the Temple of Jesus' body.

Jesus was not anywhere near 46 years old at this time; His Ministry began when He was about 30 years old (Lk 3:23). But God's work in building the Temple of the humanity of Jesus Christ began before His Incarnation and Birth. The Immaculate Conception of the Virgin Mary was the beginning of the building of the humanity of Jesus Christ. At the Immaculate Conception, God began to prepare for the Incarnation of Christ by creating the Virgin Mary and by preserving her free from all sin. God created the humanity of the Virgin Mary first, so that the Temple of the body of Jesus Christ would come from a holy and pure member of humanity. God began to build the Temple of Christ's body by creating the Virgin Mary at her Immaculate Conception.[480]

According to Blessed Anne Catherine, Jesus had this conversation with the Jews at the time of the first Passover of His ministry.[481] The Gospel of John also places this conversation near the beginning of Jesus' ministry (John 2:19-21). Since the ministry of Jesus Christ began in fall of A.D. 15, this was the Passover in spring of A.D. 16, (see chapter 7 for details).

The Virgin Mary must have been about 46 years old, counting her age from her Immaculate Conception, at the time of this Passover in A.D. 16. Sacred Scripture is telling us about the Immaculate Conception by means of the words of the Jews about the Temple, and so the 46 years are the number of years since the Virgin Mary's Immaculate Conception (as well as the number of years since the rebuilding of the Sanctuary buildings). Therefore, the Immaculate Conception occurred about 46 years before the Passover of A.D. 16. Counting back exactly 46 years would bring us to spring of 31 B.C. (Recall that there is no year zero between 1 B.C. and A.D. 1.) However, the 46 years is not necessarily counted as 46 sets of 12 calendar months.

Since the Jews were speaking about the temple buildings, the 46 years must also be counted back to some event regarding the temple buildings themselves. The Temple of

Jerusalem was rebuilt during the reign of king Herod (the Herod who was king at the time of Christ's Birth). However, it did not take 46 years to do the reconstruction work on the temple. According to the ancient Jewish Roman historian Josephus, the rebuilding of the Sanctuary itself took 1½ years, and the rebuilding of the outer enclosures took 8 years.[482] Therefore, the Jews were not referring to the number of years of reconstruction, but to the number of years since the temple was rebuilt.

Even so, some work related to the temple did continue up to and beyond the time of Jesus Christ's Ministry. Josephus counts the rebuilding of the Temple as taking 8 years, but he also places the completion of all the work related to the Temple at a much later date, after the martyrdom of the Apostle James the Lesser.[483] So, after the reconstruction work on the Temple was completed, some work related to the Temple must still have continued for many years afterwards, even to the time of this conversation between the Jews and Jesus.

This verse of Sacred Scripture (Jn 2:20) has a dual meaning; it refers both to the Temple of Jesus' body and to the temple buildings. The wording of this verse can be taken in two ways—that the process of building the Temple has taken 46 years, or that the Temple has stood for 46 years since its rebuilding. Both of these meanings are correct. First, over the course of 46 years something was built, the Temple of Christ's body, and second, it had been 46 years since the Temple Sanctuary had been rebuilt.

This dual meaning is natural when referring to the Temple of Jerusalem, since this Temple (called the Second Temple of Jerusalem) was a symbol and a foreshadowing of the Messiah. The first Temple of Jerusalem, built by Solomon, was also a symbolic representation of the Messiah. That is why Sacred Scripture gives us such a detailed description of the first Temple (2 Chron 3:1 to 5:1, 2 Kings 6)—because it is a symbolic and prophetic description of the Christ. For this reason, it is also fitting that the completion of the rebuilding of the Sanctuary of the Temple coincided with the Immaculate Conception, which laid the foundation for the Sanctuary of Christ's humanity.

The Rebuilding of the Temple

Since the Jews were not counting the 46 years as the time it took to rebuild the temple, but instead were counting the number of years since its rebuilding, the 46 years should be counted from the completion of the reconstruction work on the Temple. Blessed Anne Catherine Emmerich tells us that the Jews, whom Jesus was speaking to after He drove the sellers and money-changers out of the temple, were "a crowd of priests from the Sanhedrin."[484] These Jews must have been speaking about the completion of the work done on the Sanctuary itself, which took 1½ years, not the work on the outer areas, which took 8 years. The work on the Sanctuary itself was done solely by the priests, since none but priests were allowed to enter this holy place.[485] A group of Jewish priests would certainly consider the number of years since the Sanctuary itself was rebuilt to be important. The sacrifices which the priests offered to God took place in this Sanctuary. They would not concern themselves as much with the number of years since the completion of the outer areas of the Temple.

Furthermore, God chose to put these words in Sacred Scripture, counting 46 years since the rebuilding of the Temple. The Sanctuary itself is the holiest part of the entire

Temple, so God counts the 46 years from the completion of the Sanctuary itself, not from the completion of the work done on the outer areas. Similarly, if a church parish today were rebuilt and rededicated to God, the dedication ceremony would take place when the work on the Sanctuary was completed. The parish would not wait for work on other parish buildings to be completed before dedicating God's holy Sanctuary.

Since it did not take 46 years to rebuild the Temple of Jerusalem, the Jews were not saying that the Temple required 46 years of work to be ready to use. Instead, they were saying that, after the Temple Sanctuary had been rebuilt and rededicated to God, the Temple was in use for 46 years. The temple of Jerusalem was being spiritually rebuilt by prayer and sacrifice for the 46 years of its use since the physical reconstruction of the Temple Sanctuary was completed. Thus, the period of 46 years is to be counted from the completion of the work on the Temple Sanctuary.

According to Josephus, the rebuilding of the Temple Sanctuary took 1½ years and there was a great festival upon its completion. This festival also coincided with the anniversary of the day of the inauguration of Herod as king over the Jews.[486] Herod gained his kingship over the Jews through a war which ended on the Fast Day, that is, the Day of Atonement on Tishri 10.[487] (The month of Tishri occurs in early fall, in Sept./Oct.) His inauguration ceremony must have taken place not too soon and not too long after the war was won. Herod would not have tolerated a hastily thrown together inauguration ceremony, for he was vain and self-important. Nor would he, for much the same reason, have waited too long before holding a ceremony to declare his kingship. Thus the inauguration of king Herod likely occurred while it was still the fall season, within several weeks of Tishri 10. This reasoning places the festival at the completion of the rebuilding of the temple also in the fall, since the anniversary of the inauguration ceremony coincided with this festival.

Since the work on the Temple Sanctuary was completed in the fall, the work must have begun in springtime, a year and a half earlier. And it stands to reason that spring would be the most likely time for this rebuilding work to begin. The best time to begin a major building project is when the best weather begins, in spring, not in fall or winter. This also means that the 46 years is to be counted from the fall of one year (when the work was completed) to the spring of another year (when Jesus spoke to the Jews at Passover, in the spring). The exact length of time (by our modern way of counting) would then be either 46½ years (from fall of 32 B.C. to spring of A.D. 16) or 45½ years (from fall of 31 B.C. to spring of A.D. 16).

Blessed Anne Catherine Emmerich states, based on her visions from God, that "just seventeen years before the Birth of Christ, Herod ordered that work should be done in the Temple."[488] Since Christ was born in 15 B.C., the beginning of this work would then be in 32 B.C. So then, the work on the Temple Sanctuary was completed 1½ years later, in fall of 31 B.C., which is 45½ years before the Passover of A.D. 16.

The chronology of Herod's reign, as detailed in chapter 12 of this book, indicates that the reconstruction work on the Temple began in 11th year of Herod's reign and was completed in the 18th year of his reign. Herod captured Jerusalem in autumn of 43 B.C., so that 42 B.C. was the first calendar year of his reign. For this reason, 32 B.C. must have been the 11th year of Herod's reign, and 25 B.C. was the 18th year of his reign. So, the work on the Temple began in spring of 32 B.C.; the Sanctuary itself was completed 1½ years later in autumn of 31 B.C.; and the outer enclosures were completed sometime in 25 B.C.

Since the Immaculate Conception of the Virgin Mary coincided with the completion of the rebuilding of the Temple Sanctuary (Jn 2:20-22), the Immaculate Conception must also have occurred in fall of 31 B.C. At the time of the first Passover of Jesus Christ's ministry then, the Virgin Mary was in her 46th year of life since conception, (and it had been about 45½ years since the Immaculate Conception). She was about one half year away from completing 46 years of age from conception and a few months away from completing 45 years of age from birth. The Temple of Jerusalem is a symbol and foreshadowing of the Messiah, therefore it was fitting for the Immaculate Conception, which prepared the way for the Christ, to correspond with the physical and spiritual renewal of the Temple of Jerusalem.

In my booklet, *the Virginity of Jesus and Mary*, I state that the Immaculate Conception of the Virgin Mary occurred "at the time of the beginning of the rebuilding of the Second Temple of Jerusalem."[489] These words are correct because Sacred Scripture counts the beginning of the rebuilding of the Temple from the completion of the physical work on the Sanctuary itself, when the spiritual rebuilding of the Temple began anew: " 'It has taken forty-six years to build this temple' " (Jn 2:20). However, let the reader understand that, as concerns the rebuilding of the physical structure of the Temple, the Immaculate Conception began at the completion of the rebuilding of the holy Sanctuary of the Temple of Jerusalem.

The Count of the 46 Years

The Jews were counting the age of the Temple as 46 years since the completion of the work on the Sanctuary, because that is were the holy sacrifices took place. Their words mean that the Temple had been rebuilt since 46 years ago, and that the Temple was continually being spiritually rebuilt by all of the prayers and sacrifices in the Sanctuary of the Temple since that time.

The length of time since the Immaculate Conception was not exactly 46 years (i.e. not 12 months times 46, as one might count today), but was 46 years as the Jews counted the years. Jesus was speaking to the Jews about the Temple on the occasion of the 46th Passover since the completion of the rebuilding of the Sanctuary itself. That is why the Jews counted the length of time as 46 years; they were speaking to Jesus during the Passover.

From fall of 31 B.C. to spring of A.D. 16 is 45½ years, yet the Jews speaking to Jesus gave the time as a whole number, 46 years (John 2:20). The Sanctuary itself was, at that time, in its 46th year since the rebuilding was completed. One could argue that the Jews were herein counting a partial year as a full year, as was their custom.[490] In other words, the rebuilding of the Temple began during the middle of a certain year (the sacred calendar year beginning with Nisan in 31 B.C.), and that partial year was counted as year 1 of the 46 years. The Jewish calendar year beginning with Nisan of A.D. 16 (when this conversation about the Temple occurred), would not be counted because it had just begun.

But I conclude that the Jews were counting the number of Passovers since the Temple Sanctuary had been rebuilt. There were 46 Passovers between fall of 31 B.C. and spring of A.D. 16, including the Passover of A.D. 16 when this conversation occurred. Since the new year of the sacred calendar begins with the month of Nisan (Ex 12:2), and the Temple Sanctuary is sacred, they must have been keeping track of the number of years by the sacred calendar. They would then have counted either the number of Passovers, or the number of Nisan 1 dates, which had passed since the rebuilding of the Temple itself was completed.[491] Because the Passover is of much greater importance in the Jewish religious calendar than the first day of Nisan, (and easier to mark in one's memory), they simply counted the number of Passovers since an important event, like the rebuilding of the temple, rather than counting the number of Nisan 1 dates which had passed. In this way, the Jews counted the 46 years with each Passover marking the completion of a year, and with the first partial year, in effect counting as a full year. (See chapter 6 for a similar example in the counting of Christ's age in Sacred Scripture.)

Notice also that the length of time, 46 years, is given to us in Sacred Scripture without the word "about" and without any words to indicate that this was an approximate length of time. Since Sacred Scripture is entirely true, accurate, and without error, the time of the Passover must have been counted as 46 years exactly, not 45½ years, nor as some other approximation. If the years were counted by the number of Passovers, then the first Passover of Christ's Ministry was exactly the 46th year, because it was exactly the 46th Passover.

The Festival at the Completion of the Temple

Blessed Anne Catherine Emmerich describes the events surrounding the Immaculate Conception of the Virgin Mary. Saint Joachim and Saint Ann, the Virgin Mary's parents, had been apart for several months. They did not meet again until the end of a feast in Jerusalem.[492] Joachim and Ann met in a passageway under the Temple of Jerusalem. They held one another in a holy and chaste embrace. "Both Joachim and Anne were in a supernatural state. I learned that, at the moment in which they embraced and the light shone around them, the Immaculate Conception of Mary was accomplished."[493] Blessed Anne Catherine is saying here, and I also say, that the Virgin Mary was conceived of both Saint Joachim and Saint Ann, in a miraculous and virginal manner, solely by a miracle of God and not in the usual way, in a passageway under the temple.[494] For more details on this point of theology, see my booklet, *the Virginity of Jesus and Mary.*[495]

"I saw that because of the feast the whole Temple was open and decorated with garlands of fruit and greenery...."[496] Blessed Anne Catherine tells us that the Immaculate Conception occurred at the end of a religious feast involving the Temple of Jerusalem. At one time, she said that this was the Feast of Tabernacles.[497] But on another occasion she thought it was the Feast of the Dedication of the Temple (Hanukkah).[498] In her visions from God, Blessed Anne Catherine saw the Immaculate Conception of the Virgin Mary occurring sometime in the autumn, and earlier than December 8 (the day of the celebration in the Church's liturgical calendar).[499] But she does not give the exact day or month for the Immaculate Conception. She does state that the Immaculate Conception occurred in Jerusalem, in a passageway under the temple, at the end of a some type of religious festival related to the Temple of Jerusalem.[500]

The Feast of Tabernacles generally ends no later than the end of October (and then only when Passover begins at its latest, in late April). In the year 31 B.C., the Feast of

Tabernacles (Tishri 15-22) fell in early October (Oct. 4-11).[501] The Immaculate Conception could not have occurred at the end of the Feast of Tabernacles, in mid October, as this is too early to account for an August 5 birthday for the Virgin Mary. The length of time from Oct. 11 to Aug. 5 is 298 days, which is closer to 10 months, than to 9. Also, 90% of all births today take place 266 days from conception, plus or minus two weeks. The time period of 298 days is more than four weeks (32 days) beyond 266 days. Therefore the Virgin Mary was not conceived at the end of the Feast of Tabernacles.

On the other hand, the feast of the Dedication of the Temple (Hanukkah) begins on Kislev 25, and occurs no earlier than the last week in November. However, in 31 B.C., the feast of Hanukkah began on Dec. 12 and ended Dec. 19.[502] Blessed Anne Catherine does describe the Immaculate Conception as taking place at the end of a celebration at the Temple in Jerusalem. But this celebration could not have been the feast of Hanukkah, because Hanukkah occurs too late in the year to fit the date of August 5 for the Virgin Mary's birthday. There are less than 8 months (229 days) from Dec. 19 and August 5. This time period is over four weeks (37 days) less than 266 days. Therefore the Virgin Mary was not conceived at the end of Hanukkah.

Now Sacred Scripture indicates that the Immaculate Conception coincided with the completion of the rebuilding of the Temple. And the ancient historian Josephus describes a great festival which occurred at that time.[503] This festival in honor of the completion of the rebuilding of the Sanctuary of the Temple was certainly a type of dedication of the Temple. This feast was a very special rededication of the Temple to God after its rebuilding.

According to Josephus, the festival at the completion of the rebuilding of the Sanctuary of the Temple coincided with the anniversary of Herod's inauguration as king. As shown in chapter 12, Herod captured Jerusalem on the Fast Day (Yom Kippur; Tishri 10) in 43 B.C. In that year, the Passover began relatively early, on March 24 (Nisan 14), resulting in a relatively early date for the Fast Day, Sept. 13.[504] The Feast of Tabernacles (Tishri 15-22) began only 5 days after the day that Herod captured Jerusalem (Tishri 10). This was too soon after the capture of Jerusalem for Herod to organize an acceptable inauguration ceremony. Also, there were probably some number of additional days needed, after the city was captured, to secure the city militarily. On the other hand, the Feast of the Dedication of the Temple on Kislev 25 fell on November 26 that year. That date is more than two months after the capture of Jerusalem and is too late a date for Herod's inauguration.

The most probable time frame for the inauguration ceremony is the month of Heshvan. This time frame is long enough after the capture of Jerusalem for Herod to have secured his capture of the city, and have taken the time needed to prepare a ceremony fit for a king. It is also not too long after the capture of the city. Herod would not have tolerated too much delay before the ceremony which declared his kingship.

For the above reasons, the feast which Blessed Anne Catherine described was neither the Feast of Tabernacles, nor the dedication feast on Kislev 25 (Hanukkah), but rather some other feast associated with the Temple and occurring between those two dates. That very time frame coincides with the time of the completion of the rebuilding of the Second Temple of Jerusalem, a time when the Temple was rededicated to God. It is fitting that the Immaculate Conception of the Virgin Mary should occur at the time of that singular Feast for the dedication of the Temple Sanctuary, because both were singular, joyful, and holy events. And the Temple itself is a symbol and foreshadowing of the Messiah, Who came into the world through the Virgin Mary.

"But the temple itself was built by the priests in a year and six months,—upon which all the people were full of joy.... They feasted and celebrated this rebuilding of the temple: and for the king, he sacrificed three hundred oxen to God; as did the rest, everyone according to his ability: the number of which sacrifices it is not possible to set down...."[505]

Josephus here describes the feast at the completion of the rebuilding of the Temple Sanctuary, (he calls the Sanctuary portion of the Temple, "the temple itself"). This feast may have been mistaken by Blessed Anne Catherine for the Feast of Tabernacles, since both were a celebration at the Temple of Jerusalem, with many sacrifices offered to God. They both also occurred about the same time of year; the Feast of Tabernacles occurs in early fall, from Tishri 15 to 22. And this feast at the completion of the Temple rebuilding coincided with the anniversary of the king's inauguration, which also occurred in the fall. (For further details on the chronology of the Temple of Jerusalem, see chapter 12.)

The Age of the Virgin Mary

Another way to determine the year of the Immaculate Conception is to first determine the age of the Virgin Mary at Christ's Incarnation or at His Birth. Blessed Anne Catherine said that "the Blessed Virgin had reached the age of fourteen," when she was dismissed from her years of service as one of the temple virgins at Jerusalem. Blessed Anne Catherine counts the ages of Jesus and Mary from birth, so Mary had passed her 14th birthday at the time she was dismissed from the temple. Soon after leaving the temple, in late January, Mary was betrothed to Joseph.[506] And about a month later, the Incarnation of Jesus Christ occurred, on February 25.

After describing the Incarnation, Blessed Anne Catherine tells us the Virgin Mary's age. "Mary was at this time a little over fourteen years old."[507] Mary must have been born in 30 B.C., for then she would complete her first year from birth in 29 B.C. and her 14th year from birth in 16 B.C. She would then still be 14 years old early in 15 B.C., when the Incarnation occurred (Feb. 25). Therefore, the Virgin Mary was born in 30 B.C., and was conceived about nine months earlier in 31 B.C.

At the Holy Birth of Jesus Christ, the Virgin Mary was just over 15 years old, counting her age from birth. The Virgin Mary's age ought to be counted from her Immaculate Conception, though, for this was the beginning of her life. So, at the Virgin Birth of Jesus Christ, the Virgin Mary had completed just over 16 years of life since her Immaculate Conception. And, at the Virgin Conception of Jesus Christ, the Virgin Mary had completed over 15 years of life since her Immaculate Conception.

In another place, when speaking about the Birth of Christ, Blessed Anne Catherine says that the Virgin Mary was conceived 15 years before the Birth of Christ.[508] But if Mary was conceived 15 years before Christ's Birth, then she would have been born just over 14 years before Christ's birth, and she would have been about 13 years old at the Incarnation of Christ. Blessed Anne Catherine here contradicts what she herself said at another time, that Mary was just over 14 years old at the Incarnation. She tells us, in discussing the star of Jacob, that the three wise men had first seen this indication of the future Birth of Christ, 15 years before Christ was born. When speaking about the star, she then mentions that the Immaculate Conception of the Virgin Mary occurred at that time, 15 years earlier than Christ's birth. This must be a slight confusion on her part. She usually gives dates and ages in the lives of Jesus and Mary counting from birth. So, she may have inadvertently given the number of years from Mary's Birth to Christ's Birth, or Mary's Immaculate Conception to Christ's Holy Conception (in either case, about 15 years), when she was speaking about the number of years from Mary's Immaculate Conception to Christ's Birth (about 16 years).

The Month and Day of the Immaculate Conception

The Church currently celebrates the Immaculate Conception on Dec. 8 and the Virgin Mary's birthday on Sept. 8. The celebration of Mary's Birth, in the liturgical calendar, is placed 9 months after the celebration of the Immaculate Conception. The Virgin Mary revealed at Medjugorje that her true birthday is August 5.[509] So, if she was conceived about nine months before her true birthday on August 5 (see chapter 9), then the Immaculate Conception occurred sometime in early November, not in December. (Blessed Anne Catherine did say that the Virgin Mary was born a number of days short of nine full months,[510] but this would still place the Immaculate Conception sometime in November.)

According to Josephus, the celebration of the completion of the work on the Temple Sanctuary coincided with the anniversary of king Herod's inauguration as king over Jerusalem: "...for at the same time with this celebration for the work about the temple, fell also the day of the king's inauguration, which he kept of an old custom as a festival, and it now coincided with the other; which coincidence of them both made the festival most illustrious."[511]

Josephus also states that Herod completed his capture of Jerusalem on the Fast Day, that is, the Day of Atonement, on Tishri 10.[512] Herod's initial inauguration as king over the Jews must have been held sometime after the capture of Jerusalem, in the autumn. There may have been some additional time required to finish any minor skirmishes on the battlefield and complete Herod's conquest of the area before his inauguration ceremony. Some length of time would then be needed to prepare for the inauguration of Herod so soon after a war had ended. And this ceremony would have been fairly elaborate, since Herod was vain and liked to exalt himself. Thus, his inauguration would not likely have occurred as early as the Feast of Tabernacles (Tishri 15-22), five days after the capture of Jerusalem, but could have occurred a month later, during the Jewish month of Heshvan. The month of Heshvan contains no major Jewish religious celebration that would conflict with a yearly celebration of the king's inauguration. And so, Heshvan, which generally falls in November, is a plausible time frame for Herod's inauguration ceremony.

The celebration of the completion of the rebuilding of the Temple Sanctuary coincided with the annual celebration of the king's inauguration ceremony, and so most likely fell in Heshvan, about a month after the Feast of Tabernacles and more than a month before Hanukkah. In the year 31 B.C., Heshvan began on Oct. 19 and ended on Nov. 17.[513] But at what time of the month would a Jewish feast in celebration of the rebuilding of the Temple Sanctuary be held?

In the Jewish religious calendar, celebrations such as the Feast of Tabernacles and the Feast of Passover begin on the 15th of the Jewish month. Passover lasts for 7 days, until the 21st of the month, and the Feast of Tabernacles lasts for 8 days, until the 22nd of the month (Ex 12; Lev 23). The Jews in ancient times kept track of the days by observing the phases of the moon. The new moon is the beginning of the month, and the full moon falls in the middle of the month, about the 15th. The Jewish calendar wisely begins major celebrations on the 15th because this date is clear to everyone by observation of the full moon. So, for example, if someone was traveling a long distance to Jerusalem for a religious feast, they would be able to tell by watching the phases of the moon approximately how soon the feast would begin. For this reason, the feast celebrating the completion of the rebuilding of the Temple Sanctuary most likely began about the time of the full moon, on the 15th of the month in the Jewish calendar. Therefore, Heshvan 15 is the most likely date for the start of this feast at the completion of the rebuilding of the Sanctuary.

Important celebrations in the Jewish faith usually lasted for 7 or 8 days, (e.g. the Feast of Tabernacles, Passover, Hanukkah). People traveled from all over Israel to attend important celebrations in Jerusalem. Since the journey to the feast might take several days to a week (one way), it made sense to have the celebration last about a week. The same reasoning applies to betrothal (wedding) ceremonies, such as the wedding of Tobias: "And for seven days they feasted, and all were rejoicing with great joy." (Tobit 11:19). And, according to Blessed Anne Catherine, Joseph and Mary's betrothal ceremony "lasted for seven or eight days."[514] Therefore, a celebration as important as the rededication of the Temple Sanctuary must have lasted for 7 or 8 days.

In 31 B.C., Heshvan 15 coincided with Nov. 2, a Saturday.[515] So, the last day of the rededication festival would then have been Friday, Nov. 8 (for a 7 day festival), or Saturday, Nov. 9 (for an 8 day festival). Blessed Anne Catherine indicates that Saints Joachim and Ann met in the passageway under the Temple at the end of the feast, which would then have been either Friday, Nov. 8, or Saturday, Nov. 9.[516] When Joachim and Anne met at the very foundation of the Temple of Jerusalem, the Immaculate Virgin Conception of the Virgin Mary was accomplished by a miracle of God.

Before Saint Joachim met Saint Ann under the Temple, he offered a sacrifice to the priests of the Temple (two lambs and three young goats). Joachim then was taken by a priest to the altar of incense (the same place where Zechariah met the angel), and left there alone.[517] "He remained shut up in the Temple all night, praying with great and ardent desires."[518] Afterwards, some priests led Saint Joachim to the entrance of the passageway under the temple, where he met his wife, Saint Ann. Since Joachim was in prayer all night, they probably met in that passageway sometime in the morning. Therefore, the Immaculate Conception occurred in the morning, on either Friday, Nov. 8, or Saturday, Nov. 9, in the year 31 B.C.

Afterwards, Joachim and Ann were led by priests to the Temple above, which was open and decorated still. "Divine service was performed under the open sky."[519] Next, Joachim and Ann visited at a priest's house in Jerusalem, and then began the journey back to Nazareth. The day of the Immaculate Conception must also have been the last day of the festival, because Joachim and Ann left for home soon afterwards, on the same day.

If the Divine service, which Joachim and Ann attended after the Immaculate Conception, was a Sabbath service, then this last day of the festival was a Saturday. Joachim and Ann, being devout Jews would not have traveled on the Sabbath. They may have visited at the priest's house in Jerusalem until the close of the Sabbath, at sunset, and then begun their journey home. Similarly, Blessed Anne Catherine describes Saint Joseph and the Virgin Mary's journey to Bethlehem as beginning in the evening also.[520] This line of reasoning places the Immaculate Conception on the morning of Saturday, Nov. 9.

On the other hand, if Joachim and Ann met early on the morning of Friday, Nov. 8, they could have begun their journey back to Nazareth before the Sabbath began at sunset. After attending a religious service and visiting at the priest's house, they may still have had sufficient time left in the day to travel for several hours before the Sabbath began. In this case, the festival would have been 7 days long, instead of 8 days, and the Divine service mentioned by Blessed Anne Catherine would be a service on the last day of the feast, not the Sabbath service. Either of these scenarios is plausible.

According to Blessed Anne Catherine, the Holy Conception and Birth of Jesus Christ are each celebrated by the Church on the correct day of the month (the 25th), but one month later, than the date the actual events occurred. She places the Incarnation on Feb. 25, instead of the liturgical calendar's date of March 25, and she places Christ's Birth on Nov. 25, instead of Dec. 25. The Church celebrates the Immaculate Conception on the 8th day of December, yet, according to the argument presented above, the Immaculate Conception occurred in early November. Perhaps the correct date for the Immaculate Conception is also on the same day of the month, but one month earlier, as was the case with Christ's Holy Conception and Birth. Furthermore, the date of the Virgin Mary's entrance into the Temple of Jerusalem, as one of the Temple virgins, was also Nov. 8 (see chapter 9). For these reasons, I hold that the Immaculate Conception occurred on Nov. 8, not Nov. 9.

The Immaculate Virgin Conception of the Blessed Virgin Mary occurred on the morning of November 8 of 31 B.C. at the end of the singular and holy feast celebrating the completion of the rebuilding of the Temple Sanctuary. The very first entrance of the Virgin Mary into the Temple of Jerusalem occurred at her Immaculate Conception, in a passageway under the consecrated part of the Temple. At her Immaculate Conception, the Virgin Mary entered into existence, entered into the unfailing Grace of God, entered into the human race, and entered into the Temple of Jerusalem, a symbol and foreshadowing of the Messiah, all in the same instant. And who on earth at that time understood this great event? It went mostly unnoticed.

Chapter 9
The Virgin Birth of the Virgin Mary

The Virgin Mary's Real Birthday

"Do you know my real birthday is August fifth?"[521]

The Virgin Mary has appeared and spoken many times to the visionaries of Medjugorje. On one occasion she told them that her real birthday is August 5th. By this, she meant that she was actually born on August 5, even though the Church currently celebrates her birthday on September 8. At Medjugorje, the Virgin Mary also asked Christians to celebrate her birthday on August 5, and to fast for three days at that time.[522] It doesn't take a long and complex argument to determine the month and day of the Virgin Mary's birthday. I believe her own words, given at Medjugorje; Mary was born August 5.

Why does the Church currently celebrate the Virgin Mary's birthday on September 8? The Sept. 8 celebration of Mary's birthday is placed 9 months after our celebration of her Immaculate Conception, in the current liturgical calendar. And the celebration of her Immaculate Conception, on Dec. 8, is the correct number of days from our celebration of Jesus' Birth, on Dec. 25. The current liturgical calendar places these holy days about the correct number of days apart from one another, but also about 1 month earlier than the events actually occurred.

Why are the dates in the liturgical calendar off from the true dates by about a month? Blessed Anne Catherine explains the answer this way: "The reason why the Church keeps the feast exactly a month later than the actual event is because at one time, when an alteration in the calendar was made, some days and seasons were completely omitted."[523] Here she refers to the Birth of Christ, but she plainly states that other events, such as the Incarnation, also occurred one month earlier than their celebration in the liturgical calendar.[524]

On which three days should Christians fast at the time of the Virgin Mary's birthday? At Lent, we fast to prepare our souls for the celebration of Christ's Resurrection on Easter Sunday. We also fast on Good Friday in union with the sufferings of Christ on the Cross. We should fast before the Virgin Mary's birthday, so as to prepare our souls by self-denial for that holy celebration. We should also fast on the day of the Virgin Mary's birthday, because self-sacrifice is a holy offering presented to God through the Virgin Mary. The three days of fasting does not include the day after the Virgin's birthday, because that day is the Feast of the Transfiguration of the Lord in the Church's liturgical calendar. Therefore, the three days of fasting for the Virgin Mary's birthday should be August 3, 4, and 5.

August 5 is also the day celebrating the dedication of a basilica in Rome, Saint Mary Major Basilica (also called Santa Maria Maggiore or Great St. Mary's). This basilica was founded in the fourth century, and restored in the fifth century, at which time it was consecrated to the Blessed Virgin Mary.[525] By the Providence of God and the guidance of God's Grace within the Church, the day given to us to celebrate the Virgin Mary's basilica in Rome is also the day on which the Virgin Mary was born, August 5. In this way, God brings the faithful to reflect upon the Virgin Mary on the true date of her birth.

The Year of Mary's Birth

At Medjugorje, the Virgin Mary has appeared and spoken to six visionaries. The Virgin Mary told one of them, Ivan Dragicevic, that her 2000th birthday would occur on August 5 of 1984.[526] This day was celebrated with much joy, fasting, and conversion.[527] Does this mean that we can find the year of Mary's birth by counting back 2000 years (inclusive) from 1984? No, the Virgin Mary was referring to the current liturgical calendar when she said that 1984 was her 2000th birthday. In the same way, when Christians talk about the year 2000 as the 2000th anniversary of the Birth of Jesus Christ, they do not necessarily think that Jesus was born in 1 B.C.—it is the 2000th anniversary according to the liturgical calendar.

The number system used for the years in the current Christian liturgical calendar was devised in the sixth century by an abbot named Dionysius Exiguus. He was a theologian with additional expertise in astronomy and mathematics. The Pope asked Dionysius to determine the dates for Easter for the coming years. But when Dionysius had determined those dates, he did not want to write the number of the years using the usual system of his day—counting the number of years since the reign of the emperor Diocletian—because that Roman emperor persecuted and killed many faithful Christians. So, he decided that the years should be numbered according to the years since the Incarnation of Jesus Christ: "ab incarnatione Domini" (from the Incarnation of the Lord).[528]

Dionysius began the count of the years with the first calendar year after the Incarnation and Birth of Christ; this became A.D. 1. He believed that the Incarnation and Birth of Jesus Christ occurred in the previous year, now called 1 B.C. This system places the first anniversary of Christ's Incarnation in the year A.D. 1. That same year, A.D. 1, would then contain both the first anniversary of the Incarnation and the first anniversary of the Birth of Christ. If Dionysius chose correctly, then the years of the Christian calendar would match the years of Christ's life. In such a case, A.D. 1 would be the year in which Christ completed one year of life from His Incarnation and A.D. 2000 would be the year that Christ completed 2000 years from His Incarnation. However, scholars today do not generally believe that Dionysius chose the correct year for the Incarnation of Jesus Christ.

So, when the Virgin Mary spoke about her 2000th birthday, she was referring only to the date in the liturgical calendar, not to the actual date. The Virgin Mary knows that the year A.D. 2000 is not the actual 2000th anniversary of the Birth of Jesus Christ, but she spoke according to the liturgical calendar currently in use. In a similar way, the Church celebrates the Birth of Jesus Christ on Dec. 25 in the liturgical calendar, even though the Church does not teach that Jesus was born on Dec. 25. In asking Christians to celebrate her 2000th birthday in 1984, the Virgin Mary was not, in effect, telling us the actual year of her birth. However, she does in this way reveal that the year of her actual birth was a certain number of years before the birth of her Divine Son Jesus Christ.

Now the first anniversary of someone's birth is the year after they were born. But we should count the actual day of someone's birth as their first birthday because it is their birthday in the fullest sense of the word—the day of their birth. Counting this way (including the day of one's birth), Christ's first birthday in the liturgical calendar would be 1 B.C., then His second birthday would occur in A.D. 1. Thus, A.D. 1999 would be Christ's 2000th birthday, inclusive, according to the current liturgical calendar; and A.D.

2000 would be the 2000th **anniversary** of Christ's Birth. In the same way, 1984 would be Mary's 2000th birthday, counting the actual day of her birth as her first birthday, but only within the current liturgical calendar system.

Why would the Virgin Mary speak about her 2000th birthday as including the day of her birth, rather than using the more familiar way of counting birthdays starting with the first anniversary of her birth? First, the day of Mary's birth was a very holy and special day. We should not leave that day out of our count of the number of the Holy Virgin's birthdays. Second, we are told that the Virgin Mary said 1984 was her "2000th birthday," not the "2000th anniversary" of her birth.[529] Third, the Virgin Mary was conceived in the calendar year before the year of her birth. She was conceived in November and so was born in the following calendar year (in August). As a result, the year of the Virgin Mary's 2000th birthday (inclusive) is also the year of the 2000th **anniversary** of her Immaculate Conception. That same year contains those two important events, so the Virgin Mary pointed out that year, rather than the year of the 2000th anniversary of her birth, as deserving special devotion.

Using the current liturgical calendar, the Virgin Mary placed her 2000th birthday in 1984, which is 15 years before Christ's 2000th birthday in 1999, (counting inclusively). Therefore, the actual year of the Virgin Mary's birth occurred 15 years before the actual year of Christ's Birth. Since Christ was born in 15 B.C., the Virgin Mary must have been born in 30 B.C. Therefore, the Virgin Mary was born on August 5 of 30 B.C.

The Blessed Virgin Mary also revealed at Medjugorje that a large cross, which was built on a hilltop in Medjugorje in 1933, was to commemorate the 1900th anniversary of the Crucifixion of Jesus Christ. If Christ was crucified in A.D. 33, the 1900th anniversary would be in A.D. 1933, the year the large cross was built at Medjugorje. However, the Virgin Mary did not say that Christ was crucified in A.D. 33. She said that A.D. 1933 was the 1900th anniversary of the Crucifixion because she was speaking in terms of the current liturgical calendar.

Again, these words of the Virgin Mary about the anniversary of the Crucifixion do not directly reveal the date of the Crucifixion. However, she does, by these same words, reveal the length of the life of her Divine Son Jesus. Mary was speaking in terms of the current calendar, which was set up so that A.D. 1 would be the year that Christ completed one year of life from His Incarnation, and A.D. 33 would be the year that Christ completed 33 years of life from His Incarnation. Therefore, speaking in terms of that calendar system, if Christ died in A.D. 33, then He would have completed just over 33 years of life from His Holy Conception to His Crucifixion. The visions given to Blessed Anne Catherine Emmerich also indicate that Jesus was just over 33 years old, counting from the Incarnation, when He was crucified.

The Time of Mary's Birth

According to Blessed Anne Catherine, the Virgin Mary was born about midnight. "Anna did not go to bed, but prayed, and at midnight woke the other women to pray with her."[530] Saint Ann and the other women prayed, and during their prayers, the Virgin Mary was born by a miracle of God. Blessed Anne Catherine clearly describes the birth of the Virgin Mary as both miraculous and virginal, and clearly not the usual manner of birth. (The theology of the Virgin Birth of Mary is described in greater detail in my booklet, *the Virginity of Jesus and Mary*.)[531] The Virgin Mary's birth occurred at the same hour as the Birth of Jesus Christ, at about midnight, which is the beginning of the day according to the Christian calendar.

Notice that the time of Mary's birth (midnight) and the time of her death (3 p.m.; see chapter 10), as well as the time of her Resurrection (before dawn; see chapter 10), are the same as the time of day for these events in the life of her Divine Son Jesus Christ. Mary's life is a reflection of the life of Jesus Christ, even to the extent that some of the important events of her life happened at the same time of day as with her Son Jesus. In God's plan, the life of the Virgin Mary is a perfect imitation of the life of Jesus Christ.

The Day of the Week

The Virgin Mary was born on a Tuesday. This may surprise some people who expect that important events in Jesus and Mary's lives most likely occurred on Christian or Jewish Sabbaths. But the month and day of the Virgin Mary's birth is quite certain, since she said so herself at Medjugorje. And the year, 30 B.C., is clear from the arguments presented in this book about the rebuilding of the Temple and the year of Christ's Birth. In 30 B.C., August 5 was a Tuesday.[532]

Further support for Tuesday as the day of the Virgin Mary's birth is found in Blessed Anne Catherine's descriptions of the events surrounding that day. She mentions that Joachim and his servants went out to work in the fields the day before.[533] That day could not have been a Sabbath, because devout Jews did not work on the Sabbath. And there is no mention of a refrain from work, or of particular Jewish religious celebrations, in her description of the three days after the Virgin Mary's birth. Also, many people are said to have traveled to visit the new-born Virgin Mary in the 3 days after her birth, with no mention of a cessation of travel for the Sabbath. There is also no indication in Blessed Anne Catherine's words that the day of Mary's birth was a Jewish Sabbath. If the day before, the three days after, and the day of the Virgin Mary's birth were not a Sabbath (Saturday), then she must have been born on either a Monday or a Tuesday. August 5 of 30 B.C. was a Tuesday.[534]

In 30 B.C., August 5 coincided with the Jewish date of Av 26.[535] The fifth month of the Jewish sacred calendar is called Av. (The first month of the sacred calendar is Nisan, the month containing Passover.)

The Virgin Mary's Naming Day

Sacred Scripture describes the day on which John the Baptist was given his name:

"Now the time for Elizabeth to give birth arrived, and she brought forth a son. And her neighbors and relatives heard that the Lord had magnified his mercy with her, and so they congratulated her. And it happened that, on the eighth day, they arrived to circumcise the boy, and they called him by his father's name, Zechariah. And in response, his mother said: 'Not so. Instead, he shall be called John.' And they said to her, 'But there is no one among your relatives who is called by that name.' Then they made signs to his father, as to what he wanted him to be called. And requesting a writing tablet, he wrote, saying: 'His name is John.' And they all wondered. Then, at once, his mouth was opened, and his tongue loosened, and he spoke, blessing God." (Lk 1:57-64).

Notice, in this passage from Sacred Scripture, that the child of Zechariah and Elizabeth was given the name John on the day of his circumcision. Zechariah and Elizabeth knew that they would have a child and would name him John, even before John was conceived, for an angel had revealed this to them (Lk 1:13). Yet they waited until the day of his circumcision to name him.

"And after eight days were ended, so that the boy would be circumcised, his name was called JESUS, just as he was called by the Angel before he was conceived in the womb." (Lk 2:21).

Here again, the name of Jesus was not formally given to the Christ-child until the eighth day, the day of the circumcision. Even though the angel had revealed His name before He was conceived (Lk 1:31), the Jewish custom was to formally give a male child their name on the eighth day. This custom is clearly seen in both the births of John the Baptist and Jesus the Christ.

In Leviticus 12, Jewish custom concerning newborn children is described. When a woman gives birth to a son, she is unclean for seven days, then on the eighth day the child is circumcised. The custom to formally name the child on this day is not mentioned here, but is made clear in the above quoted passages from Luke's Gospel. Then 33 days later "the days of her purification are completed" and the child's mother is now able to enter the sanctuary of the temple on the 40th day (Lev 12:1-4). Note the division of the 40 days into the first 7 days, followed by the remaining 33 days. The child's naming occurs after the first 7 days, after the time when the mother is considered unclean, and on the first of the 33 days, the time of the mother's purifying. The ceremony for the naming and circumcision of a male child occurs on the first day that the mother is considered clean.

"But if she will bear a female, she shall be unclean for two weeks, according to the custom of her monthly flow, and she shall remain in the blood of her purification for sixty-six days." (Lev 12:5).

The custom for naming a female child was different, as can be inferred from this passage of Sacred Scripture. The time from the birth of a daughter to the end of the time of purifying is 80 days, twice the time for a son.[536] As with a son, the time after the birth of a daughter is also broken into two time periods, a time when the mother is unclean and a time for her purifying. A son would be named at his circumcision, but there is no circumcision for the daughter. However, the custom for naming a male child was to do so after the time when the mother was considered unclean, on the first of the days for her purifying. For the male child this coincides with the circumcision on the eighth day. For the female child, the mother is considered unclean for two weeks instead of one, so that the corresponding day for the daughter, the first day of the mother's purifying, would be the 15th day. (Visitors would not have been allowed to come near a Jewish mother for the first 14 days, when she was considered unclean, so the ceremony could not occur until the 15th day.) Therefore, if the custom of naming the child on the mother's first day of purifying was followed for both sons and daughters, then daughters were first formally given their names on the 15th day from birth.

The words of Blessed Anne Catherine confirm that the ancient Jewish custom was to name daughters on the 15th day from their birth. She saw visions of various events in the lives of Jesus and Mary, sometimes on the actual month and day of the event, sometimes on the day of the celebration in the liturgical calendar, and sometimes on both days. So, for example, she received visions of the Birth of Jesus Christ on both November 25 (the actual day) and December 25 (the liturgical celebration).[537] She saw visions pertaining to the birth of the Virgin Mary, on September 8, the day of the liturgical celebration of Mary's birth. And on Sept. 22 – 23, she saw visions of the Virgin Mary's naming ceremony.[538] September 22 is the 15th day counting inclusively from September 8.

Blessed Anne Catherine also said that, on the day of the Virgin Mary's birth, she heard angels announcing that on the 20th day the child would be given the name Mary.

"They announced the child's name, singing: 'On the twentieth day, this child shall be called Mary.' Then they sang *Gloria* and *Alleluia*. I heard all these words."[539]

But the Jewish custom was to formally give a name to a daughter on the 15th day from her birth, as is indicated in Sacred Scripture, and not on the 20th day. Nor could the 20th day have meant the 20th day of the Jewish month, for the Virgin Mary was born near the end of the month of Av. Counting forward 15 days would not bring us to the 20th day of the next month. And, even though Blessed Anne Catherine mistakenly believed that the Virgin Mary was born on September 8, she does not describe the events of the naming ceremony as having occurred on the 20th of the September.

On the other hand, if we count forward 15 days from the Virgin Mary's actual birth date on August 5, we arrive at August 19 (counting inclusively). The Virgin Mary was born very early in the day, about midnight, so we must include in the count of the 15 days the day of her birth.[540] According to Blessed Anne Catherine, there were many preparations which had to be made beforehand on the day of the ceremony, and after the ceremony there was a meal.[541] Thus the naming ceremony described by Blessed Anne Catherine most likely occurred near the close of the 15th day, before sunset. Since the Jewish day begins and ends at sunset, the 16th day (August 20) would be seen by the Jews as beginning at sunset just after the ceremony on August 19. Also, August 20 would be the first full day after the Virgin Mary's naming ceremony, the first full day when she was called Mary.

The 8th and the 15th day inclusive from birth always fall on the same day of the week as the birth. This timing made it convenient for the Jews in ancient times to determine and remember the day of the naming ceremonies for newborns. Thus the counting of these days is inclusive, counting the day of birth as day one.

The above explanation for the date and time of the Virgin Mary's naming ceremony agrees with both the indications of Sacred Scripture, that a daughter would be named on the 15th day from birth, and the words of Blessed Anne Catherine, that the angels sang of the 20th day as the day she would be called Mary. To accord with the date and time of the actual event and with the words of the angels, I suggest that the Church place the celebration of the Virgin Mary's Naming Day on August 20, but begin the celebration with a vigil service on the evening of August 19, the time and day of the actual event.

(More suggested changes to the Christian liturgical calendar are found in chapter 15 of this book.)

The Naming Ceremony

It may seem strange to some that the Jews had a special ceremony for naming the child, and that it was held some length of time after the child's birth. Yet we have a similar custom in the Christian Faith. The holy Sacrament of Baptism also includes the formal naming of the child, called the child's christening, and this Sacrament is generally given some length of time after the child's birth. The ancient custom of the Jews is not so different from our custom today.

"Joachim then laid the child in the hands of the high priest, who, lifting her up in offering as he prayed, laid her in the cradle on the altar. He then took a pair of scissors which, like our snuffers, had a little box at the end to hold what was cut off. With this he cut off three little tufts of hair from the child's head...and burnt them in a brazier. Then he took a vase of oil and anointed the child's five senses, touching with his thumb her ears, eyes, nose, mouth, and breast. He also wrote the name Mary on a parchment and laid it on the child's breast.... Hymns were sung and after that the meal began...."[542]

Blessed Anne Catherine describes the Naming Ceremony of the Virgin Mary. Notice that a few tufts of the infant Mary's hair are cut off and burnt. The ancient custom of the Jews was to burn lambs and other animals offered as a sacrifice to God (e.g. Numbers 29). The burning of three little tufts of the Virgin Mary's hair, while she was in a cradle on the altar, symbolizes the offering of the child Mary as a living sacrifice to God. This ceremony included writing the child's name on a parchment while she was on the altar and laying it upon the child. This action signifies that the child is given a name before God, as if to say, "This is the name that God gives you, the name that God will speak when He calls to you."

Saint Ann's Purification

"And after the days of her purification were fulfilled, according to the law of Moses, they brought him to Jerusalem, in order to present him to the Lord ... and in order to offer a sacrifice, according to what is said in the law of the Lord, 'a pair of turtledoves or two young pigeons.' " (Lk 2:22, 24)

Sacred Scripture here describes the Presentation of Our Lord Jesus Christ in the Temple of Jerusalem on the 40th day from His Birth. This day is also called the Purification of the Virgin Mary, since the Jewish law required each woman to present a sacrifice in the temple on the 40th day, inclusive, from the birth of a son. (The celebration of this event in the Catholic Church is sometimes called 'Candlemas' because of an ancient tradition to carry candles in a procession as part of this celebration.)

But when a Jewish woman gave birth to a daughter, as when Saint Ann gave birth to the Virgin Mary, the length of time was double that for a son (Lev 12:5). So, on the 80th day, inclusive, from the birth of a daughter, the mother was required to bring a sacrifice to the Temple of Jerusalem.

"And when the days of her purification have been completed, for a son or for a daughter, she shall bring to the door of the tabernacle of the testimony, a one-year-old lamb as a holocaust, and a young pigeon or a turtledove for sin, and she shall deliver them to the priest ... And if her hand has not obtained or been able to offer a lamb, she shall take two turtledoves or two young pigeons: one as a holocaust, and the other for sin. And the priest shall pray for her, and so she shall be cleansed." (Lev 12:6, 8).

Notice that the Virgin Mary and Joseph offered "a pair of turtledoves, or two young pigeons" as their sacrifice, rather than offering one lamb and one bird. This was the offering to be given by those who were too poor to offer a lamb. Sacred Scripture does not tell us directly about the Purification of Saint Ann on the 80th day after the birth of the Virgin Mary. However, Saint Ann and Saint Joachim were devout Jews, so they certainly would have followed the Law and presented their daughter to God in the Temple on the 80th day. And the sacrifice they offered would not have been the two white birds offered by the poor. Blessed Anne Catherine repeatedly describes Saint Joachim and Saint Ann as having herds of sheep and as being fairly well off.[543] Therefore, Saint Ann would certainly have offered a lamb from their herds and a turtledove or young pigeon.

The Purification of Saint Ann is described briefly by Blessed Anne Catherine. She does not give the day or time of this event, except to say that it occurred: "Some weeks after Mary's birth...." [544] Since Sacred Scripture required Saint Ann to present her offering at the Temple on the 80th day, the date must have been October 23, the 80th day inclusive from August 5. The Virgin Mary was born on a Tuesday, so the Purification of Saint Ann occurred on a Thursday.

In 30 B.C., October 23 coincided with the Jewish date of Heshvan 16.[545] Recall that the Immaculate Conception occurred at the end of the feast celebrating the rededication of the Temple Sanctuary after its rebuilding—that feast occurred from Heshvan 15 until Heshvan 21 or 22. So, this event, called the Purification of Saint Ann, occurred about one Jewish calendar year after the Immaculate Conception. (It was not a Jewish leap year, so the length of time was 12 lunar months, which is somewhat less than one solar year.)

The Presentation of the Virgin Mary

The day of the Virgin Mary's Purification, when she presented the Christ-child in the Temple of Jerusalem on the 40th day from His Birth, is called the Presentation of the Lord. Jewish Law required that a male child be presented to God in the Temple on the 40th day (Lev 12). This celebration is also called the Entrance of the Lord into the Temple, because it was the first time that Jesus Christ, as God Incarnate, entered the Temple of Jerusalem.

The same passage from Sacred Scripture, which requires a woman to present her new-born son to God in the Temple on the 40th day from birth, also requires a woman to present her new-born daughter to God in the Temple on the 80th day from birth (Lev 12). This event, the day of Saint Ann's Purification, should be called the Presentation of the Virgin Mary, because it is the same type of Jewish religious ceremony, required by the same passage of Sacred Scripture, as the Presentation of the Lord Jesus Christ. This event could also be called the Entrance of the Virgin Mary into the Temple, just as the

Presentation of the Lord is also called the Entrance of the Lord into the Temple, because it is the first time since her Immaculate Conception that the Virgin Mary entered the Temple of Jerusalem. (The Immaculate Conception occurred in a passageway under the Temple of Jerusalem. The Virgin Mary was created within the Temple of Jerusalem, so that she could be the Temple in which God Incarnate would dwell.)

There is currently no feast in the Church, that I know of, celebrating the 80th day from the Birth of the Virgin Mary, which was the day of Saint Ann's Purification in the Temple. There should be such a celebration in the Church's liturgical calendar, because this event was required by Sacred Scripture (Lev 12) and because this event paralleled and foreshadowed the day of the Virgin Mary's Purification in the Temple, called the Presentation of the Lord. Since the Virgin Mary was born on August 5 of 30 B.C., the 80th day inclusive from her birth was Oct. 23 of 30 B.C. This new feast should be celebrated on Oct. 23 in the liturgical calendar. (See chapter 15 for more suggested changes to the liturgical calendar.)

Mary, Virgin of the Temple

There is a feast celebrated in the Latin Rite of the Catholic Church under the name of "The Presentation of the Blessed Virgin Mary," which falls on Nov. 21. However, this feast is generally thought of as a celebration of the Virgin Mary's entrance into the Temple of Jerusalem when she began her years of service in the Temple as one of the Temple virgins. The Church is correct in celebrating as a feast the day the Virgin Mary began her service in the Temple. However, the name of this feast should be changed to avoid confusion with the day of Saint Ann's Purification in the Temple.

In the Eastern Rite of the Catholic Church, this feast is celebrated under the name of the "Feast of the Entrance of the Theotokos into the Temple."[546] The Eastern Orthodox Churches also celebrate this feast under the same name, "Entrance of the Theotokos into the Temple."[547] The liturgies of the Eastern Churches explicitly recognize this feast as the remembrance of Mary's entrance into the service of the Temple when she was a young child. Perhaps the universal Church should adopt the Eastern Churches tradition of calling this feast the "Entrance of the Theotokos into the Temple."

When the Virgin Mary was quite young, she went to live in the Temple of Jerusalem as one among many young girls dedicated to the service of God.[548] She and the other girls lived in one of the buildings surrounding the Temple Sanctuary.[549] The Virgin Mary's entrance into her years of prayer, worship, and service in the Temple is sometimes called "the Presentation of the Virgin Mary," and is commemorated in the current liturgical calendar, in the Latin Rite of the Catholic Church on Nov. 21. The Eastern Rite of the Catholic Church, and many other Eastern Churches, celebrate this same event under the title, "Feast of the Entrance of the Theotokos into the Temple."

The Virgin Mary lived and served at the Temple of Jerusalem until shortly before her betrothal to Saint Joseph, when she was some months past 14 years of age counting from birth.[550] She was still 14 years old when the Annunciation occurred, on February 25 of 15 B.C.[551] Counting from her Immaculate Conception, the Virgin Mary was just over 15 years of age when she was dismissed from the Temple and betrothed to Saint Joseph. At the Birth of her Divine Son Jesus Christ, the Virgin Mary was about 15 years and 3 months old counting from birth, and about 16 years old counting from the beginning of her life at the Immaculate Conception.

"Mary was three years and three months old when she made the vow to join the virgins in the Temple." [552]

Here Blessed Anne Catherine explains that the Virgin Mary began her service in the Temple of Jerusalem when she was three years and three months old. Blessed Anne Catherine always figures the ages of Mary and Jesus in the usual way, counting from birth. She received her visions of the day that the Virgin Mary entered the service of God at the Temple of Jerusalem on November 8.[553] Although she does not explicitly tell us the date of Mary's entrance into the Temple, she usually received her visions either on the same day of the month as the event occurred, or on the day of the liturgical celebration of the event. The day of the liturgical celebration is Nov. 21, therefore Nov. 8 was most likely the actual month and day of the event.

Notice that November 8 is both the date of the Immaculate Conception and the date of the Virgin Mary's entrance into the Temple. The Virgin Mary's first entrance into the Temple was at her Immaculate Conception, which took place in a passageway under the Temple.[554] Her second entrance into the Temple of Jerusalem was at Saint Ann's Purification on the 80th day from her birth, when she was presented to God. The Virgin Mary entered the Temple of Jerusalem a third time, to serve God as a Temple Virgin, on the same month and day when she was created by God within the Temple.

Blessed Anne Catherine gives the Virgin Mary's age at her entrance into the Temple, on November 8, as three years and three months old. Yet Blessed Anne Catherine thought that the Virgin Mary was born on September 8. Here is an indication that the information given by her comes from God, not merely from her own mind. For even though she did not know that the Virgin Mary was born on August 5, she was able to correctly state her age at her entrance into the Temple, 3 years and 3 months later, on November 8. Thus the year of Mary's entrance into the service of God at the Temple of Jerusalem was 27 B.C.—3 years, 3 months, and 3 days after her birth on August 5 of 30 B.C., and 4 years to the day after her Immaculate Conception on November 8 of 31 B.C. (Since Mary was born about midnight at the start of August 5, and entered the Temple sometime during the day on November 8, the exact length of time would be some number of hours greater than 3 years, 3 months, and 3 days.)

Since the Virgin Mary entered the Temple at the age of 3 years and 3 months, and left the Temple to be betrothed to Saint Joseph when she was a few months past 14 years of age, she must have been in the service of God at the Temple for about 11 years. The Virgin Mary was betrothed to Saint Joseph not long after leaving the Temple (she was dismissed from the Temple for that purpose).[555] Their betrothal ceremony occurred in late January.[556] The Virgin Mary's dismissal from the Temple most likely occurred in November, when new Temple virgins were admitted to the service of the Temple (see chapter 5, "The Betrothal of Joseph and Mary," for more on this point).

Blessed Anne Catherine states that the Virgin Mary entered the Temple "eleven years before Christ's Birth,"[557] but this cannot be correct. The Virgin Mary entered the Temple when she was 3 years and 3 months old, and was dismissed from the Temple when she was over 14 years of age, a total of about 11 years. The Incarnation of Jesus Christ occurred in February, after the betrothal of Saint Joseph and the Virgin Mary, and the

Birth of Christ occurred in November, nine months later. Therefore, Christ was born just over 12 years after the Virgin Mary entered the Temple, not 11.

Blessed Anne Catherine also said that the Virgin Mary's entrance into the Temple occurred 15 years before the Birth of Christ, and 2 years after the work rebuilding the Temple began.[558] This could not possibly refer to Mary's entrance as one of the Temple virgins when she was about 3 years old.[559] She gives the age of Mary at the Incarnation of Christ as just over 14 years of age (counting from birth).[560] The Virgin Mary was just over 15 years old (counting from her birth) at the time of Christ's Birth, not 18 years of age (15 + 3). Therefore, the entrance of the Virgin Mary into the Temple, 15 years before the Birth of Jesus (15 B.C.), must instead have occurred during the year of Mary's Birth (30 B.C.). That year, the Virgin Mary entered the Temple of Jerusalem at the time of her Presentation, that is, at the time for the Purification of Saint Ann on the 80th day from Mary's Birth. The rebuilding of the Temple of Jerusalem began in spring of 32 B.C., which was 2 calendar years prior to the Virgin Mary's Entrance into the Temple at St. Ann's Presentation in 30 B.C. By 30 B.C., the rebuilding of the Temple Sanctuary had been completed (in Nov. of 31 B.C., the time of the Immaculate Conception), but work on the other areas of the Temple still continued. Thus the Entrance of the Virgin Mary into the Temple (at St. Ann's Presentation) did occur about 2 years after the work rebuilding the Temple had begun and about 15 years prior to the Birth of Christ.

"Then, in the sixth month, the Angel Gabriel was sent by God, to a city of Galilee named Nazareth, to a virgin betrothed to a man whose name was Joseph, of the house of David; and the name of the virgin was Mary." (Lk 1:26-27).

Sacred Scripture calls Mary, the mother of Jesus Christ, a virgin because she was truly, fully, and perfectly a Virgin throughout her entire life, from her Immaculate Conception to her Assumption into Heaven. But there is a second, lesser meaning when Sacred Scripture calls Mary a virgin. The meaning is also that Mary was a Virgin of the Temple of Jerusalem, so that she had the title of Virgin, even among the Jews. Christians throughout the history of the Church have spoken of Mary as a Virgin, not merely as a description of her life, but also as a most fitting title: "Blessed Virgin Mary." But because Mary was one of the Temple Virgins when she was a child, she had the title of "Virgin of the Temple," even before Christians called her by the title "Virgin."

The Virgin Mary served God in the Temple of Jerusalem for 11 years. In the twelfth year, she left the service of God in the Temple of Jerusalem to become a living Temple for the Son of God. She, who was one of many temple virgins, was in truth the perfect Virgin of virgins and the living Temple for the Son of God. The Temple of Jerusalem was a symbol and foreshadowing of the Messiah. When the Virgin Mary's time of service within the Temple had ended, the human life of the Messiah began within her womb. Within the Virgin of the Temple, God created the Cornerstone of the New Temple, the Humanity of the Eternal Son of God. The Virgin Mary is Virgin of the Temple, and that Temple is Christ Jesus, her Savior. The Virgin Mary conceived and gave birth to Jesus Christ, who is the fulfillment of all that is symbolized by the Temple of Jerusalem. "And I saw no temple in it. For the Lord God Almighty is its temple, and the Lamb." (Rev 21:22).

Chapter 10
Dormition, Resurrection, Assumption

At the end of her life on earth, the Blessed Virgin Mary died, was resurrected from the dead, and was assumed into Heaven. Some Catholics doubt that the Virgin Mary died and was resurrected before being assumed into Heaven. But the Apostolic Constitution of Pope Pius XII, *Munificentissimus Deus*, (also titled, "Defining the Dogma of the Assumption"), clearly and repeatedly refers to the death of the Virgin Mary.[561] In no less than seven separate paragraphs this Apostolic Constitution refers, in one way or another, to the death of the Virgin Mary:

1. "In the same way, it was not difficult for them to admit that the great Mother of God, like her only begotten Son, had actually passed from this life." (para. 14)

2. " 'Venerable to us, O Lord, is the festivity of this day on which the holy Mother of God suffered temporal death....' " (paragraph 17)

3. " 'As he kept you a virgin in childbirth, thus he has kept your body incorrupt in the tomb and has glorified it by his divine act of transferring it from the tomb.' " (paragraph 18)

4. "...this feast shows, not only that the dead body of the Blessed Virgin Mary remained incorrupt, but that she gained a triumph out of death...." (paragraph 20)

5. " 'It was fitting that she, who had kept her virginity intact in childbirth, should keep her own body free from all corruption even after death.' " (para. 21)

6. " '...she has received an eternal incorruptibility of the body together with him who has raised her up from the tomb and has taken her up to himself in a way known only to him.' " (paragraph 22)

7. "Hence the revered Mother of God...finally obtained, as the supreme culmination of her privileges, that she should be preserved free from the corruption of the tomb and that, like her own Son, having overcome death, she might be taken up body and soul to the glory of heaven...." (paragraph 40)

This Apostolic Constitution also clearly refers to the Resurrection of the Virgin Mary, not only by saying she was raised up from the tomb (e.g. #6 above), but also by stating that her soul was reunited with her body: "...the Virgin Mary's flesh had remained incorrupt—for it is wrong to believe that her body has seen corruption—because it was really united again to her soul and, together with it, crowned with great glory in the heavenly courts." (paragraph 28). Death is the separation of the soul from the body. Resurrection is the re-uniting of the soul with the body. Here is a clear reference to the Resurrection of the Virgin Mary.

Furthermore, nowhere within this Apostolic Constitution does Pope Pius XII in anyway suggest even the possibility that the Virgin Mary may not have died at the end of her life on earth. Therefore, it is the teaching of the Catholic Church that the Virgin Mary died, was resurrected from the dead, and was thereafter assumed into Heaven.

This teaching is well understood among the Eastern Churches, where many Christians observe the 14-day Fast of the Dormition prior to their celebration of the Virgin Mary's Assumption into Heaven. The Dormition of the Virgin Mary is her "falling asleep" in Christ (cf. Jn 11:11-14), in other words, her death.

The present chapter begins with the above understanding and goes on to examine the chronology of these events at the end of Mary's life on earth. A detailed theology of the end of the Virgin Mary's life can be found in my booklet, *The Dormition, Resurrection, and Assumption of the Blessed Virgin Mary*.[562]

Saint Bridget of Sweden had a vision in which the Virgin Mary said, "After my Son ascended to Heaven, I lived in the world fifteen years—the time from my Son's Ascension to my death."[563] Why does the Virgin Mary mark the length of time from her Divine Son Jesus' Ascension, instead of His Crucifixion or Resurrection? Because she is counting the length of time from the day Christ left her side to go to Heaven, to the day that her soul left this world (at her death) to be at Christ's side in Heaven. Still, the 15 years is not exact to the day, but only to the year. Thus, the Virgin Mary died about fifteen years after Christ's Ascension to Heaven.

The visions of Blessed Anne Catherine Emmerich confirm this length of 15 years in several ways. First, she tells us: "After Our Lord's Ascension Mary lived for three years on Mount Sion, for three years in Bethany, and for nine years in Ephesus...."[564] The total number of years was then 15, in agreement with Saint Bridget.

Second, Blessed Anne Catherine tells us that, when Jesus was speaking about his death shortly before the Passover, the disciples asked Jesus whether He would take His Blessed Mother with Him. Jesus answered that the Virgin Mary would remain with them for a number of years before her own death. Blessed Anne Catherine states, "He mentioned the number, and in it there was a five. I think He named fifteen years...."[565] And soon after she again describes Jesus speaking about the death of His Holy Mother: "...that with Him she would die His bitter death, and still would have to survive Him fifteen years."[566]

Third, Blessed Anne Catherine was once asked how old the Virgin Mary was when she died. She then immediately received a vision from God of the number 64 (written in Roman numerals). As was the case with her vision revealing the age of Christ at His death, this vision also should be interpreted to mean the entire length of Mary's life on earth, from conception to death. The Immaculate Conception occurred in fall of 31 B.C., and so, counting forward 64 years, we arrive again at A.D. 34 as the year of the Virgin Mary's death. (There is no year zero between 1 B.C. and A.D. 1, and so counting from 31 B.C. to A.D. 34 gives us 64 years, not 65.) Since Christ died in A.D. 19, and the Virgin Mary died in A.D. 34, there were 15 years from Christ's death to Mary's death.

Fourth, Blessed Anne Catherine received a vision that further confirms the year of the Virgin Mary's Dormition. She saw the number 48, revealing the number of years from Christ's Birth to the Virgin Mary's death. "It means that the year 48 after Christ's Birth is the year of the Blessed Virgin's death."[567] So, counting forward 48 years from 15 B.C. brings us once more to A.D. 34.

These numbers revealed to Blessed Anne Catherine can be checked against the other lengths of time in this chronology. For example, since the Virgin Mary was about 64 years old (counting from conception), at her death, and 48 years had passed since the year of the Holy Conception and Birth of Christ, then the Virgin Mary must have completed her 16th year of life since conception in the year of Christ's Birth (64 – 48 = 16). This result agrees with the conclusion of chapter 8 of this book, that the Virgin Mary completed 16 years of age from conception in the year of Christ's Birth. Also, if the Virgin Mary died 15 years after the Crucifixion, Resurrection, and Ascension of Jesus, then the length of Christ's life from the year of His Holy Conception and Birth (48 years before Mary's death) to the year of the Crucifixion, Resurrection, and Ascension would be 33 years (48 – 15 = 33). Again, this agrees with the conclusions of previous chapters of this book.

The Hour of the Dormition

"The Blessed Virgin died after the ninth hour, at the same time as Our Lord."[568]

The ninth hour is about 3 p.m. (see Chapter 2). The Virgin Mary died at the same time of day as Jesus Christ died, because her death was a part of her complete and unerring imitation of the life of her Divine Son Jesus. According to Blessed Anne Catherine, the Virgin died after receiving Holy Communion, at a Mass said by the Apostle Saint Peter, with most of the other Apostles in attendance.[569]

The Month and Day of the Dormition

"Mary died in the year 48 after the Birth of Christ, thirteen years and two months after Christ's Ascension. This was shown me in numbers, not in writing. First, I saw IV [4], and then VIII [8], which denoted the year 48; lastly, I saw XIII [13], and two full months."[570]

"It means that the year 48 after Christ's Birth is the year of the Blessed Virgin's death. Then I see X [10] and III [3] and then two full moons as they are shown on the calendar, that means that the Blessed Virgin died thirteen years and two months after Christ's Ascension into Heaven."[571]

"After Christ's Ascension, she lived fourteen years and two months."[572]

After being shown a vision telling her the year of the Blessed Virgin Mary's death, given as 48 years after the Birth of Christ, Blessed Anne Catherine was shown the number 13 and then two full moons. She interpreted this to mean that Mary died 13 years and 2 months after Christ's Ascension. However, her interpretation of the vision is in error. She was already told the year of the Virgin Mary's death, the 48th year after the Birth of Christ. Thus, the next numbers must indicate days and months, not years.

If the Virgin Mary had died 13 years after Christ's death, and also 48 years after Christ's Birth, then the length of Christ's life would be (48 – 13 = 35) 35 years, not the 33 years which was revealed to her by God (see chapter 2).[573] Also, she must have, at another time, seen a vision of 14 plus two months, because she also stated Christ lived for 14 years and two months after His Ascension. She contradicts herself and Saint Bridget, so her interpretation of the vision must be mistaken.

The correct interpretation of the vision is the following. First God showed Blessed Anne Catherine the number 48, to indicate the year of the Virgin Mary's death, then

God showed her the number 13 and 2 full moons, to indicate the month and day of the Virgin's death. The second set of numbers was not a redundant indication of the year. The reason she was shown 13 plus 2 full moons (meaning 2 full months), but at another time was shown 14 plus 2 full months, is that the number of days can be counted two different ways.

One can count inclusively, counting both the day of the Ascension and the day of Mary's death, which gives us 14 days plus 2 months. Or, one can start the count with the day after the Ascension, that is, count the number of days since the Ascension to the Virgin Mary's death, which gives us 13 days plus 2 months. As concluded in chapter 3 of this book, Jesus ascended to Heaven on May 18 of A.D. 19, sometime before noon.[574] Counting inclusively, so that the remainder of the day of Christ's Ascension is the first day, there are 14 days to the end of the month (May 18 to May 31). But if you start the count at the first full day after the Ascension, May 19, then there are only 13 days to the end of the month.

The count of the number of days must bring us to the end of one month, so that two more full months can then be added. So the numbers 13 or 14 complete the month of May, then June and July are the two full months. Blessed Anne Catherine was not shown a vision that added another day after the 2 full months. The numbers she was shown encompasses the total number of days. Therefore the date of the Virgin Mary's death was not the first day of August, but the last day of July.

One could also count the exact length of time. From the Ascension of Christ in late morning (on May 18) to the Dormition of the Virgin Mary in mid afternoon (on July 31) is 2 months, 13 days, and a few hours. In any of these methods of counting the length of time, the answer is the same: the Virgin Mary died on July 31. The Dormition of the Blessed Virgin Mary occurred on July 31 of A.D. 34, a Saturday. The length of time that the Virgin Mary lived in the world from Christ's Ascension to her own death was 15 years, 2 months, 13 days, and a few hours.

Notice also that this interpretation agrees with the conclusion that Jesus Christ died on April 7 and rose from the dead on April 9. If Christ had died on any other day of March or April (at the start of Passover, which falls approximately between March 22 and April 23), adding 13 or 14 days to the date of the Ascension (40 days inclusive from Easter Sunday) would not bring us to the end of a month, so that two full months could then be added.

When Blessed Anne Catherine was shown the number 64, indicating the length of the Virgin Mary's life from conception to death, she was also informed that Mary died some number of days short of 64 full years. "She reached the age of sixty-four years, all but three and twenty days...."[575] In other words, the Virgin Mary did not die on the same day and month that she was conceived, but a number of days prior to that date. Although July 31 is not 23 days prior to the date of the Immaculate Conception on Nov. 8, there are 23 days from the 8th to the 31st of any month. Perhaps this vision of "three and twenty days" was meant to convey information about the day of the month, not a length of time. Another possibility is that the "three and twenty days" is actually three months and twenty days. The exact length of time from the day and month of Mary's Birth on August 5, to the day and month of Christ's Birth on Nov. 25, is three months and 20 days.

The Virgin Mary's age, counting from conception to the time of her death, was 63 years, 8 months, 23 days, plus several hours.[576] Perhaps Blessed Anne Catherine was shown the number 23 in reference to Mary's exact age at her Dormition.

Another possible explanation is that Blessed Anne Catherine was informed in her vision only that the Virgin Mary died before reaching 64 full years. She does not say that she was shown the number 23. She may have determined that the length of time was 23 days by counting from August 15 to September 8, the day of the celebration of the Birth of Mary in the Church's liturgical calendar. Blessed Anne Catherine never plainly stated the month and day of the conception or birth of Mary as having been revealed to her by God. So, since she saw the vision of the events of the Virgin Mary's birth on the day of the liturgical celebration, she may have mistakenly thought that Mary was born on that day, September 8.

The Virgin Mary told Saint Bridget of Sweden that there were 15 days from her Dormition to her Assumption to Heaven. However, Blessed Anne Catherine was shown the vision of the Assumption of the Virgin Mary soon after the vision of her Dormition, and so she mistakenly concluded that one event occurred soon after the other (for she did not fully comprehend every vision which was shown to her). But she did state that she was uncertain of the month and day of the Virgin Mary's death and Assumption.[577]

The Hour of the Resurrection of the Virgin Mary

The death of the Virgin Mary occurred at about 3 p.m., the same time that Jesus died. The Birth of the Virgin Mary also occurred at about the same time as the Birth of her Divine Son Jesus (about midnight). Perhaps then the Resurrection of the Virgin Mary also occurred at the same time of day as the Resurrection of Jesus. According to Sacred Scripture, the Resurrection of Jesus Christ occurred just before dawn (Mt 28:1; Mk 16:1-2; Lk 24:1-2; Jn 20:1).[578] Blessed Anne Catherine saw the Resurrection and Assumption of the Blessed Virgin Mary as occurring sometime during the night.[579] But she does not specifically say at what hour of the night. Since the Virgin Mary died at the same time of day that Jesus Christ died, perhaps she also was resurrected from the dead at the same time of day that Jesus Christ rose from the dead, just before dawn. The hour before dawn is the very end of the night, so Blessed Anne Catherine's words do not contradict the conclusion that the Virgin Mary was resurrected from the dead and was assumed into Heaven just before dawn.

The Day of the Resurrection and Assumption of the Virgin Mary

"For fifteen days my body lay buried in the earth; then, with a multitude of angels, it was assumed into Heaven."[580]

"And when dead, I lay in the sepulcher three days; then I was taken up to Heaven with infinite honor and joy...."[581]

The Virgin Mary described her Assumption into Heaven to St. Bridget of Sweden as occurring 15 days after her death and burial. She also told Saint Bridget that her body lay in the sepulcher for 3 days before her Assumption to Heaven. Since these are the words of the Virgin Mary, both of these statements must be true. Saint Bridget herself probably had some understanding of how these two statements fit together, for she wrote these close to one another in her book of revelations. How then could the Virgin Mary's body lay buried in the earth for fifteen days, and yet lay in the sepulcher for only three days?

The length of time between the Virgin Mary's death and her Assumption to Heaven must have been 15 days, for the Virgin Mary clearly said so to Saint Bridget. Also, the visions given to Blessed Anne Catherine Emmerich indicate that the Virgin Mary died at the end of July, but she saw the visions of the Virgin Mary's death, Resurrection, and Assumption about 15 days later, in the middle of August. Thus, the Virgin Mary was assumed into Heaven about 15 days after her death.

After the Virgin Mary's death, her body was placed in the earth, in a sepulcher or tomb of some kind.[582] That is why the Virgin Mary told Saint Bridget that she was buried in the earth for 15 days, because her body was in a tomb hollowed out of the earth for that length of time.

So then, why did the Virgin Mary also say that her body lay in the sepulcher for three days? Blessed Anne Catherine describes the Virgin Mary's tomb as being large enough for several persons to enter and move about (the tomb of our Lord was similar, see John 20:1-13).[583] So I suggest that the tomb of the Virgin Mary was left open after her burial, so that devout persons could visit the body. This event would be something like the custom today to hold a "wake" after someone's death. Similarly, after the death of Jesus Christ, the holy women went to Our Lord's tomb, bringing spices and ointments, with the intention of reverencing His body (Lk 23:55 – 24:1). The three days then would be counted from the end of the time for visiting the body of Mary, when the coffin was covered and the sepulcher closed, to the time when she was assumed into Heaven. Thus the wake for the body of the Virgin Mary lasted about 12 days.

The Virgin Mary's body "lay buried in the earth" for 15 days, meaning that her body was in the tomb for that length of time. The tomb is said to be "in the earth" because, according to Blessed Anne Catherine, it was a cave-like burial chamber hollowed out of a rock, perhaps on a hillside.[584] And the Virgin Mary's body "lay in the sepulcher three days," meaning that her body was in the closed-up tomb (or sepulcher) for 3 days, the last 3 days of the entire 15 day period from her death to her Resurrection and Assumption into Heaven.

The Virgin Mary must have been Resurrected from the dead sometime between her death and her Assumption to Heaven. At her death, the soul of the Virgin Mary went directly to Heaven, but her dead body remained on earth in the tomb. Death is the separation of body and soul. At her Assumption, the Virgin Mary was brought up to Heaven with her body and soul united. Therefore, her Resurrection, when her soul came down from Heaven to be reunited with her body, must have occurred sometime after her death, but before her Assumption.[585]

Blessed Anne Catherine describes the Resurrection of the Virgin Mary as occurring immediately before her Assumption to Heaven. "Then I saw the soul of the Blessed Virgin . . . float down into the tomb. Soon afterwards I saw her soul, united to her transfigured body, rising out of the tomb far brighter and clearer, and ascending into the heavenly Jerusalem with Our Lord and with the whole glory."[586] Thus the day and time of the Virgin Mary's Resurrection was also the day and time of her Assumption to Heaven.

The Virgin Mary died about 3 p.m. on July 31. She was resurrected from the dead and assumed into Heaven about 15 days later. But the Resurrection and Assumption of the Virgin Mary occurred at night, most likely just before dawn. So the length of time from Mary's death to her Resurrection and Assumption could not be exactly 15 days (as in 15 x 24 hours). The exact length of time must have been either 14 days plus some number of hours or 15 days plus some number of hours.

On August 15 of A.D. 34, the sun rose at about 04:59 hours Jerusalem Standard Time (JST).[587] The sky begins to brighten about an hour or more before sunrise. So, if the Virgin Mary's Resurrection occurred sometime during the hour before sunrise (about the same time that Jesus Christ's Resurrection occurred), then there were about 13 to 14 hours, plus some number of days, from her death at about 3 p.m. to her Resurrection at about 04:00 to 05:00 hours JST.

The Virgin Mary died on July 31. If the length of time from Mary's death to her Resurrection was 14 days and about 14 hours, then her Resurrection and Assumption occurred on August 15, just before dawn.[588] If the length of time were 15 days and about 14 hours, then her Resurrection and Assumption would have occurred on August 16, just before dawn. The Virgin Mary's Resurrection and Assumption must have occurred on August 15, shortly before dawn, for the following reasons.

First, the count of various events in the lives of Jesus and Mary, and the length of time between the events is usually counted inclusively, so that a partial day counts for a full day. Thus 14 days and about 14 hours would count as 15 days, in agreement with Saint Bridget. Second, the length of time of 14 days and about 14 hours is closer to 15 days than to 14 days. Third, August 15 of A.D. 34 was a Sunday, the same day of the week that Jesus rose from the dead. Fourth, the Church celebrates the Assumption of the Virgin Mary on August 15. For all of these reasons, it is clear that the Virgin Mary was resurrected from the dead and assumed into Heaven on August 15, just before dawn.

The Virgin Mary died on Saturday, July 31. (On Saturdays, Holy Mass is often celebrated in honor of the Virgin Mary. Perhaps this is because the Virgin Mary died on a Saturday.) She was buried in a tomb the evening of July 31, and her body lay in the tomb for 15 days. The sepulchre and the tomb were closed up after 12 days. The sepulchre and tomb were closed for about 3 days, Friday, Saturday, and (part of) Sunday—the same three days of the week as the Crucifixion, death, and Resurrection of Jesus Christ. The Virgin Mary was resurrected from the dead and assumed into Heaven, by the power of Jesus Christ, before dawn on August 15, a Sunday.

The Fast of the Dormition

The Churches of the East have long celebrated the Dormition of the Virgin Mary, as well as her Assumption. The 15 day length of time, from the death of the Blessed Virgin Mary to her Assumption to Heaven, is in harmony with the liturgical calendars of the Eastern Churches. Many Christians in the Eastern Churches commemorate the death of the Virgin Mary with the Fast of the Dormition, which lasts from August 1 to 14. This length of time reflects the length of time from the death of the Virgin Mary to her Resurrection and Assumption. The fasting begins on the first full day after the Virgin Mary's death and continues through August 14, the last full day before the Virgin Mary was resurrected from the dead and assumed into Heaven. The Church in the East fasts to mark the period of time between Virgin Mary's death and her Resurrection and Assumption. This fast commemorates her death and also looks forward to her Resurrection and Assumption. (I think that most Christians, even in the East, do not know that this is the reason for the timing of the fast.)

Another reason for celebrating the Assumption of the Virgin Mary on the day of August 15 is because the Apostles discovered her Resurrection and Assumption on that day. According to Blessed Anne Catherine, the Apostle Thomas arrived too late to attend at the death and burial of the Virgin Mary. He was upset that he had missed the event, and he wanted to see the body of the Virgin Mary in the tomb. But when the Apostles opened the tomb and went inside, they found the coffin empty, and the body of the Virgin Mary gone.[589] According to Blessed Anne Catherine, the discovery of the empty tomb occurred during the daytime following the night of the Virgin Mary's Assumption to Heaven.[590] The Virgin Mary was assumed into Heaven on Sunday, August 15 of A.D. 34, before dawn, and her empty tomb was discovered later that day. Therefore, it is fitting that the celebration of the Virgin Mary's Assumption take place on the day that her Resurrection and Assumption were discovered and made known to the Apostles.

But why does the Virgin Mary find it important to also tell Saint Bridget that she was in the sepulcher for three days, (the length of time that the sepulcher was closed)? The Virgin Mary was resurrected from the dead on the same day of the week, and perhaps about the same hour, that Jesus Christ rose from the dead. The count of the three days, when the sepulcher was closed, is a reflection of the three days from the Crucifixion to the Resurrection of Jesus Christ. Therefore, the count of the three days, when the Virgin Mary's tomb was closed, should begin with the Friday before the Assumption. In this way, the tomb was closed up for the same three days of the week, Friday to Sunday, which mark the death and Resurrection of Jesus Christ. And the discovery of Mary's empty tomb by Saint Thomas and the Apostles is like the discovery of Christ's empty tomb by the holy women and the Apostles. That is why the Virgin Mary made a point of telling Saint Bridget about the three-day length of time, because it mirrors the three days from Christ's death to His Divine Resurrection. In this way, the Apostles more easily understood the meaning of the empty tomb—that the Blessed Virgin Mary had been raised from the dead—because these events were similar to those surrounding the Resurrection of Christ.

The Beginning and the End

There is an interesting parallel found in comparing the beginning and the end of the Virgin's life on earth. The Virgin Mary's life began, at the Immaculate Conception, just over 15 years before Christ came into the world at the Incarnation, and she lived in the world for just over 15 years after the Ascension of Jesus to Heaven. The Virgin Mary spent 15 years of her life waiting for the Divine Son of God to arrive (at the Incarnation) and she spent 15 years of her life waiting to rejoin her Divine Son after His Ascension to Heaven. The beginning and the end of the Blessed Virgin Mary's life were in this way similar.

Chapter 11
Early Church History

The First Deacons

In the early Church, some Christians had converted from among the Greek-speaking Jews, called Hellenists, while others had converted from among the Hebrew-speaking Jews. Some of the Hellenists complained that their widows were not receiving their fair share in the daily distribution of food and other necessities within the Christian Community (Acts 6:1). The most likely time for such a dispute would be during a Jewish Sabbatical year, when the Jews would neither sow nor harvest their crops (Lev 25:1-7). During such times, particularly towards the end of the Sabbatical year, food would be in short supply. The general shortage of food would put a strain on the resources of the Community, which could naturally result in some complaints about unequal distribution of food.

The Acts of the Apostles describes the Twelve Apostles settling this dispute together: "And so the twelve, calling together the multitude of the disciples...." (Acts 6:2). Therefore, the Twelve Apostles had not yet dispersed to distant lands to spread the Gospel. This dispute occurred soon after the year of the Crucifixion.

The first Sabbatical year after the Crucifixion, Resurrection, and Ascension of Jesus Christ was A.D. 20/21. (See chapter 16 for details on Jewish Sabbatical and Jubilee years.) Each Sabbatical year (during this period of time) began in the autumn, in the month of Tishri, and ended the following autumn. Early in the Sabbatical year, food was still available from the harvest of the previous year. Thus, in the Sabbatical year of A.D. 20/21, the shortage of food would reach its peak in A.D. 21. So A.D. 21 is most likely time for this dispute over the distribution of food and for the appointment of the first seven deacons.

The Stoning of Saint Stephen

Stephen was one of the first seven deacons in the Church (Acts 6:1-7). He disputed with the Jewish leaders (Acts 6:8 - 7:57). "And driving him out, beyond the city, they stoned him. And witnesses placed their garments beside the feet of a youth, who was called Saul." (Acts 7:57). The Jewish people were under Roman occupation and were not allowed to put anyone to death. When the Jewish leaders wanted to put Jesus to death, they could not stone Him, but had to convince Pilate to put Him to death through Roman crucifixion (Jn 18:31). So how could the Jewish leaders stone Stephen to death, when the Romans forbid them from doing so?

According to Josephus, at the end of his ten-year rule over Judea, Pilate was accused of murder by the Samaritan Senate. The Roman general Vitellius ordered Pilate to go to Rome to answer to the charge of murder. He also sent his friend Marcellus to govern Judea in Pilate's absence.[591] Because of this change in leadership, the Romans had less control over Judea. Marcellus was never officially given the title of procurator over Judea; he was appointed by a Roman general, not by the Roman Emperor.[592] He was like a substitute teacher in a classroom—the students see that the substitute has less authority than his predecessor, so they feel more free to break the rules. Also, the Jews saw that by their complaint against Pilate, he was both removed from office and charged with a serious crime. This apparent power to remove a Roman leader from office emboldened them. Furthermore, there may have been a space of time between the departure of Pilate and the arrival of Marcellus. For Josephus says that Pilate "made haste to Rome" and did not dare to contradict the orders of Vitellius.[593] This hasty departure under pressure from a Roman general means that Pilate might not have waited for the arrival of Marcellus before leaving for Rome.

Saint Stephen could only have been stoned to death during this change in leadership from Pilate to Marcellus. Pilate's rule ended just prior to the death of the emperor Tiberius.[594] In my revised chronology of the reigns of the Roman emperors, Tiberius died in March of A.D. 22 (see chapter 13 for details). The trip to Rome was made by a long journey by sea and was more difficult in the winter months. Pliny tells us that Feb. 8 was the date when the Mediterranean Sea was considered open for travel after the harsh winter weather.[595] But Pilate may have departed sooner, being under pressure from Vitellius.[596] The trip to Rome by sea is roughly 2500 miles. Ships followed the coastline for safety and to be able to stop at various ports for supplies, so the journey was longer than one might at first imagine. The trip from Judea to Rome would take perhaps 1½ to 2 months during the good sailing season (i.e. not in winter). However, with the adverse sailing conditions in wintertime, the trip might take 3 months or longer. So, Pilate could have left for Rome as late as February, or as early as December or January, and still have arrived in Rome after the death of Tiberius in mid March.

Notice that St. Stephen was not a deacon for long before he was martyred. He was ordained sometime during the Sabbatical year of A.D. 20/21, most likely in the latter part of the Sabbatical year (A.D. 21). And he was put to death in the winter of A.D. 21/22, sometime between December and February (inclusive). Stephen was a deacon for perhaps less than a year before he was stoned. This short time frame is reflected in Sacred Scripture. The ordination of Stephen is in Acts 6:5 and his dispute with the Jews which resulted in his stoning begins in Acts 6:9. Eusebius also testifies to the brevity of Stephen's service as a deacon. He states that Stephen was the first after the Lord to be put to death, "almost as soon as he was ordained, as if this was the real purpose of his advancement."[597]

The Beheading of James the Greater

The Apostle James the Greater was one of the Twelve Apostles. He was the brother of John (the Apostle and Gospel writer). Jesus gave James and John a special place among the Twelve, beside Peter, their leader. Only Peter, James, and John were present for the Transfiguration (Mk 9:2). These three were also closer to Jesus during His agony in the garden (Mk 14:33). James was the first of the Twelve to follow Christ in martyrdom and John was the last of the Twelve to die and join Christ in Heaven.

James the Greater was martyred during the time of the Passover (the Feast of Unleavened Bread), sometime after Herod Agrippa I received authority over Judea (Acts 12:19), and sometime before Herod went to Caesarea, where he died (Acts 12:19-23). After the death of Philip (Herod the Great's son), the emperor Gaius (Caligula) gave

Philip's tetrarchy (Lk 3:1) to Herod Agrippa I.[598] Josephus tells us that Herod Agrippa I ruled only over the area of Philip's tetrarchy for the first three years of Gaius' reign, then in the fourth year, Gaius gave him the territory of Herod Antipas (Galilee and Perea).[599] Gaius' reign lasted just under four years, so Herod Agrippa I began to rule soon after Gaius became emperor. (See chapters 12 and 13 for details on the reigns of Philip, Tiberius, Gaius, et al.)

According to Josephus, Herod Agrippa I died in the 7th year of his reign after governing for four years under the emperor Gaius and three years under the emperor Claudius.[600] After succeeding Gaius as emperor, sometime during the first year of his reign, Claudius gave Herod Agrippa I the regions of Judea, Samaria, and Caesarea to add to his government. Since Herod killed the Apostle James the Greater in Judea and then went to Caesarea (Acts 12:19), the martyrdom of James must have occurred during the last three years of Herod's reign and during the first three years of Claudius' reign. Herod's reign began with the death of Tiberius and the succession of Gaius as emperor in A.D. 22 (revised date; see chapter 13). Philip also died about this time (see chapter 12). If A.D. 22 was the first year of Herod Agrippa I's reign, then A.D. 28 was his seventh year (counted inclusively) and the year in which he died. Claudius became emperor upon the death of Gaius in Jan. of A.D. 26 (revised date).

Josephus quotes an edict of the emperor Claudius as saying that the previous emperor, Caligula, did not favor the Jews because they would not worship him as a god. Claudius had a low opinion of Caligula (Gaius) and he said that Caligula had a "great madness."[601] But Claudius favored the Jews, at least during the early years of his reign, and issued an edict giving their religion a protected status within the Roman Empire.[602] These edicts were issued when Claudius was consul for the second time.[603] According to Dio, Claudius was consul once before he became emperor, and for the second time in the second year of his rule as emperor.[604] In this revised chronology, Caligula died in Jan. of A.D. 26, so that the second year of Claudius' reign was A.D. 27. According to Dio, Claudius was consul for the second time only for 2 months.[605] (The Roman emperors liked the honor of being elected consul, but they didn't like to do the work of a consul. Thus they often held the office for only the first portion of the year, then turned the duty over to someone else.) Consuls began their term with the new year on Jan. 1. Thus the edict giving the Jewish faith a protected status in the Roman Empire was issued in Jan. or Feb. of A.D. 27.

James was not stoned by the Jews, but beheaded by the Roman leader Herod Agrippa I. Herod received an increase in power because Claudius gave him a greater territory, adding Judea to the other areas he governed. According to Josephus, Herod was given this additional territory at the time of the edict favoring the Jews. Herod was in Rome at the time, and after the edict was issued he was sent to Israel to take control of the additional territories and to enforce the edict.[606] Herod was emboldened by his increase in authority when the emperor gave him additional territories to govern. He also saw an opportunity. The edict that Claudius issued gave the Jews, whom Herod now governed, protected and favored status. Herod realized that he could please the emperor and obtain his favor by pleasing the Jews. That is why Herod sided with them in their disputes with the Christians and had the Apostle James the Greater put to death. "Then he killed James, the brother of John, with the sword. And seeing that it pleased the Jews, he set out next to apprehend Peter also. Now it was the days of Unleavened Bread." (Acts 12:2-3).

Herod Agrippa I killed the Apostle James sometime after he was given authority over Judea (A.D. 26), and before he died in A.D. 28. His reason for killing James and imprisoning Peter was probably to please the Jews, whom he had recently begun to rule over (A.D. 26), and thereby to please the emperor Claudius, who had issued an edict favoring the Jews. This edict was issued in the second year of Claudius' reign, in Jan. or Feb. of A.D. 27. The killing of James took place in the spring at the Passover, not long after the edict had been issued and Herod had arrived in Judea by boat. The sailing season on the Mediterranean begins on Feb. 8 (according to Pliny[607]) and so, with good weather, Herod could easily travel to Judea from Rome by boat in less than 2 months, in time for the Passover of A.D. 27, which began on April 9 (Nisan 14) that year.[608] Therefore, the most probable date for the death of the Apostle James the Greater is the Passover of A.D. 27, between the evening of Wednesday April 9 and of Wednesday April 16, the seven days of unleavened bread (Exodus 12:14-20).[609]

After he killed James, Herod Agrippa I arrested Peter (Acts 12:3) for the same reason, to please the Jews and so please the emperor. Peter escaped with the help of an angel and left Jerusalem (Acts 12:6-17). Jerome places Peter in Rome for the first time in the second year of Claudius (A.D. 27).[610] Peter must have made his way to Rome after escaping the arrest by Herod Agrippa I earlier that same year. Peter then began his 25-year rule over Rome (during which he traveled to many other cities and nations).

The Conversion of Saul

Saul persecuted the Church, put the disciples in prison, and voted for their deaths (Acts 8:3, 9:1-4, 26:9-11; Galatians 1:13). He consented in the killing of Saint Stephen (Acts 7:58-8:1). Afterwards, Saul was converted and became the Apostle Paul (Acts 9:3-22, 13:9). Stephen was martyred during the winter of A.D. 21/22, so Saul must have been converted sometime after Stephen's death. Also, in the Acts of the Apostles, Stephen's death occurs at the end of chapter 7, but, by the first few verses of chapter 9, Saul is "still breathing threats and beatings against the disciples of the Lord...." (Acts 9:1). More than one chapter intervenes between Stephen's death and Saul's conversion, indicating that some length of time passed before Saul was converted. Thus the earliest date for Saul's conversion would be sometime in early A.D. 22.

Saul Visits Jerusalem

The latest date for Saul's conversion can be determined by comparing the Apostle Paul's letter to the Galatians to the Acts of the Apostles. Paul writes in Galatians a brief chronology of his conversion and his ministry. First, he persecuted the Church (Gal 1:13-14), then he was converted (Gal 1:15-16). Next, Paul specifically states that he did not go to Jerusalem after his conversion, but went to Arabia and then back to Damascus (Gal 1:17). His first visit to Jerusalem after his conversion occurred after his return to Damascus.

"And then, after three years, I went to Jerusalem to see Peter; and I stayed with him for fifteen days. But I saw none of the other Apostles, except James, the brother of the Lord. Now what I am writing to you: behold, before God, I am not lying." (Gal 1:18-20).

The 3 years could be counted from either Paul's conversion or from his return to Damascus. Paul visited Jerusalem again long after his conversion. "Next, after fourteen years, I went up again to Jerusalem, taking with me Barnabas and Titus." (Gal 2:1). The 14 years could be counted either from Paul's conversion or from the previous trip to Jerusalem. Paul's visit to Jerusalem after 14 years is often called his second visit, since it is the second visit to Jerusalem, after his conversion, described in Galatians. Paul specifically states that he did not visit Jerusalem between his conversion and his first visit, the one after 3 years (Gal 1:17). However, he does not say whether or not he visited Jerusalem between the visit after 3 years and the one after 14 years (Cf. Gal 2:1). Some commentators conclude that Paul did not, but an analysis of Acts of the Apostles indicates that Paul did visit Jerusalem between the visit after 3 years and the visit after 14 years.

Acts of the Apostles describes Paul's first visit to Jerusalem. In Acts 9:26-30, Paul, who is still called Saul at this point in time, visits Jerusalem and tries to join the disciples. At first they distrust him, but, with the help of Barnabas, he is accepted and preaches the Gospel among them. Clearly this is Saul's first visit to Jerusalem. He seeks acceptance from the brethren of Jerusalem because they have not yet met with him since his conversion. Also, he is still called "Saul," so this visit to Jerusalem occurred closer to his conversion. Only later in Acts, after some length of time has passed, is he called "Paul."

In Acts 9, Barnabas introduces Saul to the apostles. But in Galatians, Paul emphatically states that he saw only Cephas and James the Less (Gal 1:19-20). The reason is that Paul, in Galatians, is using the word "apostles" (Gal 1:19) to refer only to the Twelve, since he uses the expression "to those who were Apostles before me." (Gal 1:17). The expression "before me" could have a similar meaning to the expression used by John the Baptist, "He who is to come after me, has been placed ahead of me...." (Jn 1:15). Thus Paul is not only referring to the fact that the Twelve Apostles came before him in time, but also that they have a greater authority in the Church than he does; they rank ahead of him. In contrast, Acts of the Apostles seems to use the word "apostles" in the more general sense. Thus, Acts 9 is describing the same visit to Jerusalem as the first visit of Galatians, the one after three years (Gal 1:18).

Paul's visit to Jerusalem after 14 years (Gal 2:1) is the one described in Acts 15:1-35, where the leaders of the Church resolve a dispute as to whether or not Christians had to follow Mosaic Law. Paul refers to this conflict in Galatians 2:3-7. He tells us that he presented his teachings among the Gentiles (which certainly did not require them to follow Mosaic Law) to the apostles (Gal 2:2) and that as a result even Titus was not required to follow Mosaic Law by being circumcised (Gal 2:3). Acts 15 relates this same controversy about Mosaic Law and circumcision (Acts 15:1-2), and specifically mentions Paul's role in debating these issues (Acts 15:12). Furthermore, in the text of Galatians, Paul mentions that Barnabas went to Jerusalem with him on this visit, which also agrees with the text of Acts 15. In addition, Acts 15:36-41 describes a disagreement between Paul and Barnabas, which caused them to go their separate ways. Paul's visit to

Jerusalem after 14 years must have occurred before this disagreement, since Barnabas was still with Paul at that time.

Acts of the Apostles agrees well with Galatians concerning the visit by Paul to Jerusalem after 3 years and the one after 14 years. However, Acts of the Apostles describes an additional visit by Paul to Jerusalem, though mainly to the surrounding area of Judea. In Acts 11:27-30 and 12:25, Saul and Barnabas are sent to Judea during a famine (Acts 11:28), during the reign of Claudius (Acts 11:28), and about the time of the death of Herod Agrippa I (Acts 12:1-23). Their purpose is to bring relief to the brethren of Judea. The city of Jerusalem itself is not mentioned until Acts 12:25, which states: "Then Barnabas and Saul, having completed the ministry, returned from Jerusalem, bringing with them John, who was surnamed Mark." (Acts 12:25). Saul spent most of his time during this mission traveling around Judea, bringing relief to various Christians affected by the famine. He likely visited Jerusalem, at least briefly, to communicate with the leaders of the Church in Judea about this mission, resulting in the reference to Jerusalem in Acts 12:25.

Notice that the verse stating that Barnabas and Saul had been to Jerusalem (Acts 12:25) occurs after the passage in which Herod died (Acts 12:23). The intervening verse (Acts 12:24) is about the spread of the Gospel and indicates that there was some time between Herod's death and Saul's visit to Jerusalem. Saul spent most of his time bringing relief to those in need in the surrounding area of Judea. He and Barnabas likely avoided Jerusalem, the seat of Roman authority in the area, lest they be put to death as James the Greater had been, or imprisoned as Peter had been. But, once Herod died, they could freely go to and from Jerusalem, as Acts 12:25 indicates.

Why doesn't Paul, in Galatians, mention this visit to Jerusalem during the time of famine? In Galatians, Paul is talking about his authority to preach the Gospel. First, Paul states that the Gospel he preaches comes from a revelation of Jesus Christ, not from men (Gal 1:11-12). Then he makes the point that he preached the Gospel for years before going to Jerusalem to meet with some of the apostles (Gal 1:16-20), and, as Acts tells us, to obtain their acceptance (Acts 9:26-30). Next, he describes his visit to Jerusalem after 14 years in which he presented the Gospel he preached to the Gentiles to the leaders of the Church and obtained their approval (Gal 2:1-10). Paul describes these two visits to Jerusalem in the context of his authority to preach and his approval by the other leaders of the Church. His brief visit to the city of Jerusalem at the time of his mission to the needy of Judea was not related to his authority to preach the Gospel nor to the approval of his teachings by the other apostles, and so it is not mentioned. The assumption that the second visit to Jerusalem mentioned in Galatians was absolutely his second visit (after his conversion) is unwarranted; rather, it was Paul's third visit to Jerusalem, as is clear from Acts.

The date of Saul's actual second visit to Jerusalem, at the time of the famine, is now clear. Herod Agrippa I died in the third year of the reign of Claudius, after his own reign of seven years (see above). In my revised chronology, the third year of Claudius' reign was A.D. 28. That year was also a Sabbatical year (per Wacholder, A.D. 27/28). During Sabbatical years, food shortages and outright famine were common because the Jews would neither sow nor harvest crops (Lev 25:1-7)—and because the Jews changed the

Sabbatical year to begin in autumn, instead of in spring, as God intended (see chapter 16). The year A.D. 28, then, fits the criteria of Acts 11:28 – 12:25, a famine due to the Sabbatical year, during the reign of Claudius, about the time of the death of Herod Agrippa I.

It is not clear how long Saul was in Judea. In Acts, his arrival (Acts 11:27-30) is placed before the description of Herod Agrippa I's death (Acts 12:20-23), and his departure is placed afterwards (Acts 12:25). This arrangement of the text gives the impression that Saul's visit to Judea during the famine was lengthy. The text about Saul's arrival is also placed before the text about the death of James the Greater (during the Passover of A.D. 27). However, it is unlikely that Saul arrived in A.D. 27, before James the Greater's death, because the Sabbatical year began in the autumn of A.D. 27. Food shortages during Sabbatical years would not occur early in the Sabbatical year (in this case, late A.D. 27), because stored supplies of food from prior harvests would still be available. Rather, the food shortages would generally occur later in the Sabbatical year, when stored supplies had been exhausted (in this case, sometime during early A.D. 28). Saul came to Judea because of the shortage of food. Thus, the events of Acts 11-12 are not entirely arranged in chronological order. Acts 12:1-19 tells the story of Herod Agrippa I's cruelty to the Church and to James and Peter, as an introduction to the story of Herod Agrippa I's death (Acts 12:20-24). Saul most likely arrived in Judea in mid A.D. 28, after the food shortages began. And he probably completed his mission in early A.D. 29, after the death of Herod (in late A.D. 28), and after the harvest of the first crops planted at the end of the Sabbatical year (planted in autumn of A.D. 28 and harvested, some months later, in early A.D. 29).[611] Saul, Barnabas, and John Mark could then have departed Judea by boat in early A.D. 29.

Paul in Corinth

The dates of Paul's conversion and of his visits to Jerusalem after 3 years and after 14 years can be determined based on the date of his visit to Corinth, described in Acts 18:1-18. Paul stayed in Corinth, which is located within the area called Achaia, for "a year and six months" (Acts 18:11). Sometime during that time period, when Gallio was proconsul of Achaia, the Jews of Corinth made accusations against Paul before Gallio, but to no avail (Acts 18:12-17). The office of proconsul was generally held for a singe year, beginning in late spring or early summer.[612] Jack Finegan dates the proconsulship of Gallio from mid A.D. 51 to mid A.D. 52.[613] This date is based on the usual dates for the reigns of the Roman emperors, so that Gallio's reign over Achaia occurred within the 11th and 12th years of Claudius' reign as emperor. In my revised chronology, this places the proconsulship of Gallio from A.D. 36 to A.D. 37, which are the 11th and 12th years of the revised dates for Claudius' reign.

After describing the conflict with the Jews before Gallio, Acts states plainly: "Yet truly, Paul, after he had remained for many more days…." (Acts 18:18). Therefore, this conflict during Gallio's proconsulship did not occur near the end of the year and six months that Paul was in Corinth, but rather at the beginning or in the middle of that time period. The earliest date for the conflict before Gallio would be summer of A.D. 36, when Gallio first arrived. And so the earliest date for Paul's arrival in Corinth would be about a year earlier (so that there would still be "many more days" after the conflict under Gallio), in mid A.D. 35. (As shown below, A.D. 35 turns out to be too early a date, since Paul was in Antioch for a long while after the Council of A.D. 35.) And the latest date for the conflict before Gallio, and also for Paul's arrival in Corinth, would be late spring of A.D. 37, at the end of Gallio's year as proconsul.

The events of Acts 18 are placed after the events of Acts 15, which is the same visit to Jerusalem Paul describes in Galatians 2 (the visit after 14 years). Therefore, Paul visited Jerusalem "after fourteen years" (Gal 2:1) sometime before spring of A.D. 37 (the latest date for Paul's visit to Corinth).

If we count back 14 years from spring of A.D. 37, we find the latest possible date for the conversion of Saul, A.D. 24. If the 14 years were counted from his previous visit to Jerusalem, the one after 3 years, then Saul's conversion would have to be placed in A.D. 21 or earlier, before the death of St. Stephen. Since this is not possible, the 14 years must be counted instead from the conversion of Saul, and so also the 3 years must be counted from his conversion.

The earliest date for Saul's conversion is in early A.D. 22, soon after St. Stephen's martyrdom. Counting forward 14 years, inclusive, from A.D. 22 brings us to A.D. 35 as the 14th year from the conversion of Saul to his third visit to Jerusalem. This earliest date for Saul's third visit allows sufficient time between the events of Acts 15 (the third visit) and Acts 18 (conflict before Gallio) for the events described in Acts between those events. Placing Saul's conversion even one year later, in A.D. 23, moves his third visit to Jerusalem to A.D. 36, which does not leave sufficient time for all of the events of Acts 15:22 – 18:1 to occur before Gallio's proconsulship (mid A.D. 36 to mid A.D. 37) and the events of Acts 18. Therefore, Saul was converted in A.D. 22, in the first part of the year so that A.D. 22 counts as the first of the 14 years and A.D. 35 counts as the 14th year, when he visited Jerusalem for the third time (Gal 2 and Acts 15). The length of time between St. Stephen's death and Saul's conversion was at least a few weeks (Acts 8:1 – 9:1) and as much as a few months.

Saul's first visit to Jerusalem occurred 3 years after his conversion (as concluded above). Counting forward 3 years from early A.D. 22 places his first visit either sometime in mid to late A.D. 24 or, more likely (see below), in early A.D. 25. The 3 years length of time, as also the 14 years, need not be exact to the day or month.

Sabbatical Years

Some of the most important events in the early Church coincided with the Jewish Sabbatical years. Partly because of the shortage of food in the first Sabbatical year after the Ascension of Christ, the first Deacons of the Church were chosen to provide for those in need (A.D. 21). The Twelve Apostles made this decision along with "the multitude of the disciples" (Acts 6:2). This gathering of Church leaders to make an important decision was the first Council of the Church and occurred during a Jewish Sabbatical year.

In the second Sabbatical year, A.D. 27/28, after the Ascension of Christ, there were again shortages of food, particularly in the latter part of the Sabbatical year (A.D. 28). This year included Saul's second visit to Jerusalem, though he mainly spent his time bringing relief to those in the surrounding area, and the death of Herod Agrippa I, who had been persecuting the Church. There may also have been a Council of the Church soon after this second Sabbatical year ended (as explained below).

In the third Sabbatical year, A.D. 34/35, the events of Acts 15 occurred. The leaders of the Church gathered in Jerusalem, including Paul and Barnabas and Titus (Gal 2:1-3), to decide whether or not Christians had to keep Mosaic Law. Peter and James the Less were present (Acts 15:7, 13). James the Greater had been martyred years earlier. This gathering was another of the earliest Councils of the Church and took place in the Sabbatical year in A.D. 35, just prior to the Jubilee year of A.D. 35/36. (See chapter 16 for an explanation of Sabbatical and Jubilee years; see also Appendix I, Chart 7.) The issue raised at this Council, whether or not to follow all of the rules of the Jewish Law, fit this time period particularly well. Christians had to decide whether or not to keep the laws and traditions of the Sabbatical year and also the imminent Jubilee year (Lev 25). The social and cultural pressure on Christians to keep Mosaic Law must have increased due to this combination of the Sabbatical and Jubilee years.

The Virgin Mary's Dwelling Places

Blessed Anne Catherine tells us that the Virgin Mary, after the Ascension of Christ, lived for three years on Mount Zion (Jerusalem), three years at Bethany (just outside Jerusalem), and nine years at Ephesus.[614] The three years she spent living at Jerusalem would then extend from A.D. 19 to sometime in late A.D. 21 (counting the years inclusively), or in A.D. 22. In the winter of A.D. 21/22, Pilate was recalled to Rome and replaced by Marcellus, St. Stephen was martyred, and subsequently, in March of A.D. 22, the emperor Tiberius died. These political changes, and the persecution which accompanied Stephen's death (Acts 8:1), may have been the reason that the Virgin Mary moved out of the city, to the town of Bethany on the other side of the Mount of Olives from Jerusalem. Her move to Bethany, then, could have occurred as early as Dec. of A.D. 21 or as late as March of A.D. 22. Most likely, she moved along with many of the disciples at the time when the disciples were scattered by the persecution of Acts 8:1. Since Stephen's death is placed in winter of A.D. 21/22, this would also be the time that the Virgin Mary moved to Bethany.

After living in Bethany for about three years, from winter of A.D. 21/22 to late A.D. 24 or early A.D. 25, the Virgin Mary moved with St. John to Ephesus (cf. Jn 19:27).[615] To reach Ephesus from Judea, one must travel by boat on the Mediterranean. But the winter was considered a dangerous time to travel on the Mediterranean Sea. Pliny states that the sailing season would not begin until Feb. 8.[616] Sacred Scripture also refers to the difficulty of sailing the Mediterranean in winter. The Apostle Paul was taken to Rome by boat to appeal to the emperor (Acts 26:32 – 27:1). "Then, after much time had passed, and since sailing would no longer be prudent because the Fast Day had now passed...." (Acts 27:9). The "fast day" is the Day of Atonement, often called the fast day, which occurs in the autumn. Here Sacred Scripture is saying that the winter was a dangerous time to sail on the Mediterranean. Paul therefore advised them not to set sail (Acts 27:10), but he was ignored (Acts 27:11-12). The result was that they were caught by a storm, tossed about for many days, and then shipwrecked on an island (Acts 27:14-44). Therefore, the Virgin Mary would not have traveled to Ephesus in the winter of A.D. 24/25, but rather in the spring of A.D. 25 (sometime after Feb. 8) at the earliest.

This chronology has Mary leaving Bethany, which is near Jerusalem, for Ephesus about the same time that Paul visited Jerusalem for the first time. John the Gospel writer generally lived in the same town or area as the Virgin Mary (Jn 19:27). Yet, when Paul writes about his first visit to Jerusalem after his conversion, he emphatically states that the only apostles he saw were Cephas (Peter) and James the Less. If the Virgin Mary and the Apostle John were in Jerusalem or Bethany at the time, Paul would likely have taken the opportunity to meet with them. Since he did not, it is likely that the Virgin Mary and John had left for Ephesus sometime before Paul arrived.[617] If we count forward three years from Paul's conversion to his first visit to Jerusalem, we arrive at either mid/late A.D. 24 or early A.D. 25. But, since Paul did not run into John when visiting Jerusalem (Gal 1:19-20), the date of early A.D. 25, after the Virgin Mary and John had departed for Ephesus, is more likely. Saint Paul's first visit to Jerusalem after his conversion occurred in early A.D. 25.

Why did the Virgin Mary leave Judea for Ephesus in early A.D. 25? In that year, Herod the tetrarch was banished to Spain and control over Galilee was given to Herod Agrippa I.[618] Also in A.D. 25, but probably beginning later in the year, the Roman emperor Gaius (Caligula) decided to have his statue placed in the Temple of Jerusalem, so he could be worshipped as if he were a god.[619] When Mary left Judea for Ephesus, Herod Agrippa I's persecution of the Church had not yet begun. And Caligula's army had not yet arrived in Galilee on their way to try to install his statue in the Temple of Jerusalem. But she made her departure not long before these tumultuous events occurred. In this way, Grace and Providence guided her to a safe place to be nourished by God (cf. Rev 12:6).

The Virgin Mary Visits Jerusalem

"After three years' sojourn here Mary had a great longing to see Jerusalem again, and was taken there by John and Peter. Several of the Apostles were, I believe, assembled there: I saw Thomas among them and I think a Council was held at which Mary assisted them with her advice."[620]

Here Blessed Anne Catherine tells us about the Virgin Mary's return to Jerusalem after she had been living at Ephesus for about three years. Since she went to Ephesus in early A.D. 25, three years would be completed in early A.D. 28. The length of time may have been more or less than three exact years. However, in early A.D. 27, Herod Agrippa I began a persecution of the Church during which James the Greater was put to death and Peter put in prison. Mary's visit to Jerusalem most likely occurred after the death of Herod Agrippa I (in late A.D. 28), when Peter, John, and Mary could stay in Jerusalem without concern of imprisonment or death. Also, Blessed Anne Catherine believed there was a Council of the Church at the time that Peter, John, and Mary visited Jerusalem. A gathering of the leaders of the Church, including Peter, John, Thomas, and other Apostles, along with the Virgin Mary, would not be held in Jerusalem during a time when Herod Agrippa I was still in authority and willing to kill or imprison Christian leaders. When Herod Agrippa I died, there was a respite from persecution (Acts 12:24) during which the Church grew and prospered. The leaders of the early Church took advantage of this respite in order to meet in (what was most likely) the second Council of the Church. This Council and Mary's visit to Jerusalem occurred after the death of Herod Agrippa I.

Saul and Barnabas' mission to bring relief to those suffering from the famine in Judea ended soon after Herod's death (Acts 12:23-25). Herod Agrippa I died sometime in A.D. 28 (as shown above). The Sabbatical year was also completed that same year, in autumn of A.D. 28, after which the Jews could plant and harvest again. The end of the Sabbatical year must have been a major factor in ending the famine. Therefore, the famine likely ended in early A.D. 29, (the plantings from autumn of A.D. 28 would be harvested in early A.D. 29). Herod's death occurred not long before the end of the famine, and so he died in the latter part of A.D. 28. The Virgin Mary's visit to Jerusalem and the Council occurred after Herod's death, in late A.D. 28 or early A.D. 29. But, since the Mediterranean is dangerous to travel in winter, early A.D. 29 is the most likely time for both the Council and the visit of Mary to Jerusalem. Thus, the length of time that Mary lived in Ephesus before visiting Jerusalem was somewhat greater than three years.

Saul and Barnabas were in Judea and Jerusalem until sometime after the death of Herod, when their mission to bring relief to those suffering from famine had ended. Their mission ended with the end of the famine, which likely ended with the harvest of early A.D. 29. But, in his Letter to the Galatians, Paul doesn't mention a meeting with the leaders of the Church in Jerusalem. If he had been present at such a Council, he would have mentioned it, because his topic in Galatians 1-2 is his authority to preach and how his authority relates to the authority of the other Apostles. He makes this point repeatedly: his authority is from God, not men (Gal 1:1), anyone preaching a contrary gospel has gone astray (Gal 1:6-9), the Gospel he preaches is also from God, not men (Gal 1:10-12), he did not have to confer with the other apostles and leaders of the Church (Gal 1:16-17), he met with only a couple of the Apostles (Gal 1:18-20), and, when he did finally meet with the leaders of the Church as a group, they fully approved of the Gospel he had been teaching (Gal 2:1-10). He also mentions his role in correcting an error found in the actions of Cephas (Peter), which further shows his authority to preach the Gospel and his relationship with others in authority in the early Church (Gal 2:11-21). Therefore, if Paul had still been in Judea and Jerusalem at the time of the Council (the one after Herod's death), he surely would have added this to his thorough treatment of his place among those in leadership and authority in the Church. Since he does not mention this Council at all, he was not present at that Council. The famine had ended and Paul had departed, before this Council occurred. Again, this places the Council and Mary's visit in early A.D. 29, after she had been in Ephesus closer to four years than to three years.

At that time, Paul was still called "Saul" (Acts 12:25) because he was still seen more as new convert to Christianity and less as an established Apostle and leader among the brethren. Paul did not have as much authority in the Church then as he later had, and so he was not a part of this Council. His authority reached its maturity at the subsequent Council (the one about 14 years after his conversion) when he explained to Peter and the other Apostles the Gospel message he had been preaching to the Gentiles and they gave their full approval (Gal 2:7-10).

Only then did they understand that Paul had been entrusted with the Gospel to the uncircumcised, as Scripture says: "they had seen that the Gospel to the uncircumcised was entrusted to me, just as the Gospel to the circumcised was entrusted to Peter." (Gal 2:7). And only then did they acknowledge the grace that was given to the Apostle Saint Paul (Gal 2:9).

Thus, the Council and the Virgin Mary's visit to Jerusalem occurred after the famine had ended and after Paul with Barnabas had left Jerusalem and Judea. Since the famine most likely ended in early A.D. 29, the Virgin Mary visited Jerusalem, at the time of this second Council of the Church, in early A.D. 29. I speculate that the topics discussed at the Council may have included the recent persecution under Herod Agrippa I, how to deal with future persecutions, the recent famine, and the attention which the Church must always give to the poor (even after the famine had ended).

Peter in Rome

As explained above, Peter was imprisoned at the time of the martyrdom of James the Greater, in spring of A.D. 27. He soon escaped and left the area (Acts 12:4-17). Since Herod Agrippa I had imprisoned Peter, perhaps with the intention of eventually putting him to death, Peter would have gone to a place not under Herod's authority. At that time, in A.D. 27, Herod controlled the areas formerly controlled by Philip (cf. Lk 3:1) and Herod the tetrarch, as well as Judea, Samaria, and Caesarea.[621] Herod Agrippa I controlled a large area.[622] And so, Peter had to go far to escape from the threat of imprisonment and death at Herod's hands.

According to Saint Jerome, Peter went to Rome in the second year of Claudius (in this chronology, A.D. 27), and he reigned as bishop there for 25 years. "Simon Peter…pushed on to Rome in the second year of Claudius to over-throw Simon Magus, and held the sacerdotal chair there for twenty-five years until the last, that is the fourteenth, year of Nero."[623] The second year of Claudius is the same year as the martyrdom of James the Greater. So, after he escaped from prison, Peter made his way to Rome and arrived there in the same year, A.D. 27.

Peter fled for Rome about the time of the Passover (Acts 12:3). The length of Peter's bishopric at Rome is given in several different sources as 25 years, 1 month, and 8 or 9 days.[624] Since Peter died on June 29, one might conclude that he arrived in Rome about May 20. There is sufficient time between the Passover of A.D. 27 (which began April 9) and the date of May 20 for a trip to Rome by boat in the spring, when the sailing weather on the Mediterranean is good. Now this date for Peter's arrival is not certain. He may have taken longer to make the trip to Rome, especially since he had to avoid detection by Roman officials under Herod's authority as well as by Jewish leaders (who might turn him over to the Romans). But, in any case, Peter would have been able to arrive in Rome, even if his journey had difficulties and delays, at least by mid A.D. 27.

Several different sources give the length of Peter's reign as bishop of Rome as 25 years.[625] These sources are not counting the years inclusively, because they attempt to give the exact length of Peter's reign (25 years, 1 month, and 8 or 9 days).[626] If we count forward 25 years from A.D. 27, we arrive at A.D. 52 as the year of Peter's martyrdom. The emperor Nero died in the 14th year of his reign, on June 9 of A.D. 53 (see chapter 13). In this chronology, then, Peter died in the 13th year of the reign of Nero, which is A.D. 52. Why then does Saint Jerome give the 14th year of Nero as the year of Peter's death?

The Martyrdoms of Peter and Paul

Finegan reasonably places the death of Peter on June 29, based on a number of ancient sources.[627] According to Jerome, as well as Eusebius, Peter and Paul were both put to death on the same day, during the reign of Nero.[628] Since Nero died on June 9, it is unlikely that Peter and Paul were put to death 20 days later. It was Nero who undertook the first major persecution of the Church by the Roman Empire. When he died, there was a succession of three emperors (Galba, Otho, Vitellius) whose reigns were brief and who did not have the time, power, or inclination to give attention to the Christians. Therefore, the 13th year of Nero, 25 years after Peter came to Rome, is the most likely time for the deaths of Peter and Paul.

Jerome calls the year in which Peter and Paul died: "the last, that is the fourteenth, year of Nero."[629] Peter and Paul did die less than a year before the death of Nero, so they died literally in Nero's last year. It was not the 14th calendar year, but rather the 13th calendar year. Furthermore, Jerome also states that Peter and Paul died two years after the death of the poet Seneca. "He [Seneca] was put to death by Nero two years before Peter and Paul were crowned with martyrdom."[630] The usual date for Seneca's death is A.D. 65, which is A.D. 50 in this revised chronology, and which is in any case the 11th year of Nero's reign. Counting forward 2 years brings us to the 13th year of Nero's reign and this according to Jerome's own words.

Peter's Reign

Peter was leader of the Apostles and of the Church from the time of Christ's Ascension to the time of his martyrdom. Christ's Ascension took place on May 18 of A.D. 19 and Peter's martyrdom took place on June 29 of A.D. 52. The length of Peter's reign as the first leader of the Church on earth after Jesus Christ was 33 years plus 42 days (May 19 to June 29, inclusive, which is exactly six weeks). This length of time is exactly the same as the length of time in this chronology for Christ's life, from His Incarnation to His Crucifixion (see chapter 2). Christ was conceived on Feb. 25 of 15 B.C., and He was crucified on April 7 of A.D. 19, a time period of exactly 33 years and six weeks (see chapters 2 and 5). Other writers have claimed that the length of Peter's reign was more or less; they are mistaken. [631]

The Gospel of Mark

Herod Agrippa I began to persecute the Church in spring of A.D. 27, after receiving the edit from Claudius giving the Jewish religion protected and favored status in the Roman Empire.[632] James the Greater was put to death; Peter was imprisoned. Peter escaped from prison and eventually made his way to Rome. Certainly other disciples in Jerusalem and Judea were persecuted at that time and may have followed Peter, the leader of the Apostles, to Rome.

Peter mentions Mark in his first Epistle: "The Church which is in Babylon, elect together with you, greets you, as does my son, Mark." (1 Peter 5:13). Mark is called Peter's son because he was Peter's disciple. Saint Jerome calls Mark, Peter's "disciple and interpreter," and he states that the Gospel of Mark is, for that reason, sometimes attributed to Peter.[633] When Peter escaped from prison, "And as he was considering this, he arrived at the house of Mary, the mother of John, who was surnamed Mark, where many were gathered and were praying." (Acts 12:12). John Mark is the Gospel writer Mark. Peter was at Mark's house just before he fled Jerusalem for Rome. And Mark, a disciple of Peter, was at Rome with Peter for many years sometime thereafter. Thus John Mark most likely fled with Peter to Rome at that time, both to escape the general persecution under Herod Agrippa I, and to be with Peter, his teacher in the Faith. And this is how the close association between Peter and Mark began.

On the other hand, Acts of the Apostles does not specifically say that Mark fled with Peter (Acts 12:17). It is possible that Mark joined Peter in Rome at a later date. Acts does say that Mark was in Jerusalem with Saul and Barnabas at the time that they had completed their mission to those suffering from the famine. They then took Mark with them on their missionary journeys (Acts 12:25). Mark was at this time with Saul, not in Rome with Peter. Saul and Barnabas completed their mission sometime after the death of Herod Agrippa I. He died in A.D. 28, probably late in the year.[634] This places Mark in Jerusalem sometime in late A.D. 28 or early A.D. 29.

But Peter had fled Jerusalem for Rome in early A.D. 27. So Mark could easily have left Jerusalem with Peter in early A.D. 27, spent considerable time in Rome, and still visited Jerusalem 1½ to 2 years later. Since Herod had died, Peter could have visited Jerusalem at this time, along with Mark. A more likely scenario, though, is that Saul and Barnabas completed their mission not long after the death of Herod. Peter would not then have been in Jerusalem, since he would not have had time to hear about Herod's death and then travel to Judea from Rome. But Peter may have sent his disciple John Mark on his behalf, even before Herod died, to bring relief to the poor during the famine. In any case, both Peter and Mark certainly traveled extensively during the time that they were both based in Rome.

Mark was also with Paul and Barnabas in Antioch (Acts 15:30-39), sometime after the Council of the Church at the time of Paul's third visit to Jerusalem (the one after 14 years). At that time, there was a dissension between Paul and Barnabas about Mark. Paul and Barnabas had decided to continue their missionary journeys, but Paul did not want Mark to continue to travel with them. So Barnabas and Paul went their separate ways, with Mark accompanying Barnabas instead of Paul. Paul's third visit to Jerusalem (for the Council of Acts 15) occurred in A.D. 35. So Mark's journey with Barnabas must be placed either later in A.D. 35 or in early A.D. 36. Paul's missionary journeys prior to his arrival in Corinth (where the conflict under Gallio occurred) must also have begun in A.D. 35, after the Council, or in early A.D. 36. This later date of A.D. 36 still allows sufficient time for Paul's travels prior to Corinth, if Paul arrived in Corinth sometime after Gallio's reign had begun. (Gallio ruled Achaia from mid A.D. 36 to mid A.D. 37.)

Acts describes a period of time after the Council of A.D. 35, when Paul and Barnabas were in Antioch (Acts 15:22-35). Then, "after some days," Paul suggested to Barnabas that they resume their missionary journeys (Acts 15:36). This phrasing implies that they spent some significant amount of time in Antioch, long enough to constitute a break in their missionary journeys, so that they would have to reach a decision to resume those journeys. The most likely time for such resumption in traveling would be the spring of A.D. 36. The winter was a difficult and dangerous time for travel on the Mediterranean.

So, Paul often wintered in one location. As spring approached, it would be natural for any Apostle who traveled frequently spreading the Gospel to consider a missionary journey. This time frame also allows sufficient time after the Council of A.D. 35 for the events in the latter part of Acts 15. Therefore, Mark took his journey with Barnabas to Cyprus (Acts 15:39), and Paul began his journeys (Acts 15:40 to 18:1), in the spring of A.D. 36.

In addition to his missionary journeys with Paul and Barnabas, Mark spent much time in Rome and taught there under Peter's guidance for many years. The fact that Mark was based in Rome and was more a disciple of Peter than of Paul or Barnabas is well attested to by Jerome and Eusebius (see below). Also, Peter mentions Mark in his first Epistle (1 Peter 13). And, when Peter escaped from prison, he went to "the house of Mary, the mother of John, who was surnamed Mark...." (Acts 12:12). So Peter and Mark were well acquainted even before Peter went to Rome. This is not to say that Mark remained at Rome and never traveled. Many of the Apostles and disciples of Christ during this time period travel far and wide to spread the Gospel and to visit established churches. Mark most likely spent time traveling with Paul, and later with Barnabas, while he was based in Rome. The same it true for Mark's later missionary journey to Egypt. After Mark moved to Egypt to preach the Gospel, he very likely traveled back and forth from Egypt to various other established churches in the greater Mediterranean area.

Saint Jerome tells us how Mark came to write his Gospel:

> "Mark the disciple and interpreter of Peter wrote a short gospel at the request of the brethren at Rome embodying what he had heard Peter tell. When Peter had heard this, he approved it and published it to the churches to be read by his authority as Clemens in the sixth book of his Hypotyposes and Papias, bishop of Hierapolis, record."[635]

Eusebius adds that the faithful in Rome had to pester Mark quite a bit to convince him to write the Gospel:

> "So brightly shone the light of true religion on the minds of Peter's hearers that, not satisfied with a single hearing or with the oral teaching of the divine message, they resorted to appeals of every kind to induce Mark (whose gospel we have), as he was a follower of Peter, to leave them in writing a summary of the instruction they had received by word of mouth, nor did they let him go till they had persuaded him, and thus became responsible for the writing of what is known as the Gospel according to Mark. It is said that, on learning by divine revelation of the spirit what had happened, the apostle was delighted at their enthusiasm and authorized the reading of the book in the churches."[636]

Notice, in both Jerome and Eusebius, Peter was initially unaware that Mark was writing his Gospel. Eusebius even says that Peter had to be informed by divine revelation. Therefore Peter was not in Rome at the time that Mark wrote his Gospel. If Peter had been in Rome, he would surely have known of the repeated appeals by the faithful to Mark and would have known how his follower, Mark, had responded. Instead, Peter had to be informed as to what had occurred. Also, Peter must have been away from Rome for some length of time, long enough for the faithful to spend some time trying to convince Mark to write, then also long enough for Mark to write the whole of his Gospel before Peter even knew anything about it. Peter was most likely on a missionary journey to spread the Gospel, while Mark stayed behind and wrote the Gospel. And why would Peter's missionary journey take so long? Peter was probably spending the winter somewhere, because traveling the Mediterranean in winter was dangerous (Acts 27:10-12). It was quite common for the Apostles to spend the winter in one place, preferring to travel in the other seasons (see Acts 28:11; 2 Tim 4:21; 1 Cor 16:5-6; Titus 3:12).

Eusebius also tells us that the faithful of Rome not only "resorted to appeals of every kind," but also did not "let him go till they had persuaded him."[637] Where was Mark going that the faithful of Rome should detain him until he agreed to write the Gospel? Clearly Mark intended to go on a long journey, for if it were a short journey, the faithful of Rome would not have been so anxious to have the Gospel in writing. Could this journey have been one of Peter's missionary journeys to those places mentioned in 1 Peter 1:1 (modern-day Turkey)? No, if Mark did not accompany Peter, because the faithful had already persuaded him before Peter departed, then Peter would have known that Mark was writing the Gospel, which was not the case. Furthermore, Peter certainly returned to Rome after journeying to various places to preach Christ. If Mark had journeyed with Peter, he also would have returned, so that the faithful would not have been so anxious to have his teaching in writing.

Where did Mark intend to go after he wrote the Gospel? Mark likely intended to go on a long journey without Peter, a journey from which he might not return. For this reason, the faithful of Rome were anxious to persuade him to write the Gospel. Eusebius wrote that they sought to convince Mark "to leave them in writing a summary of the instruction they had received by word of mouth."[638] This phrasing indicates that Mark intended to go somewhere distant and perhaps never return, so that the faithful would no longer have access to Mark's teaching by his spoken words. Since Peter was away on a long journey of his own, and Mark was about to depart also, the faithful of Rome wanted Peter and Mark's teaching in writing. In this way, the Gospel of Mark came to be written.

Mark did make a long journey from which he did not return; he traveled to Egypt to preach the Gospel. "So, taking the gospel which he himself composed, he went to Egypt and first preaching Christ at Alexandria he formed a church so admirable in doctrine and continence of living that he constrained all followers of Christ to his example."[639] Mark completed his Gospel before going to Egypt, and, after preaching there for many years, he suffered a martyr's death. Mark's Gospel was written sometime before Mark traveled to Egypt. One possibility, then, is that the faithful of Rome delayed Mark's missionary journey to Egypt by convincing him to first write the Gospel of Mark.

It is not possible that Mark's missionary journey of Acts 15:39 was the journey delayed by the writing of the Gospel. Just prior to that time, Peter was in Jerusalem for a Council of the Church (A.D. 35:1-21). A journey to Rome with Peter could not have been the journey which Mark delayed taking in order to write the Gospel, because then Peter would have known that Mark was kept from journeying with him in order to write the Gospel, which was not the case. Thus the delayed journey could not have been one which Peter and Mark intended to take together, but rather one which Mark intended to take alone (and one from which he was not likely to return).

Nor was the delayed journey the one where Mark joined Barnabas in traveling from Antioch to Cyprus (Acts 15:39). Mark is not mentioned in the earlier passage about the Council, but Paul and Barnabas are mentioned (Acts 15:1-21). Mark does not seem to have been with Paul and Barnabas at this time. He is also not mentioned in the subsequent passage, the one that names those sent to Antioch (Acts 15:22-35). More significantly, Paul and Barnabas were in Antioch for some length of time teaching before they decided to set out on a missionary journey. Yet Paul would not accept Mark to accompany them on that journey. Paul's reason for not accepting Mark was that Mark "withdrew from them at Pamphylia, and he had not gone with them in the work." (Acts 15:38). If Mark had been teaching and serving along with Paul and Barnabas in Antioch, Paul would have been very unlikely to reject Mark for withdrawing and not doing the work of spreading the Gospel. If Paul had accepted Mark to preach with them in Antioch, then he would have accepted Mark to preach with them elsewhere. On this basis, I conclude that Mark was not at the Council in Jerusalem with Peter, nor did he spend much time with Paul and Barnabas in Antioch. Rather, Mark was elsewhere and came to Antioch at a later time, about the time that Paul and Barnabas were planning another journey. This journey most likely occurred in spring of A.D. 36, rather than late A.D. 35. Paul and Barnabas spent time in Jerusalem in A.D. 35 for the Council. Then they spent much time in Antioch preaching—so much time that it seemed to them a break from their missionary journeys, and thus did they decide to begin missionary journeys anew, as Acts 15:36 tells us. The spring would be a likely time to begin traveling again, after wintering in Antioch. Thus, Mark was in Antioch in early A.D. 36, but he was probably not in Jerusalem or Antioch in A.D. 35.

In summary, Mark wrote his Gospel before going on a long journey, from which he might never return, at a time when Peter was away for a longtime (perhaps wintering elsewhere). Mark intended to go on this journey, but delayed his trip in order to write the Gospel for the faithful of Rome. Peter did not know that Mark was writing the Gospel, and so the journey was not one that Peter and Mark had intended to take together. Neither is it likely that the delayed journey was one of Mark's journeys with Paul or Barnabas. Mark journeyed with Paul and Barnabas on a number of occasions, but did so while he was based in Rome. Mark often went on missionary journeys with Peter or with Paul and Barnabas, but he also returned from those journeys to Rome. The faithful of Rome would not have been so anxious to compel Mark to write the Gospel, if he was leaving on one of his usual trips from which he would soon return. Thus, the only missionary journey undertaken by Mark that fits the above criteria is Mark's missionary journey to Egypt.

Mark's Journey to Egypt

Mark's journey to Egypt was fundamentally different from his other trips. When he went to Egypt, Mark either traveled alone or was the leader of those who traveled with him. He was no longer tagging along with Peter or Paul or Barnabas. Mark founded the Christian community at Alexandria (in Egypt on the Delta of the Nile River), whereas, in his previous missionary journeys, he mainly visited existing Christian communities.

Eusebius tells us that Mark was the first to make a missionary journey to Egypt and the first to establish churches in Alexandria.[640] Traveling from Rome to Egypt to establish a new community of Christians was a major undertaking, perhaps the first under Mark's leadership, and clearly one from which he might never return to Rome. That is not to say that Mark never left Egypt once he arrived there. On the contrary, he likely journeyed to other Christian communities to communicate with, and to obtain support from, the other parts of the Church. However, he never did return to Rome to stay.

When did Mark make his first missionary journey to Egypt? One ancient source tells us that, in the 15th year after Christ's Ascension, Mark received a revelation that he should journey to Egypt.[641] Other sources place Mark in Egypt at various later dates.[642]

In any case, Mark could not have journeyed to Egypt too soon after arriving in Rome, for a number of reasons. Peter and Mark left for Rome from Jerusalem about the time of the Passover of A.D. 27 (early April that year), and they arrived on or about May 20 (see above). They did not have time to visit all of the places to which Peter addressed his first Epistle (1 Peter 1:1) before arriving in Rome. Yet Peter clearly had visited those places (in modern-day Turkey) before writing his first Epistle. Throughout his first Epistle, Peter speaks to them as one who knows them well. In 1 Peter 5:1, he states that he is a fellow elder along with the other elders of their churches. And in the close of the letter, Peter mentions that "my son, Mark" sends them greetings, implying that they also knew Mark (1 Peter 5:13). Thus Peter and Mark had visited those places sometime after they had arrived at Rome.

Numerous places are mentioned (Pontus, Galatia, Cappadocia, Asia, and Bithynia) in the first Epistle of Peter. But Peter first traveled to Rome from Jerusalem, and spent time preaching the Gospel and building up the church at Rome. Then Peter made at least one, and more likely several, long missionary journey to the areas mentioned in 1 Peter 1:1. Only after these events could he have written his first Epistle. Yet Mark was still with Peter when the first Epistle was written (1 Peter 5:13). Therefore, Mark journeyed to Egypt, and wrote his Gospel shortly before departing for Egypt, sometime after the first Epistle of Peter was written and many years after arriving in Rome. Mark could not have written his Gospel and departed for Egypt soon after arriving at Rome. He first had to spend much time learning from Peter, before he could write a Gospel that summarized Peter's teaching.[643]

Also, Mark was quite young when he journey to Rome with Peter. In 1 Peter 5:13, Peter refers to Mark as his "son," indicating that Mark was a young disciple of his. And in Acts of the Apostles, the house to which Peter fled after escaping from prison in Jerusalem is called, "the house of Mary, the mother of John, who was surnamed Mark" (Acts 12:12). In the culture and society of Israel at that time in history, a house would not be referred to as belonging to the woman living in that house, unless she had no husband and her son was still of a young age. Otherwise, the man of the house would be recognized by that society as the leader of that household. Therefore, the mother of John Mark was a widow and her son was still quite young, perhaps in his teens or early twenties, when Peter and Mark fled for Rome. Mark was too young, soon after arriving in Rome, to go the Egypt and found a community of Christians.[644]

The 15th year after Christ's Ascension (A.D. 34) was the year of the Virgin Mary's Dormition, Resurrection, and Assumption, according to Saint Bridget and Blessed Anne

Catherine Emmerich (see chapter 10). According to Blessed Anne Catherine, Peter attended the Dormition of the Virgin Mary and John Mark accompanied him.[645] An ancient source, *The History of the Patriarchs of the Coptic Church of Alexandria*, states that Mark decided, because of a revelation from God, to make his missionary journey to Alexandria in the 15th year after the Ascension of Christ.[646] But notice that this source does not say that Mark arrived that year, but only that he came to his decision that year.

The 15th year after the Ascension of Christ was a likely time for Mark to be inspired to leave Peter and undertake a missionary journey of his own. It was by then the 9th year of Claudius' reign. Mark had been Peter's student and assistant for over seven years, since journeying with Peter from Jerusalem to Rome during the spring of Claudius' 2nd year. He had also followed Paul and Barnabas on some of their missionary journeys. And he had attended the Dormition of the Virgin Mary at Ephesus, along with the remaining Eleven of the Twelve Apostles. Perhaps the Dormition of the Virgin Mary, as well as her Resurrection and Assumption, inspired Mark to take the next step in following Christ, to go on his own to a distant land and preach the Gospel.

Now it was the faithful of Rome who delayed Mark's missionary journey so that he would first write down the teachings of Christ for them. But the Gospel of Mark must have taken more than a few days or weeks to write. Peter and Mark probably went to Ephesus to attend the death of the Virgin Mary on relatively short notice (unless they knew long in advance the date of Mary's departure). They also had something of a deadline for beginning this journey. Therefore, this was not the journey that was delayed at the request of the faithful of Rome so Mark could write his Gospel. Yet at least one ancient source places Mark's decision to go to Egypt in that same year, the 15th since the Ascension.

For the above reasons, I conclude the following. Mark returned to Rome after the Assumption of the Virgin Mary. He was greatly inspired by the Virgin Mary's Dormition, Resurrection, and Assumption, and he may have also received some kind of revelation concerning God's will for him. The result was that he then decided to undertake his mission to preach the Gospel in Egypt. His journey to Egypt became associated with the 15th year after the Ascension because that was the year of the Assumption of the Virgin Mary and the year of his decision. But the faithful of Rome, knowing that he might never return from this mission to Egypt, delayed his journey by convincing him first to write the Gospel. Mark then took the Gospel, which he himself had recently written, to Egypt and founded the first community of Christians there, at Alexandria. In fact, the phrasing used by both Eusebius and Saint Jerome seems to imply that Mark had written his Gospel not long before journeying to Egypt: "So, taking the gospel which he himself composed, he went to Egypt...."[647] Eusebius also mentions the writing of the Gospel of Mark in the same sentence in which he tells us of Mark's journey to Egypt.[648] The Gospel of Mark was most likely written just prior to Mark's journey to Egypt and about the time of the 15th year after Christ's Ascension.

When did Mark actually arrive in Egypt? He could not have arrived in the same year as the Assumption of the Virgin Mary, which was the 15th since the Ascension of Christ and the 9th year of Claudius' reign (A.D. 34). The Assumption occurred in mid August in Ephesus (see chapter 10). But Mark wrote his Gospel in Rome, prior to leaving for Egypt. Mark must first have traveled back to Rome from Ephesus, a journey that may have taken a month or more, even in good weather. Mark could have arrived back in

Rome in September or early October. He reached his decision to undertake a missionary journey to Egypt at the time of the Assumption, or soon after.

There is not enough time between late September and the end of the season for safe travel on the Mediterranean (Nov. 11, according to Pliny[649]; see also Acts 27:9ff) to account for Mark's journey to Egypt and the preceding events. First, the faithful of Rome made numerous appeals to Mark to convince him to write, then Mark spent some length of time writing the Gospel, and, when he finally departed, Mark's journey to Egypt from Rome must have taken at least a couple of months. Therefore, the most reasonable conclusion is that Mark wanted to journey to Egypt soon after returning from the Dormition of the Virgin Mary, but the faithful of Rome delayed his journey by convincing him to first write the Gospel. Because he was writing his Gospel, Mark missed the end of the good sailing weather and had to winter in Rome. And Peter was not present in Rome during the writing of the Gospel of Mark because Peter was wintering elsewhere. Thus the delay spoken of by Eusebius was not a matter of days or weeks, but of a whole season. During that time, in late fall and winter of A.D. 34/35, Mark wrote his Gospel. He then departed for Egypt at his next opportunity, sometime in the spring of A.D. 35.

When Mark wrote his Gospel, Peter was not present, nor did Peter even know that the faithful of Rome were pestering Mark to write the Gospel. Peter could have left on a missionary journey soon after returning to Rome from attending the Dormition of the Virgin Mary at Ephesus. But, more likely, Peter did not return to Rome from Ephesus. Instead, he may have visited the churches mentioned in 1 Peter 1:1, which are in the same general area as Ephesus, and decided to winter in that region. Peter's extended absence from Rome (when he did not return from Ephesus with Mark), combined with Mark's intention to soon depart on a long missionary journey of his own, made the faithful of Rome anxious to obtain the Gospel in writing.

In summary, Mark decided to go to Egypt to preach Christ soon after the Dormition of the Virgin Mary. But when the faithful of Rome insisted he write the Gospel before leaving them, he was not able to leave before the sailing season ended and had to pass the whole winter in Rome, writing the Gospel and all the while persevering in his intention to make a missionary journey to Egypt. Since Mark wrote the Gospel without Peter's prior knowledge, Peter must have passed that winter somewhere other than Rome. Then, sometime after the good sailing weather resumed in early February, Mark set out for Egypt. He probably arrived in Egypt in spring of A.D. 35, the 16th year since the Ascension and the same year as the third Council of the Church (Acts 15). The Gospel of Mark was written in the winter of A.D. 34/35, just over 15 years since the Ascension of Christ to Heaven. The Jewish civil calendar year of A.D. 34/35 was a Sabbatical year (see chapter 16).

Acts of the Apostles records (Acts 15:36-41) that Mark made a missionary journey with Barnabas from Antioch, sometime after the Council of Acts 15 (A.D. 35). This journey probably occurred in early A.D. 36 (as concluded above). Mark's journey with Barnabas in A.D. 36 does not rule out Mark's earlier journey to Egypt in early A.D. 35. After spending about a year preaching the Gospel and establishing a new Christian community in Alexandria, Mark certainly could have returned to Antioch. In fact, it is both likely and reasonable that Mark would return to a city with a long-established Christian community after spending some time in a distant mission. Establishing a new church in a distant area is a difficult endeavor, which would benefit from periodic trips to cities with established Christian communities. There, Mark could seek advice and assistance, recruit additional workers in the faith, and perhaps also obtain financial or material support.

In addition, the Gospel of Mark had only recently been written and approved of by Peter. The distribution of this Gospel to Antioch and to other established Christian communities would have resulted in a desire by those communities to hear and meet with the Gospel writer, Mark. Thus Mark's presence was in demand, giving him another reason to make occasional trips away from his mission in Egypt.

The Gospel of Matthew

Eusebius records his understanding of the order in which the Gospels were written:

> Matthew had begun by preaching to Hebrews; and when he made up his mind to go to others too, he committed his own gospel to writing in his native tongue, so that for those with whom he was no longer present the gap left by his departure was filled by what he wrote. And when Mark and Luke had now published their gospels, John, we are told, who hitherto had relied entirely on the spoken word, finally took to writing....[650]

Here Eusebius tells us the order in which the Gospels were written. He clearly places the writing of Mark and Luke's Gospels after that of Matthew's. Also, notice that Matthew wrote his Gospel for much the same reason that Mark wrote his. Each was about to leave to preach the Gospel in a far off place. Each left behind his Gospel in writing, so that the Gospel would continue, after the preacher of the Gospel was gone.

Saint Jerome tells us that Matthew's Gospel was originally written in Hebrew.

> Matthew, also called Levi, apostle and aforetimes publican, composed a gospel of Christ at first published in Judea in Hebrew for the sake of those of the circumcision who believed, but this was afterwards translated into Greek though by what author is uncertain. The Hebrew itself has been preserved until the present day in the library at Caesarea which Pamphilus so diligently gathered. I have also had the opportunity of having the volume described to me by the Nazarenes of Beroea, a city of Syria, who use it.[651]

Jerome's assertion is confirmed by Eusebius, who was a student of Pamphilus. Eusebius actually studied under Pamphilus at the library of Caesarea.[652] Eusebius himself must have seen, read, and studied the Hebrew version of Matthew's Gospel. Thus he states unequivocally and without need to cite any evidence that Matthew's Gospel was originally written in Matthew's native tongue, Hebrew.

Jerome gives us further evidence that Matthew's Gospel was originally written in Hebrew. He tells us that copies of the Hebrew version were to be found in Alexandria: "Pantaenus...was sent to India by Demetrius bishop of Alexandria, where he found that Bartholomew, one of the twelve apostles, had preached the advent of the Lord Jesus according to the gospel of Matthew, and on his return to Alexandria he brought this with him written in Hebrew characters."[653] The name Pantaenus refers to Saint Pantaenus, who lived about 100 years before Eusebius.[654] The name "India," during the time of

Pantaenus, was used to refer to various areas east of the Red Sea, including Arabia, Persia, and Parthia, but not present-day India.[655]

Matthew originally wrote his Gospel in Hebrew and published it first in Judea, so that, when he went on a long missionary journey, they would have a written record of the life and teaching of Christ. But, if most of the other Twelve Apostles were still in Judea teaching, Matthew would have had much less incentive to make a written record of the Gospel for the Hebrew-speaking Christians of Judea. Thus, Matthew wrote his Gospel, not only because he was about to leave Judea on a missionary journey, but also because most of the other Apostles had left or were soon to leave on missions of their own. Determining the time frame for Matthew and the other Apostles' departures from Judea is the key to dating his Gospel. The Apostle Bartholomew, for example, seems to have left Judea soon after Matthew completed his Gospel, since he took the Hebrew version of Matthew's Gospel with him when he left Judea for his missionary journeys east of Judea.

According to Blessed Anne Catherine Emmerich, at the time of the Virgin Mary's Dormition, Bartholomew was already in Asia, east of the Red Sea,[656] which is one area where this apostle is believed to have preached the Gospel.[657] The other Apostles also came to Ephesus for the Virgin Mary's Dormition from various far off places where they were preaching the Gospel. Thus, by this time (A.D. 34), Matthew, Bartholomew, and the other Apostles had already left Judea on various missionary journeys. Matthew must have written the Hebrew version of his Gospel sometime before A.D. 34, since he wrote the Gospel before he and most of the other Apostles left Judea. But the Gospel of Mark was most likely written after the Dormition of the Virgin Mary (A.D. 34), just prior to Mark's missionary journey to Egypt. Therefore, Matthew's Gospel was written before Mark's Gospel.

When did Matthew leave Judea for his missionary journeys? According to Acts, all of the Twelve Apostles (Matthias, who replaced Judas Iscariot, being the 12th Apostle) were still in Judea (Acts 5:27 – 6:6) at the time of the appointment of the first Deacons of the Church. The Twelve gathered together and decided to appoint these deacons in the year A.D. 21, a Sabbatical year (as explained above). Matthew was still in Judea in A.D. 21. There was some persecution of the early Church in Judea about the time of the martyrdom of Saint Stephen (Acts 8:1). However, Acts specifically states that "they were all dispersed throughout the regions of Judea and Samaria, except the Apostles." (Acts 8:1). Notice here that even the disciples who fled this persecution did not go far. They were only scattered throughout Judea and Samaria. And the Apostles themselves were not scattered at all, that is, they remained in Jerusalem and Bethany. This minor persecution occurred about the time that Pilate left Judea for Rome in late A.D. 21 or early A.D. 22.

Tiberius died in March of A.D. 22 (see chapter 13). Gaius (Caligula) succeeded him as emperor. The nearly four-year reign of Gaius is not a likely time for any major persecution of the early Christian community. Gaius hated the Jews because he thought himself to be a god and they refused to worship him.[658] Those Jewish leaders who might wish to harm the Christians did not have the support of the Roman government at this time. After Gaius died (Jan. A.D. 26, my revised date), Claudius became emperor. In the second year of his reign (A.D. 27), when Claudius issued his edit favoring the Jews,

Herod Agrippa I tried to gain favor with the Jews and with the emperor by putting James the Greater to death and imprisoning Peter. This event was the first major persecution of the Apostles in the early Church. In the earlier minor persecution at the time of Stephen's stoning, the Apostles did not even flee from Jerusalem. But at this time, even Peter, the leader of the Apostles, fled as far away as Rome. But how many of the Twelve Apostles were in Judea at that time?

When Saul came to Jerusalem in early A.D. 25, he did not see any of the Twelve Apostles, except Cephas (Peter) and James, the Lord's brother (Gal 1:18-20). This was James the Less who, according to Eusebius and Jerome, was appointed as bishop of the Church at Jerusalem and remained the spiritual leader there until his martyrdom during Nero's reign.[659] James was still in Jerusalem, and so was Peter, but the other Apostles were not in Jerusalem in early A.D. 25. If they were, Saul would surely have met them because, during this first visit of his to Jerusalem, Saul was at first distrusted, but soon after accepted, by the leaders of the Church (Acts 9:26-30). The reference to "apostles" in Acts 9:27 does not refer specifically to the Twelve, but to apostles of Christ in general. He would not have been accepted without the approval of those members of the Twelve who were still at Jerusalem. Therefore, most of the Twelve (including Matthew) had left Jerusalem by early A.D. 25. And they must have left on long missionary journeys, because most were also not present in Jerusalem in early A.D. 27, during the persecution under Herod Agrippa I.

This major persecution (in A.D. 27) most likely scattered many of the other disciples to regions beyond the territory ruled by Herod Agrippa I. However, Acts does not say that any of the other Twelve Apostles fled with Peter from Jerusalem. James the Less is referred to, as the leader of the brethren in Jerusalem, when Peter is about to flee the area: "And he said, 'Inform James and those brothers.' " (Acts 12:17). So James did not flee with Peter, but remained with the brethren in Jerusalem. Yet it also seems clear that others of the Twelve Apostles were not in Jerusalem, nor even in Judea, at the time of this persecution. Otherwise their flight or their sufferings would have been worthy of mention by the Acts of the Apostles.

Also, A.D. 27 is not a likely time for Matthew to have left Judea to spread the Gospel in distant lands. Matthew wrote the Gospel because he "had made up his mind" to go to distant lands to preach Christ.[660] This phrasing implies that he was not forced to leave by a persecution, but that he reached a decision without compulsion. Furthermore, if he had left Judea suddenly, due to the unexpected arrival from Rome of Herod and the Claudius edict in A.D. 27, he would not have had time to write the Gospel before leaving. Rather, Matthew decided to leave and also had the time to write the Gospel down before leaving. He did not leave during a time of severe persecution, as Peter did.

Matthew was not in Judea in early A.D. 27 (during Herod's persecution), nor in early A.D. 25 (during Saul's visit). Most of the other Twelve Apostles also had left Judea by early A.D. 25, for they also were not seen by Saul (early A.D. 25) and not mentioned by Acts during Herod's persecution (early A.D. 27). The departure or impending departure of other Apostles about the same time that Matthew was preparing to leave would have added urgency to the need to have a written version of the Gospel in Hebrew for the Christians of Judea. The Apostle James the Less never left Judea on any permanent mission to preach the Gospel; his was the task to continue to preach in the Holy Land. And Peter did not leave for Rome until the persecution of A.D. 27. But others among the

Twelve Apostles, including Matthew, clearly had left Judea by early A.D. 25. Since Matthew wrote his Gospel before he and the other Apostles (including Bartholomew) left Judea for their missionary journeys, the Gospel of Matthew must have been written before early A.D. 25. The Twelve were still in Judea in A.D. 21, for the choosing of the first seven deacons of the Church, and they were still in Judea for the minor persecution of early A.D. 22, when Saint Stephen was martyred. Therefore, the Gospel of Matthew was written between early A.D. 22 and early A.D. 25, during the reign of the emperor Gaius. This time frame for the writing of Matthew's Gospel is well before the time when Peter and Mark fled from Judea to Rome. Since Mark wrote his Gospel at Rome, Mark's Gospel was certainly written after Matthew's Gospel.

Now I know that most scholars today say that Mark's Gospel was written first. They base this conclusion on their analysis of the language of the Gospels. But they ignore the historical evidence completely, including the testimony of Eusebius and Jerome. And their analysis of the text of Matthew's Gospel is based on the Greek version of Matthew's Gospel, which was written later than the Hebrew version. Furthermore, many scholars believe, or at least admit the possibility of, an earlier version of Matthew's Gospel, written well before the Greek text.

The Gospel of Luke and The Acts of the Apostles

As noted above, Eusebius places the writing of Luke's Gospel after Matthew's Gospel and before John's Gospel. Luke's Gospel is referred to as the Gospel to the Gentiles. Luke was a disciple of Paul (Col 4:14; 2 Tim 4:11) and often traveled with him. Luke also wrote Acts of the Apostles.

In Acts of the Apostles, Luke records many events that he himself either witnessed or learned directly from Paul.[661] Acts of the Apostles ends abruptly at a point in time 2 years after Paul had been in Rome, preaching the Gospel, but guarded by a Roman soldier (Acts 28:16, 30).

If Luke were living in a major Christian community, such as Rome or Jerusalem or Antioch, he would likely have included events occurring within that community. Yet Luke has little to say about those two years. Perhaps, then, Luke spent those two years in relative isolation from the larger Christian community, not traveling from place to place as he did formerly with Paul. He could have been living in a small town, some distance from Rome and other major centers of Christianity, focusing on writing.

The time frame for Paul's stay in Rome, awaiting his appeal before the emperor, is discussed below. Since Acts describes nothing beyond Paul's two-year stay in Rome, we may reasonably conclude that Acts was completed about two years after Paul arrived in Rome. Luke may have spent much of those two years working on Acts of the Apostles. He may even have had some portion of Acts written well in advance (notes he had taken along the way, and the like). However, this two-year period of time is the most likely time frame for the writing of the bulk of Acts and for its completion.

Not much detail is given about Paul's activities in Rome during those two years (Acts 28:30-31). Luke gives us great detail and precision in the order and timing of the events in the latter part of Acts (e.g. Acts 28:11-15), but he has very little to say about the two years described by Acts 28:30-31; he uses only one sentence to describe two whole years. Luke was with Paul when he arrived in Rome (Acts 28:16), but Luke must have lived somewhere distant from Rome for the greater part of those two years. Otherwise, he would have had some communication with Paul and more information to give about Paul's first two years in Rome.

From Acts 27:1 to the end of Acts, Luke uses the first person plural, "we," to describe events which he and Paul and perhaps others experienced together. But in the last two verses of Acts, the ones describing the first two years that Paul spent in Rome, Luke changes from using "we" to using "he" (Paul). Acts ends with these two verses: "Then he remained for two whole years in his own rented lodgings. And he received all who went in to him, preaching the kingdom of God and teaching the things which are from the Lord Jesus Christ, with all faithfulness, without prohibition." (Acts 28:30-31). This choice of words implies that Luke was elsewhere at the time of those two years.

According to Saint Jerome, Saint Luke wrote the Gospel while living in the region of Achaia. "He was himself a disciple of the Apostle Paul, and composed his book in Achaia and Boeotia."[662] Achaia is the ancient region roughly in the location of modern-day Greece. Boeotia is a region within Greece, just northeast of the Gulf of Corinth. It is still referred to as Boeotia today. This location makes sense in the context of the other information we have about Luke. He was not in Rome with Paul during those two years. He was not in the center of a large Christian community (he lived some distance from Corinth); otherwise he might have added events from that community to the last two years described in Acts.

In addition, Luke most likely wrote the Gospel and Acts while he was living in the same location. The Gospel of Luke is addressed to Theophilus with the expression: "most excellent Theophilus" (Luke 1:3). This phrasing indicates that Theophilus was a Roman official, and not merely a friend or associate of Luke's.[663] Both the Gospel of Luke and Acts of the Apostles are addressed to this Theophilus. Yet he could not have been very high up in the Roman government because nothing is known about him from other historical evidence. Why then would Luke address two works of such length and importance (both the Gospel and Acts were fairly lengthy works for that time period) to Theophilus?

Perhaps this Roman official expressed an interest in learning about Christ and about the Apostles. He may have been interested in converting to the Faith. Even so, Luke would only address both of these important works to a minor Roman official if Luke were living in the area ruled by that official when he was writing. Since Acts of the Apostles was most likely written sometime during the two years after Paul arrived for his appeal to the emperor, the Gospel of Luke was also written about that same time. At other times, Luke had been traveling with Paul and would not have been in one place, where Theophilus held office, for the length of time needed to write his Gospel. Thus the Gospel of Luke was written early in that two-year period of time and Acts of the Apostles was written in the latter part of those two years.

Luke's Gospel and Acts are both addressed to the same Roman official, Theophilus. Luke uses the formal term "most excellent" to address Theophilus in his Gospel (Lk 1:3). This language was commonly used in addressing Roman officials. Examples of this same expression are found in Acts, where it is used to address both Felix and Festus (Acts 24:2; 26:25). But, at the beginning of Acts, Luke no longer calls Theophilus "most excellent Theophilus," instead he calls him "O Theophilus" (Lk 1:3; Acts 1:1). This indicates that Theophilus was no longer in office by the time that Luke was writing, or had completed writing, Acts. Yet Luke still addresses Acts to Theophilus. He must still have been living in the same area and had continued respect and (unofficial) authority at that time. Minor Roman officials often held office for only a year. For example, Gallio (mentioned above) was proconsul of Achaia, probably for only one year.[664] Theophilus could have been proconsul of Achaia, the region in which Jerome tells us Luke was living when he wrote the Gospel, or he could have held some other office within the region of Achaia or Boeotia, (but there is no direct historical evidence as to where Theophilus held office).

Why would Almighty God allow two inspired works of Sacred Scripture to be addressed to a minor Roman official named Theophilus? From a spiritual point of view, the Gospel of Luke and Acts of the Apostles were both addressed to the name Theophilus because of the meaning of that name. The name Theophilus means "one who loves God" — 'Theo' refers to God (as in 'Theology'), and 'philus' is from the Greek word 'philos' meaning 'loving.' Thus Luke's Gospel is addressed, in the spiritual sense, not to one Roman official, but to all those who love God. Luke's Gospel was not written only or primarily for the Hebrews, who converted to Christ, but for all who love God, including the Gentiles.

Paul Leaves Corinth

As concluded above, Paul was in Jerusalem for the Council of A.D. 35, his visit 14 years after his conversion. He then went to Antioch and probably wintered there (A.D. 35/36) with Barnabas. Then, in spring of A.D. 36, Mark arrived in Antioch resulting in a dissension between Paul and Barnabas. Paul resumed his missionary journeys in spring of A.D. 36 without Barnabas. The events of Acts 15:40 to 18:1 followed. After these travels, Paul spent 1½ year in Corinth (within the region of Achaia).

Why did Paul spend 1½ year in Corinth, rather than a longer or shorter length of time? At least several months is required to account for all of the events of Acts 16 to 17. So, after traveling from place to place during much of A.D. 36, Paul arrived in Corinth in late fall of A.D. 36. When some of the Jewish leaders tried to have him brought to trial before the proconsul of Achaia, a Roman official named Gallio, they failed. Gallio would not even consider their accusations (Acts 18:12-17). Thus, Paul was able to stay in Corinth for a longer period of time, and was able to winter in Corinth. The length of 1½ year means that Paul spent two winters in Corinth, before resuming his travels in spring of A.D. 38. Gallio's rule over Achaia most likely ended in late spring or early summer of A.D. 37, but apparently the Roman official who replaced Gallio was no more willing to persecute the Christians than Gallio. So Paul was able to spend a second winter in Corinth, finally departing in the spring of A.D. 38.

Why didn't Gallio or his successor take the Jews part in their dispute with the Christians? Herod Agrippa I killed James the Greater and imprisoned Peter to please the Jews and so to please the emperor Claudius. But, by this time, Claudius had had a change of heart about the Jews. He expelled the Jews from Rome in the 9th year of his reign (A.D. 34).[665] Gallio was ruler over Achaia for only one year, and then he would have had to report back to Rome; so also with his successor. He was unwilling to favor the Jews because the emperor no longer favored the Jews. Gallio's refusal to assist the

Jews in their dispute with the Christians was due not only to judicial insight into the case before him, but also to self-interest.

The statements in Acts about Paul's travels after leaving Corinth support the conclusion that he departed from Corinth in the springtime. Paul left Corinth by boat; he first "sailed into Syria" (Acts 18:18), then spent time in Cenchreae and Ephesus. He then left Ephesus by boat again (Acts 18:21). He continued to travel from city to city, declining a request from the church at Ephesus to stay longer. If Paul had left Achaia in summer or fall, he would not have had sufficient time to sail from place to place before the sailing season ended on the Mediterranean (Acts 27:9-10). Spring is the most likely time for a series of missionary journeys, because the sailing weather allows many months of travel before the winter sets in. And, since Paul stayed in Corinth for about 1½ year (Acts 18:11), he must have arrived in Corinth in the fall season.

Paul in Asia

One way of determining the earliest date for Paul's arrest at Jerusalem is to examine the events of Acts between the time that Paul left Corinth, after his visit of 1½ years (Acts 18:11), and the time that Paul arrived in Jerusalem, where his conflict with Ananias and his arrest occurred. As concluded above, Paul left Corinth in spring of A.D. 38. He sailed for Syria, but along the way stopped at Cenchreae, Ephesus, and Caesarea (Acts 18:18-22). Now Ephesus is located in that area of the world which was, at that time in history, called Asia (modern-day Turkey). After spending some time in Antioch, which is in Syria, Paul traveled though Galatia and Phrygia, areas located just northeast of Asia (Acts 18:23). Paul soon returned to Ephesus (Acts 19:1), probably in the same calendar year, A.D. 38. At Ephesus, Paul taught in the synagogue "for three months" (Acts 19:8).

This period of time, 3 months, is not 3 times 30 days, nor is it necessarily three calendar months. Rather, the term "three months" means 'a season,' that is, a time of roughly three months and corresponding to some season of the year. Elsewhere in Acts, the term three months is used to signify winter. For example, when Paul was shipwrecked on his way to Rome and they had to winter on the island of Malta, the length of time is described as "three months" (Acts 28:1, 11). Thus, Paul wintered in Ephesus and spent his time teaching in the synagogue. The people of Ephesus had requested that Paul remain with them at the time of an earlier visit (Acts 18:19-21). At that time Paul declined, but now he acceded to that request.

When some of the Jews rejected his teaching, Paul withdrew from them and taught "in a certain school of Tyrannus" (Acts 19:9). Paul began by teaching the Jews in the synagogue. He moved to the hall of Tyrannus, a secular place where anyone might gather, so as to expand the reach of Christ's teaching to the Gentiles. "Now this was done throughout two years, so that all who were living in Asia listened to the Word of the Lord, both Jews and Gentiles." (Acts 19:10). If the three months that Paul taught in the synagogue were the winter of A.D. 38/39, then the two years that Paul taught in the hall of Tyrannus would be A.D. 39 and 40. Since the two years is not called "two whole years," an expression used later in Acts (Acts 28:30), the two years could have been somewhat less that two full years, ending in late A.D. 40. This conclusion is confirmed by the subsequent passages in Acts.

Paul left Asia and traveled to Macedonia, then he spent three months in Greece. Here again the term "three months" is used to signify winter (Acts 20:3). This conclusion is made obvious by the subsequent verses, which refer to the "days of Unleavened Bread" (Acts 20:6) and to various journeys by boat on the Mediterranean. The days of Unleavened Bread are the days of Passover in the spring. Thus, after wintering in Greece, Paul began his travels again by boat about the time of the Passover. Paul's winter in Greece was therefore the winter of A.D. 40/41, making the two years of Acts 19:10 the nearly two years of A.D. 39 and 40 (not including the winter of A.D. 38/39 or the winter of A.D. 39/40).

After passing through Macedonia, Paul returned to Asia, to the cities of Troas, Assos, and Mitylene.[666] While in Mitylene (a city not far from Ephesus), he sent for the elders of the church at Ephesus and spoke to them at length. He spoke about the time he spent in Asia, " 'You know that from the first day when I entered into Asia, I have been with you, for the entire time, in this manner....' " (Acts 20:18). He called the length of time he spent teaching them in Asia three years: "Because of this, be vigilant, retaining in memory that throughout three years I did not cease, night and day, with tears, to admonish each and every one of you." (Acts 20:31). The three years would then be counted from the first time that Paul set foot in Asia, that is, when he arrived in Ephesus in early A.D. 38, to the time of this speech, in early A.D. 41, shortly after the time of Passover (Acts 20:6) and before the day of Pentecost (Acts 20:16).

Claudius died in October of A.D. 39 (see chapter 13) and Nero succeeded him. The year A.D. 40 was Nero's first full year as emperor and A.D. 41 was Nero's 2nd year. The Romans generally counted the years of an emperor's reign from the first full calendar year after he gained the throne. (The main exception to this rule is found in the reign of Claudius, who became emperor so early in the year A.D. 26, in January, that his first year is counted as that same year.

Paul left Asia to journey to Jerusalem, hoping to arrive there before Pentecost, that is, in late spring/early summer. His journey seems to have had no unexpected or lengthy delays (Acts 21:1-15), so Paul likely arrived in Jerusalem in late spring/early summer of A.D. 41. Nero was then emperor of Rome and Felix was governor of Judea. Ananias was the high priest of the Jews.

Paul's Arrest

Acts of the Apostles mentions a two-year period of time that Paul spent in Rome awaiting his appeal to the Roman emperor (Acts 29:30-31). Now it should be obvious, since Acts ends at that point, that Paul may have spent more than two years awaiting a hearing before the emperor Nero. But the reason for fixing this two-year time frame is that Luke most probably wrote his Gospel and Acts during those two years.

Paul's arrest and his transfer to Rome were the result of events which began with a visit by Paul to Jerusalem in late spring/early summer A.D. 41. According to Acts, when Paul was at Caesarea, he stayed with "Philip the evangelist, who was one of the seven." (Acts 21:8). This Philip was not the Philip who was one of the Twelve Apostles, but rather one of the first seven deacons of the Church (Acts 6:5), referred to in ancient times as 'the Seven.' He was called 'evangelist' because he preached the Gospel with the spoken word; the word 'evangelist' does not here refer to a written Gospel. While staying with Philip, a prophet named Agabus predicted that Paul would be taken captive while at Jerusalem (Acts 21:10-11). The brethren pleaded with Paul not to go to Jerusalem. But Paul wanted to do God's will, even if it meant imprisonment and death, and so Paul went to Jerusalem (Acts 21:12-15).

At Jerusalem, Paul and his traveling companions met with James the Less, one of the Twelve and the leader of the church at Jerusalem. They were afraid that the Jews of Jerusalem would do violence to Paul. For it was by that time well known that Paul was teaching the Jews who converted to Christ not to follow the Law of Moses (Acts 21:20-22). And so it happened that some Jews from Asia recognized Paul and a crowd seized him, beat him, and tried to kill him (Acts 21:27-31). Paul was rescued by Roman soldiers and so had to answer to the accusations of the Jews before the Roman authorities (Acts 21:32-36).

When the Roman tribune found out that Paul was born a Roman citizen, he was afraid lest he be accused of depriving a Roman citizen of his legal rights (Acts 22:25-29). The Jewish leaders who opposed Paul came to understand that they were not going to be able to prevail over him by making accusations against him before the Roman tribune (Acts 23:6-10). So some of the Jews contrived a plan to ambush Paul and murder him; the chief priests and elders gave their assent to this plan (Acts 23:12-15). But the Roman tribune discovered their plan and sent Paul to Felix, the governor of Judea, with many soldiers to guard him. He also sent word to Felix of the plot against Paul (Acts 23:16-35).

Now the Jewish high priest at that time was named Ananias (Acts 23:2). Jewish high priests during this time in history were frequently replaced by the Roman authorities as often as the Romans wished to replace them. They needed little or no reason to replace one high priest with another. When the Romans uncovered this plot against Paul, the high priest must certainly have lost favor with the Roman leaders, with the tribune at Jerusalem, with the governor, Felix, and with king Herod Agrippa II. This plot was approved by the Jewish chief priests and elders, and involved lying to the tribune and ambushing Paul when he would be traveling with Roman soldiers to guard him. In order to kill Paul, they would also have had to kill the Roman soldiers guarding him. The plot was made known to Felix the governor through the tribune, and so the high priest, Ananias was likely removed from office soon after this scandal.

When speaking to the high priest, Ananias, Paul admits that he did not know he was the high priest (Acts 23:5). Therefore, Ananias became high priest sometime after Paul had been in Jerusalem for his previous visit, that is, for his visit after 14 years and the Council of the Church of Acts 15 (A.D. 35). Ananias' reign as high priest began after A.D. 35 and ended soon after the conflict with Paul and the failed ambush plot.

Josephus tells us that Claudius sent Felix to be governor of Judea. Immediately after making this statement, Josephus adds that Claudius, "when he had already completed the twelfth year of his reign," gave Herod Agrippa II additional areas to govern.[667] This phrasing implies that Felix became governor of Judea before Agrippa was given those additional areas, perhaps sometime during Claudius' 12th year. According to Josephus, Ananias was appointed high priest before Felix became governor.[668] But Felix was appointed governor at the recommendation of Jonathan, one of the Jewish leaders.[669] So, sometime after Felix and Agrippa learned of the plot against Paul, Ananias was removed as high priest and was replaced by Jonathan. Felix undoubtedly favored Jonathan for high priest, since Jonathan helped Felix get appointed as governor of Judea. Jonathan's appointment as high priest must be placed sometime after Felix became governor and after the conflict between Paul and the Jewish leaders.

During Felix's reign, Agrippa removed Ananias as high priest and replaced him with Jonathan. Now Jonathan had supported Felix as the choice for governor of Judea. Even so, Felix because angry with Jonathan and successfully plotted his murder, as Josephus relates.[670] Herod Agrippa II then chose Ismael to be the next Jewish high priest, while Felix was still in office.[671] Thus the high priests during Felix's reign were Ananias, Jonathan, and Ismael.

When speaking before Felix the governor of Judea, Paul states that Felix had been ruler over this nation "for many years." (Acts 24:10). Since Felix became governor of Judea about the 12th year of Claudius' reign (A.D. 37), he would had to have been governor for at least 4 or 5 years for Paul to call that length of time "many years." Claudius died during his 14th year as emperor of Rome; Nero succeeded him. This places Paul's arrest in Jerusalem no earlier than the first year or two of Nero's reign, so that the "many years" of Felix's reign would, at the least, refer to Claudius' 12th, 13th, and 14th years and to the first year or two of Nero's reign. The second year of Nero's reign, in this revised chronology, is A.D. 41. Since we concluded above that that Paul left Asia for Jerusalem in spring of A.D. 41, the term "many years" would then refer to the approx. 5 years that Felix had been governor up to that point in time.

According to Acts, Felix kept Paul in prison for about 2 years (Acts 24:27). Paul was arrested very soon after he arrived in Jerusalem (Acts 24:11). He arrived in Jerusalem about the time of Pentecost, in late spring/early summer. So the 2 years that Paul was imprisoned under Felix would then run from early summer of A.D. 41 to about the same time of year in A.D. 43. Nero replaced Felix with Festus (Acts 24:27), as Josephus also relates.[672] Festus heard Paul's case promptly, and soon afterwards king Herod Agrippa II also heard Paul's case (Acts 25:1-12; 25:13-32). But Paul wished to avoid being sent back to Jerusalem for trial, where the leaders of the Jews would have tried to have him put to death (Acts 25:7-12). So Paul made an appeal to be heard before the emperor, and Festus granted his appeal. Since there are no long delays mentioned by Acts and since Festus was of a mind to dispense Paul's case promptly (unlike his predecessor), Paul's journey to Rome must have begun that same year, in A.D. 43.

Festus and Agrippa decided to send Paul to Rome by boat (Acts 26:32 – 27:1). But the voyage was delayed and the fast day (the Day of Atonement, which is in the fall) had already gone by (Acts 27:9). Clearly, this voyage began in early fall. Paul then warned them that they should not continue the journey, because the Mediterranean is dangerous to sail upon in winter, but they continued on anyway (Acts 27:10-15). The result was that they were shipwrecked and had to spend the winter on the island of Malta (Acts 27:10 – 28:11). Since the sailing season opens again, after the winter, in early February, they could have set sail for Rome from Malta in February and arrived in Rome in late February or early March. The winter they spent on Malta took place from late A.D. 43 to early A.D. 44, and Paul arrived in Rome early in the year A.D. 44.

According to Acts, Paul then spent "two whole years" in Rome, preaching the Gospel quite freely, living in his own residence, but with a soldier to keep watch over him (Acts 28:16-31). Those two whole years must have been early A.D. 44 to early A.D. 46, that is, until early in the 7th year of Nero. As concluded above, the Gospel of Luke and Acts of the Apostles were both most likely written during these first two years that Paul spent in Rome, between early A.D. 44 and early A.D. 46.

The Martyrdom of James the Less

Saint Jerome tells us that James the Less suffered martyrdom about the time of the Passover, in the 30th year since Christ's Ascension and in the 7th year of Nero. "And so he ruled the church of Jerusalem thirty years, that is until the seventh year of Nero...."[673] In this chronology, the 7th year of Nero is A.D. 46. If James died at Passover in the spring of Nero's 7th year, then one would expect Luke to have mentioned this at the end of Acts, which was completed about A.D. 46. Luke mentions James the Less repeatedly in Acts of the Apostles (Acts 1:13; 12:17; 15:13-21), yet no mention is made in Acts of James' martyrdom.

In this chronology, and in many other modern chronologies, the number of the years from Christ's Ascension to Nero's 7th year does not add up to 30 years. First we add 7 years of Nero's reign to the 14 calendar years of Claudius' reign, and then we add the 4 calendar years of Gaius' reign (Caligula), to reach a total of 25 years. In this revised chronology, Tiberius reigned just over 21 years (A.D. 1 to March of A.D. 22), so that the last full calendar year of his reign was A.D. 21. Christ died in A.D. 19. There are only three additional years, counting inclusively, to add to the 25 years; there were not 30 years from Tiberius' 19th year to Nero's 7th year.

In other modern chronologies, Tiberius' last full calendar year would be A.D. 36. To obtain 5 additional years to add to the 25, one would have to place Christ's Crucifixion in A.D. 32 (counting inclusively), or in A.D. 31. Modern scholars do not accept either of those dates as a possible year for the Crucifixion, mainly because the Passover did not begin on a Friday in A.D. 31 or 32 (see Appendix I, chart 1). Therefore, either Jerome was mistaken that James died in the 30th year after Christ's Ascension, or, he was mistaken that he died in Nero's 7th year.

Luke brings Acts of the Apostles to a close in the spring of Nero's 7th year, and no mention is made of James the Less' martyrdom. This evidence supports the conclusion that James the Less died, not in Nero's 7th year, but later, in the 30th year since Christ's Ascension. Since Christ died in A.D. 19, and James ruled the church at Jerusalem for 30 years after Christ, the 30th year would either be A.D. 48 or 49, depending on whether or not one counts inclusively. Nero's 9th year was A.D. 48 and his 10th year was A.D. 49. I would count the length of time not inclusively. Jerome gives us the length of time that James the Less reigned over Jerusalem, much as Josephus gives us the length of time for various emperors' reigns. Also, Christ's Ascension and James the Less' martyrdom each occurred in the springtime, so that one would naturally count the length of time from spring of one year to each spring of subsequent years. So James the Less was martyred in the 10th year of Nero. (Further support for this conclusion comes from a comparison between the martyrdoms of James the Less and Mark the Evangelist, discussed below.)

Eusebius quotes Hegesippus as stating that the conflict between the Jews and the Romans, which ended in the destruction of Jerusalem, began immediately after James' death. " 'Immediately after this Vespasian began to besiege them.' "[674] Eusebius also quotes Josephus as writing that the sufferings of the siege of Jerusalem were a punishment against the Jews for unjustly putting James the Less to death.[675] If James had died in Nero's 7th year, these statements could not be correct, for the conflict between the Jews and the Romans began in Nero's 12th year.[676] Since Hegesippus lived in the first generation after the time of the Apostles,[677] his statement is to be believed and James' martyrdom must be placed at the later date, the 30th year since Christ's Ascension and Nero's 10th year, not his 7th year.

Although the war began in Nero's 12th year, the government of Florus over Judea began a year earlier, in Nero's 11th year. And this choice by Nero to put Florus over the Jews was, according to Josephus, the main cause of the revolt of the Jews against the Romans.[678] James died in the year just previous to the beginning of the conflict, Nero's 10th year, in accordance with Hegesippus. Of course, some years passed before the conflict actually led to the besieging of Jerusalem by Vespasian. (See chapter 14 for the chronology of the destruction of Jerusalem.)

Details of James the Less' martyrdom are found in the writings of Josephus, Eusebius, and Jerome. When Festus, the governor of Judea, died, Nero replaced him with Albinus. About the same time, Herod Agrippa II replaced the Jewish high priest Joseph with Ananus.[679] After Festus died and before Albinus had arrived in Judea to replace him, the new high priest decided to pressure James the Less to deny that Jesus is the Messiah and the Son of God.[680] Ananus was taking advantage of a lapse in leadership at the end of Festus' reign. Similar circumstances at the end of Pilate's reign over Judea led to the stoning of Saint Stephen. The Jewish high priest made James stand at a high point on the Temple wall, asking him to speak against Jesus to the crowds gathered for the Passover. James instead spoke in favor of Jesus as the Christ; many heard him and many were converted. So the Jewish religious leaders threw James down from the Temple wall. Yet he did not die from the fall, so they began to stone him. Still he did not die from the stoning, so a man took a fuller club (used to beat out clothing) and clubbed him to death.[681] In this way died James the Less, one of the Twelve Apostles and the leader of the Church at Jerusalem for 30 years.

The Christian Martyrs of Rome

Nero's 10th year marked the beginning of several years of persecution of Christians by the Roman Empire. This was the first major persecution against Christians that proceeded from a Roman emperor. Previous persecutions had been initiated by various Jewish leaders, or by lesser Roman leaders (such as Herod Agrippa I). The persecution began with a great fire in Rome. Dio Cassius tells us that Nero himself sent out men to start fires in the city, deliberately to destroy the city and so to increase his greatness by being the last emperor of Rome.[682] Tacitus gives a different reason, that Nero wanted to found a new city in place of Rome, and name it after himself.[683] Perhaps they were both correct. In any case, as the people of Rome began to suspect that Nero was the instigator of this great fire of Rome, he tried to deflect their suspicions by blaming the Christians.[684] Many Christians in Rome were arrested, charged with "hatred of the human race," and put to death in torturous ways.[685]

The Martyrdom of Mark

Mark journeyed to Alexandria in Egypt and established a community of Christians there. The holiness of the church he founded is extolled by Eusebius, Philo, and Jerome.[686] According to Jerome: "He died in the eighth year of Nero and was buried at Alexandria, Annianus succeeding him." In this revised chronology, the 8th year of Nero was A.D. 47.

The above reassessment of Jerome's date for the death of James the Less places some doubt on the statement of Jerome and Eusebius that Mark the Gospel writer died in Nero's eighth year.[687] "In the eighth year of Nero's reign Annianus was the first after Mark the evangelist to take charge of the see of Alexandria."[688] Despite this assertion, Mark's martyrdom may have been placed in Nero's 8th year because it was the year after James the Less' martyrdom. Note that Albinus, who took office at the time of James the Less' death, came to Jerusalem directly from Alexandria, so that the dates of those two events, James' death in Jerusalem and Mark's death in Alexandria, may have become connected.[689] If so, then Mark's death should be placed in Nero's 11th year. This conclusion fits into the political events of the time. Nero began to openly persecute Christians after the fire at Rome during his 10th year. Once people learned that the Roman Empire was persecuting and killing Christians, there would have been an implied permission for them to do the same.

How soon would the people of Alexandria in Egypt have found out that Nero was persecuting Christians? The burning of Rome occurred in Nero's 10th year, in July.[690] After the fire, people began to talk among themselves about the cause of the fire. Many suspected that Nero had ordered the burning of Rome. This idea took time to be formulated and to spread among the people. Eventually, Nero began to realize that people were accusing him. Though the fire occurred in July of Nero's 10th year, Nero's persecution of Christians was not immediate. According to Tacitus, at first Nero tried other strategies to end these accusations. "But neither human help, nor imperial munificence, nor all the modes of placating Heaven, could stifle scandal or dispel the belief that the fire had taken place by order."[691] After these other strategies failed, Nero hit upon the idea of accusing the Christians.

He blamed the Christians for starting the fire and for other problems in society. In Rome at that time, Christians were a minority; their religious beliefs were considered strange; their ideas were unpopular and not generally accepted. Tacitus says that the Christians were "loathed for their vices," and he calls Christianity, "the pernicious superstition," and, "the disease."[692] He says that Christianity spread to Rome, "where all things horrible or shameful in the world collect and find a vogue."[693]

So Nero began to torture and to put to death some of the Christians of Rome. When, after a time, he saw that this strategy worked to distract people from blaming him for the fire, he continued and increased his efforts to persecute and kill Christians in Rome.

All of these events took time. He may have begun to put Christians to death by the beginning of autumn, but it took time for him to realize that his strategy was working for him. The people of Egypt would not have heard of this persecution of Christians right away. The trip by boat from Rome to Egypt may have taken 2 months, in favorable weather. And in winter the Mediterranean was essentially closed to travel by boat because of winter storms and unfavorable sailing conditions. Thus, it was probably not until the spring of Nero's 11th year that the people of Alexandria received repeated and reliable reports that a sustained persecution of Christians was occurring in Rome with the instigation and full approval of the emperor. Once they realized that the emperor allowed and encouraged such treatment of Christians, they would have wondered if they could get away with the same.

Mark the Gospel writer had been leader of the church at Alexandria for many years. Some of those who worshipped the pagan gods would have liked to have killed him much sooner than they did. But the Roman government did not permit the peoples under their jurisdiction to put anyone to death, especially for reasons of solely a religious disagreement. That is why they did not put Mark to death on the first day that they mistreated him. On Easter Sunday, they dragged Mark through the streets with a rope around his neck. They had him under their control and could have killed him that day, but they did not. They waited a day to see how the Roman government at Alexandria would react. They were testing the limits of what they could get away with. Did Nero's persecution of Christians mean that the Roman government would not intervene if they attacked Mark? By the next day they realized that the Romans would not stop them from harming Mark. So, on the day after Easter Sunday, they again dragged Mark through the streets of the city with a rope around his neck. But this time they did not stop until he was dead.[694]

Finegan asserts that Mark died in a year when Easter Sunday coincided with the feast day of a particular pagan god, Sarapis, on Barmudah 29 in the Egyptian calendar.[695] Chronologists generally hold that Mark was put to death because of this coincidence of dates. The idea is that the pagans were afraid that the Christians were going to put an end to their religion by holding Easter on the same day as their celebration. However, the Romans would not have allowed anyone to be put to death by a mob and without the intervention of Roman authority. The killing of Mark could not have occurred before Nero began to order the death of Christians, thus creating an implied permission for others to do the same.

The usual year given for the martyrdom of Mark is Nero's 8th year, before the fire at Rome. That year in the generally-accepted chronology is A.D. 68, a year in which, according to Finegan, Barmudah 29 coincided with April 24.[696] Easter Sunday, at that time in history, (before the Council of Nicaea), was placed on the first Sunday after the first full moon after the spring Equinox. In A.D. 68, the Spring Equinox was March 22 and the first full moon after that date was April 6, a Wednesday.[697] Therefore, Easter that year was the following Sunday, April 10th, not April 24. April 10 that year coincided with Pharmuthi (Barmudah) 16 in the Egyptian calendar.[698]

Furthermore, in the usual chronology, Nero's 11th year is A.D. 71. Easter Sunday that year fell on April 7, not April 24.[699] April 7 of A.D. 71 coincided with Pharmuthi 13 in the Egyptian Alexandrian calendar.[700]

On the other hand, in my revised chronology, Easter Sunday fell on April 2 in Nero's 8th year (A.D. 47, revised).[701] Easter Sunday fell on March 29 in Nero's 11th year (A.D. 50, revised).[702] None of the above dates comes anywhere near Pharmuthi (Barmudah) 29 in the Egyptian calendar.[703]

Therefore, the reason for Mark's death was not because Easter happened to coincide with Barmudah (Pharmuthi) 29, a pagan religious day; it did not. Rather, pagan religious leaders had wanted to kill Mark for many years and did not have the opportunity until they heard that Nero had undertaken a sustained and severe persecution of Christians. Mark the Gospel writer was killed in the spring of Nero's 11th year.

In my revised chronology, Nero's 11th year was A.D. 50. Easter Sunday that year occurred, earlier than usual, on March 29. This date coincides with the 4th day of the month of Barmudah (Pharmuthi) in the Egyptian Alexandrian calendar. (Saint Athanasius, Bishop of Alexandria, writes in one of his letters about the same date, March 29 and Pharmuthi 4, which also coincided with Easter Sunday in the year about which he wrote, A.D. 347.)[704] Mark did not die on the day after Pharmuthi 29 (as is generally claimed), but rather on the day after March 29, in the month of Pharmuthi (Barmudah). Saint Mark the Evangelist died on March 30 of A.D. 50, less than a year after Nero began his persecution of Christians.

Implied permission to persecute Christians was a major factor in Mark's death. In contrast, such implied permission was clearly not present at the time of James the Less' death. Albinus rebuked the Jewish high priest, Ananus, for killing James. And Herod Agrippa II promptly removed the high priest from office for the same reason.[705] James was killed in the spring, about the time of Passover, in Nero's 10th year. The burning of Rome occurred in the summer of Nero's 10th year, beginning, according to Tacitus, on July 19.[706] Nero's persecution of Christians began after the fires in Rome and so after the death of James the Less. Thus, at the time that the Jewish high priest ordered James' death, the Roman government did not support or permit the killing of Christians.

Saint Jerome places the deaths of James the Less and Mark the Gospel writer in adjacent years.[707] In the year that James was killed, the Roman government did not support the killing of Christians. Albinus threatened the Jewish high priest who killed James and Agrippa removed the high priest from office promptly.[708] Yet, in the very next year, a mob in Alexandria could drag Mark through the public streets without Roman intervention and kill him the next day with impunity. This change in attitude on the part of the Roman government shows that James died before the burning of Rome and Mark died afterwards. Thus James' death must have occurred in the spring of Nero's 10th year, and Mark's death must have occurred in the following year, Nero's 11th year.

There is additional evidence that Mark died in Nero's 11th year. Eusebius states that Mark's successor in Alexandria, Annianus, ruled for 22 years, until his death during the 4th year of the emperor Domitian.[709] In this revised chronology, the 4th year of Domitian's reign is A.D. 72. Counting back 22 years brings us to A.D. 50, the 11th year of Nero's reign. Based on the above considerations, Mark the Gospel writer died in the 11th year of Nero's reign, not his 8th year. Luke did not include the martyrdoms of James the Less and Mark in Acts of the Apostles because they died about three years after Acts was completed.

Mark arrived in Egypt in spring of A.D. 36 and died in spring of Nero's 11th year, A.D. 50. He died about 14 years after he first came to Egypt to preach the Gospel and to establish the church at Alexandria.

Paul's Martyrdom

Peter and Paul were both put to death on the same day. Eusebius tells us that Peter was crucified and Paul was beheaded in Rome and at the same time.[710] Saint Jerome also states that Peter and Paul were martyred on the same day.[711] Both Eusebius and Jerome describe Peter and Paul's martyrdoms as occurring during Nero's reign. As explained above, the date of their death was June 29, A.D. 52, during the summer of Nero's 13th year as emperor, less than one full year before Nero died. As Jack Finegan so clearly explains, Nero was probably not in Rome directly presiding over the deaths of Peter and Paul. Rather, they died as a result of the persecution that Nero initiated, encouraged, and oversaw.[712]

Saul was converted to Christ in the year A.D. 22, sometime after Saint Stephen's martyrdom. Paul was martyred for Christ in the summer of the year A.D. 52. Therefore, Paul's service to Christ as an Apostle of the Faith lasted about 30 years.

The Gospel of John

Saint Jerome wrote that the Gospel of Mark was sometimes ascribed to the Apostle Peter.[713] Jerome is not claiming that Peter wrote the Gospel of Mark. In fact, Peter only found out that Mark had written the Gospel after it was completed.[714] Rather, Peter is given some credit for the content of Mark's Gospel because Mark learned much about Christ from Peter. Something similar can be said about the Gospel of John.

After the Ascension of Christ to Heaven, John the Gospel writer, one of the Twelve Apostles, took care of the Virgin Mary. "And from that hour, the disciple accepted her as his own." (Jn 19:27). During the 15 years from Christ's Ascension to Mary's Assumption, John spent more time with the Virgin Mary than did any of the other Apostles or Gospel writers. A devout disciple of Christ who spends much time with the Virgin Mary could not help but learn much about Christ from his holy Mother and closest Imitator. Thus the Gospel of John was undoubtedly influenced by the Virgin Mary. She did not write the Gospel of John, nor was she even living on earth when it was written. The Gospel of John was written long after Mary's Assumption to Heaven. Yet her influence is unmistakable within the depth and breadth of the understanding of Christ found in the fourth Gospel.

Saint Jerome describes the circumstances surrounding the writing of the Gospel of John:

> When he was in Asia, at the time when the seeds of heresy were springing up (I refer to Cerinthus, Ebion, and the rest who say that Christ has not come in the flesh, whom he in his own epistle calls Antichrists, and whom the Apostle Paul frequently assails), he was urged by almost all the bishops of Asia then living, and by deputations from many Churches, to write more profoundly concerning the divinity of the Saviour, and to break through all obstacles so as to attain to the very Word of God (if I may so speak) with a boldness as successful as it appears audacious. Ecclesiastical history relates that, when he was urged by the brethren to write, he replied that he would do so if a general fast were proclaimed and all would offer up prayer to God; and when the fast was over, the narrative goes on to say, being filled with revelation, he burst into the heaven-sent Preface: "In the beginning was the Word, and the Word was with God, and the Word was God: this was in the beginning with God."[715]

When was the Gospel of John written? Both Eusebius and Jerome state that John's Gospel was written last.[716] Eusebius even tells us that John had copies of each of the three other Gospels. "The three gospels already written were in general circulation and copies had come into John's hand."[717] The Gospel of Luke was written after Matthew and Mark's Gospels, and was most likely completed sometime between early A.D. 44 and early A.D. 46 (as concluded above). By the time that John wrote his Gospel, Luke's Gospel had not only been written, it had been in general circulation and a copy had made its way to John. At least several years must have passed for Luke's Gospel to enter general circulation.

The last verses of John's Gospel present themselves as having been written, not by John, but by some of his disciples. "This is the same disciple who offers testimony about these things, and who has written these things. And we know that his testimony is true." (Jn 21:24). The expression "we know that his testimony" shows that this verse was written by a group of persons who knew John well, persons to whom John had testified about his faith in Christ. Such persons are referred to as John's disciples. The present tense is used to signify that John was still alive at the time that these last verses were added to the Gospel of John: "This is the same disciple who offers testimony about these things...." No mention is made of John's actual death, even though the idea of his future inevitable death is discussed in these last verses (Jn 21:20-23). John's disciples completed his Gospel while he was still alive.

On the other hand, Peter's actual death is mentioned (Jn 21:18-19). This text is not proof that John's Gospel was written after Peter's death. Jesus was making a prophecy of Peter's future martyrdom. However, part of verse 19, placed within the description of Jesus' future prediction, could be a comment on that prediction, a comment added after Peter had died. "Now he said this to signify by what kind of death he would glorify God." (Jn 21:19). Here is one indication that John's Gospel was written after the death of Peter, and probably after the end of Nero's reign.

Some assert that John wrote his Gospel after he wrote the Apocalypse, and after the Roman emperor Domitian died and John had been released from the island of Patmos and had returned to Ephesus.[718] However, I find evidence that John wrote his Gospel before he wrote the Apocalypse (the Book of Revelation). First, the comments at the end of John's Gospel do not refer to any other writings of John (Jn 21:24-25). John's disciples refer, in those words, to John's testimony, to his bearing witness, and to other books that could be written. The subject of other writings is raised, yet no mention is made of any book, other than the Gospel, written by John. This indicates that the Apocalypse had not yet been written.

Second, the beginning of the Apocalypse refers to the Gospel of John: "...to his servant John; he has offered testimony to the Word of God, and whatever he saw is the testimony of Jesus Christ." (Rev 1:1-2). John bore witness to the Word of God in his Gospel, which begins: "In the beginning was the Word, and the Word was with God, and God was the Word." (Jn 1:1). John's Gospel is his testimony to Jesus Christ and to all that John saw. The first and second verses of the Apocalypse refer to the last verses of John's Gospel, which refer to John offering "testimony about these things, and who has written these things. And we know that his testimony is true." (Jn 21:24). A little further in the Apocalypse, John states that he was exiled to the island of Patmos because of "because of the Word of God and the testimony to Jesus." (Rev 1:9). Here again John refers to the Gospel of John, which is the written word of God and which testifies to Christ as the living Word of God. John is saying that the reason for his exile to Patmos was because of the Gospel he wrote.

Third, Eusebius' words support the idea that the Gospel of John was written before the Apocalypse. "There is ample evidence that at the time the apostle and evangelist John was still alive, and because of his testimony to the word of God was sentenced to confinement on the island of Patmos."[719] John was exiled to Patmos by the emperor Domitian because of his testimony to the Word of God, that is, because of the Gospel he wrote. John wrote the Apocalypse while he was confined to Patmos. Therefore, the Apocalypse was written after the Gospel of John. Since Domitian banished John to the island of Patmos because of his Gospel, John most likely wrote his Gospel during Domitian's reign.

Saint Jerome relates an ancient story about John the Gospel writer. "Tertullian, more over, relates that he was sent to Rome, and that having been plunged into a jar of boiling oil he came out fresher and more active than when he went in."[720] The Church commemorates this event on May 6, under the title "St. John before the Latin Gate."[721] John's miraculous preservation from the boiling oil is the reason that Domitian only banished him to an island, rather than putting him to death as many others had been put to death.

According to Jerome, John wrote his Gospel at the request of the bishops of Asia (modern-day Turkey). "John…the son of Zebedee and brother of James…most recently of all the evangelists wrote a Gospel, at the request of the bishops of Asia…."[722] John lived at Ephesus, within the region known as Asia, for many years. Eusebius quotes Irenaeus as saying that John lived at Ephesus until the reign of the emperor Trajan.[723] Since John lived at Ephesus and wrote the Gospel at the request of the bishops of that area, John most likely wrote the Gospel at Ephesus.

The Four Gospels

Matthew's Gospel was written during Gaius' reign. Mark's Gospel was written during Claudius' reign. Luke's Gospel was written during Nero's reign. John's Gospel was written during Domitian's reign. Each Gospel was written during a different period of time and during a different political administration.

Matthew's Gospel was written in Judea. Mark's Gospel was written in Rome. Luke's Gospel was written in Boeotia within Achaia (modern-day Greece). John's Gospel was written at Ephesus in Asia (modern-day Turkey). Each Gospel was written in a different area of the world, in four different locations around the Mediterranean.

The four living creatures in the Book of Revelation (The Apocalypse) each represent one of the four Gospels. Those four creatures are presented in this order: a lion, an ox, the face of a man, a flying eagle. The usual interpretation is that Matthew's Gospel is symbolized by the man, Mark's Gospel is symbolized by the lion, Luke's Gospel is symbolized by the ox, and John's Gospel is symbolized by the eagle. But I am not convinced as to which symbol represents which Gospel.

The Book of Revelation (The Apocalypse)

"I, John, your brother, and a sharer in the tribulation and in the kingdom and in patient endurance for Christ Jesus, was on the island which is called Patmos, because of the Word of God and the testimony to Jesus." (Rev 1:9).

John goes on to say that he had a vision while on Patmos and that he was told to write down what he saw in the vision (Rev 1:10-11). Clearly the Book of Revelation was written on the island of Patmos. This small island is located about 50 kilometers (about 30 miles) off the coast of modern-day Turkey. According to Saint Victorinus, John was "condemned to the labour of the mines by Caesar Domitian."[724] Condemned persons were sent to this island to work in forced labor camps mining ore.

Saint Jerome places John's exile on the island of Patmos during the persecution of Christians under Domitian. "In the fourteenth year then after Nero, Domitian having raised a second persecution, he was banished to the island of Patmos, and wrote the Apocalypse...."[725] This persecution is called the second because it was the second major persecution of Christians approved of, and proceeding from, an emperor of Rome. The first such persecution occurred under Nero; the third occurred under Trajan.

The phrase "the fourteenth year then after Nero" seems refer to the beginning of the persecution under Domitian. Jerome believed that Domitian's reign began in the 14th year after Nero. His calculation goes as follows: about one year for the reigns of Galba, Otho, Vitellius put together, plus about ten years for the reign of Vespasian (as was generally believed), plus about 2 years for the reign of Titus, equals about 13 years, making the first year of Domitian the 14th year after Nero.[726] (Note that, in my revised chronology, the reign of Domitian began more than 14 years after the end of Nero's reign.) Apparently, Jerome associated the persecutions of Christians under Domitian with that emperor's entire reign. It may well have been the case that Christians were mistreated under Domitian throughout his reign. Suetonius portrays Domitian as a cruel and unpredictable ruler.[727] He did not hesitate to put to death whomever he chose, even Roman Senators who were ex-Consuls.[728]

However, this does not mean that John was sent to Patmos at the very beginning of Domitian's reign.[729] According to Eusebius, the persecutions and martyrdoms reached their height near the end of Domitian's reign. "They also indicated the precise date, noting that in the fifteenth year of Domitian, Flavia Domitilla, who was a niece of Flavius Clemens, one of the consuls at Rome that year, was with many others, because of the testimony to Christ, taken to the island of Pontia as a punishment."[730] Though Eusebius claims this was the 15th year of Domitian, the consulship of Flavius Clemens is generally placed in the 14th year of Domitian (A.D. 95 in the usual chronology; A.D. 82 in my revised chronology).[731] And this may be the reason that Jerome associates the exile of John to Patmos with the 14th year, though it was Domitian's 14th year, not the 14th year after Nero. Therefore, the most likely year that John was sent to Patmos, given the above evidence, is the 14th year of Domitian, A.D. 82, the same year that "many others" were also sent into exile on an island. Domitian's reign ended with his death the following year, in September of A.D. 83, the 15th calendar year of his reign and just over 15 years after the death of the previous emperor, Titus.

After the death of Domitian, John was released from Patmos and allowed to return to Ephesus. "But Domitian having been put to death and his acts, on account of his excessive cruelty, having been annulled by the senate, he returned to Ephesus under Pertinax [the emperor Nerva Pertinax] and continuing there until the tithe of the emperor Trajan, founded and built churches throughout all Asia...." John's stay on Patmos lasted perhaps two years; he arrived on Patmos sometime during Domitian's 14th year (A.D. 82), Domitian died during the 15th year of his reign (A.D. 83), and John was released under the reign of the very next emperor, who ruled for only a little more than a year (late A.D. 83 to Jan. A.D. 85). Therefore, John was probably in exile on the island of Patmos for roughly two years. Still, it is possible that John was sent into exile earlier than Eusebius indicates, for the persecution of Christians under Domitian did begin earlier than Domitian's 14th year.[732] If this was the case, then John's stay on the island of Patmos could have been somewhat longer than three years.

The Death of Saint John

John survived the persecution under Domitian and his sentence to work the mines on the island of Patmos. Eusebius quotes Clement of Alexandria as saying that after "the tyrant" (Domitian) had died, John moved "from the island of Patmos to Ephesus," and that he traveled to neighboring areas, but kept Ephesus as his home.[733] Eusebius quotes Irenaeus as saying that John lived at Ephesus until sometime during the reign of the emperor Trajan.[734]

Jerome is more specific about the death of John. He tells us that John "returned to Ephesus...continuing there until the tithe of the emperor Trajan, founded and built churches throughout all Asia, and, worn out by old age, died in the sixty-eighth year after our Lord's passion and was buried near the same city." The tithe of the emperor Trajan was the third year of his reign.[735] In this revised chronology, Domitian died September 18 of A.D. 83 (see chapter 13). According to Dio, the next emperor, Nerva, reigned for only one year, 4 months, and 9 days.[736] Nerva, then, died near the end of January in the year A.D. 85. Trajan actually took over as emperor before Nerva died, for, according to Dio, Nerva resigned from the throne.[737] Thus A.D. 85 was the first year of Trajan's reign and A.D. 87 was his third year. John died in Trajan's third year, at Ephesus, in the year A.D. 87.

According to Saint Jerome, John died in the 68th year after the year of Christ's Passion. Since Christ died in A.D. 19, the 68th year after His Passion would be A.D. 87 (19 + 68 = 87). The length of time from Christ's Passion to John's death matches the year given by Jerome, Trajan's third year. (Note that Jerome does not correctly match year and length of time in the cases of James the Less, Mark the Gospel writer, and the Apostle Peter's deaths.) Since the year and the length of time agree in this case, the date Jerome gives for John the Gospel writer's death is confirmed.

According to Saint Epiphanius, John was 94 years old at the time of his death.[738] If so, then John was about 26 years old at the time of Christ's Passion (68 years earlier), and was about 23 when he became an Apostle (see chapter 7 for details on when the Apostles where chosen). This fits the description of John in the Gospels, which portray him as the youngest of the Apostles. On the other hand, Jesus would not have chosen a boy or a teenager to be an Apostle, for He Himself, the Living Word of God, did not presume to begin his Ministry teaching adults until He was in His adult years.

It is difficult to confirm Saint Epiphanius' assertion the John lived to the age of 94. However, John could not have died much younger than the age of 94. If John had died even at the age of 89, he would have been barely 21 years old at the time of Christ's Passion and would have been only 18 when chosen as an Apostle. If John had died at the age of 84, he would have been only 16 years old when Christ died and only 13 when chosen as an Apostle. For this reason, the assertion that John died in his mid-nineties must be correct, at least to a good approximation.

Chapter 12
The Reign of King Herod

The Days of Herod the King

"And so, when Jesus had been born in Bethlehem of Judah, in the days of king Herod, behold, Magi from the east arrived in Jerusalem, saying: 'Where is he who was born king of the Jews? For we have seen his star in the east, and we have come to adore him.' Now king Herod, hearing this, was disturbed, and all Jerusalem with him." (Mt 2:1-3).

Jesus was born during the reign of king Herod (called "Herod the Great"). It is useful to determine when Herod's reign began and ended, and when various events occurred during his reign. These dates are helpful in finding the dates of various events, such as the year when the rebuilding of the Temple began and the year of Christ's Birth.

Herod's reign over Judea began with his capture of the city of Jerusalem in a war between the Romans and the Parthians. Herod's reign ended with his death, which occurred about 34 years later, according to Josephus.[739] However, there is currently no agreement among scholars as to when Herod died. In past years, many scholars thought that Herod died in 4 B.C. You may see the years of Herod's reign stated in reference books, as if it were known with certainty, as 37 B.C. – 4 B.C. However, the disagreements among scholars about the chronology of Herod's reign are clear to anyone reading recent texts on the subject.[740]

The Beginning of Herod's Reign

Herod was appointed as king of the Jews by the Roman Senate, at the request of Marc Antony.[741] However, the Romans did not control Jerusalem and the surrounding area of Judea at that time, so they sent Herod with an army to capture the area from the Parthians. Herod won this war and captured Jerusalem and Judea, so that his effective reign as king began a few years after he was officially appointed as king. For this reason, the reign of Herod over the Jews is counted from the capture of Jerusalem.

Josephus states that the city of Jerusalem was captured by Herod "on the hundred eighty-fifth olympiad, on the third month, on the solemnity of the fast...."[742] The solemnity of the fast is the Day of Atonement (Yom Kippur), one of the holiest days in the Jewish faith (Lev 23:26-32). The Olympiad year begins on July 1, so that the third month is September. Thus, Josephus tells us that Jerusalem was captured by Herod in a year when the Day of Atonement (which is Tishri 10) occurred in September.

The Day of Atonement occurs on the tenth day of the Jewish month of Tishri, which is the first month of the Jewish civil calendar, but the seventh month of the Jewish sacred calendar. The sacred calendar begins in springtime with the month of Nisan, which contains the feast of Passover. The civil calendar begins in autumn with the month of Tishri, which contains the Day of Atonement and the Feast of Tabernacles (also called the Feast of Booths).

In most years, Tishri 10 does fall in September. But every 2 or 3 years, Tishri 10 will fall in early October. This occurs whenever the month of Nisan begins later than about March 28, and the Passover begins (Nisan 14) later than about April 10, so that the subsequent months also begin later than usual. Typically, this happens in years following a Jewish leap year, because an extra month has been added to the Jewish calendar, but it can also happen in years which are not leap years.

Now, as explained in chapter 17, it was not until sometime after Herod captured Jerusalem that the Jewish calendar switched from using an observation of the crescent new moon, to using a calculation of the new moon date in determining the start of each month. Since we are in the process of determining when Herod captured Jerusalem, we must consider that in any proposed year for the capture of the city that the calendar was still determined by observation.

Thus, in 37 B.C., Passover began (on Nisan 14) on April 16 (if determined by observation), so that the start of the next Jewish civil calendar year (on Tishri 1) began in late September. As a result, in 37 B.C., the solemnity of the fast (Tishri 10) fell in early October.[743] Since Tishri 10 did not fall in September in 37 B.C., this could not have been the year that Herod captured Jerusalem.

Several other years can be ruled out as the year when Herod captured Jerusalem, because Tishri 10 fell in October in those years also. In the years 34, 37, 40, 42, and 45 B.C., Tishri 10 fell in October.[744] Therefore, Herod's reign over Jerusalem could not have begun in any of those years. The astronomical new moon dates which determine the start of Nisan in those years are: March 29 at 20:23 JST (Jerusalem Standard Time) in 34 B.C., April 1 at 07:19 JST in 37 B.C., April 4 at 01:08 JST in 40 B.C., March 28 at 01:24 JST in 42 B.C., and March 30 at 22:12 JST in 45 B.C. From these dates we can easily see that the observation of the new crescent would occur a day or two later making Nisan 1 (the start of the sacred calendar year) late enough to push the date for Tishri 10 into early October.

Josephus describes the battle for the city of Jerusalem as occurring during the summertime.[745] Next he explains that, in those last months of the war, the Jews "were distressed by famine and the want of necessaries, for this happened to be a Sabbatic Year."[746] In the Sabbatical Year, which occurs every seventh year, the Jews were forbidden by Jewish religious law from planting or harvesting (Lev 25:1-7). Sabbatical years, in later practice, began in the autumn, on Tishri 1, and lasted until Tishri 1 of the following year. However, until sometime after Herod began to rule over Jerusalem, the Sabbatical years still began, as in ancient times, in the springtime with the month of Nisan (see chapter 16 on this point).

So, the Sabbatical year was going on in the summertime, during the siege and before the capture of Jerusalem. However, after the city was captured on Tishri 10, Josephus again states that their distress at that time was caused "in part by the Sabbatic Year, which was still going on, and forced the country to lie still uncultivated, since we are forbidden to sow the land in that year."[747] If the Sabbatical year began and ended with Tishri 1, then the Sabbatical year would have ended before the capture of Jerusalem on Tishri 10.

The usual interpretation of this passage is that the Sabbatical year ended on Tishri 1, but the people were still in distress because it would be some time before they could plant crops and obtain food from the harvest. However, this interpretation is incorrect. Josephus specifically says, not merely that they still lacked food, but that the land still had to be left uncultivated and that they still could not sow. My interpretation is that the Sabbatical years during this earlier time period (up to and including this first year of Herod's reign) were counted from Nisan to Nisan, not from Tishri to Tishri. This interpretation makes sense of Josephus' account as well as the words of Sacred Scripture in the book of Leviticus (see chapter 16). Thus, when the war ended with the capture of Jerusalem by Herod in September, on Tishri 10, the Sabbatical year was still ongoing and continued until the following spring.

In any case, it is clear that the year in which Herod captured Jerusalem was both **a Sabbatical year** (which must include the summer before the capture of the city) and a year in which **Tishri 10 fell in September**. To determine the year of the capture of Jerusalem, we must take both these factors into consideration.

There are two prevalent views on the chronology of Sabbatical years during this time period.[748] Zuckermann and Blosser have a Sabbatical year beginning in fall of 45 B.C. and ending in fall of 44 B.C. (45/44), and also, a Sabbatical year running from 38 to 37 B.C. (38/37). The year 44 B.C. was a year in which Tishri 10 fell in September, and may have been the end of a Sabbatical year, so this is a possible year for the capture of Jerusalem by Herod, if Zuckermann is correct.[749] But 37 B.C. is ruled out because Tishri 10 fell in October that year, as explained above. Notice that, according to Zuckermann and Blosser, the Sabbatical year began, rather than ended, in the autumn of both 45 and 38 B.C. But Josephus states that the Jews lacked food during the summer of the battle for Jerusalem because it was the Sabbatical year. Thus, neither 45 B.C. and 38 B.C. could have been the year of the capture of Jerusalem, according to the chronology of Zuckermann and Blosser.

On the other hand, Wacholder holds that the Sabbatical years during this time period were 44/43 B.C. and 37/36 B.C., a year later than Zuckermann and Blosser's dates.[750] In both 43 B.C. and 36 B.C. Tishri 10 fell in September, and so either of these years is also a plausible year for the capture of Jerusalem by Herod.

My (not so prevalent) view on the chronology of the Sabbatical years is that Wacholder is generally correct, but that the Sabbatical years were counted from Nisan to Nisan, not Tishri to Tishri, until sometime after Herod captured Jerusalem. Thus, for the year of the capture itself, the Sabbatical year would begin and end in springtime. Changing the start of the Sabbatical year to Nisan has the effect of changing the dates given by Wacholder by several months. If the capture of the city occurred at the earlier date, the Sabbatical year would be 43/42 B.C. (Nisan to Nisan), instead of 44/43 B.C. (Tishri to Tishri). Now, if the Sabbatical year occurred at the later date, then the years would be 36/35 B.C. (Nisan to Nisan). This turns out not to be the case, so the next Sabbatical year becomes 37/36 B.C. (Tishri to Tishri), due in part to the influence of Herod over the selection of the Jewish high priests (see chapter 16).

For the purposes of this chapter's argument, we will consider all of the above chronologies of the Sabbatical years. The chart below summarizes the years which can be ruled out as the year of the capture of Jerusalem.

Years	Possible year for capture of Jerusalem?
45 B.C.	No; not the summer of a Sabbatical year; and Tishri 10 fell in Oct.
44	Maybe; it is the summer of a Sabbatical year per Zuckermann
43	Maybe; it is the summer of a Sabbatical year per Wacholder/Conte
42	No; Tishri 10 fell in Oct., and not the summer of a Sabbatical year.
41	No; not a Sabbatical year;
40	No; Tishri 10 fell in Oct., and not a Sabbatical year.
39	No; not a Sabbatical year;
38	No; not the summer of a Sabbatical year
37	No; Tishri 10 fell in Oct.
36	Maybe; it is the summer of a Sabbatical year per Wacholder
35	No; not a Sabbatical year;
34 B.C.	No; Tishri 10 fell in Oct., and not a Sabbatical year.

In 44 B.C., the new moon of March 20 at 06:46 JST would be visible as a new crescent on the evening of March 21, placing Nisan 1 on March 22. The result is that Tishri 1, in the subsequent autumn, occurs early enough so that Tishri 10 would still fall in September.[751]

In 43 B.C., the astronomical new moon of March 9 at 08:38 hours JST would not be visible as a crescent until the evening of March 10, after sunset, at the earliest. Thus, Nisan 1 would coincide with March 11 and Nisan 14 would coincide with March 24, not long after the Spring Equinox of March 23 at 07:59 hours JST. This early date for Passover leads to an early date for the start of Tishri in the following autumn. The new moon of September 2 at 06:21 hours JST would be visible by the evening of September 3, after sunset. This makes Thursday, Sept. 4 the first day of Tishri. The Day of Atonement on Tishri 10 would then coincide with September 13 in 43 B.C.

In 36 B.C., the new moon of March 21 at 20:36 JST would be visible as a new crescent on the evening of March 22 or 23, placing Nisan 1 on March 23 or 24. The result is that Tishri 1, in the subsequent autumn, occurs early enough so that Tishri 10 would still fall in September.[752]

Based on the above considerations, the years **44, 43** and **36 B.C.** are the only years during this time period (from 45 B.C. to 34 B.C. inclusive) which fit the details given by Josephus for the capture of Jerusalem at the beginning of Herod's reign. To choose between these dates, we must now look at the evidence for the year of Herod's death.

The Length of Herod's Reign

Josephus describes Herod's reign as lasting 34 years, from his capture of Jerusalem to his death. At the time that Herod captured Jerusalem, he also took prisoner its former ruler, Antigonus, and sent him to Marc Antony, who eventually had him beheaded.[753] Josephus counts Herod's actual reign over Jerusalem as beginning with his capture of Jerusalem and Antigonus' death, and ending with Herod's own death. "When he had done those things he died…having reigned, since he had procured Antigonus to be slain, thirty-four years…." [754]

When speaking of the deaths of the emperors of Rome, Josephus gives the exact length of their reign in years, months, and days. For example, he wrote that the reign of Augustus Caesar lasted "fifty-seven years, besides six months and two days...." [755] Notice that Josephus is not here using any kind of system by which he would count a partial year as if it were a full year. He concerns himself with recording the exact length of the ruler's reign.[756]

In contrast to his writings about the emperors of Rome, Josephus does not tell us the exact length of Herod's reign. He clearly states the exact day that Herod's reign began, on the solemnity of the fast in the third month of the Olympiad year (when Jerusalem was captured). But he does not give any indication that he knew the exact day of Herod's death. Perhaps Josephus did not know on which day Herod died, and so did not know the exact length of his reign. So, when he tell us that Herod reigned for 34 years, we must consider the possibility that Herod reigned for a few months more or less than 34 years.

As detailed below, Herod died in the wintertime, after the fast day (Yom Kippur, Tishri 10) in the autumn, and sometime after a lunar eclipse, but before the Passover celebration which occurs in spring. His reign began sometime in September (the 3rd month of the Olympiad year), and ended in wintertime. Thus his reign could not have ended only a few months short of 34 full years, for then he would have died in summertime. Yet, if he died more than 6 months before the completion of 34 years, Josephus would have been more likely to call the length of his reign 33 years, instead of 34. Therefore, the length of Herod's reign was 34 years plus some number of months.

By subtracting 34+ years from the possible years for the beginning of Herod's reign (**44, 43**, and **36 B.C.**), we arrive at **9 B.C., 8 B.C.**, and **1 B.C.** as the possible years for the death of Herod. Here the years are given as if the death of Herod occurred in Jan./Feb, during the latter part of the winter. If Herod had instead died in Dec., the number of the year would be one year earlier, but the winter would be the same (i.e. the winters of 10/9 B.C., 9/8 B.C. and 2/1 B.C.).

If Herod died in early 1 B.C. and reigned for somewhat more than 34 years, he must then have taken Jerusalem in 36 B.C., which gives us a reign of 34 years and about 4 or 5 months. 36 B.C. was the end of a Sabbatical year according to Wacholder, and the fast day fell in September that year, in agreement with what Josephus tells us. So, here is one possibility for the years of Herod's reign: **36 B.C. to 1 B.C.**

If Herod died in Jan./Feb. of 8 B.C., the date for the capture of Jerusalem would then be 43 B.C., a time span, again, of 34 years and a few months. The year 43 B.C. was the end of a Sabbatical year according to Wacholder, and Tishri 10 fell in September that year, not October. This fits the description given by Josephus. So, **43 B.C. to 8 B.C.** is another possible time frame for the reign of Herod over Jerusalem.

If Herod died in early 9 B.C., the date for the capture of Jerusalem would then be 44 B.C., which was the end of a Sabbatical year according Zuckermann and Blosser. Since Tishri 10 fell in September that year, here again is a set of dates that agrees with Josephus. So, **44 B.C. to 9 B.C.** is the third possible time frame for the reign of Herod over Jerusalem.

But to decide between **9 B.C., 8 B.C.** and **1 B.C.** as possible years for the death of Herod, we must next consider in detail the circumstances of Herod's death as described by Josephus. In particular, we will look at information about a lunar eclipse, which Josephus tells us occurred prior to the death of Herod.

Herod's Death

Detailed information about the death of Herod is provided by the ancient Jewish Roman historian, Flavius Josephus. He describes events which occurred on "the fast day" (Yom Kippur), then a lunar eclipse, followed by a series of events leading up to the death of Herod, then a period of mourning by Herod's son, Archelaus, followed by the Feast of Passover. Since the precise day and time of lunar eclipses can be determined from astronomy, we can compare past lunar eclipses, visible from Jerusalem, which might fit this sequence of events.

Lunar eclipses only occur about the time of the full moon, when the moon is on the opposite side of the earth from the sun and so can pass through the earth's shadow causing the reflected light from the moon to be eclipsed. Passover also always occurs about the time of the full moon, because the Jewish calendar is based on the lunar cycle. So the amount of time between the lunar eclipse and the Passover must have been approximately a whole number of lunar months. Herod's death occurred between the lunar eclipse and the Passover.

How many lunar months are needed to accommodate all of the events described by Josephus as occurring between the lunar eclipse and the Passover? The sequence of events, found in *The Antiquities of the Jews*, book 17, chapters 6-9, is as follows.

Jewish Martyrs

Some length of time before the lunar eclipse, Herod had an image of a golden eagle made and placed at the entrance to the Temple of Jerusalem. (The eagle was one of the symbols used by the Roman empire.) Two well-known Jewish teachers, Judas and Matthias, considered this a sacrilege (cf. Ex 20:4; Lev 26:1; Deut 5:8) and encouraged the young men who were their students to remove it. And so, they took down the golden eagle and broke it into pieces with axes in the middle of the day, in full view of a crowd of people. About 40 of the young men were arrested, along with the two teachers.[757]

Herod considered the act of destroying the golden eagle a personal offense against himself. He removed the man who was high priest at that time from the high priesthood. Then Herod had the two Jewish teachers and the others responsible for destroying the eagle burned alive. "And that very night there was an eclipse of the moon."[758]

Now, just before telling us about the removal of this high priest at the time of the death of the Jewish martyrs and the lunar eclipse, Josephus describes how this same high priest was unable to officiate for a single day, on the occasion of the fast day (Yom Kippur, Tishri 10, in the autumn). The very next statement by Josephus is that this same high priest was permanently removed from office by Herod, at the time of the death of these Jewish martyrs and the lunar eclipse.[759] Therefore, the lunar eclipse occurred after Tishri 10.

Herod's Illness

Several events then followed after the eclipse, leading up to Herod's death. Herod, who was already quite ill, became worse still and sent for physicians to treat him. He followed their advice and traveled "beyond the river Jordan" to receive treatments, including warm baths in water and even in oil. Since these treatments were ineffective, Herod gave up hope that he could recover and resigned himself to death.[760]

Next Herod returned to his palace at Jericho, grew even sicker, and devised an evil plan. He decided to have all of the most important Jewish leaders throughout the nation brought to him. When they arrived, he had them confined to the hippodrome (a type of sports stadium which the Romans used for horse and chariot races). He gave orders to his sister and brother-in-law that upon his death, before they revealed that he had died, they were to order the soldiers to kill every Jewish leader being held by him at the hippodrome. Herod knew that the Jews hated him. In this way, he had hoped to cause a great mourning throughout the land to coincide with his death, a mourning fit for a king.[761]

Thereafter, Herod received permission from Caesar to either banish or execute Herod's son, Antipater. Herod chose to have his son, Antipater, put to death. Five days later, Herod died.[762] But Herod's sister and brother-in-law did not carry out his evil plan to kill all the Jewish leaders being held at the hippodrome. They did not make Herod's death known until they had released the Jews from the Hippodrome and sent them to their homes.[763]

After the Jewish leaders were safely away, Herod's death was made public. His son, Archelaus, then mourned for him until the seventh day. Next, Archelaus took his father's throne and held a feast with his friends.[764] Then there was a dispute between the Jews and Archelaus about whether or not the men who carried out Herod's orders to burn to death those who had destroyed the golden eagle should be punished. This dispute occurred at the time when many Jews had come to Jerusalem for the Passover feast.[765]

The Number of Lunar Months

What number of lunar months, then, would be sufficient to accommodate all of the above described events, from the burning of the Jewish martyrs to the Passover? Herod spent some time after the eclipse trying to find some treatment which would save his life. A man does not give up easily when his own life is at stake. Herod was the king and could have access to any physician in the land. He must have spent more than a brief amount of time consulting various physicians and trying various treatments before he resigned himself to his own death. Herod must have spent many weeks trying to save his own life before he gave up hope.

Only after he realized his death was imminent did Herod devise his plan to have all of the Jewish leaders from the entire nation brought to the hippodrome. Knowing that Herod had recently burned a number of Jews to death, would they have come quickly at the call of king Herod? A man does not usually go in haste to his own death. In any case, it must have taken a week or more for word of Herod's order to travel across the nation, and at least another couple of weeks for all of the Jewish leaders to comply with his order, and to travel to the hippodrome.

Then there were five days that passed between the execution of Herod's son and Herod's own death, plus another day or two for the Jews to be released from the hippodrome and travel towards their homes. Then Herod's funeral was held, a very elaborate funeral for which it may have taken a few days to prepare.[766] Then Herod's other son, Archelaus, mourned until the seventh day and then held a feast for him and his friends (cf. Sirach 22:12). Clearly, even these few events from Antipater's death to the end of Archelaus' mourning took over two weeks.

And there are any number of days that may have passed in between the events which Josephus describes, such as, between the eclipse and Herod traveling beyond the Jordan for treatments, between Herod returning from those treatments and his decision to gather the Jewish leaders, between the confining of the Jewish leaders to the hippodrome and the execution of Herod's son, and between Archelaus assuming the throne and the Passover. Just because the amount of time between two events is not specified, does not mean it is zero.

Therefore, the time frame required for the events occurring between the lunar eclipse and the Passover feast must be at least 3, and perhaps as many as 5 or 6, lunar months. But it is unlikely that these events took longer than 6 lunar months. The reason is as follows.

Immediately before describing the burning of the Jewish martyrs and the lunar eclipse, Josephus describes events occurring on Tishri 10 (Yom Kippur). Yet the lunar eclipse could not have occurred that same month. Lunar eclipses occur about the middle of the Jewish month, which would be Tishri 14 or 15. But Tishri 15 marks the beginning of the Feast of Tabernacles (also called the Feast of Booths). Jewish religious law required all Jewish adult males to come to the Temple of Jerusalem at the Feast of Tabernacles. "Three times a year all your males shall appear in the sight the Lord your God in the place which he will have chosen: at the Feast of Unleavened Bread, at the Feast of Weeks, and at the Feast of Tabernacles." (Deut 16:16). Huge crowds of adult male Jews gathered in Jerusalem for the Feast of Tabernacles, which begins on Tishri 15 (cf. Lev 23:34).

At one point in his account of Jewish-Roman history, Josephus estimates the number of Jews who came to Jerusalem for the Passover at "not fewer in number than three millions."[767] At such times, there was not nearly enough housing for so many persons, so the Jews pitched their tents around the city. Imagine Jerusalem surrounded by millions of people and their tents, like a great army encamped around the city. Of course, Israel had no standing army. In times of war, every able-bodied man took up arms. Thus, this crowd included nearly every adult Jewish man who would become a soldier if the Jews ever rebelled against the Romans in war (as they did a couple of generations later).

For these reasons, the huge crowds that assembled in Jerusalem for Jewish feasts had power to influence the Roman rulers—as both the crowds and the rulers knew well. For example, Pontius Pilate wanted to release Jesus (cf. Mt 27:17-19; Lk 23:13-16; Jn 19:6-12), but the crowds demanded His Crucifixion. Pilate feared a riot; this is part of the reason that he released Jesus to be crucified (Mt 27:24-26; Mk 15:11-15; Lk 23:23-25).

Another such example of this influence occurred at the time of the Passover following the death of Herod, when "an innumerable multitude came thither out of the country, nay, from beyond its limits also, in order to worship God…."[768] It was then that the Jews, feeling the power of their numbers, demanded that those who had carried out Herod's order to burn alive the Jewish martyrs be punished. Some of the Jews even under took violence against Herod's soldiers.[769]

Therefore, on the earlier occasion of the Feast of Tabernacle prior to Herod's death, Herod would not have dared to anger such huge crowds by deposing the Jewish high priest, by burning alive two of the teachers of the Temple and 40 of their students, and by doing all of this at the very beginning of a sacred Jewish feast. There would have been riots or an armed rebellion. Herod had thousands of soldiers, but there were millions of Jews in and around Jerusalem for the Feast of Tabernacles. Therefore, the burning of the Jewish martyrs could not have occurred at the time of the Feast of Tabernacles, and the lunar eclipse, which accompanied the burning of the Jewish martyrs and preceded the death of Herod, could not have occurred during the month of Tishri.

Thus the lunar eclipse must have occurred sometime after the month of Tishri, but before the month of Nisan (when Passover occurs). There are usually 6 lunar months from the full moon of Tishri to the full moon of Nisan, though in a Jewish leap year (when a 13th month is added to the calendar) there would be 7 lunar months. Since the lunar eclipse must have occurred sometime after Tishri, at most there would be 5 lunar months, or 6 in a Jewish leap year, from the eclipse to the Passover.

So the length of time from the lunar eclipse to the Passover could be no more than 6 lunar months, at the very most. And, because of the number of events described by Josephus between the eclipse and the Passover, the length of time would have to be a minimum of 3 lunar months. Therefore the lunar eclipse most likely occurred in one of the 4 Jewish months following Tishri: Heshvan, Kislev, Tevet, or Shevat. However, Shevat is only a possibility during in a leap year, when AdarII is added to the calendar just before Nisan. Thus, there would be at least 3, and at most 6, lunar months between the lunar eclipse and the Passover.

In addition, Herod's death probably happened closer to the Passover than to the eclipse because the more time consuming events—Herod seeking a life-saving treatment, the gathering of all the Jewish leaders in the hippodrome—were completed before Herod died. So, if the eclipse occurred at the earliest in the middle of Heshvan (lunar eclipses always occur in the middle of the Jewish lunar month), then Herod's death most likely occurred, after at least 2 or 3 months had passed, in late Tevet, or in the months of Shevat or AdarI (or, in a leap year and at the latest, in early AdarII). Also, at least a couple of weeks, and more probably a month or so, is required for the events between Herod's death and the Passover. For these reasons, Herod's death most likely occurred in January or February (not in November, December, or March).

The Usual Dates

The most often cited lunar eclipse, which many consider to be the eclipse before Herod's death, is the lunar eclipse of March 13, in 4 B.C. However, this eclipse occurred only one lunar month before the Passover of April 11 that year. It is inconceivable that so many events as are described by Josephus could possibly be fit into one month. This is one of the most ridiculous assertions of chronologists, second only to the conclusions of some that there might be errors in Sacred Scripture, that so many events could have taken place in so small a space of time. Nevertheless, many scholars insist that Herod died in 4 B.C.[770]

There are additional reasons why the lunar eclipse of March 13, in 4 B.C. could not be the eclipse which preceded Herod's death. This eclipse began about 1:42 a.m. JST (Jerusalem Standard Time) and ended 2 hours and 20 minutes later about 4:02 a.m.[771] As John Pratt points out, at that late hour few people would have viewed the eclipse and it would have been unlikely to be remembered and associated with the death of the Jewish martyrs.[772]

Another theory is that the lunar eclipse of September 15 of 5 B.C. was the lunar eclipse preceding the death of Herod. That eclipse occurred 7 lunar months before the Passover of 4 B.C. Thus the eclipse either occurred in the month of Elul (the month before Tishri) or in the month of Tishri, but with the addition of the month of AdarII before the Nisan of 4 B.C.

In 5 B.C., with the calendar determined by calculation of the new moon date, the Passover began on March 21, two days before the Spring Equinox. In such cases, the Jewish religious leaders usually added a leap month to delay the Passover one lunar month. The decision as to which years would be leap years was a human decision, made by the Jewish religious leaders. Their decision depended mainly on three factors, the Spring Equinox, and the maturity of the grain and fruit crops.[773] These factors are not independent of one another; they are closely related. These crops were not likely to be ready before the Spring Equinox because they reach maturity in spring. Therefore, 5 B.C. most likely included the leap month of AdarII, so that the eclipse of Sept. 15, 5 B.C., occurred during the month of Elul.

But if this lunar eclipse had occurred in Elul, the month before Tishri, it could not have been the eclipse mentioned by Josephus. For that eclipse clearly occurred at the same time as the removal from office of the high priest—the same high priest whom Josephus describes as still being in office on the fast day of Tishri 10.

The other possibility is that the Passover of 5 B.C. was allowed to occur earlier than the Spring Equinox, resulting in an earlier than usual start of the month of Tishri. The Jewish religious leaders would then have added the leap month of AdarII before the Passover of 4 B.C. instead. In such a case, the lunar eclipse of Sept. 15, 5 B.C., would have fallen in the middle of Tishri, after the fast day of Tishri 10 and about the time of the Feast of Tabernacles. This scenario, though, is highly unlikely. As explained above, the lunar eclipse and burning alive of the Jewish martyrs could not have occurred in Tishri, for at that time there would have been huge crowds gathered for the Feast of Tabernacles. These crowds would not have permitted such an offense, nor would Herod have dared to outrage them and risk a riot or rebellion.

Furthermore, Josephus, a Jewish priest, would most likely have made mention if the death of these Jewish martyrs occurred at the start of the holy Feast of Tabernacles. He mentions the Day of Atonement in association with the high priest, the one whom Herod later deposed, but he does not associate the death of the Jewish martyrs at the time of the eclipse with the Feast of Tabernacles. Therefore, their martyrdom occurred after the month of Tishri.

From fall of 5 B.C. to spring of 4 B.C., there were no other lunar eclipses at all. Since neither the Sept. of 5 B.C., nor the March of 4 B.C., eclipses fit the description given by Josephus, Herod could not have died during the winter of 5/4 B.C. In addition, Josephus tells us that there were 34 years from Herod's capture of Jerusalem to Herod's death. Yet, 34 years before 4 B.C., there is no year which fits Josephus' description of the year of the capture of Jerusalem. The years 37 through 42 B.C. inclusive, do not contain the summer of a Sabbatical year coupled with a year in which the fast day of Tishri 10 fell in September. Therefore, the generally-accepted chronology wherein Herod ruled over Jerusalem from 37 to 4 B.C., cannot be correct.

Other Eclipses to Consider

As concluded above, the possible years for the death of Herod are 9 B.C., 8 B.C., or 1 B.C. There are eclipses to consider for each of those winters. Lunar eclipse data given below is from the NASA web site and from *RedShift 3* astronomy software program.[774] Eclipse times are given as Jerusalem Standard Time, which is Universal Time plus 2 hours.

In the winter of 10 B.C. to 9 B.C., there is only one lunar eclipse to consider, the eclipse of Dec. 10 in 10 B.C. There were 4 lunar months from this eclipse to the Passover in early April of 9 B.C., which is a sufficient length of time for the described events. The mid-point of the eclipse occurred at 06:58 hours (Jerusalem time).[775] This was a partial eclipse (covering, at its height, just under 70% of the moon's visible surface) which began at 05:36 and ended at 08:20 hours. The entire eclipse was not visible from Jerusalem, because moonset on that day occurred about 06:34, before the eclipse was even half way completed. Only the first hour or so of the eclipse was visible from Jerusalem.

Sunrise on the day of this lunar eclipse occurred about 06:32. The sky begins to brighten about an hour or so before the sun actually rises above the horizon. Thus this eclipse began about the beginning of the daylight hours. But the eclipse Josephus describes occurred at night. "And that very night there was an eclipse of the moon."[776] Therefore, this eclipse, and any other lunar eclipse occurring about dawn, does not fit the description given by Josephus.

In the winter of 9 B.C. to 8 B.C., there is only one lunar eclipse to consider, the lunar eclipse of Nov. 28 in 9 B.C. This total lunar eclipse lasted 3 hours and 38 minutes, reaching its height at the mid-point of 21:02 hours Jerusalem time. The eclipse began at 19:13 hours (7:13 p.m.). This eclipse would have been easily noticed by the inhabitants of Israel, because it was a long-lasting total eclipse, and because it began early in the evening, not long after sunset. A more noticeable eclipse is more likely to have been remembered and associated with the events of the previous day (the burning of the Jewish martyrs).

The length of time between the 9 B.C. lunar eclipse and the next Passover (in late March of 8 B.C.) is 4 lunar months, which is sufficient time to contain all of the events described by Josephus. This eclipse fits the chronology of events surrounding the death of Herod, and could well be the eclipse mentioned by Josephus. In this case, the date of Herod's death would most likely be Jan./Feb. of 8 B.C.

In the winter of 2 B.C. to 1 B.C., one lunar eclipse occurred, on the night of Jan. 9 to Jan. 10 of 1 B.C. This eclipse is 3 lunar months from the Passover of early April in 1 B.C., and so meets the minimum length of time established above. The eclipse began about 23:33 hours JST on Jan. 9, and lasted 3 hours and 34 minutes, ending about 03:07 hours on Jan. 10. This eclipse lasted long enough to be noticed, but occurred rather late at night. An eclipse beginning as late as 11:33 p.m. would be observed by far fewer persons than one beginning about 7:13 p.m., and so would be less likely to have been associated with the historical events of the time. Even so, this eclipse must still be considered as one possibility for the eclipse mentioned by Josephus, since it occurred during the winter, after the month of Tishri, and at least 3 months before the Passover.

In chapter 17, every eclipse from 10 B.C. to A.D. 1 is examined to see if it meets the criteria for the eclipse preceding the death of Herod. In summary, the only lunar eclipses which fit the criteria established above are the eclipses of **Nov. 28 of 9** B.C. and **Jan. 9 of 1** B.C. All of the other eclipses either did not occur during the winter months, or were not visible from Jerusalem, or were only a month away from the Passover, or occurred during or before the month of Tishri, or were brief, partial penumbral eclipses (i.e. barely noticeable as eclipses to an observer) or occurred during daylight hours (not at night, as specified by Josephus). Also, these other eclipses are not the correct number of years from a possible year for Herod's capture of Jerusalem.

Of the two possible eclipses, the Nov. 28 of 9 B.C. eclipse is the better fit, because it gives 4 months to fit all of the events described by Josephus between the eclipse and the Passover. The Jan. 9 of 1 B.C. eclipse provides only 3 months, which is less likely to have been a sufficient length of time. Also, the Nov. 28 of 9 B.C. eclipse began much earlier in the evening (7:13 p.m.) than the Jan. 9 of 1 B.C. eclipse (11:33 p.m.). An earlier evening lunar eclipse is more likely to have been noticed, associated with the events of the previous day, and become a part of the history of the time.

The date of Nov. 28 of 9 B.C. for the eclipse gives us a date for the death of Herod most likely in Jan. or Feb. of early 8 B.C. Formerly, many scholars accepted early 4 B.C. as the time of Herod's death. This new date is four years earlier than many have thought; however, the conclusions of chapter 13 of this book find that many events during this time period occurred four years earlier than the generally-accepted dates. Based on the eclipse data alone, one might try to argue that the 1 B.C. eclipse, though not the best fit, is still a possibility. But, considering the evidence given in chapter 13, that the time frame for Augustus Caesar's reign actually occurred 4 years earlier than generally believed, an early 8 B.C. date for Herod's death is the only reasonable answer. If the true dates of these events occurred 4 years earlier than has been generally accepted, then the eclipse of 1 B.C. would have to be reconciled to events generally believed to have occurred as late as A.D. 4. No scholar places the death of Herod in the context of events occurring as late as A.D. 4. On the other hand, if Herod died in early 8 B.C., and if the events of that time period occurred 4 years earlier than the generally-accepted dates, then the death of Herod coincided with the events generally believed to have occurred in 4 B.C. This is exactly the historical context for the death of Herod which has been well-accepted. (Notice that the eclipse dates are not displaced by 4 years, because the astronomical data is not subject to the same historical errors which caused the misdating of certain historical events.)

The Holy Innocents

Herod tried to kill the Christ-Child by killing male children 2 years of age or younger (Mt 2:16). At the time of the Massacre of the Holy Innocents, Herod thought that as many as 2 years might have passed since the Birth of Christ. Therefore, Herod must have lived for at least 2 years after the Birth of Christ. If Herod died in early 8 B.C., then Christ must have been born before 9 B.C. The conclusion that Herod died in 8 B.C. effectively rules out any year for the Birth of Christ later than 10 B.C.

The Rebuilding of the Temple

Josephus makes several conflicting statements about when the Temple of Jerusalem was rebuilt. In *Antiquities of the Jews*, he states that Herod undertook the rebuilding the temple in his 18th year.[777] But in *Wars of the Jews*, he states that Herod rebuilt the temple in his 15th year.[778] The generally-accepted view is that the rebuilding of the temple began in Herod's 18th year. However, there is a third possibility.

Josephus counts the beginning of Herod's reign from the time that he captured Jerusalem and brought about Antigonus' death. Book 15 of *Antiquities of the Jews* begins with the capture of Jerusalem and Antigonus' death, which was the beginning of Herod's reign over Jerusalem. In the title of book 15, Josephus writes: "BOOK 15 CONTAINING THE INTERVAL OF EIGHTEEN YEARS FROM THE DEATH OF ANTIGONUS TO THE FINISHING OF THE TEMPLE BY HEROD." Since book 15 covers a period of 18 years, from the beginning of Herod's reign to the completion of the temple, work on the temple must have been completed (not begun) in Herod's 18th year.

Also, Josephus places the description of the rebuilding of the Temple at the very end of book 15. If the rebuilding had begun in Herod's 18th year, then the description of the completion of the rebuilding would fall into the middle of book 16. But book 16 instead mentions the rebuilding of the Temple in the title of the book as having already been completed: "CONTAINING THE INTERVAL OF TWELVE YEARS FROM THE FINISHING OF THE TEMPLE BY HEROD TO THE DEATH OF ALEXANDER AND ARISTOBULUS."[779] Notice from this title that book 16 begins at the time of the completion of the rebuilding of the Temple. Therefore, the Temple rebuilding did not begin in Herod's 18th year, but rather was completed in his 18th year.

The statement by Josephus that the rebuilding of the Temple of Jerusalem began in Herod's 15th year cannot be correct.[780] Josephus describes in detail a famine which took place in Israel during Herod's 13th and 14th years.[781] The year after a two-year period of famine is a very unlikely starting point for a major building project, such as the rebuilding of the Temple of Jerusalem. However, the rebuilding took eight years, so work on the Temple did occur during Herod's 15th year, and ended in his 18th year.[782]

Further confirmation that the rebuilding of the Temple was completed in Herod's 18th year is found in Josephus' description of another major building project, Cesarea Sebaste. Josephus tells us that Cesarea Sebaste took nearly ten years to build and was completed in Herod's 28th year.[783] This building project began nearly 10 years earlier, about the 19th year of Herod's reign. But if Herod had begun to build the temple in his 18th year, he would have had two major building projects going on at the same time. This is highly unlikely, for Herod had difficulty convincing the Jewish people to participate in even the one major construction project, to rebuild their own Temple, as Josephus describes: "...but as he knew the multitude were not ready nor willing to assist him in so vast a design, he thought to prepare them first by making a speech to them, and then set about the work itself...."[784] On the other hand, if the Temple was completed in Herod's 18th year, then the extensive resources formerly used to rebuild the Temple could be brought to bear on the Cesarea Sebaste project. Again, we see that the rebuilding of the Temple of Jerusalem was completed in Herod's 18th year.

According to Josephus, the rebuilding of the Temple, including the outer enclosures, took 8 years.[785] If the work was completed in Herod's 18th year, it must have begun 8 years earlier, in Herod's 11th year. The work on the Temple itself (the Sanctuary where the sacrifices took place) took only 1½ years.[786] Josephus notes that the completion of the rebuilding of the Temple Sanctuary was celebrated with a festival which coincided with the anniversary of Herod's inauguration as king of Jerusalem.[787] Herod captured Jerusalem in the autumn and must have been inaugurated as king shortly thereafter, so the rebuilding of the Temple Sanctuary was completed in the autumn. Therefore, the work on the Temple Sanctuary began in the springtime during Herod's 11th year, continued for 1½ years, and was completed at the end of his 12th year as king of Jerusalem.

Herod captured Jerusalem in autumn of 43 B.C., on the fast day (Tishri 10), which fell in mid September that year.[788] The work on the Temple of Jerusalem began in spring of Herod's 11th year, which would be spring of 32 B.C. (Regardless of whether one counts each year of Herod's reign from the autumn at his inauguration, or from the beginning of the calendar year in January, or from the beginning of the Jewish sacred calendar in Nisan, the spring of his 11th year would still be 32 B.C.) The Temple Sanctuary was completed 1½ years later, in autumn of 31 B.C. And the entire Temple, including the outer enclosures, was completed about 8 years after the work had begun, in Herod's 18th year, which was 25 B.C.

The Olympiad Years

The modern-day Olympics has its origins and inspiration in the ancient Olympic Games held by the Romans. These Olympic Games were held, as we would count it, every 4 years. The Romans counted it as every 5th year, since they counted inclusively, that is, they counted the year of the games, plus the 3 following years, plus the year of the next games. The Olympiad year began on July 1, and ended on June 30 of the following calendar year.

The Romans kept track of events by the number given to each Olympics. This method of keeping track of the years is noticeable in the writings of Josephus. For example, Josephus places the capture of Jerusalem by Herod in the third month of the 185th Olympiad.[789] According to the argument given above, Herod captured Jerusalem in the year 43 B.C., which places the 185th Olympiad from July 1 of 43 to June 30 of 42 B.C. The usual date given for the 185th Olympiad is July 1 of 40 B.C. to June 30 of 39 B.C.[790] Thus the dates for the Olympiad years in this revised chronology differ from the generally-accepted dates by 3 years.

The Sons of Herod the Great

Herod the Great had four sons and he named them all Herod: Herod Antipater, Herod Archelaus, Herod Antipas, Herod Philip. Herod the Great killed his son Antipater shortly before Herod himself died. Herod Archelaus lost political power after a reign of about 10 years.[791] Herod Antipas was tetrarch of Galilee and is referred to in the Gospels as Herod the tetrarch (e.g. Lk 3:1). Pilate sent Jesus to Herod Antipas on the day of the Crucifixion because Herod had jurisdiction over Galilee, where Jesus had lived for many years.

The reign of Herod Philip is also mentioned in Sacred Scripture (Lk 3:1). According to Josephus, Philip was unlike his father and brothers; he was a moderate, quiet, and just ruler.[792] The chronology of Philip's reign is in agreement with my revised chronology of Herod the Great's reign.

In many modern editions of *Antiquities of the Jews* by Flavius Josephus, the text reads: "About this time it was that Philip, Herod's brother, departed this life, in the twentieth year of the reign of Tiberius, after he had been tetrarch of Trachonitis, and Gaulonitis, and of the nation of the Bataneans also, thirty-seven years."[793] However, a recent study of the most ancient editions of Josephus reveals that none of the texts published prior to 1544 reads "twentieth year of Tiberius."[794] Most of the older editions had the text as "twenty-second year of Tiberius," and the older the text, the more likely it was to read "twenty-second" rather than "twentieth."[795] Therefore, Philip died in the 22nd year of Tiberius.

In the usual chronology, the 22nd year of Tiberius' reign would be A.D. 36. In this revised chronology, the 22nd year of Tiberius is A.D. 22. Josephus also mentions that Tiberius added Philip's principality (the area he governed) to the province of Syria.[796] Therefore, Philip died before Tiberius died. This places Philip's death early in A.D. 22, prior to Tiberius' death in March.

The older versions of *Antiquities of the Jews* also give a different number for the length of Philip's reign. The oldest texts say that Philip's reign lasted either 32 or 36 years, not the 37 years found in more modern editions.[797] The Roman custom was to count the first full calendar year of a ruler's reign as year one for that ruler, and to count the calendar year in which the ruler died (in which he ruled for only part of the year) as the last year of that ruler's reign. Counting the years in this way, Philip's first year would be 10 B.C., if he ruled for 32 years (10B.C. to 1 B.C. is 10 years; A.D. 1 to A.D. 22 is 22 years; 10 plus 22 = 32 years). If Philip ruled for 36 years, counting likewise, his reign would have begun with the year 14 B.C.

This revised chronology places Herod the Great's death in early 8 B.C. So Philip ruled for about 29 years after the death of his father. However, many scholars believe that Herod's sons antedated their reigns, i.e. they counted their reigns as having begun years before Herod's death. Finegan presents ample evidence for this possibility.[798] If Philip antedated his reign from a point two years before Herod's death, the length of his reign would be given as 32 years, in agreement with some of the oldest editions of Josephus.

There are two possibilities for an antedated reign. First, a ruler may have counted his reign as beginning at a time before it actually began. An example of this is found within Dio's description of the antedating of the reigns of Galba, Otho, and Vitellius.[799] According to Dio, their reigns did not actually begin as early as they claimed. Second, a ruler may count his reign as beginning before the death of the previous ruler but with good reason, because he actually did have considerable power beginning from the earlier date. An example of this is seen in Tiberius' reign, as detailed in chapter 13. Concerning Philip's antedated reign, he counted his reign from a point beginning two years before Herod's death, but he may or may not have had much power or authority at that earlier time.

Blessed Anne Catherine's Chronology of Herod

The above chronology of Herod's reign, along with the conclusions of chapter 13, supports the second line of reasoning, the one based on historical evidence, in chapters 2 and 4 concerning the year of the Crucifixion and the year of the Birth of Christ. No reference to the writings of Blessed Anne Catherine is needed to reach the conclusions of chapters 12 and 13, nor to support this line of reasoning based on historical evidence. However, it is interesting and informative to next consider how her chronology of Herod's reign compares to the above chronology.

Blessed Anne Catherine Emmerich states: "Herod reigned forty years in all until his death. He was, it is true, only a vassal-king for seven years, but harassed the country grievously and committed many cruelties. He died about the time of Christ's sixth year."[800] At first glance, the 40 years of Herod's reign would appear to be in conflict with Josephus' statement that Herod reigned for 34 years.[801] But Blessed Anne Catherine adds that Herod was a "vassal-king" for 7 years, referring to Herod's earlier rule over Galilee, before he became king in Jerusalem. It makes sense that Blessed Anne Catherine would count the years of Herod's reign beginning with his earlier rule over Galilee. Many of Blessed Anne Catherine's visions refer to events which took place in Galilee. Also, the Virgin Mary and her parents lived in Nazareth (which is in Galilee) for much of their lives, and the Holy Family also lived there for many years, after returning from Egypt.

The chronology of Herod's reign given by Blessed Anne Catherine generally agrees with the chronology given by Josephus, except that her chronology differs from Josephus' by about six years. This is because Blessed Anne Catherine starts her count of the years of Herod's reign from his rule over Galilee, which began about six to seven years earlier than his rule as king over Jerusalem. If the seven years is not seven full years (but six years and some number of months), and the 40 years is plus a few months, then the two chronologies can be harmonized. We must then subtract 6 years from the number of any year of Herod's reign given by Blessed Anne Catherine to arrive at the same year as numbered by Josephus. For example, she states that Herod reigned for 40 years (including his rule over Galilee). Josephus gives the length of Herod's reign as 34 years (not counting his rule over Galilee). If Herod reigned over Galilee for six years and some months, then these two statements about the length of Herod's reign agree.

Blessed Anne Catherine gives the year of Christ's birth with reference to Herod's reign. "Jesus must have been born about the thirty-fourth year of Herod's reign."[802] The 34th year of Herod's reign in her way of counting would then be about the 28th year of Herod's reign by Josephus' count of the years. The 28th year of Herod's reign in Josephus was about the time that Cesarea Sebaste was completed, in the 192nd Olympiad year.[803] This corresponds to 15 B.C. in the above chronology of Herod's reign, which again agrees with the conclusion that Christ was born in 15 B.C.

"Two years before the entry of Mary into the Temple, just seventeen years before the Birth of Christ, Herod ordered that work should be done in the Temple."[804]

Since Blessed Anne Catherine places the Birth of Christ in the 34th year of Herod's reign, the work rebuilding the Temple occurred about the 17th year of Herod's reign in her way of counting the years, which would correspond to the 11th year by Josephus' way of counting the years. According to the conclusions of this book, the 11th year of Herod's reign was 32 B.C., and was the very year the rebuilding of the Temple began. Here we see that the chronological information given by Blessed Anne Catherine Emmerich is of value in determining the true dates of important events in the lives of Jesus and Mary.

"Now, when Mary came to the Temple, eleven years before Christ's birth, nothing was being built in the Temple itself, but (as always) in the outer portions of it: here the work never stopped."[805]

The expression "the Temple itself" refers to the Sanctuary portion of the Temple, which only the priests could enter. Blessed Anne Catherine states that Christ was born during the 34th year of Herod's reign. Eleven years before the Birth of Christ would correspond to Herod's 23rd year in Blessed Anne Catherine's way of counting, and Herod's 17th year by Josephus' count. But, as stated in chapter 9, Mary actually came to the Temple 12 years before the Birth of Christ, which would be Herod's 16th year by Josephus' count. Blessed Anne Catherine tells us that work on the Temple Sanctuary had been completed by this time, but work on the outer parts of the temple continued. These statements further confirm the idea that work on the Temple was completed, not begun, in Herod's 18th year (see chapter 12 for details). The work on the Temple Sanctuary took only 1½ years and so was completed well before the Virgin Mary began her service in the Temple, but the work on the outer enclosures was still going on, and would continue for two more years.

Chapter 13
The Reigns of Roman Emperors

Certain dates for events in the first century B.C. and first century A.D. are generally accepted by historians and biblical scholars without question and very much without examination. They constitute unexamined premises found within almost every chronological argument for this time period. One example is the year given for the death of Julius Caesar, 44 B.C. Another is the date for the death of Caesar Augustus, A.D. 14. In general, it is the starting and ending dates for the reigns of various Roman emperors that are both most widely accepted and least examined. But what if these generally accepted dates are not correct? This chapter examines the usual dates given for the reigns of various Roman emperors and rulers and argues for a remarkable revision of these historical dates.

Many chronologies for this time period attempt to establish the dates of various events based on evidence as to which persons were Roman consuls in that year. This methodology assumes that the generally-accepted assignment of consuls to years in the B.C./A.D. calendar is correct. It also assumes that the generally-accepted dates for the reigns of various Roman emperors are correct. If these assumed dates are not correct, then, clearly, neither are the arguments based on these dates. Such unexamined and unproved assumptions undermine the logic of many scholarly chronologies. This chapter refutes those assumptions by presenting a series of definitive points in support of an earlier chronology. One cannot refute this earlier chronology by reference to the generally-accepted dates for consuls and emperors, unless such dates are accompanied by evidence and logical arguments proving that these have been correctly assigned to the years of the B.C./A.D. calendar.

At first, when I began these chronological studies, I accepted the usual dates for the reigns of the Roman emperors. However, I noticed some inconsistencies in the historical evidence and began to consider whether the actual dates for events, such as the death of Augustus, might be other than what is so widely and unquestioningly accepted. What follows are some significant points of evidence in support of a revised chronology for the reigns of Roman emperors, beginning with Julius Caesar.

1. A solar eclipse after the death of Julius Caesar.

Pliny states that there was a solar eclipse following the death of Julius Caesar. "Portentous and protracted eclipses of the sun occur, such as the one after the murder of Caesar the dictator...."[806] Yet there was no solar eclipse visible from anywhere in the Roman Empire from Feb. of 48 B.C. through Dec. of 41 B.C., inclusive.[807] Nor is Pliny likely to have been mistaken about whether or not there was a solar eclipse, since he himself explains that eclipses were predictable by the scholars of his day.[808] On the other hand, in 49 B.C., there was a solar eclipse visible from Rome, on August 9, at 11:30 hours local time.[809]

2. A comet after the death of Julius Caesar.

Pliny quotes Caesar Augustus as saying that he saw a comet soon after the death of Julius Caesar. " 'On the very days of my Games a comet was visible for seven days in the northern part of the sky. It was rising about an hour before sunset, and was a bright star visible from all lands.' "[810] This comet is often depicted in ancient images of Julius Caesar.

Ancient Chinese astronomers observed the stars carefully and kept the most detailed records for that time period. By comparing those records, reviewed in detail by the reference work *Cometography*,[811] we can search for a comet during that time period, which fits the description given by Augustus. This comet must meet certain criteria.

The comet following the death of Julius Caesar was clearly seen from Rome **in the northern part of the sky**. The location of comets in the sky was given by Chinese astronomers in terms of the constellations. The location of the constellations, as seen from Rome during that time period, can be determined using *RedShift 3* astronomy software.[812]

Julius Caesar's comet was also seen to **rise** in the northern sky at about the time of sunset. Now comets move across the sky, but not quickly enough to appear to rise in the sky by their own motion. They appear to rise or set because of their location relative to the spin of the earth. So if the constellation, against which the comet is seen, is rising or setting, so also will the comet appear to rise or set. The constellation given as the location of the comet must have been **rising** about the time of sunset as seen from Rome.

Furthermore, the above quote from Augustus places the visibility of the comet "about an hour before sunset." However, this translation of the original Latin is flawed. The original Latin reads: "circa undecimam horam diei," which means "about the eleventh hour of the day."[813] The expression "the eleventh hour of the day" refers to the division of the daylight hours into 12 parts. The eleventh hour refers to the end of the eleventh hour, and the beginning of the twelfth and last hour of daylight. Ordinarily these 12 parts of the daylight hours were counted from sunrise to sunset. However, Augustus may not have been able to see the horizon at the time that he saw the comet. Since he saw this comet during his Games, he may have been in a stadium that did not have a view of the horizon. He would not then know exactly when the sun had set. His expression "about the eleventh hour of the day" could then be interpreted to refer to a point in time about an hour before darkness, rather than an hour before sunset. Notice also that he states the time approximately, using the word "circa" meaning "about." The time of the visibility of the comet could well have been somewhat less than an hour before the onset of darkness, rather than one hour before sunset.

Now the sky is just as bright an hour before sunset, as 2 hours before sunset, or as ½ hour before sunset. But a few minutes after sunset, roughly an hour before the sky becomes as dark as at night, the sky begins to dim and the first stars are visible. This is exactly the time of day when one should expect a comet to first become visible. It makes much more sense for the time of day when the comet was first seen to be a little after the sun had set (but about an hour before darkness), because then any objects in the sky would be made more easily visible by the dimming of the sky. Thus, the comet seen by Augustus must have been **visible beginning a little after sunset**, about an hour before darkness, not an hour before sunset.

In 44 B.C., there was indeed a comet seen and recorded by ancient Chinese astronomers, during the lunar month of May 18 to June 16.[814] They describe this comet as having been seen in the constellation Orion.[815] During that time period, as seen from Rome, Orion rose in the eastern sky after dawn and began to set in the western sky before sunset. They did not record any other comets that year, nor any in the northern part of the sky. At that time, the constellation Orion began to set in the sky well before sunset. The comet of 44 B.C. must also have been setting, not rising, about the time of sunset. Orion was rising above the horizon sometime after dawn, not at sunset.

Furthermore, the constellation Orion began to set about two hours before sunset. Orion was above the horizon all day, from the point of view of Rome. By one hour before sunset, about half of the constellation Orion had set below the horizon. So, if the comet of 44 B.C. had been seen an hour before sunset (the usual interpretation), it would also have been seen through out that day. For the sky is no dimmer an hour before sunset as two hours or more before sunset, and Orion was well above the horizon throughout most of the day.[816] But Augustus clearly states it was first seen at the end of the daylight hours, not throughout the day. On the other hand, if the correct interpretation of Augustus' words is that the comet was first seen a little after sunset (about an hour before darkness), by that time Orion had already set in the sky and the comet of 44 B.C. would not have been seen. Therefore, the comet of 44 B.C., described by Chinese astronomers as located in Orion, could not have been the comet after the death of Julius Caesar.

For the 44 B.C. date to be correct, one would have to hypothesize that there was a second comet, which Augustus described as "a bright star visible from all lands," but which the diligent Chinese astronomers missed completely. The Chinese astronomers were careful observers of the stars and kept detailed records, so this is an unlikely hypothesis and one which lacks any evidence to support it..

In 47 B.C., Chinese astronomers recorded seeing a comet during the lunar month of June 20 to July 18 near the group of stars called the Pleiades.[817] This group of stars, during that time period, viewed from Rome, set in the western sky and rose in the eastern sky. This comet does not fit the description that the comet following the death of Julius Caesar was seen in the northern sky.

The comet of 47 B.C. was seen near the group of stars called the Pleiades.[818] The Pleiades was above the horizon for some of the daylight hours, and above the horizon for some of the nighttime hours. However, during that time period, the Pleiades set about 4 hours before sunset, and did not rise above the horizon again until several hours after sunset. The interpretation that the comet was seen rising at the eleventh hour of the day does not fit the location of this comet. The comet of 47 B.C. could not be seen at all in the hours immediately before and after sunset, because it was below the horizon at that time of day when viewed from Rome. Therefore, the comet of 47 B.C. could not have been the comet associated with the death of Julius Caesar.

In 49 B.C., Chinese astronomers recorded seeing a comet during the lunar month of April 14 to May 12 in the constellation Cassiopeia.[819] This constellation, as seen from Rome during that time period, was in the northern part of the sky. The comet of 49 B.C. would also have been seen in the northern part of the sky, matching the words of

Augustus closely. Also, the time of year is the correct for the comet following the death of Julius Caesar, who died in mid March.

The comet associated with the death of Julius Caesar was seen either an hour before, or a little after, sunset. This time frame for the visibility of the comet fits the 49 B.C. comet. During this time period (April 14 to May 12), the constellation Cassiopeia was above the horizon and clearly visible from Rome before, during, and after sunset.[820] At about the time of sunset, Cassiopeia was almost exactly due north, as viewed from Rome. Thus the comet of 49 B.C. would have been clearly visible in the north, as the sky first began to dim, a little after sunset.

Augustus indicates that the comet occurring after the death of Julius Caesar was rising at about the eleventh hour of the day. But the constellation Cassiopeia was setting in the northern sky at about sunset. It never fully set below the horizon, and began to rise again soon after dark. However, as Cassiopeia began to set in the north, it was also turning. The stars which make up the edge of Cassiopeia closest to north-northwest were setting, but the stars on the northern edge of Cassiopeia were, at the same time, rising. (Of course, this apparent turning motion is due to the spin of the earth and the location of the constellation in the northern sky.) Thus a comet seen in the northern part of Cassiopeia, at this time of day, would appear to be rising about the time of sunset, even though the constellation as a whole was setting. Also, not long after sunset, the entire constellation was rising, having never fully set below the horizon.[821]

Based on the above information, the comet of 49 B.C. is the only fit for the information given by Pliny and Augustus for the comet following the death of Julius Caesar. This comet was located in the northern part of the sky, was visible about the eleventh hour of the day, and could well have been rising at that time of day. The comets of 47 and 44 B.C. do not fit these criteria at all. And there were no other comets described in the records of Chinese astronomers during this general time period, other than those of 49, 47, and 44 B.C.[822]

The above information on both comets and solar eclipses points to the same conclusion. The year of the death Julius Caesar could not have been 44 B.C. In fact, the only year that fits the above astronomical evidence is 49 B.C. Therefore, Julius Caesar died in mid March of 49 B.C., not 44 B.C.

3. The length of the reign of Caesar Augustus

Numerous points below refer to events in the reign of Augustus, which began and ended 4 years earlier than generally believed. Notice, though, that the argument above has Julius Caesar's death 5 years earlier than the usual date. The extra year is accounted for by the following explanation.

Flavius Josephus gives the length of Augustus' reign as "fifty-seven years, besides six months and two days."[823] The reign of Augustus was 57 years, six months, and two days in length, according to Josephus. Both Dio Cassius and Suetonius Tranquillus tell us that Augustus died on August 19, just 35 days short of his 76th birthday (on Sept. 23).[824] So, if his reign ended on August 19, it must have begun on February 17, six months and 2 days earlier (regardless of the number of years).

Julius Caesar died on March 15, which is called "the Ides of March." But Josephus clearly counts the reign of Augustus as beginning in February, and this is not a rough estimate, since he even gives the length of Augustus' reign exact to the day. The usual date given for the death of Augustus is Aug. 19 of A.D. 14. Subtracting 57 years brings us to August of 44 B.C.; subtracting another six months brings us to Feb. of 44 B.C. But the reign of Augustus could not have begun a month **before** the death of Julius Caesar. Augustus clearly had very little power before Julius died, and he had to engage in a protracted struggle for power after Julius Caesar died in order to become one of three men in charge of the Roman Empire. Thus, even when using the usual date for the death of Augustus (A.D. 14), we must conclude that Julius Caesar could not have died in 44 B.C. Therefore, Josephus must be counting the reign of Augustus as beginning in the February that falls 11 months **after** the March in which Julius Caesar died, not the February one month before Julius Caesar died.

Here also is the reason that the death of Julius Caesar is given a revised date (49 B.C.) of 5 years earlier than the usual date (44 B.C.), whereas the beginning of the reign of Augustus is given a revised date of 4 years earlier (A.D. 10, instead of A.D. 14). In the usual chronology, the reign of Augustus is counted as beginning upon the death of Julius (or, inexplicably, a month before). But in this revised chronology, his reign begins the year following Julius Caesar's death, 11 months later. The extra year accounts for the period of time, described in detail by Josephus,[825] when a power struggle ensued between various factions. Josephus refers to this period of time as a war: "As the war that arose upon the death of Caesar was now begun, and the principal men were all gone, some one way, and some another, to raise armies...."[826] This conflict eventually resulted in the establishment of a three-man council, called the triumvirate. Augustus (called Octavian) ruled jointly with Lepidus and Marc Anthony. In no way, then, can it be said that the reign of Augustus began a month before the death of Julius Caesar, but rather 11 months later.

The length of Augustus' reign given by Josephus fits the information given by other ancient historians. Dio gives the length of Augustus' reign, beginning with his military victory over Marc Anthony and Cleopatra, as "forty-four years, lacking thirteen days."[827] Since Augustus died on August 19, this places the beginning of his reign as sole ruler on Sept. 2.[828] Suetonius Tranquillus also gives the length of Augustus' reign as sole ruler as 44 years.[829] Josephus gives the length of Augustus' reign as 57 years and six months, but he adds that Augustus ruled with Marc Anthony for the first 14 years of that time. If we subtract the 44 years (less 13 days) of Augustus' reign as sole ruler, from the total length of his reign, 57.5 years, we arrive at 13.5 years (plus 13 days) as the length of Augustus' reign with Marc Anthony. Thus, the lengths of Augustus' reign given by these various ancient historians is in agreement.

4. The battle at Actium

From the above formula, one could calculate the end of the battle at Actium, when Augustus' reign as sole ruler began, as occurring 13.5 years after Augustus' reign, as co-ruler with Marc Anthony and Lepidus, began. If Julius Caesar died in 49 B.C., and the beginning of Augustus' reign is figured from the following February (as indicated by Josephus), then adding 13.5 years (plus 13 days) to Feb. of 48 B.C. brings us to the end of August in 35 B.C. Therefore, Augustus completed his victory over Marc Anthony at

Actium in Sept. of 35 B.C. This argument is based on the conclusion above that Julius Caesar died in 49 B.C.

This date for the battle at Actium also fits seamlessly into the chronology of Herod's reign. Josephus places the battle between Augustus and Marc Anthony in the year of the 187th Olympiad, and in the seventh year of Herod's reign.[830] As explained in chapter 12 of this book, Josephus places the capture of Jerusalem, which marked the beginning of Herod's reign, in the third month of the 185th Olympiad.[831] Chapter 12 of this book concludes that Herod captured Jerusalem in Sept. of 43 B.C., in the third month of the 185th Olympiad year. The Olympic Games were held every four years, therefore the 187th Olympiad must have begun, eight years later, on July 1 of 35 B.C.

Josephus states that the battle of Actium "fell into" the 187th Olympiad, but, with other events related to Olympiad years, he instead uses the expression "on the" Nth Olympiad (as in the case of the capture of Jerusalem). By this difference in wording, Josephus indicates that the battle at Actium began before the 187th Olympiad (before July 1 of 35 B.C.), but "fell into," that is, "continued into" the year of the 187th Olympiad. The 187th Olympiad would contain the battle at Actium if the battle ended on Sept. 2 of 35 B.C. But the battle must have begun before the 187th Olympiad year began on July 1 of 35 B.C., otherwise Josephus would have said that the battle occurred "on the" 187th Olympiad, rather than "fell into" the 187th Olympiad.

Herod's reign began in the fall of the 185th Olympiad year (in 43 B.C.) and the battle at Actium ended in the fall of the 187th Olympiad year. Since Olympiad years are spaced four years apart, this places the end of the battle at Actium in the 8th year of Herod's reign (in 35 B.C.). But Josephus states that the battle at Actium occurred during Herod's 7th year: "At this time it was that the fight happened at Actium, between Octavius Caesar and Antony, in the seventh year of the reign of Herod...."[832] Therefore, the conflict at Actium between Augustus (Octavian) and Marc Anthony was not brief, but began in Herod's 7th year (36 B.C.) and ended in his 8th year (35 B.C.), which coincided with the start of the 187th Olympiad year.

5. A solar eclipse before death of Augustus

Dio Cassius describes a solar eclipse as one of the portents occurring before the death of Caesar Augustus.[833] He does not say how long before the death of Augustus, nor at what time of year, the eclipse occurred. The usual date given for the death of Augustus is August 19 of A.D. 14. However, an analysis of the solar eclipse data for the early first century A.D. shows that there were no solar eclipses visible from anywhere in the Roman Empire from A.D. 11 through A.D. 14, inclusive.[834] (See chapter 17 for a list of solar eclipses from A.D. 10 to A.D. 14.)

The solar eclipse closest to the usual date for the death of Augustus, and visible from the Roman Empire, was an eclipse on Nov. 24 of A.D. 10. This eclipse was a partial solar eclipse visible from northern Italy and northern Europe. However, since it occurred almost 4 full years prior to Augustus' death, this eclipse could not be the eclipse referred to by Dio.

On the other hand, the solar eclipse on June 30 of A.D. 10 was a total solar eclipse, and was visible from most of Europe and most of Italy as a partial solar eclipse.[835] If Augustus died on August 19 of A.D. 10, a solar eclipse occurring less than two months earlier, visible from most of the Roman Empire, would likely have been seen as a foreshadowing of his death.

Now Dio tells us "the sun suffered a total eclipse," and he describes the eclipse in rather dramatic terms: "most of the sky seemed to be on fire; glowing embers appeared to be falling from it and blood-red comets were seen."[836] His description fits that of a total eclipse of the sun. When the moon obscures the view of the sun during a solar eclipse, the sky dims, stars can be seen, and any meteors would also be visible. So the blood-red comets could be a reference to a meteor shower.[837] And, during a total or annular eclipse of the sun, the sky might well be described as looking like it is "on fire." There was no distinction at that time in history between a total solar eclipse and an annular solar eclipse, so Dio could have been referring to either. In either case, the appearance of the sky would be quite remarkable and would fit Dio's description well.

The eclipse on June 30 of A.D. 10 was a total eclipse, but would only have appeared to be a partial eclipse from anywhere in the Roman Empire. Eclipses of the sun were predictable by the scholars of Rome.[838] So perhaps Dio, writing several generations after this event, knew from scholars of his day that the eclipse was, in fact, a total eclipse. Then, when he wrote about the eclipse, he described what a total solar eclipse would look like. Perhaps he did not have before him a text describing what people saw at the time the eclipse occurred.

The information on this solar eclipse supports the date of August 19, A.D. 10 for the death of Augustus. The information on the eclipse and comet following the death of Julius Caesar places Julius' death in 49 B.C. And, when we calculate the date for the death of Augustus from the length of his reign and the revised date of Julius Caesar's death, we arrive at the same date of A.D. 10. If only one piece of evidence pointed to an earlier date for the death of Augustus, such a conclusion would be questionable. But numerous pieces of this puzzle agree and fit together well. A solar eclipse before the death of Augustus, a solar eclipse and comet after the death of Julius Caesar, the length of Augustus' reign, the chronology of Herod's reign and the battle at Actium, all support a revision of the usual dates and all fit together. And much further evidence, presented below, also supports and fits into this revised chronology.

On the other hand, the usual dates given for the deaths of Augustus and Julius are not supported by the data on solar eclipses and comets. In general, as will be shown in the points below, the usual chronology is a poor fit for the eclipse and comet data. Additional evidence, aside from the astronomical evidence, also favors a revised chronology over the usual chronology and is discussed below.

6. The length of Augustus' life

According to Suetonius, Caesar Augustus died just short of his 76th birthday. "He died…just thirty-five days before his seventy-sixth birthday."[839] Dio Cassius confirms this age: "…he passed away, having lived seventy-five years, ten months, and twenty-six days (he had been born on the twenty-third of September)…."[840] So, both Suetonius and Dio give the date of Augustus' death as August 19.

Josephus gives the length of Augustus' life as 77 years.[841] He does not, however, give the length of Augustus' life exact to the day, as he does when giving the length of his reign or the reigns of other emperors. If one counts partial years as whole years, as was the custom among the Jews of that time, then the year of Augustus' birth and the year of his death would each be counted as a year. The length of Augustus life would then be counted as 77 years by Josephus. In this way the age of Augustus at his death, given by Josephus, does not contradict the age given by Dio and Suetonius.[842]

The year of Augustus' birth can then be determined from the year of his death. If Augustus died in A.D. 14 (usual date), then he was born in 63 B.C. But if Augustus died in A.D. 10 (revised date), then he was born in 67 B.C.

Suetonius tells us the age of Augustus at various points early in his life. "At sixteen, having now come of age, he was awarded military decorations when Caesar celebrated his African triumph, though he had been too young for overseas service. Caesar then went to fight Pompey's sons in Spain."[843] The usual date given to Julius Caesar's military victory in Africa, part of the Roman civil war which established him as sole ruler over Rome, is 46 B.C.[844] According to the usual chronology, Augustus was born in 63 B.C., and so would have reached his 17th birthday in Sept. of 46 B.C. In my revised chronology, Augustus was born in 67 B.C., 4 years earlier than the usual date, but Julius Caesar died in 49 B.C., 5 years earlier than the usual date. Julius Caesar's victory in Africa should then placed in 51 B.C., and Augustus would have celebrated his 16th birthday that same year in 51 B.C. Both chronologies can account for Suetonius' statement that Augustus was 16 at the time of Caesar's African victory.

In the usual chronology, Augustus would have been 18½ years old when Julius Caesar died, reaching his 19th birthday later that year in 44 B.C. But in my revised chronology, Augustus was 17½ when Caesar died and turned 18 years old later that year, in 49 B.C.

My revised chronology places the death of Julius Caesar 5 years earlier than the usual date, and the death of Augustus 4 years earlier than the usual date. This means that Augustus was a year younger when Caesar died in this revised chronology versus the usual chronology. However, details given about the age of Augustus during this time period are not precise enough to use this one-year difference to determine which chronology is correct. For example, it is unclear whether Augustus turned 16 the year of Caesar's African victory, or if he was already 16, and turned 17 in September later that year.

Suetonius tells us that Augustus was 19 years old when he first became a Roman Consul.[845] Dio adds that Augustus died, "on the nineteenth day of August, the day on which he had first become consul...."[846] Since Augustus was born on Sept. 23, he probably become consul (on August 19) the same year that he turned 20 years old (about a month later). In the usual chronology, Augustus first became consul in 43 B.C., the year after Julius Caesar's death, about a month before Augustus reached his 20th birthday. In this revised chronology, Augustus could have become consul in 48 or 47 B.C.

In 48 B.C., one year after the death of Julius Caesar and a few months after the start of his reign (as one of three rulers of Rome), Augustus would have turned 19 in September. He would then have been 19 years old (and in his 20th year of life) during most of his consulship. Though Suetonius implies that Augustus was 19 years old when he began his consulship (a month before his birthday), this may be a slight inaccuracy on the part of Suetonius. The other possibility is that Augustus became consul in 47 B.C., two years after the death of Julius Caesar. In this case, Augustus would have begun his consulship at the age of 19, but have been 20 years old for most of his consulship, in agreement with a strict interpretation of Suetonius. This book favors the first possibility, that Augustus became consul in 48 B.C., because new rulers of Rome typically solidified their political power by taking for themselves the office of consul at the start of their reign. Augustus began to reign in February of 48 B.C., about 11 months after Julius Caesar died, so a date of August 19, 48 B.C., for the start of his consulship is only a few months into the first year of his reign.

7. The beginning of the reign of Tiberius Caesar

The usual date given for the start of the reign of Tiberius Caesar is dependent on the belief that Augustus died in A.D. 14. Some scholars would count the year A.D. 14 as the first year of the reign of Tiberius; others would count A.D. 15 as the first year. Still other scholars would count Tiberius' reign as beginning a couple of years earlier, when Tiberius ruled Rome jointly with Augustus, in a power-sharing arrangement.[847] (When one ruler counts his reign as beginning during the reign of the previous ruler, so that their reigns overlap, this is called "antedating.")

Another theory counts the reign of Tiberius as beginning at the time that Tiberius was first chosen as heir to the throne. The grandsons of Augustus, named Lucius and Gaius, were in line to succeed Augustus as emperor of Rome. But Lucius died in A.D. 2, and Gaius in A.D. 4, according to the usual chronology. About this time, Tiberius returned from a self-imposed exile on the island of Rhodes.[848] Soon after his return, Augustus decided to choose his stepson, Tiberius, to succeed him as emperor of Rome. According to Dio: "Augustus...not only adopted Tiberius, but also sent him out against the Germans, granting him the tribunician power for ten years."[849] It was at that time also that Tiberius, whose name from birth was 'Tiberius Claudius Nero,' was given the name 'Tiberius Julius Caesar.'[850]

Tiberius had a great deal of power in the Roman Empire beginning about ten years before Augustus died. Now, in the usual chronology, Augustus died in A.D. 14, and the sudden rise of Tiberius to power occurred in A.D. 4. However, the evidence presented above places the death of Augustus in A.D. 10, four years earlier. So, in this revised chronology, the death of Gaius and the appointment of Tiberius as the successor to Augustus must also be placed four years earlier, during the year 1 B.C. Augustus appointed Tiberius as his successor by adopting him, on June 26, so that he would inherit the throne.[851] The Roman custom was to count the first full calendar year of an emperor's reign as year one. The calendar year containing the death of the previous emperor would be counted as the last year of that emperor's reign, even though he only ruled for part of the year and the remainder of the year was completed by the next emperor.[852] Therefore, we should count the antedated reign of Tiberius as beginning with the first full calendar year after he was chosen to be the successor to Augustus. The first year of Tiberius' reign would then be A.D. 1.

Tiberius had a great deal of power beginning with his adoption as heir to the emperor, and he had little or no power in the years before that time. His reign over the Roman Empire did, in a real sense, begin from this earlier time, because of this sudden increase in power when he became the chosen heir. This is one argument in support of the idea that the reign of Tiberius should be antedated, that is, that it should be counted from this earlier time (see chapter 2).

Antedating did occur in the reigns of some first century Roman emperors. Dio describes the reigns of the emperors Galba, Otho, and Vitellius as lasting, respectively, 9 month and 13 days, 90 days, and 1 year minus 10 days (for a total of about 2 years time). Yet he gives the length of time from Nero's death to the start of Vespasian's reign (the time frame containing the rules of Galba, Otho, and Vitellius) as only 1 year and 22 days. Dio's explanation is a classic example of antedating: "For they did not succeed one another legitimately, but each of them, even while his rival was alive and still ruling, believed himself to be emperor from the moment that he even got a glimpse of the throne."[853] Though he complains about antedating in the reigns of Galba, Otho, and Vitellius, Dio himself accepts antedating in the reign of Vespasian to a time several months before the death of Vitellius (see sections 16 and 17 below). Furthermore, many modern scholars accepts the idea that Tiberius antedated his reign to a point in time at least a couple of years before the death of Augustus.[854] Since antedating occurred in the reigns of these first century Roman emperors, it is entirely possible that Tiberius antedated the start of his reign ten years earlier, rather than 2 years earlier to A.D. 1. Further support for this conclusion is found in sections 8 and following, below.

The usual date for the first full year of the reign of Tiberius is A.D. 15, the year after Augustus died. My revised date for the first full year of Tiberius' reign is 14 years earlier, in A.D. 1. The 14 year difference between the usual date and the revised date for the start of Tiberius' reign is due to two adjustments to the usual chronology. First, the death of Augustus, and many other dates related to his reign, occurred 4 years earlier than generally believed. Second, the reign of Tiberius is to be counted from a point in time, A.D. 1, which is 9 years before Augustus died (in A.D. 10), rather than 1 year after he died (A.D. 11). Thus, the difference between the two chronologies, during Tiberius' reign, is 14 years (9 + 1 + 4 = 14).

8. A long gap in the account of Josephus

If the first full year of the reign of Tiberius Caesar was A.D. 1, rather than A.D. 11, (the year after the death of Augustus in A.D. 10, by my revised dates), then there was a ten-year overlap in their reigns. This ten-year overlap can be discerned in the writings of the ancient Jewish Roman historian, Flavius Josephus.

Now Josephus wrote a detailed history of this time period and he clearly believed that the reign of Tiberius began upon the death of Augustus. However, he is unable to support that belief with a description of events occurring during the first ten years of Tiberius' reign. There is a clear gap in Josephus' history—a gap lasting from the first year of Tiberius' reign until the eleventh year.

The history of the Jewish people, and their interaction with the Romans, was written by Josephus in 20 books (these resemble 20 chapters of one book) called *The Antiquities of the Jews.* Events occurring during the reigns of Julius Caesar, king Herod, Caesar Augustus, and Tiberius Caesar, are told in this work in significant detail. The time period from the beginning of Herod's reign over Jerusalem to the completion of the rebuilding of the Temple, a time period of 18 years according to Josephus, is given 425 verses in book 15, an average of 23.6 verses per year. Other books from *The Antiquities of the Jews,* which cover events from the reign of Julius Caesar to the destruction of Jerusalem, likewise give detailed descriptions of events. The average number of verses per year for each book is listed in the following chart.[855]

Book number	Years	Verses	Verses/yr.
14	32	491	15.3
15	18	425	23.6
16	12	404	33.7
17	14	354	25.3
18	32	379	11.8
19	3.5	365	104.3
20	22	268	12.2
total /average:	133.5	2686	20.1

Notice that each book gives an average of over ten verses per year for each year covered in that book. (Book 20 has a low number of verses per year because those events are described by Josephus in greater detail in a separate work, *The Wars of the Jews*.) Book 18 contains the lowest average number of verses per year. The source of this lowered average is a section of book 17, from verse 33 to verse 35, which supposedly describes the first eleven years of Tiberius Caesar's reign after the death of Caesar Augustus. Only 3 verses (containing 4 sentences) supposedly describe 11 years of history of the Jewish people and the Roman Empire. That's an average of 0.27 verses per year for this section of the history compared to 20.1 verses per year average for books 14 through 20 (98.7% less than the average). If this section of the history contained the overall average of 20.1 verses per year, then there would have been approximately 221 verses, instead of 3 verses.

Josephus wrote *The Antiquities of the Jews* in the latter part of the first century A.D., not long after these events occurred. It is therefore unlikely that he was simply uninformed as to the events that happened during this 11 year time period (from the early part of the same century). Josephus was in great favor with the Roman emperor Vespasian, who made Josephus a Roman citizen, gave him an annual pension, and let him live in Vespasian's former residence.[856] He also continued to be favored by the subsequent emperors, Titus and Domitian, (Vespasian's sons). So, it is unlikely that Josephus did not have access to information on this time period.

Were there no events of significance occurring during the first eleven years of Tiberius Caesar's reign? Were there no battles, political power-struggles, or other events in Israel and in Rome that were of concern or interest to Josephus? This eleven-year gap in the sequence of events described by Josephus is unusual because his history of the Jewish people is otherwise quite detailed. His history is also well organized chronologically—each book is even labeled with the length of time it encompasses.

The reason that this eleven-year gap occurs in Josephus' chronology of the reign of Tiberius Caesar, is that the first ten years of his reign coincided with the last ten years of Augustus' reign. Josephus writes that Valerius Gratus ruled over Judea for eleven years before Pilate, having been sent to Judea at the beginning of Tiberius' reign.[857] But all that Josephus can tell us about this time period is that Valerius Gratus was procurator of

Judea and that he appointed various persons, in succession, as Jewish high priest. Josephus did not have enough material to describe that eleven-year period of time, because he had already described the events of the last ten years of the reign of Augustus (A.D. 1 to 10). Those last ten years of Augustus' reign coincided with the first ten years of Tiberius' reign.

Once Josephus states that Pilate replaced Gratus as ruler over Judea, the noticeable lack of detail in his chronology ends. My revised chronology places the eleven-year rule of Valerius Gratus over Judea from about A.D. 1 to A.D. 11. Since Pontius Pilate replaced Gratus as procurator of Judea, the first full year of Pilate's rule over Judea would then be A.D. 12. The detail in the history of Josephus resumes at that point because the overlap in the reigns of Augustus and Tiberius has ended.

9. The Gospel of Luke

All of the Roman emperors during this time period (after the death of Julius Caesar) had the word Caesar as a title after they became emperor. None would dare to use the word Caesar as a title before becoming emperor—that would be treason. Even so, whoever was in line to inherit the throne of emperor of Rome was customarily given the word Caesar as a part of their name. For example, Tiberius had the name "Tiberius Claudius Nero" from birth. Then, when he was adopted by Augustus and made next in line to inherit the title of Caesar, his name was changed to "Tiberius Julius Caesar."[858] Tiberius used the *name* Caesar from the time of his adoption by Augustus (usual date, A.D. 4; revised date, 1 B.C.), but he could not use the *title* Caesar until he actually became emperor, after the death of Augustus. Other examples are Lucius Caesar, Gaius Caesar, and Drusus Caesar, who all were at one time in line to become emperor of Rome.[859] None of these three actually became emperor (they died prematurely), so it is clear that the word Caesar was being used in these cases only as a name, not a title.

Now the Gospel of Luke refers to Augustus as "Caesar Augustus," so that the word Caesar is used as a title (Lk 2:1). But the same Gospel also refers to Tiberius as "Tiberius Caesar," using the word Caesar as a name rather than a title (Lk 3:1). The passage referring to Tiberius gives the year of the beginning of John the Baptist's ministry:

"Then, in the fifteenth year of the reign of Tiberius Caesar, Pontius Pilate being procurator of Judea, and Herod tetrarch of Galilee, and his brother Philip tetrarch of Ituraea and of the region of Trachonitis, and Lysanias tetrarch of Abilene, under the high priests Annas and Caiaphas: the word of the Lord came to John, the son of Zechariah, in the wilderness. And he went into the entire region of the Jordan, preaching a baptism of repentance for the remission of sins...." (Lk 3:1-3).

In this way, Sacred Scripture indicates that the 15th year of the reign of Tiberius is to be counted from the time he received the *name* Caesar, rather than from that later time when he received the *title* Caesar. Tiberius received the name Caesar when he was adopted by Augustus on June 26 of 1 B.C. (usual date, A.D. 4).[860] As a result, the first year of Tiberius' reign is the first full calendar year (A.D. 1) after Tiberius received the name Caesar.

Notice here that the 15th year of Tiberius Caesar's reign mentioned by Sacred Scripture coincides with A.D. 15. In this way, God is able to tell us a date in the later

B.C./A.D. calendar system, even though the Gospel of Luke was written long before that system was devised.

10. Errors of the early historians

Why did Josephus and other early historians mistakenly believe that Tiberius' reign began when Augustus died? First, most other Roman emperors counted their reigns from the death of the previous emperor. The assumption that Tiberius did the same would have been difficult to avoid. Second, the ancient historians whom we rely on for information about Tiberius' reign (Josephus, Dio, Tacitus, Suetonius) were not contemporary to Tiberius' reign. Tiberius ended his reign with a long series of murders and political assassinations.[861] Perhaps those persons contemporary to Tiberius' reign feared to write about it. Only years later did historians put together a history of the time period. Third, the system used by the Romans to keep track of the years was susceptible to this type of error. The years were counted from the start of each emperor's reign. When a new emperor came to power, the count was started anew. It would have been easy to lose track of the count of the years, if an emperor, such as Tiberius, counted the start of his reign from his rise to power years before the previous emperor died. This practice of antedating, counting the start of one ruler's reign from before the end of the previous ruler's reign, was not uncommon in ancient times.[862]

Josephus wrote during the latter part of the first century A.D. Suetonius and Tacitus wrote about a generation or so later than Josephus. Of these three, only Tacitus attempts to divide up the events of Tiberius' reign year by year. He even gives the names of the consuls matched to each year and set of events. (Dio wrote during the early third century A.D., and perhaps followed Tacitus for his consular dates). But Tacitus also wrote about the difficulties he encountered in the history of the consuls. "As to the consular elections, from this year's—the first—down to the last of the reign, I can hardly venture a single definitive assertion: so conflicting is the evidence, not of the historians alone, but of the emperor's own speeches."[863] Tacitus goes on to say that Tiberius sometimes suppressed information about candidates for the position of consul. Also, it is well known that many consuls did not hold that office for the entire one-year term. For example, Tiberius held the position of consul, on more than one occasion, for only a brief portion of a year.[864] Furthermore, Finegan notes that consular lists sometimes contained omissions or errors. "Lists of the consuls were compiled at an early date but often contained discrepancies or gaps."[865] Therefore, the consular lists are of limited value in assigning years to historical events in this time period.

According to Josephus, Agrippa and Gallo were the consuls in the year Herod took Jerusalem.[866] The generally-accepted list of consular dates places Agrippa and Gallo as consuls in 37 B.C. However, as shown clearly in chapter 12, Herod could not have taken Jerusalem in 37 B.C. Therefore, the assignment of consuls to the years B.C. contains some significant errors.

According to Pliny the Elder, the third consulship of the emperor Vespasian coincided with the second consulship of his son, Titus.[867] (Two Roman consuls held office at the same time.) Since Pliny lived and wrote during Vespasian's reign and was a member of Vespasian's inner circle, he could hardly be mistaken about the emperor and his son's consulships. Yet the usual list of consuls places Vespasian's third consulship with the consulship of Nerva, and Titus' second consulship with Vespasian's fourth consulship.[868] Thus the generally-accepted list of consular dates cannot be assumed to be correct. If a chronological argument depends upon a consular date, that argument must prove that the consuls actually held office that year. But many chronological arguments are based on the consular dates, without offering any evidence that those dates are correct.

Concerning the error in the year assigned to the death of Augustus, A.D. 14 instead of A.D. 10, this was not the error of the early Roman historians. They did not yet have the B.C./A.D. system of numbering the years. This error occurred when later historians tried to assign dates in the calendar system of Dionysius Exiguus to events in the centuries before that calendar system began. And the same is true for the consular dates. The years when various consuls held office were only assigned to particular years in the B.C./A.D. calendar system many years afterwards.

That error of four years time was inevitable, once the previous error of ten years time had become accepted and entrenched in the accounts of Roman historians. Several significant events in Roman history concerning the Jewish people, such as the capture of Jerusalem by Herod and the subsequent fall of Jerusalem many years later, coincided with the end or beginning of Jewish Sabbatical years. The Sabbatical year occurs every seven years. So, if an historical account is off from the correct dates by 10 years, one must add four years or subtract 3 years to bring the dates of events into agreement with the seven-year cycle of Sabbatical years. It is no coincidence, then, that some of the revised dates in this chronology differ from the usual dates by 14 years (a multiple of 7 years).

Dionysius placed the Incarnation and the Birth of Christ in 1 B.C. However, taking into account the above-mentioned 14-year error places Dionysius' date for the Incarnation and Birth of Christ in agreement with this book's conclusion (15 B.C.).

11. The death of Germanicus

Josephus places Gratus' rule over Judea during the first eleven years of Tiberius' reign, so that the first year of Pilate's rule over Judea began in the 12th year of Tiberius' reign. Eusebius, a bishop and historian of the early Church, interprets Josephus to the same conclusion: "it was actually in the twelfth year of the reign of Tiberius that Pilate was appointed procurator of Judea by Tiberius."[869] Now Josephus places the death of Germanicus during the reign of Pontius Pilate.[870] (Germanicus was a Roman general, at one time a Roman consul, and was the grand-nephew of Augustus.) But Dio and Tacitus both place the death of Germanicus in the fifth year after the death of Augustus.[871]

The only way that Germanicus could have died during the reign of Pontius Pilate (following the 12th year of Tiberius' reign), and in the 5th year after Augustus died, is if the reign of Tiberius began long before the death of Augustus. In this revised chronology, the 5th year after the death of Augustus coincided with Pilate's rule over Judea because Pilate's reign began during the 2nd year after the death of Augustus, which was the 12th year of the reign of Tiberius (antedated). Josephus is correct in placing the death of Germanicus during Pilate's rule over Judea and sometime after Tiberius' 12th year, because the beginning of Tiberius' reign overlapped the end of Augustus' reign by about

10 years. The first full year of Tiberius' reign was A.D. 1 (his first full year after adoption by Augustus), and Augustus died in A.D. 10. Pilate ruled over Judea beginning about A.D. 12. Germanicus died in A.D. 15.

The generally-accepted chronology for this time period cannot account for the timing of Germanicus' death. If the reign of Tiberius began with the death of Augustus, then Germanicus could not have died after Pilate began to rule Judea, that is, after the 12th year of Tiberius' reign, and yet have died in the 5th year after the death of Augustus.

12. Tiberius' death coincided with the end of Pilate's reign

According to Josephus, Tiberius died shortly after Pilate completed his ten-year reign over Judea. "So Pilate, when he had tarried ten years in Judea, made haste to Rome, and this in obedience to the orders of Vitellius, which he durst not contradict; but before he could get to Rome, Tiberius was dead."[872] In *The History of the Church*, (also called *Ecclesiastical History*),Eusebius agrees with Josephus that Pilate's reign ended shortly before Tiberius died.[873]

Eusebius also concludes that Pilate's reign began in the 12th year of the reign of Tiberius, which in my revised chronology would coincide with A.D. 12. So Pilate's reign over Judea began in early A.D. 12 (or possibly late A.D. 11). The 15th year of Tiberius thus coincided with the 4th year of Pilate's reign over Judea.[874] Since Pilate's reign lasted ten years, the end of his reign should be placed during the winter of A.D. 21–22. In this revised chronology, the 21st year of Tiberius' reign was A.D. 21.

Now Josephus states that Pilate, after ten years rule over Judea, was relieved of his authority and recalled to Rome to answer to accusations of murder made against him by the Samaritans. But before Pilate could arrive in Rome, Tiberius was dead.[875] Immediately after describing this situation, Josephus mentions the Passover feast in Jerusalem (which fell in early April in A.D. 22). Also, Dio and Suetonius both place Tiberius' death in the month of March. So, if the trip to Rome from Jerusalem ended in March, Pilate must have left for Rome during the winter of A.D. 21-22.

The Mediterranean Sea was difficult to travel during winter for the ships of that time period.[876] However, such trips were certainly made during wintertime as is clear from Josephus, *The Wars of the Jews*, where Petronius sent word to Rome and Rome replied twice (by ship), all during the winter time.[877] The distance from Israel to Rome, traveling by sea and following the coastline, is roughly 2500 miles. (Ships during that time period followed the coastline for safety and to be able to stop at various ports for supplies). A good voyage from Israel to Rome would take 1 to 2 months, but a typical voyage during wintertime, when the weather and seas were adverse to sailing, might take 3 months or longer (as explained in section 16 below). Pilate's voyage to Rome, in winter of A.D. 21-22, arrived in Rome after mid March of A.D. 22, and so that voyage could have begun as early as Dec. of A.D. 21, or as late as Feb. of A.D. 22. Pilate would certainly have preferred to wait until mid February, when the Mediterranean was more easily and more safely traveled, to return to Rome. However, Pilate returned to Rome "in obedience to the orders of Vitellius, which he durst not contradict...."[878] So Pilate may well have begun his journey to Rome in December or January.

The ancient historians Josephus, Dio, and Suetonius disagree about the exact length of Tiberius' reign, but they all give the length of his reign as greater than 22 years and less than 23 years.[879] However, in this revised chronology, Tiberius' death is placed in March of A.D. 22, after a reign of somewhat less than 22 years from his adoption as heir to the throne in June of 1 B.C. The ancient historians mistakenly thought that Tiberius' reign began with the death of Augustus, when it actually was counted from Tiberius' adoption as heir to Augustus. I think that this point of confusion led them to err also in stating the length of Tiberius' reign. The date of Tiberius' death in this revised chronology could not be placed a year later, because of the start date and length of Pilate's reign, and because of the dates and lengths of the reigns of subsequent emperors (see below).

Josephus states that Tiberius appointed only two procurators over Judea during his reign as emperor.[880] He tells us in one and the same sentence that Tiberius became emperor and that he sent the first of these two procurators, Gratus, to Judea.[881] Thus the reign of Gratus over Judea began about the time that the reign of Tiberius began. Gratus ruled Judea for 11 years; then Tiberius sent Pontius Pilate to replace Gratus as ruler over Judea.[882] Pilate ruled Judea for about 10 years, until the time that he was recalled to Rome to answer to an accusation of murder. But before Pilate arrived in Rome, Tiberius had died.[883] There were then about 21 years from the start of Gratus' reign to the end of Pilate's reign over Judea. Tiberius' reign began about the time Gratus' reign began and ended about the time Pilate's reign ended. Therefore, Tiberius' reign lasted about 21 years.

Now, one might lengthen those 21 years by supposing that Gratus' reign was a little longer than 11 years or that Pilate's reign was a little longer than 10 years or by other suppositions. But in the usual chronology, the length of Tiberius' reign is 22 years and about 7 months; quite a few suppositions are needed to reach to this length of time. On the other hand, in this revised chronology, the length of Tiberius' reign is only 21 years and just under 9 months, if one counts from Tiberius' adoption in June of 1 B.C., or only 21 years and less than three months, if one counts from the first full year (A.D. 1) after Tiberius' adoption by Augustus. This revised chronology is a better fit for the statements by Josephus about the lengths of the reigns of Tiberius, Gratus, and Pilate.

Tiberius died just after the end of Pilate's 10-year reign over Judea. Pilate's reign began during the 2nd year after the death of Augustus. Since Augustus died in A.D. 10, the death of Tiberius occurred only about 11½ years later, in March of A.D. 22. Pilate's rule over Judea must then have occurred from late A.D. 11 or early A.D. 12 to late A.D. 21 or early A.D. 22, about 15 years earlier than the usual time frame of A.D. 26 to 36. (Notice here that the revised dates of events from the death of Tiberius onward are now off by 15 years from the usual dates, because of this difference in the length of Tiberius' reign.)

Josephus clearly states that Pilate's reign lasted ten years.[884] Yet the generally-accepted chronology has Pilate's reign from A.D. 26 to 36, a total of eleven years. The first year of Pilate's reign is usually given as A.D. 26, and Pilate's arrival in Rome placed sometime after mid March of A.D. 37. The usual chronology contradicts Josephus in lengthening Pilate's reign by one year. In this revised chronology, Pilate's reign is accepted as 10 years, not eleven, and Tiberius' reign is one year shorter at just over 21 years.

The ministry of John the Baptist began in the 15th year of Tiberius' reign (Lk 3:1), which was also the 4th year of Pilate's reign over Judea. According to Eusebius, Christ was crucified less than 4 years later.[885] This calculation places the Crucifixion in the 19th year of Tiberius and the 8th year of Pilate's rule over Judea.

Tiberius was adopted as heir to Augustus on June 26,[886] of 1 B.C. (revised). The first full calendar year after this rise to power would then be counted as the first year of his antedated reign, A.D. 1. This conclusion places the start of John the Baptist's ministry in A.D. 15, the 15th year of Tiberius' reign, and the Crucifixion in A.D. 19, the 19th year of Tiberius' reign and the 8th year of Pilate's reign.

13. Josephus refers to Jesus

Josephus tells us about the death of Germanicus shortly before his description of the Ministry of Jesus Christ.[887] The only account intervening between the death of Germanicus and this mention of Jesus is a description of two conflicts between Pilate and the Jews. The number of verses intervening is only eight. The overall average number of verses per year in *The Antiquities of the Jews* is 20.1 (see section 8 above), and no single book in that work (from the time of Julius Caesar's reign and thereafter) has an average number of verses per year of less than 11. Since there are only 8 verses between the account of Germanicus' death and the mention of Christ's Ministry, Germanicus must have died close to the time of the Ministry of Christ, no more than a year before His Ministry began (although he could have died sometime soon after Christ's Ministry began).

The death of Germanicus is placed by both Dio and Tacitus in the fifth year after the death of Augustus.[888] The usual date for the death of Augustus is A.D. 14 and the usual date for the death of Germanicus is A.D. 19. Even with the generally-accepted dates for the deaths of Augustus and Germanicus, the Ministry of Christ must have begun at least a decade earlier than has been generally believed. But, with the conclusion of this chapter that Augustus died in A.D. 10, the death of Germanicus must be placed in A.D. 15 and the time of Christ's Ministry shortly thereafter (fall of A.D. 15 to spring of A.D. 19, as concluded in chapters 2 and 7 of this book).

14. The census under Quirinius

Josephus places the second census/taxation under Quirinius at the beginning of book 18 of *The Antiquities of the Jews.* The length of time from the beginning of book 15, when Herod's reign began, to the beginning of book 18 is given by Josephus as 44 years (see chart in section 8 above). The usual date for the capture of Jerusalem is 37 B.C., and the usual date for the second census under Quirinius is A.D. 6. But, with the conclusion of chapter 12 that Herod captured Jerusalem in 43 B.C., and the conclusion of this chapter that Augustus' reign began and ended 4 years earlier than the usual chronology, the date for this census would also be four years earlier, in A.D. 2.

Also, Josephus gives the date of this second census as "the thirty-seventh year of Caesar's victory over Antony at Actium."[889] The first year in this count of 37 years is the year containing the victory. As section 4 above concludes, the battle at Actium ended in

35 B.C. Counting forward 37 years (inclusive) to the date of the census again gives us A.D. 2, not A.D. 6.

Under Caesar Augustus, a census of the occupied countries, such as Syria and Israel, was held every 17 years.[890] So if the second census under Quirinius began in A.D. 2, then the first census began in 16 B.C., seventeen years earlier (there is no year zero, so the number of years from 16 B.C. to A.D. 2 is 17, not 18). A census took two years to complete.[891] The census of 16 B.C. ran from mid 16 B.C. to mid 14 B.C. This first census under Augustus and Quirinius was the census at the time of Christ's birth (Luke 2:1-2).

After the second census of Quirinius, a census was taken after every 14 years.[892] Thus the first census under Tiberius' rule as emperor (after the death of Augustus) began 14 years after the census of A.D. 2, and ran from mid A.D. 16 to mid A.D. 18. In this revised chronology, the Ministry of Christ began in fall of A.D. 15, and lasted 3½ years to the Crucifixion in spring of A.D. 19. Here we see that the time frame for the Ministry of Christ encompasses a Roman census, in agreement with the numerous Gospel references to tax collectors and the collecting of the tax.

15. *The Memoranda* and Eusebius

In his book, *The History of the Church*, Eusebius complains that some persons during his lifetime published a tract, called *The Memoranda*, (or *The Reports*), which claimed that Christ's Crucifixion occurred about the time of Tiberius' fourth consulship. This time frame for the Crucifixion was significantly earlier in Tiberius' reign than Eusebius thought correct.[893] According to Eusebius, *The Memoranda* placed the Crucifixion in the year that Tiberius was consul for the fourth time, in the seventh year of his reign. The usual date for Tiberius' fourth consulship is A.D. 21. However, Eusebius lived in the 4th century A.D., well before Dionysius devised the A.D. system of numbering the calendar years in the 6th century, so Eusebius was not figuring the date of the Crucifixion by the years of the B.C./A.D. calendar system. Eusebius believed that the Crucifixion occurred much later in the reign of Tiberius than his fourth consulship and seventh year. He placed the beginning of Pilate's rule over Judea in Tiberius' 12th year, and the beginning of Christ's Ministry in Tiberius' 15th year. He also stated his understanding that Jesus was crucified before the completion of the 4th year of His Ministry, which places the Crucifixion in Tiberius' 19th year, not his 7th year.[894]

In the usual chronology, the first year of Tiberius' reign is the first full year after the death of Augustus, A.D. 15, and the seventh year would then be A.D. 21, about two years after the usual date for the death of Germanicus. Now Eusebius is correct in saying that the Ministry and Crucifixion of Christ could not have occurred so soon as the 7th year of Tiberius' reign, for Luke 3:1 clearly places the Ministry of John as beginning in Tiberius' 15th year. However, *The Memoranda* may have contained a partially-correct understanding of the time frame for Christ's Ministry and Crucifixion. Notice that the year called the 7th of Tiberius falls about 2 years after the death of Germanicus. Josephus places the beginning of the Ministry of Christ soon after the death of Germanicus (see sections 11 and 13 above). Germanicus died about 5 years after Augustus died. Thus, *The Memoranda* contained the correct insight that the Ministry of Christ occurred closer to the deaths of Augustus and Germanicus than Eusebius believed.

Both Eusebius and *The Memoranda* were working from the assumption that the reign of Tiberius began at the death of Augustus. *The Memoranda* correctly pointed out that Christ's Ministry and Crucifixion occurred not long after the deaths of Augustus and Germanicus. Eusebius correctly pointed out that the Ministry and Crucifixion of Christ occurred in the latter part of Tiberius' reign, not long before the death of Tiberius. *The Memoranda* made the mistake of counting the start of Tiberius' reign from the death of Augustus, so that it incorrectly placed the Crucifixion early in Tiberius' reign. Eusebius objected to this mistake, without realizing that it contained an aspect of the truth, because he too assumed that Tiberius' reign began at the death of Augustus. This disagreement shows that, during the lifetime of Eusebius, the chronology of events during Tiberius' reign was in dispute, and that some persons during that time period believed that the Ministry of Christ occurred soon after the deaths of Augustus and Germanicus.

16. Sabbatical Years: Zuckermann versus Wacholder

Near the end of his reign, Gaius (Caligula) decided that he was a god and that his statues should be placed inside the Sanctuary of the Temple of Jerusalem. He sent Petronius with an army to carry out this purpose. The Jews were greatly alarmed at this event. A large number of Jewish men, with their wives and children, gathered in the plain of Ptolemais (in Galilee, near the Mediterranean Sea) and met the army sent by the emperor. They pleaded with Petronius and refused to be dissuaded by even the threat of force against them and their families. Josephus writes: "But as they could no way be prevailed upon, and he saw that the country was in danger of lying without tillage (for it was about seed-time that the multitude continued for fifty days together idle)...."[895] This dispute ended happily for the Jews, when Petronius received word that the emperor Gaius was dead.[896]

Notice here that the period of time when the Jews were in the plain of Ptolemais could not have coincided with a Sabbatical year. During Sabbatical years, the Jews were not permitted to sow seed nor to till the land. If it had been a Sabbatical year, Josephus would not have commented that the land was in danger of going without tillage and without seed being sown.

Josephus states that the Jews were in the plain of Ptolemais for about 50 days "about seed-time." The season for planting in ancient Israel occurred in November and December.[897] Yet he does not say that the land went without being planted or tilled, but only that it was in danger of this. Therefore, the Jews were in the plain of Ptolemais about Oct./Nov., just before and at the beginning of seed-time. After about 50 or so days, Petronius dismissed the multitudes and wrote a letter to Gaius to dissuade him placing his statues in the Temple of Jerusalem. That letter would have taken a month or two to arrive in Rome (from Nov. to Dec. or Jan.).

In both the usual and revised chronologies, the date for the death of Gaius is Jan. 24. Josephus tells us that two letters were sent from Rome to Petronius. In the first letter, Gaius threatened Petronius with death for not carrying out his orders, but in the second, Rome informed Petronius that Gaius had died. The first letter must have been sent in Dec. or Jan., for this was a reply to the letter Petronius had sent about November. And, since Gaius died in late January (of A.D. 41, usual, or A.D. 26, revised), the letter about

Gaius' death must have been sent in late January or early February. Josephus explains that the letter which was sent first, the one from Gaius to Petronius, was delayed on the sea for three months (the winter being a difficult time for sailing on the Mediterranean), and so the letter informing Petronius that Gaius was dead arrived 27 days ahead of the other letter.[898] Therefore, these events occurred in the winter leading up to the death of the emperor Gaius.

The Jews were in the plain of Ptolemais for 50 days or more sometime in Oct./Nov. of A.D. 40 (usual), or A.D. 25 (revised). And that winter, A.D. 40/41 (usual) or A.D. 25/26 (revised), could not have been a Sabbatical year since the Jews intended to till the soil and plant seed. Yet, according to Zuckermann, the Sabbatical year occurred from Sept. of A.D. 40 to Sept. of A.D. 41.[899] The usual date for the end of the reign of Gaius conflicts with Zuckermann's theory about the Sabbatical years. However, if one accepts the revised chronology of this book (placing Gaius' death in Jan. of A.D. 26), this conflict does not occur. Zuckermann has a Sabbatical year from fall of A.D. 26 to fall of A.D. 27, and Wacholder has it from A.D. 27 to A.D. 28. The winter of A.D. 25/26 was not a Sabbatical year in either Zuckermann or Wacholder. The dates for the Sabbatical years given by Wacholder are one year later than those by Zuckermann. Wacholder's Sabbatical years do not conflict with the year for Gaius' death in either the usual or the revised chronology. Zuckermann's Sabbatical years conflict with the usual chronology. Thus one must favor Wacholder over Zuckermann in the usual chronology. In my revised chronology, Wacholder's chronology of the Sabbatical years is overall a better fit, particularly when one looks at events during the reign of king Herod (see chapter 12), and at the time frame for the destruction of the Temple (see chapter 14), and so I must favor Wacholder over Zuckermann. (See chapter 16 for a detailed discussion of the Sabbatical years.)

17. Comets, Eclipses, Emperors

The ancient Romans considered comets to be omens indicating impending misfortune, warfare, or a change in leadership. Tacitus refers to a comet seen during Nero's reign as one of several "omens of impending misfortune."[900] In speaking about an earlier comet seen during Nero's reign, Tacitus also tells us: "The general belief is that a comet means a change of emperor. So people speculated on Nero's successor as though Nero were already dethroned."[901] Other ancient Roman historians also mention comets in connection with various important historical events. These comet sightings can be correlated to the comet sightings recorded by the ancient Chinese and Korean astronomers. Information on ancient comets, including sightings by the ancient Chinese and Korean astronomers, is taken from the reference work *Cometography*, by Gary W. Kronk.[902] Locations of constellations, used to mark the locations of comets, was determined using *RedShift 3* astronomy software.

The ancient Romans considered solar and lunar eclipses to be likewise omens related to political events. Several significant examples of eclipses coinciding with historical events are mentioned by the ancient Roman historians. As shown in chapter 12, the lunar eclipse which preceded the death of Herod is very helpful in determining the time frame for his death. In section 1 above, a solar eclipse following the death of Julius Caesar is helpful in determining the year of his death. In section 5 above, a solar eclipse preceding the death of Augustus clearly indicates that he did not die in A.D. 14, as is generally believed. The eclipse data, along with other evidence, points to A.D. 10 as the year of Augustus' death.

The following paragraphs review the evidence from comet and eclipse data in support of my revised chronology for the reigns of Roman emperors. Notice that these revised dates, supported by comet and eclipse data, fit together within the larger framework of this revised chronology. On the other hand, the comet and eclipse data does not fit well, and in several points clearly refutes, the usual chronology.

Julius Caesar's Comet

This comet is perhaps the most famous one associated with the death of an emperor. It was seen after the death of Julius Caesar and was interpreted as meaning that Julius had taken his place with the gods. The dating of this comet is important to determining the year of Julius Caesar's death. Augustus' eye-witness description of Julius Caesar's comet fits the comet of 49 B.C. very well, and does not fit the comet of 44 B.C. at all (see section 2 above).

The solar eclipse that Pliny says followed the death of Julius Caesar further supports the revised date for his death, 49 B.C., since there was a solar eclipse visible from the Roman Empire in that year. The information about a solar eclipse after Julius' death further undermines the usual date for Julius' death, 44 B.C., since there was no solar eclipse visible from anywhere within the Roman Empire from 44 B.C. through 41 B.C., inclusive (see section 1 above).

Augustus' Comets

The Christmas Star, which appeared at the time of the Birth of Jesus Christ and assisted the Magi in finding the Christ-Child (Mt 2:1-12), was most likely a comet (see chapter 4). This comet appeared at the time of the census/taxation under Caesar Augustus and Quirinius (Lk 2:1-2). Cassius Dio does mention a comet at the time of the census (about 16/15 B.C., revised).[903] He states that this comet occurred at about the time of Agrippa's death. Dio places his description of the comet after his description of Agrippa's death. He does not tell us that the comet was an omen which foreshadowed the death of Agrippa, as he typically does with a comet seen before the death of a Roman leader (e.g. Vespasian), but states merely that it was one of many events "connected with Agrippa's death."[904] Thus, the comet may have been seen after the death of Agrippa. As explained in chapter 4 of this book, my revised date for the death of Agrippa is spring of 15 B.C. (the usual date is 11 B.C.). This comet was therefore seen in 15 B.C., most likely sometime between March and December, after Agrippa died.

There is no record of a comet, seen by the ancient Chinese and Korean astronomers, in 15 B.C. However, there are gaps in the extant records of these ancient astronomers, during which time we have no record of any comet observations (e.g. 31 B.C. to 13 B.C., and 4 B.C. to A.D. 12, inclusive). Also, there is no extant record of a comet observation by Chinese astronomers from A.D. 40 to A.D. 53, inclusive; but ancient Korean astronomers did record the sighting of a comet in A.D. 46. This recorded sighting by the Korean astronomers reveals the gap in the recorded sightings of the Chinese astronomers. These gaps may have resulted from either the loss of some records as the centuries passed or from an interruption in the work of observing and recording comets (perhaps caused by political or social disruptions). The usual chronology would place the death of Agrippa in spring of 11 B.C., and use Halley's comet as the comet at the time of his death. However, Dio's description indicates that the comet was seen after the death of Agrippa (spring 11 B.C., usual), whereas Halley's comet (Aug. to Oct. of 12 B.C.) was seen before that date.

Pliny the Elder lists four comets seen the western sky, one of which he places "during the civil disorder during the consulship of Octavius…."[905] The consulship of Octavius is not the consulship of the Octavius who became Caesar Augustus, but of some other person. When writing about the comet seen by Augustus after the death of Julius Caesar, Pliny refers to Augustus as "His late Majesty Augustus," even though he had not yet received the title Augustus at the time of that comet.[906] Again, when writing about this same time-period, Pliny calls him "Augustus Caesar," though he had not yet even become part of the triumvir (three-man council) that governed Rome after Julius Caesar's death.[907] Pliny refers to him only as "Augustus," not as Octavius, even when referring to periods of time before he was actually called Augustus. Later on, Pliny refers to the consulship of a different Octavius (clearly not Augustus): "In the consulship of Gnaeus Octavius and Gaius Scribonius…."[908] Furthermore, Pliny's list of four comets seen in the western sky appears to be in chronological order. The second comet in the list took place during the war between Julius Caesar and Pompey. The first comet in the list is the one placed during the consulship of someone named Octavius. This consulship must have taken place before Julius Caesar died and before his war with Pompey. Augustus Caesar did not have a consulship before the death of Julius Caesar (he had no real power before Julius died and he was too young to be consul). Therefore, this comet sighting did not take place during Augustus Caesar's reign.

A comet is described by Dio as one of the omens associated with the war between Augustus and Marc Anthony: "…and for many days a flaming torch was seen to rise over the sea in the direction of Greece, and to soar aloft in the sky."[909] A comet recorded by the ancient Chinese astronomers, which occurred in the lunar month beginning on Feb. 6 of 32 B.C., fits this description well. That comet had a long tail, which might be described as a torch, and was seen against the constellation Pegasus.[910] From the point of view of Rome in that month and year, Pegasus would be visible rising in the east beginning just before dawn.[911] Greece is east-southeast of Rome. This comet does fit the usual chronology, which places the defeat of Marc Anthony in Sept. of 31 B.C., about one year and 6 months after the comet.

On the other hand, my revised chronology places the defeat of Marc Anthony at Actium in Sept. of 35 B.C. There is no record of a comet in 36 or 35 B.C. in the records of the ancient astronomers. The comet seen in Feb. of 32 B.C. fits Dio's description well, but occurred about 2 years and 5 months after the defeat of Anthony at Actium in my revised chronology. However, the deaths of Anthony and Cleopatra occurred in August of 34 B.C., revised, nearly a year after their defeat at Actium in September of 35 B.C.[912] This places the comet of 32 B.C. only a year and six months after the death of Marc Anthony and Cleopatra in my revised chronology. By comparison, the comet of 32 B.C.

falls almost the same length of time before the usual date for the defeat of Marc Anthony and Cleopatra at Actium. Therefore, the comet of 32 B.C. fits this revised chronology just as well as it fits the usual chronology.

A number of conspicuous comets were recorded by the ancient astronomers as occurring during the years coinciding with Caesar Augustus' reign, but these were not mentioned by the ancient Roman historians. For example, the comets of 5 B.C. and A.D. 13 are not found in the writings of Dio or Suetonius, neither in the usual chronology nor in my revised chronology. Part of the reason for this omission is that the reign of Augustus was long and fairly prosperous. The people were not hoping for a sign in the sky that would indicate the end of his reign (as was the case with Nero). So, certain comets may have been seen during Augustus' reign, but not recorded by the Roman historians, because these did not coincide with any significant event, such as a change in leadership.

The comet of A.D. 13 occurred in the lunar month between Nov. 22 and Dec. 21, only about 8 months before the usual date given for the death of Augustus (Aug. 19, A.D. 14).[913] This comet was described as a "broom star," meaning that it had a conspicuous tail, and it was seen for over 20 days. Dio lists a series of omens that foreshadowed the death of Augustus, yet this comet is not mentioned among them. He does refer to "blood-red comets" in the plural, but only in association with a solar eclipse; these are most likely meteors that can be seen, along with the stars, when the sky is darkened by a solar eclipse.

On the other hand, in my revised chronology, the comet of A.D. 13 falls over three years after the death of Augustus, and over nine years before the death of Tiberius. This comet was not mentioned by the ancient Roman historians because it did not coincide with the death of an emperor or some other significant event.

No Comets for Tiberius

The only comets recorded by the ancient astronomers that coincided with Tiberius' reign (in either chronology) were the comets of A.D. 13 and A.D. 22. Neither is mentioned by the ancient Roman historians. Both fall well before the usual date for the death of Tiberius in March of A.D. 37. The comet of A.D. 22 was seen about 8 months after my revised date for the death of Tiberius in March of A.D. 22. However, this comet was not very conspicuous; it is described as a "sparkling star" and was seen for only 5 days.[914] Comets with long tails were described by the ancient astronomers as "broom stars" or as having "rays" of a particular length. But the expression "sparkling star" indicates that this comet had no noticeable tail, and much resembled an ordinary star. Such a comet would not have been recognized by the Romans as a comet, and may not have been noticed at all by the Roman people in general.

Gaius' Comet

No comet is described by the ancient Roman historians as occurring during the reign of the emperor Gaius (Caligula). The revised dates for his reign are March of A.D. 22 to Jan. of A.D. 26. Only one comet is found in the records of the ancient astronomers from

A.D. 22 to well after A.D. 26. A comet was briefly seen, for about 5 days, during the lunar month of Nov. 13 to Dec 12 in A.D. 22, by the ancient Chinese astronomers.[915] This comet may not have been noticed by the Romans because it appeared only briefly and did not have a conspicuous tail. The Chinese astronomers described this comet as a "sparkling star," whereas they described comets with noticeable tails using terms such as "broom star" or "long-tailed star."[916]

On the other hand, the usual dates for Gaius' reign are March of A.D. 37 to Jan. of A.D. 41. Ancient Chinese astronomers observed a very conspicuous comet in A.D. 39, for 49 days from mid March to late April. This comet was easily noticed, even by a casual observer, since it had rays measuring 30 degrees, in other words, a very long tail.[917] The ancient Chinese astronomers referred to this comet as a "broom star," because of its conspicuous tail.[918] Yet there is no mention of this very obvious comet during the time period that the usual chronology assigns to the reign of Gaius. This comet sighting does not fit the usual chronology, but does fit well in the revised chronology (see below).

Claudius' Comet and Eclipse

According to Suetonius, the "main omens of Claudius' death included the rise of a long-haired star, known as a comet...."[919] Dio adds that this comet was "seen for a very long time...."[920] Pliny the Elder lists four comets which were seen (during the reigns of various emperors) "in the western sky," including the comet seen "about the time of the poisoning" of Claudius Caesar.[921] Seneca gives a different description of this comet: "The Claudius comet rose from the north into the zenith and moved east, always growing dimmer."[922] Later, he reiterates that the comet was seen in the north, then rose straight up until it disappeared.[923]

According to the generally-accepted chronology, Claudius died in Oct. of A.D. 54. A comet sighting was recorded by the Chinese astronomers in A.D. 54, sometime between the full moon of June 9 and that of July 9.[924] This comet was likely first seen in Gemini, but, because the sun was also in Gemini, its tail would not have been visible. The Romans would not have recognized this object as a comet, at this point in time, because the tail was not visible and the comet itself was difficult to see in the glare of the sun. However, the comet moved out of Gemini and became visible with its tail as it approached Ursa Minor. The location of Ursa Minor, as seen from Rome during that time period, was in the northern sky. When seen after sunset, Ursa Minor is also higher in the sky than Gemini. The Chinese astronomers described this comet as moving toward the northeast.[925]

The comet of A.D. 54 fits Seneca's description of the Claudius comet fairly well, since it was seen in the northern sky and moved higher in the sky (from Gemini to Ursa Minor), and then moved eastward. However, it conflicts with Pliny's description of a comet in the western sky. The Romans would have been unlikely to recognize this object as a comet when it was first seen in Gemini (northwest sky), since the sun's glare would have kept the comet's tail from being seen. In fact, according to Kronk, the ancient Chinese astronomers themselves did not recognize this object as a comet when it was in Gemini (they mistook it for Mercury until it moved away from the sun and the tail became visible).[926]

In this revised chronology, Claudius died in Oct. of A.D. 39. A comet sighting was recorded by the ancient Chinese astronomers in A.D. 39, from March 13 to April 30. This comet had a conspicuous tail, with rays as long as 30 degrees.[927] This very noticeable comet occurred about six months before the death of Claudius. This length of time is certainly close enough to the time of Claudius' death for the comet to have become associated with the later event. The comet was seen for about 49 days by the Chinese astronomers, a fairly lengthy observation period for a comet. Because this comet was very noticeable, was seen for many days, and occurred not long before the death of Claudius, the Romans would certainly have associated this comet with the emperor's death.

The ancient Chinese astronomers first saw the comet of A.D. 39 in the group of stars called the Pleiades.[928] As seen from Rome at that time, the Pleiades were in the western sky after sunset. This location fits the description given by Pliny for the Claudius comet (seen in the western sky). According to the ancient astronomers, the comet then moved towards the northeast between the constellations Andromeda and Pegasus. This location would have been visible before dawn in the eastern sky. These constellations, and the comet, would then appear to rise higher in the sky as the hours passed and to dim as the sun began to rise. Also, when seen in the east about dawn, Andromeda and Pegasus are higher in the sky than the Pleiades, and the Pleiades are slightly further north.[929] This location fits Seneca's description that the comet rose in the sky and grew dimmer, and that it moved eastward, but it conflicts with Seneca's statement that the comet was first seen in the north.

The details we have about the location of Claudius' comet fit both the description of the A.D. 39 and the A.D. 54 comet to a certain extent. However, there is a conflict between the locations of Claudius' comet given by Pliny and Seneca. Pliny places the comet in the west, but Seneca places it first in the north, then moving towards the east. It is therefore unlikely that any comet could accurately and completely fit both Pliny and Seneca's descriptions. One could make a case for either comet (A.D. 39 or A.D. 54) as being a better fit for the observed location of Claudius' comet.

On the other hand, Suetonius describes Claudius' comet as "a long-haired star, known as a comet."[930] This description can only fit a comet with a long tail. The A.D. 39 comet's tail was 30 degrees in length, but the A.D. 54 comet's tail was only 5 degrees.[931] The comet of A.D. 39 is therefore a much better fit for Suetonius' description of a long-haired comet.

Dio tells us an interesting story about a solar eclipse that occurred during the reign of Claudius.[932] The emperor Claudius knew from the calculations of Roman astronomers that a solar eclipse would coincide with his birthday. The Roman people considered eclipses in general to be omens of impending events, either of a change in leadership or of some misfortune. An eclipse coinciding with the birthday of an emperor is a very rare event and would have been interpreted by the Romans as very significant. They would likely have interpreted this event as indicating either an end to Claudius' reign, or the beginning of some misfortune or disaster during his reign.

In order to forestall any disturbance among the people as a result of this eclipse, Claudius issued a proclamation about the eclipse. His proclamation explained when the eclipse would occur and how long it would last, and gave a fairly scientific explanation as to why eclipses occur.[933] Dio's description of this proclamation shows us that the Roman scholars of that time period could predict eclipses with a fair degree of accuracy. Dio is therefore unlikely to have been mistaken that a solar eclipse coincided with Claudius' birthday, both because the proclamation about the eclipse was an historical event and because the scholars of Dio's time period could have verified when the eclipse occurred.

In the usual chronology, the solar eclipse on August 1 of A.D. 45 is considered to be this eclipse mentioned by Dio. That eclipse occurred in the morning and was centered in Africa, but would have been visible from much of Europe, including Rome, as a partial eclipse. Claudius' birthday was August 1 and the usual chronology has his reign extending from Jan. of A.D. 41 to Oct. of A.D. 54. The generally-accepted chronology places this eclipse a few years into the reign of Claudius. Dio apparently believed that this eclipse occurred a few years into Claudius' reign, for he places it in that context.[934]

In my revised chronology, the solar eclipse on August 1 of A.D. 26 is the eclipse mentioned by Dio. That eclipse also occurred in the morning and was centered in Africa, but would not have been visible from Europe. The scholars of Claudius' time could predict the day and time when a solar eclipse would occur. However, it is another matter altogether to be able to predict where on earth the shadow of the moon will fall during a solar eclipse. To predict the day and time, one must know the relative positions of the sun, earth, and moon. This same information is also used to predict lunar eclipses and the moon's phases. Lunar eclipses and the moon's phases are generally visible from any location on earth from which the moon would be visible. So, predicting the day and time of a lunar eclipse or a lunar phase is sufficient to predict whether the event will be visible from a particular location. Not so with solar eclipses. A solar eclipse is not visible from everywhere on earth where the sun is visible.

The Roman scholars could predict the day and time of the solar eclipse, and they knew that the eclipse would occur in the morning, when the sun would be above the horizon, so they assumed that the eclipse would be visible. They could not accurately predict the places on earth where the solar eclipse would be seen. In order to predict where the shadow of the moon will fall during a solar eclipse, one needs to know the distance of the moon from the earth (which varies within a certain range), the size of the moon, and the shape and size of the moon's shadow. They did not have this precise information (as is clear from Pliny's explanation of the solar system).[935]

This eclipse coincides with the first year of Claudius' reign in my revised chronology (A.D. 26, revised). Dio, however, places the eclipse in the context of the fifth year of Dio's reign (A.D. 45, usual). Did Dio have documents indicating that the eclipse occurred in the fifth year of Claudius' reign? Or, did Dio check with Roman scholars to find out (by means of their calculations) when an eclipse coincided with Claudius' birthday during the time period he believed contained Claudius' reign? It is likely that he did check with Roman scholars, since he follows this story about the eclipse on Claudius' birthday with a fairly scientific explanation of both solar and lunar eclipses (this explanation seems to have come from Roman scholars).[936] I conclude that he placed this eclipse in the incorrect time frame because he did not account for the overlap between Tiberius and Augustus' reigns. In looking for an August 1 eclipse, he inevitably decided upon the A.D. 45 eclipse, since it was the only one that fit his time frame for Claudius' reign.

But why was Claudius concerned enough about a possible future solar eclipse to inquire of Roman scholars when the next one would occur? Dio states only that "some other portents had already occurred."[937] In the usual chronology, there were no other solar eclipses visible from the Roman Empire for more than a year previous to the August 1, A.D. 45 eclipse. But in the revised chronology, there was a solar eclipse visible from Rome on Feb. 6 of A.D. 26. This eclipse occurred only a couple of weeks after Claudius became emperor. This first eclipse of A.D. 26 was a partial solar eclipse that was visible from Rome at, and well after, dawn. This impressive eclipse would have been seen by the Roman people as an omen associated with the reign of Claudius, because it occurred so soon after he became emperor. Thus, the revised chronology offers a clear explanation as to why Claudius consulted scholars about future solar eclipses in the first place.

The first solar eclipse (Feb. 6 of A.D. 26) caused a stir among the Roman people, who were quite superstitious about eclipses. This caused Claudius to inquire when the next solar eclipse would occur. When Roman scholars informed Claudius of a second solar eclipse later that year, and one coinciding with his birthday, he became concerned about how the Roman people would interpret such an omen. For this reason, he issued his famous proclamation about the eclipse, in an attempt to prevent people from interpreting that eclipse as also an omen against him. Now, if the eclipse mentioned in the proclamation had actually been visible from the Roman Empire, a proclamation by the emperor would not have been likely to cause the Roman people as a whole to abandon their belief that celestial events are meaningful omens. Yet Dio mentions no reaction by anyone to the eclipse of the proclamation. The August 1, A.D. 45 eclipse was visible from Rome and much of the Empire, but the August 1, A.D. 26 eclipse was not visible from the Roman Empire, but only from central and southern Africa. The reason there is no mention by Dio of any reaction to the eclipse is that it was not visible to the Roman people. The revised chronology can explain why Claudius sought information about a future solar eclipse (his reaction to the Feb. eclipse) and can explain the lack of any response from the Roman people after the August eclipse (it was not visible to them). The usual chronology offers no explanation of either of these points.

Nero's Comets

Tacitus mentions two comet sightings during the reign of Nero. "A brilliant comet now appeared."[938] This sighting is described alongside the events usually placed in A.D. 60; my revised date for this comet sighting is A.D. 46. There are recorded comet sightings from Chinese and Korean astronomers in A.D. 60, and from Korean astronomers only in A.D. 46.[939]

The poet Seneca describes a comet during the reign of Nero, when Paterculus and Vopiscus were consuls, usually dated to A.D. 60. This comet began in the north, passed through the west, and ended in the southern sky.[940] The path of this comet is similar to the comet described by Chinese astronomers for the year A.D. 60, which was first observed in the northeast and last seen in the southern sky.[941]

My revised date for this comet sighting is A.D. 46. Korean astronomers recorded a comet sighting in the southern sky in A.D. 46.[942] This location matches the final location of the comet described by Seneca. More details are available from the Chinese astronomers about the A.D. 60 comet, but the available information for the A.D. 46 comet does not conflict with any details given by Seneca. The description given by Seneca could refer to either the A.D. 46 or the A.D. 60 comet.

Tacitus reports a second comet a few years later, at the end of the year of the burning of Rome, (A.D. 64, usual; A.D. 49, revised).[943] Tacitus does not give many details about this comet, but he does tells us that this comet was "atoned for by Nero, as usual, by aristocratic blood...."[944] The phrase 'as usual' indicates Nero had previously killed members of the aristocracy in reaction to a comet or other celestial sign. Thus, Nero most likely killed members of the aristocracy in response to both comets.

There was a sighting recorded in A.D. 64 by Chinese astronomers, which was thought to be either a comet or a nova (a new star). This object did not have a visible tail, hence the dispute as to whether it was a comet or a nova. It was seen from early May to mid July, in A.D. 64. This comet or nova does not fit the description given by Tacitus of the second comet during Nero's reign. Tacitus tells us that the fire that destroyed Rome began on July 19, yet he does not make any association between the comet and the fire. If the comet had been seen from early May to mid July of A.D. 64, Tacitus and the Roman people in general would surely have seen the comet as a foreshadowing of the fire that destroyed Rome. Instead Tacitus notes that the second comet was seen near the end of the year and was interpreted as a bad omen for events occurring after the burning of Rome.

Furthermore, Tacitus states that Nero killed members of the aristocracy to atone for this comet sighting.[945] But the sighting of A.D. 64 had no visible tail and may have been either a comet or a nova, and so it probably would not have been categorized as a comet by the ancient Romans and would not have elicited any response from Nero.

Nero was so concerned about each of these two comet sightings (A.D. 60 and A.D. 64, usual dates; A.D. 46 and 49, revised dates), supposing it to be an omen of the end of his reign, that he massacred the Roman nobility in an attempt to divert this result. In the year A.D. 65, a very conspicuous comet was seen, one much more noticeable than the comet/nova recorded by the ancient astronomers in A.D. 64. The A.D. 65 comet had a long tail and remained visible for almost 2 months (Aug.-Sept.), according to the Chinese astronomers.[946] Yet there is no mention of any reaction by Nero to this much more obvious comet sighting, nor is any such sighting even mentioned by any of the ancient Roman historians during Nero's reign. In my revised chronology, Nero's reign is placed years earlier and so the comet of A.D. 65 did not occur during his reign. But there is no explanation in the usual chronology as to why Nero would decide to kill members of the Roman aristocracy in reaction to the comet of A.D. 60 and the comet/nova of A.D. 64 (which had no tail), yet show no reaction the very next year, A.D. 65, to a much more conspicuous comet with a long, very visible tail.

Again, in A.D. 66, a very conspicuous comet was recorded by Chinese astronomers—Halley's Comet. This comet had a long tail and was seen over the course of about 2½ months, from Jan. 31 to April 11, by Chinese astronomers.[947] Yet there is no mention of a comet sighting alongside the events usually assigned to A.D. 66 in Roman history. Nero was so concerned about the sightings of comets in A.D. 60 and 64 (usual dates) that he massacred members of the nobility. Yet in A.D. 65 and 66, two much more conspicuous comets were recorded by the ancient astronomers, but with no mention of any reaction by Nero by the ancient Roman historians. This omission further supports my conclusion that the usual dates given to the reign of Nero are not correct.

My revised chronology places the burning of Rome and the reign of Nero as a whole, 15 years earlier than the usual date. There is no record of a comet in A.D. 49, my revised year for the burning of Rome, in either the ancient Chinese or Korean comet sightings.[948] However, the recorded observations of the Chinese astronomers do show a gap during this time period. There are no comet sightings in the extant Chinese records from A.D. 40 to A.D. 53, inclusive, yet Korean astronomers recorded a comet sighting during the year A.D. 46.[949] Also, there are other apparent gaps in the recorded observations of the Chinese and Korean astronomers. Some periods of time, as long as 10 or more years, have no recorded sightings of comets by either Chinese or Korean astronomers, for example 31 B.C. to 13 B.C., inclusive, and 3 B.C. to A.D. 12, inclusive, contain no recorded observations of comets. During such gaps, records may have been lost or the observation and recording of comet sightings may have been interrupted.

Suetonius mentions a comet observation before he describes the burning of Rome.[950] But he makes no association between the comet and that great fire, so the comet did not immediately precede the fire, and must have occurred many months, or even a few years, earlier. He also states that Nero consulted an astrologer and was advised to kill members of the aristocracy to atone for the comet. This description of the decision to atone for the comet indicates that this was the first time that Nero atoned for a comet by killing aristocrats. Therefore, this comet was the first comet of Nero's reign, occurring a few years before the burning of Rome, in the year A.D. 46.

Tacitus describes a second comet a few years later, at the end of the year of the burning of Rome, (A.D. 64, usual; A.D. 49, revised).[951] He tells us that this comet was "atoned for by Nero, as usual, by aristocratic blood...."[952] Nero again followed the advice he received at the time of the previous comet.

Pliny also describes a comet during Nero's reign. He does not give enough information to place the comet in a particular month or year. However, he does say that the comet was seen in the western sky. Pliny also states that this comet was seen "during Nero's principate shining almost continuously and with a terrible glare."[953] The phrase "shining almost continuously" probably means that this comet was seen during daytime as well as at night, since he adds that the comet's glare was terrible. Not enough information is given by Pliny to determine whether this comet was the first or second comet of Nero's reign.

In his play *Octavia*, Seneca described a comet in the constellation Boötes. The events in this play surrounding this sighting are generally placed about the year A.D. 62 (A.D. 47, revised). Boötes is located adjacent to the constellation Virgo, in the southern sky. There is no record of a comet sighting in A.D. 47. However, the comet of A.D. 46 was seen in the southern sky, and so fits the description of this comet. Thus, this comet could well be the comet of A.D. 46.

Vitellius' Comet

"While he was behaving in this way, evil omens occurred. A comet was seen, and the moon, contrary to precedent, appeared to suffer two eclipses, being obscured on the fourth and on the seventh day."[954]

Dio first explains that Vitellius behaved very badly after he became emperor. Then he describes a comet, followed by two lunar eclipses. Now it is quite impossible for two lunar eclipses to occur only three days apart, so we must conclude that a lunar eclipse occurred only on one of those days, either on the 4th or the 7th day, and not both. The 4th and 7th days must refer to the day of the month (not of the week), because the date of any lunar eclipse is calculated as a day of the month (the day of the week being irrelevant).

After describing these omens, Dio goes on to detail the beginnings of Vespasian's aspiration to become emperor. Vitellius held office for less than a year, and during the largest part of that time Vespasian sought to displace him as emperor. Vespasian fought against Vitellius to obtain the throne during the autumn and into the winter. Therefore, the comet and the lunar eclipse occurred in the summertime, after Vitellius had become emperor and had behaved badly, but before Vespasian fought against Vitellius during the fall of that year.

In A.D. 54, a comet was observed and recorded by the ancient Chinese astronomers. This comet had a tail measuring about 5 degrees and was seen between June 9 and July 9 of that year.[955] In the following month, on August 7, a lunar eclipse occurred, which was visible from Rome before and during sunrise.

There is no other year, in either the usual or my revised chronology, when a comet observation is followed by a lunar eclipse on either the 4th or 7th of the month. The usual year for the summer of Vitellius' reign is A.D. 69. There is no record of a comet observation by the ancient astronomers for the years A.D. 67 through 70, inclusive.[956] Two lunar eclipses visible from Rome did occur in A.D. 69, one on April 25 and the other on Oct. 18. Neither of these eclipses fits Dio's description, since neither occurred on the 4th or 7th of the month. Thus the pairing of a comet with a lunar eclipse (on the 4th or the 7th of the month) is rare enough so as to establish A.D. 54 as the only reasonable fit to Dio's description.

Vespasian's Comet and Eclipses

Both Suetonius and Dio describe a comet that appeared before the death of Vespasian. The comet had a long, conspicuous tail and so was described as having long hair. The Roman people interpreted this as an omen that Vespasian would soon die. But Dio tells us: "To those who said anything to him about the comet he said: 'This is an omen, not for me, but for the Parthian king; for he has long hair, whereas I am bald.' "[957] Dio adds that the comet "was visible for a long time."[958] The identification of this comet is important in determining the year of Vespasian's death.

If Dio was correct in giving the length of Vespasian's reign as ten years, then the revised dates for his reign would be A.D. 55 to 65. However, the long-haired comet observed by Chinese astronomers in A.D. 65 was first sighted near the end of July, whereas Vespasian died in June.[959] There was no comet observed in the earlier months of

A.D. 65, and the comet of A.D. 64 did not have a long tail (and may have been a nova rather than a comet).

Furthermore, there is no mention of a comet foreshadowing the death of the emperor Titus, who died only a little more than 2 years after Vespasian. If Vespasian died in A.D. 65, then Titus' death would be placed in A.D. 67. There were two conspicuous comets in A.D. 65 to 66: a long-tailed comet seen from July to Sept. of A.D. 65, and Halley's comet (also with a noticeable tail), seen from Jan. to April of A.D. 66.[960] Neither of these is mentioned as having been seen during Titus' reign. These were two very noticeable comets. Since the Romans believed comets were ill omens, they would have associated these with the death of Titus, if they had been seen during his reign. They also would have likely associated these comets with the eruption of Mount Vesuvius, a major fire in Rome, and an outbreak of the plague, all of which occurred during Titus' reign. Yet there is no mention of these comets. Therefore, the observation of these comets did not occur during the reign of Titus.

However, both of these two comets (A.D. 65 and A.D. 66) fit well the description of the comet preceding the death of Vespasian. They both had long tails and so could be described as "long-haired" comets. And Dio makes a point of saying that the comet preceding the death of Vespasian was visible for a long time. The two comets of A.D. 65 and A.D. 66 were seen from July to Sept. of A.D. 65 and Jan to April of A.D. 66. These two could easily have been mistaken as one comet, which seemed to be visible for an unusually long time. Thus the long-haired comet at the end of Vespasian's reign was actually two comets, seen over much of the year preceding his death. Vespasian's death must then be placed in June of A.D. 66, after an antedated reign of nearly 12 years (July of A.D. 54 to June of A.D. 66), not ten years as Dio stated. (Further evidence in support of a longer reign for Vespasian is presented below.)

As occurred with Tiberius' reign, here again is a case where the antedating of an emperor's reign may have resulted in confusion over when that reign began and ended. The antedating of the reigns of Vespasian and the three emperors before him (Otho, Galba, Vitellius) may have been the cause of this misunderstanding as to the length of Vespasian's reign.

The usual year given for the end of Vespasian's reign is A.D. 79. There was a comet recorded by Korean astronomers in A.D. 79, which was described as a "broom star," meaning that it had a conspicuous tail.[961] However, that comet was only visible for about 20 days, and so does not fit Dio's statement that Vespasian's comet was visible for a long time. Also, there is no record of the comet of A.D. 79 from the observations of the Chinese astronomers. Thus there is no comet fitting Dio's description within the usual chronology of Vespasian's reign.

Pliny states that an unusual celestial event occurred during the reign of Vespasian—a pairing of solar and lunar eclipses. "For the eclipse of both sun and moon within 15 days of each other has occurred even in our time, in the year of the third consulship of the elder Emperor Vespasian and the second consulship of the younger."[962] Vespasian, the emperor, had a son named Titus, whose surname was also Vespasian.[963] So the year referred to here is the year in which the two consuls were the emperor Vespasian and his son, the younger Vespasian, who is usually called Titus.

In the usual chronology, Titus held his second consulship in the year A.D. 72, which coincided with Vespasian's fourth consulship.[964] Now, perhaps Pliny is counting Vespasian's fourth consulship as his third, since, in the usual chronology, it was his third consulship after he became emperor. However, the pairing of a solar and lunar eclipse occurred in A.D. 71, not 72. There was a lunar eclipse on March 4, A.D. 71, visible from Rome, beginning just after sunset and lasting over 2 hours. A partial solar eclipse, visible from Rome, followed on March 20.[965] Notice the incongruities here: these eclipses were 16 days apart, not 15 as Pliny states, and they occurred in a year in which Titus was not consul.

In my revised chronology, the fall of Jerusalem occurred in A.D. 56, the year of Vespasian's third consulship. In A.D. 56, a lunar eclipse on June 16 was visible from Rome before and during dawn. A partial solar eclipse followed, 15 days later, on July 1.[966] This solar eclipse was not visible from Rome, but was visible from all of Spain, most of northern Africa, southern France, and the island of Sicily. Pliny was not, however, relying on calculation to determine when this eclipse pair occurred. Pairs of lunar and solar eclipses occurring 15 days apart are common; what is rare, and what Pliny was referring to, is a pair of lunar and solar eclipses, 15 days apart, which are both **visible**. Pliny was stationed in Spain from the latter part of Nero's reign until Vespasian became emperor. But during the time of this solar eclipse, Pliny had left his post in Spain and was probably in living in Rome. Pliny was a part of Vespasian's inner circle at Rome and was eventually put in command of the Roman fleet at Misenum on the Bay of Naples.[967] Though the solar eclipse was not visible from Rome or Naples, it was visible from the sea and the islands to the west and south of Rome and Naples. Pliny may have received reports from those locations, or from Spain where he was formerly Procurator, so that he knew about the eclipse but did not view it himself.

Titus' Comet

The reign of the emperor Titus was brief, lasting just over 2 years and 2 months. According to the usual chronology, Titus ruled from June of A.D. 79 to Sept. of A.D. 81. The ancient Chinese and Korean astronomers recorded no comets during this time period. The Roman historians also mention no comets during Titus' brief reign. My revised chronology places Titus' reign from June of A.D. 66 to Sept. of A.D. 68. Here again, there are no recorded observations of comets by the ancient astronomers.

Pliny mentions a comet associated with Titus, but seen before he became emperor. " 'Javelin-stars' quiver like a dart; these are a very terrible portent. To this class belongs the comet about which Titus Imperator Caesar in his 5th consulship wrote an account in his famous poem, that being its latest appearance down to the present day."[968] The usual date for Titus' 5th consulship is the year A.D. 76, during the reign of Vespasian. My revised date for Titus' 5th consulship is A.D. 60, four years after his second consulship in A.D. 56.

In the usual chronology, Titus' 5th consulship fell in the year A.D. 76. There was a comet seen during the year A.D. 76 (Oct.-Nov.), which is generally believed to be the comet of Titus' poem. Chinese astronomers described it as a "broom star" with a tail of about 2 degrees, visible for 40 days.[969] But Pliny does not say that the comet was seen during Titus' 5th consulship, but rather that Titus wrote about the comet during his 5th consulship. Since this comet was seen near the end of the year, Titus could have written about it during or just after it was seen, at the end of his 5th consulship.

In my revised chronology, Titus' 5th consulship fell in A.D. 60. Ancient Chinese astronomers recorded sighting a comet for 135 days (Aug.-Dec.) in A.D. 60. This comet was described as a "broom star" with a tail of about 2 degrees.[970] This description fits Pliny's description of a "Javelin-star," and the length of its visibility makes it very likely that the comet was noticed by the Romans. This comet sighting began in August of A.D. 60, during Titus' 5th consulship. Titus could have written about this comet before the end of his 5th consulship. Thus the comet of A.D. 60 fits Pliny's description at least as well as the comet of A.D. 76.

The eruption of Mount Vesuvius occurred in the first year of the reign of Titus, only a couple of months after the death of Vespasian. Pliny the Elder died as a result of that disaster. The usual date for the eruption of Mount Vesuvius is August 23-24 of A.D. 79. However, in this revised chronology, the death of Vespasian is placed in June of A.D. 66, so that the revised date for the eruption of Mount Vesuvius is August 23-24 of A.D. 66.

No Comets for Domitian

Roman historians do not mention any comet sightings during the reign of the emperor Domitian. There are two reasons for this omission. First, according to Suetonius, Domitian disliked astrology and considered it to be false. He even executed an astrologer who had given an unfavorable prediction about him.[971] Second, no comet sightings coincided with the end of his reign, neither in the usual nor in the revised chronology. The usual chronology has Domitian's reign from A.D. 81 to 96. My revised chronology has Domitian's reign from A.D. 68 to 82. The ancient astronomers have left us no record of any comet sightings from A.D. 80 – 83, inclusive, nor from A.D. 85 to 100, inclusive.[972]

18. Twelve Roman Emperors

Julius Caesar (Sept. 53 B.C. to Mar. 49 B.C.)

As argued above, Julius Caesar died on March 15 of 49 B.C., not 44 B.C. (the usual date). According to Josephus, Julius reigned for only 3 years and six months.[973] He does not give the length of Julius' reign exact to the day, as he does for other emperors, so perhaps he did not know the exact start of Julius' reign. In any case, this places the start of Julius Caesar's reign in Sept. of 53 B.C. (revised).

The evidence concerning the comet seen after the death of Julius supports the date of 49 B.C. for Julius Caesar's death and does not support the later date of 44 B.C. The evidence concerning a solar eclipse after the death of Julius Caesar gives further support to a date of 49 B.C. for the death of Julius Caesar. (See sections 1 and 2 above.)

Augustus (Feb. 48 B.C. to Aug. A.D. 10)

As explained above, Josephus counts the reign of Augustus as beginning in Feb. of the year following the death of Julius Caesar, which is Feb. of 48 B.C. in this revised chronology. Josephus gives the length of Augustus' reign as 57 years, 6 months, 2 days.[974] The death of Augustus occurred on August 19 of A.D. 10 (revised). The usual dates for Augustus' reign are March of 44 B.C. to August of A.D. 14.

The solar eclipse data supports this earlier date of A.D. 10 for Augustus' death and clearly does not support the usual date of A.D. 14 (see section 5 above). Other evidence, such as the year of Julius Caesar's death, the years for the reign of king Herod, and the date for the battle at Actium, also reinforce this earlier chronology for the reign of Augustus.

Tiberius (A.D. 1 to Mar. A.D. 22)

As argued above, Tiberius' reign was antedated to A.D. 1 and his reign of less than 22 years ended in early A.D. 22. There is some disagreement among the ancient historians as to the exact date of Tiberius' death. Perhaps they are each counting Tiberius' reign as if it began at the death of Augustus on August 19, yet still they disagree as to its length. Josephus gives the length of Tiberius' reign as 22 years, 5 months, 3 days (in *The Antiquities of the Jews*), but in another place gives it as 22 years, 6 months, 3 days (in *The Wars of the Jews*).[975] If we follow Josephus, and count from the death of Augustus on August 19, then Tiberius' would be placed in either Jan. or Feb., about the 22nd day of the month. On the other hand, Suetonius states that Tiberius died on March 16, but without stating the exact length of his reign.[976] Dio agrees with Suetonius as to the month but not the day, since he states that Tiberius died on March 26, after a reign of 22 years, 7 months, and 7 days.[977] The generally-accepted date for the death of Tiberius is March 16 of A.D. 37. In this revised chronology, the date of Tiberius' death is March 16 of A.D. 22. The length of Tiberius' reign is shorter in this revised chronology than is stated by the ancient historians (as explained in section 12 above).

Gaius (Caligula) (Mar. A.D. 22 to Jan. A.D. 26)

The death of Tiberius Caesar, in March of A.D. 22, marked the beginning of the reign of the next emperor, Gaius (Caligula), who ruled for less than four years. Josephus gives the length of his reign as 3 years and 8 months.[978] Suetonius, however, gives the length of Gaius' reign as 3 years, 10 months and 8 days.[979] Dio gives the length of his reign as 3 years, 9 months and 28 days.[980] Now Josephus is less certain here than Suetonius and Dio, since he gives the length of time in years and months, but not exact to the day. Also, Josephus is counting from the death of Tiberius, but he gives conflicting information as to the length of Tiberius' reign.[981] Dio and Suetonius seem to disagree on when Gaius died. But, they also differ as to the date of Tiberius' death: March 16 for Suetonius versus March 26 for Dio. When one adds their differing lengths for Gaius' reign to their differing dates for the death of Tiberius, the result is the same month and day for the death of Gaius: Jan. 24. The usual date for the death of Gaius is Jan. 24 of A.D. 41.[982] My revised chronology places the death of the Roman emperor Gaius (Caligula) on Jan. 24 of A.D. 26, just under 4 years after Tiberius died.

Claudius (Jan. A.D. 26 to Oct. A.D. 39)

Josephus gives the length of Claudius' reign as 13 years, 8 months, and 20 days.[983] Suetonius gives the date of his death as Oct. 13 in the 14th year of his reign.[984] Tacitus agrees that Claudius died on Oct. 13.[985] It is difficult to determine what starting point Josephus was using, since he gives two different lengths for the reign of Tiberius and his length for Gaius' reign is not exact to the day. However, he does agree with Suetonius that Claudius' died before completing the 14th year of his reign. So, if Gaius died on Jan. 24 of A.D. 26, then the 14th year of Claudius' reign would begin Jan. of A.D. 26, and his death should then be placed on Oct. 13 of A.D. 39. The length of his reign would then be 13 years, 8 months, and 20 days, in agreement with Josephus. The usual date for the death of Claudius is Oct. 13 of A.D. 54,[986] fifteen years later than my revised date.

In the year A.D. 39, a comet with a long tail was seen, which agrees with the information we have for the comet seen after the death of Claudius (see section 17 above). This time frame for Claudius' reign, A.D. 26 to A.D. 39, also contains the rare event, mentioned by Dio, of a solar eclipse coinciding with the birthday of Claudius on Aug. 1 (see section 17 above).[987]

Nero (Oct. A.D. 39 to June A.D. 53)

Suetonius gives the length of Nero's reign as "nearly fourteen years."[988] He also tells us that Nero was 17 years old when Claudius died, and that Nero died at the age of 31.[989] These statements agree with a length of just under 14 years for the reign of Nero. Dio states the length of Nero's reign as 13 years and 8 months.[990] Josephus gives the length of Nero's reign as 13 years and 8 days (perhaps an error for 8 months).[991] The usual date for the death of Nero is June 9 of A.D. 68, which gives a length of 13 years, and nearly 8 months.[992] My revised date for the death of Nero is June 9 of A.D. 53 (a little more than a year before the antedated start of Vespasian's reign in July of A.D. 54).

Suetonius places the birth of Nero on Dec. 15, "nine months after Tiberius' death."[993] He places the death of Nero just before the completion of the 14th year of his reign, at the age of 31.[994] Since Nero was born in Dec. and died in June, Suetonius could be referring to either June of the year that Nero would have turned 31 (in Dec. of that same year), or June of the year following Nero's 31st birthday. The summer of Vitellius' reign is clearly established (by the comet and eclipse described in section 17) as A.D. 54. Since Nero died in the June previous to Vitellius' reign, Nero died in A.D. 53. This line of reasoning would place Nero's birth and Tiberius' death in either the year A.D. 21 or 22, depending on whether Suetonius meant that Nero was about to turn 31, or had already turned 31, at his death. Now, if we add up the lengths of the reigns of the emperors from Tiberius' death to Nero's death (just over 31 years), we find that Tiberius must have died in A.D. 22. Thus Nero died in the year that he would have turned 31, which was A.D. 53.

Galba (June A.D. 53 to Jan. A.D. 54)

The next three emperors after Nero had very short reigns. According to Josephus, Galba reigned for only 7 months and 7 days.[995] Tacitus also states that Galba reigned for about seven months, and places his death in mid January.[996] Suetonius tells us that Galba died "before he had reigned seven months."[997] On the other hand, Dio states that Galba rules for 9 months and 13 days.[998] But Dio also states, about Galba, Otho, and Vitellius, that each one counted his reign as beginning while the previous emperor was still ruling.[999] Thus Galba's reign ended in January, after an actual reign of about seven months, but he likely antedated his reign, adding about two months. That is why Dio states the length of Galba's reign as about 9 months, but the other ancient historians have it as about 7 months. The usual date for the death of Galba is January of A.D. 69. My revised date for the death of Galba is January of A.D. 54.

Otho (Jan. A.D. 54 to Apr. A.D. 54)

The next emperor, Otho, held a very brief reign. The exact length of his reign is in dispute, with Dio calling it 90 days,[1000] Suetonius 95 days,[1001] and Josephus 3 months and 2 days (92 days).[1002] Within this disagreement is a general consensus that Otho reigned about 3 months. Dio includes Otho among the emperors who antedated their reigns, so Otho's actual reign may have been even less than 90 days. If we place the death of Galba in mid Jan. of A.D. 54, Otho's death most likely occurred sometime in April of A.D. 54. According to Tacitus, the festival of Ceres, which is held in mid April, was being celebrated at the time of Otho's death.[1003] The usual year for Otho's death is A.D. 69. My revised chronology places Otho's death in April of A.D. 54.

Vitellius (Apr. A.D. 54 to Dec. A.D. 54)

Josephus states the length of Vitellius' reign as only 8 months and 5 days. Suetonius is not clear as to when the death of Vitellius occurred, but he places the revolt of several of his legions sometime during the 8th month of his reign.[1004] Since Otho died in April, the 8th month of Vitellius' reign would occur about November/December. He then goes on to describe a series of efforts by Vitellius to hold on to power despite this revolt.[1005]

Dio seems to give an even longer reign to Vitellius (whose reign began in April), for he states the length of his reign as "a year lacking ten days."[1006] On the other hand, Dio also tells us that Vitellius (along with other emperors) antedated his reign,[1007] so this period of nearly a year may overlap with a portion of the previous emperor's reign.

Tacitus places the attempted abdication of Vitellius on Dec. 18, and his death a few days thereafter, making the length of his reign also about 8 months.[1008] Tacitus' description of the events leading up to Vitellius' death has more chronological detail than that of other ancient historians. The death of Vitellius should be placed in late December, in agreement with Tacitus and Josephus.

Dio states that a comet was seen, followed by a lunar eclipse on the 4th or 7th of the month, during the summer of Vitellius' reign.[1009] The summer of A.D. 54 included the sighting of a conspicuous comet.[1010] This sighting was followed by a lunar eclipse on the seventh of the month, visible from Rome. This unusual pairing of events is not found in any other year that could possibly be the year of Vitellius' reign. The usual chronology has Vitellius' reign in A.D. 69, but no comet was seen that year and no lunar eclipse occurred in summer nor on the 4th or 7th of the month (see section 17 above). This combination of comet and eclipse constitutes yet another significant point of evidence in support of this revised chronology and against the generally-accepted chronology.

This revised chronology places Otho's death in April of A.D. 54. The summer of A.D. 54 contained the comet and eclipse associated with Vitellius' reign. Consequently, the death of Vitellius must be placed in late December of A.D. 54. The exact date of Vitellius' death is not clear. The usual year given for the death of Vitellius is late A.D. 69.

Vespasian (July A.D. 54 to June A.D. 66)

Contrary to the statements of Josephus and Tacitus, Dio gives the length of Vitellius' reign as "a year lacking ten days."[1011] However, he later states that the emperors between Nero and Vespasian (Galba, Otho, Vitellius) counted their reigns as overlapping with the reigns of the previous emperor.[1012] This statement also explains why Dio counts Galba's reign as two months longer than other ancient historians. Thus, in Dio's chronology, the beginning of Vespasian's reign cannot be calculated by adding the lengths of the reigns of Galba, Otho, and Vitellius.

Dio states, "from the death of Nero to the beginning of Vespasian's rule a year and twenty-two days elapsed."[1013] If Nero's death is placed on June 9, then Vespasian's reign began on July 1, just over a year later. However, Vitellius did not die until December of that same year (A.D. 54), about 8 months after the death of Otho (April of A.D. 54). Clearly, Dio antedates the start of Vespasian's reign to July 1, months before the death of Vitellius.

Several comments by Dio illustrate this point. Not long after relating the death of Otho, Dio tells us that Vespasian was considering seeking to become emperor, in place of Vitellius. "The soldiers, on perceiving all this, surrounded Vespasian's tent and hailed him as emperor."[1014] A little later, some soldiers were persuaded to switch their allegiance from Vitellius to Vespasian. "So at the time they removed the images of Vitellius from their standards and took the oath that they would be ruled by Vespasian."[1015] These events occurred at the beginning of the conflict between Vespasian and Vitellius, months before the death of Vitellius.

According to Dio, then, Galba, Otho, Vitellius, and Vespasian all antedated their reigns to a time before the previous emperor died. These are examples of antedating in the Roman emperors of the first century A.D. Each of these emperors counted his reign as beginning before the death of the previous emperor, at whatever point in time he first gained the power that led him to the throne. Dio describes the antedating used by the emperors from Galba to Vespasian with disdain. "For they did not succeed one another legitimately, but each of them, even while his rival was alive and still ruling, believed himself to be emperor from the moment that he even got a glimpse of the throne."[1016]

In this revised chronology, the reign of Vespasian is counted from July 1 of A.D. 54, overlapping with the reign of Vitellius, rather than from the death of Vitellius in Dec. A.D. 54. The usual year for the start of Vespasian's antedated reign is A.D. 69.

According to Suetonius, Vespasian's reign ended with his death on June 23.[1017] Dio gives the length of his reign as "ten years lacking six days."[1018] Both Suetonius and Dio count Vespasian's reign as beginning on July 1 (before the death of Vitellius), so they are in agreement that Vespasian died in June. In the usual chronology, Vespasian's antedated reign began in A.D. 69 and ended in A.D. 79. In this revised chronology, Vespasian's reign began on July 1 of A.D. 54, but ended in June of A.D. 66, a length of nearly 12 years from the antedated start of his reign on July 1, but a length of just over 11 years when not antedated.

Several pieces of evidences support the conclusion that Vespasian's reign was two years longer than Dio stated it to be. First, the summer of Vitellius' reign included a comet sighting followed by a lunar eclipse on the 4th or 7th day of the month (see above). The only year fitting these criteria is A.D. 54; consequently, Vespasian's antedated reign must have begun in A.D. 54. Second, Suetonius places the birth of Titus (Vespasian's son) in the same year as the death of Gaius (Caligula), and he states that Titus died at the age of 41.[1019] This information gives us two additional years to account for between the deaths of Gaius and Titus (as explained below in the section on Titus' reign). Third, the comet data presents us with a very good fit for the comet preceding the death of Vespasian if he died after a reign of nearly 12 years, rather than nearly 10 years (see section 17 above). Fourth, information concerning the date of the destruction of the Temple of Jerusalem points to the year A.D. 56 (see chapter 14). A reign of 12 years, rather than 10 years, for Vespasian brings all of these points into agreement.

Titus (June A.D. 66 to Sept. A.D. 68)

The emperor Titus was one of the sons of Vespasian. His reign was brief and both Suetonius and Dio agree on its length: 2 years, 2 months, 20 days.[1020] Suetonius also gives the day and month of the end of Titus' reign at his death as September 13. This determination agrees with the date for the death of Vespasian on June 23—there are 2 months and 20 days from June 23 to September 13. Thus, the emperor Titus died in the month of September after a reign of just over 2 years. This revised chronology, therefore, places his death in the year A.D. 68; whereas the usual year for his death is given as A.D. 81.

Notice that the difference between the usual and revised chronologies is now 13 years, not 15 years. The reason is that Vespasian's reign in this revised chronology is 2 years longer than in the usual chronology.

Suetonius states Titus was born on Dec. 30 of the year that the emperor Gaius (Caligula) died, and that Titus died in Sept. at the age of 41 years.[1021] In the usual chronology, Gaius died in January of A.D. 41. If Titus was born in Dec. of that year (11 months later), then he would then turn 41 in Dec. of A.D. 82, and he would still be 41 years of age if he died the following Sept., in A.D. 83. But the usual chronology places Titus' death in Sept. of A.D. 81. Thus, there is a two-year error in the usual chronology between the death of Gaius and the death of Titus.

My revised chronology has the death of Gaius in A.D. 26. If Titus were born in Dec. of A.D. 26, then he would turn 41 in Dec. of A.D. 67 and would still be 41 (plus about 9 months) when he died in Sept. of A.D. 68. Since Titus' reign was only 2 years, 2 months, 20 days long, this line of reasoning further supports the date for the end of Vespasian's reign as June of A.D. 66. That date for Vespasian's death also follows closely the recorded observations of Chinese astronomers of two very conspicuous comets: Halley's Comet (Jan.-April of A.D. 66) and another "long-tailed star" (July-Sept.) A.D. 65. Thus the comet information and the information on the length of Titus' life both support the same year for the death of Vespasian—A.D. 66.

The two-year error in the usual chronology is found in the length of the reign of Vespasian. The generally-accepted length for Vespasian's reign is based on Dio's plain statement that he reigned for "ten years lacking six days."[1022] However, a reign of just under 12 years (counting from Vespasian's antedated accession to the throne on July 1) is necessary to account for the comet data and the length of Titus' life and reign. By comparison, the usual chronology cannot make these two criteria fit together. If Vespasian's reign were 2 years longer in the usual chronology, there would be no comet preceding his death. But if Vespasian's reign is kept the usual length of about 10 years, the length of Titus' life does not fit. Furthermore, the comet that coincided with Vespasian's death in the usual chronology does not match Dio's description. That comet was observed in A.D. 79 by the ancient Korean astronomers for only 20 days, and not for a long time, as Dio stated.

Domitian (Sept. A.D. 68 to Sept. A.D. 83)

The emperor Domitian was a son of Vespasian and brother of Titus. The emperor Titus was regarded as wise and conscientious; yet his reign was short. The emperor Domitian was regarded as cruel, avaricious, and self-indulgent; yet his reign was long. Suetonius tells us that Domitian died on Sept. 18, "in the fifteenth year of his reign."[1023] This phrase means that Domitian died during 15th full calendar year of his reign. In the Roman system of numbering the years, the first partial year of an emperor's reign was not counted. Thus Domitian's first year would be A.D. 69, even though he began his reign upon the death of Titus in Sept. of A.D. 68. The 15th year of Domitian's reign would then be A.D. 83.

Dio plainly states that Domitian reigned for "fifteen years and five days."[1024] Counting forward 15 years and 5 days from Sept. 13 of A.D. 68 brings us to Sept. 18 of A.D. 83. Therefore, Dio and Suetonius agree about the length of Domitian's reign and the date of his death.

The usual chronology has Domitian's reign from A.D. 81 to A.D. 96, a reign of just over 15 years. This revised chronology places Domitian's reign from Sept. A.D. 68 to Sept. A.D. 83, also a reign of just over 15 years.

Suetonius gives one additional clue as to the year of Domitian's death. He tells us that, just before his death, Domitian spoke about the moon entering Aquarius as if it was a bad omen for himself. "There will be blood on the Moon as she enters Aquarius, and a deed will be done for everyone to talk about throughout the entire world."[1025] The moon entered Aquarius, prior to Domitian's death, in both Sept. of A.D. 83 and Sept. of A.D. 96.[1026]

19. The Destruction of the Temple in A.D. 56

In this revised chronology, the reigns of Nero and Vespasian are placed years earlier than in the generally-accepted chronology. Thus the war between the Jews and the Romans, as well as the destruction of the Temple, must also be placed in an earlier time frame. Chapter 14 of this book presents an explanation of the timing of these events. Though the widely-accepted date for the destruction of the Temple is A.D. 70, the above conclusions, and the further evidence found in chapter 14, clearly support A.D. 56 as the correct year for that event.

20. Errors of modern historians

How could so many historians and Biblical scholars be wrong about the dates for the reigns of these Roman emperors? The vast majority of historians and scholars accept the usual chronology for these events, such as 44 B.C. as the year of Julius Caesar's death and A.D. 14 as the year of Augustus' death, without examination. They have accepted what has been handed down to them as if it were proven fact; they have not arrived at these dates by means of their own study of the evidence. Some may examine the evidence in an attempt to support what they have already accepted. But I know of no modern historian or Biblical chronologist (other than myself) who has attempted to determine the year of Julius Caesar's death, or the year of Augustus' death, or similar dates, starting from scratch, with no predetermined conclusion in mind. Modern chronological arguments for this time period are typically based on the assumption that Julius Caesar died in 44 B.C., Augustus died in A.D. 14, etc.

I myself began this study accepting the usual dates for the reigns of the Roman emperors. Only when I noticed some discrepancies in the data on eclipses and comets was I drawn to determine these dates anew, without relying on the usual assumptions. I think that if historians and Biblical scholars were to examine the evidence (which I review in chapters 12, 13, and 14 of this book) with an open mind, they would at least conclude that the generally-accepted dates are reasonably in dispute. Furthermore, I believe that the evidence presented above is sufficient to establish this revised chronology as the correct one.

Chapter 14
The Fall of Jerusalem

Josephus, Eyewitness Account

Josephus was one of the leaders of the Jews in the revolt against the Romans. He was eventually captured by the Romans and put in prison. When he was captured, he met Vespasian, the Roman general in charge of the war against the Jews. At that time, Josephus predicted that Vespasian would become emperor. Dio describes a number of portents which foreshadowed the rise of Vespasian to power. "These portents needed interpretation; but not so the saying of a Jew named Josephus: he, having earlier been captured by Vespasian and imprisoned, laughed and said: 'You may imprison me now, but a year from now, when you have become emperor, you will release me.' "[1027] Josephus himself gives an account of this prediction (but he does not mention a one-year time frame).[1028] When Vespasian became emperor, he remembered the prediction of Josephus and had him released.[1029] Josephus became a Roman citizen and for the rest of his life had the favor of the emperor Vespasian, as well as his sons Titus and Domitian (subsequent emperors of Rome).

Josephus was an eyewitness to the war between the Jews and the Romans, the war which ended with the destruction of the Second Temple of Jerusalem. Josephus even went to Jerusalem, to speak to the Jews on behalf of the Romans, during the siege, after he had been released from prison. His eyewitness account provides strong evidence, which cannot be ignored in any chronology of the fall of Jerusalem.

The Timeline of Events

Most of what Josephus tells us about this war is found in his work *The Wars of the Jews.* A few comments are found at the end of his work, *The Antiquities of the Jews.* The war began in Nero's 12th year, which was the second year of the reign of Florus over Judea. "Now this war began in the second year of the government of Florus, and the twelfth year of the reign of Nero."[1030] In his work *The Wars of the Jews*, Josephus give a more precise account of the start of this war. He places the start of the war in the spring of Nero's 12th year: "...at the same time began the war, in the twelfth year of the reign of Nero...in the month of Artemissus [Iyar]."[1031] In this revised chronology, the 12th year of Nero was the year A.D. 51.

Josephus then details a number of events in this conflict, often citing the month, or month and day, when an event occurred. He mentions the month of Lous [Ab][1032] (in the summer), the subsequent month of Gorpieus [Elul],[1033] and the Feast of Tabernacles during the month of Hyperbereteus [Tishri][1034] (in the fall). These months must be contained within the 12th year of Nero's reign, for he mentions a subsequent event, a battle, which happened "on the eighth day of the month of Dius [Marhesvan], in the twelfth year of the reign of Nero."[1035] The month of Marhesvan (or Heshvan) is in the late fall.

Josephus then describes his own actions in preparing the Jews of Galilee for an all-out war with the Romans.[1036] These lengthy preparations must have occurred during the winter of Nero's 12th to 13th years, A.D. 51/52. Spring is the time when kings go to war, so winter is the time when they prepare for war. Book 2 of *The Wars of the Jews* ends with these preparations for war. Book 3 begins with Nero sending Vespasian to fight the war against the Jews, which therefore occurred in the spring of Nero's 13th year, A.D. 52. As the events of Book 3 progress, Josephus mentions the month of Artemisius [Iyar],[1037] and the month of Desius [Sivan].[1038] These dates are followed by the date for the capture of the city of Jotapata, "in the thirteenth year of the reign of Nero, on the first day of the month of Panemus [Tamuz]."[1039] Thus Jotapata fell in the summer of A.D. 52. Book 3 then ends with the mention of the month of Gorpiaeus [Elul].[1040] Thus Book 3 ends in the late summer of Nero's 13th year, A.D. 52.

Book 4 states in its title, "CONTAINING THE INTERVAL OF ABOUT ONE YEAR."[1041] Yet the timeline contained therein is clearly more than two years. Book 3 ends in late summer of A.D. 52, so Book 4 must begin in the fall of A.D. 52. Book 4 contains the death of Nero[1042] (June A.D. 53), the death of Galba seven months later[1043] (Jan. A.D. 54), the death of Otho three months later[1044] (April, A.D. 54), the declaration of Vespasian as emperor by his troops, but before he obtained the throne[1045] (summer A.D. 54), and the wintertime battle that resulted in Vitellius' death[1046] (Dec. A.D. 54). Thereafter, Book 4 describes Vespasian setting out for Rome "as the winter was now almost over."[1047] In the view of Josephus, a Jewish priest, the winter would end about the time of the Spring Equinox and the month of Nisan, in late March. But Book 4 does not end with Vespasian departing from Alexandria. The end of Book 4 describes Titus and his troops traveling to Caesarea.[1048] How long this journey took is discussed in detail below.

Thus Book 4 begins in the fall of A.D. 52 and it ends no earlier than March of A.D. 55. The length of time encompassed by Book 4 is clearly more than 2 years: late A.D. 52, plus all of A.D. 53 and 54, and the early part of A.D. 55 as well. Even in the usual chronology (dating these events in the late A.D. 60's), the length of time must be given as well over two years. Therefore, the title of Book 4, which states the length of time as about one year, is in error.

Near the end of Book 4 of *The Wars of the Jews*, a battle is described between the troops of Vitellius and those loyal to Vespasian.[1049] Josephus places the death of Vitellius at the time of this battle. The date Josephus gives is "the third day of the month of Apelleus [Casleu]."[1050] The month name in brackets is the translator's comment giving the equivalent month, Kislev, in the Jewish calendar. Josephus wrote the month name Apelleus, which is from Macedonian calendar. Tacitus places this same battle, and the death of Vitellius, not long after Dec. 18.[1051] A common interpretation of Tacitus places this same battle described by Josephus on Dec. 20.[1052]

For the year A.D. 69, the third day of the month in the Jewish or Macedonian calendars would occur in early December, a couple of weeks before the date given by Tacitus.[1053] For the year A.D. 54, the third day of the month in the Jewish and Macedonian lunar calendars coincides with Dec. 20, in agreement with Tacitus.[1054] The month, though, is Tevet, not Kislev. In no year does the month of Kislev begin as late as Dec. 18. This would mean that the previous Nisan 14, the start of Passover, would have fall on or about May 10—too late a date for the Passover, even following a Jewish leap year (when a 13th month is added to the calendar just before Nisan). However, Josephus did not write the month name of Kislev, rather he wrote the Macedonian calendar month name of Apelleus. Usually, during this time period, the month of Apelleus would correspond to the month of Kislev.[1055] But this correlation could easily have been out of synch for brief periods.

The Macedonian calendar uses the month of Artemissus as the leap month (the month to be repeated for the 13th month in a leap year), but the Jewish calendar uses the month of Adar (repeated as AdarII in leap years). If the Macedonian calendar, in a particular year, adds a second Artemissus for a leap year, and if the Jewish calendar does not make that year a leap year, then the correlation of the months between those two calendars will change. In such a case the Macedonian month of Apelleus would correspond to the month of Tevet, not Kislev. Tevet is the month after Kislev; Tevet 3 coincided with December 20 in the year A.D. 54. The months would then return to their usual synchronization when the Jewish calendar added a Second Adar during a Jewish leap year. (See Appendix I, Chart 5 for an example of the correlation between the Jewish and Macedonian calendars.)

The Macedonian calendar did not always have the same leap years as in the Jewish calendar. The reason is that the Jews chose their leap years based on certain religious considerations. For example, the grain had to be ready for harvest so that it could be offered to God as first fruits during the Passover. If the grain was not ready, the Jews would add a leap month of AdarII and so delay the start of Passover. The Macedonians did not have such considerations affecting their choice of leap years.

In this way, the correlation of the months between the Macedonian and Jewish calendars could have varied, in some years, by one month. The differences between the leap years in the Macedonian and Jewish calendars can also explain another chronological problem in the writings of Josephus about the fall of Jerusalem. There appears to be an extra month in Josephus' detailed, eyewitness account of the siege of Jerusalem (see below, "The Siege of Jerusalem").

There is another possible explanation for Josephus' statement that Vitellius was defeated on Apelleus 3. Perhaps Josephus' date is simply off by one month. Josephus was an eyewitness to the siege of Jerusalem, but at this point in time, before Vespasian became emperor, Josephus was still in prison. He was released from prison by Vespasian after he became emperor. It is therefore possible that the date was Audynaios 3 (the month after Apelleus in the Macedonian calendar). The month of Audynaios in the Macedonian calendar usually coincides with the month of Tevet in the Jewish calendar.

Either of the above explanations is possible, but I favor the latter explanation. My reconstruction of the Macedonian/Jewish calendars for that time period, based on the analysis of the siege of Jerusalem below, places Audynaios 3 on Tevet 3 and December 20 in the year in question, A.D. 54. See Appendix I, Chart 5 for the correlation between these calendars.

From Alexandria to Caesarea

Vespasian's troops were successful in defeating Vitellius' troops at Rome in late December of A.D. 54. Tacitus places this victory about Dec. 20.[1056] But Vespasian himself was not in Rome at the time. According to Josephus, Vespasian was at Alexandria, in Egypt, when the news of his troops' victory reached him.[1057] It would have taken 6 to 8 weeks for a ship to travel from Rome to Alexandria in winter (when sailing the Mediterranean is difficult and dangerous).[1058] Their mission to inform Vespasian that he was now emperor of Rome was important enough to justify this risk. So Vespasian would not have learned of his troops' success in Rome until sometime in February of A.D. 55 (6 to 8 weeks after his victory in late December).

Now, according to Josephus, Vespasian did not travel immediately to Rome, but spent some time in Alexandria receiving emissaries from various nations and celebrating his accession to the throne.[1059] These event would occupy at least a few weeks, placing Vespasian's departure from Alexandria no earlier than March of A.D. 55. Josephus also states that Vespasian departed from Alexandria for Rome when winter was nearly over, which would again seem to be sometime in March. For a Jewish priest such as Josephus, the end of winter would be the days leading up to the Spring Equinox and the month of Nisan. The Spring Equinox occurred about March 22 or 23 during this time period.

On the other hand, Tacitus describes Vespasian spending a longer amount of time at Alexandria. "In the course of the months which Vespasian spent at Alexandria, waiting for the regular season of summer winds when the sea could be relied upon...."[1060] Tacitus here places Vespasian's departure from Alexandria at least a few months later than Josephus. If Vespasian waited months before returning to Rome, and if he waited for the summer winds, this would seem to place his departure later than March, in perhaps May or June. Dio seems to agree with Tacitus on this point. He tells us that Vespasian had intended to wait for Titus to capture Jerusalem before returning to Rome, but that time dragged on and so Vespasian set out for Rome anyway.[1061]

When Vespasian heard the good news that he was now emperor of Rome, he did not immediately send Titus to capture Jerusalem. According to Josephus, Titus remained at Alexandria to assist his father "in settling that government which had been newly conferred upon them by God...."[1062] Vespasian heard of his victory at Rome sometime in February, and Titus remained with Vespasian at Alexandria for some length of time before setting out to capture Jerusalem. Thus the earliest that Titus could have set out for Jerusalem would be sometime in March, as Josephus seems to indicate.[1063] Dio places Vespasian's departure for Rome at a later date, but he also indicates that Titus departed for Judea before Vespasian left Alexandria, so there is no real conflict between Josephus and Dio on this point.

How long did it take Titus to travel from Alexandria to Jerusalem? Neither Tacitus nor Dio give us any detailed information on the time period between Titus departing from Alexandria and the beginning of the siege of Jerusalem. Josephus details a series of locations within Egypt through which Titus marched with his army.[1064] From Egypt, Titus traveled along the coast, stopping to rest with his army at a series of cities: Rhinocolura, Raphia, Gaza, Ascalon, Joppa, and Caesarea.[1065] According to Josephus, Titus gathered his forces at Caesarea.[1066] The journey was mainly on foot; boats were used only for one short portion of the journey while they were still in Egypt. The journey from Alexandria to Caesarea is between 350 and 400 miles.[1067] To march an army on foot for most of that distance, stopping to rest at several places along the way, would take 4 weeks or longer. So, if Titus left Alexandria in mid to late March, he would have arrived at Caesarea in mid to late April, in the year A.D. 55. On the other hand, if we follow Dio and Tacitus on this point, Titus may have left Alexandria, and arrived at Caesarea, a month or two later.

Preparations at Caesarea

At Caesarea, Titus had to gather his forces from other areas. According to Tacitus, the Twenty-Second and Third legions were brought up from Alexandria. The Twelfth legion joined Titus from Syria. The Fifth, Tenth, and Fifteenth legions joined Titus from various areas within Judea. In addition to these forces, there were additional infantry and cavalry, plus troops sent from king Agrippa II, king Sohaemus (from Emesa, north of Phoenicia), and "supporting forces offered by King Antiochus."[1068] There were also soldiers from Rome and Italy, and some Arab soldiers. "This then was the army with which Titus entered enemy territory."[1069]

This army was assembled from many different places, some at a considerable distance from Caesarea. Notice also that this army was assembled before Titus entered enemy territory (Judea). Titus assembled his forces, prepared his strategy, and built his engines of war, at Caesarea. Titus also had to obtain information about the preparedness and condition of Jerusalem. How long would it take to complete these tasks and assemble such a vast army gathered from many locations? These tasks must have taken at least several months. Yet the usual chronology allows little or no time for this task.

Tacitus tells us that Titus, when Vespasian chose him to complete the conquest of Judea, "received added support and recognition, as provinces and armies vied in displaying their enthusiasm."[1070] The distant provinces had to hear the news that Titus was assembling an army to capture Jerusalem, then respond by sending their support. Again, the time required would be months, not days.

From Caesarea to Jerusalem

After preparing his legions, and readying the engines of war (machines used to besiege a city, such as catapults and battering rams), he then had to travel with this larger army and its engines of war from Caesarea to Jerusalem. This distance, in a straight line on a map, is about 60 miles. The distance actually traveled by the army would be more like 80 miles. This trip would proceed much more slowly than the trip from Alexandria for several reasons. First, the army was much larger, having been joined by forces from other areas. Josephus gives a detailed description of all the portions of the army that traveled to Jerusalem; it was a large and diverse group, but well organized.[1071] Second, the army traveled with its engines of war.[1072] Third, they had to travel with greater caution, prepared for imminent battle. As Tacitus put it, Titus "advanced in an orderly fashion, maintaining good reconnaissance and a state of readiness for battle...."[1073] Titus and his army did not travel with haste to Jerusalem. For these reasons, this journey from Caesarea to Jerusalem would have taken perhaps 2 weeks or longer.

Titus Arrives at Jerusalem

Josephus describes the Roman army as arriving at Jerusalem well before the Passover, which begins on Nisan 14. "As now the war abroad ceased for a while, the sedition within was revived; and on the feast of unleavened bread, which was come, it being the fourteenth day of the month Xanthicus [Nisan]....”[1074] Here Josephus mentions the start of Passover on the 14th day of the month Xanthicus, a month in the Macedonian calendar, which in this year must have coincided with the Jewish month of Nisan.

Prior to Nisan 14, there was “the war abroad,” meaning the battles between the Jews and the Romans away from Jerusalem.[1075] Josephus describes these battles in some detail earlier in this same book.[1076] Then there was a cessation in the fighting, during which the internal conflicts among the Jews within the city were revived.[1077] Dio also mentions both the battles outside the city and a cessation in the hostilities.[1078] During this respite from the fighting, Titus tried to convince the Jews “by certain representations and promises” to surrender the city.[1079] After the battles outside the city, during this respite from the fighting, the Passover began. Therefore, the arrival of Titus at Jerusalem must have preceded the Passover by some length of time, perhaps 2 weeks or longer. Thus Titus arrived at Jerusalem either at the start of the month of Xanthicus (Nisan), or during the previous month of Dystros (Adar).

Near the end of Book 5, Josephus summarizes events by saying that the Romans pitched their camp by the city of Jerusalem on the 14th day of Xanthicus [Nisan]. However, this is not to say that they arrived on that day. They had to fight a number of battles, and defeat the Jews outside the city walls, before they could pitch camp and thereafter begin the siege. This point is clear from the detailed description of events that Josephus gives before his mention of the start of Passover on Nisan 14.[1080]

In the usual chronology, Titus arrived at Jerusalem before the Passover of A.D. 70, which began on began on Friday, April 13.[1081] Titus could not have traveled from Alexandria to Caesarea, assembled his army, then traveled from Caesarea to Jerusalem, and arrived before the Passover in A.D. 70, as the usual chronology asserts. Even if one compresses these events into the shortest imaginable time, the time required for Titus to travel from Alexandria to Caesarea, gather his forces at Caesarea, and then travel to Jerusalem with a vast and well-prepared army is longer than can be fit into the usual chronology. The attempt to fit events into the shortest possible amount of time is a common error in Biblical chronology. Titus could not have left Alexandria in early A.D. 70 and arrived at Jerusalem with his well-prepared and vast army before Passover that same year.

In my revised chronology, Titus departed from Alexandria in March or April of A.D. 55. That year the Passover could have begun either on March 30 or on April 29. The later date is only possible if the Jews added a leap month of AdarII in A.D. 55 in order to avoid having to add a leap month during the Sabbatical year of A.D. 56 (fall of A.D. 55 to fall of A.D. 56). Placing a leap year in the year prior to a Sabbatical year was commonly done to avoid having an extra month in a Sabbatical year, a year when Jews could neither plant nor harvest. But even with the latest possible date for the Passover, on April 29, the Roman army could not have arrived at Jerusalem before the Passover. At least a month is needed to account for the journey of Titus and two Roman legions from Alexandria to Caesarea. Two weeks more accounts for the journey of Titus (and the full army he had assembled) from Caesarea to Jerusalem. Titus arrived at Jerusalem perhaps 2 weeks or more in advance of the Passover and fought a number of battles outside the city walls before being able to make camp and begin the siege. A minimum of 8 weeks can account for these events. But add to those 8 weeks the length of time needed to assemble and prepare such a huge army while Titus was at Caesarea, and the length of time clearly cannot be fit into the same year. Therefore, Titus did not arrive at Jerusalem in spring of A.D. 55, but the following year, in spring of A.D. 56.

This revised chronology allows sufficient time for Titus to complete all of the following: to remain in Alexandria for a while assisting his father with his new government; to move two full Roman legions from Alexandria to Caesarea; to assemble many additional legions, troops, and equipment at Caesarea; to receive support from the Roman provinces; to prepare the engines of war, strategies, and information about the current condition of Jerusalem; to move this large army in a cautious and orderly fashion to Jerusalem; and to arrive at Jerusalem in advance of the Jewish Passover.

The Length of the War

The usual chronology has the war between the Jews and the Romans beginning in the spring of Nero's 12th year (A.D. 66, usual) and ending in the summer of A.D. 70. This length of time is just over 4 years. But, in this revised chronology, the length of the war is one year longer because Titus could not have besieged Jerusalem in the spring of the same year as he departed from Alexandria. See Appendix II, Section D, for a comparison of the revised and usual chronologies of the siege and destruction of Jerusalem.

How could a year's time be lost from the usual chronology of the fall of Jerusalem? The Roman historians did not write at length about the war with the Jews. Consequently, there are not enough chronological details in Dio or Tacitus to establish the length of the war as 4 years or 5 years. The Roman historians do not state the length of the war. Josephus also never states that the war lasted 4 years, nor does he state that it lasted 5 years. The length of the war is determined by various details given by the ancient historians, but it is never stated outright.

In my revised chronology of the war between the Jews and the Romans, there is one additional year than in the usual account of events. This additional year takes place, in the writings of Josephus, from the end of Book 4 of *The Wars of the Jews* through the early part of Book 5. During that year Titus traveled to Caesarea and gathered a vast array of soldiers, weapons, and resources, in order to prepare to capture Jerusalem. Also during that year, there was an internal conflict, a near civil war, within Jerusalem. This last event occupies most of the interest and the words of Josephus for that period of time (early in Book 5).[1082]

As shown above, Book 4 states in its title that it covers events lasting about a year, but it actually covers events lasting about 2½ years (fall of A.D. 52 to spring of A.D. 55). Book 5 states in its title, "CONTAINING THE INTERVAL OF NEAR SIX MONTHS."[1083] Yet, here again, the length of time encompassed by this book appears to be significantly longer than the title states. Josephus tells us little about Titus' preparations for war while he was at Caesarea. Instead, he describes events during that time period occurring at Jerusalem, namely the internal conflicts between three groups of Jews within the city.[1084] Thus Book 5 actually contains the interval of about a year, but the main focus of the book is the assault on Jerusalem, which occupied nearly 6 months.

The Siege of Jerusalem

Josephus was present at the siege of Jerusalem. He gives us a detailed eyewitness account of events, even telling us the exact days and the exact lengths of time for various events. His account of the months of the siege itself must be reasonably accurate. However, there is a problem with his chronology of the siege. There seems to be one more month of events described than can be accounted for by the dates Josephus gives.

As noted above, Titus and his army arrived at Jerusalem in advance of the Passover by perhaps two weeks or longer. In A.D. 56, the Passover would ordinarily have begun on April 17 (Nisan 14). However, A.D. 55/56 was a Sabbatical year and the Jews would not have added a leap month during a Sabbatical year. Doing so would prolong the length of time that they could neither plant nor harvest. To prevent leap years from coinciding with Sabbatical years, the Jewish religious leaders would often make the year prior to the Sabbatical year a leap year.

However, in A.D. 55, the nation of Israel was divided. Only Jerusalem had not yet fallen to the Romans; Jerusalem was divided from the rest of Israel. And within Jerusalem there was a kind of civil war, with the Jews being divided into three factions, as Josephus recounts in some detail.[1085] Because of the war and the internal strife, the Jewish leaders may not have had the foresight to add a leap month of AdarII to the calendar in spring of A.D. 55. This would place the Passover of A.D. 55 on March 30 (Nisan 14). This date falls after the Spring Equinox and so is late enough in the season not to cause any immediate problems with the calendar. But the following year, the dilemma would be that the Passover would either begin before the Spring Equinox or they would have to add a leap month, Second Adar, to the calendar during a Sabbatical year.

Since it was a time of war, they lacked an easy supply of grain from the surrounding countryside. The Jews would have been particularly unwilling to add an extra month to this Sabbatical year. They would have been much more willing to tolerate a Passover occurring before the Spring Equinox. As a result, the Passover of A.D. 56, which should have begun on April 17, most likely began on Friday, March 19.[1086] The Spring Equinox that year fell on the morning of March 22.[1087] This early date for Passover also allows for the additional month found in Josephus' chronology of the siege of Jerusalem (more on this below).

Given this early date for the Passover of A.D. 56, Titus and his army most likely arrived at Jerusalem in early March. This timing makes sense, in terms of the Roman strategy of war. Titus would not encamp his army around Jerusalem during the colder and wetter winter months.[1088] In mid February, with warmer weather approaching, Titus would have began the journey from Caesarea. He would then arrive at Jerusalem about two weeks or so later, in early March. This would be the best time of year to begin a prolonged siege. It would be unwise to begin the siege of such a well fortified city (perhaps the best fortified city the Romans ever captured) in summer or fall. The siege could have lasted for many months. If the Romans had to continue the siege during winter, they would be at a disadvantage. In fact, according to Josephus, if the Jews had not destroyed most of their supply of grain during fighting among themselves, they might have been able to withstand the siege for a much longer period of time.[1089] Thus Titus planned this siege to begin as early as possible in spring.

Josephus recounts a number of events which occurred about the time of the Passover, during the month of Xanthicus [Nisan].[1090] The month-name Xanthicus comes from the Macedonian calendar. Josephus tells us that Passover at Jerusalem began on the 14th of Xanthicus, so this month must have corresponded to the month of Nisan in the Jewish calendar that year. A number of battles occurred outside of the city of Jerusalem during this month.[1091]

After a series of battles outside the walls of Jerusalem, Titus made an assault on the first wall, which is the outer-most wall around the city. Josephus gives the date when the Roman army breached the first wall and took possession of the area between the second wall and the first wall: "the seventh day of the month of Artemisius [Iyar]."[1092] He also tells us that it took the Romans 15 days to breach this first wall.[1093] The date of Artemisius [Iyar] 7 coincided with Saturday, April 10, in A.D. 56. Counting the 15 days inclusively, the assault on the first wall began on Saturday, March 27 and Xanthicus [Nisan] 22. This timing makes sense in the context of the Roman strategies of war. Josephus tells us that the Jews would not attack on the Sabbath (Saturday), but they would fight defensively on that day. So the Roman strategy was to refrain from attacking on the Sabbath, so as to be able to concentrate all of their efforts on raising their siege works and embankments.[1094] Thus the Romans deliberately began the siege against the first wall on a Sabbath. Now the Romans also were able to complete the siege on a Sabbath, and this was not entirely by coincidence. They could put more time and effort into their siege works on the Sabbath and so they were more likely to complete this task on the Sabbath.

Titus was able to breach the second wall on the fifth day after the first wall had been taken.[1095] The date of this event must then be Wednesday, Artemisius [Iyar] 12 and April 15. But breach in the second wall was narrow, and the Romans were not able to hold their position against the Jews attacks.[1096] The Jews then defended the breach in the second wall for three days. On the fourth day, the Romans took the wall again, and the Jews retreated to the third wall.[1097] The 4th day would then be either Artemisius [Iyar] 15 or 16, and April 18 or 19, depending on whether or not Josephus counted the day the breach occurred as the first day of the four.

After the second wall was taken, for the second time, Titus demolished the second wall and began to determine how best to take the third wall.[1098] The task of demolishing the second wall, that is, of making the breach in the wall very large, may have taken at least several days. Titus did not immediately thereafter assault the third wall, rather he decided to "relax the siege for a little while" to see if the loss of the second wall and the famine might soften the Jews resolve to fight.[1099] The length of this respite from the siege is not given by Josephus, but it must have been at least several days. So, adding the time needed to demolish the second wall to the time for this respite from the siege brings us to late April or early May and to the end, or nearly the end of Artemisius [Iyar].

Then Josephus tells us that the usual time for paying the soldiers had arrived. The end of April, and perhaps part of early May, were taken up with the above-described events, so the distribution of pay most likely occurred in early to mid May. Since there were several Roman legions present, it took 4 days to distribute the money.[1100] On the 5th day, since the Jews had still not surrendered, Titus began to raise the siege works against the third wall. Clearly by now, the month of Artemisius [Iyar] has been completed, and we should be in the subsequent month of Daisios [Sivan]. However, Josephus gives the date of the raising of the siege works against the third wall as "the twelfth day of the month of Artemisius [Iyar]."[1101]

Notice that this date for the start of the siege against the third wall conflicts with the dates given for the fall of the second wall. The second wall was taken on Artemisius 12 [Iyar], then lost for a few days, then finally taken again on Artemisius [Iyar] 15 or 16. There are numerous events described between this final capture of the second wall and the start of the siege against the third wall. The assault on the third wall must have taken place on the 12th of the month after Artemisius. Yet Josephus was an eyewitness to these events, a Jewish priest (knowledge of the calendar is an integral part of the role of Jewish priest), and a Roman historian. So, we cannot suppose that he was in error. Furthermore, his description of subsequent events in no way supports the idea that this month was not Artemisius (as we shall see).

The only conclusion which fits the description given by Josephus is that there were two months named Artemisius, one after the other, in this particular year. This surprising conclusion is easily supported. Josephus doesn't give the month names by the Jewish calendar (Nisan, Iyar, etc.), instead he uses the month names of the Macedonian calendar (Xanthicus, Artemisius, etc.). The Jewish month names in the quotations from Josephus are in brackets because they were added by the translator/editor, not by Josephus himself. In the Jewish calendar, during a leap year, a 13th month is added by repeating the month of Adar. First Adar is followed by Second Adar (AdarI and AdarII). In the Macedonian calendar, the calendar is similarly arranged, but the leap month was the month of Artemisius.[1102] In a leap year, in the Macedonian calendar, the month of Artemisius would be followed by a second month called Artemisius. The year A.D. 56 would have been a leap year in the Jewish calendar, except that it coincided with the Sabbatical year. In the Macedonian calendar, A.D. 56 would also have been a leap year. That is why Josephus seems to describe two months worth of events all within the month called Artemisius.

The siege against the third wall began on the 12th of ArtemisiusII, which coincided with May 15, a Saturday. This timing accords with the Roman practice of beginning to raise siege works against the Jews on a Sabbath, when the Jews would not attack them. Notice that now the Macedonian and Jewish calendars are out of their usual synchronization, such that ArtemisiusII coincides with Sivan in the Jewish calendar, and the subsequent month of Daisios will now coincide with Tammuz. (See Appendix I, Chart 5.) According to Josephus, the siege works were completed on the 29th day of the same month, ArtemisiusII [Sivan].[1103] That date coincided with Tuesday, June 1, in A.D. 56.

Next followed a series of attempts by the Jews to destroy the siege works (embankments built to scale the wall). These attempts occupied about three days.[1104] The Jews were successful in destroying and damaging the siege works, so that the capture of the third wall was delayed. This brings us to about the third day of June and the second day of Daisios [Tammuz].

Titus then put his soldiers to work raising a wall around the city, to prevent the Jews from coming out to obtain food or to fight against the Romans. This task took only three days.[1105] Since Titus may have taken a day or two to decide on this course of action, this brings us to approximately June 7 and Daisios [Tammuz] 6 as the date for the completion of the Roman's wall.

The wall built around the city by the Romans did not suffice to cause the Jews to surrender. So Titus ordered the soldiers again to build siege works against the third wall.[1106] Josephus does not tell us how long Titus waited before determining this new course of action. However, he does say that these new siege works took 21 days to complete.[1107] These 21 days, plus the previous events, take up the entire month of Daisios. The building of the siege works probably began on the first Saturday (June 12; Daisios 11) after the Romans wall was completed, in accordance with the Roman practice. This timing also allows sufficient time, after the completion of the Roman's wall around the city, for Titus to decide that the wall was not working and that additional siege works needed to be built. Furthermore, Josephus tells us that the Jews made an attack on these new siege works, after they had been completed, "on the first day of the month Panemus."[1108] That date is the 21st day inclusive from Saturday, June 12 and Daisios 11. The first day of Panemus coincided with July 2 in A.D. 56.

Note: Because the Macedonian calendar included the second month of Artemisius due to the leap year, the Jewish calendar no longer had the usual synchronization with the Macedonian calendar. For this reason, the Jewish calendar month name, placed in brackets or parentheses next to the Macedonian calendar name by the translator/editor of *The Wars of the Jews*, ceases to be correct beginning with the second Artemisius. So, where Josephus wrote "the twelfth day of the month Artemisius," referring to the second instance of that month, the corresponding Jewish month would be Sivan, not Iyar.[1109] For the following month, which is Daisios in the Macedonian calendar, Josephus happens not to mention the month name at all. Instead, he simply gives the number of days each event occupied. Daisios would usually correspond to the Jewish month of Sivan, but, because of the second Artemisius, in this year Daisios corresponded to Tammuz. The next month name Josephus mentions is Panemus, which would usually correspond to Tammuz, but in this year corresponded to the Jewish month of Av (or "Ab").

When the siege works against the third wall were completed, about Panemus [Av] 1 and July 2, there began a series of battles at the place where the Roman embankment allowed them access to the part of the city within the third wall.[1110] The Romans first fought to get over the third wall, then they fought battles within the wall, including a battle at the entrance to the Temple of Jerusalem.[1111] Josephus mentions the dates of Panemus [Av] 1, Panemus 3, and Panemus 17, which correspond to July 2, July 4, and July 18 of A.D. 56.[1112] The date of Panemus [Av] 17 is given as the first day when Titus ordered his soldiers to dig up the foundations of the tower of Antonia.[1113]

Later on, Josephus describes a long battle that took place at the entrance to the Temple.[1114] Then he immediately states that the soldiers had spend 7 days overturning a part of the foundation for the tower of Antonia.[1115] The battle at the Temple therefore occurred on the seventh day from Panemus [Av] 17. Counting these 7 days inclusively brings us to Panemus [Av] 23, which is July 24, a Saturday. The battle began before dawn, about the ninth hour of the night, which would be about 3 hours before dawn. (The Jews divided the night into 12 hours and the day into 12 hours.) Notice that, here again, the Romans took account of the Jewish Sabbath when fighting against the Jews. They attacked the Temple before dawn on the Jewish day of rest, when they thought that the Jews would be off-guard.

Next the Romans brought their banks (the embankments they built for getting over the walls) to the wall around the Temple precincts.[1116] There followed several days of battles at the top of the walls.[1117] Then on the date of Panemus [Av] 27, which is July 28, the Jews set fire to an area near the cloisters, (buildings surrounding the Temple Sanctuary), in order to trap and kill some of the Roman soldiers.[1118] This fire destroyed one of the cloisters.[1119] The next day (Panemus 28/July 29), the Romans burnt down the northern cloister entirely.[1120] The month of Panemus here corresponds to the Jewish month of Av, not Tammuz (as has been generally believed).

The next prominent date mentioned by Josephus is Loos 8 (the month following Panemus in the Macedonian calendar). This month has been generally thought to correspond to the Jewish month of Av, but in this year, because of the previous addition of ArtemisiusII, Loos corresponded to the Jewish month of Elul. Josephus tells us that the Romans completed their siege works against the wall around the Temple precincts on Loos 8. They then moved their battering rams to a new location on that wall and they fought battles at the top of the wall on that day.[1121] Loos [Elul] 8 in A.D. 56 coincided with Saturday, August 7. Here again, the completion of Roman siege works fell upon a Saturday.

When Titus saw that his soldiers could not successfully get over the wall, because of strong resistance from the Jews, and that the walls were too strong for the Roman battering rams, he gave orders for the Temple gate to be set on fire.[1122] Details about the burning of the Temple are discussed below. After the Temple and many of the surrounding buildings were burned down, the Romans made an assault against the upper-most portion of the city of Jerusalem. This was the last area left to be conquered.

The embankments against the upper city began to be built on Loos [Elul] 20, August 19, and were completed in 18 days time on Gorpieus [Tishri] 7 and September 5.[1123] The next day, Gorpieus [Tishri] 8 and September 6, the upper city was captured by the Romans and the siege of Jerusalem was completed.[1124] In A.D. 56, the month of Gorpieus in the Macedonian calendar corresponded to the month of Tishri in the Jewish calendar. Thus the fall of Jerusalem was completed on Tishri 8 in A.D. 56. But the generally-accepted date give for the fall of Jerusalem is Elul 8. The generally-accepted date assumes the usual synchronization between the Macedonian and Jewish calendars, which was actually put out of synch by the addition of the month of ArtemisiusII in the leap year.

The Burning of the Temple

Now we come to an interesting problem in the chronology of the destruction of the Temple of Jerusalem. Rabbinical tradition holds that the Temple was burned in the month of Av. But Josephus, an eyewitness to these events, never states that the month was Av, but rather that the month was Loos (using the Macedonian calendar, not the Jewish calendar). Also, as shown above, the Macedonian calendar must have added a second Artemisius, due to a leap year, in A.D. 56. Thus the month in the Jewish calendar was Elul, not Av.

Why then would Rabbinical tradition call this month Av? First, the year A.D. 55 should have been a leap year in the Jewish calendar. Ordinarily, the Jews would have added a Second Adar to the spring of A.D. 55 in order to prepare the calendar for the coming Sabbatical year (A.D. 55/56). This would prevent Nisan 14 from falling before the Spring Equinox and would prevent a leap year from coinciding with a Sabbatical year. Leap years in the Jewish calendar have an extra month, a 13th month. But, in a Sabbatical year, the Jews could neither plant nor harvest. Sabbatical years often resulted in food shortages. The Jewish calendar would typically be adjusted to avoid adding the extra leap month to the Sabbatical year, so as not to lengthen the time when food would be in short supply. However, as explained above, the war with the Romans and the internal conflicts among the Jewish leaders within Jerusalem resulted in a lack of foresight concerning the calendar. Usually, the Jewish calendar would be controlled by the religious leaders at Jerusalem. But, at that time, Jerusalem was cut off from the rest of the Jewish nation. So, they did not add a Second Adar in the spring of A.D. 55 and they would have been unwilling to add an extra month in the spring of A.D. 56, during the war and the Sabbatical year. So, if we reconstruct the Jewish calendar of this time period, as it ought to have been arranged, the month the Temple burned down would have been Av (if the leap years had been arranged correctly. But, as the above analysis of Josephus' eyewitness account shows, the calendar was not arranged according to custom and tradition (due to the war). Thus the Temple actually burned down in the month of Elul.

Rabbinic tradition holds that the Temple burned in the month of Av because a proper reconstruction of the calendar, in accord with the usual way the calendar would be arranged, would call that month Av. Another reason is that the month in which the Temple burned, the Macedonian month of Loos, is usually equivalent to the Jewish month of Av. Also, the First Temple of Jerusalem was burned down in the month of Av (2 Kings 25:8; Jer 52:12).[1125] The parallel between those two events is given greater emphasis by considering the month of the burning of the Second Temple to be the same month, the month of Av.[1126] One can truly say that the Temple burned down in the month of Av, because that is the way the calendar should have been arranged. However, the month in which the Temple burned down was most likely observed as the month of Elul.

The Sabbatical Year

Every seventh year in the Jewish calendar is a Sabbatical year, a year like the seventh day, a Sabbath-like year. There are two prevalent theories about which years were Sabbatical years, one proposed by Ben Zion Wacholder, the other proposed by Benedict Zuckermann and Donald Blosser. These two competing theories differ from one another by only one year. Wacholder has the Sabbatical years as one year later than Zuckermann/Blosser.

My revised chronology places the destruction of the Second Temple of Jerusalem in A.D. 56, a Sabbatical year (A.D. 55/56) according to Wacholder. The usual chronology places the destruction of the Temple 14 years later, in A.D. 70, which was also a Sabbatical year (per Wacholder), or the year after a Sabbatical year (per Zuckermann).

Ancient Rabbinical tradition holds that the first and second Temples of Jerusalem were destroyed on the same month and day, Av 9.[1127] Sacred Scripture states that the First Temple was destroyed on the tenth day of the fifth month (Jer 52:12), which is Av 10. Josephus gives the date for the destruction of the Second Temple as also the tenth day of the fifth month: "and now that fatal day was come, according to the revolution of ages; it was the tenth day of the month Loos, upon which it was formerly burnt by the king of Babylon...."[1128] The month of Loos is the fifth month (Xanthicus, Artemisius, Daisios, Panemus, Loos...), though in a leap year the month of Artemisius is repeated. Josephus is able to correlate the timing of the destruction of the First and Second Temples by not counting the leap month of second Artemisius (which would make Loos the sixth month in a leap year). Thus the destruction of each Temple occurred in the fifth calendar month.

The apparent disagreement, as to whether the Second Temple was burnt on Loos 9 or 10, is resolved by the detailed description given by Josephus of the burning of the Temple. He explains that the fire started on Loos 8, beginning with the gates to the Temple.[1129] On the next day, Loos 9, though the Roman soldiers had been setting on fire the buildings around the Sanctuary of the Temple, such as the cloisters, Titus commanded his soldiers to put out the fire.[1130] Then, on Loos 10, a soldier set a window leading to the Sanctuary of the Temple (the "holy house") on fire and it spread to the Sanctuary. Titus then sent soldiers to stop the fire and went into the Sanctuary himself to order the soldiers to put out the fire, but they would not all follow his orders. The Temple then burnt to the ground.[1131] The Temple fire started on Loos 8 at the gates, spread on Loos 9 to the outer buildings of the Temple, and reached the Sanctuary of the Temple on Loos 10. That is why Rabbinical tradition counts the Temple as burning down on Loos 9, but Josephus counts the day as Loos 10. Of course, the Rabbinical tradition is that Loos coincided with the Jewish month of Av, whereas this revised chronology shows that Loos coincided with Elul.

Rabbinical tradition also states that Loos 9, the day the Temple burned down, was "immediately after the Sabbath," and "immediately after the Sabbatical year."[1132] The description given by Josephus fits this idea that Loos 8 was the Sabbath (Sat.). The Romans completed building the works they used to assault the Temple walls: "two of the legions had completed their banks on the eighth day of the month Loos."[1133] Earlier in this same work, Josephus explains that the Jews would not make an attack on the Sabbath, but they would repel an attack on the Sabbath.[1134] So the Romans took advantage of the Jews refusal to attack on the Sabbath by building their embankments, battering-rams, and other devices of war on that day.[1135] On Loos 8 two full Roman legions (3,000 to 6,000 troops per legion) were used on that day to work on the banks (artificial embankments constructed in warfare to scale walls). Furthermore, Dio states that the destruction of Jerusalem coincided with a Jewish Sabbath.[1136] The day he refers to was Loos 8, the day the Roman soldiers first entered the Temple's outer courts and the day the fire began. In A.D. 56, Loos 8 coincided with Saturday, August 7.[1137]

The generally-accepted year for the destruction of the Second Temple is A.D. 70. In that year, Loos 8 [Av 8] would fall on the Sabbath if the Jewish calendar months were determined by observation, rather than calculation. My revised year of the destruction of the Temple is A.D. 56. In that year, Loos 8 [Elul 8] coincides with the Sabbath if the calendar months were determined by calculation, not observation. Support for the idea that the Jewish calendar was determined by calculation, not observation, during this time period is found in chapter 17.

The Rabbinic tradition that the Temple was destroyed in the year immediately after the Sabbatical year can be interpreted two ways. Sabbatical years begin and end in the fall (and so any Sabbatical year will overlap with two Christian calendar years). According to Zuckermann, A.D. 68/69 was a Sabbatical year; but, according to Wacholder, A.D. 69/70 was the Sabbatical year.[1138] Thus, if one follows Zuckermann, the month of Av in the summer of A.D. 70 falls in the 11th month after the end of the Sabbatical year (A.D. 68/69). But, if one agrees with Wacholder, the month of Av in A.D. 70 was near the end of the Sabbatical year (A.D. 69/70). Both theories could be argued as fitting the Rabbinical tradition. The above considerations also apply to the year A.D. 56. Wacholder has A.D. 55/56 as the Sabbatical year, whereas Zuckermann has A.D. 54/55.

My revised chronology generally follows Wacholder for the Sabbatical years, with some modifications (see chapter 16). The expression "immediately after the Sabbatical year" fits Wacholder best, since the month of Av is the 11th month of the Sabbatical year and falls after the largest part of that time. On the other hand, the month of Av falls 11 months after the end of the Sabbatical year according to Zuckermann, which is rather long after the end of the Sabbatical year to fit well the expression "immediately after the Sabbatical year." Also, Zuckermann's chronology of the Sabbatical years conflicts with Josephus' assertion that the Jews intended to till and plant seed in the winter before the death of the emperor Gaius (see section 16 in chapter 13).

The Second Year of Vespasian

Josephus places the fall of Jerusalem in Vespasian's second year. "And thus was Jerusalem taken, in the second year of the reign of Vespasian, on the eighth day of the month of Gorpieus."[1139] According to the Roman method of counting the years of an emperor's reign, the first full calendar year of that emperor's reign was counted as year one.[1140] Vespasian antedated his reign to July 1 of the year after Nero's death (A.D. 54). At that time, Vitellius was still in power and Vespasian first began his attempt to become emperor. However, even with this antedating, the first full calendar year of Vespasian's reign was the calendar year beginning after that July 1, A.D. 54, starting point. This makes A.D. 55 the first year of Vespasian's reign. The second year of Vespasian's reign was therefore A.D. 56.

Josephus places the start of the war in Nero's 12th year.[1141] This 12th year is always counted from the first full calendar year after Nero became emperor. Josephus uses this method of counting the years of Nero's reign when giving us the date for the start of the war. Therefore, when he gives us the date for the end of the same war, Vespasian's second year, he would not suddenly switch to a different method of counting the years.

The usual chronology places the fall of Jerusalem in A.D. 70, which is the first full calendar year of Vespasian's reign in that chronology. That year is interpreted as Vespasian's second by counting the previous year as his first year. But the Roman custom was to count the first full calendar year as the first year of any emperor's reign. And Vespasian only antedated his reign to July 1, not January 1, of the year before he actually obtained the power and role of emperor. By comparison, my revised chronology places the fall of Jerusalem in the second full calendar year of Vespasian's reign.

The Comet of Jerusalem

Josephus does not mention those comets which the Romans associated with the deaths of various emperors. However, he does mention a comet associated with the destruction of Jerusalem and the Temple. "Thus there was a star resembling a sword, which stood over the city, and a comet, that continued for a whole year."[1142] Comets are not generally visible to the naked eye for an entire year; the longest period of time that any comet would be visible is several months. Perhaps the star appeared for a whole year (the sighting of a nova, or new star, is not too rare an event), or perhaps the star and the comet together took up about a year. In any case, the exact time of this comet's appearance is not clear from the text.

Josephus places this comet sighting during the war, not long before the destruction of the Temple. He writes about "the signs that were so evident and did so plainly foretell their future desolation."[1143] But these words refer to the future desolation of the destruction of the Temple, not to the beginning of the war. This conclusion is supported by the title of chapter 5 in book 6 of *The Wars of the Jews*, which specifically mentions the destruction of the Temple and the signs that preceded it: "...the Conflagration of the Holy House....the Signs that Preceded this Destruction."[1144] Also, Josephus separates the comment about the comet from his next comment, about the events occurring before the war began, by saying: "Thus also, before the Jews' rebellion, and before those commotions which preceded the war...."[1145] This comet then was observed well after the war began, and was interpreted as a foreshadowing of the destruction of the Temple at the end of the war.

According to Josephus, the rebellion of the Jews against the Romans began "in the twelfth year of the reign of Nero...in the month of Artemissus [Iyar]."[1146] The Jewish month of Iyar is in the spring; it is the month after Nisan. Nero's 12th year, in the usual chronology, was A.D. 66 and is considered year one of the Jewish rebellion. The usual date for the destruction of Jerusalem, near the end of this war, is the summer of A.D. 70. However, there is no extant record, from the ancient Chinese or Korean astronomers, of a comet sighting from May of A.D. 66 to Feb. of A.D. 71 inclusive, a period of time that encompasses the war between the Jews and the Romans. Two very conspicuous comets were sighted prior to the usual date given for the start of the Jewish rebellion. The comets of A.D. 65 and 66 (discussed in detail in chapter 13) were observed from July-Sept. of A.D. 65 and Jan.-Apr. of A.D. 66. Yet Josephus does not mention a comet sighting prior to the war (which would have foreshadowed the start of the war), but rather one during the war which foreshadowed the destruction of the Temple, well after the war began. The usual chronology does not fit the comet sighting as described by Josephus.

In my revised chronology, the Jewish rebellion began in the spring of A.D. 51, and the destruction of Jerusalem occurred in summer of A.D. 56. There are a number of comets mentioned in the records of the ancient astronomers during these years.[1147] However the comet most closely fitting Josephus' description was sighted by the ancient Chinese astronomers from Dec. of A.D. 55 to March of A.D. 56. The length of the observation was fairly long, 113 days. And the sighting was not long before the destruction of the

Temple in summer of A.D. 56. The length of the observation of this comet is not near to a year, but Joseph may have been referring to the star (nova), or to the combination of star and comet, when he gives the length of time as about a year.[1148]

Jesus, Son of Ananus

This Jesus is not Jesus of Nazareth, the Messiah, but another man named Jesus who lived years after Christ died and rose from the dead. This Jesus, son of Ananus, predicted the destruction of Jerusalem years before the war even began. Josephus tells us that this prediction began four years before the war began, at the time of the Feast of Tabernacles, which is in the autumn.[1149] Now the war began, according to Josephus, in the spring of Nero's 12th year, in the Jewish month of Iyar (the month after Nisan).[1150] So, when Josephus says that this man began making this prediction four years earlier, he is referring to Nero's 8th year as being 4 years before Nero's 12th year. But the predictions began in the autumn, whereas the war began in the spring. So the length of time was not four full years before the war began, but 3.5 years (fall of Nero's 8th year to spring of his 12th year).

Josephus states the entire length of time during which this man continued proclaiming the impending destruction of Jerusalem, both before and during the war, as 7 years and 5 months.[1151] Counting forward 7 years from the fall of Nero's 8th year (A.D. 47 revised), at the time of the Feast of Tabernacles, brings us to the fall of the year after Nero's death (A.D. 54 revised). Counting forward 5 more months brings us to early in the first full calendar year of Vespasian's reign (A.D. 55 revised), just after he defeated Vitellius and became emperor of Rome in fact. At that time, Vespasian had sent his son Titus to besiege and capture Jerusalem.[1152] But by this early date, the siege itself had not yet begun. Yet, according to Josephus, the man who made this prediction of the destruction of Jerusalem died during the siege.[1153]

Josephus calculates the length of time that this man was making the prophecy of the destruction of Jerusalem as 7 years and 5 months. In the title of Book 4 of *The Wars of the Jews*, Josephus writes "CONTAINING THE INTERVAL OF ABOUT ONE YEAR."[1154] Yet Book 4 clearly contains the interval of just over two years. Book 3 ends with the date of Elul 8 (late summer) during the 13th year of Nero's reign (A.D. 52).[1155] Book 4 contains the death of Nero[1156] (June A.D. 53), the death of Galba seven months later[1157] (winter A.D. 53/54), the death of Otho three months later[1158] (spring A.D. 54), the declaration of Vespasian as emperor by his troops, but before he obtained the throne[1159] (summer A.D. 54), and the wintertime battle which resulted in Vitellius' death[1160] (winter A.D. 54/55). Thus Book 4 begins in the fall of A.D. 52 and it ends in the winter of A.D. 54/55. The length of time encompassed by Book 4 is clearly more than 2 years: late A.D. 52, plus all of A.D. 53 and 54. Even in the usual chronology (dating these events in the late A.D. 60's), the length of time is over two years. Here is a one year error in Josephus' counting of the length of time for these events. The length of time that the man was predicting the destruction of Jerusalem could have been 8 years and 5 months, owing to this one year error.

Alternately, the length of time could be correct and the starting point off by one year. Perhaps he began his predictions in the fourth year inclusive before the war, so that the four years were Nero's 9th, 10th, 11th, and 12th. The 7 years and 5 months length of time would then extend well into the time when the siege of Jerusalem was underway, in early A.D. 56.

Chapter 15
Calendar Suggestions

Read This Twice

This chapter contains suggestions for changes to the liturgical calendar of the Church. These suggested changes are based on my understanding of the true dates of important events in the lives of Jesus and Mary. I myself currently ignore this suggested calendar. I follow the current liturgical calendar of the Catholic Church. I am **not** asking anyone to follow this suggested calendar instead of the Church's calendar. If anyone thinks that I have correctly understood the true dates of events in the life of Christ, let them nevertheless follow the Church's calendar, not this suggested calendar, until such time, if any, that the Church adopts some of these suggestions.

I expect that the Church will eventually put some of these changes into effect in the liturgical calendar. I do not expect all of these suggestions to be adopted by the Church. I will follow the liturgical calendar of the Catholic Church in any case. I believe that the teaching of the Holy Catholic Church is God's teaching, without exception.

Should the Liturgical Calendar Be Changed?

The Christian liturgical calendar should be ordered according to Christ's life. The liturgical calendar is not merely a method of keeping track of time, it is a reflection of our participation in the life of Christ. As we follow the holy days of the liturgical calendar, we are following and becoming a part of events in the life of Jesus, our Savior. In this chapter, I make suggestions for changes in the liturgical and civil calendars, so as to bring the calendar in closer conformity to the life of Christ.

This chapter is meant to be read by all Christians, not only by those leaders who might have some influence over the liturgical calendar. The liturgical calendar is a part of the life and worship of all Christians, and so any changes to the calendar must both conform to the will of God and be understood by the ordinary Christian. May the members of the Church consider the liturgical calendar and its relationship to the lives of Jesus and Mary.

The current liturgical calendar places the celebration of events in the lives of Jesus and Mary, in many cases, on days other than the days when these events occurred. This book presents a comprehensive set of evidence for the true dates of these events. The liturgical calendar should be changed so that the date for each celebration matches the true date, as much as possible. The liturgical calendar must be based on the truth because we worship Jesus Christ, Who is Truth.

Change is difficult for stubborn and sinful human beings such as ourselves. We say, "The old wine is good." People don't like to change. We often resist change, even when changing is the right thing to do. In this case, the difficult path is the correct path to follow, so follow it we must. Yes, I know that some people will oppose changing the liturgical calendar. But Truth is First. The liturgical calendar must change to conform to the true dates and to the will of God.

Will the Liturgical Calendar Be Changed?

For those readers who believe, I offer this proof that the liturgical calendar will certainly be changed to conform more closely to the true dates of events in the lives of Jesus and Mary. At Medjugorje, the Virgin Mary revealed that the true date of her birth is August 5 (see chapter 9 for details). She asked Christians to celebrate her birthday on August 5, with three days of fasting. At Medjugorje, the Virgin Mary's birthday is celebrated on August 5 and many pilgrims to Medjugorje also accept this as the true date of Mary's birth.

The Virgin Mary is asking the people of Medjugorje, and Christians all over the world, to celebrate her birthday on August 5. Yet the Church celebrates the birth of the Virgin Mary on September 8. The Virgin Mary is not opposing or contradicting the Church. The Virgin Mary is leading the Church and the faithful according to the plan of Jesus Christ. She is leading the Church to an eventual change in the liturgical calendar. The Virgin Mary is God's Holy Servant. She tells us the true date of her birth because God wants us to know the true date of her birth and the true dates of other important events in the lives of Jesus and Mary. The date for the celebration of Mary's birth in the liturgical calendar will be changed to August 5. Mary's plan is God's plan and God's plan cannot fail.

The Virgin Mary dwells in Eternity with the Most Holy Trinity. The Virgin Mary's request from Heaven to the Church is God's request. It is the will of God that the liturgical calendar be eventually changed so that the Virgin Mary's birthday be celebrated on August 5, the actual day of her birth. The Church will follow Mary's request to celebrate her birthday on August 5, because the Church is responsive to the will of God. When Mary leads the Church to change the liturgical calendar in this way, she is leading us according to God's plan. The Virgin understands.

Other Changes in the Calendar

The liturgical celebration of the birth of the Virgin Mary will be moved to August 5. I expect that this inevitable change in the Christian liturgical calendar will be accompanied by at least several other changes, as detailed in this chapter. Since the celebration of the Virgin Mary's birth must be moved to the true date, about a month earlier on August 5, the celebration of her Immaculate Conception must also be moved to the true date, a month earlier. We must celebrate both her conception and her birth on the correct dates. Since Mary was in the womb of her mother Saint Ann about nine months, the date for the celebration of Mary's Immaculate Conception must be placed about nine months earlier than the date for her birth on August 5. If the date for Mary's birth is changed to the true date, then so also must the date for her Immaculate Conception be changed to the true date.

Notice that the Virgin Mary herself, in revealing that her real birthday is August 5, is also revealing that the dates in the Church's liturgical calendar do not necessarily match the true dates of the events. If you believe what the Virgin Mary revealed at Medjugorje, then you must conclude that both the true date for her birth and the true date for her Immaculate Conception are different than the date for their celebration in the liturgical calendar. And you must also admit the possibility that other dates in the liturgical calendar do not match the true dates. In leading us to celebrate her birthday on the true date, she is leading the Church to make changes throughout the liturgical calendar, so as to match the true dates of events, as closely as possible. I believe that God wants most of the important events in the lives of Jesus and Mary to be celebrated on the actual month and day that they occurred, including the births and conceptions of Mary and Jesus.

However, I do not believe that God wants every event to be celebrated on the same day of the month as the event actually occurred. For example, our celebration of the death and Resurrection of Jesus Christ should take place on the same day of the week as these events happened (Good Friday and Easter Sunday), instead of on the same day of the month (April 7 and 9). Most years April 7 does not fall on a Friday, so we must choose between celebrating on the same day of the week, or on the same day of the month as these events occurred. In any year when April 7 falls on a Friday, as in the year of Christ's death, the Church should celebrate Good Friday on that day, Friday, April 7, and Easter Sunday on Sunday, April 9. Otherwise, Good Friday and Easter Sunday should be celebrated on a Friday and Sunday close to the dates of April 7 and 9.

When Will the Liturgical Calendar Be Changed?

I am suggesting changes to the liturgical calendar of the Catholic Church. But I say more. Before these suggested changes are accepted and made a part of the calendar, all Christians will be united in one Holy Catholic Church. If the Church is not yet One, then it is not yet time to change the liturgical calendar.[1161]

The Spring Equinox

August 5th—what does that date mean? Is the placement of August 1 or January 1 on a particular day arbitrary? In the ancient Jewish calendar (and the modern one as well), the placement of the months is determined by the placement of the Passover celebration, during the month of Nisan, after the spring Equinox. This placement was chosen so that the harvest of the first fruits of grain would coincide with the Passover celebration (Lev 23) and so that the completion of the harvest would coincide with the Feast of Weeks (Lev 23:15-17).

During the time of Christ's Ministry, the Spring Equinox fell between noon on March 22 and noon on March 23, Jerusalem time.[1162] Currently (A.D. 2001-2010), the Spring Equinox falls before or after noon on March 20, Jerusalem time.[1163] (In some years in the 21st century, the Spring Equinox would fall after noon on March 19, in other years it would fall very early on March 21.) The Spring Equinox is currently placed about three days earlier (just over 2½ days earlier, to be more precise) than it was during the time of Christ's Ministry.

The Spring Equinox was used during Christ's time on earth to help determine the date for the Jewish Passover (and hence the rest of the calendar year). In the early Church, the Spring Equinox (of the Northern Hemisphere) was used to determine the date for Easter. Therefore, I suggest that the Spring Equinox be used in the revised liturgical calendar to determine the date for Easter and all the days of the calendar year. The date for January 1 should be set so that the Spring Equinox for the location of Jerusalem generally falls on March 23, Jerusalem time.[1164] Occasionally, the date for Spring Equinox will fall late in the day on March 22, or (more rarely) early in the day on March 24, but most years it can and should remain on March 23. To accomplish this, three days must be subtracted from the calendar.

The revised date for the Spring Equinox of Jerusalem should be generally March 23, so that it only occasionally falls on March 22. During Christ's Ministry, the Spring Equinox fell on either March 22 or 23, but never on March 21. This statement is true for all of the years that various scholarly opinions have considered to be the years of Christ's Ministry (A.D. 15 to A.D. 36, see Appendix I, Chart 1). Placing the Spring Equinox of Jerusalem generally on March 22 would result in the Spring Equinox falling on March 21 in quite a few years, which would not be in conformity with the years of Our Lord's Ministry.

In the Gregorian calendar, the Spring Equinox of Jerusalem usually falls on March 20 and is preceded by March 19. If the Spring Equinox is called March 23 and the preceding day would have been called March 19, then three days have been taken away to make this adjustment. When Pope Gregory changed the calendar from Julian to Gregorian, he adjusted the date of the Spring Equinox by subtracting ten days from the calendar (Oct. 4 was followed by Oct. 15). Choosing which three days should be removed from the calendar is a practical matter and is not for me to decide. Once the adjustment is made, following Pope Gregory's existing system for determining leap years should be sufficient to maintain the date of Spring Equinox for the location of Jerusalem on or about March 23 for hundreds of years....[1165]

Why Change the Date of the Spring Equinox?

There are two compelling reasons for changing the date of the Spring Equinox of Jerusalem to March 23. First, the Christian calendar should be a reflection of the life of Christ. During Christ's life on earth, the Spring Equinox generally fell on March 23 (or late in the day on March 22). So, when we say that Christ died on a particular day (April 7), we mean that he died a certain number of days after the Spring Equinox. If the date of the Spring Equinox in the calendar we use is not in the same place as it was during Christ's Ministry, then the dates of events will not be in the correct place throughout the calendar year.

For example, if we celebrate the Virgin Mary's birth on August 5, but we move the Spring Equinox of Jerusalem to a place 3 days earlier (March 20) than it was in the year of her birth (March 23), then all of the dates in our calendar are off by 3 days. So we end up celebrating her birth 3 days later than the actual date. We call the Spring Equinox March 20, but it really should be called March 23. We call a particular day August 5, but it is a certain number of days after the Spring Equinox and so it really should be called August 8. The true date of August 5 occurs three days earlier than the date for August 5 in the current Gregorian calendar, because the true date of March 20 should be placed three days before the Spring Equinox, not on the same day as the Spring Equinox. The day we have been calling August 5 should really be called August 8, because the day we have been calling March 20 (the day of the Spring Equinox in the Gregorian calendar) should really be called March 23. Moving the date for the Spring Equinox to March 23 solves this misalignment of the calendar dates. Once the date of March 23 is moved to coincide with the Spring Equinox, then the day of August 5 will be the correct day for the celebration of Mary's birth. And the other days of the liturgical calendar will be able to be placed in their proper month and day also.

Second, moving the Spring Equinox to March 23 removes a current obstacle to the unification of all the Christian Churches in One Holy Catholic Church. Orthodox Christians still follow the Julian calendar system, which places leap years every four years without exception. This system results in a calendar year which, on average, is slightly longer than the true solar year. The result is that the date given for the Spring Equinox has receded through the Julian calendar. Currently, the Julian calendar calls the day of the Spring Equinox, March 7. In the Gregorian calendar, the same day is called March 20. During the time of Christ's Ministry, the day of the Spring Equinox was generally called March 23. In order to have a unified Christian Church, we must have a unified Christian calendar. All Christians should be able to agree that the day of the Spring Equinox of Jerusalem should be given the same calendar day as it was during Christ's Ministry.

A Uniform Date for Easter

In the early Church, there was a controversy about when to celebrate the Crucifixion and Resurrection of Christ. Christ died on a Friday, which was also the 14th day of the Jewish month of Nisan. Since Nisan 14 does not always fall on a Friday, Christians had to decide whether to celebrate the Passion of Christ always on a Friday, regardless of the number of the day, or always on the 14th of the month, regardless of the day of the week. The eventual decision of the Church was to celebrate the Crucifixion always on a Friday, Good Friday, and so also to celebrate the Resurrection always on a Sunday, Easter Sunday.[1166]

Similarly today, the Christian Church is divided concerning when to celebrate Good Friday and Easter Sunday. We all celebrate these events on a Friday and a Sunday, but not on the same Friday and Sunday. The basis for such a decision must be the life of Christ. Since Christ's death and Resurrection occurred at the beginning of Passover, and Passover was determined by the Spring Equinox and the lunar cycle, Easter should be determined by mean of the Spring Equinox and the lunar cycle.

The current date for Easter is determined based on the date of the Spring Equinox of Jerusalem from the year A.D. 325 (the year of the Council of Nicaea), which was March 20 in the Julian calendar. The date for Easter used by Catholics and Protestants does not depend on the current date for the Spring Equinox, but rather still uses the fixed date of March 20, in the Gregorian calendar. Easter is the first Sunday after the first full moon after March 20. However, the date used for the full moon is not the exact astronomical full moon for Jerusalem, nor for any specific location, but is based on charts giving an approximate date for the full moon (termed the Ecclesiastical Full Moon).[1167]

In the Julian calendar, the date given for the Spring Equinox of Jerusalem has gradually changed to its current date of approx. March 7. This change from March 23 to March 7 for the Spring Equinox occurred because the Julian calendar system has too many leap days, approximately 3 too many leap days for every 400 years. The excessive number of leap days leads to a calendar year which is, on average, longer than the true solar year. Thus the date given to the Spring Equinox of Jerusalem in the Julian calendar now differs by 13 days from the Gregorian calendar date of March 20, and by 16 days from the date during the time of Christ's Ministry (March 23).

The Orthodox Church still uses the date of March 20 in the Julian calendar to determine the date of Easter, even though the Spring Equinox in the Julian calendar now falls on March 7. The date of March 20 in the Julian calendar was the date established by the Council of Nicaea in determining dates for Easter. Since the date of March 20 in the Julian calendar now falls 13 days later than the date of March 20 in the Gregorian calendar, the dates for Easter in the East and West usually do not agree. Easter is generally celebrated at a later date in the East than in the West.

The main source of the different dates for Easter is the use of the fixed date of March 20 in place of the date of the Spring Equinox. If all Christians would agree to use the actual date for the Spring Equinox, then all Christians will be able to agree on a uniform date for Easter. The correct placement of the Spring Equinox is essential to any calendar system which seeks to conform itself to the true dates of events in the life of Jesus Christ. All Christians should agree on when to celebrate the Crucifixion and Resurrection of our Lord Jesus Christ. A uniform date for Easter requires a uniform date for the Spring Equinox. The date for the Spring Equinox should be the same as the date during the Ministry of Jesus Christ. The date for the Spring Equinox should be calculated based on the location of Jerusalem, where Christ died and rose from the dead.

The reason that the Council of Nicaea used the date of March 20 is because that was the date of the Spring Equinox in the year of the Council. In the spirit of that great Council's decision, let us continue to use the Spring Equinox as the basis for determining Easter Sunday. In these modern times, we have quick and easy methods of determining both the exact time and date of the Spring Equinox and the exact time and date of the full moon, for any location. Therefore, let us use this increase in our knowledge of the times and the seasons to determine the date for Easter using the exact time and date for the Spring Equinox and for the full moon for the location of Jerusalem.

I suggest to the One Christian Church the following. Let Easter be celebrated everywhere on the same day, on the first Sunday after the first full moon after the Spring Equinox of Jerusalem. The Spring Equinox will be determined as the exact time and date of the astronomical Spring Equinox for the location of Jerusalem (Jerusalem Standard Time). The full moon will be likewise determined as the exact time and date of the astronomical full moon for the location of Jerusalem. The first full moon whose exact time and date occurs after the exact time and date of the Spring Equinox of Jerusalem will be the Paschal Full Moon and will be used to determine the date of Easter. Thus the Spring Equinox and the Paschal Full Moon could occasionally occur on the same calendar day, as long as the time for the full moon follows after the time for the Spring Equinox. Easter Sunday will be the first Sunday after the exact time and date of the Paschal Full Moon. If the Paschal Full Moon falls on a Sunday, Easter shall be the next Sunday, one week later. Easter Sunday must not begin before the exact time and date of the Paschal Full Moon of Jerusalem. Easter Sunday must not be celebrated on the same calendar day as the Spring Equinox, nor as the Paschal Full Moon, because then the day of Sunday would begin before the Spring Equinox or before the Paschal Full Moon. Easter should be celebrated on the first Sunday, which begins after the time and date of the first full moon, which begins after the time and date of the Spring Equinox, for the location of Jerusalem. This revised Christian calendar does not place the Spring Equinox on March 7 (Julian) or March 20 (Gregorian), but rather on March 23, in agreement with the Julian calendar during the time of the Ministry of Christ.

One Church with Seven Parts

The current Roman Catholic Church (A.D. 2001) has two parts, the Latin Rite and the Eastern Rite. Here is an example of division within unity. Both Rites are under one Shepherd, the Pope, and both Rites believe all that the Catholic Church teaches without exception. When all Christians are united in One Holy Catholic Church, there will be more than two divisions within the unity of the One Church. The Book of Revelation is addressed to *the* seven churches (Rev 1:4, 11-16, 20) because the Church will be restructured into one Church with seven parts not long after the events of the Book of Revelation begin. The Restructuring of the Church and the Unification of all Christians will begin in A.D. 2020 and be completed in A.D. 2023.[1168]

I tell you solemnly, all Christians shall be united in One Holy Catholic Church. God wills that the Church on earth be One and God never fails. Jesus prayed that his disciples would be one (Jn 17:11) and His prayer shall bear fruit. By the Mercy and Grace of God shall this be done.

The True Dates and the Liturgical Dates

The dates in the liturgical calendar for the celebration of various events in the lives of Jesus and Mary should conform, as much as possible, to the true dates when those events actually occurred. Based on the dates presented in this book, I suggest to the One Church the following revisions for the celebrations in the liturgical calendar.

Jesus Christ:

The Incarnation of Jesus Christ (February 25)

The true date for the Incarnation of Jesus Christ is February 25 (see chapter 5). This celebration is currently referred to as the Annunciation. It is our remembrance of the angel Gabriel's announcement to the Virgin Mary of the Incarnation of Christ. Christians celebrate this day as the first holy day of the human life of our Savior Jesus Christ, the day when Jesus was conceived solely by a miracle of God within the womb of the Virgin Mary, the day when God became Incarnate in Christ. Jesus is more important than Mary. Since Christ is before Mary, this day should be named according to the event in Christ's life, His Blessed Incarnation and Virgin Conception. This celebration should be renamed "The Incarnation of Jesus Christ," or "The Virgin Conception of Jesus Christ," or similar wording, to emphasize the Incarnation. On this day we also recall the event in the Virgin Mary's life of the angel's announcement to her, but the focus must be first and foremost on Jesus the Messiah. The Annunciation should be called The Incarnation, since this name points to the most important event of that day.

Currently, the Church gives too little emphasis to this day when God became man. Greater emphasis should be placed on this event by the Church, since this was the beginning of the life of Jesus Christ as a human being. The Solemnity of the Annunciation is not currently a holy day of obligation. I suggest making this day a holy day of obligation, if it falls on a day other than Sunday. And when February 25 falls on a Sunday, the Solemnity of the Incarnation should still be observed. And when February 25 falls (as it occasionally will) during the days of Lent, the Solemnity of the Incarnation should still be observed.[1169]

The Virgin Birth of Jesus Christ (November 25)

Our celebration of the Birth of Jesus Christ is an important and holy day in the liturgical calendar of the Church. This celebration should take place on the true date of Christ's Birth, November 25 (see chapter 4). The Virgin Mary asked us to celebrate her birthday on the true date, about a month earlier than the date in the liturgical calendar. Her request to the Church cannot be denied. Nor can anyone deny that the celebration of the Birth of Christ is even more important than our celebration of Mary's birth. Therefore the celebration of the Birth of Christ must also take place on the true day (Nov. 25), a month earlier than the current date (Dec. 25) for that celebration. Yes, the date for our celebration of Christmas should be moved to the true date for the Birth of Christ, November 25.

There are cultural obstacles to accomplishing this change. The secular culture in most parts of the world has adopted Christmas as if it were a pagan holiday, a holiday about gifts and food and fictional stories told to children. Gift buying in advance of Christmas plays a significant role in the current retail economy. Changing the date for the celebration of Christmas will likely be opposed by those who are devoted more to the pagan holiday than to the Christian Holy Day. Even so, we must remember and celebrate Christ's Birth on the true date.

The Birth of Jesus Christ was a true Virgin Birth, occurring solely by a miracle of God and not in the usual way.[1170] Christmas is a remembrance and celebration of the Virgin Birth of Jesus Christ. The Birth of Christ must be known and celebrated everywhere in the Church as a true Virgin Birth.

Martyrdom of Holy Innocents

The Church (in the West) currently celebrates the martyrdom of the Holy Innocents on Dec. 28, three days after Christmas. In the East, this celebration is placed on Dec. 27. But, in either case, no one thinks that the infants were killed so soon after the birth of Christ. The celebration is placed close to Christmas because it is closely connected to the Birth of Christ. Herod was trying to kill the Christ-child by killing all of the male children two years of age and younger in Bethlehem and in all that region (Mt 2:16). I believe that the martyrdom of the Holy Innocents occurred in the spring of 13 B.C., about 1½ year after the Birth of Christ (see chapter 6). However, I think that the celebration of this event should remain close to Christmas in the calendar, because its meaning is connected with the Birth of Christ. Since Christmas will be moved to Nov. 25, our celebration of the martyrdom of the Holy Innocents should remain soon after November 25.

In the same way, other celebrations closely connected with the Birth of our Lord, such as the feast of the Holy Family (Catholic) or the Veneration of St. Mary (Orthodox), which have been traditionally celebrated close to Christmas, should remain close to the date of Christmas. Some differences in the liturgical calendar, from one part of the Church to another, are acceptable—as long as they have been approved by competent Church authority.

The Circumcision of Christ (December 2)

This Holy Day could also be called the Naming Day of Jesus Christ, for it was on the 8th day inclusive from birth that Jewish boys were both circumcised and given their name. A similar tradition for newborn girls gave them their name on the 15th day (see 'The Naming Day of the Virgin Mary' below). This day must be celebrated on the 8th day inclusive from Christmas, the Octave of Christmas, which is Dec. 2 in this revised liturgical calendar.

Flight to Egypt (February 29)

According to Blessed Anne Catherine Emmerich, the Holy Family fled to Egypt beginning on February 29.[1171] This event is described in Sacred Scripture (Mt 2:13-15). Since this date of February 29 only appears in the revised calendar every 4 years (with some exceptions), the remembrance of this event should be kept in the liturgical calendar only in leap years. And there is a good reason for keeping this celebration only in leap years.

This holy day can help to seal the unity of the One Christian Church in following one and the same calendar system. Formerly, different Churches followed different rules for leap years (Julian, Gregorian). When the Church is One, the calendar must be one. Placing this holy day on February 29, only in leap years, will be an outward sign of our inward unity. This holy day can show that all Christians are following the same calendar system.

The leap year system for the one calendar must be the system used in the Gregorian calendar. This system for determining leap years will maintain the Spring Equinox of Jerusalem on the correct date. Those faithful Christians in the East, who have long followed the Julian system for leap years, must accept change. Christians in the West will also be required to accept many changes. The revised calendar, though, is not the same as the Gregorian calendar, because the date of the Spring Equinox of Jerusalem is to be placed on the Julian calendar date for the Spring Equinox during the Ministry of Christ. The revised calendar should not be called Julian or Gregorian, but rather, Christian.

The Return from Egypt (September)

The Return of the Holy Family from their exile in Egypt is described in Sacred Scripture (Mt 2:19-21). This event should be remembered in the Church's liturgical calendar. The event actually occurred in the fall, most likely in September (see chapter 6). This celebration could be placed on any appropriate day within the liturgical calendar, but most appropriately on some day in September. I have no suggestion as to which day in September.

The Presentation of the Lord (January 3)

On the 40th day from the Birth of Christ, the Virgin Mary presented her new-born male child at the Temple in Jerusalem (Lk 2:22-24), as the Jewish Law required (Lev 12). The celebration of this event is called The Presentation of the Lord. Since Christ was actually born very early in the day on November 25, the 40th day from His Birth is January 3 (see chapter 6). The liturgical celebration of this event should be placed on the 40th day inclusive from the true date of Christ's Birth.

The Finding in the Temple

The Gospel of Luke describes an event when Jesus, at the age of 12 years, was lost to Joseph and Mary for three days. On the third day, He was found in the Temple (Lk 2:41-51). This event foreshadowed Jesus' death and Resurrection. By God's Providence, Jesus was left behind by Joseph and Mary on April 7, and found by them on April 9,—the same calendar dates as Jesus' death and Resurrection (see chapters 2 and 6).

The liturgical celebration in remembrance of the Finding of the Christ-child in the Temple should take place on the date of the event, April 9, except in years when such a celebration would conflict with the holy days of Lent and Easter. For example, when Easter Sunday falls on April 15, then April 9 will be the Monday of Holy week (the week of Holy Passion). The Finding of the Child Jesus in the Temple could be celebrated at such a time, because this event foreshadowed Jesus' death and Resurrection. However, if April 9 coincides with the first day of Lent, or Palm Sunday, or any day from Holy Thursday (Thursday of the Holy Mysteries) to Easter Sunday, then the celebration of this event could either be omitted or transferred to April 7 (if this date does not also conflict).

Baptism of Christ (October 4)

Jesus Christ was baptized by John on October 4 (see chapter 7). The Ministry of Jesus Christ lasted about 3½ years, beginning in the fall and ending in the spring (at the Passover). The Baptism of the Lord is currently celebrated in early January, but it would be more appropriately placed in the fall. The liturgical celebration of the Baptism of Jesus should be moved to October 4.

Ash Wednesday and Lent (February/March)

Lent should be kept the same length as it has been. Lent is 40 days from Ash Wednesday to Holy Saturday, not including the Sundays within Lent. Sunday is a day of celebration of the Resurrection of Jesus Christ, a celebration of our salvation, and so Sundays are not usually days of fasting, even during Lent. Easter is always a Sunday, and Ash Wednesday always a Wednesday, 46 days before Easter. In the Eastern Rite, Lent can be of a different length and need not begin on a Wednesday, according to the traditions of the East.

Good Friday and Easter Sunday (March/April)

Good Friday will always be the Friday before Easter Sunday. Easter Sunday should be determined, as stated above, according to the Spring Equinox of Jerusalem and the Paschal Full Moon.

Divine Mercy Sunday

The Sunday after Easter is Divine Mercy Sunday in the Catholic Church and should be celebrated in the revised calendar by all Christians throughout the world. All Christians must acknowledge and celebrate the great Mercy of God (see chapter 3).

The Ascension of Christ

Currently (A.D. 2001), in some places, the Ascension of Christ to the right hand of the Father in Heaven is celebrated on a Sunday. Christians everywhere agree that Christ ascended to Heaven on a Thursday, on the 40th day from the Resurrection (Acts 1:3). I understand that the reason for transferring the celebration to a Sunday is to include as many of the faithful as possible in the celebration of this event. However, this accommodation is not the ideal, not the fullness of the will of God, and shows a lack of faith among the faithful. Those who follow Christ should be willing to go to church on a Thursday to celebrate so important an event as Christ's Ascension to Heaven. When God gives the world the Day of Repentance, many of the faithful will live up to their name and become more faithful to God. The Ascension of Christ should be celebrated on a Thursday, the 40th day inclusive from Easter Sunday.

Pentecost

Pentecost Sunday should remain the 50th day from Easter Sunday and the 10th day from Ascension Thursday. The celebrations of Good Friday, Easter Sunday, Ascension Thursday, and Pentecost Sunday should remain on the same days of the week as they actually occurred. And the number of days from one celebration to the next should remain the same as with the events themselves.

The Virgin Mary:

The Immaculate Virgin Conception (November 8)

The Immaculate Conception of the Virgin Mary occurred on the morning of November 8 (see chapter 8). The birth of the Virgin Mary must be celebrated on August 5, in compliance with her own request at Medjugorje. The true date of her birth (Aug. 5) is about a month earlier than the current date for the celebration of her birth in the liturgical calendar (Sept. 8). The true date of the Virgin Mary's Immaculate Conception (Nov. 8) is also a month earlier than the current date for this celebration in the liturgical calendar (Dec. 8). The date for the celebration of the Virgin's Conception must be moved to November 8. In this way, the length of time between our celebrations of her conception and her birth will remain about 9 months and the days on which we celebrate these events will be the correct calendar dates.

The Immaculate Conception of the Virgin Mary was a Virgin Conception, occurring solely by a miracle of God and not in the usual way.[1172] This teaching is certain and true; let no one have any doubts about the perfect, complete, and all-encompassing Virginity of the Mother of Christ. Our celebration of the Virgin Mary's Immaculate Conception must also include a celebration of her Perfect Virginity and her Virgin Conception. Let this event be known and celebrated everywhere in the Church as the Immaculate Virgin Conception.

The Virgin Birth of the Virgin Mary (August 5)

August 5 is the true date of the Virgin Mary's birth, as she herself revealed at Medjugorje (see chapter 9). The date for the celebration of Mary's birth must be moved to August 5, for this is the day on which she asked us to celebrate her birth. But there is more. The birth of the Virgin Mary was a true Virgin Birth, occurring solely by a miracle of God and not in the usual way. It cannot be otherwise.[1173] The birth of the Virgin Mary must be known and celebrated everywhere in the Church as a true Virgin Birth, like the true Virgin Birth of her Divine Son Jesus Christ.

The Naming Day of the Virgin Mary (August 20)

As explained in chapter 9, on the 15th day inclusive from the birth of the Virgin, she was formally given the name Mary, in a Jewish religious ceremony. This ceremony was most likely held on the evening of August 19, before sunset. The Jewish day begins and ends at sunset, so the beginning of Saint Ann's time of purifying according to Jewish Law (Lev 12:5) would have been the 15th day from Mary's birth. This 15th day began at sunset on August 18 and ended at sunset on August 19. According to Blessed Anne Catherine, the naming ceremony occurred late in the day on August 19. The celebration of the Naming Day of the Virgin Mary should therefore be placed on August 20, with a vigil celebration permitted on the evening of August 19. August 20 was the first full day after the naming of the Virgin Mary (see chapter 9 for more information).

This new feast for the Church is similar to an existing feast, celebrated more in the East than the West, remembering the Circumcision of Jesus. "And after eight days were ended, so that the boy would be circumcised, his name was called JESUS, just as he was called by the Angel before he was conceived in the womb." (Lk 2:21). The day for the circumcision was also the day He was formally given His name, Jesus.

The Presentation of the Virgin Mary (October 23)

The day on which Saint Ann presented her newborn child to God in the Temple of Jerusalem, in obedience to Jewish Law (Lev 12), was the 80th day inclusive from the birth of the Virgin Mary. October 23 is the 80th day inclusive from August 5. A similar celebration, when the Virgin Mary presented her newborn child Jesus to God in the Temple of Jerusalem on the 40th day, is called the Presentation of the Lord. The day on which Saint Ann presented the Virgin Mary to God in the Temple should be called by a similar name, the Presentation of the Virgin Mary. This new celebration should be added to the liturgical calendar of the Church.

This day could also be called the Purification of Saint Ann, just as the Presentation of the Lord is also referred to as the Purification of the Virgin Mary. The term Purification comes from the Jewish Law, which requires this visit to the Temple by the mother of a new-born child "when the days of her purification have been completed" (Lev 12:6). This day could also be called the Entrance of the Virgin Mary into the Temple, just as the Presentation of the Lord is also called the Entrance of the Lord into the Temple.

There is currently no celebration of Saint Ann's Purification in the liturgical calendar of the Church. There is a feast celebrated in the Church under the name of "The Presentation of the Blessed Virgin Mary," which falls on Nov. 21. However, this feast is a celebration of the Virgin Mary's entrance into the Temple of Jerusalem, when she began her years of service in the Temple as one of the Temple virgins. The Church is correct in celebrating as a feast the day the Virgin Mary began her service in the Temple. However, the name of this feast should be changed to avoid confusion with the day of Saint Ann's Purification in the Temple. The day for celebrating Saint Ann's purification should be called 'The Presentation of the Virgin Mary.' The other feast should be called 'Entrance of the Theotokos into the Temple,' just as it is called in the Eastern Churches.

Entrance of the Theotokos into the Temple (November 9)

The Virgin Mary is Virgin of the Temple, and that Temple is Christ Jesus, her Savior. The Virgin Mary entered the service of the Temple of Jerusalem on November 8, the same day as her Immaculate Virgin Conception (see chapters 8 and 9). Her first full day as a Temple Virgin was therefore November 9. Since the Immaculate Virgin Conception will be celebrated on November 8, the beginning of the Virgin Mary's service to God as the Temple Virgin should be celebrated on the following day, November 9.

In the current liturgical calendar, November 9 is the feast of the Dedication of the Lateran Basilica in Rome. I suggest dropping this feast from the calendar or moving it to another day. The events of Mary's Immaculate Conception and her service to God as Temple Virgin are far more important to the Church than the dedication of any Basilica.[1174]

The Virgin Mary, Perfect Virgin (January 1)

The first day of the (civil) calendar year should be dedicated to the Virgin Mary, so that we begin each year with her blessings. But the celebration of Mary as the Mother of God should remain close to the date of Christmas. This celebration on January 1 can be dedicated to the Virgin Mary under whatever title or purpose the Church decides. I suggest dedicating this day to the Perfect Virginity of the Virgin Mary.[1175]

The Dormition of the Virgin Mary (July 31)

In the East, Christians know well that the Virgin Mary died and was resurrected from the dead before she was assumed into Heaven (see chapter 10). At the present time (A.D. 2001), many Catholics do not know or understand this truth. Those who still doubt, I refer to the Apostolic Constitution of Pope Pius XII, *Munificentissimus Deus*, (also titled, "Defining the Dogma of the Assumption"), which clearly and repeatedly refers to the death of the Virgin Mary.[1176]

The Virgin Mary died on July 31; she was resurrected from the dead and was assumed into Heaven by the power of Jesus Christ early in the day on August 15. The Dormition (death) of the Virgin Mary should be remembered on July 31, the actual day of her death. The Church should place the Solemnity of Mary's Dormition on the same calendar day as it actually occurred, July 31.

The Fast of the Dormition (August 1 to 14)

In the East, many Christians fast from August 1 to August 14, inclusive. This fast is a remembrance of the time between the Virgin Mary's death and her Resurrection and Assumption. I ask the Church to consider making this 14-day fast a part of the liturgical calendar for the entire worldwide Church. Fasting is not only for Lent, but for other times of the year as well. All Christians should observe this fast in remembrance of the Virgin Mary's death and in preparation for the celebration of the Virgin Mary's Resurrection and Assumption.

The Resurrection and Assumption of the Virgin Mary (August 15)

The Resurrection of the Virgin Mary re-united her soul with her body, so that she could then be assumed into Heaven, body and soul. Just as Christ died, rose from the dead, and ascended to Heaven, so also the Virgin Mary died, was resurrected from the dead by Jesus Christ, and was brought up to Heaven by Jesus Christ. Unlike her Divine Son Jesus, the Virgin Mary did not remain on earth between her Resurrection and her Assumption. Immediately upon being raised from the dead by Christ, she was also brought up to Heaven, body and soul, by Christ. Thus the Resurrection and the Assumption of the Virgin Mary occurred at the same hour and on the same day.

According to Saint Bridget of Sweden, there were 15 days from the death of the Virgin Mary to her Resurrection and Assumption (see chapter 10). The Church currently celebrates the Assumption of the Virgin Mary on August 15, which is the true date of this event and the correct date for this celebration. The Virgin Mary was resurrected from the dead and assumed into Heaven early in the morning, shortly before sunrise, on August 15. The Assumption of the Virgin Mary should continue to be celebrated on August 15. However, this celebration should also include the clear and authoritative teaching of the Church that the Virgin Mary was both resurrected from the dead and assumed into Heaven on this day.

No theologian or teacher in the Church should ever assert even the possibility that the Virgin Mary did not die, as Christ died, and did not rise, as Christ rose, before being assumed into Heaven. Anyone who speaks or writes against the Dormition and Resurrection of the Virgin Mary is speaking or writing against Truth and against Christ. May such persons be ignored by the faithful and rebuked by God.

The Coronation of the Virgin Mary

The Virgin Mary was made Queen of Heaven upon her entrance into Heaven, which is in Eternity. Since Eternity is beyond of Time, one cannot say "when" she was crowned Queen of Heaven—it happened within Eternity and beyond Time. The Catholic Church currently celebrates the Coronation of the Virgin Mary one week after the celebration of her Assumption. It is appropriate to place the celebration of Mary's Coronation near the celebration of her Assumption, when she entered Heaven body and soul.

John the Baptist:

The Annunciation to Zechariah (September 13)

In the Orthodox church, Christians celebrate the event described in Luke 1:5-23, when the angel Gabriel announced to Zechariah that he and his wife would soon be able to conceive a child, John the Baptist. This event is described at some length in Sacred Scripture and was an important preparatory step for the coming of the Messiah. Therefore, this event should be celebrated throughout the One Christian Church.

According to Saint John Chrysostom, Zechariah was serving in the Temple of Jerusalem at the time of the Day of Atonement and the Feast of Tabernacles when this annunciation occurred. In chapter 5 of this book, I confirm this statement by Saint John Chrysostom and give further evidence that the exact day of the annunciation to Zechariah was the Day of Atonement, which fell on September 13 in that year. The celebration of the annunciation to Zechariah should be placed on Sept. 13 in the revised liturgical calendar. The memorial for Saint John Chrysostom, who is remembered on Sept. 13, can fittingly remain on the same day.

The Conception of John the Baptist (September 27)

The most likely time for the conception of John the Baptist was Tishri 24, which was Sept. 27 in that year (see chapter 5). John's conception is referred to in the Gospel of Luke directly (Lk 1:24) and also indirectly in the angel's statement to Mary that Elizabeth was in her sixth month (Lk 1:36). This event should be added to the revised liturgical calendar. The day for this memorial should be September 27 in the liturgical calendar.

The Visitation of Mary to Elizabeth (April 20)

At the time of the Visitation, Jesus was in the womb of the Virgin Mary and John the Baptist was in the womb of Elizabeth. The Visitation of Mary to Elizabeth is also the Visitation of Jesus to John the Baptist. The Visitation occurred on April 20, after Mary and Joseph had attended the Passover celebrations at Jerusalem (see chapter 5). The Visitation should be celebrated on the actual day of the event, on April 20.

The Birth of John the Baptist (June 27)

I do not know the exact date for the birth of John the Baptist. However, I conclude in chapter 5 that the most probable date for John's birth falls within an 11-day time frame, from June 27 to July 7, of 15 B.C., inclusive. Since the celebration of John's conception is placed on Sept. 27 in this revised calendar, the celebration of his birth should fittingly be placed nine months later on June 27.

John's birth is currently celebrated on June 24. But the Spring Equinox is currently placed on March 20 (Gregorian). So, when the Spring Equinox is called March 23, then the day on which we now celebrate John's birth, June 24, will be called June 27. The celebration is actually remaining on the same day, but the numbers of the days of the calendar are being adjusted by 3 days to accord with the Julian calendar during the Ministry of Christ.

The Beheading of Saint John the Baptist (January 25)

The beheading of John the Baptist is currently celebrated on August 29. But John the Baptist was martyred for Christ about the middle of the month of Tevet in the third year of Christ's Ministry. According to Blessed Anne Catherine, John was beheaded about ten days before Tevet 29, which gives us the approximate date of Tevet 19 (see chapter 7). In the third year of Christ's Ministry (A.D. 18), Tevet 19 coincided with January 25. Since this is the best information that we have for the date of John's martyrdom, the beheading of John the Baptist should be remembered and celebrated on January 25.

The Martyrdom of Zechariah and Elizabeth

Zechariah and Elizabeth died on different days, perhaps even in different years. But both Zechariah and Elizabeth were martyrs for the sake of John the Baptist and Jesus Christ (see chapter 6). The Church should celebrate their martyrdoms on the same day. I do not have a suggestion as to which day.

Other Celebrations:

All Saints Day and All Souls Day

All Saints Day, currently Nov. 1, and All Souls Day, currently Nov. 2, could remain on those same days, if the Church so decides. There is no chronological reason (that I know of) to place these celebrations on any other days. These celebrations could be moved to another month, such as early October, if the Church wishes, so as not to have too many important celebrations all in one month (in November).

Saint Mark's Feast Day

Mark the Gospel writer's feast day is currently celebrated on April 25. As explained in chapter 11, Saint Mark the Evangelist died on March 30 of A.D. 50. The feast day for Saint Mark should be moved to March 30. In some years, this feast day will not be celebrated because March 30 will sometimes coincide with Holy Week. But, in most years, this day will not conflict with Holy Week and so can and should be celebrated in remembrance of Saint Mark.

Other Holy Days

Not every event within the liturgical calendar has been mentioned above. It is not my place to make a decision about every day of the liturgical calendar. Other celebrations and memorials not mentioned in this chapter should still remain in the calendar, on appropriate days with respect to the other celebrations, in accordance with the decisions of the Church.

Secular Holidays

In the United States, the secular holiday of Thanksgiving is celebrated in late November. This celebration would conflict with the revised date for Christmas of Nov. 25. I suggest that the holiday of Thanksgiving be moved to another date, so that it does not interfere with the sacred days of the liturgical calendar. It is also possible that, at some point in the future, the holiday of Thanksgiving might be replaced by other holidays of thanks and remembrance.

On the other hand, Christians should give little time or attention to the pagan holiday called Halloween (Oct. 31). How is it that many more Christian children know Halloween than know All Saint's Day? Halloween should not be celebrated in the Holy Sanctuary (in churches) nor in conjunction with the Holy Mass, nor should any pagan-like holiday. Children should be discouraged from giving too much time or preparation or money or effort to this base holiday. Halloween occurs on the eve of All Saint's Day, but the current popular use of that eve is not at all religious in nature. It is permissible for Christians to celebrate such non-religious holidays, in a manner in keeping with the Christian Faith, but they should not give the holiday much emphasis. The same is true for other non-religious holidays, such as Mardi Gras (Fat Tuesday). Christians should give little attention to such days and should be careful not to offend God in anything they choose to do. And such pagan-like celebrations must not be memorialized by being combined with truly religious celebrations.

Some important religious celebrations, including Easter and Christmas, have been partially secularized by the culture of our day. People have added non-religious elements, including fictional characters and events, to these holy celebrations. These non-religious elements take the focus away from God and Jesus Christ. Faithful Christians should mostly ignore these non-religious elements and focus on the true meaning of these religious Holy Days.

Even the secular holiday of Thanksgiving has become somewhat cheapened in our modern culture and society. The emphasis in more recent years has been on eating and watching sports, with little thought or time for giving thanks to God.[1177] Christians can and should celebrate certain secular holidays, such as Thanksgiving, Veteran's Day, and other days, but when they do the emphasis should be on remembering God and our place in God's creation. Also, unlike some of the other secular holidays, Thanksgiving can be celebrated in the context of religious celebrations, including the Sacred Mass. Christians must always give thanks to God for all they have received.

The Decision of the Church

The decision of competent authority within the Holy Roman Catholic Church, and within the One Christian Church once all Christians are united, is above and beyond this book. No one should use my writings to argue against the decisions of the Church regarding the liturgical calendar, once those decisions have been made. I myself cheerfully follow the current liturgical calendar of the Catholic Church. I intend always to adhere to the decisions of the Church regarding the liturgical calendar and all teachings on faith and morals.

I am certain that some of the above suggested revisions to the liturgical calendar will be accepted and made official by the Church. I am equally certain that only some, not all, of my suggestions will be implemented. So be it. Not my will, but God's will be done. If anyone rejects the official liturgical calendar of the Church, or any official teaching of the Church, they are not my students or imitators—may God rebuke them.

Variations within the One Liturgical Calendar

The restructured Catholic Church will have Seven Rites and each Rite will have some variations within their version of the liturgical calendar. Each Rite must decide for itself about these variations. However, the main liturgical holy days shall remain the same for all Christians, including (but not limited to) the dates for Christmas, Good Friday, and Easter. For example, in the Orthodox Church, there are currently a number of differences in the liturgical calendar: the three-day Lent, Golden Friday, Renewal of the Church, Revelation to St. Joseph. These differences and others can remain as long as they conform, as much as possible, to the true dates and are based on the revised Christian calendar. Unification does not require complete uniformity. One Lord, One Faith, One Pope; many traditions, many cultures, many languages.

Changes to the Liturgical Calendar

This book presents, not only a chronology for the lives of Jesus and Mary, but also suggestions to the Church for changes in the liturgical calendar. These suggested changes are based on the chronology of the life of Jesus Christ found in this book. The Church does have the authority to make changes to the liturgical calendar. Such changes should be made in accordance with the Church's understanding of the life of Christ and the will of God. The suggestions for a new liturgical calendar found in this book are suggestions made to the Church. These suggestions should not be followed by the faithful until such time, if any, that the Church makes official changes to the liturgical calendar. It is for the Church to decide which changes to make in the calendar and when to make those changes, and it is for the faithful to accept those changes. Through this book, I teach and advise the Church, but I have no authority to make decisions for the Church. As the Church grows in faith and holiness, the people of God will grow in their understanding of the lives of Jesus and Mary. Faithful Christians believe and follow the teaching of the Church; unfaithful Christians reject the teaching of the Church.

The Numbers of the Years

The Incarnation of Jesus Christ occurred in 15 B.C. The current liturgical calendar gives numbers to the years as if Christ had been born in 1 B.C. The year A.D. 1 was numbered by Dionysius Exiguus as if it were the year in which Christ completed one year since the Incarnation. If we were to number the years of the revised liturgical calendar according to this system, we would call 14 B.C. the year in which Christ completed one year since the Incarnation. The number of the years would then tell us the number of years since the Incarnation, that is, they would tell us Christ's age from conception. To obtain this number, one can simply add 14 to the A.D. calendar date. For example, the year A.D. 2000 was not the completion of 2000 years since Christ's Incarnation, but rather the completion of 2014 years since Christ's Incarnation.

The Christian calendar ought to be changed so that the number of the year corresponds to the amount of time since the Incarnation. However, this change is too much for many of you to accept at this point in Time. I do not suggest making this change in the near future. May the Church eventually use a calendar system which, in agreement with the idea presented to the Church by Dionysius Exiguus, counts the years *ab incarnatione Domini*, from the Incarnation of the Lord.

Chapter 16
Sabbatical and Jubilee Years

Jewish Sabbatical Years

"And the Lord spoke to Moses on mount Sinai, saying: Speak to the sons of Israel, and you shall say to them: When you will have entered into the land which I will give to you, rest on the Sabbath of the Lord. For six years you shall sow your field, and for six years you shall care for your vineyard, and you shall gather its fruits. But in the seventh year, there shall be a Sabbath of the land, a resting of the Lord. You shall not sow your field, and you shall not care for your vineyard. What the soil shall spontaneously produce, you shall not harvest. And you shall not gather the grapes of the first-fruits as a crop. For it is a year of rest for the land. But these shall be yours for food, for you and for your men and women servants, and for your hired hands, and for the newcomers who sojourn with you...." (Lev 25:1-6).

Every seventh day is a day of rest and worship of God. The seventh day is called the Sabbath. In the Jewish faith, every seventh year is a day of rest and worship of God. The seventh year is called the Sabbatical year. Each set of seven years is a week of years, with the seventh year a Sabbath year, just as the seventh day in each week of days is a Sabbath day.

"For six years, you shall sow your land and gather its produce. But in the seventh year, you shall release it and cause it to rest, so that the poor of your people may eat. And whatever remains, let the beasts of the field eat it. So shall you do with your vineyard and your olive grove." (Ex 23:10-11).

The Sabbatical year was good news for the poor who did not own land. During this year, the land was neither sown nor harvested, but the poor could eat from the produce of the land, even if they did not own the land.

On the Sabbath day, we rest from work because we know that the things we need in life come from God, not from our own efforts. The Sabbath day is a day of trust in God. Likewise, the Sabbatical year was a year of rest from certain types of work, such as working the land, and a year of trust in God. The Jews trusted that God would provide for them, even though they would neither plant nor harvest in the Sabbatical year.

Jewish Jubilee Years

"You shall also number for yourselves seven weeks of years, that is, seven times seven, which together makes forty-nine years. And you shall sound the trumpet in the seventh month, on the tenth day of the month, at the time of the atonement, throughout all your land. And you shall sanctify the fiftieth year, and you shall proclaim a remission for all the inhabitants of your land: for the same is the Jubilee. A man shall return to his possession, and each one shall go back to his original family, for it is the Jubilee and the fiftieth year. You shall not sow, and you shall not reap what grows in the field of its own accord, and you shall not gather the first-fruits of the crop, due to the sanctification of the Jubilee. But you shall eat them as they present themselves."
(Lev 25:8-12).

The usual understanding of the timing of the Sabbatical year is that each of the seven years is to be counted from Tishri 1, in the autumn. This calendar is called the Jewish civil calendar. The Jewish sacred calendar begins with Nisan 1, in the spring.

There is some disagreement among Rabbis as to which year is meant to be the Jubilee year. The usual idea is that the 49th year (the 7th year in the 7th week of years) is a Sabbatical year and the next year, the 50th year, is the Jubilee year. Some Rabbis place the 50th year between the count of each set of 49 years; whereas other Rabbis count the 50th year as also the first year in the next set of 49 years. In the former case, adding 50 to the year of one Jubilee would give the year of the next Jubilee; in the latter case, adding 49 to the year of one Jubilee would give the year of the next Jubilee. On the other hand, still other Rabbis count the 49th year as also the 50th (since it is the 50th year inclusive from the previous Jubilee year). In that case, the Sabbatical year and the Jubilee year would be the same year and the length of time from one Jubilee to the next would be 49 years, not 50. The reason for the lack of agreement about the Jubilee years is that the ancient Israelites did not keep the Jubilee years consistently. The observance of the Jubilee years fell in and out of practice.[1178]

The practice among Jews has long been to count both Sabbatical and Jubilee years from the month of Tishri, the first month of the civil calendar, not from the month of Nisan, the first month of the sacred calendar. However, I believe that the Sabbatical years were originally counted using the Jewish sacred calendar, beginning with the month of Nisan in the spring, not with the month of Tishri in the autumn.[1179] My reasons for this conclusion are as follows.

1. Jubilee years are to be counted from the month of Tishri, as Sacred Scripture clearly states: "And you shall sound the trumpet in the seventh month, on the tenth day of the month, at the time of the atonement, throughout all your land." (Lev 25:9). But Sacred Scripture does not specify the seventh month as the start of a Sabbatical year, nor as the start of the count of the years leading up to the Sabbatical year.

2. One verse describes the count of the seven weeks of years, a total of 49 years (Lev 25:8). The very next verse calls the month of Tishri (when the Day of Atonement occurs) the seventh month (Lev 25:9). Tishri is only the seventh month when counting the months according to the sacred calendar, beginning in the spring with the month of Nisan. This indicates that the word "year" in the previous verse (Lev 25:8) is also to be counted according to the sacred calendar, with the year beginning in Nisan. Thus the Sabbatical years should be, and originally were, counted from the month of Nisan.

3. "And the Lord spoke to Moses on mount Sinai, saying: Speak to the sons of Israel, and you shall say to them: When you will have entered into the land which I will give to you, rest on the Sabbath of the Lord."
(Lev 25:1-2).

Sacred Scripture tells the Israelites when to begin the counting of Sabbatical years, beginning from the time that they would come into the Promised Land. Joshua led the Israelites across the Jordan river and into the Promised Land in the spring, in the month of Nisan. "Then the people ascended from the Jordan, on the tenth day of the first month, and they made camp at Gilgal, opposite the eastern section of the city of Jericho." (Joshua 4:19). The first month here is certainly the month of Nisan, since, a few days later, the Israelites celebrated the Feast of Passover. "And the sons of Israel remained in Gilgal, and they kept the Passover, on the fourteenth day of the month in the evening, in the plains of Jericho." (Joshua 5:10). Thus the Sabbatical years were to be counted from the month of Nisan, when the Israelites came into the land which God gave to them.

4. "But if you will say: 'What shall we eat in the seventh year, if we do not sow and do not gather our produce?' I will give my blessing to you the sixth year, and it shall yield the produce of three years. And in the eighth year you shall sow, but you shall eat from the old produce, until the ninth year, until what is new matures, you shall eat what is old." (Lev 25:20-22).

Notice here that the crop planted in the 8th year produces its harvest in the 9th year. This timing, where the planting of one year is harvested in the next year, only occurs when the years are counted according to the sacred calendar, with the year beginning in Nisan. Grain is planted in Nov./Dec. in Israel.[1180] The harvest of grain in the spring is a part of the religious ceremonies during the Passover. The harvest of grain begins during the Passover, when the first fruits are cut from the field and offered to God (Lev 23:9-10). Thus, planting occurs in one sacred calendar year, but harvesting cannot occur until the Passover at the start of the next sacred calendar year. And this is exactly the timing of planting and harvesting described in the passage from Leviticus 25—sowing in late autumn of the 8th year (the year after the Sabbatical year) and harvesting in the spring of the 9th year. Here again, the sacred calendar is used in referring to the counting of the Sabbatical years.

The planting in the 8th year and harvest in the 9th year clearly does not refer to a crop harvested in the 8th year and kept in storage for use in the 9th year. This passage from Leviticus refers to the 9th year as the year when "what is new matures," meaning when the grain sown in the 8th year is ready to be harvested.

Also, the grain could not be planted near the end of the year in the civil calendar (which begins with the month of Tishri in the autumn) and harvested in the next civil calendar year. This would require the grain to be planted in the summer, when there is no rain, and harvested in the fall. Such a crop would not grow due to lack of rainfall. The rainy season in Israel is the winter time, from November through March. October and April generally have a little precipitation. The remainder of the year, especially the summertime, has practically no appreciable rainfall.[1181]

5. If the Sabbatical year began in the autumn, the fields would not have been sown with any grain seed, because planting occurs in late autumn. Some grain would still grow, since some seed from the previous years plantings would not germinate until a year or two had passed. Seeds from wild plants commonly germinate in different years; some seed will germinate in the first year and some in subsequent years. Modern domesticated grains, such as wheat and barley, mostly tend to germinate soon after planting, since the seed is taken from plants that germinated soon after planting. The genes which allow for delayed germination have been mostly removed from the gene pool of modern domesticated grains by this process of selection. But this effect would have been less

pronounced in Biblical times. So there still would be some grain growing in the fields from grain seed of previous years' plantings, but the harvest would be significantly less.

Sacred Scripture says that the sixth year will produce a harvest with enough abundance to last the 6th, 7th, and 8th years—until the crop sown in the 8th year is harvested at the start of the 9th year. This could mean that the crop of the 6th year would produce triple the usual harvest. Or, it could mean that the crop sown in the 6th year would continue to provide during the 7th and 8th years by growing again, on its own, each year. And this exact result would naturally occur, if the Sabbatical years were counted by the sacred calendar, beginning in spring with the month of Nisan.

If the Sabbatical year began in the spring, the previous year's planting (from late in the 6th year) would still be in the field. It could not be harvested, but the grain would be plentiful in the field and the people could eat from the field at the start of the Sabbatical year (7th year). Then, because the grain stood in the field unharvested, it would self-sow. Many grains of the wheat or barley would naturally drop to the ground and, during the rains of the following winter, would germinate and produce another abundant crop. Then in the spring, at the start of the 8th year, when the Sabbatical year had ended, this self-sown crop could be harvested.

Here we see that, with the Sabbatical years counted from Nisan, the fields would consistently produce sufficient grain for the Israelites. The Sabbatical and Jubilee years were not intended by God to be years of privation and famine. Rather, these are years when God provides for the people so that they can turn their hearts and minds to God. Sabbatical years often were years of food shortages or outright famine, because the Israelites changed the start of the Sabbatical years from the spring to the autumn.

6. The Sabbatical years were meant to be counted from Nisan in the spring. But the Jubilee year was clearly meant to be counted from Tishri in the autumn. Sacred Scripture plainly states that the start of the Jubilee year is in the seventh month, the month containing the Day of Atonement (Lev 25:9). The preceding verse describes the counting of 49 years (7 sets of Sabbatical years). Thus the Jubilee year begins in the seventh month, Tishri, during the 49th year. The Jubilee year is not the same year as the 49th year, nor is it a separate 50th year. The Jubilee year overlaps the 49th and 50th years, with the 50th year being also the first year of the next cycle of 49 years. The Jubilee year sanctifies both the end of one cycle of 7 weeks of years and the start of the next cycle of 7 weeks of years. Jubilee years therefore occur every 49 years.

Since the Jubilee year overlaps with the 49th year, at such times there would be a period of about 1½ year when the Israelites could neither reap nor sow. The Sabbatical year would begin in the spring (7th year), the Jubilee year would begin in the autumn of that same year. Though the Sabbatical year would end in spring with the start of the 8th year, the Jubilee year would not end until the autumn of the 8th year. After month of Tishri in the 8th year, crops could again be planted. Those crops would then come in and be harvested in the spring of the 9th year. This situation is specifically described in Sacred Scripture (Lev 25:22). The 8th year is the first year of the next cycle of 49 years; the 9th year is the second year of the next cycle of 49 years.

7. What caused this change in practice concerning the count of the Sabbatical years and when did this change occur?

Josephus describes the siege and capture of Jerusalem by Herod during the latter half of the first century B.C. First he describes the siege, during the summer before Jerusalem fell. He plainly states that the Jews at that time "were distressed by famine and the want of necessaries, for this happened to be a Sabbatic Year."[1182] Then he describes the capture of Jerusalem in the autumn, on the fast day (the Day of Atonement), in Tishri. If the Sabbatical years at that time were according to the civil calendar, beginning and ending in autumn, then the Sabbatical year would have ended by the time Jerusalem was captured on Tishri 10. Yet, after the capture of Jerusalem, Josephus plainly states that the Sabbatical year was still going on: "…in part by the Sabbatic Year, which was still going on, and forced the country to lie still uncultivated, since we are forbidden to sow the land in that year."[1183]

This may be an example of a year where the Sabbatical year was counted from the spring, according to the sacred calendar. The Sabbatical year began in the spring, prior to the capture of Jerusalem, and was still going on after Herod captured the city, and did not end until the following spring. Josephus was a Jewish priest and would not have been likely to make a mistake about when the Sabbatical year ended. So, this mention of a Sabbatical year occurring before and after the month of Tishri is not likely to be a simple error or misunderstanding on the part of Josephus.

The food shortages in this Sabbatical year were not caused merely by the Sabbatical year, since the proper observance of the Sabbatical year should provide sufficient produce from the land. Rather, the famine was caused by the war, which had been disrupting agriculture during the 3 years of Herod's attack on Judea and Jerusalem. The inability to plant and harvest during the Sabbatical year made the situation more difficult, but was not the cause of the lack of food.

After Herod captured Jerusalem, he controlled who became high priest of the Jews. And he chose the Jewish high priests from a different group of men. "Herod was then made king by the Romans, but did no longer appoint high priests out of the family of Asamoneus; but made certain men to be so that were of no eminent families, but barely of those that were priests…."[1184] This change in leadership among the Jews could easily have resulted in changes to policies set by the Jewish high priest, who had authority over decisions about the religious calendar. This is the most likely time for the Jewish high priest to have changed the start of the Sabbatical year from spring to autumn. The change in leadership could also have brought other changes to the calendar, such as a change to using the calculated date of the new moon, rather than the observation of the crescent new moon, to determine the start of each month (see chapter 17 for details).

I cannot be certain whether the change in the way Sabbatical years were counted occurred at this time or at some other time. However, based on the words of Sacred Scripture, the Sabbatical year clearly was counted from the month of Nisan at some point in the history of the Jews.

The assertion that there were changes in the Jewish calendar from time to time is not such an unusual idea. Certainly the ancient calendar of the Jews was determined by observation of the crescent new moon. But the modern calendar is determined by calculation of the astronomical new moon date. Changes have occurred to the Jewish calendar. Also, even the Rabbis cannot agree about which year is supposed to be the Jubilee year. Nor is there agreement on when the Jubilee years were kept in ancient times.

The above evidence provides substantial support for the idea that Sabbatical years were originally kept beginning in the spring, with the Jubilee year overlapping the 49th and 50th years. However, the practice of how the Sabbatical and Jubilee years were counted in later times was different. Sabbatical years in later practice were counted from Tishri in the autumn. And Jubilee years were most likely counted as the full year after the end of the Sabbatical year, so that there were two full civil calendar years when the Jews could neither plant nor harvest.[1185]

Chronology of the Jewish Sabbatical Years

The Sabbatical years began to be counted from Tishri in the autumn, probably no later than the early part of Herod's reign over Jerusalem. This made the previous practice, whereby the Jubilee year overlapped the 7th and 8th years, impossible. So the Jubilee year became the same as the 8th year.

There are two prevalent theories about which years were Sabbatical years, one proposed by Ben Zion Wacholder, the other proposed by Benedict Zuckermann and Donald Blosser.[1186] These two competing theories differ from one another by only one year. Wacholder has the Sabbatical years as one year later than Zuckermann/Blosser. Are either of these two theories correct?

According to Josephus, the Jews camped out in the plain of Ptolemais in order to block the advance of an army sent by the emperor Caligula to install his statue in the Temple of Jerusalem.[1187] This event occurred "about seed-time," during the late fall/early winter before Caligula's death.[1188] It was the time of year when the Jews would plant grain, and so Josephus states that the land was "in danger of lying without tillage."[1189] The stand-off on the plain of Ptolemais caused the Jews to be in danger of missing the season for planting grain. In a Sabbatical year, the Jews would neither plant nor harvest grain; they were forbidden from this type of work by Mosaic law.

In the usual chronology, Caligula died in January of A.D. 41, so that this conflict would have taken place in Nov./Dec. (planting season) of A.D. 40. Zuckermann and Blosser have the year A.D. 40/41 as a Sabbatical year.[1190] But Josephus, a Jewish priest, clearly indicates that the Jews intended to plant in that year. Therefore, Zuckermann and Blosser's Sabbatical years do not fit the usual chronology. In my revised chronology, the winter of Caligula's death was A.D. 25/26, which does not conflict with either Zuckermann or Wacholder. For details on this point, see chapter 13, section 16, "Sabbatical Years: Zuckermann versus Wacholder".

The chronology of Herod's reign again raises questions about the timing of the Sabbatical years. According to Josephus, Herod's siege of Jerusalem occurred in a Sabbatical year and ended with the capture of the city in the autumn (on Tishri 10).[1191] In chapter 12 of this book, I determine that the capture of Jerusalem by Herod occurred in 43 B.C., which was the end of a Sabbatical year in Wacholder. The details given by Josephus do not fit any year in which Zuckermann has a Sabbatical year. The usual chronology places the capture of Jerusalem by Herod in 37 B.C., but this would place

Herod's death in 4 B.C. The year of 4 B.C. is ruled out as a possible year for Herod's death because that year does not fit the other details given by Josephus (see chapter 12). Also, in 37 B.C., the fast day (Yom Kippur) fell in October, whereas Josephus tells us that the fast day fell in September (3rd month of the Olympiad year) at the time that Herod captured Jerusalem.[1192] Only Wacholder's chronology of the Sabbatical years fits the information given to us by Josephus about the capture of Jerusalem by Herod.

The Sabbatical year at the time of the capture of Jerusalem by Herod may have been the last Sabbatical year counted as originally intended, starting with the month of Nisan. This would make that Sabbatical year run from Nisan of 43 B.C. to Nisan of 42 B.C. Wacholder, though, has this Sabbatical year from Tishri of 44 B.C. to Tishri of 43 B.C. In either case, the 14th year of Herod's reign, 29 B.C., would be a Sabbatical year. That Sabbatical year began in autumn of the 13th year of Herod's reign (30 B.C.) and ended in autumn of the 14th year of Herod's reign (29 B.C.). By that time, the Sabbatical year was counted from Tishri to Tishri (in autumn), so that Wacholder's dates are correct for this time period.

In support of Wacholder's chronology, note that Josephus gives several indications that the Jewish civil calendar year of 30/29 B.C. was a Sabbatical year. First, he describes a famine, in the 13th year of Herod's reign due to "perpetual droughts."[1193] He does not blame the famine on the occurrence of a Sabbatical year, as he does at other points in his history,[1194] so the 12th to the 13th year of Herod's reign (31/30 B.C.) was not a Sabbatical year. Zuckermann/Blosser have a Sabbatical year from 31/30 B.C., which conflicts with Josephus in this revised chronology.[1195] However, in Wacholder, the Sabbatical year (30/29 B.C.) did not begin until the autumn of 30 B.C., in agreement with Josephus in this revised chronology.

The people were in great distress because "the fruits of that year were spoiled."[1196] The grain harvest occurs in the springtime, so the spring of Herod's 13th year (30 B.C.) was the harvest ruined by droughts. The famine continued into Herod's 14th year (29 B.C.) because the seed that had been sown did not produce "its fruits on the second year."[1197] This refers to the seed sown in Herod's 12th year (31 B.C.), which should have produced its first harvest in spring of Herod's 13th year (30 B.C.). The seed was expected to produce a harvest for a second year, in spring of Herod's 14th year (29 B.C.), because 30/29 B.C. was a Sabbatical year. The grain sown in one year could produce an additional harvest in the second year because some grains would not germinate until the second year, as explained above. This expectation was typical of a Sabbatical year, when, instead of planting another crop, the Jews would depend on the seed sown in previous years to germinate a year or more later. The only reason that one planting would be expected to produce fruits in two consecutive years would be if the second year was a Sabbatical year. Some seed would germinate in the first year and some in the second year, as is naturally the case with many types of seed. Therefore, 30/29 B.C. was a Sabbatical year, in agreement with Wacholder, (see Appendix I, Chart 7).

The planting, which did not produce well because of the drought, was the seed sown in Nov/Dec of 31 B.C. (late in Herod's 12th year). This crop was to be harvested in April/May of 30 B.C. (13th year). When it did not produce well, after the food that had been in storage was used up, there was a famine beginning in Herod's 13th year. So, 31/30 B.C. could not have been a Sabbatical year (as Zuckermann has it), because seed was sown and expected to be harvested in that civil calendar year.

Furthermore, Herod's attempts to relieve the famine included sending seed to the Syrians.[1198] Yet there is no mention of seed being given to the Israelites, whom Herod most wanted to help. There was no sense in giving seed to the Israelites at that time, because they would not sow the seed in a Sabbatical year. Instead, he gave them grain to make bread with, and for those who were unable to prepare the grain, he hired others to bake bread for them.[1199]

Then, when the next harvest time was approaching (this would be spring of 29 B.C., still within the Sabbatical year of 30/29 B.C.), Herod send 50,000 of his Roman men to harvest the fields.[1200] So many men were needed because it was a Sabbatical year and the Jews could not harvest the fields themselves. These men could harvest whatever lesser amount of grain the fields did produce, since they were not bound by Jewish Law. Perhaps Herod also sent out Romans (non-Jews) to sow seed in the Sabbatical year. Since he sent out men to harvest, he may well have sent out men to sow (though Josephus does not mention the sowing, only the harvest).

Wacholder's chronology of the Sabbatical years also fits certain events in the early Church. Food shortages due to the Sabbatical year (A.D. 20/21) caused tensions between Hebraic Christians and Greek Christians about the distribution of food to those in need (Acts 6:1). The solution was the appointment of the first Deacons. Subsequently, a Sabbatical year during Claudius' reign (A.D. 27/28) caused food shortages which brought Barnabas and Saul to Judea (Acts 11:28-29). The next Sabbatical year (A.D. 34/35) was followed by a Jubilee year (A.D. 35/36) and was the occasion for disputes among Christians as to whether or not to keep Mosaic law. This dispute brought about one of the first Councils of the early Church and was the time of Saul's visit to Jerusalem after 14 years (Acts 15; Gal 2:1). For details on these points, see chapter 11.

The chronology of the capture of Jerusalem by Titus also raises questions about the Sabbatical year. In this revised chronology, Jerusalem was captured in the summer of A.D. 56, which was the end of a Sabbatical year in Wacholder (A.D. 55/56). Zuckermann has a Sabbatical year in A.D. 54/55, which is too early to fit into this chronology. For details on these points, see chapter 14.

In summary, Wacholder's chronology of the Sabbatical years fits my revised chronology well, whereas Zuckermann and Blosser's chronology of the Sabbatical years does not fit. Wacholder, of course, has his own evidence and arguments in support of his ideas, which are separate from, and in addition to, my reasons for accepting his chronology of the Sabbatical years.[1201] Wacholder, Zuckermann, and Blosser all count the Sabbatical year as beginning in autumn, which I agree was the practice of the Jews during the time period of the New Testament. See Appendix I, Chart 7 for a list of Sabbatical and Jubilee years.

Chronology of the Jewish Jubilee Years

Jubilee years occur at the end of a cycle of seven Sabbatical years. So the determination of when Jubilee years occurred is based on when Sabbatical years occurred. I conclude above that Wacholder's dates for the Sabbatical years are generally correct, with the exception that the Sabbatical years were originally counted from the month of Nisan (and only later changed to the timing described by Wacholder). My conclusions about the chronology of the Jubilee years are also based on Wacholder's chronology, but with some differences.

Zuckermann and Blosser, as far as I know, have not arrived at a conclusion about which years were Jubilee years.[1202] August Strobel does reach a conclusion about the Jubilee years, but this depends on the same chronology of the Sabbatical years as Zuckermann and Blosser, which cannot be reconciled with the conclusions of this book.

Wacholder has the Jewish civil calendar year of 16/15 B.C. as both a Sabbatical year and a Jubilee year.[1203] However, during this time period, I believe that the Jews placed the Jubilee year in the year following the Sabbatical year, the 50th year, not the 49th. Josephus refers to the Jubilee year, calling it the 50th year.[1204] I agree with Wacholder that the year 16/15 B.C. was the seventh Sabbatical year (49th year), but the Jubilee year would then be 15/14 B.C. (50th year).

Wacholder's chronology of the Jubilee years fits my revised chronology well. He has a Jubilee year in the Jewish civil calendar year of A.D. 34/35 (coinciding with a Sabbatical year). Though I place the Jubilee year in A.D. 35/36, the year after the Sabbatical year, this timing fits my chronology of the early Church (chapter 11).

One of the early Church Councils settled a controversy as to whether or not Christians had to follow all of the rules of the Jewish Law (Acts 15). My chronology of the early Church places that Council in A.D. 35. Why did this controversy reach a high point in A.D. 35, rather than some years sooner or later? Because A.D. 34/35 was a Sabbatical year and A.D. 35/36 was a Jubilee year. Early Christians who converted from Judaism would have had to decide whether or not to follow those portions of the Jewish Law which apply to Sabbatical and Jubilee years. Such issues would include who owned the land, whether or not one could plant and harvest (for two years in a row), and whether or not other types of work could be done (Lev 25).

Messianic Prophecy

The Jubilee year was associated in Jewish thought with the Messiah. The Jubilee year was a holy year, a year of favor from God, which foreshadowed the coming of the Messiah. Jesus also made this association between the Jubilee year and Himself, when He quoted Isaiah: " 'The Spirit of the Lord is upon me; because of this, he has anointed me. He has sent me to evangelize the poor, to heal the contrite of heart, to preach forgiveness to captives and sight to the blind, to release the broken into forgiveness, to preach the acceptable year of the Lord and the day of retribution.' " (Lk 4:18-19; cf. Isaiah 61:1-2). What is the association between the timing of the Jubilee years and the timing of the arrival of the Messiah? Jesus became Incarnate, at His Virgin Conception, in early 15 B.C., during the Sabbatical year of 16/15 B.C. Jesus was born in late 15 B.C., during the Jubilee year of 15/14 B.C. The combination of a Sabbatical year with a Jubilee year was the holiest of times in the Jewish faith and fittingly coincided with the Incarnation and Birth of the Messiah.

There was a widespread belief among the Jews that the Messiah would arrive during a Sabbatical year.[1205] The Jubilee year too was associated with Messianic prophecy, as seen in Isaiah 61:1-4. These expectations turned out to be true. Jesus Christ was conceived in the Sabbatical year 16/15 B.C. and born in the Jubilee year of 15/14 B.C. The Sabbatical year is not only an image of the Sabbath day, it is a preparation for, and a celebration of, our salvation by the Messiah; so also with the Jubilee year. Thus it was fitting that Christ's Incarnation should occur in a Sabbatical year and His birth in a Jubilee year.

Eschatology

Jesus quoted the first part of the passage from Isaiah which refers to the Jubilee year and to the Messiah. That first part refers to the arrival of the Messiah at the time of a Jubilee year. But the next part refers to the more distant future: "to proclaim the acceptable year of the Lord and the day of vindication of our God.... And they will rebuild the deserted places of past ages, and they will raise up the ruins of antiquity, and they will repair the desolate cities, which had been dissipated for generation after generation." (Isaiah 61:2, 4). This part of the passage, referring to both the day of vindication of God and the rebuilding of ruined cities and former devastations, does not refer to Christ's Ministry, nor to anytime in the past. It refers to the Second Coming of the Messiah, after the devastations predicted by Daniel (Daniel 11) and by the book of Revelation. The prediction that there will be a time of rebuilding after those great sufferings is clear from Revelation 20:1-6. That time of peace, holiness, and rebuilding is sometimes called the Millennium (because it lasts for over a thousand years).

Jesus the Messiah arrived at the time of Sabbatical and Jubilee years. And, at His First Return, after the sufferings described by the book of Revelation, Jesus will again arrive at the time of Sabbatical and Jubilee years.

The Sabbatical year is the 7th year; but 7 sets of 7 years are also counted, so that the 49th year, a Sabbatical year, contains the start of the Jubilee year (in the 7th month of that 7th year, counted from Nisan, as it ought to be). The Jubilee years are 49 years apart from one another, but the Jubilee year is the 50th year. So, if we count 50 sets of 49 years (50 x 49 = 2450), the last year of those 2450 years would be the 50th Jubilee year. If we start the count of this Jubilee of Jubilees from the Jubilee year at the Birth of the Messiah (15/14 B.C.), adding 2450 years brings us to the year A.D. 2436 as the start of the 50th Jubilee year. That Jubilee year begins in fall of A.D. 2436 and ends in fall of A.D. 2437. (This counting of 50 Jubilee periods does not include the Jubilee at the time of Christ's Birth, for that year is the end of the previous Jubilee period.)

If the length of time from Christ's arrival at His Birth to Christ's arrival at the end of the tribulation is 50 Jubilees, a Jubilee of Jubilees, then Christ's Second Coming will occur sometime during the Jubilee year of 2436/2437, most likely during the year 2437. Does this accord with other prophecies about the future found in Sacred Scripture?

According to Saint Paul, the lawless one (Antichrist) will be destroyed by the arrival of Christ at His Second Coming. "And then that iniquitous one shall be revealed, the one whom the Lord Jesus shall bring to ruin with the spirit of his mouth, and shall destroy at the brightness of his return...." (2 Thess 8). Thus the arrival of Christ occurs about the time of the end of the Antichrist's reign.

According to Daniel, "Seventy weeks of years are concentrated on your people and on your holy city...from the going forth of the word to build up Jerusalem again, until the Christ leader, there will be seven weeks of years, and sixty-two weeks of years...." (Dan 9:24-25). A week of years is seven years; seventy weeks of years is 70 x 7 = 490 years. The going forth of the word to rebuild Jerusalem refers to the founding of the State of

Israel, which began in 1948. Counting 490 years, with 1948 as the first year, brings us to exactly A.D. 2437 as the last of the 490 years. Furthermore, Daniel reveals that the last week of years, the last 7 years, are the time of the reign of Antichrist (Dan 9:27). And what happens at the end of the 490 years?—"so that transgression shall be finished, and sin shall reach an end, and iniquity shall be wiped away, and so that everlasting justice shall be brought in, and vision and prophecy shall be fulfilled, and the Saint of saints shall be anointed." (Daniel 9:24). Thus at the end of the 490 years, and at the end of Antichrist's reign (the last 7 of the 490 years), Christ returns, punishes the wicked, and then establishes a reign of peace and holiness on earth.

This date for the Return of Christ, the last year of Daniel's 490 years, is exactly the year of the end of 50 Jubilees (A.D. 2437) since the Birth of Christ. The Second Coming of Jesus Christ will occur in the year A.D. 2437. For more on the timing of these future events, see my book, *The Bible and the Future of the World.*[1206]

The Messianic Kingdom

The Sabbath, the Sabbatical year, and the Jubilee year also anticipate the establishment of the Messiah's kingdom on earth. In that future time, which we Christians also look forward to, there will be rest for the faithful and rest for the land. Sowing and reaping will not be needed, because God will provide for His people. The command of Holy Scripture to the ancient Israelites not to sow or reap the land during a Sabbath (on which one could do no work), nor in the Sabbatical or Jubilee years, foreshadows that future time when sowing and reaping will never be needed. Since sowing and reaping were not needed for a whole year even during a time of sinfulness, these will not be necessary at all during a time of great holiness, when Christ's kingdom is established over all the earth (cf. Rev 20:4-6).[1207] During the time of the Messianic kingdom on earth, God will provide for His people, just as He provided for them on the Sabbath and in the Sabbatical and Jubilee years.

The First Jubilee after the Birth of the Messiah

The Dormition, Resurrection, and Assumption of the Virgin Mary occurred in A.D. 34 (see chapter 10). The year A.D. 34/35 was a Sabbatical year in Wacholder's chronology. The year A.D. 35/36 was a Jubilee year, the first Jubilee year after the Jubilee year of Christ's Birth. Thus the period of time from the Incarnation and Birth of Christ to the death, Resurrection, and Assumption of the Virgin Mary begins and ends with a combination of a Sabbatical year followed by a Jubilee year. The first Jubilee period after Christ's Birth encompassed many important spiritual events. Important events in Christ's life, in His Ministry, and in the early Church occurred within that first Jubilee period. And the end of the Virgin's life on earth also fell within that first Jubilee.

Not Yet Fifty Years Old

"And so the Jews said to him, 'You have not yet reached fifty years, and you have seen Abraham?' " (John 8:57). The Jews used the number 50 because they kept track of time, not by centuries, but by the Sabbatical and Jubilee years (see also, "Anna,

Daughter of Phanuel," below). They meant that Jesus had not yet seen a Jubilee year in His adult life. Since He had not yet lived for even the length of one Jubilee period, they were asking him how he could have seen Abraham.

The Jews counted a person's age by how many Passovers had occurred since that person's birth (see chapter 6). Similarly, they considered it a significant milestone in a man's life when he had lived for at least the length of time from one Jubilee year to the next (50 years inclusive). The liturgical calendar was an integral part of their lives.

Anna, Daughter of Phanuel

"And there was a prophetess, Anna, a daughter of Phanuel, from the tribe of Asher. She was very advanced in years, and she had lived with her husband for seven years from her virginity. And then she was a widow, even to her eighty-fourth year. And without departing from the temple, she was a servant to fasting and prayer, night and day." (Lk 2:36-37)

Why does Sacred Scripture tell us the age of Anna and how many years she lived with her husband until she was widowed? Scripture does not usually tell us each person's age. And why would her age be generally known, so that her age and the years of certain events in her life would become a part of Luke's description of her?

Notice that her age, 84 years, is a multiple of 7 years. And she lived with her husband for 7 years from the time of her marriage to the time she became a widow at her husband's death. The Jews kept track of the passage of the years by Sabbatical and Jubilee years. Every 7th year is a Sabbatical year; every 50th year is a Jubilee year (but the length of time from one Jubilee to another is 49 years). If these events in her life—her marriage, her husband's death, and her visit with the Christ-child—all occurred at the time of Sabbatical or Jubilee years, then the number of years would be generally remembered and associated with her.

Now Anna was constantly in the Temple of Jerusalem worshiping God.[1208] The women who served God in the Temple of Jerusalem were the Temple virgins (who were young girls) and the women who taught and governed them. Whether any other women served God in the Temple, besides those who had charge of the Temple virgins, I do not know.[1209] But, in any case, Blessed Anne Catherine tells us that Anna was indeed one of the women who took care of the Temple virgins and taught the Virgin Mary when she was a Temple Virgin.[1210] According to Blessed Anne Catherine, the women who served at the Temple were generally from the Essenes, so Anna may well have been one of the Essenes also.[1211]

Anna, who taught in the Temple as a widow, was most likely a Temple virgin as a child. In ancient Israel, not many girls received an education, but the Temple virgins were well taught. So, then, which women would be best qualified to be teachers of the Temple virgins?—women who had themselves been educated in the Temple when they were young girls.

When Anna's husband died, who would take her in? She could have returned to her family, or even been taken in by her late husband's family. Or, she returned to her religious family, where she was raised and educated, at the Temple of Jerusalem. I think, though, that there was likely a space of time between the death of her husband and her return to the Temple.[1212]

Now the Temple virgins, in general, were not vowed to be virgins their whole lives. "Upon reaching a certain age, they were given in marriage, for there was among the more enlightened Israelites the pious, though secret hope that from such a virgin dedicated to God, the Messiah would be born."[1213] (cf. Isaiah 7:14). Blessed Anne Catherine also tells us that the Virgin Mary left the Temple to be given in marriage to Joseph at the age of 14 years. "When the Blessed Virgin had reached the age of fourteen and was to be dismissed from the Temple with seven other maidens to be married...."[1214] Thus, the age of marriage for the Temple virgins was generally 14 years.[1215]

Anna "had lived with her husband for seven years from her virginity," (Lk 2:36) meaning that she was married for seven years after she ceased to be a virgin and so also after she ceased to be a Temple virgin. If her marriage took place at the customary age for Temple virgins, then she was married at the age of 14 years.

Notice that the important events in Anna's life occurred after some multiple of seven years. And these events did coincide with Sabbatical years, so that these lengths of time would have been not only easily remembered, but also seen as having special religious meaning. A Temple virgin, born in a Sabbatical year (99 B.C., beginning in Nisan), left the Temple to be married in a Sabbatical year (85 B.C.), was widowed in a Sabbatical year (78 B.C.), lived as a widow for the same length of time she lived as a virgin, 14 years, until the Sabbatical year followed by the Jubilee year (64/63 B.C., Sabbatical [Nisan to Nisan]; 64/63 B.C., Jubilee [Tishri to Tishri]), then she served God 49 more years, until the next Jubilee when the long-awaited Messiah was born, entered the Temple of Jerusalem, and was seen by Anna, who had waited so long for that one blessed day (in 15/14 B.C., a Jubilee year).

The lengths of time in her life are also full of meaning. Two Sabbatical years (14 years) as a virgin, one Sabbatical year (7 years) as a wife, two more Sabbatical years (14 years) as a widow, and then from one Jubilee year to the next spent serving God in the Temple (49 years) until the Messiah arrived. The total length of time is 84 years—Anna's age in Luke 2:37. The length of time is also 12 Sabbatical years (12 x 7 = 84). The Sabbatical and Jubilee years looked forward to the arrival of the Messiah, and Anna's life looked forward to the arrival of the Messiah. So it was fitting that the events of Anna's life should coincide with the Sabbatical and Jubilee years.

Christian Sabbatical and Jubilee Years

One of the earliest Church Councils declared that Christians do not have to follow the majority of the Jewish laws found in the Old Testament (Acts 15). Christians must always follow the moral law and the teachings of the Church. And Christians must still "restrain themselves from the defilement of idols, and from fornication, and from whatever has been suffocated, and from blood." (Acts 15:20). But we do not have to follow the other laws of Moses, such as keeping a year of rest for the land in the Sabbatical and Jubilee years. This judgment was of particular interest to Christians at that time, for this decision was made in the year A.D. 35, at the time of a Sabbatical year (A.D. 34/35) followed by a Jubilee year (A.D. 35/36).

Though Christians do not have to follow many aspects of the Jewish Law, we are still bound by all of the teachings on Faith and Morals found in the Old Testament. The ancient laws about Sabbatical and Jubilee years teach us to dedicate our time, efforts, and attention to God. The example of the Jews in ancient times, when they kept the Sabbatical and Jubilee years, teaches us to trust God and to set aside time to intensify our worship of God.

Catholics keep a Jubilee year when one is declared by the leadership of the Church. At such times, there are no Jubilee laws preventing Christians from working the land or from doing other work (nor should there be). The Church should continue to set aside particular years as Jubilee years. But Christians should also keep Sabbatical years. I offer the following suggestions to the Church concerning Christian Sabbatical and Jubilee years.

Suggestions to the Church

Every seventh year should be a Sabbatical year in the Church. The Sabbatical year should be a year with special emphasis on repentance and renewal. The Sabbatical year should be a year of increase in prayer, self-denial, and works of mercy. The Sabbatical year should be like the Sabbath day, a time dedicated to the worship of God. As in the Christian Jubilee year, there would be no additional laws or restrictions placed on Christians, only encouragement and opportunity to move closer to God.

The cycle of seven years should be counted beginning with the Christian Sabbatical year of A.D. 2009. That year will have special significance in the salvific history of the Church. This timing of the Christian Sabbatical years also follows from the ancient timing of the Jewish Sabbatical years, (when the year was counted from Nisan in the spring). So, for example, Wacholder has a Sabbatical year from autumn of 44 B.C. to autumn of 43 B.C. But if the Sabbatical year at that time in Jewish history was from Nisan to Nisan, the year would begin in spring of 43 B.C. and end in spring of 42 B.C. (in accord with Josephus' description). In the first century A.D., Sabbatical years were observed from autumn to autumn, so the Sabbatical year was from autumn of A.D. 34 to autumn of A.D. 35. But if that Sabbatical year had been observed as in ancient times, it would have begun in spring of A.D. 35 and ended in spring of A.D. 36. The Jubilee year would still have begun in the autumn of A.D. 35 and ended in autumn of A.D. 36, overlapping half of the Sabbatical year, as originally intended. Thus the Sabbatical year, in the A.D. calendar, should begin in the spring of each year whose number is evenly divisible by seven. (The spring and autumn of the year should be according to the seasons in Jerusalem, in the northern hemisphere.)

Christian Sabbatical years should begin with our celebration of the Incarnation of Christ, February 25, near the start of the season of Lent. (See my suggested revisions to the Christian liturgical calendar in chapter 15 of this book.) Our celebration of the Holy Virgin Conception of Jesus Christ is a good starting point for a Sabbatical year because it reminds us of the starting point for the human life of Christ, whom we seek to imitate. The season of Lent occurs about that same time of year and is also a fitting time for the start of a year of repentance and renewal. Jewish Sabbatical years in ancient times began in the spring, so Christian Sabbatical years should also begin about that time of year.

Christian Sabbatical years should begin on the holy day of the Incarnation of Christ in each year which is evenly divisible by seven: A.D. 2009, 2016, 2023, 2030, 2037, 2044, etc. This means that the Sabbatical year which begins early in A.D. 2009 will end early in the year A.D. 2010, and so on.

The Jubilee year should be every 49 years; it is called the 50th year because it begins in the autumn of the seventh Sabbatical year (the 49th year) and overlaps the 49th and 50th years. The 50th year is also the first year of the next cycle of 49 years. The Jubilee years should keep the same cycle as in ancient times. Since autumn of A.D. 35 was the start of a Jubilee year, the next Jubilee year should be A.D. 2044. For Jubilee years, when you subtract 35 from the number of the year (in which the Jubilee year begins), the result should be evenly divisible by 49 (e.g. (2044 - 35) / 49 = 41). This keeps the Jubilee years in synch with the Jubilee year at the time of Christ's Birth (Jubilee year of 15/16 B.C.) and at the time of His Return (Jubilee year of A.D. 2436/2437).

Jubilee years should begin in the autumn with our celebration of the Immaculate Virgin Conception of the Blessed Virgin Mary. The day of the Immaculate Conception was the day of the beginning of the building of the Body of Christ. And so that day is a fitting start to the celebration of a Jubilee year. This timing of the start of the Jubilee year means that the Jubilee year will begin some number of days after the start of the liturgical year in the season of Advent (in my suggested revised liturgical calendar). The Jewish Jubilee year in ancient times began on the 10th day of Tishri, on the Day of Atonement, even though the Jewish civil calendar began on the first of Tishri. So it is fitting that the Christian Jubilee year also begin a number of days after the start of the liturgical calendar, on the holy day of the Immaculate Conception, November 8. (See chapter 15 of this book for my suggested revisions to the liturgical calendar.)

Christian Jubilee years should begin on the holy day of the Immaculate Virgin Conception of the Blessed Virgin Mary, every 49 years, beginning in the year A.D. 2044, as follows: A.D. 2044, 2093, 2142, 2191, 2240, 2289, 2338, 2387, 2436. The Jubilee year which begins in November of A.D. 2044 will end in November of A.D. 2045, and so on. The Jubilee year which begins in the year A.D. 2436 will end in the year A.D. 2437, when Christ returns.

Suggestions for Sabbatical and Jubilee years

No type of honest work should be prohibited in a Sabbatical or Jubilee year. However, Christians should try to find some way to spend less time working. This might include (for those who are able): taking a sabbatical, arranging for more paid or unpaid time off from work, shortening your work day, using vacation time to go on a retreat or to do some special work for God, or taking on a special project for God within your line of work.

Another way to apply the Sabbatical year to the workplace would be to change jobs to something more pleasing to God. All honest work done with prayer and integrity is pleasing to God. But you might know of a different line of work, or a change in your job position, which would be more pleasing to God than your current work. During the Sabbatical year, each Christian should reflect on ways to make their work more pleasing to God. Even those Christians who cannot lessen their work, can make extra efforts to do their work more prayerfully and with greater integrity and honesty.

Sabbatical and Jubilee years should be a time of repentance and spiritual renewal. During such times, we Christians should make extra efforts to identify the sins in our lives. Many people commit sins and do not realize or care that they are sinning. Before you can repent of sin, you must first know which things are sinful. Christians should use the Sabbatical and Jubilee years to conform their consciences to the teachings of the Church. After identifying sin in our lives, we must admit to ourselves and to God that we are at fault and seek God's merciful forgiveness in the Sacrament of Reconciliation. Sabbatical and Jubilee years should be a time of increased use of the Sacraments by the faithful, especially the daily Sacraments of Confession and Communion. During such years, we Christians should seek to do Penance for our sins. God desires penance from us in the form of prayer, self-denial, and works of mercy. However, the best penance is not prayer or self-denial, or works of mercy; the best penance is change.

Change. Become more like Christ. Admit you were wrong and give up your sins and your sinful tendencies and attitudes. Give up all that pertains to sin. The penance that God most wants most from each of us is that we change and become new persons in Christ Jesus. We must make extra efforts to free ourselves from sinful habits and attachments. We must root out the causes and near-occasions of sin in our lives. We must look more closely at our own moral failings. Christian Sabbatical and Jubilee years are particularly good times for increased emphasis on the penance of abandoning sin and becoming more like Christ.

Prayer: Christian Sabbatical and Jubilee years should be a time when we seek to move closer to God in prayer. There are many holy ways to approach God in prayer; all of these ways include sincerity and humility and the desire to seek God's will. The Rosary and the Divine Mercy Chaplet are particularly good forms of recited prayer. The Sacred Mass as a whole is a kind of prayer to God. And there are other good ways to pray. Prayer is essential to the spiritual life. Whoever prays little, loves little. Whoever loves little, loves God little. To grow in love for God, you must pray and pray and pray.

Self-denial: Christian Sabbatical and Jubilee years should be times of self-denial. Much has been said about fasting in the spiritual life. Fasting from food is one good type of self-denial. But if you only practice self-denial in food, then you are not carrying your cross as Christ asked you. Christians must practice self-denial in all things, in all things, in all things. Every aspect of your life must include self-denial. Even the things in your life that you call "good" and "for God" must include self-denial.

Mercy: Christian Sabbatical and Jubilee years should be a time of forgiveness and release from debt. Works of mercy towards others should be increased and emphasized during these years. I refer the reader to the spiritual and corporeal works of Mercy, as taught by the Church. There are many ways to show mercy to others. You must seek opportunities within the events of your daily life. Seek to be merciful in all things; then God will be merciful to you in all things.

The Sabbatical and Jubilee years are not only times when we should do certain things, but times when God will do certain things. God will give the Church special blessings in these years. So much is said about what Christians should do and say. But we should always rely primarily on what God will do and say, and not so much on ourselves. The Prayer of the Faithful, during the Sacred Mass, should be primarily requests to God, asking God to grant specific requests and favors. Sometimes the Prayer of the Faithful at Mass emphasizes what we should do, asking God to grant that we may help others and accomplish whatever is needed. On the contrary, faith relies primarily on God, and only secondarily on oneself, to accomplish the tasks of life. In the same way, the Christian Sabbatical and Jubilee years should be primarily times to rely on God and receive God's blessing. Only secondarily should these years be times to accomplish goals and tasks through our own efforts. These holy years are **not** a call to be in charge, organize groups of people, gather money and power, and tell others what to do. In any year, such behavior is not the will of God and is contrary to the meekness and humility to which we are all called.

Prayer in all things, self-denial in all things, mercy in all things—such is the Way of Christ.

Chapter 17
Technical Notes

The Modern Jewish Calendar

The months in the Jewish calendar follow the cycles of the moon. Each month begins with the new moon. The length of each month is either 29 or 30 days, because the length of each lunar cycle (from new moon to new moon) is between 29 and 30 days. Lunar cycles do not have one set length; they vary in length. The usual number cited for the length of the lunar cycle is 29.5306 days. However, that number is an average of the length of the lunar cycle over a number of years. The actual length of the lunar cycle goes through a cycle of its own. The lunar month increases in length as each month passes, then the lunar month decreases in length, and then the cycle repeats itself. Any particular lunar cycle will rarely have an exact length of 29.5306 days; but rather, the length of the lunar cycle moves through sets of months that are longer or shorter than that average length.

The length of 12 lunar months is approximately 354.37 days, which is approximately 11 days less than the length of the solar year, 365.25 days. In a purely lunar calendar, the months would recede though the seasons. Each month would begin about 11 days earlier each year, compared to the solar year. The months would move in relation to the seasons, so that a month which occurred in spring would occur earlier each year, eventually moving from spring to winter to fall to summer and back to spring again.

The Jewish calendar has 12 months of 29 or 30 days, leading to a year which is about 11 days shorter than the solar year. As a result, every 2 or 3 years, the Jewish calendar must add a 13th month, otherwise the feast of Passover would gradually move from spring into winter, and the other feasts and holy days would recede through the seasons also.

To prevent this from occurring, the Jewish calendar is periodically adjusted to stay in synch with the solar year. Every 2 or 3 years, a 13th month is added to the calendar. The month of Adar, which usually occurs just before the month of Nisan (when Passover occurs, in the spring) is repeated as Second Adar (AdarII). In the modern Jewish calendar, 7 of every 19 years are leap years. Thus 12 of every 19 years are about 11 days short of a solar year, but 7 of every 19 years have an additional 30 days added to the calendar. In those leap years, AdarI has 30 days (instead of the usual 29) and AdarII has 29 days, causing 30 days total to be added to the calendar in a leap year. Thus leap years are about 19 days longer than the solar year (instead of 11 days shorter). Those 7 leap years add enough days to the calendar, so that every 19 years has an average calendar year which is about the same length as the solar year. The cycle of 19 years, used to determine leap years, is called the Metonic Cycle.

The exact length of each common year and each leap year, in the modern Jewish calendar, varies. A common year can actually be 353, 354, or 355 days in length (12, 11, or 10 days shorter than a solar year) and a leap year can actually be 383, 384, or 385 days in length (18, 19, or 20 days longer than a solar year). The reason for the variation in a year's length is that certain months can be either 29 or 30 days (such as Heshvan and Kislev), so that adding a leap year is not the only way to adjust the length of the year.

The end result is that the Jewish calendar stays more or less in synch with the solar year and the Passover remains in the springtime (when grain is harvested in Israel).[1216]

The Ancient Jewish Calendar

In ancient times, the Jewish calendar was adjusted periodically by the addition of the leap month of AdarII every 2 or 3 years. However, the leap years did not follow the Metonic Cycle. The decision as to which years would be leap years was a human decision, so that leap months were added as needed to keep the Passover celebration from receding from spring to winter.[1217]

Similarly, in ancient times, the Jewish calendar did not have a set length for each month. Any month, including leap months, could be 29 days or 30 days, as needed to keep the months in synch with the lunar cycle.[1218] The length of each month, 29 or 30 days, was also determined in part by the desire to keep certain holy days (on which Jews could not work) from interfering with the Preparation Day of the Sabbath (on which work is done to prepare for the Sabbath day of rest from work). The decision as to whether a month had 29 or 30 days was a human decision. In the modern Jewish calendar, the months generally have set lengths. For example, Av is always 30 days long and Elul is always 29 days. But some months will vary in length, even in the modern calendar. For example, Heshvan and Kislev can each be either 29 or 30 days in length, depending on the year; and AdarI is usually 29 days, but has 30 days during any leap year.

New Moons

In the modern Jewish calendar, the start of each month is determined mainly by the date and time of the new moon, as determined by astronomical calculation. One cannot view the moon at the time of the astronomical new moon (except during a solar eclipse) because the moon is too close to the sun. Calculation, rather than observation, is used to determine the start of the months in the modern Jewish calendar.

In the ancient Jewish calendar, the start of each month was determined mainly by observation of the new crescent moon. This calendar system is called the observation-based calendar. Sometime after the astronomical new moon, usually one or two days later, the new moon has moved far enough away from the sun to be visible just after sunset. The new moon at this time has a thin crescent shape.

At some point in time, the Jewish people made a transition from an observation-based calendar to a calculation-based calendar. There is no clear agreement among scholars as to when this transition occurred. However, most scholars believe that in the first century A.D. the calendar was still observation-based. My belief is that the transition to a calculation-based calendar occurred in the first century B.C., during the reign of king Herod the Great.

Transition to a Calculation-based Calendar

When Herod the Great captured Jerusalem (43 B.C., my revised date), the Roman conquest of the Jewish people was completed. Roman politics, culture, and science then became more influential in the land of Israel, because the Romans controlled the country.

Roman scholars could calculate lunar eclipses and solar eclipses. Pliny the Elder explains that, as far back as the 6th century B.C., scholars could predict solar and lunar eclipses. He also states that, 200 years before Pliny the Elder's time, Hipparchus also made significant contributions to the study and prediction of eclipses.[1219] Hipparchus (a Greek astronomer) lived during the 2nd century B.C. Thus, Roman scholars had knowledge of eclipses and how to predict them, well before Herod's capture of Jerusalem in the first century B.C.

The Romans knew that solar eclipses always coincided with new moons. Pliny mentions his understanding of this fact.[1220] And Cassius Dio states the same: "for it [the moon] is eclipsed only at full moon, just as the sun is eclipsed at the time of the new moon."[1221] If one can calculate solar eclipses, one can also calculate new moons. To know when a solar eclipse will occur, one must be able to determine the future positions of the sun, moon and earth relative to one another. This is the same information needed to determine new moons.

Also, solar eclipses offer a way to verify calculations of new moons. The astronomical new moon is not generally visible because of its proximity to the sun. But during a solar eclipse the astronomical new moon is visible. In this way, the Roman's calculation of astronomical new moons could be periodically verified. Thus Roman scholars could calculate new moons as well as eclipses.

Once Herod captured Jerusalem, Roman and Jewish societies coexisted. Jewish scholars and Roman scholars became part of the same Roman empire. Jewish scholars were almost exclusively men of religion, either priests or Levites, or else scribes who were closely connected to the leaders among the priests. Jewish scholars could now more easily obtain knowledge from Roman scholars. (While the war was going on, this would have been much more difficult.)

Sometime within a few years after the capture of Jerusalem by Herod, Jewish religious leaders would have been able to calculate new moons. The Romans could calculate the relative positions of sun, moon, and earth closely enough to know if the moon would eclipse the sun, or merely pass nearby. Thus, the Jewish leaders, using the same knowledge, would be able to calculate new moons with a fairly high degree of precision. The Jewish religious leaders valued knowledge about new moons, as this was needed to make decisions about their liturgical calendar. It is reasonable to conclude that any knowledge about new moons the Romans had would be desired and obtained by the Jewish religious leaders soon after the Roman occupation of Israel began.

The Jewish religious leaders were able to calculate new moons, using knowledge obtained from the Romans. But what would cause them to apply that knowledge to the liturgical calendar, changing the way that the start of each month was determined?

Herod's capture of Jerusalem brought changes to the Jewish religion. Herod now controlled who was high priest, and, according to Josephus, Herod began to choose high priests from a different group of men among the Jews. "Herod was then made king by the Romans, but did no longer appoint high priests out of the family of Asamoneus; but made certain men to be so that were of no eminent families, but barely of those that were priests...."[1222] The Jewish high priest had authority over calendar decisions. When Herod brought about a change in leadership among the Jews, he may have unwittingly brought about changes to the Jewish calendar. The new high priests were from a different group and so likely had somewhat different ideas about religious issues, including calendar decisions. When you have someone from a different group making decisions, the decisions are likely to be different. This change in leadership was likely the cause of the change in the calendar, from an observation-based to a calculation-based calendar system. This change in leadership also brought other changes to the calendar, such as changing the start of the Sabbatical year from spring to autumn (see chapter 16).

The Jewish Calendar in the Writings of Blessed Anne Catherine

The writings of Blessed Anne Catherine Emmerich contain various references to Sabbaths, Jewish calendar dates, and dates in the Julian calendar, which would only fall in place as she describes them if the basis for the start of each Jewish month was a calculation of the astronomical new moon, and not the observation of the lunar crescent.

For example, when speaking about the days following the Birth of Jesus Christ, Blessed Anne Catherine said that the feast of Hanukah on Kislev 25 (the "Feast of the Consecration of the Temple") would have coincided with a Sabbath that year, and so was postponed a day (to avoid a conflict between the Sabbath day of rest and the celebration of Hanukah).[1223] In 15 B.C., Kislev 25 (by calculation) would have fallen on a Saturday (Dec. 15), and so Hanukah that year may well have been postponed until Sunday. If the calendar was determined by observation, Kislev 25 would have fallen one day later, on Sunday, Dec. 16.

In 15 B.C., the new moon which began the month of Kislev occurred on Nov. 20 at 12:39 p.m. Jerusalem time. Since the new moon fell after noontime, the next calendar day, Nov. 21, was Kislev 1, by the calculation-based system. The Jewish day begins at sunset, so Kislev 1 began at sunset on Nov. 20 and ended at sunset on Nov. 21. In calculating the first day of any month, if the time of the new moon began after apparent solar noon, the next calendar day would begin the month. If the time of the new moon began before noon, that same calendar day would begin the month. Since this was determined by calculation, it could be known in advance which day began the month. And, of course, noontime in the ancient Jewish calendar was determined by the sun, so that noontime was not 12:00 hours, but rather 'solar transit,' when the sun is at its highest point in the sky. The Jews called this time 'the sixth hour,' astronomers today call this time 'apparent solar noon.' This time of day is noon by a sundial.

If the calendar in 15 B.C. had been determined by observation, then Kislev 1 would have coincided with Nov. 22. The new crescent moon would have been visible the evening of Nov. 21 after sunset. Thus Kislev 1 would have begun at sunset on Nov. 21 and ended at sunset on Nov. 22. This would make Kislev 25 a Sunday, in contrast to Blessed Anne Catherine's statement that Kislev 25 was a Saturday.[1224]

Other mentions of dates and days of the week in Blessed Anne Catherine's writings fit well into this revised chronology, with the start of each month begin determined by calculation, not observation. In general, my revised chronology and the chronological comments made by Blessed Anne Catherine are complementary and support one another.

This book establishes that Christ was crucified in A.D. 19. Support for this year is found in the revised dates for the reigns of the Roman emperors (see chapter 13). All four Gospels tell us that Christ died on a Friday. The Gospel of John adds that the day was both Friday, the preparation day of the Sabbath, (Jn 19:31), and Nisan 14, the Preparation Day of the Passover, (Jn 19:14). Yet Nisan 14 would have only fallen on a Friday that year if Nisan 1 was determined by calculation and coincided with March 25. In A.D. 19, the astronomical new moon of March 25 occurred at 06:11 hours JST, and the new crescent moon would have been visible the evening of March 26 (see Appendix I, Chart 1). So, Nisan 1 would have been March 25 by calculation, but March 27 by observation. The year of A.D. 19 for Christ's death fits my understanding that the Jewish calendar at that time was determined by calculation, not observation.

Calendar Rules

In the modern Jewish calendar, sometimes the start of a month in the Jewish calendar is delayed a day, or even two days, to prevent the Sabbath (Saturday) or the preparation day of the Sabbath (Friday) from interfering with a holy day. For example, the start of the month of Tishri is not permitted to occur on Wednesday, Friday, or Sunday. If Tishri began on Wednesday, then Tishri 10 (Yom Kippur) would fall on Friday. This would cause a conflict between the obligation to rest and worship God on the Day of Atonement (Lev 23:26-32), and the need to prepare for the Sabbath, working on Friday, so as to be able to rest and worship on Saturday (Lev 23:3).

Tishri 1 is also not permitted to fall on a Friday, because then the first and last days of the Feast of Tabernacles, days of solemn rest (Lev 23:33-36), would also fall on Fridays. This situation would present a conflict between the need to work on the preparation day of the Sabbath, and the holy days of rest at the start and end of the Feast of Tabernacles. Tishri 1 is also not permitted, in the modern calendar, to fall on a Sunday, because then the first and last days of the Feast of Tabernacles, days of solemn rest, would also fall on a Sunday. Having two days in a row when one cannot do any work (Saturday and Sunday) would be difficult. To avoid such conflicts, the modern Jewish calendar is arranged so that Tishri does not fall on Wednesday, Friday, or Sunday.

In the ancient Jewish calendar, both before and after the transition to a calculation-based start of each month, there were similar rules affecting the start of Tishri and other months. The rule that Tishri cannot start on a Wednesday or Friday is an obvious necessity, due to the obligation, on Friday, to prepare for the Sabbath and the obligation to rest on certain feast days. This rule must have been observed, even in ancient times, for the obligations of those days have always been held in high regard by the Jews. The rule that Tishri cannot begin on a Sunday was, I suggest, not observed in ancient times. If Tishri 1 falls on Sunday, then the first and last days of the Feast of Tabernacles also fall on Sundays. This results in two days of rest in a row. People must prepare well on the preparation day of the Sabbath, so that they have food and necessities for two consecutive days. But there is no essential conflict with the obligations of faith.

My reconstruction of the Jewish calendar during the Ministry of Christ (A.D. 15-19) shows that Tishri 1 fell on a Sunday in A.D. 16. Blessed Anne Catherine states: "the people were still busied with preparations, because with the close of the coming Sabbath, the Feast of Tabernacles began."[1225] Since the Feast of Tabernacles that year began on Sunday, the first day of Tishri must also have been a Sunday.

Similar considerations affect the start of the month of Nisan, in both the ancient and modern Jewish calendars. The first day of Passover, Nisan 15, is a holy day of rest and worship of God (Lev 23:5-7). This day is not permitted to fall on a Friday, because then the preparation day of the Sabbath would interfere with the first holy day of Passover. Thus Nisan cannot begin on a Friday. On the other hand, the preparation day of the Sabbath, Friday, can coincide with the Preparation Day of the Passover, Nisan 14. This was the case in the year of Christ's Crucifixion (Jn 19:14, 31).

Since Nisan 15 cannot fall on Friday, Nisan 14 cannot fall on Thursday. Since the Passover meal is held on the evening of Nisan 14, the Passover meal does not ever occur on a Thursday evening in the modern calendar. And, even in ancient times, Nisan 14 could not fall on a Thursday. So, when Jesus and the disciples held the Passover meal on Thursday evening, they were celebrating the Passover meal a day early. According to Blessed Anne Catherine, this was permitted to the Jews from Galilee since ancient times, due to the large number of sacrifices of lambs required at the Passover at Jerusalem.[1226]

Astronomy and Chronology

Astronomy provides useful information in the study of Biblical chronology. With modern-day computer programs, scholars can determine the past dates and times of various astronomical events, including solar eclipses, lunar eclipses, equinoxes, and lunar phases. We can also determine where each eclipse was visible, how long it lasted, and its general appearance.

The Jewish calendar is based on the phases of the moon and, to some extent, the Spring Equinox. In reconstructing the Jewish calendar of ancient times, we need information on the date and time of new moons and of the Spring Equinox. With such information, we can determine when the important feasts, such as Passover, the Feast of Weeks, and the Feast of Tabernacles, occurred. In some cases, we can be fairly certain about such determinations. For example, some scholars think that Christ was crucified in A.D. 30, and some think A.D. 33, but no scholar thinks Christ died in A.D. 31 or 32. A reconstruction of the Jewish calendar for A.D. 31 and 32 shows, with a high degree of certainty, that Passover did not begin on a Friday in those years.

On the other hand, for certain years in the ancient Jewish calendar, a human decision was made by the leaders of the Jewish faith whether or not to make a particular year a leap year. The ancient Jewish calendar did not follow the modern pattern of leap years, called the Metonic Cycle. Rather, the religious leaders decided when to have a leap year, adding a 13th month to the calendar just before the month of Nisan, based on a number of factors. Those factors included whether or not the grain crop was ready for harvest, whether or not the fruit trees were ready for harvest, and whether the start of Passover would fall before or after the Spring Equinox.[1227] If the crops were ready for harvest and the Passover would fall after the Spring Equinox, a leap year was not needed. Since we have no way of knowing what the state of the harvest was in particular years in ancient times, whenever the date for the start of Passover is close to that of the Spring Equinox we end up with some uncertainty about the leap year.

An example of uncertainty in reconstructing the Jewish calendar is seen in the year 5 B.C. If a 13th month, AdarII, was added to the calendar in spring of 5 B.C., then the dates of Passover and the Feast of Tabernacles would be a month later than their dates without the addition of a leap month. Because the Passover would fall close to the Spring Equinox without a leap year, we cannot determine with certainty whether or not the Jewish leaders decided to add the leap month of AdarII. This results in two possibilities for dates in a reconstructed calendar (see chapter 12).

The ancient Roman historians often recorded astronomical events, such as eclipses and comet sightings, because they associated these with historical events. If a comet was sighted, or if an eclipse occurred, the Roman people generally believed that this had some meaning for the Roman empire. Comet sightings were often interpreted as foreshadowing the death of the Roman emperor. See chapter 13 of this book for numerous examples.

Lunar eclipses are visible from anywhere on earth where it will be dark at some point during the eclipse. Lunar eclipses can last for several hours and can also be visible at dawn and dusk. There are anywhere from 2 to 4 lunar eclipses each year. However, some of these lunar eclipses are very brief, partial eclipses where the shadow of the earth passes over only a small portion of the visible disc of the moon. Such eclipses (called partial penumbral lunar eclipses) are not generally observable without a telescope.

Solar eclipses are generally more helpful than lunar eclipses in determining an historical date. Any particular solar eclipse can be seen from only a small portion of the earth's surface, whereas any lunar eclipse can be seen from any place on earth where it is dark during the eclipse, and from places where is it dusk or dawn. As a result, there are more lunar eclipses visible from the Roman empire than solar eclipses. Since a solar eclipse is less likely to have been seen, its mention in relation to an historical event is more specific and more likely to help us determine the date of the historical event.

Comet sightings were also mentioned by the ancient Roman historians. Computer astronomy programs are of limited value in determining when ancient comet sightings occurred. Many comets are seen only once; only a few comets return century after century, as Halley's comet does. However, ancient Chinese and Korean astronomers observed the stars closely and kept careful records of the date, location, and appearance of comets. Since the ancient Chinese calendar system (a lunar calendar) is unrelated to the B.C./A.D. system, this provides a way to independently verify the dates of sightings mentioned by the Roman historians.

The best modern source of information on these ancient comet sightings is undoubtedly *Cometography, A Catalog of Comets, Volume 1,* by Gary W. Kronk. This book covers every ancient comet from 675 B.C. to A.D. 1799, and consolidates all of the often quoted sources for ancient comet data, such as the Han shu (an ancient Chinese text), J. Williams, Ho Peng Yoke, A. G. Pingré, and others. Treatment is even given to mentions of comets found in ancient Roman texts.

Comets are typically visible (with the naked eye) for a period of a few days to a few weeks. They travel in an arc around the sun and should be visible, at some point in their path, from both Europe and China. Thus, any noted comet in Roman history would likely have been observed and mentioned by the ancient astronomers of China. It should then be possible, in a given chronology for dates in the reigns of Roman emperors, to match the mention of comets in Roman texts to those in Chinese texts. Comet data is examined in chapter 13 of this book, along with a revised chronology of the reigns of the Roman emperors, from Julius Caesar to Domitian.

Astronomers use a slightly modified version of the usual B.C./A.D. calendar. The B.C./A.D. calendar system does not have a year zero. For this reason, one cannot simply add or subtract to find the number of years from a date B.C. to a date A.D. (or vise versa). Astronomers give the year 1 B.C. the number zero; 2 B.C. is given the number negative 1; 3 B.C. is negative 2, and so on. This allows one to easily calculate the number of years between dates by addition and subtraction. This numbering system for the years in the B.C./A.D. calendar is called the astronomical dating system.

Sources for Astronomy Calculations

This book relies on two sources for the dates and times of solar eclipses, lunar eclipses, and lunar phases. The first source is the astronomy software program *RedShift 3*, developed by Maris Multimedia, Ltd (ISBN 1-888023-22-8). *RedShift 3* not only provides the date, time, and duration for each eclipse, but also displays a realistic view of the sky from any point on earth, at any point in time stretching back for thousands of years. One can use this software to watch an eclipse much as it might have been seen from Jerusalem, or Rome, or some other location. This software provides dates, times, and other information for eclipses, lunar phases, and the Spring Equinox.

The second source for data on solar and lunar eclipses and lunar phases is Fred Espenak's Eclipse Home Page at the NASA/GSFC Sun-Earth Connection Education Forum:

NASA/GSFC Sun-Earth Connection Education Forum
http://sunearth.gsfc.nasa.gov/eclipse/eclipse.html

Five Millennium Catalog of Solar Eclipses
http://sunearth.gsfc.nasa.gov/eclipse/SEcat/SEcatalog.html

Five Millennium Catalog of Lunar Eclipses
http://sunearth.gsfc.nasa.gov/eclipse/LEcat/LEcatalog.html

Five Millennia Catalog of Phases of the Moon
http://sunearth.gsfc.nasa.gov/eclipse/phase/phasecat.html

Eclipse predictions are provided courtesy of Fred Espenak, NASA/Goddard Space Flight Center. "All eclipse calculations are by Fred Espenak, and he assumes full responsibility for their accuracy."[1228]

The *Five Millennia Catalog of Phases of the Moon* provides: "...the date and time (Greenwich Mean Time) of all phases of the Moon for a period covering five millennia. This data is provided primarily to assist in historical research projects."[1229]

Fred Espenak is a scientist at NASA's Goddard Space Flight Center. He is the author of the book, *Fifty Years of Canon of Lunar Eclipses 1986-2035* (Sky Publishing Corp.), and co-author of the book, *Totality : Eclipses of the Sun*, (Oxford University Press). No endorsement of the premises or conclusions of this book by Fred Espenak or by NASA is implied, nor should be inferred.

The dates and times for eclipses and lunar phases given by Fred Espenak on the NASA/GSFC web site correlate well with the data given by the *RedShift 3* software. The correlation between the data from *RedShift 3* and from the NASA/GSFC web site on eclipses and phases of the moon is not exact, but differs for the times of eclipses and new moons by about 9 to 12 minutes. This small difference is not enough to affect the date of an eclipse or the date for the start of a month in the Jewish lunar calendar.

The fact that a difference occurs at all indicates that a somewhat different calculation method was used by these two sources of data. If the same method is used by two different sources to arrive at the exact same conclusion, this is not like two witness, but one, since the method is one and the same. But when two different methods are used to arrive at nearly the same conclusion, this provides further support for the conclusion, since two different approaches gave essentially the same result.

The difference between the *RedShift 3* data and the NASA/GSFC web site data, a difference of 9 to 12 minutes or so, does not affect the calculation as to whether or not an eclipse was visible. The difference of 12 minutes or so is only a matter of what time one gives to a particular event. For example, the NASA/GSFC web site has a solar eclipse on June 30 of A.D. 10 at 11:19 hours Universal Time (U.T.). *RedShift 3* has a solar eclipse on June 30 of A.D. 10 at 11:08 U.T.

The difference in calculations is not a difference in the relative positions of the sun, moon, and earth on any one day. If it were, then 11 minutes would be the difference between whether an eclipse occurred or not. Rather, both sources have the sun, moon, and earth in the same positions relative to one another. The difference is basically the amount of time which has lapsed since the moon, sun, and earth were in such a position relative to one another. This is clearly seen when one compares the data on solar eclipses from the two sources. They both agree in every case as to whether or not there was an eclipse and as to what kind of eclipse it was (total or partial). If there was a difference in the positions of the sun, moon, and earth relative to one another, then one set of data would be saying that there was a total eclipse, and the other set of data would be saying that there was no eclipse at all, or that it was only a partial eclipse. Since that is not the case, the fact that two different sets of calculations arrived at very much the same conclusions is reassuring and constitutes the evidence of two witnesses who agree.

The evidence of two or three witnesses is needed to decide a case (Mt 18:16; Deut 17:6; 2 Cor 13:1). Since the data from both the NASA/GSFC web site and *RedShift 3* software are in close agreement, we can have confidence is this data and use it to assist in determining the dates of events in the first century B.C. and first century A.D.

Solar Eclipses and Augustus Caesar's Death

From A.D. 10 to A.D. 14, inclusive, there is only one solar eclipse that fits the description given by Dio for the eclipse prior to Augustus Caesar's death—the eclipse of June 30, A.D. 10. Below is a list of eclipse dates and times, taken from the *Five Millennium Catalog of Solar Eclipses* on the NASA/GSFC web site.[1230] Beside each eclipse is noted the area of the earth's surface which was covered by the shadow of the moon during the solar eclipse, according to *RedShift 3* software.[1231]

Date	U.T.	Mag.	Lat./Long.	Visible from
0010 Jan 04	05:13	0.914	75.5S 103.0E	Antarctica
0010 Jun 30	11:19	1.060	82.9N 13.5W	Europe
0010 Nov 24	13:49	0.119	63.3N 12.3E	Northern Europe
0010 Dec 24	05:48	0.218	65.8S 73.5W	Antarctica
0011 May 21	15:05	0.980	56.3S 12.8W	South America, South Africa
0011 Nov 14	00:48	1.020	27.2N 177.2W	Pacific Ocean
0012 May 09	19:05	0.953	4.4N 102.6W	Central and South America
0012 Nov 02	16:07	1.049	11.5S 63.7W	South America
0013 Apr 28	19:35	0.951	41.7N 132.5W	North America
0013 Oct 23	07:10	1.019	44.6S 46.0E	Antarctica
0014 Mar 19	12:57	0.186	60.9S 80.5E	Antarctica
0014 Apr 18	00:01	0.528	61.2N 71.1E	Russia
0014 Sep 13	02:12	0.105	60.8N 115.1W	Alaska, Western Canada
0014 Oct 12	17:23	0.298	61.0S 173.7E	Antarctica

The first two columns above are the year, month, and day of the solar eclipse. The next column is the time, using a 24-hour clock, in Universal Time (essentially equivalent to Greenwich Mean Time). The time in Rome would be 1 hour later than U.T.; the time in Jerusalem would be 2 hours later than U.T. The time of the eclipse is given at the point when the eclipse is greatest. The next column is the magnitude of the eclipse. If the magnitude is 1.0 or greater, the eclipse is a total eclipse. The next columns have the location of the eclipse, in latitude and longitude, at the time of its greatest magnitude. The last column is the location on earth from which the eclipse was visible, at any point in time during the eclipse. Please note that an eclipse whose latitude and longitude places it in one location during its greatest magnitude could easily be visible from other locations before and after the time of its greatest magnitude. The last column's information was determined using *RedShift 3* software to view a simulation of the surface of the earth during the entire solar eclipse.

Only two eclipses were visible from anywhere in the Roman empire during the years A.D. 10 to 14. Both of those eclipses occurred in A.D. 10. The first was the eclipse of June 30, A.D. 10, which was visible from Italy and most of Europe. This total eclipse would have been seen from most of the Roman empire as a partial, but still substantial, eclipse. It occurred less then two months prior to my revised date for the death of

Augustus, August 19 of A.D. 10. This is the only eclipse from A.D. 10 to 14 which fits Dio's description of the eclipse before Augustus' death.[1232]

The second eclipse visible from Europe during that time period occurred on Nov. 24 of A.D. 10. It was a very partial eclipse, at best covering less than 12% of the visible disk of the sun. This eclipse was visible from northern Europe, specifically from England, northern France, and Germany. It was not visible from most of Italy, nor from Spain. In the areas of the Roman empire where it was visible, it would have affected much less than 12% of the sun's visible disk and been a very brief, very partial eclipse. A brief, very partial eclipse does not fit Dio's description of a substantial eclipse.[1233] Since this eclipse occurred after August 19, not before, it does not fit Dio's description of a solar eclipse which preceded the death of Augustus.

Lunar Eclipses and Herod the Great's Death

As discussed in chapter 12 of this book, Josephus describes a lunar eclipse occurring after the fast day (Yom Kippur; the Day of Atonement) and well before the Passover. The following is a list of every lunar eclipse from 10 B.C. to A.D. 1. The list is taken from the *Five Millennium Catalog of Lunar Eclipses*.[1234] This data was also compared to simulations of these eclipses in the astronomy software, *RedShift 3*.[1235]

Date	U.T.	Pen. /Umb. Mag.		S.D. Partial/Total	
-0009 Jan 19	00:43	0.305	-0.713	-	-
-0009 Jun 15	22:08	0.741	-0.348	-	-
-0009 Dec 10	04:58	1.691	0.697	82m	-
-0008 Jun 03	23:12	2.147	1.075	106m	22m
-0008 Nov 28	19:02	2.844	1.813	109m	50m
-0007 May 24	05:51	2.202	1.181	104m	32m
-0007 Nov 18	03:15	1.544	0.455	75m	-
-0006 Apr 14	12:17	0.267	-0.698	-	-
-0006 May 13	19:26	0.843	-0.129	-	-
-0006 Oct 08	09:31	0.048	-1.070	-	-
-0006 Nov 07	04:26	0.257	-0.869	-	-
-0005 Apr 04	05:09	1.557	0.579	77m	-
-0005 Sep 27	11:19	1.374	0.298	62m	-
-0004 Mar 23	18:32	2.850	1.821	111m	51m
-0004 Sep 15	20:22	2.730	1.715	109m	50m
-0003 Mar 13	00:52	1.456	0.370	70m	-
-0003 Sep 05	11:18	1.723	0.745	84m	-
-0002 Jan 31	07:55	0.293	-0.814	-	-
-0002 Mar 02	01:18	0.126	-0.983	-	-
-0002 Jul 27	18:56	0.550	-0.447	-	-
-0002 Aug 26	03:44	0.435	-0.549	-	-

-0001 Jan 20	12:04	1.646	0.587	82m	-
-0001 Jul 17	05:25	1.880	0.829	95m	-
0000 Jan 09	23:20	2.801	1.794	107m	50m
0000 Jul 05	08:49	2.537	1.448	115m	48m
0000 Dec 29	14:43	1.570	0.581	76m	-
0001 Jun 24	09:25	1.150	0.069	32m	-
0001 Nov 19	16:47	0.364	-0.683	-	-
0001 Dec 19	05:38	0.318	-0.700	-	-

The first column above is the year, month, and day. The year is given using astronomical dating, where 0001 is A.D. 1; 0000 is 1 B.C.; -0001 is 2 B.C.; etc. The next column is the time in Universal Time (which uses a 24-hour clock). The next two columns are the penumbral and umbral magnitudes of the eclipse.

The umbra of a lunar eclipse is the area of darkest shadow of the earth, seen on the visible disk of the moon during an umbral lunar eclipse. The penumbra is the area of partial shadow of the earth. The magnitude of each of these two types of shadows is the percentage of the visible surface of the moon covered by the shadow. A magnitude of 1.0 or greater means that the entire visible disk of the moon is covered by the earth's shadow (at the time of greatest magnitude). If the umbral magnitude is greater than or equal to 1.0, the eclipse is a total eclipse. If the umbral magnitude is less than 1.0 and greater than zero, the eclipse is a partial eclipse. If the umbral magnitude is less than zero, then the eclipse is a penumbral eclipse. If the umbral magnitude is less than zero and the penumbral magnitude is 1.0 or greater, the eclipse is a total penumbral eclipse. (If both the umbral and penumbral magnitudes are less than zero, then there is no eclipse at all.) A negative number for the umbral magnitude means that the umbra (the darkest part of the earth's shadow) does not affect the visible disk of the moon for that particular eclipse at all. Such eclipses are called penumbral eclipses.

The last two columns are the semi-duration of the partial and total eclipses. The semi-duration of the partial eclipse is one half the time that any portion of the umbral shadow is seen on the moon's surface. The partial eclipse begins when the umbral shadow is first seen on the visible disk of the moon, and ends when it is last seen. The semi-duration of the total eclipse is one half the length of time that the visible surface of the moon is completely covered by the umbra. Every total lunar eclipse will have a semi-duration number for both the partial and total phases of the eclipse. Partial lunar eclipses will only have a semi-duration number for the partial eclipse.

Penumbral eclipses will not have a semi-duration number at all, because semi-durations refer only to the umbral shadow, not the penumbral shadow. Penumbral eclipses are difficult to observe and may not be noticeable to the casual observer at all. This is because the penumbral shadow is only a partial shadow. It is darkest close to the umbral shadow and progressively lighter away from the umbral shadow. For this reason, brief or partial penumbral eclipses would not have been noticed by observers in ancient times and would not be recorded by the ancient historians as lunar eclipses.

None of the penumbral lunar eclipses (those with two dashes in the last columns), listed above, could have been the lunar eclipse prior to the death of Herod. Penumbral eclipses are not noticeable to the casual observer and may be difficult or impossible to discern with the naked eye, even for a knowledgeable observer. This is particularly true for penumbral eclipses with small magnitudes. In penumbral eclipses with smaller magnitudes, only the lighter portion of the penumbra covers a portion of the moon's surface. Furthermore, the penumbral eclipses above that are of greater magnitude (> 0.4) did not occur between the Day of Atonement (Tishri 10, in the autumn) and the Passover (Nisan 14, in the spring), as required by Josephus' description (see chapter 12).

Several of the remaining eclipses, those that are umbral rather than penumbral, can also be ruled out because they did not occur between the months of Tishri and Nisan: -0008 Jun 03, -0007 May 24, -0003 Sep 05, -0001 Jul 17, 0000 Jul 05, and 0001 Jun 24. In addition, the eclipse of -0005 Apr 04 (6 B.C.) is ruled out because it occurred during the Passover that year. According to Josephus, a number of time-consuming events occurred between the lunar eclipse and the death of Herod and the subsequent Passover (see chapter 12). Thus the eclipse could not have occurred during the Passover.

Interestingly, we can also rule out any eclipse which occurred immediately after the Day of Atonement at the start of the Feast of Tabernacles. Every able-bodied adult Jewish man was required by the Jewish Law to attend the Feast of Tabernacles (Deut 16:16). With so many devout Jews staying in and around Jerusalem for the feast, Herod would not have chosen such a time to put to death 40 students of the Temple and two of their teachers.[1236] Furthermore, Josephus, a Jewish priest, would most likely have made mention, if the deaths of these Jewish martyrs occurred at the start of the holy Feast of Tabernacles. He mentions the Day of Atonement (Tishri 10) in association with the high priest, the one whom Herod later deposed, but he does not associate the deaths of the Jewish martyrs (at the time of the eclipse) with the Feast of Tabernacles. On this basis, the following eclipses are ruled out: -0005 Sep 27 and -0004 Sep 15. In addition, the Sept. 27 eclipse in 6 B.C. (-0005) occurred during the daylight hours in Jerusalem (UT + 2 hours), and so was not visible.

Note also that the Sept. 15, 5 B.C. eclipse (-0004) would have preceded the month of Tishri if spring of 5 B.C. contained the leap month of AdarII. In 5 B.C., the decision as to whether or not to add a leap month before the month of Nisan could have gone either way (because the Passover would begin close to the Spring Equinox). With the leap month of AdarII added, the eclipse would be ruled out because it would have occurred before Tishri. Without the leap month added, the eclipse would have occurred during Tishri, at the start of the Feast of Tabernacles. In either case, the eclipse is ruled out as the eclipse at the time of Herod's death.

As explained in detail in chapter 12 of this book, one lunar month is not a sufficient length of time to contain all of the events Josephus describes from the eclipse to the death of Herod to the subsequent Passover. On this basis, the eclipses of -0004 Mar 23 and -0003 Mar 13 are ruled out. Note that the March 13, 4 B.C. (-0003) eclipse is often cited as the eclipse before the proposed date for the death of Herod in 4 B.C.

The March 13, 4 B.C. (-0003) eclipse has two additional problems. First, it began very late at night. The umbral shadow could first be seen on the moon at about 01:42 hours on Mar. 14, Jerusalem Standard Time (JST): the time of greatest eclipse (00:52) minus

S.D. partial (70 min.) and adjusted for Jerusalem Standard Time (by adding two hours). Second, this eclipse at its time of greatest magnitude (02:52 JST) covered only 37 percent of the moon's visible disk. An eclipse such as this one, occurring very late at night and affecting considerably less than that 37% of the moon for most of the time of the eclipse (the 37% was at the time of greatest magnitude) would not have been likely to have been noticed by many persons, remembered in association with the events of the previous day, and recorded in the history of Josephus.

An ideal candidate for the eclipse before Herod's death would be a total eclipse of the moon beginning in the early evening when many persons are still awake and outside. Such an eclipse would have at least 3, and preferably 4 or more, months between the eclipse and the Passover, in order to allow for all of the events described by Josephus.

There are six remaining lunar eclipses, in the period 10 B.C. to 1 A.D., to be considered. The -0009 Dec 10 eclipse (10 B.C.) was an early morning eclipse. The time of greatest eclipse was 04:58 hours U.T., that is, 06:58 hours Jerusalem time. The eclipse would have first been visible about 82 minutes earlier (05:36 hours), when the umbral shadow began to move across the moon. Sunrise that day occurred about 06:32 hours.[1237] But the sky begins to brighten an hour or more before the visible disk of the sun is seen above the horizon at sunrise. And much of this eclipse occurred after sunrise. Thus the visibility of this eclipse was reduced by the brightness of the sky. More importantly, Josephus describes the eclipse before Herod's death in this way: "And that very night there was an eclipse of the moon."[1238] The eclipse of Dec. 10 in 10 B.C. did not even begin to be visible until morning had arrived with the brightening of the sky which precedes sunrise. This was not a nighttime lunar eclipse and so this was not the eclipse before Herod's death.

The eclipse of -0007 Nov 18 (8 B.C.) has much the same problem. It began while the sky was still dark, but much of the eclipse took place after the sky began to brighten, and the eclipse ended after sunrise. The time of greatest eclipse was 03:15 hours U.T. (05:15 hours, JST). The eclipse began to be visible about 75 minutes earlier, at about 04:00 hours, JST (Jerusalem Standard Time). Sunrise occurred about 06:13 hours.[1239] But the sky began to brighten an hour or more before sunrise. And the eclipse ended about 06:30 hours JST, that is, about 75 minutes after the time of greatest eclipse. This eclipse was also a morning eclipse, partially obscured by the brightening of the sky prior to sunrise. This was not the eclipse described by Josephus.

The eclipse of 0000 Dec 29 (1 B.C.) has a similar problem, but at the other end of the daylight hours. Most of this eclipse occurred before moonrise, while the moon was still below the horizon. As the moon rose, the eclipse was ending and the sun was setting, but the sky was still bright and by the time the sky was dark, the umbral shadow was no longer on the moon. The time of greatest eclipse was 14:43 hours U.T., which is 16:43 hours JST. Sunset that day was approx. 16:48 hours, but the sky remains bright for sometime after sunset.[1240] Josephus describes the eclipse before Herod's death as occurring at nighttime, but this eclipse was over by the time darkness set in.

The eclipse of -0001 Jan 20 (2 B.C.) can be ruled out simply because it was not visible from Jerusalem. The time of greatest eclipse is 12:04 hours U.T., which is 14:04 hours Jerusalem time. By the time the eclipse ended, 82 minutes or so later, the moon was still below the horizon, from the point of view of Jerusalem.

The two remaining eclipses are, in and of themselves, eclipses which fit the description given by Josephus. These eclipses occurred on -0008 Nov 28 (9 B.C.) and 0000 Jan 09 (1 B.C.). Each occurred between the Feast of Tabernacles and the Feast of Passover, 3 or more months before the Passover, at nighttime. Each was an impressive total lunar eclipse, lasting over 3.5 hours.

The Nov 28 of 9 B.C. eclipse has the advantage of having occurred somewhat earlier in the night. The time of greatest eclipse was 19:02 hours U.T., which is 21:02 hours JST. The eclipse began 109 minutes before the time of greatest eclipse, at about 19:13 hours JST. Sunset that day occurred at approx. 17:21 hours. This eclipse began less than 2 hours after sunset. Thus the eclipse began after the sky had become dark, but soon enough in the evening to be seen by many persons (about 7:13 p.m.).

The Jan 09 of 1 B.C. eclipse occurred somewhat later in the night. The time of greatest eclipse was 23:20 hours U.T., which is 01:20 hours Jerusalem time. The eclipse began 107 minutes before the time of greatest eclipse, at about 23:33 hours J.S.T. Sunset that day occurred at approx. 16:55 hours. This eclipse began more than 6 hours after sunset (about 11:33 p.m.), when fewer persons were likely to have seen it.

An earlier eclipse is more likely to have been noticed, remembered, and recorded by Josephus. However, both of the above eclipses are a plausible fit for Josephus' description. In chapter 12 of this book, I conclude that the Nov 28 of 9 B.C. eclipse was the eclipse before Herod's death and that Herod died in early 8 B.C. The basis for this conclusion is discussed in chapters 12 and 13 in great detail. In summary, numerous pieces of evidence point to an earlier date for the reigns of various Roman emperors and rulers (see chapter 13). The earlier eclipse of 9 B.C. fits that earlier chronology, whereas the later eclipse of 1 B.C. does not. Also, the information we have from Josephus about the length of Herod's reign and the start of his reign at the capture of Jerusalem fit the earlier date for Herod's death, but not the later date (see chapter 12).

The Start of Passover: A.D. 15 to A.D. 36

Christ was crucified at the start of Passover, on a Friday and Nisan 14 (Jn 19:14, 31). Passover does not always begin on a Friday, so we must determine which years could have had a Nisan 14 Friday. See Appendix I, Chart 1 for a summary of this information.

My conclusion, detailed above, is that the start of each month in the Jewish calendar, during the time of Christ's life, was generally according to the calculated day and time of the new moon. In other words, the astronomical new moon, not the observed new crescent moon, was used to determine the first day of each month. However, due to the contrary opinion of many scholars, I have included in Chart 1 the possible dates for Nisan 14 according to either method.

The only years, in this date range, which could possibly have had a Nisan 14 Friday are A.D. 15, 16, 19, 22, 23, 26, 27, 30, 33, 34, and 36. If the start of Nisan was by calculation, the list of Nisan 14 Fridays is narrowed to A.D. 15, 16, 19, 22, 26, 33, and 36 (most probably ruling out A.D. 23, 27, 30, and 34). The year A.D. 16 could still have had a Nisan 14 Friday, due to the need to delay the start of Nisan (so that Nisan 15 would not conflict with Friday, the preparation day of the Sabbath). The same consideration applies to the year A.D. 33.

If the start of Nisan was by observation of the crescent new moon, then the years A.D. 15, 19, 22, 26, and 36 are most probably ruled out, leaving us with the years A.D. 16, 23, 27, 30, 33, and 34. Notice that A.D. 33 has a Nisan 14 Friday regardless of whether the start of the month was by calculation or observation. If by calculation, a day's delay is needed to prevent Nisan 15 from falling on a Friday. This pushes the date by calculation ahead enough to coincide with the date by observation. A similar consideration applies to A.D. 16, but with less certainty. See Appendix I, Chart 1, for further information.

In chapter 2, I conclude that Christ was crucified on Friday, April 7 and Nisan 14, in A.D. 19. This year falls within my revised dates for the reign of Pontius Pilate (see chapters 2 and 13). It meets the criteria for a Passover beginning on a Friday, Nisan 14. And it is long enough into the reign of Pilate to account for the 3½ year Ministry of Jesus Christ and for the ministry of John the Baptist, both of which began after Pilate began his rule over Judea. John's ministry began in the 15th year of Tiberius Caesar's reign (Lk 3:1). According to the conclusions of chapter 13, Tiberius' 15th year was A.D. 15. This leaves us with A.D. 19 as the only year fitting our criteria for the year of the Crucifixion of Jesus Christ.

Appendix I: Chart 1
Passover Dates, A.D. 15 – 36: Notes

Age (of moon) = amount of time from the astronomical new moon to sunset (hours : minutes). Lag1 = time of moonset minus time of sunset (in minutes) on the first evening (at sunset) after the astronomical new moon. Lag2 = time of moonset minus time of sunset (in minutes) on the second evening after the astronomical new moon. Times are given below in Jerusalem time (GMT + 2 hours). Day of **first** indisputable opportunity to view the crescent new moon after sunset is given in **bold type**, (borderline cases are underlined). Most probable Nisan 14 Passover dates, using observation-based calendar, are also in **bold**.

This book concludes that Nisan 1 and Passover dates were determined by calculation, not observation (see chapter 17). An astronomical new moon date prior to solar transit (noon sun time) would place Nisan 1 on the same day as the new moon date; if after solar transit, Nisan 1 would begin the next day. The first date in the column for Nisan 14 range is the one accepted in this book's conclusions.

Jewish leap years were determined in ancient times by three factors: the date for the Spring Equinox, the maturity of the grain harvest, the maturity of the fruit trees harvest.[1241] Since we can only determine the date of the Spring Equinox, we cannot be certain which years were leap years. The decision as to which years would be leap years, in ancient times, was a human decision made by the Jewish religious leaders. For this reason, in some years two sets of dates are given in Chart 1, to take into account the possibility of a Jewish leap year.

Nisan 14 was not allowed to fall on a Thursday (to avoid conflict between Nisan 15 and Friday, the preparation day of the Sabbath). In such a case, Nisan 1 would be delayed a day, from Friday to Saturday, and Nisan 14 would fall on a Friday instead of a Thursday. The above ranges for Nisan 1 and Nisan 14 take this consideration into account. For this reason, there should not be any Friday Nisan 1 dates or Thursday Nisan 14 dates in Chart 1.

New moon and Spring Equinox dates and times taken from *RedShift 3* astronomy software. New moon dates were checked against data from NASA web site. Days of the week taken from Universal Calendar Calculator

(See the Chart on the following two pages.)

Appendix I: Chart 1
Passover Dates, A.D. 15 - 36

Year	New Moon	Nisan 1 (range)	1st Evening Lag1, Age, Date
A.D. 15	Mar. 9, 04:46	Mar. 9 (Sat.), 10 , 11	31, 12:57, Mar. 9
Or	Apr. 7, 13:43	Apr. 8 (Mon.), 9, 10	9, 4:17, Apr. 7
A.D. 16	Mar. 27, 06:00	Mar. 28 (Sat; delayed), 29	32, 11:54, Mar. 27
A.D. 17	Mar. 16, 22:22	Mar. 17 (Wed.), 18	52, 19:26, **Mar. 17**
Or	Apr. 15, 06:34	Apr. 15 (Thurs), 17 (Sat.)	34, 11:31, Apr. 15
A.D. 18	Apr. 4, 21:28	Apr. 5 (Tues), 6, 7	55, 20:31, **Apr. 5**
A.D. 19	Mar. 25, 06:11	Mar. 25 (Sat.), 26, 27	27, 11:41, Mar. 25
A.D. 20	Mar. 13, 8:00	Mar. 13 (Wed.), 14, 16	20, 9:46, Mar. 13
Or	Apr. 11, 23:54	Apr. 13 (Sat.; delayed), 13	41, 18:09, Apr. 12
A.D. 21	Apr. 1, 00:23	Apr. 1 (Tues.), 2, 3	37, 17:34, Apr. 1
A.D. 22	Mar. 21, 03:14	Mar. 21 (Sat.), 22, 23	32, 14:36, Mar. 21
A.D. 23	Mar. 10, 13:03	Mar. 11 (Thurs.), 13 (Sat.)	10, 4:40, Mar. 10
Or	Apr. 8, 23:49	Apr. 9 (Sat.), 10, 11	41, 18:53, Apr. 9
A.D. 24	Mar. 28, 13:08	Mar 29 (Wed.), 30	7, 4:47, Mar. 28
A.D. 25	Mar. 18, 05:52	Mar. 18 (Sun.), 19, 20	29, 11:56, Mar. 18
A.D. 26	Apr. 6, 06:34	Apr. 6 (Sat.), 7, 8	24, 11:26, Apr. 6
A.D. 27	Mar. 26, 20:03	Mar. 27 (Thurs.), 29 (Sat.)	48, 21:51, **Mar. 27**
A.D. 28	Mar. 15, 02:32	Mar. 15 (Mon.), 16, 17	27, 15:15, Mar. 15
Or	Apr. 13, 16:17	Apr. 14 (Wed.), 15	5, 1:47, Apr. 13
A.D. 29	Apr. 2, 19:36	Apr. 3 (Sun.), 4, 5	42, 22:22, Apr. 3
A.D. 30	Mar. 22, 19:53	Mar. 23 (Thurs.), 25 (Sat.)	42, 21:58, Mar. 23
A.D. 31	Mar. 12, 00:25	Mar. 12 (Mon.), 13, 14	36, 17:19, Mar. 12
Or	Apr. 10, 13:38	Apr. 11 (Wed.), 12	4, 4:24, Apr. 10
A.D. 32	Mar. 29, 22:06	Mar. 30 (Sun.), 31, Apr. 1	46, 19:50, Mar. 30
A.D. 33	Mar. 19, 12:45	Mar. 21 (Sat; delayed), 22	9, 5:05, Mar. 19
A.D. 34	Mar. 9, 05:32	Mar. 9 (Tues.), 10, 11	30, 12:11, Mar. 9
Or	Apr. 7, 13:48	Apr. 8 (Thurs.), 10 (Sat.)	10, 4:12, Apr. 7
A.D. 35	Mar. 28, 06:12	Mar. 28 (Mon.), 29, 30	31, 11:42, Mar. 28
A.D. 36	Mar. 16, 17:53	Mar. 17 (Sat.), 18, 19	58, 23:55, **Mar. 17**

(Continued on the next page)

Appendix I: Chart 1
Passover Dates, A.D. 15 - 36
(Continued from the previous page)

2nd Evening Lag2, Age, Date	Nisan 14 (range)	Equinox
100, 36:57, **Mar. 10**	Mar. 22 (Fri.), 23, **24**	Mar. 23, 09:11
76, 28:18, **Apr. 8**	Apr. 21 (Sun.), **22**, 23	[same]
103, 35:55, **Mar. 28**	Apr. 10 (Fri.), **11**	Mar. 22, 14:55
122, 43:26, Mar. 18	Mar. 30 (Tues.), **31**	Mar. 22, 20:42
108, 35:32, **Apr. 16**	Apr. 28 (Wed.), **30 (Fri.)**	[same]
124, 44:31, Apr. 6	Apr. 18 (Mon.), **19**, 20	Mar. 23, 02:40
85, 35:42, **Mar. 26**	Apr. 7 (Fri.), 8, **9**	Mar. 23, 08:24
73, 33:46, **Mar. 14**	Mar. 26 (Tues.), 27, **29 (Fri.)**	Mar. 22, 14:13
96, 42:10, **Apr. 13**	Apr. 26 (Fri.), **27**	[same]
90, 41:34, **Apr. 2**	Apr. 14 (Mon.), 15, **16**	Mar. 22, 20:10
87, 38:37, **Mar. 22**	Apr. 3 (Fri.), 4, **5**	Mar. 23, 01:58
72, 28:41, **Mar. 11**	Mar. 24 (Wed.), **26 (Fri.)**	Mar. 23, 07:47
99, 43:52, **Apr. 10**	Apr. 22 (Fri.), 23, **24**	[same]
74, 28:47, **Mar. 29**	Apr. 11 (Tues.), **12**	Mar. 22, 13:36
97, 35:57, **Mar. 19**	Mar. 31 (Sat.), Apr. 1, **2**	Mar. 22, 19:26
92, 35:26, **Apr. 7**	Apr. 19 (Fri.), 20, **21**	Mar. 23, 01:22
111, 45:51, Mar. 28	Apr. 9 (Wed.), **11 (Fri.)**	Mar. 23, 07:03
83, 39:15, **Mar. 16**	Mar. 28 (Sun.), 29, **30**	Mar. 22, 12:49
54, 25:48, **Apr. 14**	Apr. 27 (Tues.), **28**	[same]
96, 46:23, **Apr. 4**	Apr. 16 (Sat.), 17, **18**	Mar. 22, 18:46
95, 45:59, **Mar. 24**	Apr. 5 (Wed.), **7 (Fri.)**	Mar. 23, 00:36
94, 41:20, **Mar. 13**	Mar. 25 (Sun.), 26, **27**	Mar. 23, 06:25
61, 28:24, **Apr. 11**	Apr. 24 (Tues.), **25**	[same]
110, 43:50, **Mar. 31**	Apr. 12 (Sat.), 13, **14**	Mar. 22, 12:12
78, 29:05, **Mar. 20**	Apr. **3 (Fri)**, 4	Mar. 22, 17:59
101, 36:11, **Mar. 10**	Mar. 22 (Mon.), 23, **24**	Mar. 22, 23:49
82, 28:13, **Apr. 8**	Apr. 21 (Wed.), **23 (Fri.)**	[same]
100, 35:43, **Mar. 29**	Apr. 10 (Sun.), 11, **12**	Mar. 23, 05:30
121, 47:56, Mar. 18	Mar. 30 (Fri.), **31**, Apr. 1	Mar. 22, 11:14

Appendix I: Chart 2

The Birth and Crucifixion of Christ

(years compared to days of the week)

According to my interpretation of the writings of Blessed Anne Catherine Emmerich, Christ was born on Sunday, Nov. 25 and crucified on Friday, Nisan 14, which was also April 7. The length of time from Christ's Incarnation to His Crucifixion is 33 years plus six weeks. (See chapters 2 and 4.) Christ was born in the same calendar year as His Incarnation. Thus the year of Christ's Crucifixion is the 33rd year from the year of Christ's Incarnation and Birth. If Christ were born in A.D. 1, then He was crucified in A.D. 34. If Christ were born in 1 B.C., then He was crucified in A.D. 33. And so on.

This chart compares days of the week for Nov. 25 to days of the week for Nisan 14, 33 years apart. Whenever Nisan 14 would fall on a Thursday, the start of Nisan was delayed one day to prevent Nisan 15 from interfering with Friday, the preparation day of the Sabbath. Whenever there is doubt as to whether or not the 13th month of AdarII was added (prior to Nisan), both possible dates for Nisan 14 are given. At such times, Nisan 14 either falls in mid March or mid April, no where near April 7.

Leap years in the Julian calendar, prior to 4 A.D., are: 1 B.C., 5 B.C., 9 B.C., 13 B.C., 17 B.C., etc.[1242] Days of the week were determined by Universal Calendar Calculator software program.[1243] Nisan 1 new moon dates (used to determine the dates for Nisan 14 below) were determined by *RedShift 3* software and checked against data from the *Five Millennia Catalog of Phases of the Moon.*[1244]

The chart below shows that A.D. 19 and A.D. 30 are the only years which fit the details given by Blessed Anne Catherine about the Birth and Crucifixion of Christ, (i.e. that Nisan 14 coincided with both a Friday and with April 7, 33 years after a year when Nov. 25 was a Sunday). If the Jewish calendar was determined by calculation of new moon dates, then A.D. 19 is the only year which fits; but if the calendar was determined by observation of the crescent new moon, then A.D. 30 is the only year which fits. The Nisan 14 dates below are by calculation, not observation (unless otherwise noted). The date by observation would be one or two days later. See chapter 17 for my conclusion that the calendar was determined by calculation, not observation, during this time period.

Born Sunday, Nov. 25		Crucified Friday, Nisan 14		
17 A.D.	Thursday	50 A.D.	March 25	Wednesday
16 A.D.	Wednesday	49 A.D.	April 4	**Friday**
15 A.D.	Monday	48 A.D.	April 15	Monday
14 A.D.	**Sunday**	47 A.D.	March 28	Tuesday
13 A.D.	Saturday	46 A.D.	April 8	**Friday**
12 A.D.	Friday	45 A.D.	March 21	Sunday
		or	April 19	Monday
11 A.D.	Wednesday	44 A.D.	March 31	Tuesday
10 A.D.	Tuesday	43 A.D.	April 12	**Friday**
9 A.D.	Monday	42 A.D.	March 24	Saturday
		or	April 22	Sunday
8 A.D.	**Sunday**	41 A.D.	April 3	Monday
7 A.D.	Friday	40 A.D.	April 13	Wednesday

6 A.D.	Thursday	39 A.D.	March 27	**Friday**
5 A.D.	Wednesday	38 A.D.	**April 7**	Monday
4 A.D.	Tuesday	37 A.D.	April 19	**Friday**
3 A.D.	**Sunday**	36 A.D.	March 30	**Friday**
2 A.D.	Saturday	35 A.D.	April 10	Sunday
1 A.D.	Friday	34 A.D.	March 22	Monday
		or	April 21	Wednesday
1 B.C.	Thursday	33 A.D.	April 3	**Friday**
2 B.C.	Tuesday	32 A.D.	April 12	Saturday
3 B.C.	Monday	31 A.D.	March 25	Sunday
4 B.C.	**Sunday**	30 A.D.	April 5	Wednesday
			April 7	**Friday** (observation)
5 B.C.	Saturday	29 A.D.	April 16	Saturday
6 B.C.	Thursday	28 A.D.	March 28	Sunday
7 B.C.	Wednesday	27 A.D.	April 9	Wednesday
8 B.C.	Tuesday	26 A.D.	March 21	**Friday**
		or	April 19	**Friday**
9 B.C.	Monday	25 A.D.	March 31	Saturday
10 B.C.	Saturday	24 A.D.	April 11	Tuesday
11 B.C.	Friday	23 A.D.	March 24	Wednesday
		or	April 22	**Friday**
12 B.C.	Thursday	22 A.D.	April 3	**Friday**
13 B.C.	Wednesday	21 A.D.	April 14	Monday
14 B.C.	Monday	20 A.D.	March 26	Tuesday
15 B.C.	**Sunday**	19 A.D.	**April 7**	**Friday** (calculation)
16 B.C.	Saturday	18 A.D.	April 18	Monday
17 B.C.	Friday	17 A.D.	March 30	Tuesday
18 B.C.	Wednesday	16 A.D.	April 10	**Friday**
19 B.C.	Tuesday	15 A.D.	March 22	**Friday**
		or	April 21	Sunday
20 B.C.	Monday	14 A.D.	April 2	Monday
21 B.C.	**Sunday**	**13 A.D.**	**April 12**	**Wednesday**
22 B.C.	Friday	12 A.D.	March 25	**Friday**
23 B.C.	Thursday	11 A.D.	April 6	Monday
24 B.C.	Wednesday	10 A.D.	April 16	Wednesday
25 B.C.	Tuesday	9 A.D.	March 29	**Friday**
26 B.C.	**Sunday**	8 A.D.	April 8	Sunday
27 B.C.	Saturday	7 A.D.	March 21	Monday
		or	April 19	Tuesday
28 B.C.	Friday	6 A.D.	March 31	Wednesday
29 B.C.	Thursday	5 A.D.	April 11	Saturday
30 B.C.	Tuesday	4 A.D.	March 23	Sunday
		or	April 21	Monday
31 B.C.	Monday	3 A.D.	April 4	Wednesday
32 B.C.	**Sunday**	2 A.D.	April 15	Saturday
33 B.C.	Saturday	1 A.D.	March 27	Sunday

Appendix I: Chart 3
Lengths of Time in the Lives of Jesus and Mary

Ages Counting from Conception:

Mary:

1. From Mary's Conception (31 B.C., Nov. 8, morning) to Christ's Conception (15 B.C., Feb. 25, about midnight at the start of the 25th): 15 years, 3 months, 17 days, less several hours.

2. From Mary's Conception (31 B.C., Nov. 8, morning) to Christ's Birth (15 B.C., Nov. 25, about midnight): 16 years, 17 days, less several hours.

3. From Mary's Conception (31 B.C., Nov. 8, morning) to the Crucifixion (A.D. 19, April 7, 3 p.m.): 48 years, and about 5 months.

4. From Mary's Conception (31 B.C., Nov. 8, morning) to Mary's Dormition (A.D. 34, July 31, 3 p.m.): 63 years, 8 months, 23 days, plus several hours.

5. From Mary's Conception (31 B.C., Nov. 8, morning) to Mary's Resurrection and Assumption (A.D. 34, August 15, before sunrise): 63 years, 9 months, 7 days.

Christ:

1. From Christ's Conception (15 B.C., Feb. 25, about midnight) to the Flight to Egypt (13 B.C., February 29, before midnight): 2 years, 5 days.

2. From Christ's Conception (15 B.C., Feb. 25, about midnight) to the Finding in the Temple (3 B.C., April 9): 12 years, 1 month, 15 days, plus some number of hours.

3. From Christ's Conception (15 B.C., Feb. 25, about midnight) to Christ's Baptism (A.D. 15, Oct. 4, about 10 a.m.): 29 years, 7 months, 9 days, plus about 10 hours.

4. From Christ's Conception (15 B.C., Feb. 25, about midnight) to Christ's Crucifixion (A.D. 19, April 7, 3 p.m.): 33 years, 6 weeks (42 days); or, more precisely, 33 years, 41 days, 15 hours.

5. From Christ's Conception (15 B.C., Feb. 25, about midnight) to Christ's Ascension (A.D. 19, May 18, late morning): 33 years, 2 months, 23 days, plus about 10 or 11 hours.

6. From Christ's Conception (15 B.C., Feb. 25, about midnight) to Pentecost (A.D. 19, May 28): 33 years, 3 months, 3 days, plus some number of hours.

7. From Christ's Conception (15 B.C., Feb. 25, about midnight) to Mary's Dormition (A.D. 34, July 31, 3 p.m.): 48 years, 5 months, 6 days, 15 hours.

8. From Christ's Conception (15 B.C., Feb. 25, about midnight) to Mary's Resurrection and Assumption (A.D. 34, August 15, before sunrise): 48 years, 5 months, 21 days, plus several hours.

Lengths of Time from Birth:

Mary:

1. From Mary's Birth (30 B.C., August 5, about midnight) to Christ's Conception (15 B.C., Feb. 25, about midnight): 14 years, 6 months, 20 days.

2. From Mary's Birth (30 B.C., August 5, about midnight) to Christ's Birth (15 B.C., Nov. 25, about midnight): 15 years, 3 months, 20 days.

3. From Mary's Birth (30 B.C., August 5, about midnight) to Christ's Crucifixion (A.D. 19, April 7, 3 p.m.): 47 years, 8 months, 2 days, 15 hours.

4. From Mary's Birth (30 B.C., August 5, about midnight) to Mary's Dormition (A.D. 34, July 31, 3 p.m.): 63 years, less 4 days and about 9 hours; or 62 years, 11 months, 26 days, 15 hours.

5. From Mary's Birth (30 B.C., August 5, about midnight) to Mary's Resurrection and Assumption (A.D. 34, August 15, before sunrise): 63 years, 10 days, plus several hours.

Christ:

1. From Christ's Birth (15 B.C., Nov. 25, about midnight) to the Flight to Egypt (13 B.C., February 29, before midnight): 1 year, 3 months, 5 days.

2. From Christ's Birth (15 B.C., Nov. 25, about midnight) to the Finding in the Temple (3 B.C., April 9): 11 years, 4 months, 15 days, plus some number of hours.

3. From Christ's Birth (15 B.C., Nov. 25, about midnight) to Christ's Baptism (A.D. 15, Oct. 4, about 10 a.m.): 29 years, less 1 month, 20 days, and about 14 hours; or 28 years, 10 months, 9 days, plus about 10 hours.

4. From Christ's Birth (15 B.C., Nov. 25, about midnight) to Christ's Crucifixion (A.D. 19, April 7, 3 p.m.): 32 years, 4 months, 13 days, 15 hours.

5. From Christ's Birth (15 B.C., Nov. 25, about midnight) to Pentecost (A.D. 19, May 28): 32 years, 6 months, 3 days, plus some number of hours.

6. From Christ's Birth (15 B.C., Nov. 25, about midnight) to Mary's Dormition (A.D. 34, July 31, 3 p.m.): 47 years, 8 months, 6 days, 15 hours.

7. From Christ's Birth (15 B.C., Nov. 25, about midnight) to Mary's Resurrection and Assumption (A.D. 34, August 15, before sunrise): 47 years, 8 months, 21 days, plus several hours.

Lengths of Time between Events:

1. From John the Baptist's Conception (16 B.C., Sept. 26/27) to Christ's Conception (15 B.C., Feb. 25, about midnight): 5 months, less about 2 days.

Elizabeth was in her sixth month at the time of the Incarnation, but this was the sixth month by the Jewish lunar calendar. The nine months of pregnancy are actually nine lunar months (a woman's due date is 266 days from conception). See chapter 5 for more information on this point.

2. From John the Baptist's Conception (16 B.C., Tishri 24) to Christ's Conception (15 B.C., AdarI 28): 5 lunar months plus 4 days.

3. From Christ's Baptism (A.D. 15, Oct. 4, about 10 a.m.) to Christ's Crucifixion (A.D. 19, April 7, 3 p.m.): 3 years, 6 months, 3 days, plus about 5 hours. This is the length of the Divine Ministry of Jesus Christ.

4. From Christ's Baptism (A.D. 15, Oct. 4, about 10 a.m.) to John the Baptist's Martyrdom (A.D. 18, on or about Jan. 25): 2 years, 3 months, and about 21 days.

5. From Christ's Ascension (A.D. 19, May 18, late morning) to Mary's Dormition (A.D. 34, July 31, 3 p.m.): 15 years, 2 months, 13 days, plus a few hours.

6. From Christ's Ascension (A.D. 19, May 18, late morning) to Mary's Resurrection and Assumption (A.D. 34, August 15, before sunrise): 15 years, 2 months, 28 days, less several hours.

7. From Joseph and Mary's Betrothal (15 B.C., Jan. 23) to Joseph's Death (spring of A.D. 15): 29 years, and about 4 months or so. This was the length of the marriage of Joseph and Mary.

If the reader is interested in other lengths of times, the reader can make the appropriate calculations.

Appendix I: Chart 4

Months of the Macedonian, Jewish, and Julian Calendars

The columns below show the general synchronization between the Julian, Jewish, and Macedonian calendars. In a Jewish leap year, a 13th month of AdarII is added, pushing Nisan into April/May. In advance of a leap year, Tishri may fall as early as August/Sept.

The Jewish and Macedonian calendars are both lunar calendars, but the leap month in the Macedonian calendar is Artemisios (corresponding to Iyar), not Dystros (corresponding to AdarI). This results in the two calendars moving out of synch with one another for a couple of months, when the leap year is the same in both calendar systems. But if different years were chosen for the leap year in the Jewish and Macedonian calendars, then the calendars would be out of synch for more than a year. (See Charts 5 and 6 for more on this point.)

Macedonian Calendar[1245]	Jewish Calendar[1246]	Julian Calendar
Dios	Heshvan	Oct/Nov
Apellaios	Kislev	Nov/Dec
Audynaios	Tevet	Dec/Jan
Peritios	Shevat	Jan/Feb
Dystros	AdarI	Feb/March
Xanthikos	Nisan	March/April
Artemisios	Iyar	April/May
Daisios	Sivan	May/June
Panemos	Tammuz	June/July
Loos	Av (Ab)	July/August
Gorpiaios	Elul	August/Sept
Hyperberetaios	Tishri	Sept/Oct

Appendix I: Chart 5
Synchronization of the Macedonian, Jewish, and Julian Calendars

Macedonian Calendar	Jewish Calendar	Julian Calendar
Dystros	**AdarI** (not leap year)	
Xanthikos	Nisan (usual synch)	**March 23, A.D. 53 (**Passover)
Artemisios	Iyar	April
Daisios	Sivan	
Panemos	Tammuz	
Loos	Av (Ab)	
Gorpiaios	Elul	
Hyperberetaios	Tishri	
Dios	Heshvan	
Apellaios	Kislev	
Audynaios	Tevet	
Peritios	Shevat	January, A.D. 54
Dystros	**AdarI**	
Xanthikos	**AdarII** *	March
Artemisios	Nisan 14 (out of synch)	**April 10, A.D. 54** (Passover)
* **Artemisios-2**	Iyar	
Daisios	Sivan (usual synch)	
Panemos	Tammuz	
Loos	Av (Ab)	
Gorpiaios	Elul	
Hyperberetaios	Tishri	
Dios	Heshvan	
Apellaios	Kislev	
Audynaios	Tevet 3 [Wars, 4.654]	December 20, A.D. 54
Peritios	Shevat	January, A.D. 55
Dystros	**AdarI**	
Xanthikos	Nisan 14	**March 30, A.D. 55** (Passover)
Artemisios	Iyar	April
Daisios	Sivan	
Panemos	Tammuz	
Loos	Av (Ab)	
Gorpiaios	Elul	
Hyperberetaios	Tishri	
Dios	Heshvan	
Apellaios	Kislev	
Audynaios	Tevet	
Peritios	Shevat	January, A.D. 56
Dystros	**AdarI**	
Xanthikos	Nisan 14 (usual synch)	**March 19, A.D. 56** (Passover)
Artemisios	Iyar	April
* **Artemisios-2**	Sivan (out of synch)	May
Daisios	Tammuz	June
Panemos	Av (Ab)	July
Loos	Elul	August (the Temple burns)

Macedonian Calendar	Jewish Calendar	Julian Calendar
Gorpiaios	Tishri	
Hyperberetaios	Heshvan	
Dios	Kislev	
Apellaios	Tevet	
Audynaios	Shevat	January, A.D. 57
Peritios	**AdarI**	
Dystros	**AdarII** *	
Xanthikos	Nisan (back in synch)	

* indicates an extra month added to the calendar in a leap year

Appendix I: Chart 6
A Suggested Revised Christian Liturgical Calendar

January 1: Mary, Perfect Virgin
January 3: The Presentation of the Lord
January 25: The Beheading of Saint John the Baptist

February 25: The Virgin Incarnation of Jesus Christ
February 29: The Flight of the Holy Family to Egypt (only celebrated in leap years)

March 9: The Martyrdom of the Holy Innocents
March 23: Spring Equinox of Jerusalem (most years)
March 30: Saint Mark the Evangelist Feast Day (transferred or omitted if it conflicts with the Easter Triduum)

April 9: The Finding in the Temple (transferred to April 7 or omitted, if it conflicts with the Easter Triduum)
April 20: The Visitation of Mary to Elizabeth

May: The Feast of the Ascension (most years)
May: Pentecost (most years)

June 27: The Birth of John the Baptist

July 31: The Dormition of the Virgin Mary

August 1 to 14: The Fast of the Dormition
August 5: The Virgin Birth of the Virgin Mary
August 15: The Resurrection and Assumption of the Virgin Mary
August 20: The Naming Day of the Virgin Mary
August: The Coronation of the Virgin Mary (sometime after August 15)

September 13: The Annunciation to Zechariah
September 27: The Conception of John the Baptist

October 4: The Holy Baptism of Jesus Christ
October 23: The Presentation of the Virgin Mary

November 8: The Immaculate Virgin Conception of the Virgin Mary
November 9: The Entrance of the Theotokos into the Temple
November 25: The Virgin Birth of Jesus Christ

December 2: The Naming Day of Jesus Christ
December: Mary, Mother of God (sometime after November 25)

Moveable Feasts:

The Crucifixion (Good Friday): the Friday before Easter

The Resurrection (Easter Sunday): the first Sunday after the first full moon after the Spring Equinox of Jerusalem

Divine Mercy Sunday: the first Sunday after Easter

The Feast of the Ascension: Thursday, the 40th day inclusive from Easter

Pentecost (Descent of the Holy Spirit): Sunday, the 50th day inclusive from Easter

Appendix I: Chart 7
Sabbatical and Jubilee Years

Sabbatical Years:

Conte[1247]	Wacholder[1248]	Zuckermann/Blosser[1249]
64/63 B.C. (starting in Nisan)	65/64 B.C.	
57/56 B.C. (starting in Nisan)	58/57 B.C.	
50/49 B.C. (starting in Nisan)	51/50 B.C.	
43/42 B.C. (starting in Nisan)	44/43 B.C. (starting in Tishri)	45/44 (start Tishri)
37/36 B.C. (starting in Tishri)	37/36 B.C.	38/37 B.C.
30/29 B.C.	30/29 B.C.	31/30 B.C.
23/22 B.C.	23/22 B.C.	24/23 B.C.
16/15 B.C. (Incarnation)	16/15 B.C.	17/16 B.C.
9/8 B.C.	9/8 B.C.	10/9 B.C.
2/1 B.C.	2/1 B.C.	3/2 B.C.
A.D. 6/7	A.D. 6/7	A.D. 5/6
A.D. 13/14	A.D. 13/14	A.D. 12/13
A.D. 20/21	A.D. 20/21	A.D. 19/20
A.D. 27/28	A.D. 27/28	A.D. 26/27
A.D. 34/35	A.D. 34/35	A.D. 33/34
A.D. 41/42	A.D. 41/42	A.D. 40/41
A.D. 48/49	A.D. 48/49	A.D. 47/48
A.D. 55/56	A.D. 55/56	A.D. 54/55
A.D. 62/63	A.D. 62/63	A.D. 61/62
A.D. 69/70	A.D. 69/70	A.D. 68/69

Jubilee Years:

Conte[1250]	Wacholder[1251]	Strobel[1252]
		72/71 B.C. (start Tishri)
64/63 B.C. (start Tishri)	65/64 B.C. (start Tishri)	
		23/22 B.C.
15/14 B.C. (Nativity)	16/15 B.C.	
		A.D. 27/28
A.D. 35/36	A.D. 34/35	
		A.D. 76/77

Appendix II: Section A
Summary of Dates in Salvation History

1. Immaculate Virgin Conception of the Virgin Mary: Friday morning, November 8 in 31 B.C.

2. Virgin Birth of the Virgin Mary: about midnight at the start of Tuesday, August 5 in 30 B.C.

3. The Naming Day of the Virgin Mary: the evening of Tuesday, August 19 in 30 B.C.

4. The Presentation of the Virgin Mary (St. Ann's Purification): Thursday, October 23 in 30 B.C.

5. The Day the Virgin Mary began her Service in the Temple of Jerusalem: Wednesday, November 8 in 27 B.C.

6. The Annunciation to Zechariah about John the Baptist: on the Day of Atonement, Wednesday, Tishri 10 and September 13, 16 B.C.

7. The Conception of John the Baptist: earliest opportunity was the night of Tuesday/Wednesday, September 26/27 and Tishri 24, 16 B.C.

8. The End of the Virgin Mary's Service in the Temple: winter of 16/15 B.C.

9. The Betrothal of Saint Joseph and the Virgin Mary: late January of 15 B.C. (a 7 or 8 day betrothal/wedding ceremony and celebration, beginning on or about Tuesday, January 23)

10. Elizabeth's Sixth Month: about AdarI 24 (Wed., February 21) to Adar II 23 (Thurs., March 22) of 15 B.C.

11. The Incarnation of Christ: about midnight at the start of Sunday, AdarI 28 and February 25 in 15 B.C.

12. The Visitation of Mary and Elizabeth: sometime before sunset on Friday, April 20 in 15 B.C.

13. The Birth of John the Baptist: most likely between Wednesday, June 27 and Saturday, July 7, of 15 B.C.

14. The Virgin Birth of Jesus Christ: about midnight at the start of Sunday, November 25 (Kislev 5) in 15 B.C.

15. The Circumcision of Christ: about dawn on Sunday, December 2 in 15 B.C.

16. The Presentation of Jesus Christ in the Temple: on the 40th day from birth, inclusive, which was the morning of Thursday, January 3 in 14 B.C.

17. The Flight of the Holy Family to Egypt: after sunset on Saturday, February 29 in 13 B.C.

18. The Arrival of the Holy Family in Egypt: approx. Friday, March 20 in 13 B.C.

19. The Massacre of the Holy Innocents: sometime between March and June of 13 B.C., (possibly on or about March 9).

20. The Return of the Holy Family from Egypt: September in 7 B.C.

21. The Child Jesus Lost and Found in the Temple: Sunday, April 7 to Tuesday, April 9 in 3 B.C.

22. The Death of Saint Joseph: spring of A.D. 15, shortly before (or soon after) John began baptizing, and several months before Jesus began His Ministry.

23. The Beginning of the Ministry of John the Baptist: spring of A.D. 15.

24. The Baptism of Jesus: the morning of Friday, October 4 in A.D. 15.

25. The Forty Days Jesus spent in the Wilderness: Saturday, Tishri 24 and Oct. 26, to Wednesday, Kislev 5 and Dec. 4, inclusive, in A.D. 15.

26. The Wedding at Cana: Tuesday, December 31 to Friday, January 3, in A.D. 15/16.

27. The Cleansing of the Temple: Saturday, Nisan 15 and April 11, in A.D. 16.

28. John the Baptist's Arrest: early to mid June of A.D. 16 (mid to late Sivan, in the Jewish calendar).

29. The Martyrdom of John the Baptist: approximately January 25; about the middle of Tevet, and about the end of January, in A.D. 18.

30. The Last Supper: the evening of Thursday, April 6, after sunset, in A.D. 19 (Nisan 14 had just begun, since the Jewish day begins at sunset).

31. The Crucifixion of Jesus Christ: about 15:00 hours on Friday, April 7 and Nisan 14, in A.D. 19.

32. The Resurrection of Jesus Christ: before sunrise on Sunday, April 9 and Nisan 16, in A.D. 19.

33. The Ascension of Jesus Christ: mid to late morning on Thursday, May 18, in A.D. 19.

34. Christian Pentecost: coincided with Jewish Pentecost (the Feast of Weeks), Sunday, May 28 and Sivan 6, in the year A.D. 19.

35. The Appointment of the First Seven Deacons: most likely in A.D. 21.

36. The Stoning of Saint Stephen: the winter of A.D. 21/22, sometime between Dec. and Feb., inclusive.

37. The Virgin Mary moves from Jerusalem to Bethany: winter of A.D. 21/22

38. Saul's Conversion: early to mid A.D. 22, not long after the martyrdom of Saint Stephen.

39. The Writing of the Gospel of Matthew: between early A.D. 22 and early A.D. 25, during the reign of the emperor Gaius

40. The Virgin Mary moves to Ephesus: early A.D. 25

41. Saul's First Visit to Jerusalem (visit after 3 years): early A.D. 25.

42. The Beheading of James the Greater: between the evening of Wednesday, April 9, and the evening of Wednesday, April 16 (the seven days of unleavened bread), in the year A.D. 27.

43. Saint Peter's Flight from Jerusalem to Rome: departed Jerusalem about the time of the Passover of A.D. 27 and arrived in Rome on May 20 (or at least sometime in mid A.D. 27)

44. Saul's Actual Second Visit to Jerusalem (Acts 11-12): mid A.D. 28 to early A.D. 29.

45. The Virgin Mary's Visit to Jerusalem at the Time of a Church Council: early A.D. 29 (sometime after Saul's departure).

46. The Death of the Virgin Mary: about 15:00 hours on Saturday, July 31 in A.D. 34.

47. The Resurrection and Assumption of the Virgin Mary: before sunrise on Sunday, August 15 in A.D. 34.

48. The Writing of the Gospel of Mark: in late fall and winter of A.D. 34 to 35, during the reign of the emperor Claudius.

49. Saint Mark founds the Church at Alexandria: spring of A.D. 35 (after he completed the Gospel).

50. Paul's Third Visit to Jerusalem (visit after 14 years) and the Church Council on Mosaic Law (Acts 15): early to mid A.D. 35.

51. Paul (Saul) in Corinth: fall of A.D. 36 to spring of A.D. 38 (two winters).

52. Paul's Three Years in Asia (Acts 20:31): early A.D. 38 to early A.D. 41.

53. Paul's Arrest at Jerusalem: early summer of A.D. 41

54. Paul's Two Years in Prison under Felix: early summer of A.D. 41 to about the same time in A.D. 43.

55. Paul's Trip to Rome: left Jerusalem in fall of A.D. 43, shipwrecked on Malta winter of A.D. 43/44, arrived in Rome early in the year A.D. 44.

56. Paul's Two Years at Rome (Acts 28:30): early A.D. 44 to early A.D. 46

57. The Writing of the Gospel of Luke and the Acts of the Apostles: between early A.D. 44 and early A.D. 46 (while Paul was in Rome), during the reign of the emperor Nero.

58. The Martyrdom of Saint James the Less: spring, about the time of Passover, in A.D. 49, Nero's 10th year as emperor.

59. The First Christian Martyrs of Rome: the fall of A.D. 49, some length of time after the summer fire in Rome, during Nero's 10th year.

60. The Martyrdom of Saint Mark the Gospel Writer: Monday, March 30 of A.D. 50, on the day after Easter, during Nero's 11th year.

61. The Martyrdoms of Saints Peter and Paul: on June 29 of A.D. 52, during Nero's 13th year as emperor.

62. The Writing of the Gospel of John: during the reign of Domitian, sometime between A.D. 68 and A.D. 81 (most likely sometime well before A.D. 82, when he was exiled to Patmos because of the Gospel).

63. The Writing of the Book of Revelation: while John was on the island of Patmos, from approximately A.D. 82 to A.D. 83 or 84.

64. The Death of Saint John the Gospel Writer: in the year A.D. 87, at the approximate age of 94 years.

Appendix II: Section B
Summary of Dates in Roman History

The following chart summarizes the revised dates for events in Roman History presented by this book. The second column is the generally-accepted or usual date given for the event. In cases where the year is a matter of much dispute among scholars, such as the year of Herod the Great's death, a range of dates is given. See chapters 12, 13, and 14 for details on these dates and events.

Revised	Usual	Event
49 B.C.	44 B.C.	Julius Caesar dies (March 15)
43 B.C.	37 B.C.	Herod the Great captures Jerusalem (**Sept.** | Oct.)
35 B.C.	31 B.C.	Marc Anthony defeated by Octavian in the battle at Actium (Sept.)
34 B.C.	30 B.C.	Marc Anthony and Cleopatra die (August)
16 B.C.	12 B.C.	Consulship of P. S. Quirinius
8 B.C.	4 - 1 B.C.	Herod the Great dies (winter, Jan./Feb.)
1 B.C.	4 B.C.	Caesar Augustus adopts Tiberius, making him heir (June 26)
A.D. 1	A.D. 15	Year One of Tiberius Caesar's reign
A.D. 1	A.D. 15	First year of Valerius Gratus' rule over Judea
A.D. 2	A.D. 6	Second census under Quirinius
A.D. 10	A.D. 14	Caesar Augustus (Octavian) dies (August 19)
A.D. 11	A.D. 25	Eleventh and last year of Valerius Gratus' rule over Judea
A.D. 12	A.D. 26	First year of Pontius Pilate's rule over Judea
A.D. 15	A.D. 19	Germanicus, a Roman general, dies during the 5th year after Augustus died
A.D. 22	A.D. 37	Tiberius Caesar dies (March), succeeded by Gaius (Caligula)
A.D. 22	A.D. 37	Pontius Pilate returns to Rome, arriving after Tiberius died
A.D. 26	A.D. 41	Gaius (Caligula) dies (Jan.), succeeded by Claudius
A.D. 39	A.D. 54	Claudius dies (Oct.), succeeded by Nero
A.D. 50	A.D. 65	The poet Seneca dies; Nero's 11th year
A.D. 53	A.D. 68	Nero dies (June), succeeded by Galba
A.D. 54	A.D. 69	Galba dies (Jan.), succeeded by Otho
A.D. 54	A.D. 69	Otho dies (April), succeeded by Vitellius

A.D. 54	A.D. 69	Vitellius dies (Dec.), succeeded by Vespasian (antedated to July)
A.D. 66	A.D. 79	Vespasian dies (June), succeeded by Titus
A.D. 66	A.D. 79	Mount Vesuvius erupts (August), destroying Pompeii and killing Pliny the Elder
A.D. 68	A.D. 81	Titus dies (Sept.), succeeded by Domitian
A.D. 83	A.D. 96	Domitian dies (Sept.), succeeded by Nerva
A.D. 85	A.D. 98	Nerva dies (Jan.), succeeded by Trajan

Appendix II: Section C
Jewish Calendar during the Ministry of Christ

Julian Calendar	Jewish Calendar
A.D. 15:	
Friday, Feb 8	AdarI 1
Saturday, March 9	AdarII 1
Monday, April 8	Nisan 1
Wednesday, May 8	Iyar 1 (delayed)
Thursday, June 6	Sivan 1 (delayed)
Friday, July 5	Tammuz 1
Sunday, Aug 4	Av 1
Tuesday, Sept 3	Elul 1 (delayed)
Thursday, Oct 3	Tishri 1 (delayed)
Friday, Nov 1	Heshvan 1
Saturday, Nov 30	Kislev 1
Monday, Dec 30	Tevet 1
A.D. 16:	
Tuesday, Jan 28	Shevat 1
Thursday, Feb 27	Adar 1
Saturday, March 28	Nisan 1 (delayed)
Monday, April 27	Iyar 1 (delayed)
Tuesday, May 26	Sivan 1 (delayed)
Tuesday, June 23	Tammuz 1
Thursday, July 23	Av 1
Saturday, Aug 22	Elul 1 (delayed)
Sunday, Sept 20	Tishri 1
Tuesday, Oct 20	Heshvan 1
Thursday, Nov 19	Kislev 1
Friday, Dec 18	Tevet 1
A.D. 17:	
Sunday, Jan 17	Shevat 1
Monday, Feb 15	AdarI 1
Wednesday, Mar 17	AdarII 1
Thursday, April 15	Nisan 1
Saturday, May 15	Iyar 1
Sunday, June 13	Sivan 1
Monday, July 12	Tammuz 1
Wednesday, Aug 11	Av 1
Thursday, Sept 9 or 10	Elul 1 (possible delay)
Saturday, Oct 9	Tishri 1
Monday, Nov 8	Heshvan 1 (delayed)
Wednesday, Dec 8	Kislev 1 (delayed)

Julian Calendar	Jewish Calendar
A.D. 18:	
Friday, Jan 7	Tevet 1 (delayed)
Saturday, Feb 5	Shevat 1
Sunday, Mar 6	Adar 1
Tuesday, April 5	Nisan 1
Thursday, May 5	Iyar 1 (delayed)
Friday, June 3	Sivan 1
Saturday, July 2	Tammuz 1
Sunday, July 31	Av 1
Tuesday, Aug 30	Elul 1
Thursday, Sept 20	Tishri 1 (delayed)
Friday, Oct 28	Heshvan 1
Saturday, Nov 26	Kislev 1
Monday, Dec 26	Tevet 1
A.D. 19:	
Wednesday, Jan 25	Shevat 1
Friday, Feb 24	Adar 1
Saturday, Mar 25	Nisan 1
Monday, April 24	Iyar 1
Tuesday, May 23	Sivan 1
Thursday, June 22	Tammuz 1
Friday, July 21	Av 1
Saturday, Aug 19	Elul 1
Monday, Sept 18	Tishri 1
Tuesday, Oct 17	Heshvan 1
Thursday, Nov 16	Kislev 1
Saturday, Dec 16	Tevet 1

Reasons for this calendar reconstruction:

Adar II in A.D. 15: Blessed Anne Catherine Emmerich describes Jesus celebrating the Feast of Tabernacles that year sometime after His Baptism of early October.[1253] In order for the Feast of Tabernacles to occur after early October, the month of Nisan earlier that year would have had to be delayed by the addition of AdarII.

Iyar 1 in A.D. 15: delayed one day so that Nisan will have 30 days and Iyar 29 days. This causes a one day delay in the start of Sivan.

Elul 1 in A.D. 15: delayed one day so that Tishri 1 will not coincide with a Wednesday.

Nisan 1 in A.D. 16: delayed one day so that Nisan 15 will not coincide with a Friday. This results in a one day delay in the start of Iyar and Sivan, to keep the Feast of Weeks in its proper place on Sivan 6.

Elul 1 in A.D. 16: delayed one day, probably to prevent 3 months of 29 days each occurring in a 4-month period of time. Iyar and Sivan both had 29 days because of the delay in the start of Nisan. Tammuz had 30 days, but Av would have had 29 days again, without the delay in the start of Elul. The one day delay in the start of Elul provides 2 months of 30 days (Tammuz and Av) to balance the 2 months of 29 days (Iyar and Sivan). This delay also has the effect of giving Elul 29 days and Tishri 30 days, the preferred configuration and the rule eventually adopted for the modern Jewish calendar.

AdarII in A.D. 17: see chapter 7, "The Martyrdom of John the Baptist," for details on why this year was a leap year.

Elul 1 in A.D. 17: may or may not have been delayed one day. The reason for a delay would be so that Elul would have 29 days and Tishri would have 30 days. This would be the preferred configuration so that, if Tishri needed to be delayed one day, Elul could be extended by one day to 30 days.

Heshvan, Kislev, and Tevet in winter of A.D. 17 – 18: The start of the months of Heshvan, Kislev, and Tevet were each delayed a day. Heshvan could have begun on Nov. 7 of A.D. 17 (new moon at 11:00 hours JST that day; solar transit at 11:26 hours), but seems to have been delayed until Nov. 8, possibly in order to give Tishri 30 days, instead of 29. This conclusion fits the information given by Blessed Anne Catherine about the dates and days of the week for Hanukah, namely, that Hanukkah that began and ended (Kislev 25 and Tevet 2) on the Jewish Sabbath. (See chapter 7, "The Martyrdom of John the Baptist" for details.)

Iyar 1 in A.D. 18: may have been delayed to give Nisan 30 days and Iyar 29. If there was no delay, then Nisan would have 29 days, and Iyar 30 days.

Tishri 1 in A.D. 18: delayed one day (from Wednesday to Thursday), to prevent Tishri 10 from interfering with the preparation day of the Sabbath. A number of configurations for the months Elul, Tishri, Heshvan, and Kislev are possible. The simplest is to give Elul 30 days and Tishri 29. If they decided to give Tishri 30 days, then Heshvan and Kislev would each likely have been delayed by one day also.

Appendix II: Section D
Siege of Jerusalem and Destruction of the Temple

Revised	Usual	Event
A.D. 51	A.D. 66	The war between the Romans and the Jews begins in the spring.
A.D. 51/52	A.D. 66/67	Wintertime preparations for an escalation of the war. Josephus prepares for battle.
A.D. 52	A.D. 67	Vespasian is sent by Nero to make war against the Jews, in the spring.
A.D. 52	A.D. 67	The capture of the city of Jotapata by the Romans, in the summer.
A.D. 53	A.D. 68	Nero dies in June and is succeeded by Galba.
A.D. 54	A.D. 69	Galba dies in January and is succeeded by Otho.
A.D. 54	A.D. 69	Otho dies in April and is succeeded by Vitellius.
A.D. 54	A.D. 69	Vespasian's troops declare their support for his bid to become emperor (July 1).
A.D. 54	A.D. 69	Vitellius dies in December and is succeeded by Vespasian.
A.D. 55	A.D. 70	Vespasian travels to Rome from Alexandria to take over as emperor (March or later).
A.D. 55	A.D. 70	Titus and his army set out from Alexandria and travel to Caesarea (April or later).
A.D. 55		Titus prepares his forces for many months at Caesarea (summer/autumn/winter).
	A.D. 70	Titus prepares his forces very quickly and attacks/captures Jerusalem the same year.
A.D. 56		Titus and his army arrive at Jerusalem before Nisan 14 = March 19.
A.D. 56		Assault on the first wall, from March 27 to April 10 = Artemisius [Iyar] 7.
A.D. 56		Breach in the second wall, April 15 = Artemisius [Iyar] 12.
A.D. 56		Second wall captured, April 18 or 19 = Artemisius [Iyar] 15 or 16.
A.D. 56		Demolition of second wall, then relaxation in siege, until late April or early May.
A.D. 56		Roman soldiers receive their pay, early May = end of Artemisius [Iyar].
A.D. 56		Raising of the siege works against the third wall, ArtemisiusII [Sivan] 12 = May 15.

A.D. 56	Siege works against the third wall completed on ArtemisiusII [Sivan] 29 = June 1.
A.D. 56	The Jews destroy the siege works for the third wall, Daisios [Tammuz] 2 = June 3.
A.D. 56	Titus completes wall around Jerusalem, Daisios [Tammuz] 6 = June 7.
A.D. 56	Rebuilding of siege works against the third wall, Daisios [Tammuz] 11 = June 12.
A.D. 56	Completion of siege works against the third wall, Panemus [Av] 1 = July 2.
A.D. 56	Battles at the third wall, Panemus [Av] 1 to 17 = July 2 to 18.
A.D. 56	Romans dig up the foundations of the tower of Antonia, Panemus [Av] 17 to 23.
A.D. 56	Romans attack entrance to Temple on Saturday, Panemus [Av] 23 = July 24.
A.D. 56	Temple cloisters burned by Jews and Romans, Panemus [Av] 27, 28 = July 28, 29.
A.D. 56	Siege works against Temple wall completed on Saturday, Loos [Elul] 8 = August 7.
A.D. 56	The Second Temple of Jerusalem destroyed by fire, Loos [Elul] 8-10 = August 7-9.
A.D. 56	Siege works against the upper city begin to be built, Loos [Elul] 20 = August 19.
A.D. 56	Siege works against the upper city completed, Gorpieus [Tishri] 7 = September 5.
A.D. 56	Upper city taken, siege of Jerusalem completed, Gorpieus [Tishri] 8 = September 6.

Appendix III
A Word About Dr. E. Jerry Vardaman

I corresponded with Jerry Vardaman on the topic of Biblical chronology for about 2 years, prior to his death in Nov. 2000. His work was important to the development of the ideas in this book. Please note that, in the course of our correspondence, he encouraged my research in Biblical chronology, but he did not generally agree with my conclusions. Jerry Vardaman's work was helpful to me in my research on Biblical chronology in three important ways.

First, I owe Dr. Vardaman a debt of gratitude for sharing his discovery of microletters on the Lapis Venetus with me. This very important archaeological discovery of his gives the census of Luke 2:2 a clear date: year one of the consulship of P.S. Quirinius ("LA CONS P.S.QVIRINI"). While Dr. Vardaman did not agree with my earlier date for that consulship, he did place the Birth of Jesus Christ during the time of the census which began with Quirinius' consulship.

Second, Dr. Vardaman's published a theory that Tiberius Caesar's reign may have been antedated, so that it overlapped with Augustus' reign by about 10 years.[1254] From my point of view, this theory is one of his most important contributions to Biblical chronology. This book presents evidence and arguments in support of that theory. Dr. Vardaman later abandoned his theory on the antedating of Tiberius' reign in favor of a different approach. He suggested that the original text of Luke 3:1 read "In the second year of the reign of Tiberius Caesar," and that the current text, "In the fifteenth year...," resulted from a copyist error. In my view, however, his earlier theory is the correct one, as this book attempts to show.

Third, Dr. Vardaman's ground-breaking work on microletters led him to the conclusion that the Crucifixion of Jesus Christ occurred years earlier than has been generally believed. Though he placed the Crucifixion in A.D. 21 and I place it in A.D. 19, his idea that certain events occurred outside the usual time constraints assisted me in arriving at my earlier chronology for events during this time period.

Dr. Vardaman's date for the start of the Ministry of Jesus Christ was the fall of A.D. 15. He arrived at this conclusion partly through his study of microletters on ancient coins.[1255] I arrived at this same date for the start of Christ's Ministry independently and on a different basis. My conclusion depends partly on the date of A.D. 19 for the Crucifixion and a length of 3½ years for Christ's Ministry (see chapters 2 and 7).

Dr. Vardaman's work in the fields of archaeology and Biblical chronology has breathed fresh air into these fields of study. He had an ability to bring new insights to bear upon ancient questions. His work has been a great benefit to the field of Biblical chronology and his important contributions will affect the work of Biblical scholars for many years.

Appendix IV
Considering Other Dates

The Crucifixion of Jesus Christ

A.D. 36

The latest date which has been considered as a possible year for the Crucifixion of Jesus is A.D. 36. Nisan 14 fell on a Friday that year. If we go back 33 years from A.D. 36 to A.D. 3, we find that November 25 did fall on a Sunday that year, in agreement with Blessed Anne Catherine Emmerich's visions from God. However, A.D. 3 is too late a date for the Birth of Christ. Herod died well after Christ was born (Mt 2:16-19), but the evidence places Herod's death earlier than A.D. 1 (see chapter 12). If one accepts that Christ died at about the age of 33 years, A.D. 36 is too late for the Crucifixion, because the Birth of Christ cannot be placed as late as A.D. 3. On the other hand, we cannot place the Incarnation and Birth of Christ much more than 33 years before the Crucifixion, for the Ministry of Jesus Christ began when He was about 30 years old (Lk 3:23) and lasted about 3½ years (see chapters 2 and 7).

A.D. 33

Some faithful Christians hold an opinion that Jesus Christ died in A.D. 33. They give a number of reasons for this opinion. In the year A.D. 33, Passover began on a Friday at sundown, as was the case the year that Jesus was crucified. Passover began on Friday, April 3, in A.D. 33.

However, if Jesus had died in the year 33 A.D., at the age of 33 years and 6 weeks from His Holy Conception (the Incarnation), then He would have been born in 1 B.C. Blessed Anne Catherine's visions from God clearly indicate that Jesus was born in a year when November 25 fell on a Sunday. But in 1 B.C., November 25 fell on a Thursday. And if Jesus had died in 33 A.D., at the age of about 33 years counting from His Birth (rather than from His Holy Conception), then He would have been born in 2 B.C., when November 25 fell on a Tuesday, not a Sunday.

Again, if one accepts that Christ was born about 33 years before the Crucifixion, then the year for His Birth, in 1 or 2 B.C., is too late to accord with the year of the death of Herod. If Christ was born in late 2 B.C., then the latest date for the death of Herod (which has some scholarly support) is early 1 B.C. There is not, in this case, enough time between late 2 B.C. and early 1 B.C. to account for Herod's search for the new-born King of the Jews, the flight of the Holy Family to Egypt, and the Massacre of the Holy Innocents. Also, Herod chose to kill infants two years of age or younger, because he thought the Christ-child might be as old as about 2 years. He determined this date from the information given him by the wise men (Mt 2:16). The Massacre of the Holy Innocents occurred about 1½ years after the Birth of Christ (see chapter 6).

Some people assume that A.D. 33 is the correct number because it is a holy number, being the same number as the age of Christ at His Crucifixion. There is some truth to this view because, if the years of the Christian calendar had been correctly matched to the years of Christ's life as was intended, then the year of His death and Resurrection would be called A.D. 33. This is, in fact, the way that the calendar ought to be set up. However, there is no basis for assuming that the years called A.D. have been correctly matched to the age of Jesus Christ, and this book presents ample evidence to the contrary.

On April 3 of A.D. 33, there was a lunar eclipse which should have been visible from Jerusalem just as it was ending, a little after sunset. Sometimes a lunar eclipse will make the moon appear a red color (the exact shade of red varies). Some people refer to the words of Saint Peter the Apostle as evidence of a lunar eclipse associated with the Crucifixion. Saint Peter quoted the book of the prophet Joel: " 'The sun shall be turned into darkness and the moon into blood, before the great and manifest day of the Lord arrives.' " (Acts 2:20; cf. Joel 2:31). He then spoke about the Crucifixion of Jesus Christ.

There is no mention in the Gospels of a lunar eclipse occurring on the day of the Crucifixion. The sun did turn to darkness for about 3 hours when Christ was on the Cross (Mt 27:45). But the prophecy of Joel about the sun and the moon refers to signs preceding "the great and manifest day of the Lord," which is part of the sufferings which the Church must endure (cf. Rev 6:12). There is a connection between the darkness of the sun at the Crucifixion and the darkness of the sun at the time of the Church's great suffering, for the Church must suffer even as Christ Jesus suffered. However, the signs in the sun and moon which Sacred Scripture predicts are supernatural signs. These signs will occur during the time of the sufferings prophesized by the book of Revelation.[1256]

Furthermore, lunar eclipses are common events. There are at least two lunar eclipses every year, and there can be as many as three or four lunar eclipses in the same year. Also, a lunar eclipse is visible from any place on earth where it is night at the time of the eclipse, and will be visible from some places on earth at sunset or sunrise. This makes the observation of lunar eclipses from any particular place on earth fairly common. Surely the prophecy of Joel is not fulfilled every year, merely because there is a lunar eclipse. When Saint Peter spoke about the moon turning red, in a quote from the prophet Joel, he was not speaking about a common event of nature, but of future great signs and wonders from God.

There is a tendency among some Christians today to try to explain every event described by Sacred Scripture as some type of natural event. For example, some who are weak in faith try to explain the miracles of the multiplication of the loaves as being not miraculous at all, but merely a sharing of the food that each person had brought with them. Some try to explain the 3 hours of darkness when Jesus was on the Cross as being caused by a cloud or a dust storm. But Sacred Scripture refers to these and other great signs and wonders as the works of God, not as a coincidence of nature with human events. I find no basis in Sacred Scripture for the belief that a lunar eclipse coincided with the Crucifixion of Jesus Christ.

A.D. 30

At this time, there are also many faithful Christians who believe that Christ died in A.D. 30. Nisan 14 fell on Friday, April 7, in A.D. 30. (This is the same day of the month as in the year A.D. 19.) This year for the Crucifixion assumes that the usual dates given for the reign of Tiberius Caesar are correct. The revised dates for Tiberius Caesar's reign and the reign of Pontius Pilate over Judea, as presented in chapter 13 of this book, would rule out the year A.D. 30 because Tiberius and Pilate both no longer held power at that time. Also, the chronology of king Herod's reign, presented in chapter 12 of this book, places the rebuilding of the Temple of Jerusalem from 32 B.C. to 25 B.C. This time frame is too many years before A.D. 30 to agree with the Gospel of John's statement that the rebuilding of the Temple occurred 46 years earlier (than a Passover during Christ's Ministry).

Even without these revised dates, the year of A.D. 30 does not accord with various chronological statements by Blessed Anne Catherine. For example, she stated that Christ was born 7 years earlier than some year which was generally thought to be the year of Christ's Birth.[1257] Christ was conceived and born about 33 years before the Crucifixion (see chapters 2 and 7). So, a date of A.D. 30 for the Crucifixion places the Birth of Christ in 4 B.C. But the year 4 B.C. is not 7 years earlier than any proposed year for the Birth of Christ. Also, she places the death of Herod about the time of Christ's sixth year.[1258] But the latest date which scholars in general will consider for the death of Herod is 1 B.C. Further explanations on this point, as to why Christ could not have been born in any year in the last decade of the first century B.C., are presented below.

The Birth of Jesus Christ

1 B.C.

Modern scholarship places the death of Herod no later than 1 B.C., effectively ruling out the chronology given by Dionysius (the abbot who began the "A.D." system of counting the years), which places the Birth of Jesus Christ in December of 1 B.C. Jesus could not have been born in Dec. of 1 B.C., if Herod died beforehand in early 1 B.C. Then Herod would not have been alive, 1½ to 2 years later, to take the lives of the Holy Innocents, causing the Holy Family to flee to Egypt.

Also, the Gospel of Luke clearly tells us that there was an enrollment (or census) at the time of the Birth of Jesus. This census occurred during the reign of Caesar Augustus, when Quirinius was governor of (or had authority over) Syria (Lk 2:1-2). Quirinius was in charge of a later census again in the early years A.D. This type of census/taxation of the Roman occupied territories, such as Israel and Syria, took place every 17 years.[1259] Blessed Anne Catherine also describes the census at the time of Christ's Birth as a census for the purpose of taxation. There is no evidence of a census/taxation in 1 B.C., nor in any of the early years B.C. which are often suggested as possible years for the Birth of Christ. (For details on these points, see chapter 4.)

Blessed Anne Catherine tells us that God revealed to her in visions the date of the Birth of Jesus Christ as Sunday, Nov. 25. The only years, in this time frame, when Nov. 25 fell on a Sunday are A.D. 3, 4 B.C., and 15 B.C. Again, most of the commonly-suggested years for the Birth of Christ are ruled out.

The Christian liturgical calendar numbers the years based on the idea that the Incarnation occurred in the year before A.D. 1. However, the Church does not teach that this date for the Incarnation is necessarily correct. The error made by Dionysius in assigning the year of Christ's Incarnation to the year we now call 1 B.C. was due to an error in understanding the dates of various events in Roman history, such as the year of Julius Caesar's death and the start of Tiberius Caesar's reign.

8 B.C.

This year, 8 B.C., was once a commonly-held date for the Birth of Christ, because scholars long believed that there was a census in 8 B.C. However, modern scholarship describes the census of 8 B.C. as applying only to Roman citizens, not to the citizens of the occupied countries, such as Israel.[1260] Furthermore, the date of 8 B.C. is too close to the second enrollment under Quirinius, in A.D. 6 (A.D. 2, revised), to have been the enrollment of Luke 2:2. Also, in the year 8 B.C., Nov. 25 did not fall on a Sunday, as required by the information given by Blessed Anne Catherine Emmerich. However, since this date was long thought to be one of the most likely years for the Birth of Christ, the year 8 B.C. is probably the year that Blessed Anne Catherine was referring to when she said Christ was born 7 years earlier than some commonly-accepted date for Christ's Birth.[1261]

12 B.C.

This year, 12 B.C., is the year given by scholars for the first enrollment under Quirinius, which was held 17 years before the second enrollment (in the early years A.D.).[1262] These enrollments were for the purpose of taxing the territories conquered and occupied by the Roman army. It took two years to complete the whole process of counting and taxing the people.[1263] Any year after 11 B.C. could not be the year of the Birth of Christ, because a census or enrollment, such as that described by Luke 2:1-2, was only held once every 17 years under Caesar Augustus.[1264]

The conclusions of chapter 13 of this book place this census, usually dated as beginning in 12 B.C., four years earlier, beginning in 16 B.C. The process of taxation took 2 years, so that 15 B.C. falls within the time of this census/taxation. The year of 15 B.C. is the only date which fits both the revised chronology for events in the Roman empire and the chronological information given by Blessed Anne Catherine Emmerich.

Appendix V
Glossary

antedating – the practice of counting a ruler's reign as beginning before the previous ruler left office. For example, the Roman emperor Vespasian counted his reign as beginning July 1, even though the previous emperor, Vitellius, was not removed from power until several months later. (See chapter 13 for examples and references.)

A.D. – "anno Domini," which translates as: "in the year of the Lord." Originally, the Christian calendar of Dionysius was based on the year of the incarnation of the Lord: "ab incarnatione Domini," which translates as: "from the Incarnation of the Lord."[1265] This expression was later changed to "anno Domini."

apparent solar noon – midday according to a sundial, i.e. when shadows from the sun are shortest; when the sun reaches it's highest point in the sky; referred to by the Jews as 'the sixth hour.'

accession year – the year that a ruler, usually a king or emperor, receives the throne.

accession-year system – a calendar system which counts the first full year of the ruler's reign as year one. The year during which the ruler received the throne is called the "accession year" and is not numbered.[1266] Roman practice often counted the years of an emperor's reign in this way.

astronomical new moon – when the moon passes an imaginary line drawn between the earth and the sun. The moon is not visible at the time of the astronomical new moon, except when the moon passes directly between the earth and sun, resulting in a solar eclipse. The time/date of the astronomical new moon is usually determined by calculation, because the moon is not visible at that time (except during a solar eclipse).

Assumption – the raising of a human person, body and soul, to Heaven. The Assumption of the Virgin Mary occurred after her death and Resurrection. The Assumption of the Faithful occurs after the general Resurrection.[1267] Christ ascended to Heaven by His own Divine power, so this event is called the Ascension. The Virgin Mary was brought up to Heaven by Christ, so this event is called the Assumption.

A.U.C. – *ab urbe condita*, which translates as: "from the founding of the city." The city referred to is Rome.

B.C. – "before Christ;" used to specify the years prior to A.D. 1. The year 1 B.C. immediately precedes the year A.D. 1; there is no year zero.

Biblical chronology – the study of 'what happened when' in Biblical times.

Emmerich, Anne Catherine – Blessed Anne Catherine lived from 1774 to 1824, and spent most of her adult years as a nun in an Augustinian convent. She had the stigmata, the wounds of Jesus Christ, in her body, and she suffered many times with Christ while meditating on His Passion.[1268] She was certainly a devout disciple of Jesus Christ. The Catholic Church has declared Anne Catherine Emmerich to be Blessed, that is, to be an example of holiness for faithful Christians to emulate.

Blessed Anne Catherine had many visions from God about the lives of Jesus and Mary. Since she was close to God, had the stigma, and suffered much for Christ, she must have been telling the truth about her visions from God. These visions from God are not merely the meditations of a pious nun. Blessed Anne Catherine clearly and repeatedly spoke of these visions as having come from God. Her visions are private revelation, subject to error in her understanding of the visions and in the writing down of the visions, but the source of the visions is entirely reliable.

calculation-based calendar – modern calendar system used by the Jews, which counts the start of each month according to a calculation of the astronomical new moon (before the new moon can be seen as a new crescent).

Cenaculum – also referred to as the Cenacle; a small dining room, usually on an upper floor. In the context of New Testament events, this refers to the dining room on an upper floor where Christ celebrated the Last Supper and where the Apostles and disciples continued to meet after the Resurrection. This was one of the first places of meeting and prayer of the nascent Church.

centennial year – a year whose number is evenly divisible by 100; e.g. A.D. 2000, 2100, etc.

civil calendar, Jewish – The Jewish calendar year beginning with the month of Tishri in the autumn; used to count the Sabbatical year in the modern Jewish calendar (though that may not have been the case in the ancient Jewish calendar; see chapter 16).

conjunction of planets – when two planets appear close to one another in the sky. A planet can also have a conjunction with a star or with the moon. A double conjunction occurs when two planets appear close to one another on two occasions (usually a few months apart). A triple conjunction of planets is when two planets appear close to one another on three occasions (usually within the same year or the same 12 month period of time).

Consul – see **Roman Consul** below.

crescent new moon – the first visible crescent of the moon after the astronomical new moon. Generally, the crescent moon is first seen just after sunset 24 to 48 hours after the astronomical new moon. The observation of the crescent new moon was used by the Jews in ancient times to determine the start of each calendar month.

Dio – Dio Cassius was a Greek, who wrote extensively on the history of Rome. He lived from the mid second century to the early third century A.D.[1269] His work, *Roman History*, is a major source of information for historians and chronologists.

Dionysius – Dionysius Exiguus was a Roman Catholic abbot and a theologian, with expertise in astronomy and mathematics. He devised the A.D. system of numbering the years according to the life of Christ. See chapter 1 for more information.

Divine Revelation – God's Sacred Infallible Word, found in both Sacred Scripture and Sacred Tradition, (which together are called 'The Deposit of Faith'). As contrasted with private revelation, Divine Revelation refers only to God's revelation within the Deposit of Faith, even though a particular private revelation may come from God.

Dormition – the death of the Virgin Mary. The term literally means falling asleep, but was used by early Christians to refer to actual death, because of the hope of the Resurrection. Jesus uses the word "asleep" to refer to death (Jn 11:11-14). The Acts of the Apostles and the Epistles also use the word in the same way (Acts 7:60; 1 Cor 15:6,18; Eph 5:15; 1 Thess 4:13-14; 2 Peter 3:4).

EFM (Ecclesiastical Full Moon) – the date of the full moon according to a system of charts used by the early Christian Church. The EFM is not exact and can differ from the actual full moon date/time by a day or two.

Equinox – the day when the length of the daylight hours and the nighttime hours are approximately equal; the day/time when the sun appears to cross an imaginary line extending outward from the earth's equator; occurs twice per year, once in spring and once in autumn.

Essenes – a Jewish sect active in the first century B.C. and first century A.D. Flavius Josephus held them in high esteem. They are generally regarded as holy and devout Jews. Many, but not all, of the Essenes kept themselves apart from society and lived in community in the desert.

Eusebius – Bishop of Caesarea, he wrote a detailed history of the early Church which is still used by scholars and Biblical chronologists today. He lived in the late third and early fourth century A.D.

Feast of Tabernacles – also called the feast of booths; one of the three great feasts in the Jewish faith; celebrates the time of forty years the Israelites spent in the desert.

Feast of Unleavened Bread – also called the feast of Passover; one of the three great feasts in the Jewish faith; celebrates the Jews exodus from Egypt and their freedom from slavery. Bread with leavening (such as yeast) is removed from the home of devout Jews during this feast; only unleavened bread is eaten during the feast.

Feast of Weeks – also called (Jewish) Pentecost; one of the three great feasts in the Jewish faith; celebrates the giving of the Law to Moses; occurs at the end of the harvest season; occurs 7 weeks plus one day, inclusive, from the Sabbath of Passover (this can be interpreted as either the Saturday during Passover, or the first holy day of Passover, Nisan 15).

full moon – when the moon is on the opposite side of the earth from the sun; results in the largest portion of the moon's surface being lit by the sun's light and visible from earth.

GMT (Greenwich Mean Time) – the time of day, according to the modern time zone method of keeping time, within the Greenwich, England time zone; solar time (time according to the position of the sun in the sky) at the Greenwich meridian (longitude zero) is the basis for determining time in all time zones.

Gregorian calendar – reformed version of the Julian calendar in which leap years are every 4 years, except that centennial years (1700, 1800, 1900, etc.) are only leap years when evenly divisible by 400. So, 2000 was a leap year, but 2100 will not be a leap year. This calendar system began in 1582 with the removal of ten days from the month of

October (Oct.4 was followed by Oct. 15, in 1582). This calendar is currently used by most Western nations and by most Christians.

Heli – another name for Joachim, the Virgin Mary's father (Lk 3:23).

Herod the Great – made king over the Jews by the Romans; attempted to kill the Christ-Child (Mt 2:1-23); had four sons: Herod Antipater, Herod Archelaus, Herod Antipas, Herod Philip.

Herod Antipater – killed by his father Herod the Great.

Herod Archelaus – also called Herod the ethnarch; exiled after a reign of about 10 years.

Herod Antipas – also known as Herod the tetrarch (Lk 3:1); saw and questioned Christ just before the Crucifixion (Lk 23:6-12).

Herod Philip – considered a benevolent and fair ruler by Josephus (*Antiquities* 18:106-107); also mentioned in the Gospel (Lk 3:1).

Herod Agrippa I – grandson of Herod the Great.

Herod Agrippa II – great-grandson of Herod the Great; son of Agrippa I.

inclusive counting – counts the starting point (day, month, or year) as well as the end point. For example, the time from Christ's Crucifixion to His Resurrection was three days counting inclusively (Friday, Saturday, Sunday), but was actually less than 48 hours (3 p.m. Friday to before dawn on Sunday). With inclusive counting, any part of a day, month, or year is counted as a whole.

Jerome – Saint Jerome, Doctor of the Church. He lived from the mid fourth to early fifth century A.D.

Jewish calendar – a lunar calendar, where the months follow the phases of the moon, but one which is periodically adjusted according to the solar year and the Spring Equinox. The Jewish calendar generally has 12 lunar months, but adds a 13th lunar month, every 2 or 3 years, so as to maintain the months in the same season of year, and especially to maintain the Passover in the springtime, to coincide with the grain harvest. See also: Appendix I, Charts 4, 5, 7, and Appendix II, Section C.

Jewish day – the Jewish day begins and ends at sunset; each day is divided into 12 hours of daylight and 12 hours of night; no matter how long or short the daylight time, each daytime is divided into 12 parts of equal length.

Josephus – a devout Jew, Joseph son of Matthias, was the son of a Jewish priest, member of a priestly family, a Pharisee, and a priest himself (*Wars* 3:352). He was one of the leaders in the rebellion against the Romans in the first century A.D. When he was captured and imprisoned by Vespasian, he prophesied that Vespasian would become emperor. When Vespasian did become emperor, Vespasian released Joseph and made him a Roman citizen (with the favor of the Roman emperor). Joseph took Vespasian's family name, Flavius, becoming Flavius Josephus. He wrote detailed histories of Israel and the relationship between Israel and the Roman empire.

JST (Jerusalem Standard Time) – the time in Jerusalem by the modern time-zone standard, used in this book as a convenient way to specify time, even in past centuries; GMT plus 2 hours.

Julian calendar – calendar system devised under the direction of Julius Caesar; the basis for the modern Christian calendar; differs from the Gregorian calendar in that it places a leap year every 4 years without exception; used by Orthodox Christians; reformed under Pope Gregory XIII.

leap month, Jewish calendar – every 2 or 3 years, the Jewish calendar adds a 13th month, the month of Second Adar (AdarII), to keep the Jewish lunar calendar more or less in synch with the solar year. In a leap year, Second Adar (AdarII) follows First Adar (AdarI). Adar is the month before Nisan. See **Jewish calendar** above.

leap year, Jewish calendar – Leap years in the Jewish calendar have 13 months, instead of 12 months. In the modern Jewish calendar, leap years follow a specific pattern, called the Metonic cycle, but, in ancient times, leap years were decided upon by the Jewish religious leaders, every 2 or 3 years as needed.

lunar calendar – In a pure lunar calendar, each calendar month coincides with the phases of the moon. One lunar month has an average length of 29.5306 days. Twelve lunar months are approx. 11 days short of a solar year. Thus, the months of a pure lunar calendar, (e.g. the Islamic calendar), recede through the seasons. Each lunar calendar year begins about 11 days earlier compared to a solar calendar year, (e.g. Julian or Gregorian calendars).

lunar eclipse – when the shadow of the earth covers a portion of the visible disk of the moon; occurs only about the time of the full moon.

lunisolar calendar – a calendar system based on both the phases of the moon and the solar year. The Jewish calendar is lunisolar; the months are based on the phases of the moon, but the calendar is periodically adjusted (by adding a 13th month every 2 or 3 years) to keep the calendar more or less in synch with the solar year.

Mary of Heli – the Virgin Mary's older sister, also called: "Mary of Cleophas." (Jn 19:25).

Mary Cleophas – the Virgin Mary's niece; daughter of "Mary of Cleophas."

Metonic cycle – the set pattern of leap years used in the modern Jewish calendar. In this pattern, the 3rd, 6th, 8th, 11th, 14th, 17th, and 19th years are leap years.

new moon – considered the start of the lunar cycle, one half lunar cycle from the full moon, when the moon is not visible from earth because of its proximity to the sun. See also: **astronomical new moon**, **crescent new moon**.

non-accession-year system – a calendar system which counts the first partial year of the ruler's reign as year one. The next calendar year is counted as year 2 of that ruler's reign, even if year one was only a small fraction of a year.[1270] The Jewish calendar system counted the years of a king's reign in this way.[1271]

observation-based calendar – ancient calendar system used by the Jews, which counted the start of each month according to the first observation of the crescent new moon.

Passover – also called the Feast of Unleavened Bread; one of the three great feasts in the Jewish faith; celebrates the Jews exodus from Egypt and their freedom from slavery; occurs at the start of the harvest season.

Passover, preparation day of – Nisan 14; the day before the first holy day of Passover; the day on which the Pascal lambs are killed and prepared for the Pascal meal.

PFM (Pascal Full Moon) – the first EFM (Ecclesiastical Full Moon) after March 20 is called the Pascal Full Moon and is used to determine the date of Easter. In the current Christian liturgical calendar system, Easter is the first Sunday after the PFM.

Pentecost, Jewish – also called the Feast of Weeks; one of the three great feasts in the Jewish faith; celebrates the giving of the Law to Moses; occurs at the end of the harvest season; occurs 7 weeks plus one day, inclusive, from the Sabbath of Passover (this can be interpreted as either the Saturday during Passover, or the first holy day of Passover, Nisan 15).

Pentecost, Christian – the descent of the Holy Spirit upon the nascent Church; called "Pentecost" because it coincided with Jewish Pentecost and occurred on the 50th day inclusive from the Resurrection of Christ.

penumbra – an area of partial shadow; used to refer to the lighter shadow of the earth on the visible surface of the moon during a lunar eclipse; becomes progressively darker closer to the umbra.

penumbral eclipse – a lunar eclipse where only the penumbra, not the umbra, of the earth's shadow falls upon the visible surface of the moon; such eclipses are not generally visible to the naked eye, because the penumbra is a lighter shadow which does not reduce the brightness of the moon's visible surface by a significant degree. May be visible with the naked eye if the darkest part of the penumbra (the part closest to the umbra) covers a portion of the moon's surface.

Pliny the Elder – a writer and scholar who was part of the emperor Vespasian's inner circle; lived during the first century A.D.; was killed by the eruption of Mt. Vesuvius.

prima facie – at first appearance, i.e. without closer examination.

private revelation – a revelation from God other than Sacred Scripture and Sacred Tradition. Many Saints have described visions and other revelations from God. Though God is infallible, those receiving private revelation are fallible, and so private revelation is not considered infallible. Private revelation is also lacking in other ways when compared with Sacred Scripture and Sacred Tradition.

Purim – celebrates the rescue of the Jews from extermination by Haman, the chief minister of the King of Persia.[1272]

Rosh Hodesh – or Rosh Chodesh, literally "New Moon;" the first day of the lunar month in the Jewish calendar coincides with the new moon and is a holy day of worship.

Roman Consul – a position of leadership in the Roman Senate; two consuls were chosen for each calendar year. Though the term of office was one calendar year, it was common for an emperor to hold the office for a fraction of a year, in order to obtain the honor of having been Consul, and then to relinquish the position to someone else, so as not to have to do the work of Consul for a whole year.

Sabbath – the day of worship of God and holy rest from labor. In the Jewish faith, the Sabbath is Saturday, from Friday at sunset to Saturday at sunset. In the Christian faith, the Sabbath is Sunday, from midnight (Saturday/Sunday) to midnight (Sunday/Monday).

Sabbath, preparation day of – in the Jewish faith, the day before the Sabbath is a day to do the work needed to allow one to rest on the Sabbath; Friday, from sunset Thursday to sunset Friday.

sacred calendar – the Jewish liturgical calendar, beginning with the month of Nisan in the springtime.

Sacred Scripture – the Bible; God's Holy Infallible Writings.

sepulchre – a tomb for burial.

solar calendar – a calendar system based on the solar year. The Julian and Gregorian calendar systems are solar calendars.

solar eclipse – when the shadow of the moon covers a portion of the earth's surface; occurs only about the time of the astronomical new moon; occurs whenever the visible disk of the moon partially or completely blocks the view of the visible disk of the sun from anywhere on earth.

solar time – time according to the position of the sun in the sky.

solar transit – when the sun reaches the meridian in the sky; approximately the midpoint between sunrise and sunset, when the sun is highest in the sky.

Spring Equinox – see **Equinox**. Before the Spring Equinox, nighttime is longer than daytime; after the Spring Equinox, daytime is longer than nighttime. The reverse is true for the vernal equinox in the autumn.

stadia – an ancient Greek unit of measure, equal to about 600 feet.

Standard Time – time according to the modern time-zone standard.

Suetonius – Gaius Suetonius Tranquillus lived in the late first and early second century A.D. He wrote the well-known history of the Roman emperors, *Lives of the Caesars* (also called *The Twelve Caesars*).

sun time – time according to the position of the sun in the sky; time according to a sundial.

Tacitus – Cornelius Tacitus lived from the mid first to early second century A.D. He was a Roman senator and historian.

Theotokos – literally, "God-bearer." This term refers to the Virgin Mary as she who bore the Son of God in her womb. The term is accepted in both the Latin and Eastern Rites of the Catholic Church, but is primarily used by all the Eastern Churches.

tribunician power – authority given to high Roman officials; enabled them to nullify the rulings of other officials and to act as judge over any who offended them. The Roman emperors regularly gave themselves tribunician power .

umbra – an area of darkest shadow; used to refer to the dark shadow of the earth on the visible surface of the moon during a lunar eclipse.

umbral eclipse – a lunar eclipse where the darkest area of the earth's shadow covers a portion of the moon's visible surface. Such eclipses are easily visible from earth, because the dark shadow contrasts well with the lit surface of the moon.

Universal Time – abbreviated as U.T.; equivalent, within a fraction of a second, to GMT.

Victorinus – Saint Victorinus, Bishop of Pettau, martyr during the persecution under Diocletian. Victorinus wrote commentaries on Sacred Scripture and is mentioned in the writings of Saint Jerome.[1273]

Endnotes:

[1] Nikos Kokkinos, "Crucifixion in A.D. 36," *Chronos, Kairos, Christos*, ed. Jerry Vardaman and Edwin M. Yamauchi, (Winona Lake, Indiana: Eisenbrauns, 1989), p. 143-145.

[2] Blessed Anne Catherine Emmerich, *The Dolorous Passion of Our Lord Jesus Christ*, (Rockford, Illinois: TAN Books and Publishers, Inc., 1983), p. 3 - 57.

[3] Blessed Anne Catherine Emmerich, *The Life of the Blessed Virgin Mary*, trans. Sir Michael Palairet, (Rockford, Illinois: TAN Books and Publishers, Inc., 1970), p. 241.

[4] Emmerich, *The Life of the Blessed Virgin Mary*, p. 138.

[5] Emmerich, *The Life of the Blessed Virgin Mary*, p. 207.

[6] Blessed Anne Catherine did not understand the Jewish calendar well enough to calculate any date in the Jewish calendar on her own. For example, see Emmerich, *The Life of the Blessed Virgin Mary*, p. 206. She tells us she cannot remember how the Jewish leap month worked, and that maybe it was 21 or 22 days long. Yet in spite of this lack of understanding, she is able to give the feasts and holy days in the Jewish calendar their correct place in the calendar. This correctness, in spite of limited understanding, shows that her chronological information came from her visions from God, not from her own mind.

[7] Flavius Josephus, *The Works of Josephus: Complete and Unabridged, New Updated Edition*, trans. William Whiston, (Peabody, Massachusetts: Hendrickson Publishers, Inc., 1995), *The Antiquities of the Jews*, 15.380; *The Antiquities of the Jews*, title of book 15; *The Wars of the Jews*, 1.401.

[8] Jerry Vardaman, "Jesus' Life: A New Chronology," *Chronos, Kairos, Christos*, p. 55ff.

[9] Jack Finegan, *Handbook of Biblical Chronology*, revised edition, (Peabody, Massachusetts: Hendrickson Publishers, Inc., 1998).

[10] *RedShift 3*, astronomy software, (Kingston, UK: Maris Multimedia Ltd., Maris.com, 1998).

[11] Eclipse Predictions by Fred Espenak, NASA/GSFC, (Greenbelt, Maryland: National Aeronautics & Space Administration/Goddard Space Flight Center), <http://sunearth.gsfc.nasa.gov/eclipse>.

"All eclipse calculations are by Fred Espenak, and he assumes full responsibility for their accuracy." No endorsement of the premises or conclusions of this book by Fred Espenak or by NASA is implied, nor should be inferred.

NASA/GSFC Sun-Earth Connection Education Forum, NASA/GSFC, <http://sunearth.gsfc.nasa.gov/eclipse/eclipse.html>.
Fred Espenak, *Five Millennium Catalog of Solar Eclipses*, NASA/GSFC, <http://sunearth.gsfc.nasa.gov/eclipse/SEcat/SEcatalog.html>.
Fred Espenak, *Five Millennium Catalog of Lunar Eclipses*, NASA/GSFC, <http://sunearth.gsfc.nasa.gov/eclipse/LEcat/LEcatalog.html>.
Fred Espenak, *Five Millennia Catalog of Phases of the Moon*, NASA/GSFC, <http://sunearth.gsfc.nasa.gov/eclipse/phase/phasecat.html>.

[12] Fred Espenak is a scientist at NASA's Goddard Space Flight Center. He is the author of the book, *Fifty Year Canon of Lunar Eclipses: 1986-2035* (Sky Publishing Corp.), and co-author of the book, *Totality: Eclipses of the Sun*, (Oxford University Press).

[13] Fred Espenak, *Five Millennia Catalog of Phases of the Moon*, NASA/GSFC,

<http://sunearth.gsfc.nasa.gov/eclipse/phase/phasecat.html>.
"This data is provided primarily to assist in historical research projects....Algorithms used in predicting the phases of the Moon as well as eclipses are based on Jean Meeus' Astronomical Algorithms (Willmann-Bell, Inc., Richmond, 1991). All calculations are by Fred Espenak, and he assumes full responsibility for their accuracy."

[14] Easter is the first Sunday after the first Ecclesiastical Full Moon (EFM) after March 20. The EFM is an approximation of the date of the full moon developed by astronomers in A.D. 325 in order to help determine future dates for Easter. March 20 was the date of the spring Equinox in A.D. 325. See Ronald W. Mallen, Astronomical Society of South Australia, *Easter Dating Method*, <http://www.assa.org.au/edm.html>.

[15] Finegan, *Handbook of Biblical Chronology*, revised edition, no. 217, p. 113.

[16] Finegan, *Handbook of Biblical Chronology*, revised edition, no. 218, p. 113.

[17] Finegan, *Handbook of Biblical Chronology*, revised edition, no. 219, p. 114.

[18] Blessed Anne Catherine make this point clear in her descriptions of Joseph and Mary. See, for one example: Emmerich, *The Life of the Blessed Virgin Mary*, p.191.

[19] Josephus, *The Wars of the Jews*, 6.423. See also Jack Finegan, *Handbook of Biblical Chronology*, revised edition, no. 20, p. 11; and Emmerich, *The Dolorous Passion of Our Lord Jesus Christ*, p. 273.

[20] Finegan, *Handbook of Biblical Chronology*, revised edition, no. 633, p. 368. See also, Eusebius, *Ecclesiastical History*, books I–V, trans. Kirsopp Lake, Eusebius, Volume I, Loeb Classical Library, (Cambridge, Massachusetts: Harvard University Press, 1998), 5.23-25.

[21] Emmerich, *The Dolorous Passion of Our Lord Jesus Christ*, p. 160-161.

[22] An ordinary sundial can be used to keep track of sun time. In this method of time-keeping, sunrise generally marked as 6:00 a.m. and sunset as 6:00 p.m., even when the daylight hours are more than 12 times 60 minutes. So, using a sundial is the modern equivalent of the ancient Jewish method of measuring daytime hours.

[23] Standard Time, using worldwide time zones, was developed in the late 1800's.

[24] Emmerich, *The Dolorous Passion of Our Lord Jesus Christ*, p. 222.

[25] Emmerich, *The Dolorous Passion of Our Lord Jesus Christ*, p. 225.

[26] Today, one could calculate exactly how many minutes after sunrise marked the third hour of a particular day. However, this result would contain a degree of precision not in general use among the Jews of that time and not indicated by Sacred Scripture.

[27] On April 7, at Jerusalem, using the modern time zone standard, sunrise occurred at 05:23 and solar noon occurred at 11:41. The midpoint between sunrise and solar noon was therefore 08:32 standard time. Thus 9 a.m. solar time was equivalent, on that day, to 08:32 standard time.

[28] By modern time-zone method, the sixth hour (apparent solar noon) would be 11:41 hours Jerusalem standard time, when the sun reached its zenith in the sky, on April 7.

[29] Ronald L. Conte Jr., *The Bible and the Future of the World*, (Catholic Planet, 2001), <http://www.catholicplanet.com/>, chapter 5. This book contains additional comments on this point and its relationship to the future sufferings of the Church.

[30] Emmerich, *The Dolorous Passion of Our Lord Jesus Christ*, p. 273.

[31] Emmerich, *The Dolorous Passion of Our Lord Jesus Christ*, p. 268-273.

[32] Noon solar time was equivalent to 11:41 Jerusalem Standard Time, using the modern time zone method of tracking time.

[33] The length of time from the sixth hour to the ninth hour can be calculated by dividing into 12 parts the amount of time from sunrise on April 7 at 05:23 to sunset at 18:00, which is 12 hours 37 minutes. Thus each solar hour on that day was about 63 minutes long and the time from the sixth hour to the ninth hour was about 3 hours and 9 minutes. Solar transit (noon sun time) occurred that day at 11:41 hours (according to *RedShift 3* astronomy software).

[34] The longest solar eclipse, occurring between A.D. 1 and A.D. 100, was 11 minutes and 18 seconds in duration (Nov. 4, A.D. 96). Data on solar eclipses taken from the NASA/GSFC Sun-Earth Connection Education Forum. Fred Espenak, *Five Millennium Catalog of Solar Eclipses*, NASA/GSFC,
<http://sunearth.gsfc.nasa.gov/eclipse/SEcat/SEcatalog.html>.

[35] By the modern time-zone method, the third hour, measured as the midpoint between noon sun time (11:41) and sunset (18:00), would be approx. 14:50 hours (2:50 p.m.) at Jerusalem on April 7 during that time period (A.D. 1 to A.D. 50).

[36] Emmerich, *The Dolorous Passion of Our Lord Jesus Christ*, p. 294.

[37] Saint Faustina Kowalska of the Most Blessed Sacrament, *Diary: Divine Mercy in My Soul,* (Stockbridge, Massachusetts: Marians of the Immaculate Conception, 1996), margin number 1320.

[38] Saint Faustina Kowalska, *Diary: Divine Mercy in My Soul*, margin number 1572.

[39] Solar transit (noon sun time) occurred that day at 11:41 hours. The ninth hour occurred 3 hours and 9 minutes later, at 14:50 hours (2:50 p.m.). Even so, the exact time of Christ's death on the Cross was not exactly the ninth hour and is not precisely known.

[40] Emmerich, *The Dolorous Passion of Our Lord Jesus Christ*, p. 97-124.

[41] Emmerich, *The Dolorous Passion of Our Lord Jesus Christ*, p. 99. Passover always begins about the time of the full moon, because the Jewish calendar is based on the cycles of the moon. Moonrise will occur about the same time as sunset when the moon is full, since at that time the moon is on the opposite side of the earth from the sun.

[42] Blessed Anne Catherine Emmerich, *The Life of Jesus Christ and Biblical Revelations*, ed. Carl E. Schmoger, C.SS.R (Rockford, Illinois: TAN Books and Publishers, Inc., 1986), vol. 4, p. 396.

[43] Emmerich, *The Dolorous Passion of Our Lord Jesus Christ*, p. 304.

[44] Emmerich, *The Dolorous Passion of Our Lord Jesus Christ*, p. 304.

[45] Sun times from *RedShift 3*, astronomy software, (Kingston, UK: Maris Multimedia Ltd., Maris.com, 1998). Jerusalem standard time is according to the modern time zone for Jerusalem, which is GMT + 2:00.

[46] Emmerich, *The Dolorous Passion of Our Lord Jesus Christ*, p. 305.

[47] The famine had to have lasted 3½ years, rather than 3 years, because the rains in Israel occur only in winter. There is no appreciable rain, sufficient to end a famine by providing water for crops, in Israel, anytime other than in winter. That is why crops are planted in Israel in late fall/early winter, and harvested in early spring. For this reason, any dry spell would be counted as beginning in spring, after the last rainy season, and ending in fall, before the next rainy season. So every drought in Israel must be counted as some number of years **plus** one half year.

[48] Conte, *The Bible and the Future of the World*, see especially chapters 5 and 10. This book contains many explanations of the 3½ years of the Church's greatest suffering.
[49] Emmerich, *The Life of the Blessed Virgin Mary*, p. 169, 177.
[50] Emmerich, *The Life of Jesus Christ and Biblical Revelations* , vol. 1, p. 469.
[51] Emmerich, *The Life of Jesus Christ and Biblical Revelations* , vol. 1, p. 469.
[52] Emmerich, *The Life of the Blessed Virgin Mary*, p. 169, see also chapter 7.
[53] Emmerich, *The Life of the Blessed Virgin Mary*, p. 145.
[54] Emmerich, *The Life of the Blessed Virgin Mary*, p. 144.
[55] Further proof that the age of Christ, as shown to Blessed Anne Catherine, must be counted from the Incarnation, rather than the Birth of Christ, is found in the date she herself gives for Christ's Birth. She states that Christ was born on a Sunday, Nov. 25. But none of the dates when Nov. 25 fell on a Sunday fall 33 years and 18 weeks prior to a year when Nisan 14 was a Friday. The years when Nov. 25 was a Sunday are 15 B.C., 4 B.C., and A.D. 3. Counting forward 33 full years plus about 18 weeks from those years brings us to A.D. 20, A.D. 31 and A.D. 37. (You cannot calculate this by simply adding 33, because Christ was born near the end of the calendar year, and was crucified near the beginning of the calendar year. In other words, the extra 18 or so weeks pushes the date into the next calendar year.) A.D. 37 is too late a date for the Crucifixion, since, according to Josephus, Pilate left his position as ruler of Judea before Tiberius died. And Nisan 14 did not fall on a Friday in A.D. 31 (see Appendix I, Chart 1). A.D. 20 could have had a Nisan 14 Passover only if the calendar was determined by observation, not calculation, but chapter 17 concludes that the calendar was determined by calculation. So, none of these could be the year of Christ's death. Thus, the age of Christ as revealed to Blessed Anne Catherine cannot be counted from Christ's Birth, but from the Incarnation of Jesus Christ, which was certainly the beginning of Christ's human life.
[56] Emmerich, *The Life of the Blessed Virgin Mary*, p. 129-130.
[57] Emmerich, *The Life of the Blessed Virgin Mary*, p. 140. The words in brackets are from the original text; they were not added by the author of this book.
[58] Emmerich, *The Life of the Blessed Virgin Mary*, p. 144.
[59] Six weeks is 42 days (6 x 7 = 42). According to Blessed Anne Catherine, the Incarnation occurred on Feb. 25 at the beginning of that day, about midnight. So, the first whole day of Christ's human life was Feb. 25. So, there are 4 days at the end of February, plus 31 days in March, plus 7 more days in April, making 42 days total (4 + 31 + 7 = 42). Therefore, there are exactly 6 weeks from Feb. 25, the day of the Incarnation, to April 7, the day of the Crucifixion.
[60] Nikos Kokkinos, "Crucifixion in A.D. 36," *Chronos, Kairos, Christos*, p. 149. He cites U. Holzmeister, "Neuere Arbeiten über das Datum der Kreuzigung Christi," *Bib* 13 (1932) 99.
[61] Suetonius Tranquillus, *Lives of the Caesars*, ed. and trans. John C. Rolfe, Suetonius, Volume I, Loeb Classical Library, (Cambridge, Massachusetts: Harvard University Press, 1998), 1.88.1.
[62] Emmerich, *The Life of the Blessed Virgin Mary*, p. 205, 367.
[63] Emmerich, *The Life of the Blessed Virgin Mary*, p. 346.

[64] This determination includes the widest range of possible dates for the start of Passover on Nisan 14, considering possible dates both by calculation and by observation-based calendar systems.

[65] Finegan, *Handbook of Biblical Chronology*, revised edition, no. 78-81, p. 38-39.

[66] Finegan, *Handbook of Biblical Chronology*, revised edition, no. 475 and tables 128-138, p. 280-287.

[67] Finegan, *Handbook of Biblical Chronology*, revised edition, no. 570 and table 150, p. 330-331.

[68] Finegan, *Handbook of Biblical Chronology*, revised edition, no. 583, p. 340-341.

[69] Dr. E. Jerry Vardaman was a Biblical Archaeologist and New Testament Scholar. He was an editor and a contributing author of *Chronos, Kairos, Christos* and *Chronos, Kairos, Christos II*, two important books on Biblical chronology. Please note that Dr. Vardaman changed his mind about the theory that Tiberius' reign should be counted from his adoption as heir to Augustus. His later theory proposed a copyist error in Luke 3:1, which changed "in the second year of Tiberius" to "in the fifteenth year of Tiberius." See Vardaman, "Jesus' Life: A New Chronology," *Chronos, Kairos, Christos*, p. 59-61.

[70] Dio Cassius, *Roman History*, ed. Jeffrey Henderson, trans. Earnest Cary, Dio Cassius, Volume VI, Loeb Classical Library, (Cambridge, Massachusetts: Harvard University Press, 2000), 55.10a.8-10. See also, Vardaman, "Jesus' Life: A New Chronology," *Chronos, Kairos, Christos*, p. 58.

[71] Dio, *Roman History*, 55.9.5-10. See also, Vardaman, "Jesus' Life: A New Chronology," *Chronos, Kairos, Christos*, p. 58-59.

[72] Dio, *Roman History*, 55.13.1a. See also, Vardaman, "Jesus' Life: A New Chronology," *Chronos, Kairos, Christos*, p. 58-59.

[73] Dio, *Roman History*, 55.13.1a.

[74] Finegan, *Handbook of Biblical Chronology*, revised edition, no. 570, p. 330.

[75] Dio Cassius, *Roman History*, ed. G. P. Goold, trans. Earnest Cary, Dio Cassius, Volume VII, Loeb Classical Library, (Cambridge, Massachusetts: Harvard University Press, 1994), 56.30.5.

[76] Dio, *Roman History*, 55.13.1a-2.

[77] Finegan, *Handbook of Biblical Chronology*, revised edition, no. 517, p. 300-301. See also, Ernest L Martin, "The Nativity and Herod's Death," *Chronos, Kairos, Christos*, p. 90-91.

[78] Finegan, *Handbook of Biblical Chronology*, revised edition, no. 183 and table 42, p. 86.

[79] Finegan, *Handbook of Biblical Chronology*, revised edition, no. 165, p. 78. This is called the non-accession-year system. A partial year, of even a brief number of days, was counted as a full year.

[80] Finegan, *Handbook of Biblical Chronology*, revised edition, no.583, p. 340.

[81] This is called the accession-year system, a common method of dating a ruler's reign. The year that the ruler came to power is numbered as the last year of the previous ruler's reign, but is referred to as the current ruler's "accession year." See Finegan, *Handbook of Biblical Chronology*, revised edition, no. 161, p. 75.

[82] Finegan, *Handbook of Biblical Chronology*, revised edition, no. 583, p. 340. Here Jack Finegan concludes that Luke would have counted the years of Tiberius' reign beginning with the first whole calendar year. His argument is that the Gospel of Luke and the Acts of the Apostles are addressed to Theophilus (a Roman name and probably a Roman

official), and so Luke would have followed the practice of Roman historians by counting whole calendar years.

[83] Finegan, *Handbook of Biblical Chronology*, revised edition, no. 620, p. 362.

[84] Vardaman, "Jesus' Life: A New Chronology," *Chronos, Kairos, Christos*, p. 77-82. See also: Jerry Vardaman, "Were the Samaritan Military Leaders, Rufus and Gratus, at the Time of Herod's Death, the Later Roman Judean Governors Who Preceded Pontius Pilate?," *Chronos, Kairos, Christos II*, (Macon, Georgia: Mercer University Press, 1998), p. 191-202.

[85] Cf. Josephus, *The Antiquities of the Jews*, 18.89, 18.224.

[86] Eusebius, *Ecclesiastical History*, 1.9.2.

[87] Finegan, *Handbook of Biblical Chronology*, revised edition, no. 78-81, p. 38-39.

[88] Finegan, *Handbook of Biblical Chronology*, revised edition, no. 165, p. 78.

[89] Sunrise data from *RedShift 3*, astronomy software, (Kingston, UK: Maris Multimedia Ltd., Maris.com, 1998). Jerusalem Standard Time is GMT plus 2:00 hours.

[90] Also, the Resurrection occurred about the time of the full moon near the beginning of Passover. The moon was full and above the horizon for the whole night, so the sky was not completely dark at any time that night (unless it was very cloudy).

[91] Emmerich, *The Life of Jesus Christ and Biblical Revelations* , Vol. 4, p. 363.

[92] Emmerich, *The Life of Jesus Christ and Biblical Revelations*, Vol. 4, p. 365.

[93] Emmerich, *The Life of Jesus Christ and Biblical Revelations*, Vol. 4, p. 363.

[94] Emmerich, *The Dolorous Passion of Our Lord Jesus Christ*, p. 359; *The Life of the Blessed Virgin Mary*, p. 81.

[95] Emmerich, *The Life of the Blessed Virgin Mary*, Genealogical Table, p. 384.

[96] Emmerich, *The Life of Jesus Christ and Biblical Revelations*, Vol. 4, p. 365.

[97] Emmerich, *The Life of Jesus Christ and Biblical Revelations*, Vol. 4, p. 363.

[98] Emmerich, *The Dolorous Passion of Our Lord Jesus Christ*, p. 359.

[99] Emmerich, *The Life of Jesus Christ and Biblical Revelations*, Vol. 4, p. 319.

[100] Emmerich, *The Life of Jesus Christ and Biblical Revelations*, Vol. 4, p. 365.

[101] Emmerich, *The Life of Jesus Christ and Biblical Revelations*, Vol. 4, p. 364.

[102] Emmerich, *The Life of Jesus Christ and Biblical Revelations*, Vol. 4, p. 364-365.

[103] Emmerich, *The Life of Jesus Christ and Biblical Revelations*, Vol. 4, p. 366.

[104] Emmerich, *The Dolorous Passion of Our Lord Jesus Christ*, 363-364; *The Life of Jesus Christ and Biblical Revelations*, Vol. 4, p. 366-367.

[105] Emmerich, *The Dolorous Passion of Our Lord Jesus Christ*, p. 304-305.

[106] Emmerich, *The Dolorous Passion of Our Lord Jesus Christ*, p. 364; *The Life of Jesus Christ and Biblical Revelations*, Vol. 4, p. 366.

[107] Emmerich, *The Life of Jesus Christ and Biblical Revelations*, Vol. 4, p. 366-367; *The Dolorous Passion of Our Lord Jesus Christ*, p. 364-365.

[108] Emmerich, *The Life of Jesus Christ and Biblical Revelations*, Vol. 4, p. 367; *The Dolorous Passion of Our Lord Jesus Christ*, p. 365.

[109] Emmerich, *The Life of Jesus Christ and Biblical Revelations* , Vol. 4, p. 367; *The Dolorous Passion of Our Lord Jesus Christ*, p. 365.

[110] Emmerich, *The Life of Jesus Christ and Biblical Revelations*, Vol. 4, p. 367-369; *The Dolorous Passion of Our Lord Jesus Christ*, p. 365-367.

[111] Emmerich, *The Life of Jesus Christ and Biblical Revelations*, Vol. 4, p. 369-370; *The Dolorous Passion of Our Lord Jesus Christ*, p. 368.
[112] Emmerich, *The Life of Jesus Christ and Biblical Revelations*, Vol. 4, p. 370-372; *The Dolorous Passion of Our Lord Jesus Christ*, p. 368-369.
[113] Emmerich, *The Life of Jesus Christ and Biblical Revelations*, Vol. 4, p. 370-371; *The Dolorous Passion of Our Lord Jesus Christ*, p. 369.
[114] Emmerich, *The Life of Jesus Christ and Biblical Revelations*, Vol. 4, p. 371; *The Dolorous Passion of Our Lord Jesus Christ*, p. 369-370.
[115] Emmerich, *The Life of Jesus Christ and Biblical Revelations*, Vol. 4, p. 369.
[116] Emmerich, *The Dolorous Passion of Our Lord Jesus Christ*, p. 365; *The Life of Jesus Christ and Biblical Revelations*, Vol. 4, p. 367.
[117] Emmerich, *The Dolorous Passion of Our Lord Jesus Christ*, p. 303-305, 337, 361.
[118] Emmerich, *The Dolorous Passion of Our Lord Jesus Christ*, p. 360-361.
[119] Emmerich, *The Dolorous Passion of Our Lord Jesus Christ*, p. 361.
[120] Emmerich, *The Dolorous Passion of Our Lord Jesus Christ*, p. 370.
[121] Emmerich, *The Life of Jesus Christ and Biblical Revelations*, Vol. 4, p. 313.
[122] Emmerich, *The Dolorous Passion of Our Lord Jesus Christ*, p. 305, note 1.
[123] Josephus, *The Antiquities of the Jews*, 20.1.
[124] Josephus, *The Antiquities of the Jews*, 14.119; 14.271.
[125] Josephus, *The Antiquities of the Jews*, 19.362.
[126] Emmerich, *The Life of Jesus Christ and Biblical Revelations*, Vol. 4, p. 370-371; *The Dolorous Passion of Our Lord Jesus Christ*, p. 369.
[127] Emmerich, *The Life of Jesus Christ and Biblical Revelations*, Vol. 4, p. 371; *The Dolorous Passion of Our Lord Jesus Christ*, p. 369-370.
[128] Emmerich, *The Life of Jesus Christ and Biblical Revelations*, Vol. 4, p. 371.
[129] Emmerich, *The Life of Jesus Christ and Biblical Revelations*, Vol. 4, p. 371.
[130] Emmerich, *The Life of Jesus Christ and Biblical Revelations*, Vol. 4, p. 378.
[131] Emmerich, *The Life of Jesus Christ and Biblical Revelations*, Vol. 4, p. 378-382.
[132] Emmerich, *The Life of Jesus Christ and Biblical Revelations*, Vol. 4, p. 378.
[133] Emmerich, *The Dolorous Passion of Our Lord Jesus Christ*, p. 368. Cf. *The Life of Jesus Christ and Biblical Revelations*, Vol. 4, p. 370.
[134] Emmerich, *The Life of Jesus Christ and Biblical Revelations* , Vol. 4, p. 389.
[135] Emmerich, *The Life of Jesus Christ and Biblical Revelations* , Vol. 4, p. 407.
[136] Emmerich, *The Life of Jesus Christ and Biblical Revelations* , Vol. 4, p. 407; cf. p. 420.
[137] Emmerich, *The Life of Jesus Christ and Biblical Revelations* , Vol. 4, p. 405-407.
[138] Emmerich, *The Life of Jesus Christ and Biblical Revelations* , Vol. 4, p. 405-406.
[139] Emmerich, *The Life of Jesus Christ and Biblical Revelations* , Vol. 4, p. 447.
[140] Emmerich, *The Life of Jesus Christ and Biblical Revelations* , Vol. 4, p. 418.
[141] Finegan, *Handbook of Biblical Chronology*, revised edition, no. 73, p. 36.
[142] A cubit was the length of a man's forearm, from the tip of the middle finger to the elbow, or about 17 to 22 inches. So, 2,000 cubits would be between 0.54 miles and 0.69 miles, which is 0.86 to 1.12 kilometers.
[143] John Rogerson, *Atlas of the Bible*, (New York, NY: Facts on File, Inc., 1998), p. 163.
[144] Encyclopedia Britannica, (Chicago, IL: Encyclopedia Britannica, Inc., 1989), *Bethany*, Vol. 2, p. 173, 1a.

[145] Emmerich, *The Life of the Blessed Virgin Mary*, p. 183.
[146] Emmerich, *The Life of Jesus Christ and Biblical Revelations,* Vol. 4, p. 424.
[147] Emmerich, *The Life of Jesus Christ and Biblical Revelations,* Vol. 4., p. 423-425.
[148] Emmerich, *The Life of Jesus Christ and Biblical Revelations,* Vol. 4, p. 424-425.
[149] Emmerich, *The Life of Jesus Christ and Biblical Revelations,* Vol. 4, p. 425.
[150] Emmerich, *The Life of Jesus Christ and Biblical Revelations,* Vol. 4, p. 426-427.
[151] Emmerich, *The Life of Jesus Christ and Biblical Revelations,* Vol. 4, p. 427.
[152] Emmerich, *The Life of Jesus Christ and Biblical Revelations,* Vol. 4, p. 422-424.
[153] Emmerich, *The Life of Jesus Christ and Biblical Revelations,* Vol. 4, p. 427.
[154] The American Heritage Dictionary, second edition, (Boston, Massachusetts: Houghton Mifflin Company, 1985), p. 252.
[155] Emmerich, *The Life of Jesus Christ and Biblical Revelations,* Vol. 4, p. 428.
[156] Emmerich, *The Life of the Blessed Virgin Mary*, p. 191.
[157] Emmerich, *The Life of the Blessed Virgin Mary*, p. 191.
[158] Emmerich, *The Life of the Blessed Virgin Mary*, p. 190-191.
[159] Emmerich, *The Life of the Blessed Virgin Mary*, p. 183-193.
[160] Emmerich, *The Life of the Blessed Virgin Mary*, p. 194.
[161] Emmerich, *The Life of the Blessed Virgin Mary*, p. 197, 207.
[162] Emmerich, *The Life of the Blessed Virgin Mary*, p. 207.
[163] Emmerich, *The Life of the Blessed Virgin Mary*, p. 219; see also p. 207-208.
[164] Emmerich, *The Life of the Blessed Virgin Mary*, p. 105.
[165] Emmerich, *The Life of the Blessed Virgin Mary*, p. 191.
[166] By comparison, during the same time period, December 25 only fell on a Sunday in 17 B.C., 11 B.C., A.D. 1 and A.D. 7. None of these years are strongly argued by anyone as possible years for the Birth of Christ.
[167] Emmerich, *The Life of the Blessed Virgin Mary*, p. 205.
[168] Finegan, *Handbook of Biblical Chronology*, revised edition, no. 474-551, p. 279-320.
[169] Finegan, *Handbook of Biblical Chronology*, revised edition, "Dates of the Birth of Christ in Early Christian Sources," table 139, p. 291.
[170] Emmerich, *The Life of the Blessed Virgin Mary*, p. 205, footnote 1: *Catholic Commentary*, p. 676a, 1953.
[171] Nov. 25 coincided with Kislev 6 that year, if the Jewish calendar was determined by calculation. If by observation, then the date would have been Kislev 5. As explained in chapter 17, I am convinced that the Jewish calendar, during this time period, was determined by calculation, not by observation.
[172] Emmerich, *The Life of the Blessed Virgin Mary*, p. 241.
[173] Emmerich, *The Life of the Blessed Virgin Mary*, p. 138.
[174] Emmerich, *The Life of the Blessed Virgin Mary*, p. 207.
[175] Emmerich, *The Life of the Blessed Virgin Mary*, p. 240.
[176] Emmerich, *The Life of the Blessed Virgin Mary*, p. 180-181; see also p. 167.
[177] Emmerich, *The Life of the Blessed Virgin Mary*, p. 181.
[178] Emmerich, *The Life of the Blessed Virgin Mary*, p. 180.
[179] Emmerich, *The Life of the Blessed Virgin Mary*, p. 181.
[180] Emmerich, *The Life of the Blessed Virgin Mary*, p. 181.
[181] Emmerich, *The Life of the Blessed Virgin Mary*, p. 205.

[182] Emmerich, *The Life of the Blessed Virgin Mary*, p. 333.
[183] Finegan, *Handbook of Biblical Chronology*, revised edition, p. 306-320.
[184] Emmerich, *The Life of the Blessed Virgin Mary*, p. 234.
[185] Emmerich, *The Life of the Blessed Virgin Mary*, p. 233.
[186] Emmerich, *The Life of the Blessed Virgin Mary*, p. 238.
[187] Finegan, *Handbook of Biblical Chronology*, revised edition, no. 533, p. 311. This passage quotes an ancient Roman historian, Justin, concerning a comet described as being bright enough to be seen in the daytime. See also: Donald K. Yeomans, *Great Comets in History*, <http://ssd.jpl.nasa.gov/great_comets.html>, which lists several comets clearly visible in daylight hours, even when close to the sun.
[188] Emmerich, *The Life of the Blessed Virgin Mary*, p. 258.
[189] Emmerich, *The Life of the Blessed Virgin Mary*, p. 243.
[190] Emmerich, *The Life of the Blessed Virgin Mary*, p. 253, 257.
[191] Emmerich, *The Life of the Blessed Virgin Mary*, p. 245.
[192] Emmerich, *The Life of the Blessed Virgin Mary*, p. 246.
[193] Emmerich, *The Life of the Blessed Virgin Mary*, p. 196.
[194] Emmerich, *The Life of the Blessed Virgin Mary*, p. 219.
[195] Yeomans, *Great Comets in History*, <http://ssd.jpl.nasa.gov/great_comets.html>. Several comets are listed which split into two or more pieces, including the Ikeya-Seki comet of October, 1965.
[196] Only a comet fits this description of the Christmas Star. A comet can split into two or more pieces. A comet has a tail, and can therefore present a complex image that could be interpreted as a picture of a virgin and child. A conjunction of planets does not appear to have a tail, nor would two planets appearing close to one another in the sky present a complex pattern that could be interpreted as a picture of a virgin and child.
[197] Gary W. Kronk, *Cometography, A Catalog of Comets*, Volume 1: Ancient–1799, (Cambridge, United Kingdom: Cambridge University Press, 1999), p. 24-25.
[198] Emmerich, *The Life of the Blessed Virgin Mary*, p. 219-220, 257-259.
[199] Yeomans, *Great Comets in History*, <http://ssd.jpl.nasa.gov/great_comets.html>.
[200] Emmerich, *The Life of the Blessed Virgin Mary*, p. 220-221, 257-258.
[201] Kronk, *Cometography*, p. 26-27. A comet, sometimes mentioned as occurring early in the year in 4 B.C., was likely a misdated account of the 5 B.C. comet, which appeared at the same time of year. See also, John Mosley, Program Supervisor, Griffith Observatory, *Common Errors in "Star of Bethlehem" Planetarium Shows*, The Griffith Observatory Home Page, <http://www.griffithobs.org/IPSChristmasErrors.html>, reprinted from *Planetarian*, vol. 10, no. 3, 3rd quarter, (International Planetarium Society, 1981). See also, Finegan, *Handbook of Biblical Chronology*, revised edition, no. 543, p. 315.
[202] For example, Konradin Ferrari-D'Occhieppo, "The Star of the Magi and Babylonian Astronomy," *Chronos, Kairos, Christos*, p. 41-53
[203] John Mosley, Program Supervisor, Griffith Observatory, *Common Errors in "Star of Bethlehem" Planetarium Shows*, The Griffith Observatory Home Page, <http://www.griffithobs.org/IPSChristmasErrors.html>, no. 7.
[204] Finegan, *Handbook of Biblical Chronology*, revised edition, no. 550, p. 319.
[205] Emmerich, *The Life of the Blessed Virgin Mary*, p. 54, 66, 219-220, 237-239.

[206] There are several conjunctions of one planet with another planet every year. And, if one also includes conjunctions of a planet with a bright star or with the moon, there are dozens of conjunctions each year. *RedShift 3*, astronomy software, (Kingston, UK: Maris Multimedia Ltd., Maris.com, 1998).

[207] Finegan, *Handbook of Biblical Chronology*, revised edition, no. 532-533, p. 310-311.

[208] Emmerich, *The Life of the Blessed Virgin Mary*, p. 245, 246.

[209] For example, see Finegan, *Handbook of Biblical Chronology*, revised edition, no. 533-534, p. 311, on the reign of Mithridates. Also, certain events in Roman History, such as the death of Julius Caesar and the departure of Augustus for Gaul, were connected with the appearance of a comet.

[210] Kronk, *Cometography*, p. 24.

[211] Dio, *Roman History*, 54.29.8 – 30.1.

[212] Dio, *Roman History*, 54.28.2.

[213] Dio, *Roman History*, 54.28.3. Cf. Cassius Dio, *The Roman History: The Reign of Augustus*, (London, England: Penguin Books Ltd, 1987), "the festival called Quinquatrus," to Dio Cassius, *Roman History*, ed. Jeffrey Henderson, trans. Earnest Cary, Dio Cassius, Volume VI, Loeb Classical Library, (Cambridge, Massachusetts: Harvard University Press, 2000), "the Panathenaic festival."

[214] Cassius Dio, *The Roman History: The Reign of Augustus*, (London, England: Penguin Books Ltd, 1987) footnote 65, p. 288.

[215] Dio, *Roman History*, Volume VI, Loeb Classical Library, 54.29.8.

[216] Dio, *The Roman History*, Penguin Books, p. 182. Compare to: Dio, *Roman History*, Volume VI, Loeb Classical Library, 54.29.7–54.30.1. In the Loeb translation, there is a general reference to "portents…as are wont to happen to them before the greatest calamities." However, Dio does not specifically apply this to the comet's appearance. It is rather a general comment on portents in general. The Penguin Books translation has it as: "when the greatest calamities threaten the state."

[217] Dio, *Roman History*, 54.30.1.

[218] Dio, *Roman History*, 54.29.8.

[219] See, for example, Dio, *Roman History*, 54.19.7.

[220] Dio mentions the census of 28 B.C. (usual date). Dio, *Roman History*, 53.1.3.

[221] Finegan, *Handbook of Biblical Chronology*, revised edition, no. 523, p. 305.

[222] Josephus, *The Antiquities of the Jews*, 18.1ff.

[223] Josephus, *The Antiquities of the Jews*, 18.1-3; *The Wars of the Jews*, 7.253, 2.118.

[224] Cyrenius and Quirinius are merely different transliterations of the same name. See: *The Works of Josephus: Complete and Unabridged, New Updated Edition*, trans. William Whiston, p. 907.

[225] Josephus, *The Antiquities of the Jews*, 18.1-3. On the point that this Judas was a Galilean, see *The Antiquities of the Jews*, 18.23-25; *The Wars of the Jews*, 2.118.

[226] Vardaman, "Jesus' Life: A New Chronology," *Chronos, Kairos, Christos*, p. 62-63. See also, Finegan, *Handbook of Biblical Chronology*, revised edition, no.523, p. 305.

[227] E. Jerry Vardaman, "The Birth of Christ in the Light of Chronological Research," Lecture 1, *Chronology and Early Church History in the New Testament*, (Seminar given at Hong Kong Baptist Theological Seminary, June of 1998), taken from lecture notes sent to the author by Jerry Vardaman in February of 1999, p. 8-9. Vardaman dates a line of

the text to 11/10 B.C., and he dates the death of the Roman officer, A. Secundus, to 10 B.C.

[228] This microletter inscription was described in personal correspondence from E. Jerry Vardaman to the author. "The microletters (but these are clear and definite as far as I am concerned) LA CONS P.S.QVINIRI are on the line referring to the census which A. Secundus took of Apamea, being sent by Quirinius for that purpose on the Lapis Venetus (Inscription of Venice - still there in the Arch. Museum). Quirinius was only consul one time - in 12 B.C. For some it will be a problem since here Greek is mixed with Latin, but such critics will have to blame the original writer of the microletters - I am confident of my reading. (In many places on this text Greek is mixed with Latin, and Phoenician, as well - particularly the sign for year - looks like a stretched out "K")." This quote is from an e-mail sent to the author, from E. Jerry Vardaman, dated May 18, 2000.

[229] Josephus, *The Antiquities of the Jews*, 18.1ff.

[230] Dio, *Roman History*, 54.28.2.

[231] E. Jerry Vardaman, "The Birth of Christ in the Light of Chronological Research," Lecture 1, *Chronology and Early Church History in the New Testament*, (Seminar given at Hong Kong Baptist Theological Seminary, June of 1998), taken from lecture notes sent to the author by Jerry Vardaman in February of 1999, p. 9, 11.

[232] Finegan, *Handbook of Biblical Chronology*, revised edition, no. 523, p. 305.

[233] Josephus, *The Antiquities of the Jews*, 18.1.

[234] Finegan, *Handbook of Biblical Chronology*, revised edition, no. 522, p. 304, see also Table 147.

[235] Dio, *Roman History*, 54.28.2. Publius Sulpicius Quirinius is here called simply "Publius Sulpicius."

[236] Vardaman, "Jesus' Life: A New Chronology," *Chronos, Kairos, Christos*, p. 61-64.

[237] Finegan, *Handbook of Biblical Chronology*, revised edition, no. 522, p. 304-305.

[238] Vardaman, "Jesus' Life: A New Chronology," *Chronos, Kairos, Christos*, p. 62-63.

[239] Nikos Kokkinos, "Crucifixion in A.D. 36," *Chronos, Kairos, Christos*, p. 140-141.

[240] Nikos Kokkinos, "The Relative Chronology of the Nativity in Tertullian," *Chronos, Kairos, Christos II*, p. 127.

[241] Finegan, *Handbook of Biblical Chronology*, revised edition, no. 512, p. 298. See also Ernest L. Martin, "The Nativity and Herod's Death," *Chronos, Kairos, Christos*, p. 85-92. John Pratt proposes that Herod may have died in early A.D. 1, but this is the latest date argued for the death of Herod. John P. Pratt, *Yet Another Eclipse for Herod*, The Griffith Observatory Home Page, <http://www.griffithobs.org/IPSPlanPlatt.html>, reprinted from the *Planetarian*, vol. 19, no. 4, (International Planetarium Society, 1990), pp. 8-14.

[242] Finegan, *Handbook of Biblical Chronology*, revised edition, no. 525, p. 306.

[243] Josephus, *The Antiquities of the Jews*, 17.41- 42.

[244] Justin Martyr, *Apology* 1.34, Christian Classics Ethereal Library, (Wheaton, Illinois: Wheaton College, 1998), CD-ROM, <http://www.ccel.org/>.

[245] Josephus, *The Antiquities of the Jews*, 18.1-3; *The Wars of the Jews*, 7.253, 2.118.

[246] Finegan, *Handbook of Biblical Chronology*, revised edition, no. 523, p. 304.

[247] Vardaman, "Jesus' Life: A New Chronology," *Chronos, Kairos, Christos*, p. 62-63.

[248] Vardaman, "Jesus' Life: A New Chronology," *Chronos, Kairos, Christos*, p. 63.

[249] 90% of all births occur within a four week period of time, from 266 days after conception plus or minus 2 weeks. The Merck Manual of Medical Information, Home Edition, (Whitehouse Station, N.J.: Merck Research Lab, 1997), p. 1139. Other medical sources agree.

[250] Josephus, *The Antiquities of the Jews*, p. 62-63.

[251] Emmerich, *The Life of Jesus Christ and Biblical Revelations* , Vol. 1, p.180.

[252] Finegan, *Handbook of Biblical Chronology*, revised edition, no. 567, p. 327.

[253] Finegan, *Handbook of Biblical Chronology*, revised edition, no. 225-226 and table 57, p. 118-122. Finegan cites Zuckermann, *Sabbatical Cycle and Jubilee*, p. 60-64; Blosser, *Jesus and the Jubilee*, p. 113; Ben Zion Wacholder, *Essays*, p. 2-3.

[254] Josephus, *The Antiquities of the Jews*, 4.209.

[255] Finegan, *Handbook of Biblical Chronology*, revised edition, no. 241, p. 133; see also: Josephus, *The Antiquities of the Jews*, 7.365.

[256] Finegan, *Handbook of Biblical Chronology*, revised edition, no. 241, p. 133.

[257] In those days, many people would arrive several days before the beginning of a major feast, such as Passover or the Feast of Tabernacles. The Day of Atonement occurs on Tishri 10 and the Feast of Tabernacles begins on Tishri 15 (i.e. on Tishri 14 at sunset). Thus, the huge crowd which would gather for the Feast of Tabernacles would also be largely present a few days earlier for the most holy day of the year, the Day of Atonement.

[258] Emmerich, *The Life of the Blessed Virgin Mary*, p. 125.

[259] New moon and solar transit data from: *RedShift 3*, astronomy software, (Kingston, UK: Maris Multimedia Ltd., Maris.com, 1998).

In 16 B.C., Tishri 1 coincided with Sept. 4, which was a Monday. This date is based on the conclusion of chapter 17 that the ancient Jewish calendar during this time period was determined by calculation, not by observation. The new moon for that month was Sept. 3 at 13:58 Jerusalem Standard Time. The first day of Tishri would then most likely have been Sept. 4, since the new moon began after solar transit (apparent solar noon; the sixth hour). This places Tishri 10, the Day of Atonement, on Wednesday, Sept. 13; Tishri 15 on Monday, Sept. 18; and Tishri 22 on Monday, Sept. 25. Tishri 15 is the start of the Feast of Tabernacles and Tishri 22 is the last day of the Feast.

In the modern Jewish calendar, Tishri 1 is delayed to the next day if the new moon occurs after noontime, or if the new moon occurs on Sun., Wed., or Fri. In the first century B.C., these rules were not yet in place. But, I argue that these rules must have developed over a period of time, based on the experience of the Jewish leaders in making decisions about the calendar. The decision to keep certain holy days from interfering with the Sabbath, by preventing the start of the calendar year on Tishri 1 from falling on Wed., or Fri., is likely to have been one of the earliest insights which the Jewish leaders had about the calendar, since the keeping of the Sabbath was of the utmost importance. See chapter 17 for details.

During the time that the start of each month was determined by calculation, there had to have been a determination as to the time (not just the day) of the new moon. Also, it would have been necessary to determine a cut-off point, so that, if the time of the new moon fell after a certain hour of the day, not that day but the next would be the start of the month. In later times, at least for the determination of the start of Tishri, the cut-off point was noontime (apparent solar noon). Since the new moon for Tishri 1 of 16 B.C. fell on Sunday and in the afternoon, the start of Tishri 1 that year was most probably the next day, Monday, Sept. 4 of 16 B.C.

[260] Zechariah was not the high priest, nor would he have had to be high priest in order to offer sacrifice on the Day of Atonement. It may well have been the custom in that ancient time for a priest to be chosen by lot to offer the sacrifice of burning incense on that day.

[261] Days of the week determined using: *Universal Calendar Calculator*, (Clarksville, Tennessee: Cumberland Family Software, 1999), Astronomical Algorithms by Nachum Dershowitz and Edward M. Reingold.

[262] Emmerich, *The Life of the Blessed Virgin Mary*, p. 125; *The Life of Jesus Christ and Biblical Revelations*, Vol. 1, p. 179.

[263] Hammond's Atlas of the Bible Lands, ed. Harry Thomas Frank, (Maplewood, New Jersey: Hammond, Inc., 1997), p. 12. Distances are given as the straight line distance. A traveler might have to take a longer route, in order to follow roads or avoid geographical obstacles.

[264] The new moon for that month was Sept. 3 at 13:58 Jerusalem Standard Time. The first day of Tishri would then have been Sept. 4. This places Tishri 10, the Day of Atonement, on Wednesday, Sept. 13.

[265] Finegan, *Handbook of Biblical Chronology*, revised edition, no. 233, p. 127-128.

[266] In the ancient Jewish calendar, AdarI could have 29 or 30 days. In 15 B.C., AdarI probably had 30 days. The new moon occurred Jan. 28 at 22:14 hours Jerusalem Standard Time (JST), so that the first day of AdarI was January 29 of 15 B.C. The next new moon was Feb. 27 at 12:24 hours JST. Since the new moon began after noon solar time (solar transit was 11:56 hours that day), the first day of the month of AdarII would be the next day, Feb. 28 (actually, the day began Feb. 27 at sunset). Thus AdarI that year had 30 days. AdarII that year had 29 days, from Feb. 28 to March 28, inclusive. The next new moon was March 29 at 03:41 hours JST. This places the start of the month of Nisan on March 29. New moon and solar transit data from: *RedShift 3*, astronomy software, (Kingston, UK: Maris Multimedia Ltd., Maris.com, 1998). See chapter 17 for details.

[267] *The Merck Manual of Medical Information*, Home Edition, (Whitehouse Station, N.J.: Merck Research Lab, 1997), p. 1139.

[268] The new moon of Oct. 22, 15 B.C., at 01:51 hours JST places the first day of Heshvan on Oct. 22 (actually, the day starts Oct. 21 at sunset). The next new moon was Nov. 20 at 12:45 hours JST. Since this time is after solar transit (noon sun time; the sixth hour), the first day of Kislev would be the following day, Nov. 21 (beginning at sunset on Nov. 20). New moon and solar transit data from *RedShift 3*. See chapter 17 for details.

[269] Emmerich, *The Life of the Blessed Virgin Mary*, p. 140.

[270] *RedShift 3* data places the new moon of AdarI, 15 B.C., on January 28 at 22:14 Jerusalem Standard Time (GMT + 2:00). By calculation, then, the first day of AdarI would then be January 29. February 25 would then coincide with AdarI 28.

[271] The Merck Manual of Medical Information, Home Edition, p. 1139.

[272] The Merck Manual of Medical Information, Home Edition, p. 1139.

[273] Emmerich, *The Life of the Blessed Virgin Mary*, p. 206.

[274] Dates were determined using *RedShift 3* software. See chapter 17 for details. Start of the Jewish month in dates presented in this book is by calculation, not by the observation-based system. See chapter 17 for details on this point.

[275] The order of the months is: AdarI, AdarII, Nisan, Iyar, Sivan, Tammuz, Av, Elul, Tishri, Heshvan, Kislev. From AdarI 28 to AdarII 28 is one lunar month, from AdarI 28 to Heshvan 28 is nine lunar months, and adding one weeks brings us to the beginning of the month of Kislev.

[276] Emmerich, *The Life of the Blessed Virgin Mary*, p. 207.

[277] Emmerich, *The Life of the Blessed Virgin Mary*, p. 144; cf. *The Life of Jesus Christ and Biblical Revelations*, Vol. 1, p. 195.

[278] Emmerich, *The Life of the Blessed Virgin Mary*, p. 128-132.

[279] *Book of James, or Protoevangelium*, ed. Dave J. Giles, Wesley Center Online, Non-canonical Homepage,
(Northwest Nazarene University: Wesley Center for Applied Theology, 1996),
<http://wesley.nnu.edu/noncanon/gospels/gosjames.htm>, 9.1. See also: *The Gospel of Pseudo-Matthew*, <http://wesley.nnu.edu/noncanon/gospels/psudomat.htm>, 8.4.

[280] Saint Bridget of Sweden, *Revelations of Saint Bridget*, (Rockford, Illinois: TAN Books and Publishers, 1984), p. 14. Saint Bridget is here quoting the Blessed Virgin Mary, who spoke to Bridget in private revelation.

[281] Why would the Jewish priests give Joseph a dry dead branch that they could not have expected to open? Perhaps because he was much older than the other candidates; they were comparing him to a dry old branch.

[282] The Catholic Community Forum, "Patron Saints Index: Joseph," Images Gallery, <http://www.catholic-forum.com/saints/saintj01.htm>.

[283] Finegan, *Handbook of Biblical Chronology*, revised edition, no. 164, p.78.

[284] Finegan, *Handbook of Biblical Chronology*, revised edition, no. 78, p. 38.

[285] Suzanne Ashworth, *Seed to Seed*, ed. Kent Whealy, (Decorah, Iowa: Seed Saver Publications, 1991), p. 118.

[286] The Weather Channel, weather.com – Averages and Records – Jerusalem, Israel, "Monthly Averages and Records," Avg. Precip. <http://www.weather.com/weather/climatology/ISXX0010>. The monthly averages are as follows: June, July, August, September: no precipitation; Oct. 0.90 inches; Nov. 2.70 inches; Dec. 4.30 inches; Jan. 5.70 inches; Feb. 4.50 inches; Mar. 3.90 inches; Apr. 1.20 inches; May 0.10 inches.

See also: USA Today.com, Climate, Jerusalem, Israel, Average Precipitation, <http://www.usatoday.com/weather/climate/mideast/Israel/wjerusal.htm>. The monthly averages are as follows: June, July, August, September: no precipitation; Oct. 0.4 inches; Nov. 2.7 inches; Dec. 5.1 inches; Jan. 5.50 inches; Feb. 4.4 inches; Mar. 4.6 inches; Apr. 0.7 inches; May 0.2 inches.

[287] Some species of trees could have taken much longer to produce fruit, but the beginning of the cycle would have to coincide with the rainy season from late fall to early spring.

[288] Emmerich, *The Life of Jesus Christ and Biblical Revelations*, Vol. 1, p. 187; *The Life of the Blessed Virgin Mary*, p. 133.

[289] Emmerich, *The Life of Jesus Christ and Biblical Revelations*, Vol. 1, p. 187.

[290] Emmerich, *The Life of Jesus Christ and Biblical Revelations*, Vol. 1, p. 190.
[291] Emmerich, *The Life of the Blessed Virgin Mary*, p. 165-179.
[292] Emmerich, *The Life of the Blessed Virgin Mary*, p. 138, 140.
[293] Emmerich, *The Life of Jesus Christ and Biblical Revelations*, Vol. 1, p. 196.
[294] Emmerich, *The Life of the Blessed Virgin Mary*, p. 146.
[295] Details on this point, that the Virgin Mary was a descendent of David, can be found in my booklet: Conte, *the Virginity of Jesus and Mary,* (CatholicPlanet.com, 2001).
[296] Emmerich, *The Life of the Blessed Virgin Mary*, p. 146.
[297] Emmerich, *The Life of the Blessed Virgin Mary*, p. 149-150.
[298] Emmerich, *The Life of the Blessed Virgin Mary*, p. 148.
[299] The new moon occurred on March 29 at 03:41 Jerusalem Standard Time, in 15 B.C., making March 29 the first day of Nisan. New moon data from *RedShift 3.* The start of Nisan was determined by calculation, rather than by observation; see chapter 17 for details.
[300] See, for example, their travel to Bethlehem from Nazareth, when they rested from their journey for an entire day on the Sabbath. Emmerich, *The Life of the Blessed Virgin Mary*, p. 173.
[301] Emmerich, *The Life of the Blessed Virgin Mary*, p. 148.
[302] Emmerich, *The Life of the Blessed Virgin Mary*, p. 163.
[303] Tishri 24 coincided with Sept. 27 in 16 B.C., but the Jewish day begins and ends at sunset, so Tishri 24 began the evening of Sept. 26. Determination of the start of Tishri is by calculation, as explained in chapter 17.
[304] The Merck Manual of Medical Information, Home Edition, p. 1139.
[305] Counting Sept. 27 as day one, Elizabeth's due date would be June 19, day 266.
[306] June 19 would mark the end of the 38th week, June 7 would then be the start of the 37th week. The four week time frame is week 37 through week 40, inclusive. Note that, within the four-week time frame, distribution of births is greater closer to the "due date" in the middle of that time frame.
[307] A lunar month is, on average, 29.5306 days. You do the math.
[308] The new moon occurred at 01:13 hours JST on June 26 of 15 B.C. New moon data from *RedShift 3.* The start of any month in the Jewish calendar during that time period was determined by calculation, not observation, so that June 26 would be Tammuz 1; see chapter 17 for details.
[309] Summer solstice occurred at 02:02 hours on June 25 in 15 B.C. Summer solstice data from *RedShift 3.*
[310] Emmerich, *The Life of the Blessed Virgin Mary*, p. 213-214.
[311] Emmerich, *The Life of the Blessed Virgin Mary*, p. 282.
[312] Emmerich, *The Life of the Blessed Virgin Mary*, p. 282-283.
[313] Emmerich, *The Life of the Blessed Virgin Mary*, p. 282-284.
[314] Cf. Emmerich, *The Life of the Blessed Virgin Mary*, p. 286-7, footnote 1.
[315] Emmerich, *The Life of the Blessed Virgin Mary*, p. 284.
[316] Emmerich, *The Life of the Blessed Virgin Mary*, p. 288.
[317] Emmerich, *The Life of Jesus Christ and Biblical Revelations*, Vol. 1 p. 280, 283.
[318] Emmerich, *The Life of the Blessed Virgin Mary*, p. 282.
[319] Emmerich, *The Life of the Blessed Virgin Mary*, p. 295.

[320] Emmerich, *The Life of the Blessed Virgin Mary*, p. 295.
[321] Emmerich, *The Life of the Blessed Virgin Mary*, p. 295.
[322] Emmerich, *The Life of Jesus Christ and Biblical Revelations*, Vol. 1, p. 292.
[323] Emmerich, *The Life of the Blessed Virgin Mary*, p. 304.
[324] The new moon of Feb. 6 at 11:37 hours JST is about 20 min. before solar transit (noon sun time) and so Feb. 6 would be the first day of AdarII by calculation. If the new moon falls before solar transit, that same calendar day begins the month, but if the new moon falls after solar transit, the next calendar day begins the month (see chapter 17). New moon and solar transit data from *RedShift 3*. Days of the week from *Universal Calendar Calculator*.
[325] Emmerich, *The Life of the Blessed Virgin Mary*, p. 301.
[326] In the Roman (Julian) calendar, the day begins and ends at midnight.
[327] Emmerich, *The Life of the Blessed Virgin Mary*, p. 299.
[328] Emmerich, *The Life of the Blessed Virgin Mary*, p. 313.
[329] Hammond's Atlas of the Bible Lands, p. 39.
[330] Emmerich, *The Life of the Blessed Virgin Mary*, p. 304-306.
[331] Blessed Anne Catherine does tell us that the Holy Family rested for the Sabbath, even when they were fleeing to protect the life of the Christ-Child. Emmerich, *The Life of the Blessed Virgin Mary*, p. 305.
[332] Emmerich, *The Life of the Blessed Virgin Mary*, p. 319.
[333] Emmerich, *The Life of Jesus Christ and Biblical Revelations*, Vol. 1, p. 304.
[334] Emmerich, *The Life of the Blessed Virgin Mary*, p. 206.
[335] The new moon of March 6 at 21:22 hours JST makes March 7 the first day of either Adar or Nisan. If it were Nisan, the Passover would begin on Nisan 14 and March 20, which is three days before the Spring Equinox that year (March 23 at 14:24 hours JST). The Spring Equinox was one of the factors which determined when to add a leap month of AdarII, delaying the start of Nisan by a month. Generally, a leap year was added every 2 or 3 years in order to keep the start of Passover from falling before the Spring Equinox. Thus, in 13 B.C., the month of Nisan probably began a month later, with the new moon of April 5 at 07:05 hours JST, so that Nisan 14 coincided with April 18 for the start of Passover. This determination is based on data from *RedShift 3*; see chapter 17 for details.
[336] Emmerich, *The Life of the Blessed Virgin Mary*, p. 321.
[337] Emmerich, *The Life of the Blessed Virgin Mary*, p. 319.
[338] Hammond's Atlas of the Bible Lands, p. 11, 26.
[339] Emmerich, *The Life of the Blessed Virgin Mary*, p. 319.
[340] Hammond's Atlas of the Bible Lands, p. 15, 19, 26.
[341] Emmerich, *The Life of the Blessed Virgin Mary*, p. 313.
[342] Emmerich, *The Life of the Blessed Virgin Mary*, p. 314.
[343] Hammond's Atlas of the Bible Lands, p. 10, 39.
[344] Emmerich, *The Life of the Blessed Virgin Mary*, p. 323.
[345] Emmerich, *The Life of the Blessed Virgin Mary*, p. 324.
[346] Emmerich, *The Life of the Blessed Virgin Mary*, p. 326.
[347] Emmerich, *The Life of the Blessed Virgin Mary*, p. 333.
[348] Emmerich, *The Life of the Blessed Virgin Mary*, p. 322.

[349] Emmerich, *The Life of the Blessed Virgin Mary*, p. 322.
[350] Emmerich, *The Life of Jesus Christ and Biblical Revelations*, Vol. 1, p. 338.
[351] Emmerich, *The Life of the Blessed Virgin Mary*, p. 322.
[352] The Macmillan Bible Atlas, Yohanan Aharoni and Michael Avi-Yonah, Third Edition, (New York, New York: Macmillan General Reference, 1993), map 134. See also: Hammond's Atlas of the Bible Lands, p. 39.
[353] Dr. Gerald E. Aardsma, "Yeroham: the True Mt. Sinai," *The Biblical Chronologist*, vol. 6, no. 4, (Loda, Illinois: Aardsma Research and Publishing, 2000), p. 1-11.
[354] Emmerich, *The Life of the Blessed Virgin Mary*, p. 322-323.
[355] Emmerich, *The Life of the Blessed Virgin Mary*, p. 4-20.
[356] Emmerich, *The Life of the Blessed Virgin Mary*, p. 7.
[357] Josephus, *The Antiquities of the Jews*, 13.171-172, 15.373-379, 18.18-22.
[358] Emmerich, *The Life of the Blessed Virgin Mary*, p. 327, cf. p. 329.
[359] Emmerich, *The Life of the Blessed Virgin Mary*, p. 329-330.
[360] Emmerich, *The Life of the Blessed Virgin Mary*, p. 330.
[361] Emmerich, *The Life of the Blessed Virgin Mary*, p. 329.
[362] Emmerich, *The Life of the Blessed Virgin Mary*, p. 330.
[363] Emmerich, *The Life of the Blessed Virgin Mary*, p. 329.
[364] Emmerich, *The Life of the Blessed Virgin Mary*, p. 331. Cf. *The Life of Jesus Christ and Biblical Revelations*, Vol. 1, p. 319-320.
[365] Emmerich, *The Life of the Blessed Virgin Mary*, p. 333.
[366] Emmerich, *The Life of the Blessed Virgin Mary*, p. 333.
[367] Emmerich, *The Life of the Blessed Virgin Mary*, p. 329-330.
[368] Emmerich, *The Life of Jesus Christ and Biblical Revelations*, Vol. 1, p. 313. Cf. *The Life of the Blessed Virgin Mary*, p. 342.
[369] Emmerich, *The Life of the Blessed Virgin Mary*, p. 345.
[370] Emmerich, *The Life of Jesus Christ and Biblical Revelations*, Vol. 1, p. 325.
[371] For details on this point, see: Conte, *The Bible and the Future of the World.*
[372] Determined by calculation, based on *RedShift 3* data. The new moon of March 16 in 3 B.C. occurred at 22:02 hours, making March 17 the first day of Nisan by calculation.
[373] *Universal Calendar Calculator* software.
[374] Emmerich, *The Life of Jesus Christ and Biblical Revelations*, Vol. 1, p. 326.
[375] Determined by calculation, based on *RedShift 3* data. The new moon of April 4 in 2 B.C. occurred at 23:02 hours, making April 5 the first day of Nisan by calculation and Friday, April 18, the 14th day of Nisan (the Preparation day of the Passover). Passover actually begins at sunset on Nisan 14, which is the start of Nisan 15 in the Jewish calendar. Days of the week from *Universal Calendar Calculator* software.
[376] Emmerich, *The Life of Jesus Christ and Biblical Revelations*, Vol. 1, p. 392.
[377] Emmerich, *The Life of Jesus Christ and Biblical Revelations*, Vol. 2, p. 109.
[378] Emmerich, *The Life of Jesus Christ and Biblical Revelations*, Vol. 1, p. 329.
[379] Finegan, *Handbook of Biblical Chronology*, revised edition, no. 164-167, p. 78-79.
[380] An example of this is found in Finegan, *Handbook of Biblical Chronology*, revised edition, no. 165, p. 78. He quotes from commentary by Rabbi Avadyah on the Mishna: "Like a man whose son is born on passover. He has fulfilled his first year of life on passover of the next year." Finegan interprets this quote to mean that each year of a

person's life is counted as the completion of 12 full months of the Jewish calendar (or 13 in a leap year) since the day of their birth. However, I suggest that the choice of the Passover to illustrate the counting of a person's age was not arbitrary. Thus, a man whose son is born on any day of the year would count his son's first year as being completed on the very next Passover. In this way, the number of Passovers since birth would be the count of a person's age.

[381] Finegan, *Handbook of Biblical Chronology*, revised edition, no. 165, p. 78.

[382] Emmerich, *The Life of Jesus Christ and Biblical Revelations*, Vol. 1, p. 330.

[383] Emmerich, *The Life of Jesus Christ and Biblical Revelations*, Vol. 1, p. 329.

[384] Emmerich, *The Life of Jesus Christ and Biblical Revelations*, Vol. 1, p. 329.

[385] Emmerich, *The Life of Jesus Christ and Biblical Revelations*, Vol. 1, p. 330.

[386] Emmerich, *The Life of Jesus Christ and Biblical Revelations*, Vol. 1, p. 331.

[387] Emmerich, *The Life of Jesus Christ and Biblical Revelations*, Vol. 1, p. 331.

[388] Emmerich, *The Life of Jesus Christ and Biblical Revelations*, Vol. 1, p. 332.

[389] Emmerich, *The Life of Jesus Christ and Biblical Revelations*, Vol. 1, p. 330.

[390] Emmerich, *The Life of Jesus Christ and Biblical Revelations*, Vol. 1, p. 330.

[391] Emmerich, *The Life of Jesus Christ and Biblical Revelations*, Vol. 1, p. 330. Blessed Anne Catherine often did not realize that, in visions given to her by God, the count of the ages of Jesus and Mary was from conception, rather than from birth. This error led to some incongruities in her chronological statements, which are, I think, mostly corrected in this book.

[392] Emmerich, *The Life of Jesus Christ and Biblical Revelations*, Vol. 1, p. 341.

[393] Emmerich, *The Life of Jesus Christ and Biblical Revelations*, Vol. 1, p. 316.

[394] Even though the average life-span for a man at that time in history was considerably less than 75 years, it was not so unusual for someone to live into their seventies. For example, the Roman emperor Augustus Caesar lived to be about 77 years old, according to the ancient Jewish Roman historian Josephus: *The Antiquities of the Jews*, 18.32.

[395] Emmerich, *The Life of Jesus Christ and Biblical Revelations*, Vol. 1, p. 331-332.

[396] John is referred to as "the Baptist" by Sacred Scripture (e.g. Mt 3:1) and even by the writings of the first century A.D. historian Josephus: *The Antiquities of the Jews*, 18.116.

[397] Emmerich, *The Life of Jesus Christ and Biblical Revelations*, Vol. 1, p. 417.

[398] Emmerich, *The Life of Jesus Christ and Biblical Revelations*, Vol. 1, p. 440-441.

[399] Note that the disciples of Jesus began baptizing, at His direction, in wintertime, after Christ's Baptism, after the 40 days in the desert, but before the feast of Purim (Adar 14, 15; late winter). However, when baptism was given by the disciples of Jesus, the water was poured over the person's head; they were not immersed in the water. See Emmerich, *The Life of Jesus Christ and Biblical Revelations*, Vol. 1, p. 479; Vol. 2, p. 1-22, 65-67, 98-102.

[400] Emmerich, *The Life of Jesus Christ and Biblical Revelations*, Vol. 1, p. 412-414.

[401] Emmerich, *The Life of Jesus Christ and Biblical Revelations*, Vol.2, p. 20ff, 65ff.

[402] Emmerich, *The Life of Jesus Christ and Biblical Revelations*, Vol. 1, p. 333-438.

[403] Emmerich, *The Life of Jesus Christ and Biblical Revelations*, Vol. 1, p. 341.

[404] Life of, p. 169, 177.

[405] Hammond's Atlas of the Bible Lands, p. 26.

[406] Emmerich, *The Life of Jesus Christ and Biblical Revelations*, Vol. 1, p. 416-417.

[407] Emmerich, *The Life of Jesus Christ and Biblical Revelations*, Vol. 1, p. 416. See also, Macmillan Bible Atlas, text accompanying map no. 229.
[408] Macmillan Bible Atlas, no. 229.
[409] Emmerich, *The Life of Jesus Christ and Biblical Revelations*, Vol. 1, p. 416.
[410] Emmerich, *The Life of the Blessed Virgin Mary*, p. 169.
[411] Emmerich, *The Life of the Blessed Virgin Mary*, p. 177. Blessed Anne Catherine makes an error in saying that Jesus was baptized 30 years later (i.e. 30 years after His Birth). It could be counted as 30 years inclusively (15 B.C. to A.D. 15), but was actually about 29 years later that Jesus was baptized. She makes similar mistakes in other places in the text.
[412] Emmerich, *The Life of Jesus Christ and Biblical Revelations*, Vol. 1, p. 438.
[413] Emmerich, *The Life of Jesus Christ and Biblical Revelations*, Vol. 1, p. 444.
[414] Emmerich, *The Life of Jesus Christ and Biblical Revelations*, Vol. 1, p. 477.
[415] Emmerich, *The Life of Jesus Christ and Biblical Revelations*, Vol. 1, p. 444, 473.
[416] New moon occurred on Tuesday, Oct. 1 at 22:39 hours. Ordinarily, in the calculation method of determining the start of a month, this would make the next day, Wednesday, Oct. 2, the start of the month. But the month of Tishri is not permitted to begin on a Wednesday, because then the Day of Atonement (Yom Kippur) would interfere with the Preparation Day of the Sabbath. This is the rule in the modern calendar, and must also have been the rule in ancient times also (see chapter 17 for details on this point). In such a case, Tishri 1 is delayed until Thursday. So, in A.D. 15, Tishri 1 began on Thursday, Oct. 3. New moon data from *RedShift 3* software.

Also, in the year A.D. 15, the month of Tishri could not have fallen in September, for two reasons. First, because Blessed Anne Catherine states that Jesus celebrated the Feast of Tabernacles after His Baptism, which she places between Sept. 30 and Oct. 11. Second, only if the Passover of A.D. 15 occurred before the Spring Equinox (by calculation method of determining the calendar) could Tishri have started in Sept. The Jews generally added a 13 month to the calendar, every 2 or 3 years, to prevent the Passover from beginning before the Spring Equinox.
[417] Emmerich, *The Life of Jesus Christ and Biblical Revelations*, Vol. 1, p. 444.
[418] Emmerich, *The Life of Jesus Christ and Biblical Revelations*, Vol. 2, p. 70-71.
[419] Blessed Anne Catherine also states that Jesus and his disciples did not baptize on a particular day, because a feast was being celebrated. Emmerich, *The Life of Jesus Christ and Biblical Revelations*, Vol. 2, p. 71.
[420] Emmerich, *The Life of Jesus Christ and Biblical Revelations*, Vol. 1, p. 438.
[421] Emmerich, *The Life of Jesus Christ and Biblical Revelations*, Vol. 2, p. 66.
[422] Emmerich, *The Life of Jesus Christ and Biblical Revelations*, Vol. 2, p. 67.
[423] Catechism of the Catholic Church, (New York, New York: Doubleday, 1995), no. 1239-1240.
[424] Emmerich, *The Life of Jesus Christ and Biblical Revelations*, Vol. 2, p. 67.
[425] Apostolic Constitution of Pius IX, *Ineffabilis Deus*, December 8, 1854, (Boston, Massachusetts: St. Paul Books and Media), p. 4, 21.
[426] Emmerich, *The Life of Jesus Christ and Biblical Revelations*, Vol. 1, p. 473-475.
[427] Tishri began on Thursday, Oct. 3 (see above). This places Tishri 10, the Day of Atonement, on Saturday, Oct. 12, and the Feast of Tabernacles (Tishri 15-22) from

Thursday, Oct. 17 to Thursday, Oct. 24. Notice that the Feast of Tabernacles begins on the same day of the week as Tishri 1 and the Day of Atonement falls two days of the week after Tishri 1. That is why the first day of Tishri, (even in the first century A.D.), was not permitted to fall on certain days of the week. The Jews prevented the Day of Atonement from falling on a Friday, when it would interfere with preparations for the Sabbath, by making the rule that the month of Tishri could not begin on a Wednesday. And they kept the Feast of Tabernacles from beginning and ending on a Friday, by not allowing Tishri to begin on a Friday. These calendar rules, found still today in the modern Jewish calendar, must have had their beginnings in ancient times. It does not take much calculation to determine that delaying Tishri 1 will prevent certain holy days from conflicting with the Preparation Day of the Sabbath. However, the Jews of Jesus' time did not see fit to prevent the first day of Tishri from falling on a Sunday. For example, see: Emmerich, *The Life of Jesus Christ and Biblical Revelations*, Vol. 2, p. 373. In A.D. 16 the first day of the Feast of Tabernacles fell on Sunday, the day after the Jewish Sabbath, so that the first day of Tishri must also have been a Sunday that year.

[428] Emmerich, *The Life of Jesus Christ and Biblical Revelations*, Vol. 2, p. 1.

[429] Emmerich, *The Life of Jesus Christ and Biblical Revelations*, Vol. 2, p. 22, 27, 32-33.

[430] In A.D. 15, the new moon was Nov. 30 at 08:48, placing Kislev 1 on Nov. 30, by calculation method. See chapter 17 for a detailed explanation of the method of determining calendar dates in the Jewish calendar at this time in history. New moon data from *RedShift 3* software.

[431] Emmerich, *The Life of Jesus Christ and Biblical Revelations*, Vol. 2, p. 20.

[432] Emmerich, *The Life of Jesus Christ and Biblical Revelations*, Vol. 1, p. 469-471.

[433] Emmerich, *The Life of Jesus Christ and Biblical Revelations*, repeated examples throughout the book.

[434] Emmerich, *The Life of Jesus Christ and Biblical Revelations*, Vol. 2, p. 33-35.

[435] Emmerich, *The Life of Jesus Christ and Biblical Revelations*, Vol. 2, p. 58.

[436] Emmerich, *The Life of Jesus Christ and Biblical Revelations*, Vol. 2, p. 33-59.

[437] Emmerich, *The Life of Jesus Christ and Biblical Revelations*, Vol. 2, p. 60.

[438] Emmerich, *The Life of Jesus Christ and Biblical Revelations*, Vol. 2, p. 117-121.

[439] Emmerich, *The Life of Jesus Christ and Biblical Revelations*, Vol. 2, p. 108, 110. Note that the celebration of the first day of Nisan, the feast of the New Moon (Rosh Hodesh), began in the evening and that Blessed Anne Catherine refers to the next day as the Sabbath. In the Jewish calendar, the Sabbath and any other day begins at sunset. Thus, she is referring to the same day in the Jewish calendar when she talks about one evening and the next day.

[440] *RedShift 3* software.

[441] See chapter 17, *Technical Notes*, for more on this point. See also Appendix II, Chart C.

[442] Finegan, *Handbook of Biblical Chronology*, revised edition, no. 58, p. 29.

[443] Finegan, *Handbook of Biblical Chronology*, revised edition, no. 58, p. 29.

[444] *The Life of Jesus Christ and Biblical Revelations*, Vol. 2, p. 114-121.

[445] Emmerich, *The Life of Jesus Christ and Biblical Revelations*, Vol. 2, p. 145.

[446] Tracey R. Rich, *Judaism 101: The Counting of the Omer*, <http://www.jewfaq.org/holidayb.htm>.

[447] Emmerich, *The Life of Jesus Christ and Biblical Revelations*, Vol. 2, p. 145, 155.

[448] Emmerich, *The Life of Jesus Christ and Biblical Revelations*, Vol. 2, p. 161-162.
[449] Emmerich, *The Life of Jesus Christ and Biblical Revelations*, Vol. 2, p. 121-161; the Sabbaths are mentioned on p. 121, 134, 145, and 155.
[450] Nisan 1 that year was delayed a day to prevent Nisan 15 from interfering with the Preparation Day of the Sabbath. Nisan must have had 30 days and Iyar 29 days, so that Shavuot (Feast of Weeks) would fall both on the 50th day from the second day of Passover and on Sivan 6. This places Sivan 1 on May 26, one day's delay from the ordinary start of that month by calculation of the new moon. New moon data from *RedShift 3* software.
[451] Emmerich, *The Life of Jesus Christ and Biblical Revelations*, Vol. 1, p. 469.
[452] Emmerich, *The Life of Jesus Christ and Biblical Revelations*, Vol. 2, p. 255.
[453] In A.D. 16, the new moon of Friday, August 21, at 05:41 Jerusalem Standard Time would have marked the beginning of the month of Elul. However, I believe that the start of the month of Elul was delayed for one day, to prevent 3 months of 29 days each occurring in a 4-month period of time. Iyar and Sivan both had 29 days because of the delay in the start of Nisan. Tammuz had 30 days, but Av would have had 29 days again, without the delay in the start of Elul. The one day delay in the start of Elul provides 2 months of 30 days (Tammuz and Av) to balance the 2 months of 29 days (Iyar and Sivan). This delay also has the effect of giving Elul 29 days and Tishri 30 days, which was probably the preferred configuration, even at that early date, and became the rule eventually adopted for the modern Jewish calendar.
[454] New moon data from *RedShift 3* software. Day of the week data from *Universal Calendar Calculator* software.
[455] Emmerich, *The Life of Jesus Christ and Biblical Revelations*, Vol. 2, p. 373.
[456] Emmerich, *The Life of Jesus Christ and Biblical Revelations*, Vol. 3, p. 92-105
[457] Emmerich, *The Life of Jesus Christ and Biblical Revelations*, Vol. 3, p. 92-105
[458] The start of the months of Heshvan, Kislev, and Tevet were delayed a day from their date by calculation alone. Heshvan could have begun on Nov. 7 of A.D. 17 (new moon at 11:00 hours JST that day; solar transit at 11:26 hours), but seems to have been delayed until Nov. 8, giving Tishri 30 days, instead of 29. The delay may have been because the new moon was so close to solar transit (noon sun time). In any case, a one day delay in the start of a month is not unusual in the Jewish calendar. This conclusion fits the information given by Blessed Anne Catherine about the dates and days of the week for Hanukah, namely, that Hanukkah that began and ended (Kislev 25 and Tevet 2) on the Jewish Sabbath.
[459] Finegan, *Handbook of Biblical Chronology*, revised edition, no. 77-81, p. 37-39.
[460] Finegan, *Handbook of Biblical Chronology*, revised edition, no. 78-79, p. 38.
[461] Emmerich, *The Life of Jesus Christ and Biblical Revelations*, Vol. 3, p. 170.
[462] Finegan, *Handbook of Biblical Chronology*, revised edition, no. 164, p. 78.
[463] The new moon fell on February 4 at 19:46 hours JST, which makes Feb. 5 the first day of the month by calculation. New moon data from *RedShift 3* software. Day of the week data from *Universal Calendar Calculator* software.
[464] Emmerich, *The Life of Jesus Christ and Biblical Revelations*, Vol. 3, p. 105, 148, 170.
[465] Emmerich, *The Life of Jesus Christ and Biblical Revelations*, Vol. 3, p. 245-250.
[466] Emmerich, *The Life of Jesus Christ and Biblical Revelations*, Vol. 3, p. 249.

[467] The new moon fell on March 6 at 10:17 hours JST, making Sunday, March 6 as AdarI 1 in A.D. 18. New moon data from *RedShift 3* software. Day of the week data from *Universal Calendar Calculator* software.
[468] Emmerich, *The Life of Jesus Christ and Biblical Revelations*, Vol. 3, p. xvi.
[469] Emmerich, *The Life of the Blessed Virgin Mary*, p. 286, footnote 1.
[470] Emmerich, *The Life of Jesus Christ and Biblical Revelations*, Vol. 4, p. 11-19.
[471] Emmerich, *The Life of Jesus Christ and Biblical Revelations*, Vol. 4, p. 8.
[472] Finegan, *Handbook of Biblical Chronology*, revised edition, no. 140-142, p. 65-66.
[473] Emmerich, *The Life of Jesus Christ and Biblical Revelations*, Vol. 4, p. 9.
[474] Emmerich, *The Life of Jesus Christ and Biblical Revelations*, Vol. 4, p. 10.
[475] Emmerich, *The Life of Jesus Christ and Biblical Revelations*, Vol. 4, p. 19-20.
[476] Emmerich, *The Life of Jesus Christ and Biblical Revelations*, Vol. 4, p. 21ff.
[477] Emmerich, *The Life of Jesus Christ and Biblical Revelations*, Vol. 4, p. 22-34.
[478] Emmerich, *The Life of Jesus Christ and Biblical Revelations*, Vol. 4, p. 28-29.
[479] Emmerich, *The Life of Jesus Christ and Biblical Revelations*, Vol. 4, p. 35.
[480] For more on the theology of the Immaculate Virgin Conception of the Virgin Mary, see: Conte, *the Virginity of Jesus and Mary*, <http://www.catholicplanet.com/>.
[481] Emmerich, *The Life of Jesus Christ and Biblical Revelations*, Vol. 2, p. 114-121.
[482] Josephus, *The Antiquities of the Jews*, 15.420-421.
[483] Josephus, *The Antiquities of the Jews*, 15.420; 20.200, 219.
[484] Emmerich, *The Life of Jesus Christ and Biblical Revelations*, Vol. 2, p. 120.
[485] Josephus, *The Antiquities of the Jews*, 15.419, 421.
[486] Josephus, *The Antiquities of the Jews*, 15.421-423. Josephus refers to the Temple Sanctuary as the "temple itself."
[487] Finegan, *Handbook of Biblical Chronology*, revised edition, p. 122, no. 227.
[488] Emmerich, *The Life of the Blessed Virgin Mary*, p. 206.
[489] Conte, *the Virginity of Jesus and Mary*, p. 22.
[490] Finegan, *Handbook of Biblical Chronology*, revised edition, no. 165, p. 78. It has ever been the custom of the Jews to count partial years as full years, or part of a day as a whole day, in numbering lengths of time.
[491] Finegan, *Handbook of Biblical Chronology*, revised edition, no. 165, p. 78. The lengths of the reigns of kings were numbered with any partial year, however brief, numbered just as a full year would be numbered, and with the year beginning on Nisan 1.
[492] Emmerich, *The Life of the Blessed Virgin Mary*, p. 29, 32; *The Life of Jesus Christ and Biblical Revelations*, Vol. 1, p. 134.
[493] Emmerich, *The Life of Jesus Christ and Biblical Revelations*, Vol. 1, p. 138.
[494] Emmerich, *The Life of Jesus Christ and Biblical Revelations*, Vol. 1, p. 135. Here she describes a metaphor, used by the angel when speaking to Joachim, of a shining sphere which remained clear even though Joachim breathed on it. This metaphor refers to the virginal aspect of the Immaculate Conception.
[495] Conte, *the Virginity of Jesus and Mary*.
[496] Emmerich, *The Life of the Blessed Virgin Mary*, p. 33.
[497] Emmerich, *The Life of the Blessed Virgin Mary*, p. 32.
[498] Emmerich, *The Life of the Blessed Virgin Mary*, p. 72.
[499] Emmerich, *The Life of the Blessed Virgin Mary*, p. 71-72.

[500] Emmerich, *The Life of Jesus Christ and Biblical Revelations*, Vol. 1, p. 134, 138.
[501] Dates for the start of each month were determined using lunar cycle data from *RedShift 3* software, and the calculation-based calendar system. See chapter 17, for my detailed argument that the start of the Jewish calendar months during this time period were determined by calculation, not by mere observation.
[502] For details on the determination of dates in the ancient Jewish calendar, see chapter 17.
[503] Josephus, *The Antiquities of the Jews*, 15.421-423.
[504] As explained in chapter 17, at this early date (43 B.C.), the Jewish calendar was still based on observation of the crescent new moon, rather than on calculation of the astronomical new moon. The astronomical new moon of March 9 at 08:38 hours JST would not be visible as a crescent until the evening of March 10, after sunset, at the earliest. Thus, Nisan 1 would coincide with March 11 and Nisan 14 would coincide with March 24, not long after the Spring Equinox of March 23 at 07:59 hours JST. This early date for Passover leads to an early date for the start of Tishri in the following autumn. The new moon of September 2 at 06:21 hours JST would be visible by the evening of September 3, after sunset. This makes Thursday, Sept. 4 the first day of Tishri. The Day of Atonement on Tishri 10 would then coincide with Saturday, September 13 in 43 B.C. New moon and Spring Equinox data from *RedShift 3* software. Days of the week from *Universal Calendar Calculator* software.
[505] Josephus, *The Antiquities of the Jews*, 15.421-422.
[506] Emmerich, *The Life of Jesus Christ and Biblical Revelations*, Vol. 1, p. 187.
[507] Emmerich, *The Life of Jesus Christ and Biblical Revelations*, Vol. 1, p. 195.
[508] Emmerich, *The Life of the Blessed Virgin Mary*, p. 66.
[509] The Visions of the Children, p. 89. Cf. Facts, Documents and Theology, p. 42
[510] Emmerich, *The Life of the Blessed Virgin Mary*, p. 74.
[511] Josephus, *The Antiquities of the Jews*, 15.423.
[512] Finegan, *Handbook of Biblical Chronology*, revised edition, no. 227, p. 122. See also: Josephus, *The Antiquities of the Jews*, 14.487.
[513] These dates were determined by the calculation method, with new moons on Oct. 19 at 04:10 and Nov. 17 at 18:39, making Oct. 19 the first day of Heshvan, and Nov. 18 the first day of Kislev. Not long after Herod captured Jerusalem, the Jewish calendar system made its transition from the observation-based calendar to the calculation-based calendar. See chapter 17 for details.
[514] Emmerich, *The Life of the Blessed Virgin Mary*, p. 133.
[515] Days of the week determined using *Universal Calendar Calculator* software.
[516] Emmerich, *The Life of the Blessed Virgin Mary*, p. 71.
[517] Emmerich, *The Life of the Blessed Virgin Mary*, p. 33.
[518] Emmerich, *The Life of Jesus Christ and Biblical Revelations*, Vol. 1, p. 134.
[519] Emmerich, *The Life of Jesus Christ and Biblical Revelations*, Vol. 1, p. 138.
[520] Emmerich, *The Life of the Blessed Virgin Mary*, p. 168.
[521] Janice T. Connell, *The Visions of the Children*, (New York, New York: St. Martin's Press, 1992), p. 89. See also: Michael O'Carroll, CSSp, *Medjugorje: Facts, Documents, Theology*, (Dubin, Ireland: Veritas Publications, 1986), p. 42.

[522] Steve & Ana Shawl, Medjugorje Web, *Messages From Our Lady 1984-1989*, Our Lady Of Medjugorje: Additional Messages and Conversations Between Our Lady and the Visionaries From 1984-1989, <http://www.medjugorje.org/msgmisc.htm>.
[523] Emmerich, *The Life of the Blessed Virgin Mary*, p. 207.
[524] Emmerich, *The Life of the Blessed Virgin Mary*, p. 140.
[525] *Butler's Lives of the Saints, Complete Edition*, ed. Herbert J. Thurston, S.J. and Donald Attwater, (Westminster, Maryland: Christian Classics, 1990), Vol. 3, August 5, p. 265.
[526] O'Carroll, *Medjugorje: Facts, Documents, Theology*, p. 42. See also: Shawl, *Messages From Our Lady 1984-1989*, <http://www.medjugorje.org/msgmisc.htm>.
[527] Shawl, *Messages From Our Lady 1984-1989*, <http://www.medjugorje.org/msgmisc.htm>.
[528] Finegan, *Handbook of Biblical Chronology*, revised edition, no. 217-218, p. 113.
[529] O'Carroll, *Medjugorje: Facts, Documents, Theology*, p. 42. See also: Shawl, *Messages From Our Lady 1984-1989*, <http://www.medjugorje.org/msgmisc.htm>.
[530] Emmerich, *The Life of the Blessed Virgin Mary*, p. 75.
[531] This booklet, originally titled, *the Virginity of Mary and Jesus*, was revised and expanded, then re-titled as: *the Virginity of Jesus and Mary*. It is available from CatholicPlanet.com.
[532] Days of the week determined using *Universal Calendar Calculator* software. The days of the week determined by that software and used in this book are in agreement with the determinations of other scholars. For example, April 7 of A.D. 30 was a Friday.
[533] Emmerich, *The Life of the Blessed Virgin Mary*, p. 74.
[534] Days of the week determined using *Universal Calendar Calculator* software.
[535] August 5 of 30 B.C. was Av 26, determined by calculation. The new moon of July 11 at 04:58 hours JST made July 11 the first day of Av. New moon data from *RedShift 3* astronomy software.
[536] The lengths of time for the birth of a female child are doubled because there are two females to account for, the mother and the daughter.
[537] Emmerich, *The Life of the Blessed Virgin Mary*, p. 207, 219.
[538] Emmerich, *The Life of the Blessed Virgin Mary*, p. 81.
[539] Emmerich, *The Life of Jesus Christ and Biblical Revelations*, Vol. 1, p. 151. Cf. *The Life of the Blessed Virgin Mary*, p. 76.
[540] Jewish custom was to count days, months, and years inclusively. Finegan, *Handbook of Biblical Chronology*, revised edition, no. 165, p. 78.
[541] Emmerich, *The Life of the Blessed Virgin Mary*, p. 81-82.
[542] Emmerich, *The Life of the Blessed Virgin Mary*, p. 82.
[543] Emmerich, *The Life of the Blessed Virgin Mary*, p. 26, 32, 74, 114.
[544] Emmerich, *The Life of the Blessed Virgin Mary*, p. 86.
[545] This date was determined by calculation. The new moon of Oct. 8 at 06:41 hours JST in 30 B.C. marked the beginning of the month of Heshvan. New moon data from *RedShift 3* astronomy software.
[546] Melkite Greek Catholic Information, *Great Feast of the Entrance of the Theotokos into the Temple*, <http://www.mliles.com/melkite/entrancetheotokos.shtml>. See also: Saint Therese Byzantine Catholic Church web site, *The Eastern Catholic Church, A Short Explanation*, <http://www.byzantines.net/st-therese/byzrite.htm>.

[547] Orthodox Church in America, *OCA - Worship - Entrance of the Theotokos into the Temple*, <http://www.oca.org/pages/orth_chri/Orthodox-Faith/Worship/Theo-Into-Temple.html>.
[548] Emmerich, *The Life of Jesus Christ and Biblical Revelations*, Vol. 4, p.149.
[549] Emmerich, *The Life of the Blessed Virgin Mary*, p. 115.
[550] Emmerich, *The Life of the Blessed Virgin Mary*, p. 129.
[551] Emmerich, *The Life of the Blessed Virgin Mary*, p. 129, 145.
[552] Emmerich, *The Life of the Blessed Virgin Mary*, p. 156.
[553] Emmerich, *The Life of the Blessed Virgin Mary*, p. 109.
[554] Emmerich, *The Life of Jesus Christ and Biblical Revelations*, Vol. 1, p. 177.
[555] Emmerich, *The Life of the Blessed Virgin Mary*, p. 129.
[556] Emmerich, *The Life of Jesus Christ and Biblical Revelations*, Vol. 1, p. 187.
[557] Emmerich, *The Life of the Blessed Virgin Mary*, p. 115.
[558] Emmerich, *The Life of the Blessed Virgin Mary*, p. 206.
[559] Emmerich, *The Life of the Blessed Virgin Mary*, p. 87.
[560] Emmerich, *The Life of the Blessed Virgin Mary*, p. 145.
[561] Apostolic Constitution of Pope Pius XII, *Munificentissimus Deus*, November 1, 1950, (Boston, MA: St. Paul Books & Media), paragraphs no. 14, 17, 18, 20, 21, 22, 28, 40. Furthermore, paragraph no. 28 refers specifically to the Resurrection of the Virgin Mary, after her death and before her Assumption.
[562] Ronald L. Conte Jr., *The Dormition, Resurrection, and Assumption of the Blessed Virgin Mary*, (Catholic Planet, 1998). I intend to use this booklet as chapter 3 of my third book.
[563] Saint Bridget of Sweden, *Revelations of Saint Bridget*, p. 68.
[564] Emmerich, *The Life of the Blessed Virgin Mary*, p. 346.
[565] Emmerich, *The Life of Jesus Christ and Biblical Revelations*, Vol. 4, p. 39.
[566] Emmerich, *The Life of Jesus Christ and Biblical Revelations*, Vol. 4, p. 42.
[567] Emmerich, *The Life of the Blessed Virgin Mary*, p. 367. Could she have misunderstood this vision as referring instead to the number of years since Christ's Incarnation, rather than His Birth? Perhaps, but since Christ was conceived and born in the same calendar year, the result is the same year.
[568] Emmerich, *The Life of the Blessed Virgin Mary*, p. 372.
[569] Emmerich, *The Life of the Blessed Virgin Mary*, chapter 15.
[570] Emmerich, *The Life of Jesus Christ and Biblical Revelations*, Vol. 4, p. 450.
[571] Emmerich, *The Life of the Blessed Virgin Mary*, p. 367-368.
[572] Emmerich, *The Life of the Blessed Virgin Mary*, p. 361.
[573] Emmerich, *The Life of the Blessed Virgin Mary*, p. 145.
[574] Emmerich, *The Life of Jesus Christ and Biblical Revelations*, Vol. 4, p. 424, 427.
[575] Emmerich, *The Life of the Blessed Virgin Mary*, p. 346.
[576] See Appendix I, Chart 3.
[577] Emmerich, *The Life of the Blessed Virgin Mary*, p. 368.
[578] Emmerich, *The Dolorous Passion of Our Lord Jesus Christ*, p. 359-360; *The Life of Jesus Christ and Biblical Revelations*, Vol. 4, p. 363-365.
[579] Emmerich, *The Life of the Blessed Virgin Mary*, p. 377; *The Life of Jesus Christ and Biblical Revelations*, Vol. 4, p. 467-468.
[580] Saint Bridget of Sweden, *Revelations of Saint Bridget*, p. 68.

[581] Saint Bridget of Sweden, *Revelations of Saint Bridget*, p. 68.
[582] Emmerich, *The Life of the Blessed Virgin Mary*, p. 376.
[583] Emmerich, *The Life of the Blessed Virgin Mary*, p. 379-380.
[584] Emmerich, *The Life of the Blessed Virgin Mary*, p. 376.
[585] *Munificentissimus Deus*, paragraph no. 28.
[586] Emmerich, *The Life of the Blessed Virgin Mary*, p. 377.
[587] Sunrise time from *RedShift 3* astronomy software.
[588] *RedShift 3* computer software places sunrise on August 14 of A.D. 34 at 04:58, Jerusalem Standard Time.
[589] Emmerich, *The Life of the Blessed Virgin Mary*, p. 378-380.
[590] Emmerich, *The Life of Jesus Christ and Biblical Revelations*, Vol. 4, p. 468.
[591] Josephus, *The Antiquities of the Jews*, 18:85-90.
[592] Finegan, *Handbook of Biblical Chronology*, revised edition, no. 638, 685, p. 373, 396.
[593] Josephus, *The Antiquities of the Jews*, 18:89.
[594] Josephus, *The Antiquities of the Jews*, 18:89.
[595] Pliny, *Natural History*, books I – II, ed. G. P. Goold, trans. H. Rackham, Pliny, Volume I, Loeb Classical Library, (Cambridge, Massachusetts: Harvard University Press, 1991), 2.47. Pliny states that the spring weather opened the seas to travel beginning on Feb. 8.
[596] Such trips were certainly made during wintertime as is clear from Josephus, where Petronius sent word to Rome, and Rome replied twice (by ship), all during the winter time. Josephus, *The Wars of the Jews*, 2.199-203.
[597] Eusebius, *The History of the Church*, ed. Andrew Louth, trans. G. A. Williamson, (London, England: Penguin Books, 1989), 2.1.1, p. 35.
[598] Finegan, *Handbook of Biblical Chronology*, revised edition, no. 635, p. 370. Josephus, *The Antiquities of the Jews*, 19.351.
[599] Finegan, *Handbook of Biblical Chronology*, revised edition, no. 635, p. 370. Josephus, *The Antiquities of the Jews*, 19.351.
[600] Josephus, *The Antiquities of the Jews*, 19.350-351.
[601] Josephus, *The Antiquities of the Jews*, 19.284-285.
[602] Josephus, *The Antiquities of the Jews*, 19.287-291.
[603] Josephus, *The Antiquities of the Jews*, 19.287.
[604] Dio, *Roman History*, Volume VII, Loeb Classical Library, 60.1.4 and 60.10.1.
[605] Dio, *Roman History*, Volume VII, Loeb Classical Library, 60.10.1.
[606] Josephus, *The Antiquities of the Jews*, 19.274-275, 292.
[607] Pliny, *Natural History*, 2.47.
[608] The new moon was on Mar. 26 at 20:03 hours, placing Nisan 1 on March 27 by calculation, and Nisan 14 on April 9. See Appendix I, Chart 1. New moon data from *RedShift 3* software.
[609] Nisan 1 began that year on March 27, so that Nisan 14 coincided with April 9. The new moon for Nisan was March 26 at 20:03 hours JST. New moon data from *RedShift 3* software.
[610] Saint Jerome, *Lives of Illustrious Men*, chapter 1, Christian Classics Ethereal Library, (Wheaton, Illinois: Wheaton College, 1998), CD-ROM, <http://www.ccel.org/>.

[611] Once the Sabbatical year ended, in mid September, they would have planted crops as soon as possible, because of their lack of food. Most ancient varieties of grains take 4 to 5 months to reach maturity.

[612] Finegan, *Handbook of Biblical Chronology*, revised edition, no. 675, p. 391.

[613] Finegan, *Handbook of Biblical Chronology*, revised edition, no. 674-678, p. 391-393.

[614] Emmerich, *The Life of the Blessed Virgin Mary*, p. 346.

[615] Emmerich, *The Life of the Blessed Virgin Mary*, p. 346-347.

[616] Pliny, *Natural History*, 2.47.

[617] Venerable Mary of Agreda, *A Popular Abridgement of The Mystical City of God*, trans. Fiscar Marison, (Washington, New Jersey: Ave Maria Institute, 1978), p. 688. Venerable Mary is good source for devout meditation on heavenly things, but a very poor source for chronological information. Nevertheless, her conclusion that the Virgin Mary and John left for Ephesus before Paul arrived is based on sound reasoning.

[618] Josephus, *The Wars of the Jews*, 2.181-183; *The Antiquities of the Jews*, 20:351.

[619] Josephus, *The Wars of the Jews*, 2.184ff.

[620] Emmerich, *The Life of the Blessed Virgin Mary*, p. 352.

[621] Josephus, *The Antiquities of the Jews*, 20:351.

[622] Finegan, *Handbook of Biblical Chronology*, revised edition, no. 635, p. 370-371.

[623] Jerome, *Lives of Illustrious Men*, chapter 1.

[624] Finegan, *Handbook of Biblical Chronology*, revised edition, no. 663-667, p. 384-386. Finegan quotes the *Liberian Catalog* (*Catalogus Liberianus*) and the *Book of the Popes* (*Liber pontificalis*), as well as Saint Jerome, *Lives of Illustrious Men*, chapter 1.

[625] Finegan, *Handbook of Biblical Chronology*, revised edition, no. 663-667, p. 384-386. Finegan quotes the *Liberian Catalog* (*Catalogus Liberianus*) and the *Book of the Popes* (*Liber pontificalis*), as well as Saint Jerome.

[626] Finegan, *Handbook of Biblical Chronology*, revised edition, no. 663, 666, p. 384-385.

[627] Finegan, *Handbook of Biblical Chronology*, revised edition, no. 669, p. 387. He cites the *Chronographer of the Year 354* and the *Book of the Popes* (*Liber pontificalis*).

[628] Eusebius, *The Ecclesiastical History*, trans. Kirsopp Lake, Eusebius, Volume I, Loeb Classical Library, (Cambridge, Massachusetts: Harvard University Press, 1998), 2.25.5-8. Jerome, *Lives of Illustrious Men*, chapters 1, 5, 12. See also, Finegan, *Handbook of Biblical Chronology*, revised edition, no. 669, p. 387.

[629] Jerome, *Lives of Illustrious Men*, chapter 1.

[630] Jerome, *Lives of Illustrious Men*, chapter 12.

[631] Jerome, *Lives of Illustrious Men*, chapter 5. He gives the length of Peter's reign as 37 years, which does not leave enough time, from the 15th year of Tiberius (cf. Lk 3:1) to the 14th year of Nero, for Christ to have a 3½ year Ministry (you do the math).

[632] Josephus, *The Antiquities of the Jews*, 19.286-289.

[633] Jerome, *Lives of Illustrious Men*, chapters 1, 8.

[634] Finegan, *Handbook of Biblical Chronology*, revised edition, no. 636, p. 372. Finegan cites Daniel Schwartz' book, *Agrippa I*, p. 110-111.

[635] Jerome, *Lives of Illustrious Men*, chapter 8.

[636] Eusebius, *The History of the Church*, Penguin Books, 2.15.1-2.

[637] Eusebius, *The History of the Church*, Penguin Books, 2.15.1-2.

[638] Eusebius, *The History of the Church*, Penguin Books, 2.15.1-2.

[639] Jerome, *Lives of Illustrious Men*, chapter 8.
[640] Eusebius, *The History of the Church*, Penguin Books, 2.16.1.
[641] Finegan, *Handbook of Biblical Chronology*, revised edition, p. 382, no. 658.
[642] Finegan, *Handbook of Biblical Chronology*, revised edition, p. 382, no. 658.
[643] Jerome, *Lives of Illustrious Men*, chapter 1. See also: Eusebius, *Ecclesiastical History*, Loeb Classical Library, 2.15.1-2.
[644] Recall that even Jesus did not begin His Ministry until He was about thirty years old (Lk 3:23). The culture and society of that time gave greater weight to the words of a man with greater years.
[645] Emmerich, *The Life of the Blessed Virgin Mary*, p. 358.
[646] Finegan, *Handbook of Biblical Chronology*, revised edition, no. 658, p. 382.
[647] Jerome, *Lives of Illustrious Men*, chapter 8.
[648] Eusebius, *Ecclesiastical History*, Loeb Classical Library, 2.16.1.
[649] Pliny, *Natural History*, 2.47.
[650] Eusebius, *The History of the Church*, Penguin Books, 3.24.6-7. The Loeb Classical Library translation differs by saying: "Mark and Luke had already published," rather than the "had now published" of the Penguin Books translation. The other chronological evidence presented in this chapter indicates that Matthew must have published before Mark and Luke, so the Penguin Books translation is preferred.
[651] Jerome, *Lives of Illustrious Men*, chapter 3.
[652] Eusebius, *The History of the Church*, Penguin Books, p. 401.
[653] Jerome, *Lives of Illustrious Men*, chapter 36.
[654] *Butler's Lives of the Saints*, Vol. 3, August 24, p. 392.
[655] *Butler's Lives of the Saints*, Vol. 3, August 24, p. 392.
[656] Emmerich, *The Life of the Blessed Virgin Mary*, p. 366.
[657] *Butler's Lives of the Saints*, Vol. 3, August 24, p. 392.
[658] Josephus, *The Antiquities of the Jews*, 18.257-261.
[659] Eusebius, *Ecclesiastical History*, Loeb Classical Library, 2.23. See also: Jerome, *Lives of Illustrious Men*, chapter 2.
[660] Eusebius, *The History of the Church*, Penguin Books, 3.24.6-7.
[661] *Butler's Lives of the Saints*, Vol. 3, October 18, p. 142-143.
[662] Jerome, *The Commentaries*, Matthew, Christian Classics Ethereal Library, (Wheaton, Illinois: Wheaton College, 1998), CD-ROM, <http://www.ccel.org/>.
[663] Finegan, *Handbook of Biblical Chronology*, revised edition, no. 580, p. 338.
[664] Finegan, *Handbook of Biblical Chronology*, revised edition, no. 675, p. 391.
[665] Finegan, *Handbook of Biblical Chronology*, revised edition, no. 680, p. 393.
[666] Macmillan Bible Atlas, map 252.
[667] Josephus, *The Antiquities of the Jews*, 20.137-138.
[668] Josephus, *The Antiquities of the Jews*, 20.118-136.
[669] Josephus, *The Antiquities of the Jews*, 20.162.
[670] Josephus, *The Antiquities of the Jews*, 20.162-165.
[671] Josephus, *The Antiquities of the Jews*, 20.179.
[672] Josephus, *The Antiquities of the Jews*, 20.182.
[673] Jerome, *Lives of Illustrious Men*, chapter 2.
[674] Eusebius, *The History of the Church*, Penguin Books, 2.23.18.

[675] Eusebius, *The History of the Church*, Penguin Books, 2.23.19.

[676] Josephus, *The Antiquities of the Jews*, 20.257.

[677] Eusebius, *The History of the Church*, Penguin Books, 2.23.3.

[678] Josephus, *The Antiquities of the Jews*, 20.252ff.

[679] Josephus, *The Antiquities of the Jews*, 20.197.

[680] Jerome, Illustrious, chapter 2.

[681] Eusebius, *The History of the Church*, Penguin Books, 2.23.3-19. Eusebius quotes Hegesippus extensively.

[682] Dio Cassius, *Roman History*, ed. G. P. Goold, trans. Earnest Cary, Dio Cassius, Volume VIII, Loeb Classical Library, (Cambridge, Massachusetts: Harvard University Press, 1995), 62.16.1 to 62.18.5.

[683] Tacitus, *The Annals*, ed. G. P. Goold, trans. John Jackson, Tacitus, Volume V, Loeb Classical Library, (Cambridge, Massachusetts: Harvard University Press, 1999), 15.40.

[684] Tacitus, *The Annals*, 15.44.

[685] Tacitus, *The Annals*, 15.44. Also cited by Finegan, *Handbook of Biblical Chronology*, revised edition, no. 645, p. 375.

[686] Eusebius, 2.16-17, p. 50-54. Eusebius cites and quotes Philo extensively there. See also: Jerome, *Lives of Illustrious Men*, chapter 8.

[687] Eusebius, *The History of the Church*, Penguin Books, 2.24.1. Jerome, *Lives of Illustrious Men*, chapter 8.

[688] Eusebius, *The History of the Church*, Penguin Books, 2.24.1.

[689] Josephus, *The Antiquities of the Jews*, 20.202.

[690] Tacitus, *The Annals*, 15.41.

[691] Tacitus, *The Annals*, 15.44.

[692] Tacitus, *The Annals*, 15.44.

[693] Tacitus, *The Annals*, 15.44.

[694] Finegan, *Handbook of Biblical Chronology*, revised edition, no. 658, p. 382.

[695] Finegan, *Handbook of Biblical Chronology*, revised edition, no. 658, p. 382.

[696] Finegan, *Handbook of Biblical Chronology*, revised edition, table 8, no. 49, p. 25. Barmudah is also transliterated as Pharmuthi. All the months of the Egyptian calendar have 30 days. Finegan had the 30th day of Pharmuthi as April 25.

[697] Spring Equinox and Full moon data from *RedShift 3* astronomy software. The days of the week are from Universal Calendar Calculator, Cumberland Family Software.

[698] Egyptian calendar data from UCC software.

[699] The Spring Equinox of A.D. 71 was on March 22, the next full moon was on Wednesday, April 3, making Sunday, April 7, Easter Sunday. Spring Equinox and Full moon data from *RedShift 3*. Days of the week from *Universal Calendar Calculator* software.

[700] Egyptian calendar data from *Universal Calendar Calculator* software.

[701] The Spring Equinox of A.D. 47 was on March 23, the next full moon was on Thursday, March 30, making Sunday, April 2, Easter Sunday. Spring Equinox and Full moon data from *RedShift 3*. Days of the week from *Universal Calendar Calculator* software.

[702] The Spring Equinox of A.D. 50 was on March 22, the next full moon was on Friday, March 27, making Sunday, March 29, Easter Sunday. Spring Equinox and Full moon data from *RedShift 3*. Days of the week from *Universal Calendar Calculator* software.

[703] April 2 of A.D. 47 coincided with Pharmuthi 8 in the Egyptian Alexandrian calendar. March 29 of A.D. 50 coincided with Pharmuthi 4 in the Egyptian Alexandrian calendar. Egyptian calendar data from *Universal Calendar Calculator* software.

[704] Athanasius, *Letter XVIII.* (for 346), Nicene and Post-Nicene Fathers, Series II, volume IV, Christian Classics Ethereal Library, (Wheaton, Illinois: Wheaton College, 1998), CD-ROM, <http://www.ccel.org/>. The day "iii Kal April" means three days before the Kalends (the first day) of April, which works out to be March 29. Athanasius wrote this letter in A.D. 346, on the topic of the date of Easter in A.D. 347, when March 29 was Easter Sunday.

[705] Josephus, *The Antiquities of the Jews*, 20.200-203.

[706] Tacitus, *The Annals*, 15.41.

[707] Jerome, *Lives of Illustrious Men*, chapters 2, 8.

[708] Josephus, *The Antiquities of the Jews*, 20.203.

[709] Eusebius, *Ecclesiastical History*, Loeb Classical Library, 3.14.1.

[710] Eusebius, *Ecclesiastical History*, Loeb Classical Library, 2.25.8.

[711] Jerome, *Lives of Illustrious Men*, chapter 5.

[712] Finegan, *Handbook of Biblical Chronology*, revised edition, no. 669-670, p. 387-388.

[713] Jerome, *Lives of Illustrious Men*, chapter 1.

[714] Jerome, *Lives of Illustrious Men*, chapter 8.

[715] Jerome, *The Commentaries*, Matthew.

[716] Jerome, *Lives of Illustrious Men*, chapter 9. Eusebius, 3.24, p. 86-87.

[717] Eusebius, *The History of the Church*, Penguin Books, 3.24.7.

[718] *Butler's Lives of the Saints*, Vol. 4, Dec. 27, p. 621.

[719] Eusebius, *The History of the Church*, Penguin Books, 3.18.1.

[720] Jerome, *Against Jovinianus*, 1.26, Christian Classics Ethereal Library, (Wheaton, Illinois: Wheaton College, 1998), CD-ROM, <http://www.ccel.org/>.

[721] *Butler's Lives of the Saints*, Vol. 2, May 6, p. 240-242.

[722] Jerome, *Lives of Illustrious Men*, chapter 9.

[723] Eusebius, *Ecclesiastical History*, Loeb Classical Library, 3.23.4

[724] Victorinus, *Commentary on the Apocalypse of the Blessed John*, 10.11, Christian Classics Ethereal Library, (Wheaton, Illinois: Wheaton College, 1998), CD-ROM, <http://www.ccel.org/>. See paragraph 11 of his commentary on the tenth chapter of Revelation.

[725] Jerome, *Lives of Illustrious Men*, chapter 9.

[726] Eusebius, *Ecclesiastical History*, Loeb Classical Library, 3.5.1; 3.13.1. The writings of Eusebius were well-known and accepted by Jerome.

[727] Suetonius Tranquillus, *Lives of the Caesars*, ed. G.P. Goold, trans. J.C. Rolfe, Suetonius, Volume II, Loeb Classical Library, (Cambridge, Massachusetts: Harvard University Press, 1997), 12.11.1.

[728] Suetonius, *Lives of the Caesars*, Loeb Classical Library, 12.10.2.

[729] If John had spent most of Domitian's reign on Patmos, the early Church Fathers would have spoken of his stay on Patmos as lengthy. Instead, they talk at length about his work in Ephesus and the surrounding area of Asia, giving only brief mention to his stay on Patmos.

[730] Eusebius, *The History of the Church*, Penguin Books, 3.18.4.

[731] Finegan, *Handbook of Biblical Chronology*, revised edition, no. 179, table 40, p. 85.

[732] Jerome, *Lives of Illustrious Men*, chapter 9. Jerome indicates this by referring to "the fourteenth year then after Nero," i.e. Domitian's first year, as the start of the troubles.

[733] Eusebius, *Ecclesiastical History*, Loeb Classical Library, 3.23.6-8; see also 3.20.9 and 3.23.1.

[734] Eusebius, *Ecclesiastical History*, Loeb Classical Library, 3.23.3-4.

[735] *Butler's Lives of the Saints*, Vol. 4, Dec. 27, p. 622.

[736] Dio, *Roman History*, Volume VIII, Loeb Classical Library, 68.4.2.

[737] Dio, *Roman History*, Volume VIII, Loeb Classical Library, 68.3.4 to 68.4.2.

[738] *Butler's Lives of the Saints*, Vol. 4, Dec. 27, p. 622.

[739] Josephus, *The Antiquities of the Jews*, 17.191.

[740] See, for example: Finegan, *Handbook of Biblical Chronology*, revised edition; *Chronos, Kairos, Christos*, and *Chronos, Kairos, Christos II*.

[741] Josephus, *The Antiquities of the Jews,* 14.385-386.

[742] Josephus, *The Antiquities of the Jews*, 15.487.

[743] The new moon of April 1 at 07:19 JST in 37 B.C. was first visible as a new crescent on the evening of April 2, making April 3 as Nisan 1 and April 16 as Nisan 14. The result is a later than usual start for Tishri. The date of Tishri 1 that year was probably Saturday, Sept. 28. The new moon of Sept. 24 at 13:17 JST would not have been visible as a new crescent until the evening of Thursday, Sept. 26. Ordinarily, this would make Sept. 27 the first day of the month, but Tishri 1 is not permitted to coincide with Friday to avoid a conflict between the Preparation day of the Sabbath and the holy days at the start and end of the Feast of Tabernacles. Thus, Tishri 1 would have been delayed until Saturday, Sept. 28. An alternate, but somewhat less likely, possibility was to start Tishri 1 on Thursday, Sept. 26, most probably before the new crescent was sighted. New moon and visibility data from *RedShift 3*. Days of the week determined using *Universal Calendar Calculator* software.

[744] In 42 B.C., Tishri 10 would have fallen on Sept. 30 only if the Jewish calendar at that time was determined by calculation (which was probably not the case), rather than by observation. With the other years listed, Tishri 10 would fall in October regardless of whether the calendar was by calculation or observation. I am convinced that the Jewish calendar was determined by calculation, but not until some years after the capture of Jerusalem. See chapter 17 for details on this point.

[745] Josephus, *The Antiquities of the Jews,* 14.473.

[746] Josephus, *The Antiquities of the Jews*, 14.475.

[747] Josephus, *The Antiquities of the Jews*, 15.7.

[748] Finegan, *Handbook of Biblical Chronology*, revised edition, no. 225, p. 118-119.

[749] The new moon of March 20 at 06:46 JST in 44 B.C. places the date of Nisan 1 on March 22, making the date of Tishri 1 in the subsequent autumn early enough that Tishri 10 would still fall in September. New moon data from *RedShift 3* astronomy software.

[750] Finegan, *Handbook of Biblical Chronology*, revised edition, no. 225, p. 118-119.

[751] New moon data from *RedShift 3* software.

[752] The determination of the start of Nisan is by observation here, because we are considering the possibility that Herod captured Jerusalem in 36 B.C. The switch from

observation to calculation to determine the start of each month did not occur until sometime after Herod captured Jerusalem.

[753] Josephus, *The Antiquities of the Jews*, 15.1, 15.8-9.

[754] Josephus, *The Antiquities of the Jews*, 17.191.

[755] Josephus, *The Antiquities of the Jews*, 18.32.

[756] He uses neither "ascension-year" nor "non-ascension-year" reckoning. For a succinct explanation of these terms, see: Finegan, *Handbook of Biblical Chronology*, revised edition, no. 160-161, p. 74-75.

[757] Josephus, *The Antiquities of the Jews*, 17.149-163.

[758] Josephus, *The Antiquities of the Jews*, 17.167.

[759] Josephus, *The Antiquities of the Jews*, 17.165-167.

[760] Josephus, *The Antiquities of the Jews*, 17.168-172.

[761] Josephus, *The Antiquities of the Jews*, 17.174-181.

[762] Josephus, *The Antiquities of the Jews*, 17.191.

[763] Josephus, *The Antiquities of the Jews*, 17.193.

[764] Josephus, *The Antiquities of the Jews*, 17.200-205.

[765] Josephus, *The Antiquities of the Jews*, 17.213-215.

[766] Josephus, *The Antiquities of the Jews*, 17.196-199.

[767] Josephus, *The Wars of the Jews*, 2:280.

[768] Josephus, *The Antiquities of the Jews*, 17.214.

[769] Josephus, *The Antiquities of the Jews*, 17.206-218.

[770] Those scholars who place Herod's death in 4 B.C. are partially correct, for the death of Herod did occur in the context of events usually dated to 4 B.C. But, as explained in chapter 13, events during this portion of Roman history occurred 4 years earlier than has been generally believed. Thus, events attributed to 4 B.C. actually took place in 8 B.C.

[771] Fred Espenak, *Five Millennium Catalog of Lunar Eclipses*, Eclipse Home Page, NASA/GSFC Sun-Earth Connection Education Forum, <http://sunearth.gsfc.nasa.gov/eclipse/LEcat/LEcatalog.html>.

[772] John P. Pratt, *Yet Another Eclipse for Herod*, The Griffith Observatory Home Page, reprinted from the *Planetarian*, <http://www.griffithobs.org/IPSPlanPlatt.html>, vol. 19, no. 4, (International Planetarium Society, 1990), pp. 8-14. See also: <http://www.johnpratt.com/>.

[773] Finegan, *Handbook of Biblical Chronology*, revised edition, no. 78-81, p. 38-39.

[774] Fred Espenak, *Five Millennium Catalog of Lunar Eclipses*, NASA/GSFC, <http://sunearth.gsfc.nasa.gov/eclipse/LEcat/LEcatalog.html>. See also: *RedShift 3* astronomy software.

[775] Lunar eclipse times in this book are generally given as Jerusalem Standard Time, which is Universal Time plus 2:00 hours. Jerusalem sun time is approximately Universal Time plus 2:21 hours. See chapter 17 for details.

[776] Josephus, *The Antiquities of the Jews*, 17.167.

[777] Josephus, *The Antiquities of the Jews*, 15.380.

[778] Josephus, *The Wars of the Jews*, 1.401.

[779] Josephus, *The Antiquities of the Jews*, 16.

[780] Josephus, *The Wars of the Jews*, 1.401.

[781] Josephus, *The Antiquities of the Jews*, 15.299-316

[782] Josephus, *The Antiquities of the Jews*, 15.420.
[783] Josephus, *The Antiquities of the Jews*, 16.136.
[784] Josephus, *The Antiquities of the Jews*, 15.381.
[785] Josephus, *The Antiquities of the Jews*, 15.420.
[786] Josephus, *The Antiquities of the Jews*, 15.421.
[787] Josephus, *The Antiquities of the Jews*, 15.421-423.
[788] New moon occurred on Sunday, Sept. 2 at 06:21 Jerusalem Standard Time. The start of each month at that point in Jewish history was determined by observation of the crescent new moon. The crescent new moon would have been visible by the evening of Sept. 3., making Tuesday, Sept. 4 as Tishri 1. Tishri 10 that year would then fall on Sept. 13.
[789] Josephus, *The Antiquities of the Jews*, 14.487.
[790] Finegan, *Handbook of Biblical Chronology*, revised edition, table 46, p. 97.
[791] Finegan, *Handbook of Biblical Chronology*, revised edition, no. 516, p. 300.
[792] Josephus, *The Antiquities of the Jews*, 18.106-108.
[793] Josephus, *The Antiquities of the Jews*, 18.106.
[794] Finegan, *Handbook of Biblical Chronology*, revised edition, no. 518, p. 301. Finegan cites David W. Beyer's 1995 study, reported to the Society for Biblical Literature.
[795] Finegan, *Handbook of Biblical Chronology*, revised edition, no. 518, p. 301.
[796] Josephus, *The Antiquities of the Jews*, 18.108.
[797] Finegan, *Handbook of Biblical Chronology*, revised edition, no. 518, p. 301.
[798] Finegan, *Handbook of Biblical Chronology*, revised edition, no. 517-518, p. 300-301.
[799] Dio, *Roman History*, Volume VIII, Loeb Classical Library, 66.17.5.
[800] Emmerich, *The Life of the Blessed Virgin Mary*, p. 205.
[801] Josephus, *The Antiquities of the Jews*, 17.191.
[802] Emmerich, *The Life of the Blessed Virgin Mary*, p. 206.
[803] Josephus, *The Antiquities of the Jews*, 16.136.
[804] Emmerich, *The Life of the Blessed Virgin Mary*, p. 206.
[805] Emmerich, *The Life of the Blessed Virgin Mary*, p. 115. Cf. *The Life of Jesus Christ and Biblical Revelations*, Vol. 1, p. 177.
[806] Pliny, *Natural History*, 2.30. Julius Caesar is obviously the one referred to as the dictator who was murdered. The circumstances of his death, described by Suetonius, Josephus, and others make it clear Julius Caesar was murdered. And he was long thought of, and referred to, in ancient Rome, as a dictator.
[807] Based on eclipse data from *RedShift 3* astronomy software and Fred Espenak, *Five Millennium Catalog of Solar Eclipses*, NASA/GSFC, <http://sunearth.gsfc.nasa.gov/eclipse/SEcat/SEcatalog.html>.
[808] Pliny, *Natural History*, 2.9.
[809] Fred Espenak, *Five Millennium Catalog of Solar Eclipses*, NASA/GSFC, <http://sunearth.gsfc.nasa.gov/eclipse/SEcat/SEcatalog.html>. Here the time is given as 10:30 Universal Time (GMT), which would be 11:30 hours local standard time in Rome.
[810] Pliny, *Natural History*, 2.23. The same comet is also mentioned by numerous other ancient writers. See Kronk, *Cometography*, p. 22, for a listing.
[811] Kronk, *Cometography*, p. 21-23.

[812] *RedShift 3* astronomy software. Verification of the accuracy of this software is shown by comparison with data from *NASA/GSFC Sun-Earth Connection Education Forum*, NASA/GSFC, <http://sunearth.gsfc.nasa.gov/eclipse/eclipse.html>. See chapter 17 for details.

[813] Pliny, *Natural History*, 2.23.

[814] Kronk, *Cometography*, p. 23.

[815] Kronk, *Cometography*, p. 22-23.

[816] *RedShift 3* astronomy software.

[817] Kronk, *Cometography*, p. 22.

[818] Kronk, *Cometography*, p. 22.

[819] Kronk, *Cometography*, p. 21.

[820] *RedShift 3* astronomy software.

[821] *RedShift 3* astronomy software.

[822] Kronk, *Cometography*, p. 21-24. The next earliest comet is placed in 61 B.C., and the next latest comet is placed in 32 B.C.

[823] Josephus, *The Antiquities of the Jews*, 18.32.

[824] Dio, *Roman History*, Volume VII, Loeb Classical Library, 56.30.5. See also: Suetonius, *Lives of the Caesars*, Loeb Classical Library, 2.100.1.

[825] Josephus, *The Antiquities of the Jews*, 14.271 – 305; *The Wars of the Jews*, 1.218-242.

[826] Josephus, *The Antiquities of the Jews*, 14.271.

[827] Dio, *Roman History*, Volume VII, Loeb Classical Library, 56.30.5.

[828] Dio, *Roman History*, Volume VI, Loeb Classical Library, 51.1.1-2. Here Dio specifically states that Augustus' reign as sole ruler began on Sept. 2.

[829] Suetonius, *Lives of the Caesars*, Loeb Classical Library, 2.8.3.

[830] Josephus, *The Antiquities of the Jews*, 15.109, 121.

[831] Josephus, *The Antiquities of the Jews*, 14.487.

[832] Josephus, *The Antiquities of the Jews*, 15.121.

[833] Dio, *Roman History*, Volume VII, Loeb Classical Library, 56.29.3.

[834] Data on solar eclipses from *RedShift 3* software and Fred Espenak, *Five Millennium Catalog of Solar Eclipses*, NASA/GSFC, <http://sunearth.gsfc.nasa.gov/eclipse/SEcat/SEcatalog.html>. *RedShift 3* software can be used to visualize the locations on the surface of the earth covered by the shadow of the moon during any solar eclipse. During these years, A.D. 11 to A.D. 14, no solar eclipse was visible, even as a partial eclipse, from anywhere in the Roman Empire.

[835] Solar eclipse on June 30 of A.D. 10 at 11:19 hours (time of greatest eclipse). Fred Espenak, *Five Millennium Catalog of Solar Eclipses*, NASA/GSFC, <http://sunearth.gsfc.nasa.gov/eclipse/SEcat/SEcatalog.html>. *RedShift 3* software shows that this eclipse was visible at a partial solar eclipse from Italy and most of Europe.

[836] Dio, *Roman History*, Volume VII, Loeb Classical Library, book 56.29.3.

[837] At that time in history there was no distinction given between meteors and comets. A reference to comets, plural, seen on only one occasion would mean a meteor shower; a reference to a comet or star seen over the course of several days would mean a comet.

[838] Pliny, *Natural History*, 2.9.

[839] Suetonius, *Lives of the Caesars*, Loeb Classical Library, 2.100.1.

[840] Dio, *Roman History*, Volume VII, Loeb Classical Library, 56.30.5.
[841] Josephus, *The Antiquities of the Jews*, 18.32.
[842] The ages at death for various other emperors were probably not always from records, but often from calculations the ancient historians made based on assumptions about the lengths of each emperors reign. For example, Suetonius states that Vespasian was born five years before Augustus' death, and that Vespasian died at the age of 69 years. Suetonius, *Lives of the Caesars*, Loeb Classical Library, 8.2.1, 8.24.1. But in my revised chronology, the age of Vespasian at his death would be calculated as 61 years (this difference is mainly due to the antedating of Tiberius' reign). It is unlikely that Suetonius had a record of the age of each emperor at his death, but rather, in many cases, he was merely calculating the emperor's age based on his understanding of the lengths of the reigns of previous emperors.
[843] Suetonius, *The Twelve Caesars*, trans. Robert Graves, (London, England: Penguin Books, 1989), 2.8.1.
[844] *The New Encyclopedia Britannica*, (Chicago, Illinois: Encyclopedia Britannica, Inc., 1997), Vol. 15, p. 405a.
[845] Suetonius, *Lives of the Caesars*, Loeb Classical Library, 2.26.1. The text reads, literally, "in the twentieth year of his age," meaning the year of his life ending with his 20th birthday. A person's 20th birthday marks the end, not the start, of their 20th year of life. This is the usual understanding of this text. Cf. Suetonius, *The Twelve Caesars*, Penguin Books, 2.26.1, p. 67.
[846] Dio, *Roman History*, Volume VII, Loeb Classical Library, 56.30.5.
[847] Finegan, *Handbook of Biblical Chronology*, revised edition, no. 570-578, p. 330-338.
[848] Vardaman, "Jesus' Life: A New Chronology," *Chronos, Kairos, Christos*, p. 58-59. Although Jerry Vardaman first advanced this theory that the reign of Tiberius should be counted from the death of Gaius in A.D. 4, he later abandoned this view in favor of an alternative theory.
[849] Dio, *Roman History*, Volume VI, Loeb Classical Library, 55.13.1a.
[850] Finegan, *Handbook of Biblical Chronology*, revised edition, no. 570, p. 330.
[851] Finegan, *Handbook of Biblical Chronology*, revised edition, table 42, p. 89.
[852] Finegan, *Handbook of Biblical Chronology*, revised edition, no. 580, p. 338-339. Finegan calls the method of counting the years of an emperor's reign as the "accession year" system, because the first partial year of an emperor's reign is not given a number, but is instead referred to as his year of accession.
[853] Dio, *Roman History*, Volume VIII, Loeb Classical Library, 66.17.5.
[854] Finegan, *Handbook of Biblical Chronology*, revised edition, no. 570-578, p. 330-338.
[855] Josephus, *The Antiquities of the Jews*. Each book begins with a brief statement as to the period of time covered by that book. The verse numbers were not original with Josephus, but were added at a later date.
[856] Josephus, *The Life of Flavius Josephus*, from *The Works of Josephus: New Updated Edition*, ed. William Whiston, (Peabody, Massachusetts: Hendrickson Publishers, Inc., 1995), verse 414, 423.
[857] Josephus, *The Antiquities of the Jews,* 18.33-35.
[858] Finegan, *Handbook of Biblical Chronology*, revised edition, no. 570, p. 330.

[859] Dio, *Roman History*, Volume VII, Loeb Classical Library, 56.25.4. See also: Suetonius, *The Twelve Caesars*, Penguin Books, Genealogical Tables, p. 316.
[860] Finegan, *Handbook of Biblical Chronology*, revised edition, table 42, p. 89.
[861] Tacitus, *The Annals of Imperial Rome*, trans. Michael Grant, (London, England: Penguin Books, 1996), chapter 8, "The Reign of Terror," p. 198-227.
[862] Finegan, *Handbook of Biblical Chronology*, revised edition, no. 517, p. 300-301.
[863] Tacitus, *The Annals of Tacitus*, ed. G. P. Goold, trans. John Jackson, Tacitus, Volume III, Loeb Classical Library, (Cambridge, Massachusetts: Harvard University Press, 1998), 1.81.
[864] Suetonius, *Lives of the Caesars*, Loeb Classical Library, 3.26.2.
[865] Finegan, *Handbook of Biblical Chronology*, revised edition, no. 174, p. 82.
[866] Josephus, *The Antiquities of the Jews,* 14.487.
[867] Pliny, *Natural History*, 2.10.
[868] Finegan, *Handbook of Biblical Chronology*, revised edition, table 40, p. 85.
[869] Eusebius, *Ecclesiastical History*, Loeb Classical Library, 1.9.4.
[870] Josephus, *The Antiquities of the Jews*, 18.54.
[871] Dio, *Roman History*, Volume VII, Loeb Classical Library, 57.18.6. See also: Tacitus, *The Annals of Imperial Rome*, trans. Michael Grant, (London, England: Penguin Books, 1996), p. 112-113; Tacitus, *The Annals*, Loeb Classical Library, 2.70 – 2.75.
[872] Josephus, *The Antiquities of the Jews*, 18.89.
[873] Eusebius, *Ecclesiastical History*, Loeb Classical Library, 1.9.2-3.
[874] Eusebius, *Ecclesiastical History*, Loeb Classical Library, 1.10.1.
[875] Josephus, *The Antiquities of the Jews*, 18.85-89.
[876] Pliny, *Natural History*, 2.47. Here Pliny states that the spring weather opened the seas to travel beginning on February 8.
[877] Josephus, *The Wars of the Jews*, 2.199-203.
[878] Josephus, *The Antiquities of the Jews*, 18.89.
[879] Josephus, *The Antiquities of the Jews*, 18.224 versus *The Wars of the Jews,* 2.180. See also: Dio, *Roman History*, Volume VII, Loeb Classical Library, 58.28.5; Suetonius, *Lives of the Caesars*, Loeb Classical Library, 3.73.1.
[880] Josephus, *The Antiquities of the Jews*, 18.177.
[881] Josephus, *The Antiquities of the Jews*, 18.33.
[882] Josephus, *The Antiquities of the Jews*, 18.35.
[883] Josephus, *The Antiquities of the Jews*, 18.88-89.
[884] Josephus, *The Antiquities of the Jews*, 18.89.
[885] Eusebius, *Ecclesiastical History*, Loeb Classical Library, 1.10.1-6.
[886] Finegan, *Handbook of Biblical Chronology*, revised edition, table 42, p. 89.
[887] Josephus, *The Antiquities of the Jews*, 18.54, 18.63-64.
[888] Dio, *Roman History*, Volume VII, Loeb Classical Library, 57.18.6. See also: Tacitus, *The Annals of Imperial Rome*, Penguin Books, p. 112-113; Tacitus, *The Annals*, Loeb Classical Library, 2.70 – 2.75.
[889] Josephus, *The Antiquities of the Jews*, 18.26.
[890] Vardaman, "Jesus' Life: A New Chronology," *Chronos, Kairos, Christos*, p. 63.
[891] Kokkinos, "Crucifixion in A.D. 36," *Chronos, Kairos, Christos*, p. 140.
[892] Vardaman, "Jesus' Life: A New Chronology," *Chronos, Kairos, Christos*, p. 63.

[893] Eusebius, *The History of the Church*, Penguin Books, 1.9.3-4. The Penguin Books translation uses the term "The Memoranda." Compare: Eusebius, *Ecclesiastical History*, Loeb Classical Library, 1.9.3-4. The Loeb Classical Library translation uses the phrase "Pilate's Reports," to refer to these documents; however, these are not the same as the extant documents called "The Gospel of Nicodemus or Pilate's Reports." Eusebius, *Ecclesiastical History*, Eusebius, Volume I, Loeb Classical Library, footnote 1, p. 74.

[894] Eusebius, *Ecclesiastical History*, Loeb Classical Library, 1.10. See also: Eusebius, *The History of the Church*, Penguin Books, 1.10.

[895] Josephus, *The Wars of the Jews*, 2.200.

[896] Josephus, *The Wars of the Jews*, 2.203.

[897] Finegan, *Handbook of Biblical Chronology*, revised edition, table 11, p. 29-30.

[898] Josephus, *The Wars of the Jews*, 2.199-203.

[899] Finegan, *Handbook of Biblical Chronology*, revised edition, table 57, p. 120.

[900] Tacitus, *The Annals of Imperial Rome*, Penguin Books, p. 367. See also: Tacitus, *The Annals*, Volume 5, Loeb Classical Library, 15.47.

[901] Tacitus, *The Annals of Imperial Rome*, Penguin Books, p. 324. See also: Tacitus, *The Annals*, Volume 5, Loeb Classical Library, 14.22.

[902] Gary W. Kronk, *Cometography, A Catalog of Comets*, Volume 1: Ancient–1799, (Cambridge, United Kingdom: Cambridge University Press, 1999).

[903] Dio, *The Roman History*, Penguin Books, p. 182. Compare to: Dio, *Roman History*, Volume VI, Loeb Classical Library, 54.29.7–54.30.1. In the Loeb translation, there is a general reference to "portents...as are wont to happen to them before the greatest calamities." However, Dio does not specifically apply this to the comet's appearance. It is rather a general comment on portents in general. The Penguin Books translation has it as: "when the greatest calamities threaten the state."

[904] Dio, *Roman History*, Volume VI, Loeb Classical Library, 54.30.1.

[905] Pliny, *Natural History*, 2.23.

[906] Pliny, *Natural History*, 2.33.

[907] Pliny, *Natural History*, 2.28.

[908] Pliny, *Natural History*, 2.35.

[909] Dio, *The Roman History*, Penguin Books, p. 40. See also: Dio, *Roman History*, Volume V, Loeb Classical Library, 50.8.2.

[910] Kronk, *Cometography*, p. 24.

[911] Information the location of this constellation as seen from Rome in that time period is from the astronomy software program *RedShift 3*.

[912] The usual date for the deaths of Marc Anthony and Cleopatra is August of 30 B.C. Finegan, *Handbook of Biblical Chronology*, revised edition, no. 299, p. 162.

[913] Kronk, *Cometography*, p. 27.

[914] Kronk, *Cometography*, p. 27.

[915] Kronk, *Cometography*, p. 27.

[916] Kronk, *Cometography*, p. 27, 33.

[917] Kronk, *Cometography*, p. 27-28.

[918] Kronk, *Cometography*, p. 27.

[919] Suetonius, *The Twelve Caesars*, Penguin Books, 5.46.

[920] Dio, *Roman History*, Volume VIII, Loeb Classical Library, 61.35.1.

[921] Pliny, *Natural History*, 2.23.
[922] Lucius Annaeus Seneca, *Natural Questions II*, ed. E. H. Warmington, trans. Thomas H. Corcoran, Loeb Classical Library, (Cambridge, Massachusetts: Harvard University Press, 1972), "Comets," 7.21.3.
[923] Kronk, *Cometography*, p. 28.
[924] Kronk, *Cometography*, p. 28-30. Kronk states that the comet was first seen on June 9 and last seen on July 9. The full moon dates for that period are June 9 and July 8 (as seen from China). It is probably not pure coincidence that the dates of the comets first and last appearance are the dates of the full moon. More likely, the comet was seen sometime between these two dates, i.e. between the dates for these two consecutive full moons. Full moon data from *RedShift 3* astronomy software.
[925] Kronk, *Cometography*, p. 29.
[926] Kronk, *Cometography*, p. 28-29.
[927] Kronk, *Cometography*, p. 27.
[928] Kronk, *Cometography*, p. 27.
[929] Locations of constellations, as seen from Rome, from *RedShift 3* astronomy software.
[930] Suetonius, *The Twelve Caesars*, Penguin Books, 5.46.
[931] Kronk, *Cometography*, p. 27, 29.
[932] Dio, *Roman History*, Volume VII, Loeb Classical Library, 60.26.1-5.
[933] Dio, *Roman History*, Volume VII, Loeb Classical Library, 60.26.1-5.
[934] Dio, *Roman History*, Volume VII, Loeb Classical Library, 60.26-27.
[935] See for example: Pliny, *Natural History*, 2.8-13.
[936] Dio, *Roman History*, Volume VII, Loeb Classical Library, 60.26.1-5.
[937] Dio, *Roman History*, Volume VII, Loeb Classical Library, 60.26.1.
[938] Tacitus, *The Annals of Imperial Rome*, Penguin Books, p. 324. Compare: Tacitus, *The Annals*, Loeb Classical Library, 14.22.
[939] Kronk, *Cometography*, p. 28, 33.
[940] Kronk, *Cometography*, p. 31.
[941] Kronk, *Cometography*, p. 31-32.
[942] Kronk, *Cometography*, p. 28.
[943] Tacitus, *The Annals*, Loeb Classical Library, 15.47. See also: Tacitus, *The Annals of Imperial Rome*, Penguin Books, p. 367.
[944] Tacitus, *The Annals of Imperial Rome*, Penguin Books, p. 367. See also: Tacitus, *The Annals*, Loeb Classical Library, 15.47.
[945] Tacitus, *The Annals of Imperial Rome*, p. 367; Tacitus, *The Annals*, Loeb Classical Library, 15.47. See also: Suetonius, *Lives of the Caesars*, Loeb Classical Library, 6.36.
[946] Kronk, *Cometography*, p. 33.
[947] Kronk, *Cometography*, p. 34.
[948] Kronk, *Cometography*, p. 28, 33.
[949] Kronk, *Cometography*, p. 27-28.
[950] Suetonius, *Lives of the Caesars*, Loeb Classical Library, 6.36.
[951] Tacitus, *The Annals of Imperial Rome*, p. 367; Tacitus, *The Annals*, Loeb Classical Library, 15.47.
[952] Tacitus, *The Annals of Imperial Rome*, p. 367; Tacitus, *The Annals*, Loeb Classical Library, 15.47.

[953] Pliny, *Natural History*, 2.23.
[954] Dio, *Roman History*, Volume VIII, Loeb Classical Library, 64.8.1.
[955] Kronk, *Cometography*, p. 28-30. Note that Kronk states the comet was seen from June 9 to July 9, and that the full moons of those months were June 8 and July 8. Because these dates nearly coincide with the dates for consecutive full moons, the dates of June 9 to July 9 are more likely a time frame within which the comet was seen, rather than the exact beginning and endpoints of observation. The ancient Chinese astronomers would sometimes give a time frame related to phases of the moon within which a comet was seen, rather than exact beginning and endpoints of observation (e.g. Kronk, *Cometography*, p. 27, comets dated A.D. 13 and A.D. 22). This was particularly the case with comets observed over the course of less than one month.
[956] Kronk, *Cometography*, p. 34-35.
[957] Dio, *Roman History*, Volume VIII, Loeb Classical Library, 66.17.3.
[958] Dio, *Roman History*, Volume VIII, Loeb Classical Library, 66.17.2.
[959] Kronk, *Cometography*, p. 33.
[960] Kronk, *Cometography*, p. 33-35.
[961] Kronk, *Cometography*, p. 36-37.
[962] Pliny, *Natural History*, 2.10.
[963] Suetonius, *The Twelve Caesars*, p. 292. See also: Suetonius, *Lives of the Caesars*, Loeb Classical Library, Book VIII, Titus, 1.1.
[964] Finegan, *Handbook of Biblical Chronology*, revised edition, no. 179, table 40, p. 85.
[965] Lunar and solar eclipse data from *RedShift 3* astronomy software, and from the NASA web site:
Fred Espenak, *Five Millennium Catalog of Solar Eclipses*, NASA/GSFC,
<http://sunearth.gsfc.nasa.gov/eclipse/SEcat/SEcatalog.html>.
Fred Espenak, *Five Millennium Catalog of Lunar Eclipses*, NASA/GSFC,
<http://sunearth.gsfc.nasa.gov/eclipse/LEcat/LEcatalog.html>.
[966] Lunar and solar eclipse data from *RedShift 3* astronomy software, and from the NASA web site:
Fred Espenak, *Five Millennium Catalog of Solar Eclipses*, NASA/GSFC,
<http://sunearth.gsfc.nasa.gov/eclipse/SEcat/SEcatalog.html>.
Fred Espenak, *Five Millennium Catalog of Lunar Eclipses*, NASA/GSFC,
<http://sunearth.gsfc.nasa.gov/eclipse/LEcat/LEcatalog.html>.
[967] Pliny, *Natural History*, books I – II, ed. G. P. Goold, trans. H. Rackham, Pliny, Volume I, Loeb Classical Library, (Cambridge, Massachusetts: Harvard University Press, 1991), p. vii.
[968] Pliny, *Natural History*, 2.22.
[969] Kronk, *Cometography*, p. 36.
[970] Kronk, *Cometography*, p. 31.
[971] Suetonius, *The Twelve Caesars*, p. 310-311. See also: Suetonius, *Lives of the Caesars*, Loeb Classical Library, Book VIII, Domitian, 15.3.
[972] Kronk, *Cometography*, p. 36-37.
[973] Josephus, *The Antiquities of the Jews*, 14.270.
[974] Josephus, *The Wars of the Jews*, 2.168.
[975] Josephus, *The Antiquities of the Jews*, 18.224; *The Wars of the Jews*, 2.180.

[976] Suetonius, *The Twelve Caesars*, p. 150. See also: Suetonius, *Lives of the Caesars*, Loeb Classical Library, 3.73.1.
[977] Dio, *Roman History*, Volume VII, Loeb Classical Library, 58.28.5.
[978] Josephus, *The Antiquities of the Jews*, 19.201; *The Wars of the Jews*, 2.204.
[979] Suetonius, *The Twelve Caesars*, p. 183. See also: Suetonius, *Lives of the Caesars*, Loeb Classical Library, 4.59.
[980] Dio, *Roman History*, Volume VII, Loeb Classical Library, 59.30.1.
[981] Josephus, *The Antiquities of the Jews*, 18.224, (22 years, 5 months, 3 days); *The Wars of the Jews*, 2.180, (22 years, 6 months, 3 days).
[982] Finegan, *Handbook of Biblical Chronology*, revised edition, no. 636, p. 372.
[983] Josephus, *The Antiquities of the Jews*, 20.148; *The Wars of the Jews*, 2.248.
[984] Suetonius, *The Twelve Caesars*, Penguin Books, p. 212. See also: Suetonius, *Lives of the Caesars*, Loeb Classical Library, 5.45.
[985] Tacitus, *The Annals of Imperial Rome*, p. 282. See also: Tacitus, *The Annals*, Loeb Classical Library, 12.69.
[986] Tacitus, *The Annals of Imperial Rome*, p. 282. See also: Tacitus, *The Annals*, Loeb Classical Library, 12.69.
[987] Dio, *Roman History*, Volume VII, Loeb Classical Library, 60.26.1-5.
[988] Suetonius, *The Twelve Caesars*, Penguin Books, p. 237. See also: Suetonius, *Lives of the Caesars*, Loeb Classical Library, 6.40.1.
[989] Suetonius, *The Twelve Caesars*, Penguin Books, p. 217, 246. See also: Suetonius, *Lives of the Caesars*, Loeb Classical Library, 6.8, 6.57.1.
[990] Dio, *Roman History*, Volume VIII, Loeb Classical Library, 63.29.3.
[991] Josephus, *The Wars of the Jews*, 4.491.
[992] Finegan, *Handbook of Biblical Chronology*, revised edition, no. 200, p. 105.
[993] Suetonius, *The Twelve Caesars*, Penguin Books, p. 216. See also: Suetonius, *Lives of the Caesars*, Loeb Classical Library, 6.6.1.
[994] Suetonius, *The Twelve Caesars*, Penguin Books, p. 246. See also: Suetonius, *Lives of the Caesars*, Loeb Classical Library, 6.57.1.
[995] Josephus, *The Wars of the Jews* 4.499.
[996] Tacitus, *The Histories*, trans. Kenneth Wellesley, (London, England: Penguin Books, 1995), 1.27, 1.37, p. 32, 39. See also: Tacitus, *The Histories*, ed. G. P. Goold, trans. C. H. Moore, Tacitus, Volume II, Loeb Classical Library, (Cambridge, Massachusetts: Harvard University Press, 1996), 1.27, 1.37.
[997] Suetonius, *The Twelve Caesars*, Penguin Books, p. 258. See also: Suetonius, *Lives of the Caesars*, Loeb Classical Library, 7.23.
[998] Dio, *Roman History*, Volume VIII, Loeb Classical Library, 63.6.1, p. 207.
[999] Dio, *Roman History*, Volume VIII, Loeb Classical Library, 66.17.5, p. 297.
[1000] Dio, *Roman History*, Volume VIII, Loeb Classical Library, 63.15.2, p. 219.
[1001] Suetonius, *The Twelve Caesars*, Penguin Books, p. 265. See also: Suetonius, *Lives of the Caesars*, Loeb Classical Library, book 7, Otho, 11.2.
[1002] Josephus, *The Wars of the Jews*, 4.548.
[1003] Tacitus, *The Histories*, Penguin Books, p. 114. See also: Tacitus, *The Histories*, Loeb Classical Library, 2.55.

[1004] Suetonius, *The Twelve Caesars*, Penguin Books, p. 275. See also: Suetonius, *Lives of the Caesars*, Loeb Classical Library, book 7, Vitellius, 15.1.

[1005] Suetonius, *The Twelve Caesars*, Penguin Books, p. 275-277. See also: Suetonius, *Lives of the Caesars*, Loeb Classical Library, book 7, Vitellius, 15.1-18.1.

[1006] Dio, *Roman History*, Volume VIII, Loeb Classical Library, 64.22.1.

[1007] Dio, *Roman History*, Volume VIII, Loeb Classical Library, 66.17.5.

[1008] Tacitus, *The Histories*, Penguin Books, p. 192, 206. See also: Tacitus, *The Histories*, Loeb Classical Library, 3.67, 3.85.

[1009] Dio, *Roman History*, Volume VIII, Loeb Classical Library, 64.8.1.

[1010] Kronk, *Cometography*, p. 28-30.

[1011] Dio, *Roman History*, Volume VIII, Loeb Classical Library, 64.22.1.

[1012] Dio, *Roman History*, Volume VIII, Loeb Classical Library, 66.17.4-5.

[1013] Dio, *Roman History*, Volume VIII, Loeb Classical Library, 66.17.4.

[1014] Dio, *Roman History*, Volume VIII, Loeb Classical Library, 64.9.1.

[1015] Dio, *Roman History*, Volume VIII, Loeb Classical Library, 64.10.3.

[1016] Dio, *Roman History*, Volume VIII, Loeb Classical Library, 66.17.5.

[1017] Suetonius, *The Twelve Caesars*, Penguin Books, p. 291. See also: Suetonius, *Lives of the Caesars*, Loeb Classical Library, book 8, Vespasian, 24.

[1018] Dio, *Roman History*, Volume VIII, Loeb Classical Library, 66.17.3.

[1019] Suetonius, *The Twelve Caesars*, Penguin Books, p. 292, 298. See also: Suetonius, *Lives of the Caesars*, Loeb Classical Library, book 8, Titus, chapters 1, 11.

[1020] Suetonius, *The Twelve Caesars*, Penguin Books, p. 298; Suetonius, *Lives of the Caesars*, Loeb Classical Library, book 8, Titus, chapters 11. See also: Dio, *Roman History*, Volume VIII, Loeb Classical Library, 66.26.4.

[1021] Suetonius, *The Twelve Caesars*, Penguin Books, p. 292, 298. See also: Suetonius, *Lives of the Caesars*, Loeb Classical Library, book 8, Titus, 1, 11.

[1022] Dio, *Roman History*, Volume VIII, Loeb Classical Library, 66.17.3.

[1023] Suetonius, *The Twelve Caesars*, Penguin Books, p. 312. See also: Suetonius, *Lives of the Caesars*, Loeb Classical Library, book 8, Domitian, 17.3.

[1024] Dio, *Roman History*, Volume VIII, Loeb Classical Library, 67.18.2.

[1025] Suetonius, *The Twelve Caesars*, Penguin Books, p. 311. See also: Suetonius, *Lives of the Caesars*, Loeb Classical Library, book 8, Domitian, 16.1.

[1026] *RedShift 3* astronomy software.

[1027] Dio, *Roman History*, Volume VIII, Loeb Classical Library, 65.1.4.

[1028] Josephus, *The Wars of the Jews*, 3.398-408.

[1029] Josephus, *The Wars of the Jews*, 4.626-629.

[1030] Josephus, *The Antiquities of the Jews*, 20.257.

[1031] Josephus, *The Wars of the Jews*, 2.284.

[1032] Josephus, *The Wars of the Jews*, 2.430.

[1033] Josephus, *The Wars of the Jews*, 2.440.

[1034] Josephus, *The Wars of the Jews*, 2.528.

[1035] Josephus, *The Wars of the Jews*, 2.555.

[1036] Josephus, *The Wars of the Jews*, 2.556-654.

[1037] Josephus, *The Wars of the Jews*, 3.142.

[1038] Josephus, *The Wars of the Jews*, 3.282, 315.

[1039] Josephus, *The Wars of the Jews*, 3.339.
[1040] Josephus, *The Wars of the Jews*, 3.542.
[1041] Josephus, *The Wars of the Jews*, 4.title.
[1042] Josephus, *The Wars of the Jews*, 4. 491.
[1043] Josephus, *The Wars of the Jews*, 4.499.
[1044] Josephus, *The Wars of the Jews*, 4.548.
[1045] Josephus, *The Wars of the Jews*, 4. 601.
[1046] Josephus, *The Wars of the Jews*, 4.632, 652-654.
[1047] Josephus, *The Wars of the Jews*, 4.658.
[1048] Josephus, *The Wars of the Jews*, 4.659-663.
[1049] Josephus, *The Wars of the Jews*, 5.650-653.
[1050] Josephus, *The Wars of the Jews*, 5.654.
[1051] Tacitus, *The Histories*, Penguin Books, p. 192-206. See also: Tacitus, *The Histories*, Loeb Classical Library, 3.67-86.
[1052] Tacitus, *The Histories*, Penguin Books, p. 203, n. 1.
[1053] Dec. 7 by observation method, Dec. 5 by calculation. This would assume that the month of Apelleus fell within Dec. that year.
[1054] This date in the Jewish/Macedonian calendar is determined by calculation.
[1055] Finegan, *Handbook of Biblical Chronology*, revised edition, table 25, p. 58.
[1056] Tacitus, *The Histories*, Penguin Books, p. 192-206. See also: Tacitus, *The Histories*, Loeb Classical Library, 3.67-86.
[1057] Josephus, *The Wars of the Jews*, 4.656.
[1058] See chapter 13, section 12, for a detailed discussion of this point.
[1059] Josephus, *The Wars of the Jews*, 4.656.
[1060] Tacitus, *The Histories*, Penguin Books, p. 272. See also: Tacitus, *The Histories*, Loeb Classical Library, 4.81.
[1061] Dio, *Roman History*, Volume VIII, Loeb Classical Library, 65.9.2a.
[1062] Josephus, *The Wars of the Jews*, 5.2.
[1063] Josephus, *The Wars of the Jews*, 4.658.
[1064] Josephus, *The Wars of the Jews*, 4.659-661.
[1065] Josephus, *The Wars of the Jews*, 4.662-663. See also: *Macmillan Bible Atlas*, map 265, p. 194.
[1066] Josephus, *The Wars of the Jews*, 4.663.
[1067] Several different maps were compared to arrive at this conclusion.
[1068] Tacitus, *The Histories*, Penguin Books, p. 279. See also: Tacitus, *The Histories*, Loeb Classical Library, 5.1.
[1069] Tacitus, *The Histories*, Penguin Books, p. 279. See also: Tacitus, *The Histories*, Loeb Classical Library, 5.1.
[1070] Tacitus, *The Histories*, Penguin Books, p. 279. See also: Tacitus, *The Histories*, Loeb Classical Library, 5.1.
[1071] Josephus, *The Wars of the Jews*, 5.47-49.
[1072] Josephus, *The Wars of the Jews*, 5.48.
[1073] Tacitus, *The Histories*, Penguin Books, p. 279. See also: Tacitus, *The Histories*, Loeb Classical Library, 5.1.
[1074] Josephus, *The Wars of the Jews*, 5.98.

[1075] Josephus, *The Wars of the Jews*, 5.98-99.
[1076] Josephus, *The Wars of the Jews*, 5.54-97.
[1077] Josephus, *The Wars of the Jews*, 5.98.
[1078] Dio, *Roman History*, Volume VIII, Loeb Classical Library, 65.4.1-4.
[1079] Dio, *Roman History*, Volume VIII, Loeb Classical Library, 65.4.1.
[1080] Josephus, *The Wars of the Jews*, 5.47-97.
[1081] This date for the Passover is by calculation; the date by observation would be only a day or two later.
[1082] Josephus, *The Wars of the Jews*, 5.2-98.
[1083] Josephus, *The Wars of the Jews*, 5.title.
[1084] Josephus, *The Wars of the Jews*, 5.2-98.
[1085] Josephus, *The Wars of the Jews*, 5.2-98.
[1086] There would have been 30 days in the previous AdarI, delaying the start of Nisan one day, so as to prevent Nisan 15 (a day of rest) from coinciding with Friday, the Preparation Day of the Sabbath (a day of work).
[1087] March 22, at 07:37 hours Jerusalem Standard Time, according to *RedShift 3* astronomy software.
[1088] Herod the great also waited until the end of winter before besieging Jerusalem. Josephus, *The Antiquities of the Jews*, 14.465.
[1089] Josephus, *The Wars of the Jews*, 5.24. The word 'corn' is often used, in ancient writings, to refer to grain. There was no corn (maize) in the Middle East and Europe during this time frame because corn (maize) originated in the Americas.
[1090] Josephus, *The Wars of the Jews*, 5.98.
[1091] Josephus, *The Wars of the Jews*, 5.54-97.
[1092] Josephus, *The Wars of the Jews*, 5.302.
[1093] Josephus, *The Wars of the Jews*, 5.302.
[1094] Josephus, *The Wars of the Jews*, 1.146.
[1095] Josephus, *The Wars of the Jews*, 5.331.
[1096] Josephus, *The Wars of the Jews*, 5.332, 342.
[1097] Josephus, *The Wars of the Jews*, 5.346.
[1098] Josephus, *The Wars of the Jews*, 5.347.
[1099] Josephus, *The Wars of the Jews*, 5.348.
[1100] Josephus, *The Wars of the Jews*, 5.356.
[1101] Josephus, *The Wars of the Jews*, 5.466.
[1102] Finegan, *Handbook of Biblical Chronology*, revised edition, no. 118, p. 52.
[1103] Josephus, *The Wars of the Jews*, 5.466.
[1104] Josephus, *The Wars of the Jews*, 5.469-472 (one day; perhaps the same day that the siege works were completed); *The Wars of the Jews*, 5.473 (two more days).
[1105] Josephus, *The Wars of the Jews*, 5.509.
[1106] Josephus, *The Wars of the Jews*, 5.522-524.
[1107] Josephus, *The Wars of the Jews*, 6.5.
[1108] Josephus, *The Wars of the Jews*, 6.22.
[1109] Josephus, *The Wars of the Jews*, 5.466.
[1110] Josephus, *The Wars of the Jews*, 6.22, 58ff, 68ff, 81ff.
[1111] Josephus, *The Wars of the Jews*, 6.74.

[1112] Josephus, *The Wars of the Jews*, 6.22, 67, 94.
[1113] Josephus, *The Wars of the Jews*, 6.93-94.
[1114] Josephus, *The Wars of the Jews*, 6.136-148.
[1115] Josephus, *The Wars of the Jews*, 6.149.
[1116] Josephus, *The Wars of the Jews*, 6.150ff.
[1117] Josephus, *The Wars of the Jews*, 6.177.
[1118] Josephus, *The Wars of the Jews*, 6. 178ff.
[1119] Josephus, *The Wars of the Jews*, 6.191.
[1120] Josephus, *The Wars of the Jews*, 6.192.
[1121] Josephus, *The Wars of the Jews*, 6.220-227.
[1122] Josephus, *The Wars of the Jews*, 6.228.
[1123] Josephus, *The Wars of the Jews*, 6.374, 392.
[1124] Josephus, *The Wars of the Jews*, 6.435.
[1125] Finegan, *Handbook of Biblical Chronology*, revised edition, no. 200, 203, p. 105-107.
[1126] Josephus, *The Wars of the Jews*, 6.250.
[1127] Finegan, *Handbook of Biblical Chronology*, revised edition, no. 200-203, p. 105-107.
[1128] Josephus, *The Wars of the Jews*, 6.250.
[1129] Josephus, *The Wars of the Jews*, 6.220, 228.
[1130] Josephus, *The Wars of the Jews*, 6.235-236, 243.
[1131] Josephus, *The Wars of the Jews*, 6.252-266.
[1132] Finegan, *Handbook of Biblical Chronology*, revised edition, no. 203, p. 107. Finegan there quotes Rabbi Yose from the second century A.D.
[1133] Josephus, *The Wars of the Jews*, 6.220.
[1134] Josephus, *The Wars of the Jews*, 1.146.
[1135] Josephus, *The Wars of the Jews*, 1.145-146.
[1136] Dio, *Roman History*, Volume VIII, Loeb Classical Library, 65.7.2.
[1137] *Universal Calendar Calculator* software. *RedShift 3* astronomy software.
[1138] Finegan, *Handbook of Biblical Chronology*, revised edition, no. 224-225, table 57, p. 116-121.
[1139] Josephus, *The Wars of the Jews*, 6.435.
[1140] Finegan, *Handbook of Biblical Chronology*, revised edition, no. 583, p. 340.
[1141] Josephus, *The Antiquities of the Jews*, 20.257.
[1142] Josephus, *The Wars of the Jews*, 6.289.
[1143] Josephus, *The Wars of the Jews*, 6.288.
[1144] Josephus, *The Wars of the Jews*, 6, title to chapter 5.
[1145] Josephus, *The Wars of the Jews*, 6.290.
[1146] Josephus, *The Wars of the Jews*, 2.284.
[1147] Kronk, *Cometography*, p. 29-30. Dates for comets mentioned: Feb. 27 - Mar. 27 of A.D. 54, June 9 - July 9 of A.D. 54, and possibly June 4 to July 4 of A.D. 55. These dates ranges are from full moon to full moon, with the comet sighting taking place any time with that date range.
[1148] Josephus, *The Wars of the Jews*, 6.289.
[1149] Josephus, *The Wars of the Jews*, 6.300.
[1150] Josephus, *The Wars of the Jews*, 2.284.
[1151] Josephus, *The Wars of the Jews*, 6.308.

[1152] Josephus, *The Wars of the Jews*, 6.658.
[1153] Josephus, *The Wars of the Jews*, 6.308.
[1154] Josephus, *The Wars of the Jews*, 4.title.
[1155] Josephus, *The Wars of the Jews*, 3.542.
[1156] Josephus, *The Wars of the Jews*, 4. 491.
[1157] Josephus, *The Wars of the Jews*, 4.499.
[1158] Josephus, *The Wars of the Jews*, 4.548.
[1159] Josephus, *The Wars of the Jews*, 4. 601.
[1160] Josephus, *The Wars of the Jews*, 4.632, 652-654.
[1161] For expected dates of future events in the Church, see: Conte, *The Bible and the Future of the World.*
[1162] See Appendix I, Chart 1, for examples of Spring Equinox dates. Dates for the Spring Equinox were taken from *RedShift 3* astronomy software.
[1163] Spring Equinox times/dates: 08:30 hours, March 20, 2001; 14:15 March 20, 2002; 19:59 March 20, 2003; 01:48 March 20, 2004; 07:33 March 20, 2005; 13:25 March 20, 2006; 19:06 March 20, 2007; 00:48 March 20, 2008; 06:43 March 20, 2009; 12:31 March 20, 2010. All times/dates taken from *RedShift 3* astronomy software using Jerusalem Standard Time.
[1164] Either Jerusalem Standard Time or Jerusalem sun time could be used in setting the date for the Spring Equinox.
[1165] ...unless there is some catastrophic change to the spin of the earth, or to the orbit of the earth around the sun. In such a case, additional adjustments will need to be made.
[1166] Eusebius, *The History of the Church*, Penguin Books, p. 170-174. See also: Eusebius, *Ecclesiastical History*, Loeb Classical Library, 5.23-25.
[1167] For more information, see: Ronald W. Mallen, Astronomical Society of South Australia, *Easter Dating Method*, 23 April 2000, <http://www.assa.org.au/edm.html>. See also: Calendar & Easter Topics, *How Easter Date is Determined*, GM Arts Home Page, <http://users.chariot.net.au/~gmarts/easter.htm>.
[1168] For details, see: Conte, *The Bible and the Future of the World.* The events of the book of Revelation begin in A.D. 2009-2010.
[1169] John Donne, *Upon the Annunciation and Passion Falling Upon One Day*:

> Tamely, frail body, abstain to-day; to-day
> My soul eats twice, Christ hither and away....
>
> Whose first and last concur; this doubtful day
> Of feast or fast, Christ came, and went away....
>
> How well the Church, God's Court of Faculties
> Deals, in sometimes, and seldom joining these!

[1170] For a detailed theology of the Virgin Birth of Jesus Christ, see: Conte, *The Virginity of Jesus and Mary.* This booklet will constitute chapter one of my third book.
[1171] Emmerich, *The Life of the Blessed Virgin Mary*, p. 295.
[1172] For a detailed theology of the Virgin Mary's Perfect Virginity, see: Conte, *The Virginity of Jesus and Mary*. This booklet will constitute chapter one of my third book.
[1173] Conte, *The Virginity of Jesus and Mary*.

[1174] For predictions about the churches (buildings) of Rome, see: Conte, *The Bible and the Future of the World.*

[1175] Conte, *The Virginity of Jesus and Mary.*

[1176] Pius XII, *Munificentissimus Deus*, paragraphs 14, 17, 18, 20, 21, 22, 28, 40. Furthermore, paragraph 28 refers specifically to the Resurrection of the Virgin Mary, after her death and before her Assumption.

[1177] Some people have even taken to calling this day "Turkey Day," instead of Thanksgiving, because the importance of the day for them is to eat a lot of turkey.

[1178] Finegan, *Handbook of Biblical Chronology*, revised edition, no. 232ff, p. 127ff.

[1179] It has been a subject of dispute among the Jews as to when the Sabbatical year of ancient times began, in Nisan or Tishri.

[1180] Finegan, *Handbook of Biblical Chronology*, revised edition, no. 31, p. 16; no. 58-59, p. 29-30.

[1181] The Weather Channel, weather.com – Averages and Records – Jerusalem, Israel, "Monthly Averages and Records," Avg. Precip. <http://www.weather.com/weather/climatology/ISXX0010>. The monthly averages are as follows: June, July, August, September: no precipitation; Oct. 0.90 inches; Nov. 2.70 inches; Dec. 4.30 inches; Jan. 5.70 inches; Feb. 4.50 inches; Mar. 3.90 inches; Apr. 1.20 inches; May 0.10 inches.

See also: USA Today.com, Climate, Jerusalem, Israel, Average Precipitation, <http://www.usatoday.com/weather/climate/mideast/Israel/wjerusal.htm>. The monthly averages are as follows: June, July, August, September: no precipitation; Oct. 0.4 inches; Nov. 2.7 inches; Dec. 5.1 inches; Jan. 5.50 inches; Feb. 4.4 inches; Mar. 4.6 inches; Apr. 0.7 inches; May 0.2 inches.

[1182] Josephus, *The Antiquities of the Jews*, 14.475.

[1183] Josephus, *The Antiquities of the Jews*, 15.7.

[1184] Josephus, *The Antiquities of the Jews*, 20.247.

[1185] Finegan, *Handbook of Biblical Chronology*, revised edition, no. 232, p. 127.

[1186] Finegan, *Handbook of Biblical Chronology*, revised edition, no. 225, table 57, p. 118-121.

[1187] Josephus, *The Wars of the Jews*, 2.192-200.

[1188] Josephus, *The Wars of the Jews*, 2.200.

[1189] Josephus, *The Wars of the Jews*, 2.200.

[1190] Finegan, *Handbook of Biblical Chronology*, revised edition, table 57, p. 120.

[1191] Josephus, *The Antiquities of the Jews*, 14.475, 487-488.

[1192] Josephus, *The Antiquities of the Jews*, 15.487.

[1193] Josephus, *The Antiquities of the Jews*, 15.299-302.

[1194] Josephus, *The Antiquities of the Jews*, 14.475 and 15.7.

[1195] Those who follow Zuckermann/Blosser on the Sabbatical years generally date Herod's capture of Jerusalem to 37 BC, so that Herod's 13th year would be 24 B.C. Such a chronology does not conflict with what Josephus says about the famine in Herod's 13th and 14th years, because the Sabbatical year would begin in autumn of 24 BC, according to Zuckermann/Blosser.

[1196] Josephus, *The Antiquities of the Jews*, 15.302.

[1197] Josephus, *The Antiquities of the Jews*, 15.302.

[1198] Josephus, *The Antiquities of the Jews*, 15:311.

1199 Josephus, *The Antiquities of the Jews*, 15:309.

1200 Josephus, *The Antiquities of the Jews*, 15:312.

1201 Finegan, *Handbook of Biblical Chronology*, revised edition, no. 224-231, p. 116-126.

1202 Finegan, *Handbook of Biblical Chronology*, revised edition, no. 236, p. 130.

1203 Finegan, *Handbook of Biblical Chronology*, revised edition, no. 235, p. 129.

1204 Josephus, *The Antiquities of the Jews*, 4.273.

1205 Finegan, *Handbook of Biblical Chronology*, revised edition, no. 584, p. 342. Finegan cites Wacholder's study of a wide variety of sources.

1206 Conte, *The Bible and the Future of the World*, <http://www.catholicplanet.com>. In this book, I give the date of A.D. 2437 as the last year of the Antichrist's reign and I state that Antichrist is destroyed at the end of his reign by the coming of Jesus Christ. Therefore, the reader can conclude that the Return of Jesus Christ will occur in A.D. 2437, (though I neglected to say so outright).

1207 For details on this anticipated time of peace and holiness, see: Conte, *The Bible and the Future of the World*, <http://www.catholicplanet.com>.

1208 Emmerich, *The Life of Jesus Christ and Biblical Revelations*, Vol. 1, p. 284 – 285. She mentions Anna praying in her cell and states that Anna lived in the outer courts of the Temple.

1209 Emmerich, *The Life of the Blessed Virgin Mary*, p. 107, 117.

1210 Emmerich, *The Life of Jesus Christ and Biblical Revelations*, Vol. 1, p. 176-177.

1211 Emmerich, *The Life of the Blessed Virgin Mary*, p. 117.

1212 Apocryphal literature claims that the virgins were dismissed so as not to defile the Temple once they reached menarche. *Proto-evangelium of James*, 8.2, Wesley Center for Applied Theology, Non-canonical Homepage, <http://wesley.nnu.edu/noncanon/gospels/gosjames.htm>. Though this comes from a non-canonical source, the statement accords with Jewish belief and custom concerning ritual cleanliness and the Temple. If so, then Anna might not have been admitted to service of the Temple until she reached menopause, about the age of 49 years. Thus, we cannot be certain as to when she returned to the service of the Temple.

1213 Emmerich, *The Life of Jesus Christ and Biblical Revelations*, Vol. 1, p. 177.

1214 Emmerich, *The Life of the Blessed Virgin Mary*, p. 129.

1215 Apocryphal literature claims that the virgins were dismissed so as not to defile the Temple once they reached menarche. *Proto-evangelium of James*, 8.2.

In modern times, the average age of menarche has decreased to between 12 and 13 years of age. See *Merck Manual of Diagnosis and Therapy*, Section 18, Chapter 234, "Puberty," and Figure 234-3, <http://www.merck.com/pubs/mmanual/section18/chapter234/234a.htm>. See also: U.S. Centers for Disease Control, National Center for Health Statistics, *Vital and Health Statistics*; Series 11, No. 133, <http://www.cdc.gov/nchs/data/series/sr_11/sr11_133.pdf>, p. 3.

As late as the eighteenth century, the average age of menarche was about 17 years of age. See: Cornell University, Science News, "New 'Rituals' Of Menarche May Not Be Preparing Girls For Emerging Sexuality, Cornell Scholar Argues," <http://www.news.cornell.edu/general/PRESS93/PR11109301.html>. This article cites: Joan Jacobs Brumberg, "Something Happens to Girls: Menarche and the

Emergence of the Modern American Hygienic Imperative," *Journal of the History of Sexuality*, 1993, Vol. 4.

In ancient times, if 17 years was the average, then 14 years was approximately the time when some percentage of girls in any group would reach menarche; hence the need to dismiss the Temple virgins at that age, (before any of the girls might defile the Temple).

Note that the Virgin Mary never had menarche. Conte, *the Virginity of Jesus and Mary*, PDF ebooklet, p. 10; printed booklet, p. 14, <http://www.catholicplanet.com/virgin/>.

[1216] Scott E. Lee, *Calendar Conversions Overview*, <www.genealogy.org/~scottlee/cal-overview.html>.

[1217] Finegan, *Handbook of Biblical Chronology*, revised edition, no. 78, p. 38.

[1218] Finegan, *Handbook of Biblical Chronology*, revised edition, no. 75-81, p. 37-39.

[1219] Pliny, *Natural History*, 2.9-10.

[1220] Pliny, *Natural History*, 2.10, p. 205.

[1221] Dio, *Roman History*, Volume VII, Loeb Classical Library, 60.26.5.

[1222] Josephus, *The Antiquities of the Jews*, 20.247.

[1223] Emmerich, *The Life of the Blessed Virgin Mary*, p. 240.

[1224] Dates and times of new moons taken from *RedShift 3* astronomy software.

[1225] Emmerich, *The Life of Jesus Christ and Biblical Revelations*, Vol. 2, p. 373.

[1226] Emmerich, *The Dolorous Passion of Our Lord Jesus Christ*, p. 160.

[1227] Finegan, *Handbook of Biblical Chronology*, revised edition, no. 78-81, p. 38-39.

[1228] Fred Espenak, *Five Millennium Catalog of Solar Eclipses*, NASA/GSFC, <http://sunearth.gsfc.nasa.gov/eclipse/SEcat/SEcatalog.html>.

[1229] Fred Espenak, *Five Millennia Catalog of Phases of the Moon*, NASA/GSFC, <http://sunearth.gsfc.nasa.gov/eclipse/phase/phasecat.html>.

[1230] Fred Espenak, *Five Millennium Catalog of Solar Eclipses*, NASA/GSFC, <http://sunearth.gsfc.nasa.gov/eclipse/SEcat/SEcatalog.html>.

[1231] *RedShift 3* astronomy software.

[1232] Dio, *Roman History*, Volume VII, Loeb Classical Library, 56.29.3.

[1233] Dio, *Roman History*, Volume VII, Loeb Classical Library, 56.29.3.

[1234] Fred Espenak, *Five Millennium Catalog of Lunar Eclipses*, NASA/GSFC, <http://sunearth.gsfc.nasa.gov/eclipse/LEcat/LEcatalog.html>.

[1235] *RedShift 3* astronomy software.

[1236] Josephus, *The Antiquities of the Jews*, 17:157, 167.

[1237] *RedShift 3* astronomy software.

[1238] Josephus, *The Antiquities of the Jews*, 17:167.

[1239] *RedShift 3* astronomy software.

[1240] *RedShift 3* astronomy software.

[1241] Finegan, *Handbook of Biblical Chronology*, revised edition, no. 78, p. 38.

[1242] Finegan, *Handbook of Biblical Chronology*, revised edition, p. 67, no. 144.

[1243] *Universal Calendar Calculator* software.

[1244] Fred Espenak, *Five Millennia Catalog of Phases of the Moon*, NASA/GSFC, <http://sunearth.gsfc.nasa.gov/eclipse/phase/phasecat.html>.

[1245] Finegan, *Handbook of Biblical Chronology*, revised edition, table 18, p. 52.

[1246] Finegan, *Handbook of Biblical Chronology*, revised edition, table 13, p. 35.

[1247] See chapter 16.

[1248] Finegan, *Handbook of Biblical Chronology*, revised edition, no. 225, table 57, p. 118-121.

[1249] Finegan, *Handbook of Biblical Chronology*, revised edition, no. 225, table 57, p. 118-121.

[1250] See chapter 16.

[1251] Finegan, *Handbook of Biblical Chronology*, revised edition, no. 235, table 59, p. 129-130.

[1252] Finegan, *Handbook of Biblical Chronology*, revised edition, no. 236, p. 130.

[1253] Emmerich, *The Life of Jesus Christ and Biblical Revelations*, Vol. 1, p. 477.

[1254] Vardaman, "Jesus' Life: A New Chronology," *Chronos, Kairos, Christos*, p. 58-59.

[1255] Vardaman, "Jesus' Life: A New Chronology," *Chronos, Kairos, Christos*, p. 55ff.

[1256] Conte, *The Bible and the Future of the World*, chapter 10. This book contains details and the time frames of various prophecies from the book of Revelation.

[1257] Emmerich, *The Life of the Blessed Virgin Mary*, p. 205.

[1258] Emmerich, *The Life of the Blessed Virgin Mary*, p. 205.

[1259] Vardaman, "Jesus' Life: A New Chronology," *Chronos, Kairos, Christos*, p. 62-63, table 3.

[1260] Finegan, *Handbook of Biblical Chronology*, revised edition, no. 523, p. 305.

[1261] Emmerich, *The Life of the Blessed Virgin Mary*, p. 205.

[1262] Vardaman, "Jesus' Life: A New Chronology," *Chronos, Kairos, Christos*, p. 61-63.

[1263] Nikos Kokkinos, "Crucifixion in A.D. 36," *Chronos, Kairos, Christos*, p. 140-141.

[1264] Vardaman, "Jesus' Life: A New Chronology," *Chronos, Kairos, Christos*, p. 63.

[1265] Finegan, *Handbook of Biblical Chronology*, revised edition, no. 218, p. 118.

[1266] Finegan, *Handbook of Biblical Chronology*, revised edition, no. 161, p. 75.

[1267] For more on this point: Ronald L. Conte Jr., *The Dormition, Resurrection, and Assumption of the Blessed Virgin Mary*, (Catholic Planet, 1998).

[1268] Emmerich, *The Dolorous Passion of Our Lord Jesus Christ*, p. 3 - 57.

[1269] Dio, *The Roman History*, Penguin Books, p. 1.

[1270] Finegan, *Handbook of Biblical Chronology*, revised edition, no. 161, p. 75.

[1271] Finegan, *Handbook of Biblical Chronology*, revised edition, no. 165, p. 78.

[1272] Tracey R. Rich, Judaism 101, *Purim*, <http://www.jewfaq.org/holiday9.htm>.

[1273] Butler's Lives of the Saints, Vol. 4, Nov. 2, p. 242.

Made in the USA